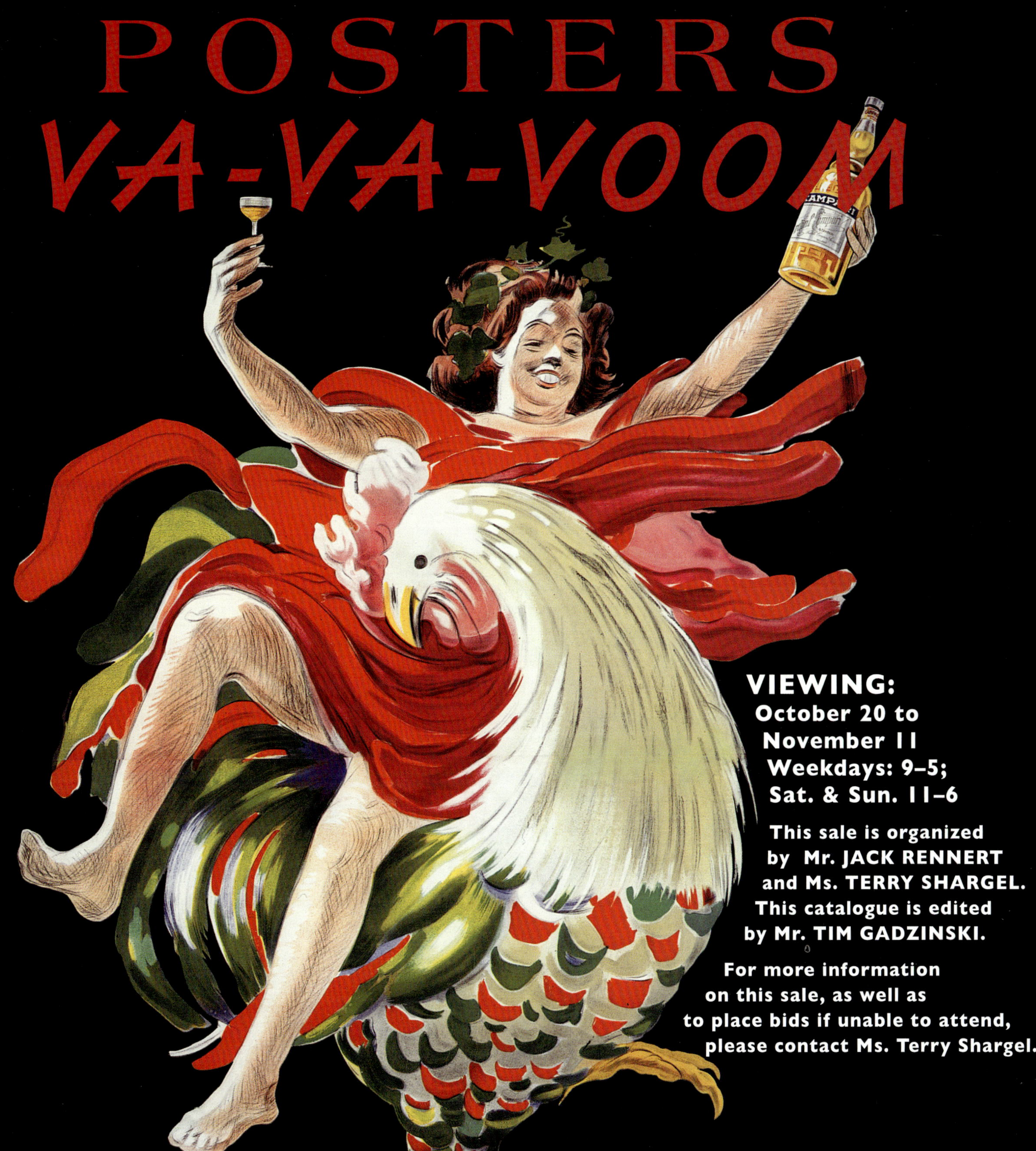
POSTERS
VA-VA-VOOM

VIEWING:
October 20 to
November 11
Weekdays: 9–5;
Sat. & Sun. 11–6

This sale is organized
by Mr. JACK RENNERT
and Ms. TERRY SHARGEL.
This catalogue is edited
by Mr. TIM GADZINSKI.

For more information
on this sale, as well as
to place bids if unable to attend,
please contact Ms. Terry Shargel.

SUNDAY, November 12, 2006 at 11AM
at The International Poster Center, 601 West 26th Street, N.Y.C.
(between 11th & 12th Ave.—13th floor)

POSTER AUCTIONS INTERNATIONAL, INC.
601 West 26th Street, New York, N.Y. 10001
Telephone (212) 787-4000   Fax (212) 604-9175
Email: info@posterauctions.com   Website: www.posterauctions.com

CONTENTS

ACKNOWLEDGMENTS

I am most grateful to the many individuals who have given their full support and assistance to us in the preparation of this POSTERS VA-VA-VOOM sale. First and foremost, our thanks to the 77 consignors in 12 states and 8 foreign countries who entrusted their finest works to us for this very special occasion.

Our staff has been materially helpful in all aspects of this auction, and I wish to especially single out the work of my associate, Ms. Terry Shargel. Our editorial department was headed once again by Mr. Tim Gadzinski, who is responsible for the lively and incisive text in this book. Helping with many of the administrative aspects were Ms. Sarah Sternick, Ms. Julie Press and Mr. Xavier Serbones. Mr. John Greenleaf, Mr. Edward Haber and Mr. Troy Hollar handled all computer and internet-related matters. And finally, a special personal note of thanks to Barbara Rennert, who helps and encourages in countless ways.

We take great pride in making all of our annotations as complete and accurate as possible, and we are helped enormously in this task by being able to call upon very knowledgeable colleagues throughout the world. Helpful in answering our many questions for this book were Mr. Chester Collins, Mr. Wiliam W. Crouse, Mr. James Dierks, Ms. Diana Dreger, Ms. Laura Kotsis, Dr. Maura Mansfield and Mr. Howard Sigman.

In the production of this catalogue, I was again fortunate to be able to call on the talents and devotion of fine craftsmen: Mr. Guenter Knop is our very able photographer; the staff of Harry Chester, Inc. was in charge of design and production, and I especially want to thank Ms. Susannah Ing; all aspects of printing and binding were again handled by Cosmos Communications and I am especially indebted to Ms. Judy Lamm of their large and able staff.

With this auction, we welcome the Cannon Group as our new public relations firm. We are certain that with their able staff, headed by Mr. Jeff Cannon, we will be reaching an even larger public.

To all of them and to all the others who offered help, suggestions and encouragement, many thanks.

—Jack Rennert

CONDITIONS OF SALE

We call your attention to the Conditions of Sale printed at the end of the book.
Those bidding at this sale should first familiarize themselves with the terms contained therein.

OUR NEXT SALE

We are pleased to announce that the PAI-XLIV sale of rare posters
will be held on Sunday, May 6, 2007.

Consignments are accepted until January 15, 2007.

BID WITH CONFIDENCE—EVEN IF YOU CANNOT ATTEND

If you cannot attend the auction of November 12, please use the Order Bid Form provided.
It should be mailed or faxed to arrive at our office no later than Friday, November 10.
Note that all illustrations in this book are of the item being sold—we never use stock photos.

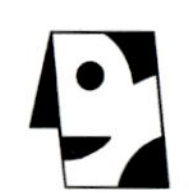

Jack Rennert—License 0797440

AUTOMOBILE POSTERS

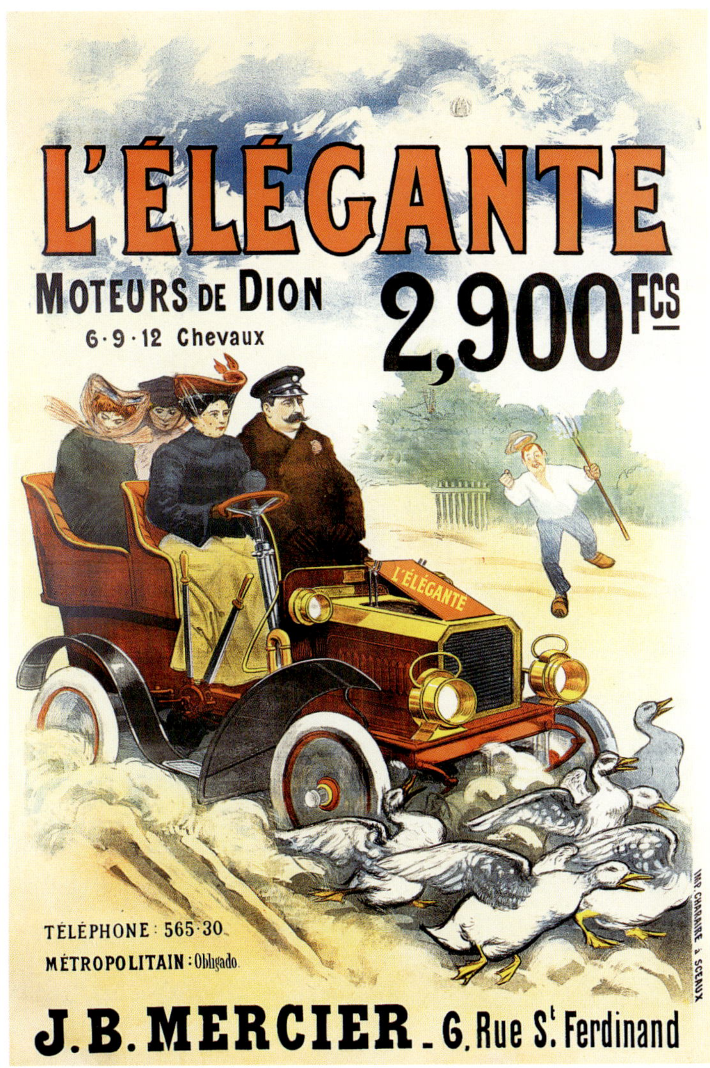

1

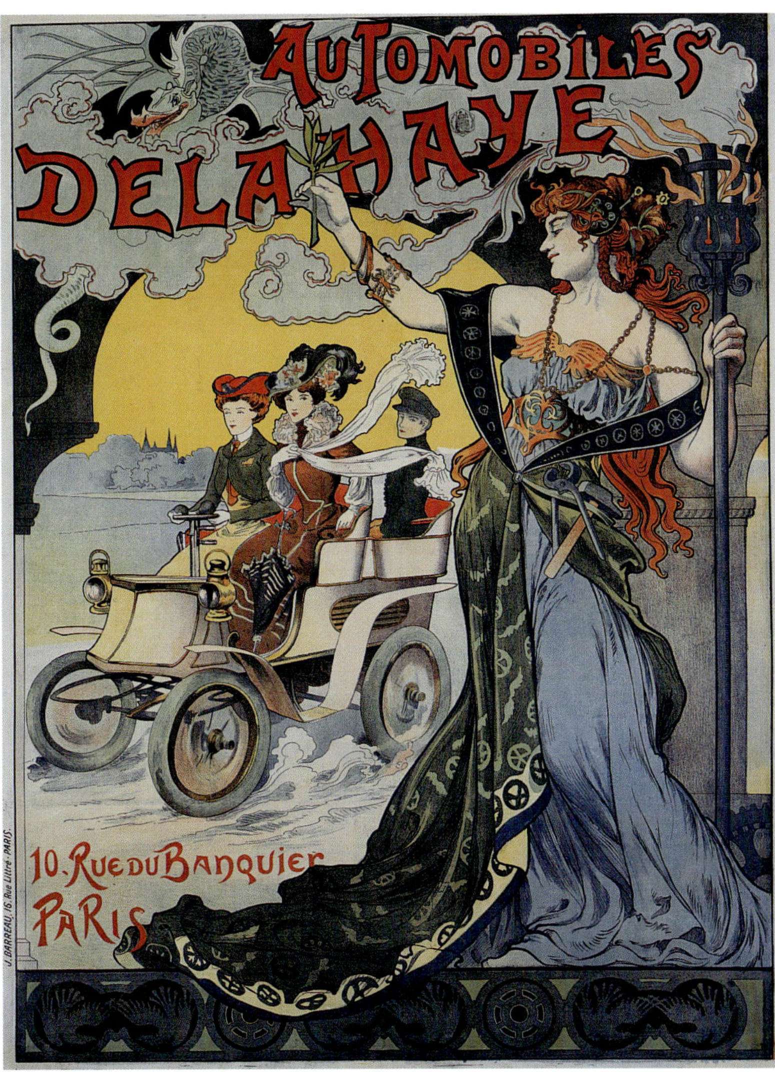

2

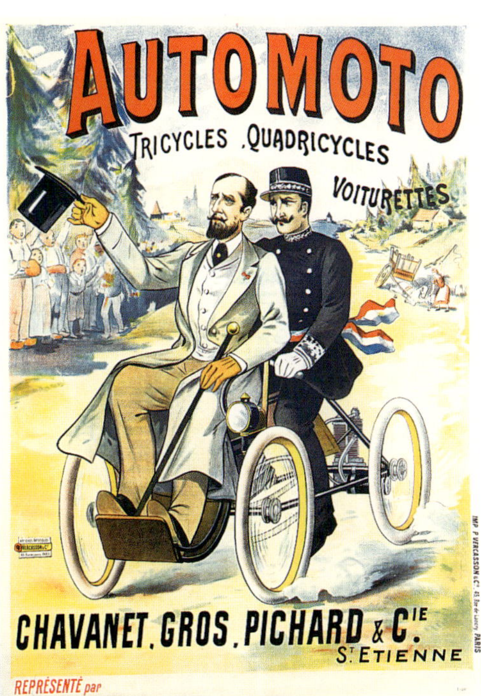

3

ANONYMOUS

1. L'Élégante.
38¹/₈ x 58 in./97 x 147 cm
Imp. Charaire à Sceaux
Cond B/Restored tears at folds and edges.
Cut from the same transportational cloth as Steinlen's Motocycles Comiot (*see* PAI-XLII, 471), this anonymous creation for Elegant motors pits machine against goose. While the Steinlen design appears to give the geese a fighting chance, we're not sure that the same can be said here. The age-old conflict of technology vs. machine is thematically appropriate for the period; what sets this design apart, however, is the seeming embarrassment of the backseat passengers and the stolid forward gaze of the frontseat military type, which would appear to be an obvious commentary regarding the driver's lack of control. Clearly bad driving skills have been a perturbation from the get-go.
Est: $3,000-$3,500.

2. Automobiles Delahaye. 1898.
37 x 50 in./94 x 127 cm
J. Barreau, Paris
Cond B+/Restored tears at folds and edges.
Ref: Auto Show I, 5; PAI-XXXIV, 156
One of the earliest posters for this particular automobile manufacturer on record. And what we see, right off the bat, is that these savvy industrialists were targeting the female populace, demographically present-ing their automobile as the natural next step in vehicular suffrage. And take note that as the goddess of technical advances smiles down on the Delahaye product, the male—albeit feminine—chauffeur has been ordered to the back seat by the woman driver and an even more accessorized companion. The message is clear—if a bicycle provides a woman with greater freedom, just imagine the boundless liberation a car could provide.
Est: $4,000-$5,000.

3. Automoto.
41³/₈ x 59¹/₈ in./105.2 x 150.2 cm
Imp. P. Vercasson, Paris
Cond A–/Unobtrusive tears at folds and paper edges.
Ref: Auto Show III, 6; Ailes, p. 82; PAI-XXXII, 104
You'd think that President Carnot could have found a more dignified way of parading himself before the excited residents of this rustic berg than to be chauf-feured about by a military official on what, by today's standards, would be considered rather precarious trans-port. The truth of the matter is, however, that these demi-cars, tricycles and quadrocycles gained nearly instant popularity upon their introduction and their pre-sence on the European roadways was fairly common-place, disappearing completely only after World War I. Automoto began operations in 1901 in St. Etienne, Loire, under the name Chavanet, Gros, Pichard & Cie.
Est: $2,000-$2,500.

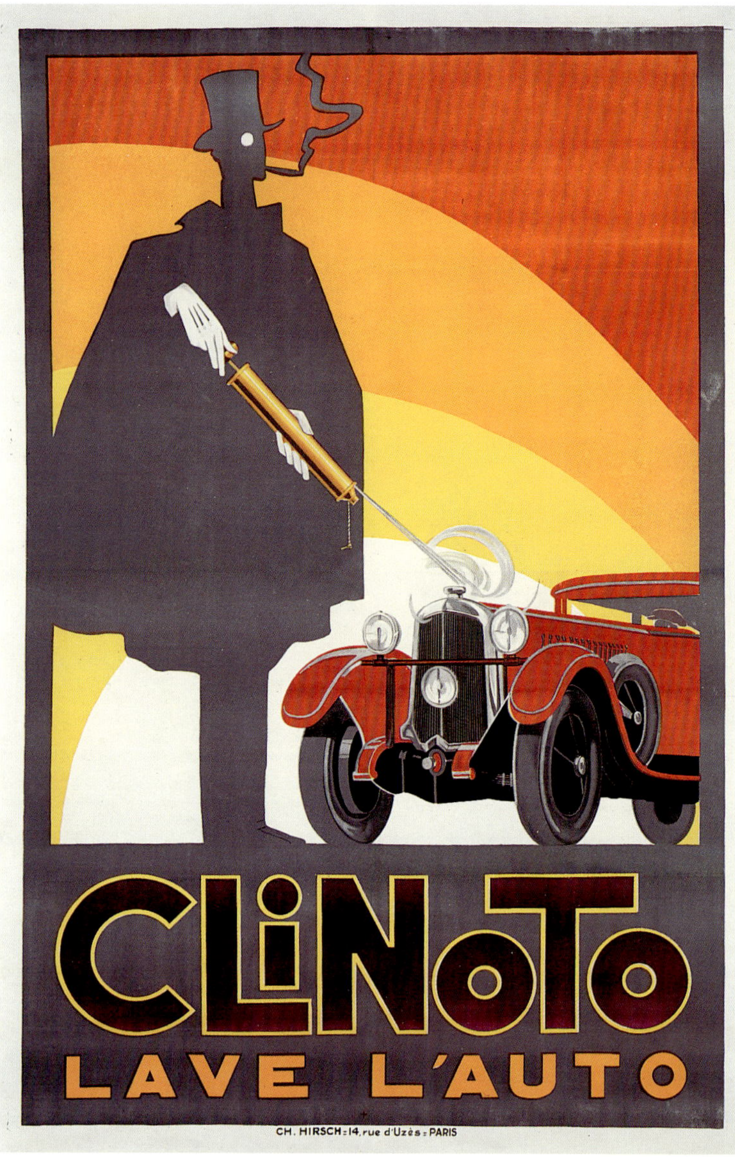

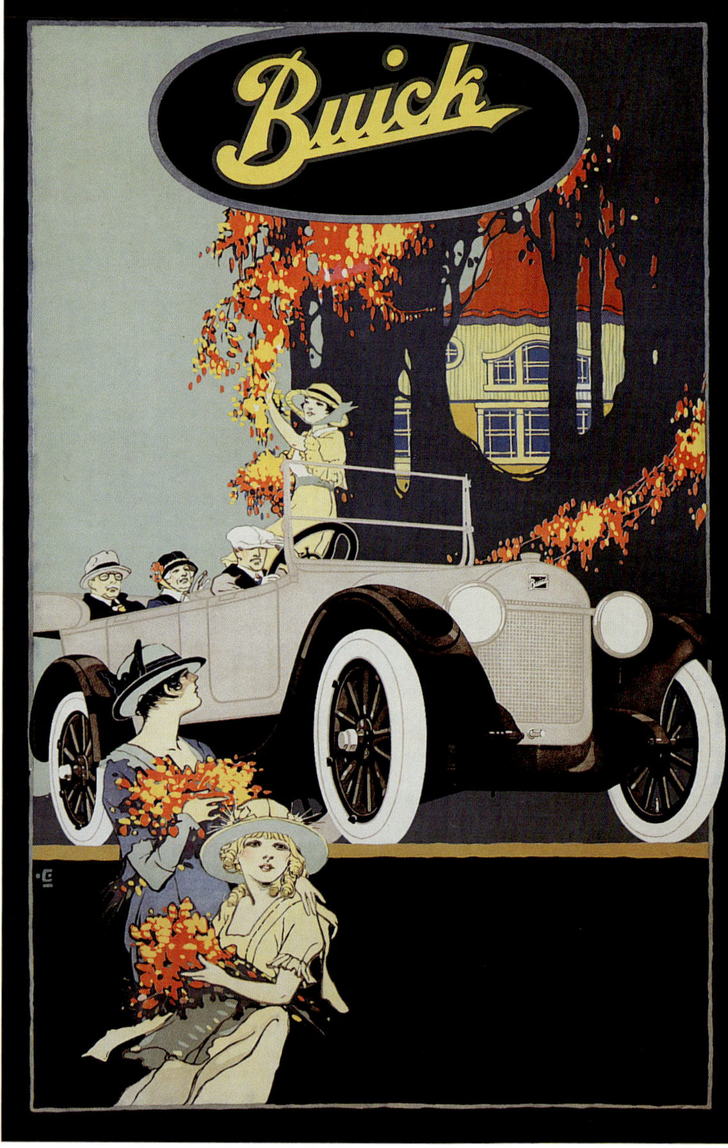

4

5

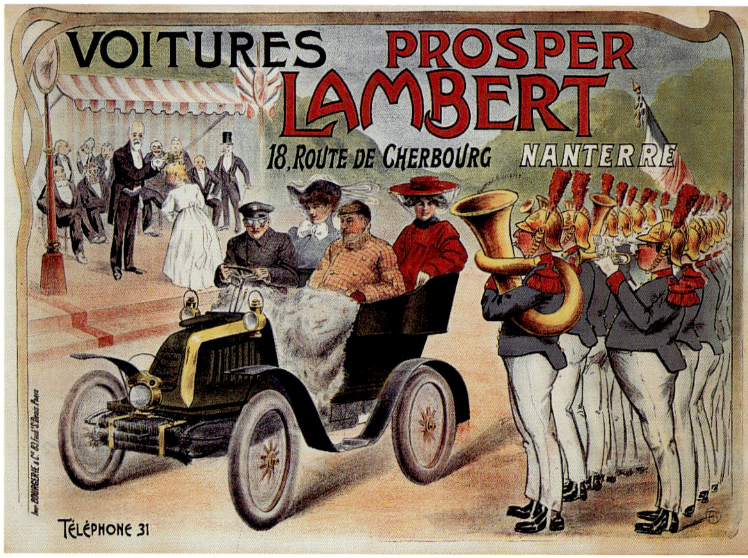

6

Regardless of his profession—spy, magician, fringe hero of automotive cleanliness—this caped fellow is doing quite a job on the limousine he's spritzing, which appears to be as lovely as the day it rolled out of the showroom. *Rare!*
Est: $5,000-$6,000.

5. Buick.
25 x 39³/₈ in./63.5 x 100 cm
Cond A-/Slight tears and creases at edges.
Ref: PAI-II, 33a
In 1899, David Dunbar Buick sold his plumbing business and began producing gasoline engines primarily for farming and marine equipment—by 1903, Buick had designed and built his first automobile. After a series of bad partnerships and superfluous experimentations he finally began production of the Buick automobile with the help of a far more clever businessman, William C. Durant. Within three years of entering into his partnership with Durant in 1904, Buick's automobile succeeded so spectacularly that the company was selling some 8,000 cars a year. David Buick, however, left the company in 1908, disgruntled by the frantic pace of the automotive industry. That very same year, Durant, using the Buick as a cornerstone, incorporated the company with General Motors—later adding Cadillac, Oldsmobile and Oakland (Pontiac). While Durant went on to make a fortune and the Buick became one of the best selling cars in the United States, the man for whom it was named went from one poor venture to another and eventually died in poverty. Artist's monogram appears left side.
Est: $2,000-$2,500.

6. Voitures Prosper Lambert. ca. 1902.
50¹/₈ x 36³/₄ in./127.3 x 93.3 cm
Imp. Bourgerie, Paris
Cond A.
Obviously, the woman being crowned with the laurel wreath is being honored for some achievement or another, but if you didn't know better you'd

AUTOS/ANONYMOUS (cont'd)

4. Clinoto. ca. 1923.
49¹/₂ x 76¹/₄ in./126 x 193.5 cm
Ch. Hirsch, Paris
Cond B+/Slight tears at folds.
Even with its happy candy-striped sunset, this anonymous creation simmers with mysterious portent—regardless of the fact that it's for a car cleaning device. The shadowy foreground figure almost appears to be operating a weapon of mass insect destruction—which potentially is intentional seeing as this product eradicates dirt and grime the way the other does bugs.

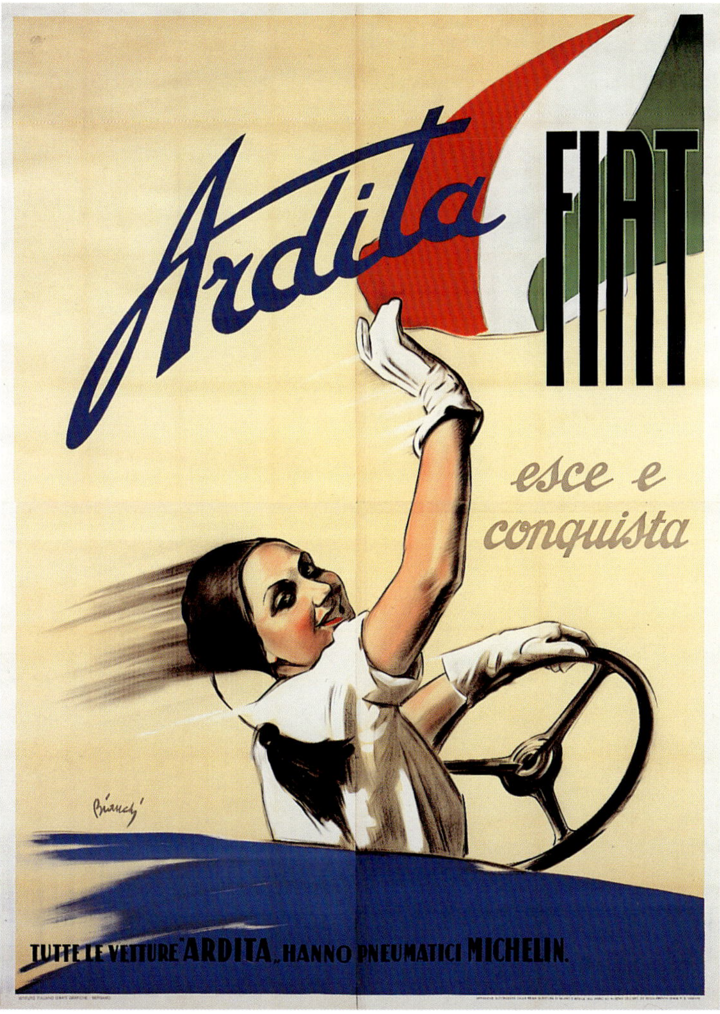

8

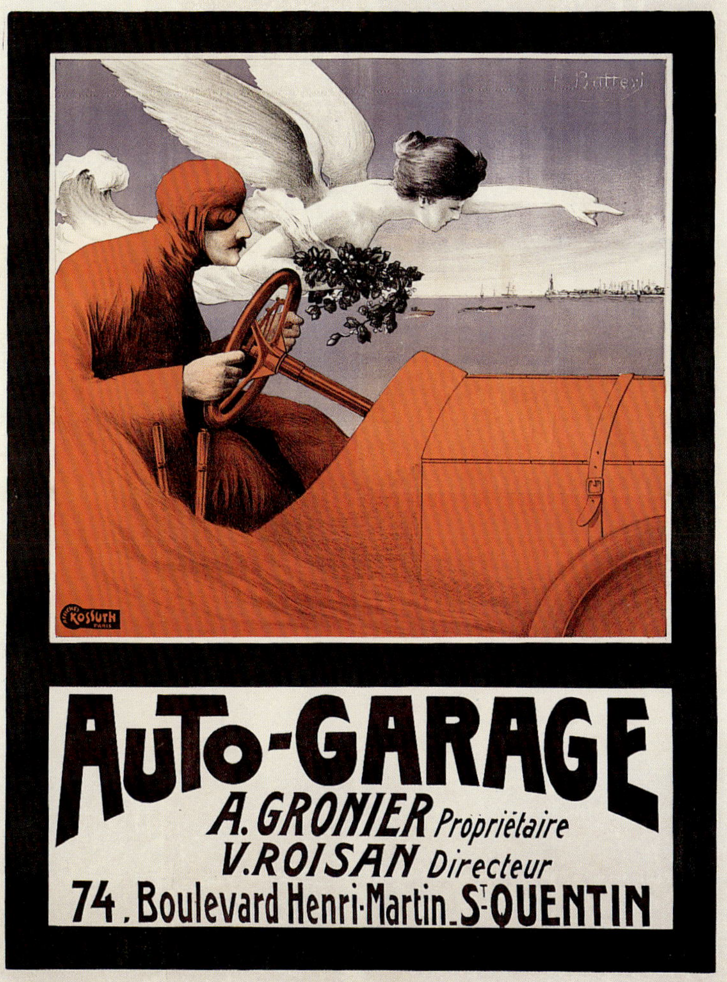

9

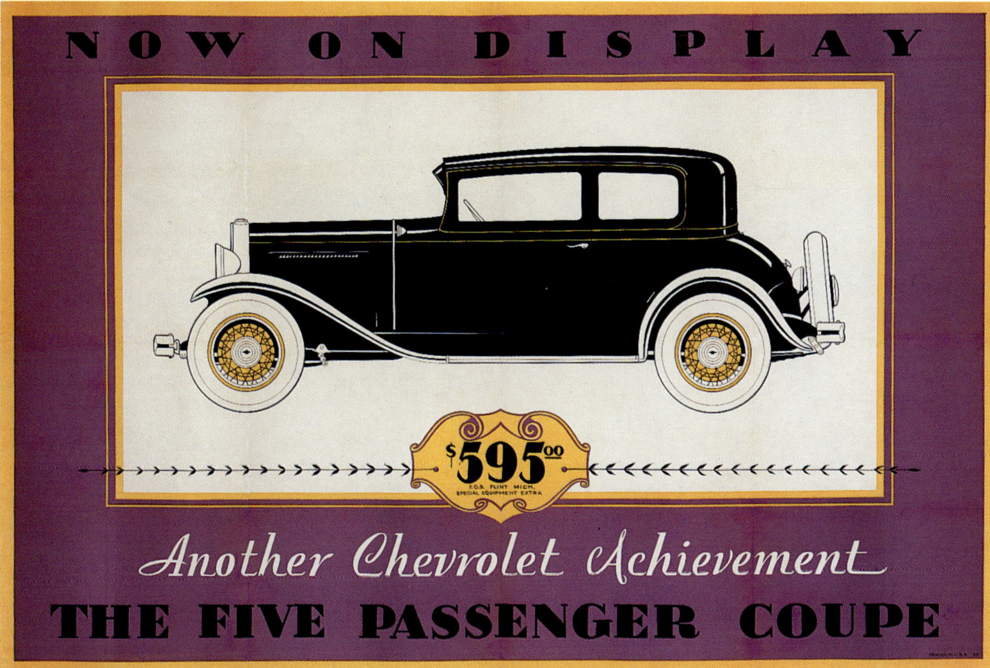

7

ALBERTO BIANCHI (1882-1969)

8. Fiat/Ardita. 1933.
77 x 108^{3}/$_{4}$ in./195.4 x 276 cm
Istituto Italiano d'Arti Grafiche, Bergamo
Cond A–/Unobtrusive folds.
Ref: Fiat, p. 151; Bolaffi, p. 19 (var)
Considering the time period during which this poster was produced, its nationalistic fervor can be somewhat unsettling. However, you have to take into consideration that Mussolini's autarchic policies forced Fiat to reconfigure its plans to become an international presence and to concentrate instead on the domestic market. To that end, the speedy lass in this 4-sheet Bianchi poster makes a "Bold" statement as she whizzes past in her Fiat (a Balilla one has to imagine), urging the viewer to do as she has done—to "get out and conquer" the road. *Rare!*
Est: $4,000-$5,000.

ACHILLE BUTTERI

9. Auto-Garage.
46^{3}/$_{4}$ x 62^{1}/$_{4}$ in./119 x 158 cm
Affiches Kossuth, Paris
Cond B+/Unobtrusive folds.
Doesn't everyone wish that they had a guardian angel who could direct them to a repair shop that would address their automotive issues without taking them to the cleaners? That's precisely the desire addressed in this dramatic Butteri poster for a St. Quentin establishment, with a blanched heavenly messenger pointing the way to the focused, somewhat futuristic crimson motorist—whose car definitely appears to be in need of assistance judging from the fiery red flow cascading from the right wheel well (the monochromatic scheme of car-and-driver, though extremely effective, makes a solid determination less than definitive). A spectacular poster for what most would consider a less-than-spectacular destination. *Rare!*
Est: $15,000-$20,000.

think that this brass band and assemblage of dignitaries had been convened in order to heap accolades upon the Prosper- Lambert four-seater that just so happens to be cruising by. Peculiarly, the words "viens, poupoule, veins" can be seen emanating from one of the horns, which is something of a bizarre incongruity. Does it indicate that the band is playing "Viens, Poupoule," a song popularized in 1902 by Felix Mayol, one of the all-time music hall greats? And if that's the case, how does it apply to either the car or the woman being honored once we translate the title and discover that it means "Come Here Little Whore"? Quite mysterious. Prosper-Lambert was a French auto produced between 1901 and 1905.

An artist's mark appears in the lower-right corner.
Est: $1,200-$1,500.

7. Another Chevrolet Achievement. 1931.
59^{1}/$_{2}$ x 40^{1}/$_{4}$ in./151 x 102.2 cm
Cond B/Restored tears at folds.
What an "Achievement," indeed! $595 may sound like quite a bargain—especially considering that the 1931 five-passenger coupe was sporting a new body style and an inline six-cylinder motor—but shipping from Flint, Michigan, and "Special Equipment"—which included front and rear bumpers—cost extra. *Rare!*
Est: $2,000-$2,500.

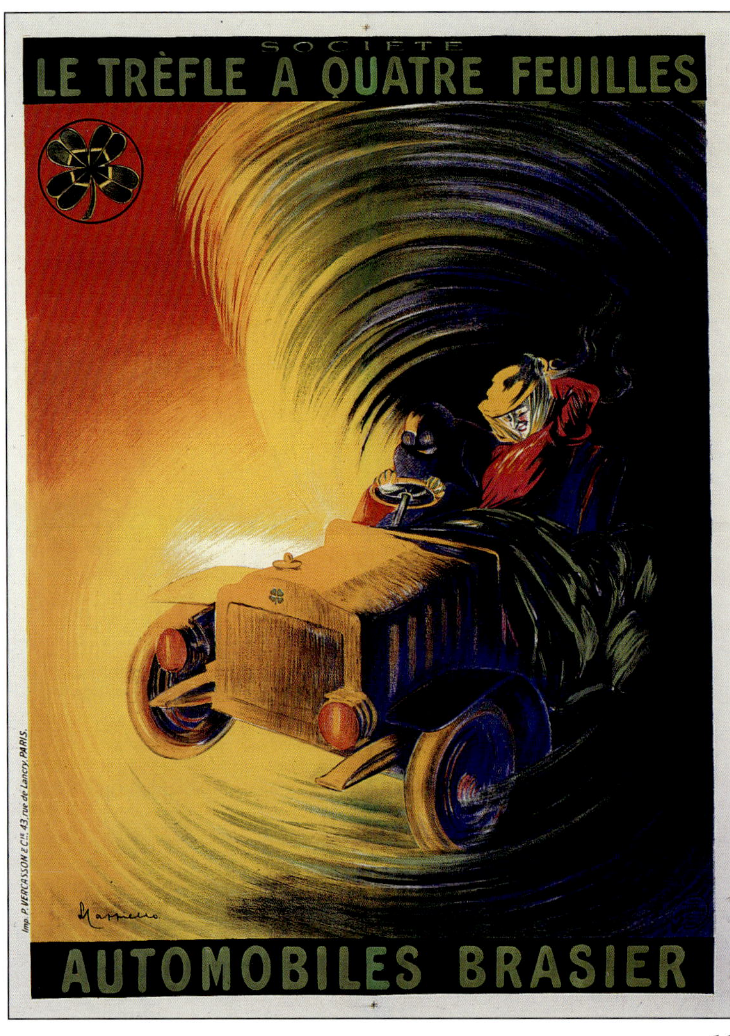

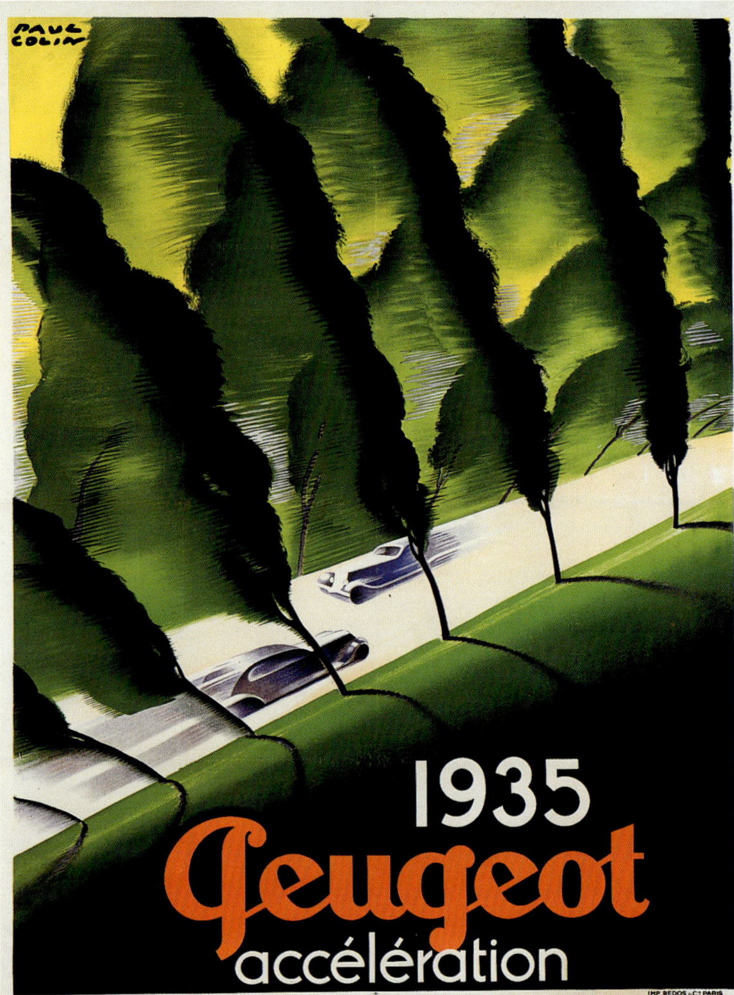

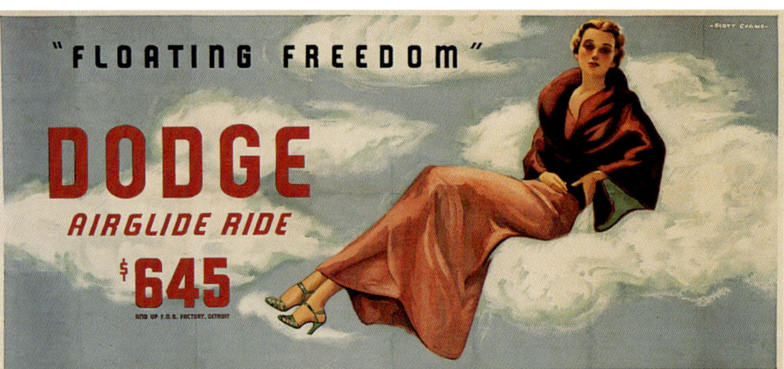

AUTOMOBILE POSTERS (cont'd)

LEONETTO CAPPIELLO (1875-1942)
For other Cappiello posters, see Nos. 190-216.

10. Automobiles Brasier. 1906.
$45^3/_4 \times 62^1/_2$ in./116.2 x 158.8 cm
Imp. P. Vercasson, Paris
Cond B+/Unobtrusive tears at folds; image and colors excellent.
Ref: Cappiello/Rennert, 100; Cappiello, 272; Cappiello/St. Vincent, 4.28;
Auto Show I, 27; Sport à l'Affiche, 26; Wine Spectator, 212; PAI XLI, 135
"There were two basic ways of selling cars in the early days of motoring.
One emphasized class . . . The other pushed speed, as seen in the swirling
cloud of rainbow-hued dust of this Automobiles Brasier poster. H. Brasier
was an engineer in the Paris firm owned by the Mors Brothers. In 1901,
he began to work with Georges Richard—whose trade name 'Le Trèfle à
Quatre Feuilles' is written at top and whose trademark four-leaf clover is
seen in the upper left—to produce cars under the name of Richard-Brasier.
After racing successes in 1904 and the following year, Richard left the firm
to found his own company, Unic. Brasier continued alone in the Paris suburb of Ivry, making good quality, classically conceived cars. After World
War I, production continued, but Brasier had fallen behind the times. The
firm was reorganized in 1926 as Chaigneau-Brasier and ultimately bought
by Delahaye in 1931" (Cappiello/Rennert, p. 90).
Est: $10,000-$12,000.

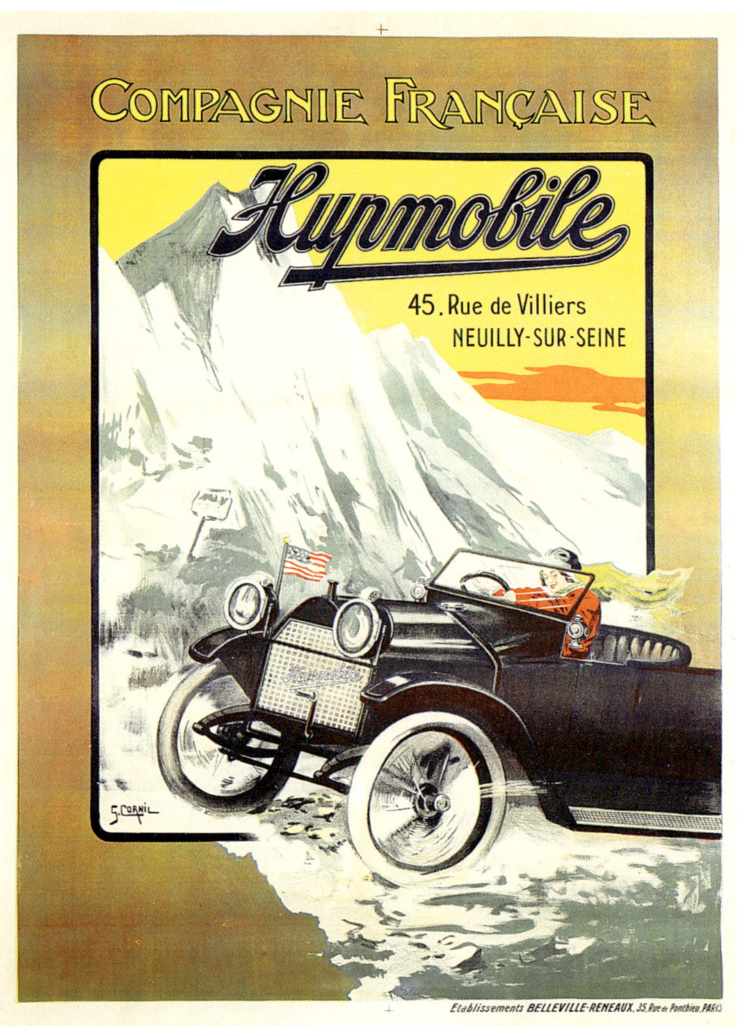

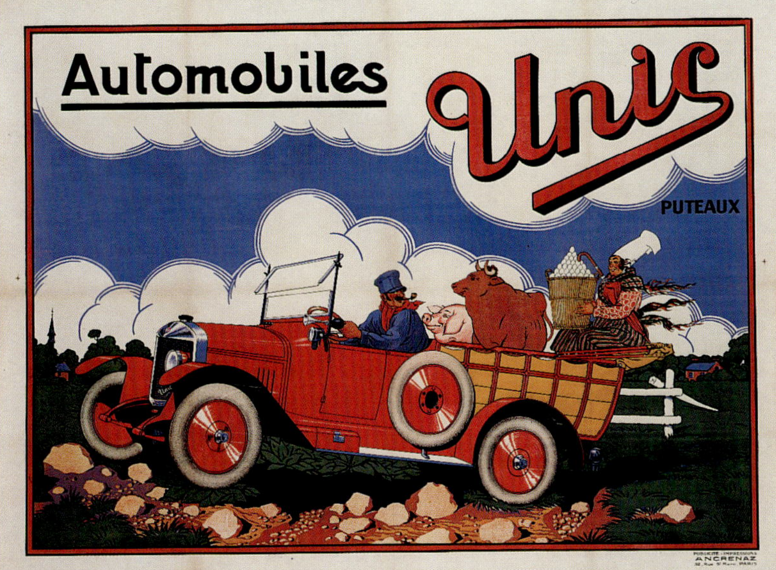

PAUL COLIN (1892-1986)

For other works of Colin, see Nos. 50, 281-288.

11. Peugeot. 1935.
$46^7/_8$ x $63^1/_4$ in./119 x 160.6 cm
Imp. Bedos, Paris
Cond B/Slight tears at folds. Framed.
Ref: Modern Poster, 173; Auto Show I, 79; Art & Auto, p. 181; PAI-XLI, 234
Stately poplars lining country roads like green sentinels are commonplace in France, and Colin makes them appear to bend and sway to the swift passage of the car zipping past them. Does it give us any technical information about Peugeot? No, but we can practically hear the rustle of the leaves stirred up in the car's wake, and that's a much more effective way to convince us of the car's merits.
Est: $10,000-$12,000.

G. CORNIL

12. Hupmobile.
45 x $61^1/_2$ in./114.3 x 156.2 cm
Imp. Belleville-Reneaux, Paris
Cond A–/Unobtrusive tears at horizontal fold.
Hupmobile was an automobile built by the Hupp Motor Company from 1909 thru 1940. The Hupp Motor Company of Detroit, Michigan, started building cars in 1908 and introduced their creation, called the Model 20, to the public at the Detroit Auto Show in February 1909. The company's philosophy was to build a car in the working man's price range. That idea, along with a strong commitment to quality and workmanship, produced many years of dependable, tough and durable machines. Here, a slyly smiling driver bears down on the wheel of her Hupmobile roadster as she enters *into* the icy mountainous landscape of the Cornil poster, demonstrating that there isn't a French condition that the import can't handle. And if the motorist's sassy attitude isn't enough to inform the viewer that she hails from the good old U. S. of A., the flag on her fender ought to do the trick.
Est: $2,500-$3,000.

FERNAND COUDERC

13. Automobiles Unic.
$62^5/_8$ x 47 in./159 x 119.4 cm
Imp. Ancrenaz, Paris
Cond B+/Unobtrusive folds.
Ref: PAI-XXXV, 68
Drawing on a theme that was obviously popular with the Unic automotive higher-ups, Couderc takes Jean Mercier's rural conceptualization (*see* PAI-XX, 68) one step further: Instead of loading up his wood-paneled open touring car with its canvas roof pulled back with a carved wooden farm playset, Couderc places the real deal in his Unic—livestock, precariously piled egg basket and all. And when a commonplace through line in automobile advertising was the inherent friction felt between progress and tradition, it's refreshing to see a designer willing to show that a harmonious balance can easily be achieved. Though the Bibliothèque Nationale credits Couderc with producing more than two-hundred thirty posters during the 1920s and '30s, this is one of only two of his designs to come our way.
Est: $3,000-$4,000.

SCOTT EVANS

14. Dodge. 1934.
60 x 28 in./152.3 x 71.2 cm
Continental Litho. Corp., U. S. A.
Cond B/Slight tears at folds.
"Floating Freedom" isn't usually a catchphrase one would immediately associate with automotive travel, but that's the image that Dodge Motors wanted the public to connect with their 1934 Business Coupe. The two-passenger, two-door model isn't reproduced in this Evans creation—who needs a picture of a car when a cloud-comfy socialite will do quite nicely—but it's important to note that 1934's Coupe was outfitted with Goodyear "Airwheel" tires—hence the "Floating Freedom" of the "Airglide Ride."
Est: $1,500-$1,800.

JULES ABEL FAIVRE (1867-1945)

15. Automobile Club de France. 1904.
$48^3/_8$ x $48^3/_4$ in./123 x 123.7 cm
Littre, Paris
Cond B–/Restored tears, largely at edges.
Ref: Auto Show II, 6; Auto Show III, 39; Art & Auto, p. 42; PAI-VII, 398
Pictured in front of the Grand Palais, an exquisite young lady in ermine goes for a spin to promote the ACF 1904 exposition. Nothing terribly elaborate, but in the incipient days of the automotive age, nothing exceedingly far flung was required to spark public interest. And Faivre executes the task he was assigned with sophisticated aplomb. Primarily an illustrator, Faivre contributed to many Paris magazines including *Assiette au Beurre, Baïonnette, Candide, Figaro, Journal* and *Rire*.
Est: $2,500-$3,000.

13

15

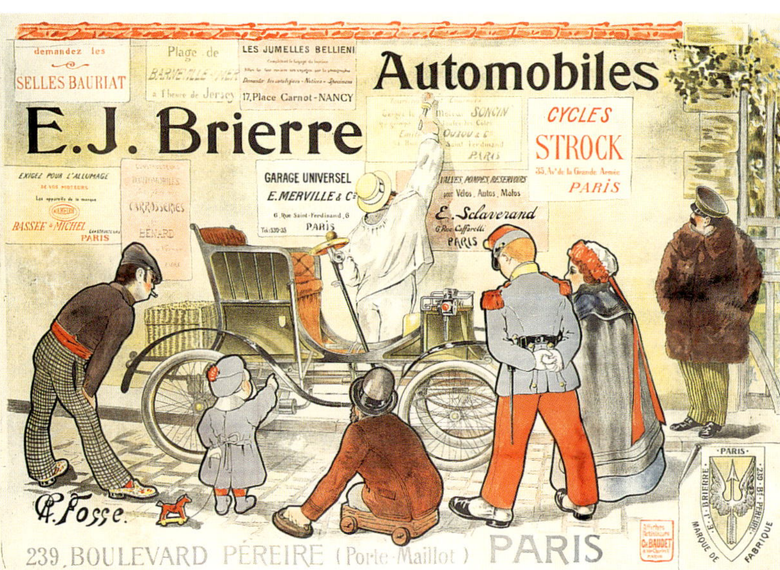

16

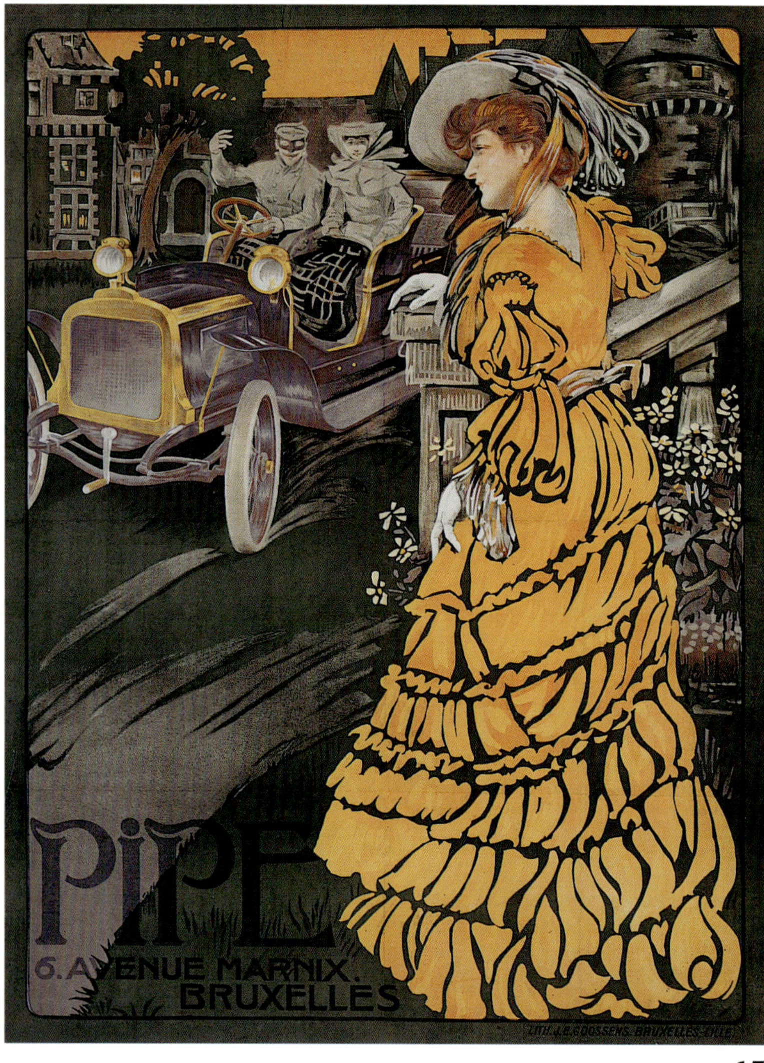

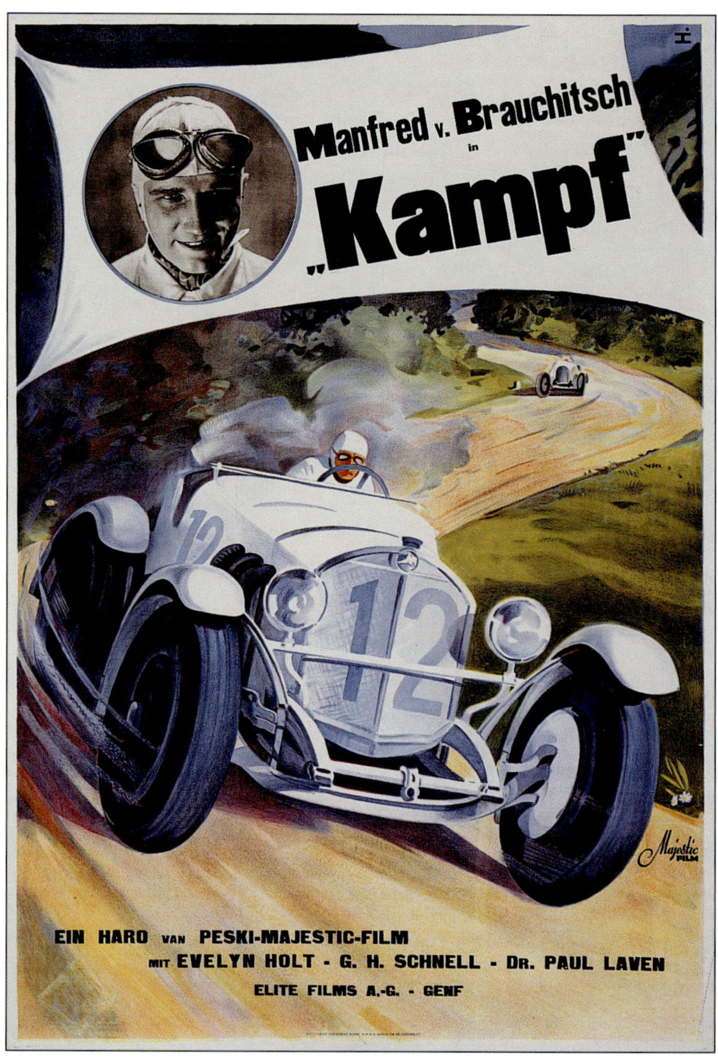

17

20

AUTOMOBILE POSTERS (cont'd)

C. R. FOSSE

16. Automobiles E.J. Brierre.
51$^1/_4$ x 37 in./130.1 x 94 cm
Ch. Baudet, Paris
Cond B/Restored tears, largely at folds.
Ref: Auto Show III, 24
"Today, would one dare to place a crippled man in the center of an advertising poster?" An excellent question, posed in the catalogue that accompanied a 1984 exhibition of automobile posters at the Musée de la Publicité, Paris (p. 59). The answer more likely than not is no, especially seeing as it's a poster for a car. However, the sentiment that Fosse exhibits in his poster for the Brierre machine is that it appeals to everyone, from children to housewives. Also noteworthy is the background wall, plastered with posters for an array of automotive services, as well as a bicycle shop and the Barneville-sur-Mer beach.
Est: $2,500-$3,000.

GEORGES GAUDY (1872-?)

17. Pipe.
34 x 46$^1/_4$ in./86.3 x 117.3 cm
J. E. Goosens, Bruxelles-Lille
Cond B+/Slight tears at folds.
Ref: Auto Show II, 16; Wallonie, 80;
    Affiche/Belgique, 53; PAI-XXIX, 15
Gaudy was a Belgian painter, magazine illustrator and posterist whose masterful handling of bicycle and automotive subjects reflected his own interests. His image here for Pipe, a major Belgian auto company of the era, founded in 1898, is nothing short of spectacular. A handsome woman and her dress—the color of the sunset—take center stage. Her presence communicates the quality, elegance and refinement Gaudy wishes the viewer to associate with the auto. This allows the "merchandise" to pass in the background in a non-

commercial role; the two are linked by the driver's friendly wave. The elaborate dress is actually unstructured—a series of unconnected areas of color—and the text sits down at the bottom so as to not distract. The whole effect is beautiful and altogether compelling.
Est: $6,000-$8,000.

R. GAUTIER

18. Alcyon. 1906.
42$^7/_8$ x 58$^3/_8$ in./109 x 148.3 cm
Imp. G. Elleaume, Paris
Cond A.
"Alcyon" is the Latin word from which "halcyon" is derived. But things don't appear that serene in this Gautier scene, what with one motorist utterly befuddled by his vehicular breakdown and another chap leading a horse that doesn't look as if it would ever entertain the idea of being mounted. However, if you're wise enough to purchase an Alcyon—we have to assume that this applies to the manufacturer's bikes as well seeing as the two cyclists have no problem keeping up with the red *voiturette*—it's easy going all the way. That doesn't mean that driving in an Alcyon will make you a better person judging from the callous disregard being displayed by the passing passenger towards the other driver's flustered state.
Est: $2,000-$2,500.

GEO HAM (Georges Hamel, 1900-1972)

19. Horsepower. ca. 1933.
13 x 9$^1/_2$ in./33 x 24.2 cm
Hand-signed gouache-and-crayon drawing. Framed.
During the early days of automotive advertising, the confrontation betwixt the then-newfangled car and the traditional trusty steed was a commonplace lithographic motif. However, by the time that Ham executed this

marvelous drawing of a country lane encounter featuring a woman out for a spin in her Renault and a gentleman enjoying a gallop around the estate, there's less animosity and more respectful acceptance—indeed the rider appears to be saluting the touring car as it passes. Granted, the scales may have tipped forever in favor of the internal-combustion engine, but that doesn't mean that rivalries need to be uncivilized.
Est: $3,000-$4,000.

ALFRED HERRMANN (1884-1962)

20. "Kampf". 1932.
37$^1/_4$ x 55$^1/_4$ in./94.6 x 140.3 cm
August Scherl, Berlin
Cond A.
Fasten your seat belts, ladies and gentlemen, because you're in for a "Battle"! The Herrmann advertisement makes it perfectly clear that a high-octane rivalry takes place on the race track, but it also extends into the personal lives of the drivers, old friends and rivals, with one's new wife being the old flame of the other. Perhaps the picture's alternate title sums up the flick more accurately: "Rivals of the Curve." Filmed at the actual Avus and Nürburgring race tracks, "Kampf" is probably most memorable for its star: Manfred von Brauchitsch (1905-2003), an actual Grand Prix racer, who drove for the factory Mercedes-Benz racing team in their famous Nazi state-backed "Silver Arrows." Despite winning forty-five races over a six-year span in the 1930s, von Brauchitsch was nicknamed "Der Pechvogel" (roughly translated: "Mr. Bad Luck") for the races he lost, his hard-driving impetuosity and his imperious Prussian officer-class mien. When he died at the age of ninety-seven, he was the last surviving winner of a prewar Grand Prix. Best known for his "Frau im Mond" poster of 1929 (*see* PAI-XXXII, 351), Alfred Herrmann created a number of distinguished posters and publicity

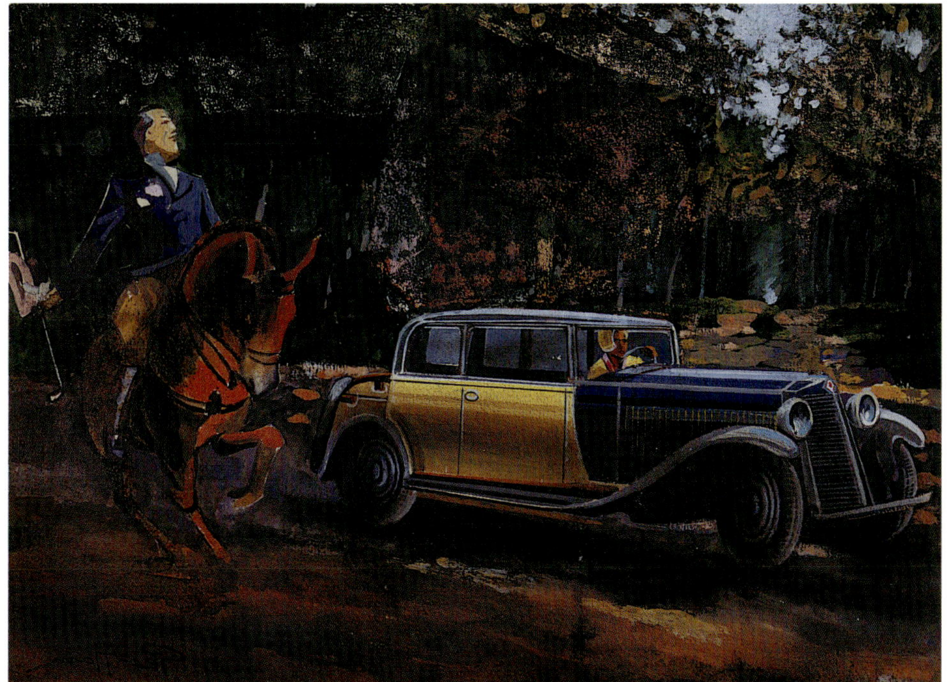

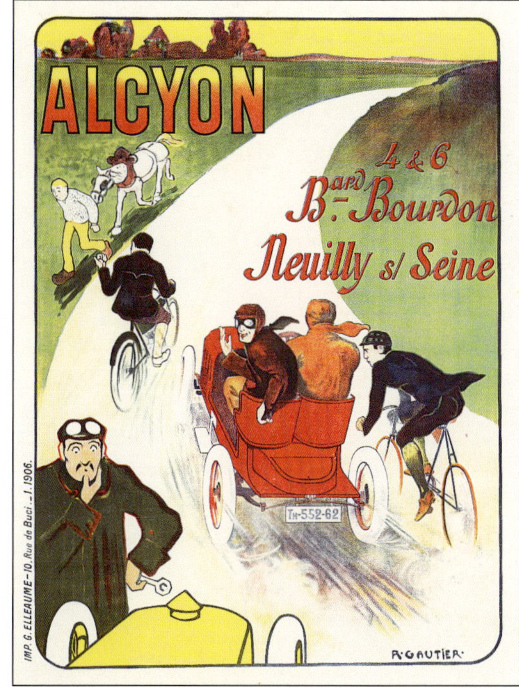

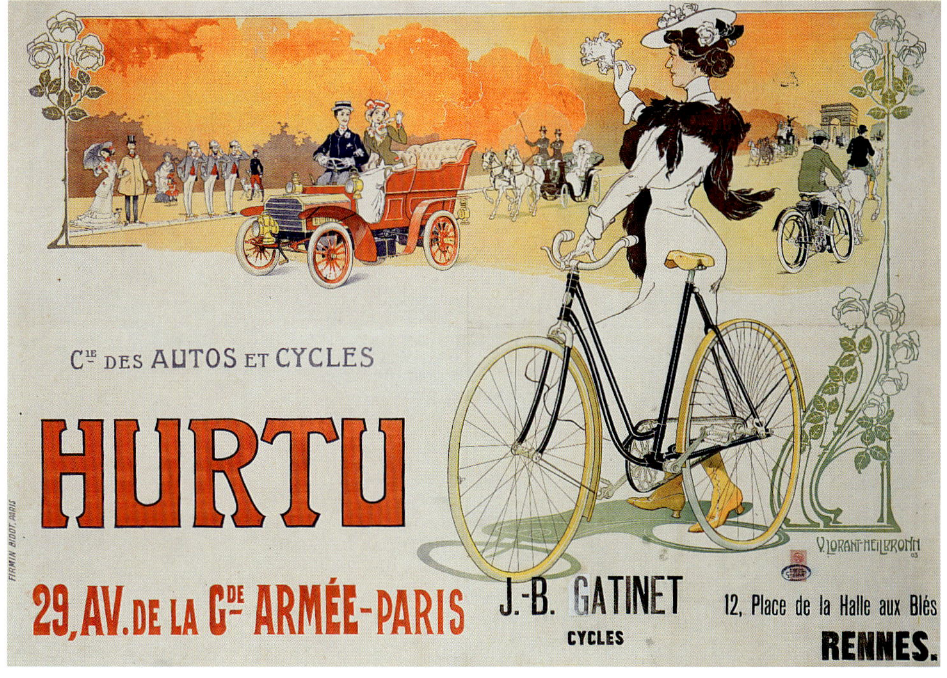

material for the UFA film distribution company from 1927 to 1939. After 1946, he taught at the Berlin School for Book and Graphic Design. *Rare!*
Est: $7,000-$9,000.

VINCENT LORANT-HEILBRONN (1874–?)

21. Hurtu. 1903.
$59^1/_4$ x $42^3/_4$ in./150.3 x 108.6 cm
Firmin Didot, Paris
Cond B/Slight tears and stains at folds and edges.
Ref: Petite Reine, 38; Auto Show I, 19; PAI-XVII, 56
An irresistible street scene of Gay Paris, the Champs-Élysées thronging with colorful characters, like the trio of curbside dandies for example, and amicably competing modes of transport, from carriages and coaches to motor bikes and people on horseback, as well as those fortunate enough to possess Hurtu bicycles or automobiles. Within a blossoming Art Nouveau border, a female cyclist waves her hanky with decorous vivacity, her friend returning the greeting from the passenger seat of her Hurtu, a firm which, like many others, began manufacturing bicycles and then added automobiles. Lorant-Heilbronn began his career as a posterist for various Paris theaters and movie halls. When films came along, he added duties as set designer and assistant director to his graphic responsibilities.
Est: $2,500-$3,000.

E. CHARLE LUCAS

22. La Marque George Richard.
$54^7/_8$ x $77^1/_2$ in./139.4 x 196.8 cm
Imp. Charles Verneau, Paris
Cond A–/Unobtrusive tear at bottom edge.
Life on the boulevard is as pleasant as can be with George Richard. Lucas loads the scene with hazy sentimentality, an idyllic reminiscence of events unfolding right before our eyes. "Georges Richard was one of quite a number of bicycle manufacturers who were hurriedly adding automobiles as a sideline around the turn of the century; within a few years, the sideline would become the main, or as here, the only product of the company" (Gold, p. 56). And of course, the four-leaf clover, the very symbol of good fortune used by the Georges Richard bicycle manufacturers as their logo, is included in the design's lower-right hand corner. Lucas, who signed all his posters E. Charle Lucas, was born Charles-Louis Lucas. Unfortunately, little else is known about him.
Est: $3,000-$3,500.

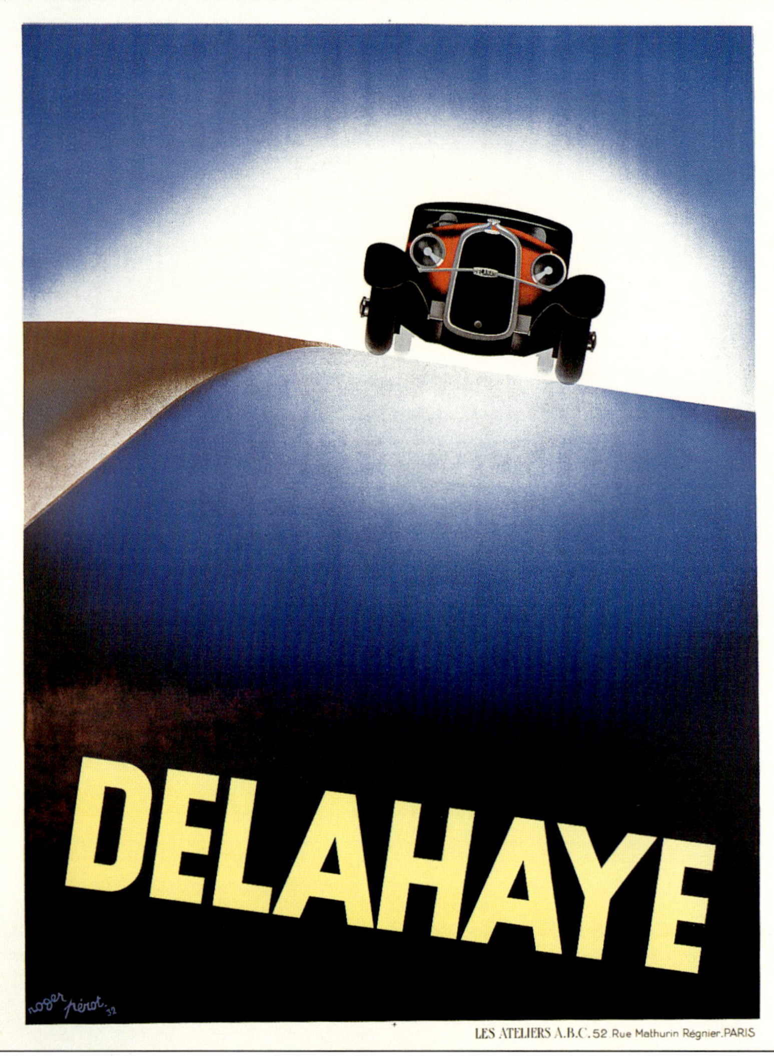

25

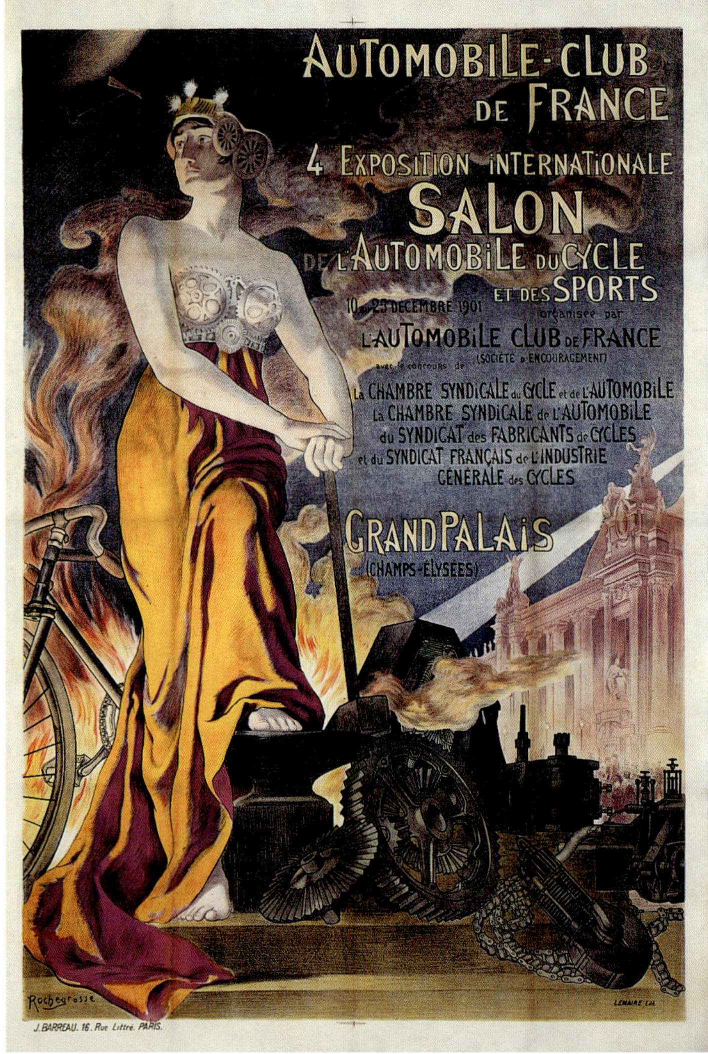

28

AUTOMOBILE POSTERS (cont'd)

MISTI (Ferdinand Mifliez, 1865-1923)
For other works by Misti, see Nos. 430-432.

23. Cycles & Automobiles Cottereau. ca. 1900.
$14^1/4$ x $19^5/8$ in./36.3 x 50 cm
Imp. P. Vercasson, Paris
Cond B/Slight tears at paper edges.
Ref: Phillips, I, 412 (var)
With the horrors of horse-and-buggy transportation haunting the background of this Misti design like the shadowy specters of an age that firmly belongs in the past, a threesome of prescient travelers hit the happy open road aboard their Cottereau machines. Louis Cottereau, born in Angers, was a speed-demon cyclist possessed of an extraordinary will that enabled him to prevail in spite of his short stature. Like Griffon and the Belgian firm Delin, Cottereau used his factory to turn out motorized vehicles as well as bicycles. Misti was a busy poster artist who, between 1894 and 1914, designed more than 100 images—many for bicycles, as well as department stores, railroads, publishing clients and the Neuilly fair. *This is the smaller format, with the local dealer's address handwritten in the blank box at bottom center.*
Est: $800-$1,000.

24. Cleveland Car. ca. 1900.
$21^3/4$ x 59 in./55.2 x 150 cm
Imp. Vercasson, Paris
Cond B+/Unobtrusive folds.
Ref: PAI-XXXIV, 174
Elmer E. Sperry of Cleveland was instrumental in establishing the electric street railway in that city. His early inventions in the 1890s included the electric arc lamp and electricity operated mining equipment, with which he made a fortune. He built his first electric carriage in 1898 and in 1899 he contracted with the Cleveland Machine Screw Company to manufacture his automobile for him. The resulting Cleveland Car had

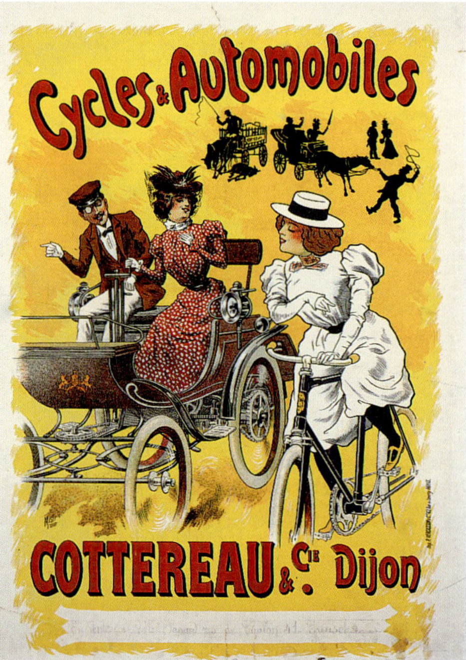

23

lamps operated by push button and a single lever for controlling the movement of the automobile. The lever was moved sideways to indicate direction, pushed downward for speed and pulled upward to remove the current and apply the brakes. The Car was ultimately known as the "Sperry" in the United States and was exported under the name "Cleveland Car." Misti, in this 2-sheet poster, shows an evening ride in the electric car beneath a midnight blue sky filled with shooting stars.
Est: $2,000-$2,500.

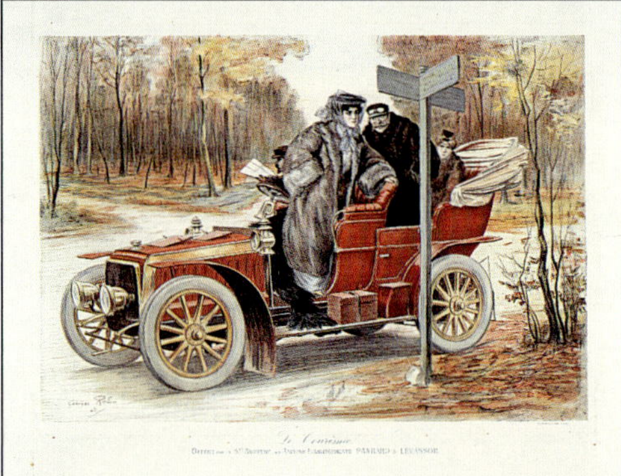

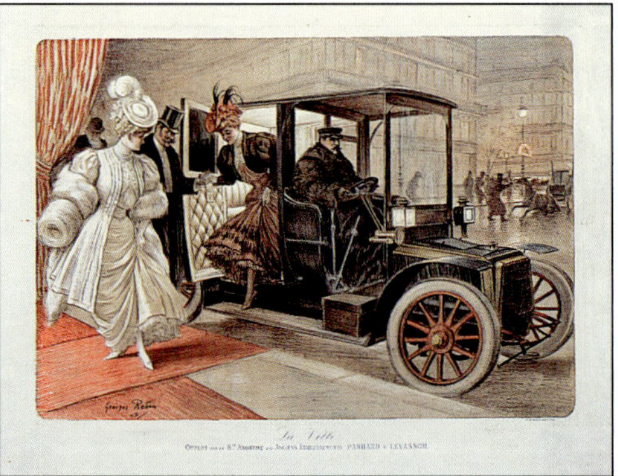

26

ROGER PEROT (1908-1976)

25. Delahaye. 1932.
$47^1/4$ x 63 in./120 x 160 cm
Ateliers A.B.C., Paris
Cond A.
Ref: Auto Show I, 72; Deco Affiches, p. 71; PAI-XXXII, 135

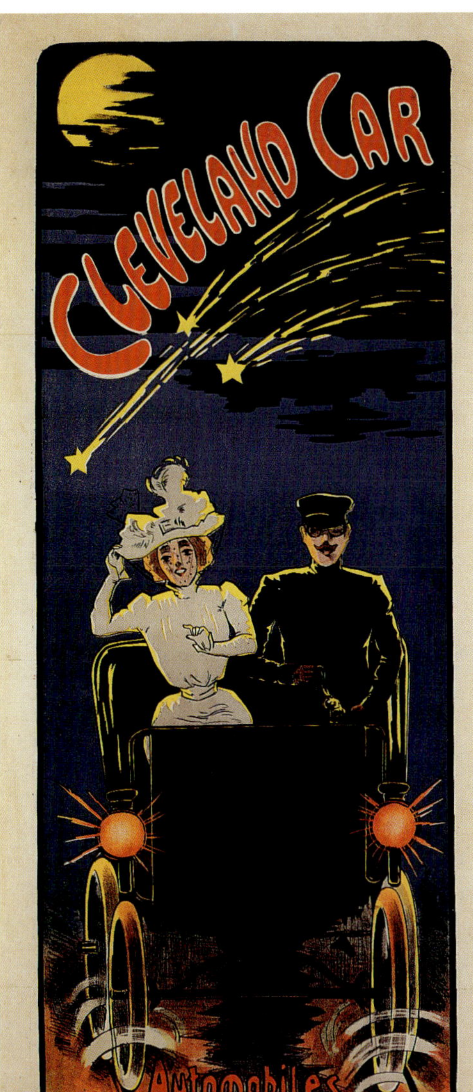

24

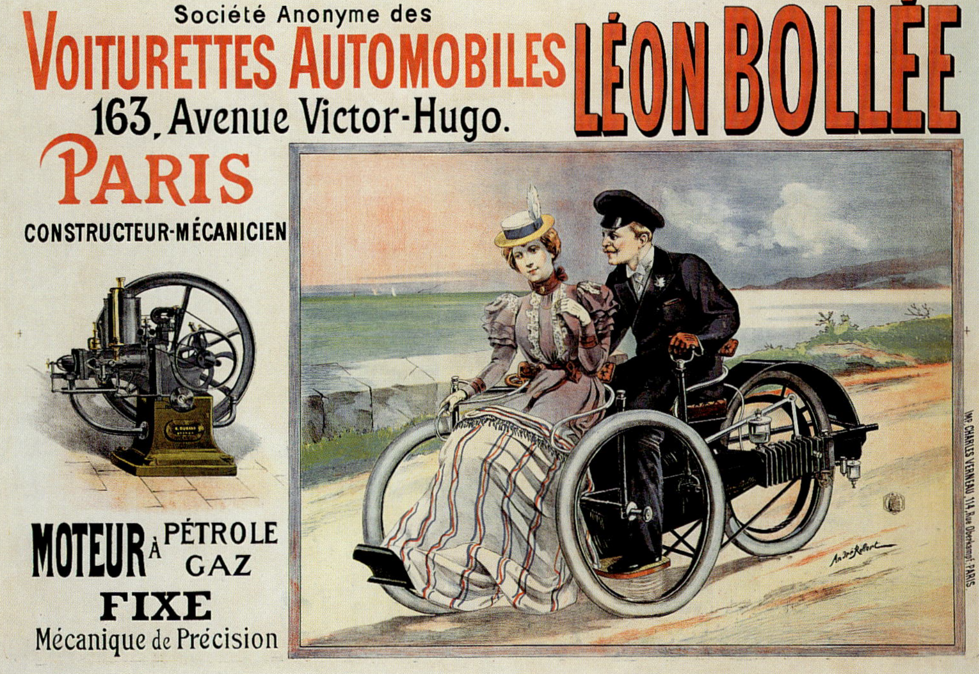

27

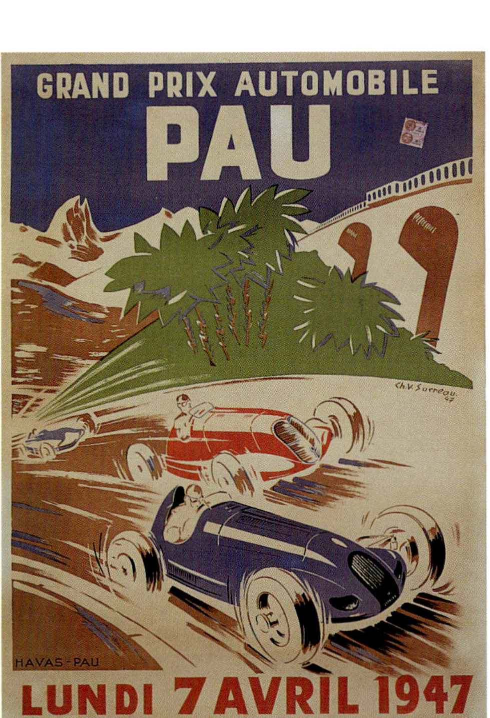

29

The Delahaye coming over the horizon makes for one of the most perfect automobile posters ever created. (The design was so popular that it was reprinted three years later with few changes other than color and an updated grille.) The positioning of the type parallel with the horizon line is especially effective. Although the public most fondly remembers Delahaye as a fast French sporting and racing car of the late 1930s, the marque actually had a sixty-year span beginning in 1894. It was dropped only in 1954 when the company was taken over by Hotchkiss, a truck maker. Little is known of Pérot, an architect who, regrettably, produced only a few posters.
Est: $7,000-$9,000.

GEORGES REDON (1869-1943)

26. Panhard & Levassor: Two Decorative Panels. 1905.
Each: 29³/₄ x 23¹/₄ in./75.5 x 59 cm
Imp. Minot, Paris
Cond B+/Slight tears and stains in borders.
Ref: PAI-XLI, 492 (b only)
These two Redon panels make one thing crystal clear: whether you're out for a night on the town or tooling around the countryside (with a difference of opinion as to which way to head), Panhard & Levassor makes the vehicle to suit your transportational needs. A charter member of the Salon d'Automne, Redon employed a lighthearted touch that showed up in his contributions to Parisian humor magazines as well as his paintings and posters.
Est: $3,000-$4,000. (2)

ANDRÉ ROBERT

27. Voiturettes Automobiles Léon Bollée. 1896.
55¹/₂ x 39 in./141 x 99 cm
Imp. Charles Verneau, Paris
Cond A–/Restored tears at paper edges.
Ref: Auto Show III, 5; PAI-XXXI, 116
Bollée was one of the mechanics and machine shop owners who, in the days before mass production was introduced into the auto industry, offered to build custom bodies for the early enthusiasts. In this three-wheeler, the fastidiously-dressed passenger is perched semi-comfortably *in front* of her chauffeur. And though the dangling blanket and lack of a safety belt might make the modern motorist a bit uneasy, it's an excellent portrayal of the devil-may-care naivety of the early automotive age.
Est: $4,000-$5,000.

GEORGES ROCHEGROSSE (1859-1938)

28. Automobile Club de France/4eme Exposition. 1901.
50¹/₈ x 76 in./127.5 x 193 cm
J. Barreau, Paris
Cond B+/Slight tears and stains at folds and egdes.
Ref: Auto Show I, 13; PAI-XLII, 31
This is the larger format poster for the fourth ACF expo held at the Grand Palais, and as was the case with Rochegrosse's previous design for the third vehicular concourse (*see* PAI-XXVI, 42), an allegorical figure once again represents technical achievement. Since at this time automobiles were still being made mostly as a sideline by bicycle manufacturers, both the expo and the poster emphasized the relation. Rochegrosse honed his illustrative technique on the books of his era's literary giants: Theophile Gautier, Gustave Flaubert, Victor Hugo, and others. He was also house artist for the magazine *La Vie Parisienne*.
Est: $7,000-$9,000.

CH. V. SURREAU

29. Pau/Grand Prix Automobile. 1947.
30⁷/₈ x 43¹/₄ in./78.5 x 109.7 cm
Cond B+/Unobtrusive tears at folds.
With a street circuit facing the Pyrénées-Atlantiques mountain range, the Pau Grand Prix is a mythic proving ground where some of the greatest legends of motor sport have been written, the first race to have been named "Grand Prix" with a circuit that has not changed its layout since its beginning in 1930. All told, Pau has played host to sixty races and Surreau promotes the 1947 running of that event with a design that unabashedly blends all of the elements that make the contest unique. This particular race marks the resumption of the competition after the hostilities of World War II.
Est: $3,000-$4,000.

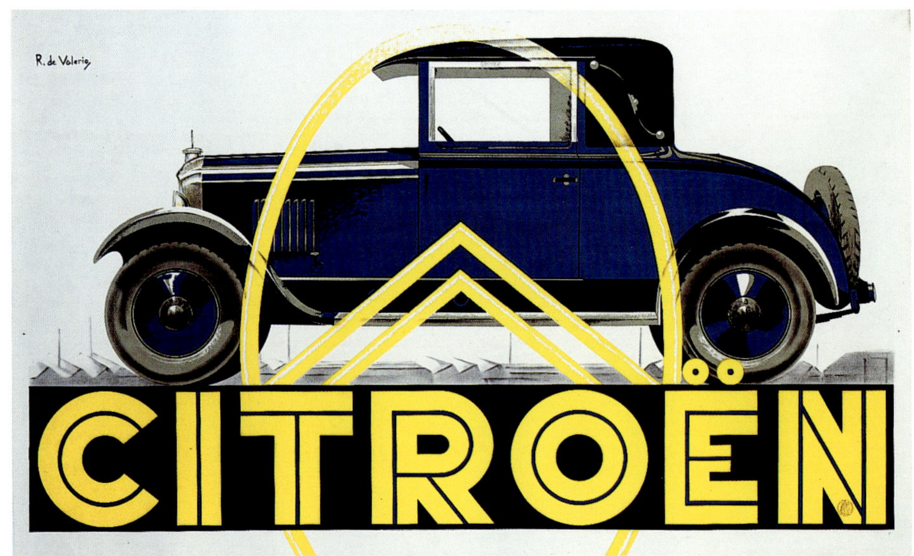

30

AUTOMOBILE POSTERS (cont'd)

ROGER DE VALERIO (1896-1951)

30. Citroën. ca. 1932.
63 x 38³/4 in./160 x 98.9 cm
Cond A.
Ref: Die Buggatis, p. 479; PAI-XXIX, 34
The electric blue of the the sedan, along with the equally stunning gold of the lettering and insignia, make for an uncluttered, eye-catching design. De Valerio, a native of Lille, worked in Paris—principally at the Devambez and Perceval agencies, whose clients, apart from Citroën, included Air France and Chrysler. He also designed over 2,000 sheet-music covers for music publisher-producer Salabert.
Est: $1,700-$2,000.

RENÉ VINCENT (1879-1936)

For another poster of Vincent, see No. 579.

31. Peugeot. ca. 1925.
62¹/2 x 46³/4 in./158.7 x 119 cm
Imp. Draeger, Paris
Cond B+/Slight tears at folds and edges.
Ref: Graphicar, 312; Auto Posters, 27; PAI-XXXIX, 518
Vincent virtually defined the snob appeal in automobile advertising, with his sleek cars, elegant women and all the trappings of good taste. He worked for a number of top magazines, from *La Vie Parisienne* to *Saturday Evening Post*, and created many posters for the Au Bon Marché department store. He adds some zip to this front view of the latest cabriolet in the Peugeot line with a pair of awe-struck, even somewhat fearful turbaned exotics. A simple concept, but a surefire eye-catcher.
Est: $3,500-$4,000.

WEILUC (Lucien-Henri Weil, 1873-1947)

32. "Bayard." 1908.
62³/4 x 47³/4 in./161.9 x 121.3 cm
Société Nouvelle d'Art et Décoration, Paris
Cond B/Tears and stains at folds and edges.
Ref: Auto Show II, 22; PAI-XXXI, 124
Clément was a hugely successful bicycle in France in the late 1800s, but in 1903, one of the family scions, Adolphe Clément, set up an auto workshop in the town of Mezieres. There is a statue in the town to Bayard, a legendary knight who supposedly saved the city from an invasion in the 16th century, and Clément chose to name his car after him. He operated the factory until 1922. Weiluc quite frequently took a humorous approach to posters for clients who appreciated it; here, he makes the Bayard fly through the air with the greatest of ease and, by gum, it works.
Est: $3,000-$4,000.

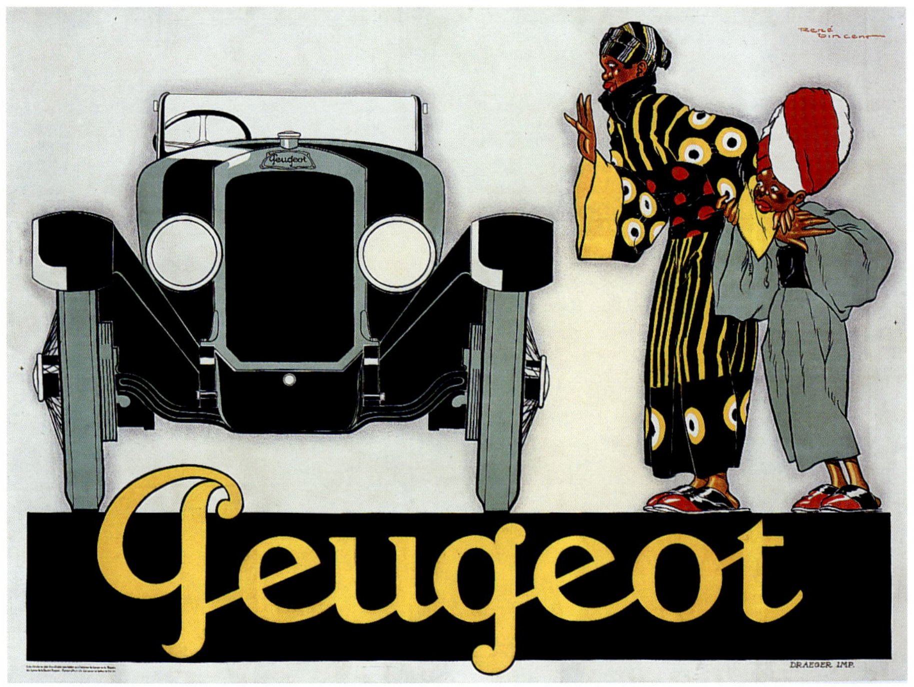

31

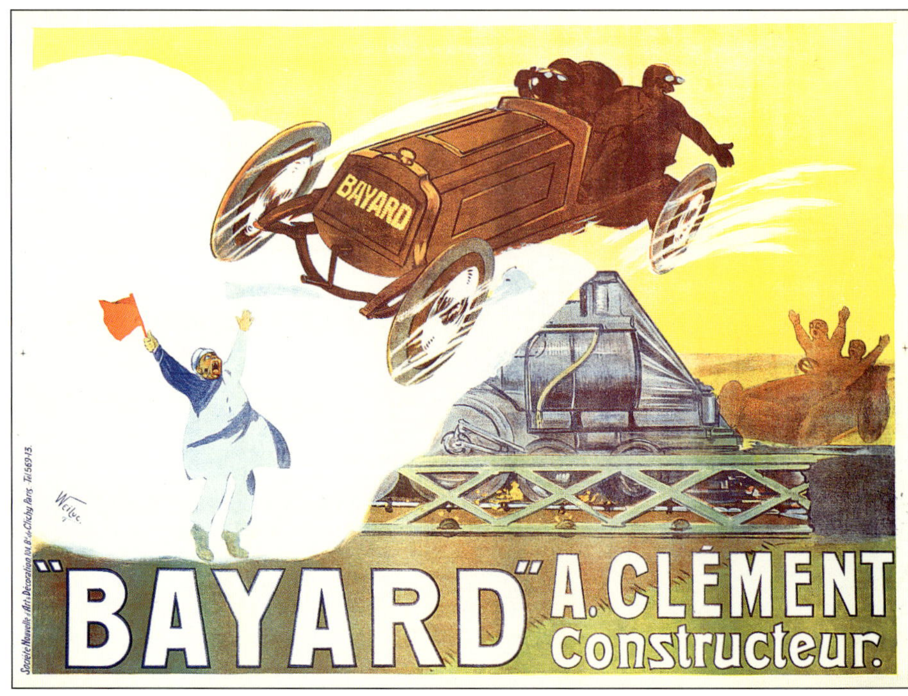

32

MONACO GRAND PRIX

The Monaco Grand Prix is the most glamorous Formula One race in the world. It is unique in its combination of state-of-the-art machines and its picturesque—even quaint—setting: its 100-lap route, unaltered over the years, goes through the ancient streets of the tiny principality, around hairpin turns and along hair-raising cliffs and spectacular coastal roads. Naturally, it's an attraction that has every hotel in Monaco and the surrounding region booked months in advance.

The Automobile Club of Monaco had been holding annual rallies before 1928, but the success of the 1929 inaugural Grand Prix was huge: the course demanded immense skill and stamina from the drivers, and strength and staying power from the cars.

The annual race was cancelled in 1938 because of a dispute over a guaranteed starting fee, and in 1939 the threat of war took care of the event; thus there was an eleven-year gap before the race was resumed in 1948.

All Grand Prix posters are quite rare and much in demand by racing and poster collectors alike. They all catch the excitement of the event and, in most cases, they also provide a fine scenic backdrop.

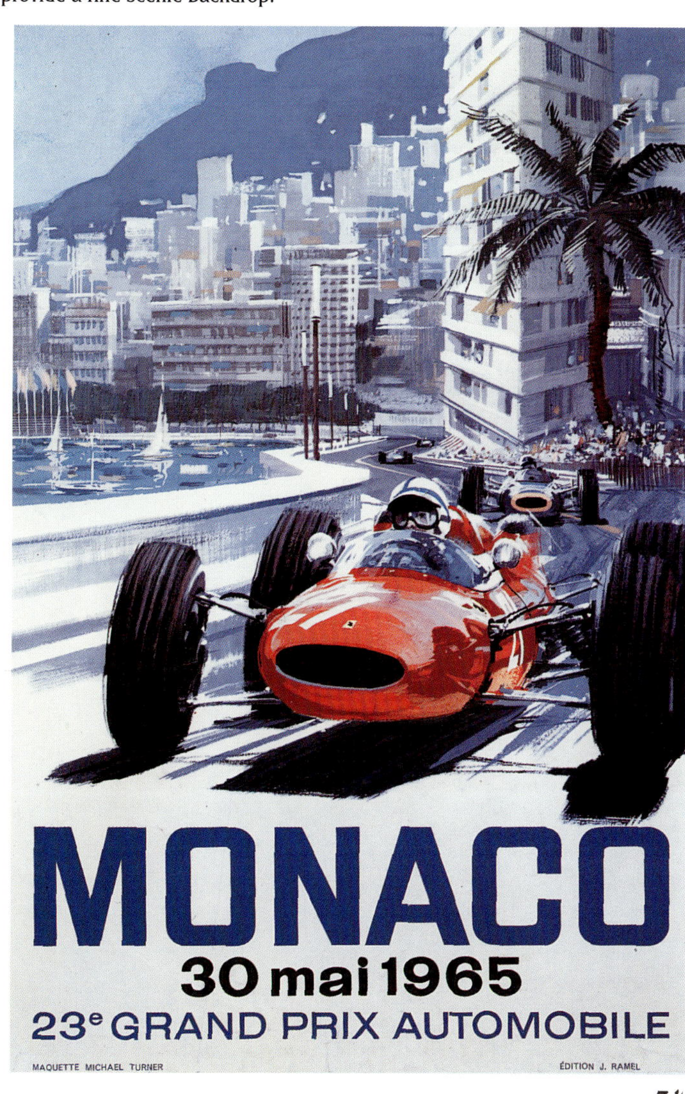

33

34

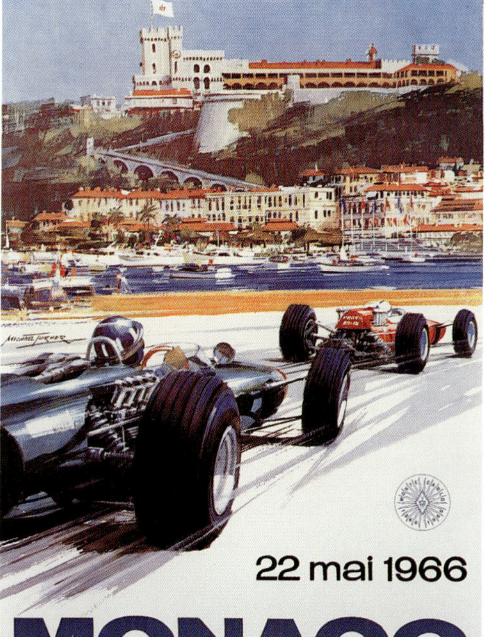

35

33. 22e grand prix/10 Mai 1964.
Artist: **J. May**
15 x 23$^{1}/_{8}$ in./38 x 58.7 cm
J. Ramel, Nice
Cond A.
The speed of the Formula 1 racer is so extreme that car and driver appear to be more liquid than solid, transformed by acceleration into an entirely different form of velocity-based matter altogether as it heads towards the heart of the principality. Graham Hill won the Grand Prix in 1964 as a member of the British Racing Motor team. Hill, the only driver to win the so-called Triple Crown of motor racing—the Indianapolis 500, the Twenty-Four Hours of Le Mans and the Monaco Grand Prix—described his life behind the wheel thus: "I'm an artist, the track is my canvas, and the car is my brush."
Est: $1,400-$1,700.

34. Monaco Grand Prix 1965.
Artist: **Michael Turner (1934-)**
15$^{1}/_{4}$ x 23$^{1}/_{4}$ in./38.8 x 59 cm
J. Ramel, Nice
Cond B/Restored tears at edges.
Ref: Ferrari, p. 300; PAI-XLII, 34

A number of the famous Monaco Grand Prix races were brought to pulse-pounding life via the brush of this highly talented draftsman. All show the racers speeding along from a vantage point that displays the way the course wends its way through the city. The 1965 race featured the debut of the Honda team from Japan, and a surprise success of the BRM V8, which won with Graham Hill at the wheel. Turner created all the posters from 1965 to 1970; however, his design for 1969 was only used as the event's program cover.
Est: $2,000-$2,500.

35. Monaco Grand Prix 1966.
Artist: **Michael Turner (1934-)**
15$^{5}/_{8}$ x 23$^{7}/_{8}$ in./39.6 x 60.7 cm
J. Ramel, Nice
Cond A.
Ref: PAI-XLI, 571
Turner keeps the racing excitement revved-up and the location sun-baked and swank in his poster promoting the 1966 Monaco Grand Prix. As was the case the year before, the BRM V8 took the checkered flag, this time piloted by Great Britain's Jackie Stewart.
Est: $2,000-$2,500.

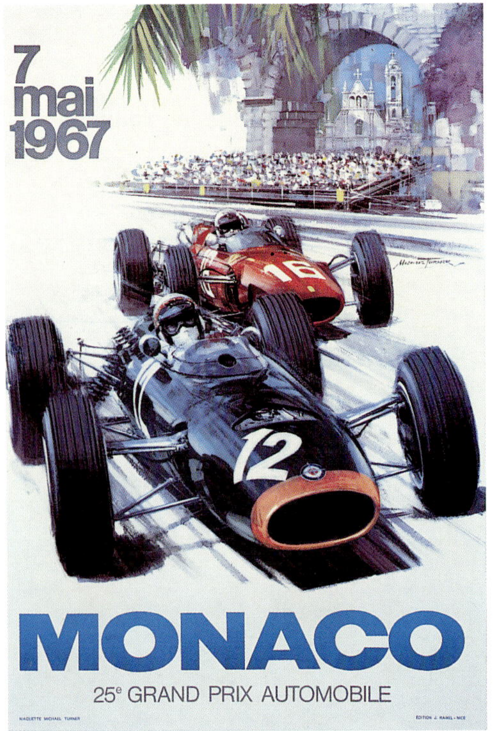

36

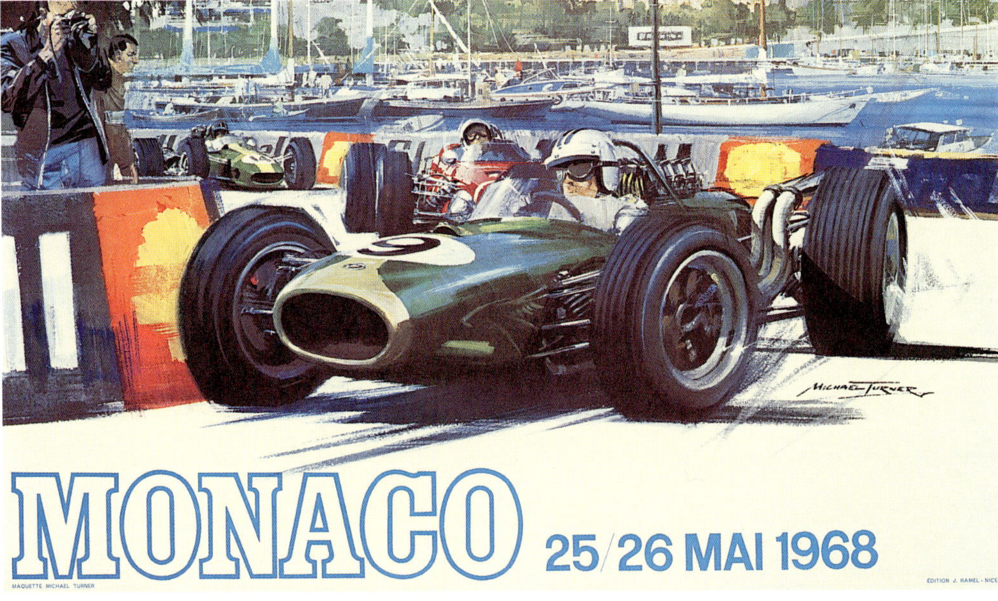

37

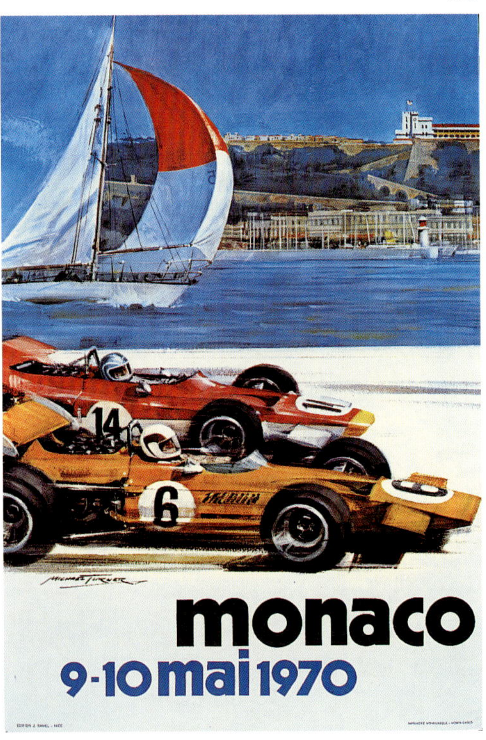

38

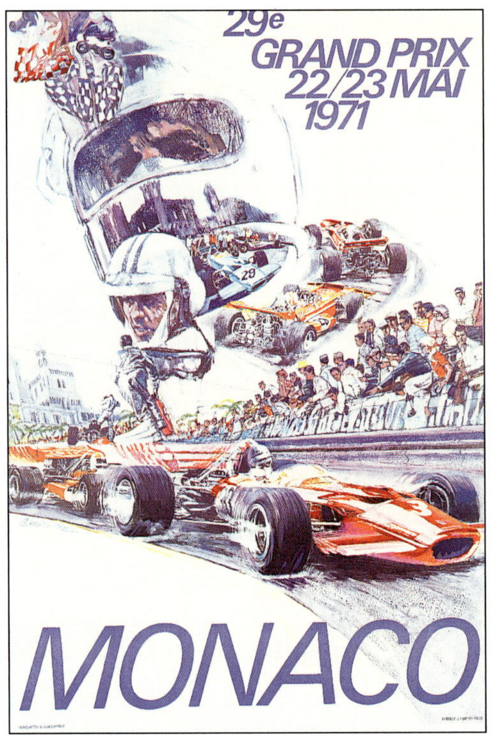

39

40

36. Monaco Grand Prix 1967.
Artist: **Michael Turner (1934-)**
15⁷/₈ x 23⁷/₈ in./40.2 x 60.7 cm
Edition J. Ramel, Nice
Cond A.
Ref: PAI-XLI, 572
For the twenty-fifth running of the road race held at the independent Riviera principality, Turner contrasts his sleek torpedo-shaped racers off of the city's 19th-century Byzantine-style cathedral, upping the tradition ante without forcing the issue. The race was won by Denny Hulme (1936-1992), who took the wheel for the Brabham Racing Organization, the only Australian team ever to carry a Formula One World Champion to victory.
Est: $1,500-$2,000.

37. Monaco 1968.
Artist: **Michael Turner (1934-)**
23³/₄ x 15¹/₂ in./60.4 x 39.4 cm
Edition J. Ramel, Nice
Cond A–/Slight tear on lower-right edge.
Ref: PAI-XXVI, 8 (var)
In 1968, British racing legend Graham Hill would take the checkered flag in a Lotus-Ford, a feat he accom-

plished a total of five times during the course of his illustrious career. Turner's poster features a Cooper in the lead, though as previously stated that vehicle would not cross the finish line first.
Est: $1,000-$1,200.

38. Monaco/9·10 mai 1970.
Artist: **Michael Turner (1934-)**
15³/₄ x 23⁵/₈ in./40 x 60 cm
Imp. Monégasque, Monte Carlo
Cond A.
Ref: PAI-XXVI, 8 (var)
The 1970 race provided down-to-the-wire excitement as Jack Brabham led the entire race only to go into the bales two turns from the finish line. He regained control of his vehicle, but not in time to catch Jochen Rindt, who took the checkered flag.
Est: $1,000-$1,200.

39. Monaco/29e Grand Prix 1971.
Artist: **Steve Carpenter (1943–)**
15⁵/₈ x 23⁷/₈ in./39.7 x 60.6 cm
J. Ramel, Nice
Cond A.
The vignettes called upon by Carpenter to illustrate the entire running of a Monaco Grand Prix race come off as somewhat surreal in combination with the more action-oriented aspects of the design. He also makes it clear just how perilously close spectators were to the

action once upon a time. The 1971 race was won by Jackie Stewart in a Tyrrell-Ford. Stewart, nicknamed "The Flying Scot," is a three-time Formula One racing champion, well-known in the United States as a commentator of racing television broadcasts where his Scottish accent made him a distinctive presence.
Est: $800-$1,000.

40. Monaco/37e Grand Prix. 1979.
Artist: **Alain Giampaoli (1946–)**
15¹/₂ x 23¹/₄ in./39.4 x 59 cm
A.I.P., Monaco
Cond A.
The action is so fast-paced in Giampaoli's advertisement for the thirty-seventh running of the Monaco Grand Prix that we only get a rearview of the racer as he enters into a turn like a bat out of hell. Jody Scheckter, a South African driver who rapidly ascended the ranks of Formula One after moving to Great Britain, took first place in the 1979 competition behind the wheel of a Ferrari. He was the last driver to win a driver's championship for Ferrari until Michael Schumacher did so twenty-one years later.
Est: $800-$1,000.

41. 38e Grand Prix/15/18 Mai. 1980.
Artist: **Jacques Grognet (1927–)**
15⁵/₈ x 23³/₄ in./39.7 x 60.5 cm
A.I.P. Monaco

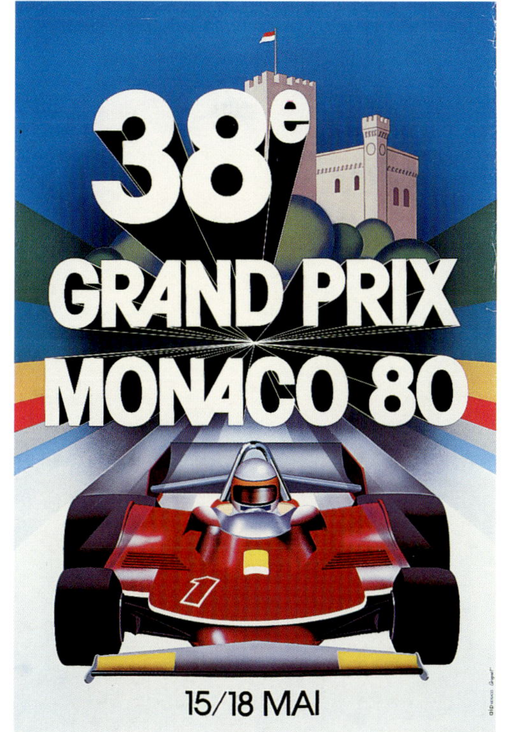

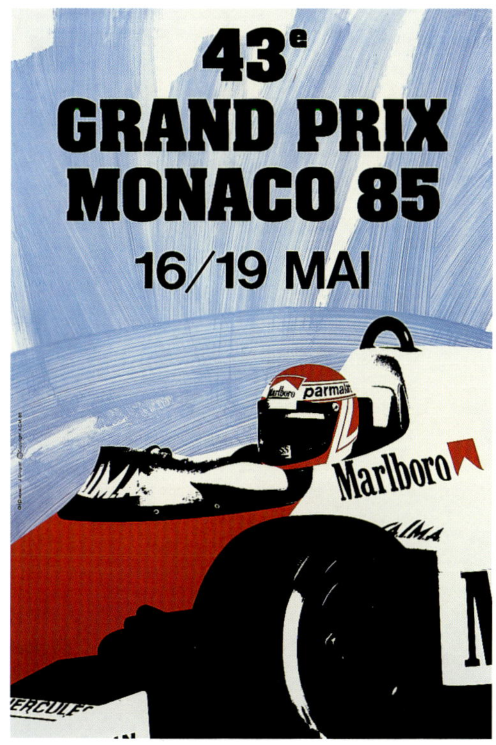

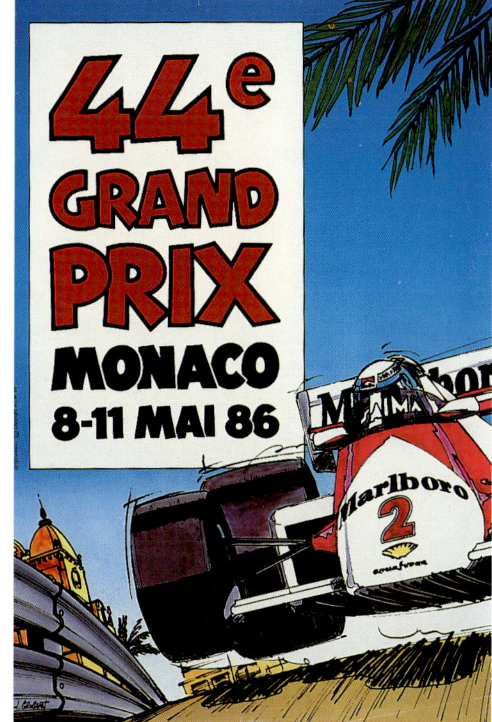

41   42   43

Cond A–/Slight tears at paper edges.
It wasn't the Ferrari driven by South Africa's Jody Scheckter that first crossed the finish line at the thirty-eighth running of the Monaco Grand Prix. Whether that was Grognet's prediction or simply his way of showing the Number One car bearing down on the passerby is left for the viewer to decide. It was, however, Carlos Reutemann who took First Prize for the Williams-Ford team that year. After his racing career came to an end, Reutemann became a prominent politician in the Santa Fe province of his native Argentina. Grognet, who produced eight Monaco posters in the 1980s and 90s, was the most prolific of the artists working for this Grand Prix; Geo Ham comes in second.
Est: $800-$1,000.

42. 43e Grand Prix/16/19 Mai. 1985.
Artist: **Jacques Grognet (1927–)**
$15^5/_8$ x $23^3/_4$ in./39.7 x 60.3 cm
A.I.P. Monaco
Cond A–/Slight creases at bottom paper edge.
As opposed to the somewhat slick futuristic angle seen in the previous design, Grognet takes a more photo-inspired approach in his promotion for the 1985 running of the Monaco Grand Prix, an approach that one can't help but notice helps to accentuate in the corporate sponsorship of the vehicle. France's Alain Prost (the first French Formula One World Champion, incidentally) took the checkered flag that year driving for the Marlboro McLaren International team.
Est: $700-$900.

43. 44e Grand Prix/8-11 Mai 86.
Artist: **Jacques Grognet (1927–)**
$15^5/_8$ x $23^3/_4$ in./39.7 x 60.3 cm
A.I.P. Monaco
Cond A–/Slight tears at paper edges.
Apart from the vehicle shaking off the shackles of gravity, Grognet stays relatively close to the formula he utilized the previous year in order to promote the forty-fourth Monaco Grand Prix, keeping the vehicle realistic and the Marlboro sponsorship conspicuous. And even though he graphically prognosticated that Keke Rosberg would dominate the race, it was once again Alain Prost, Rosberg's Marlboro McLaren International teammate who would win at Monaco for the second year running.
Est: $700-$900.

AVIATION POSTERS

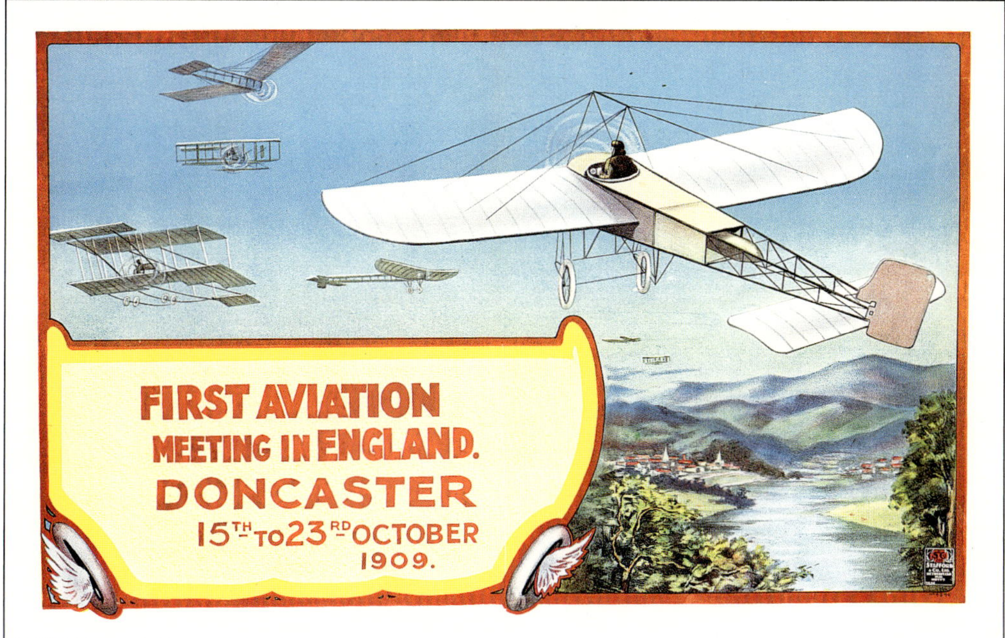

44

44. Doncaster/First Aviation Meeting in England. 1909.
$30^1/_4$ x $19^7/_8$ in./77 x 50.6 cm
Stafford & Co., Netherfield near Nottingham
Cond A–/Slight tears at edges.
A Blériot II, a Wright Type A and a Voison are among the aircraft filling the skies over the British countryside to promote England's inaugural air show. "This pioneer gathering coincided with another meeting at Blackpool-by-the-Sea. Even though the Doncaster meeting opened three days earlier, it was surrounded by an unseemly squabble as to which place would go down in history as the first to put on a flying exhibition in Great Britain. The poor timing, together with equinoxial gales and local rivalries, detracted from both occasions and did little to enhance public interest in flying. Doncaster's flights were staged on the Town Moor, scene of the classic Saint Leger horse race, and attracted a dozen airmen, mostly French and Belgian . . . The greatest height attained by any aviator was only two hundred seventy three meters, reached by Roger Sommer on a Farman biplane in what was described by one journalist as 'the worst breeze that has ever been flown in' . . . Delarange, on a Blériot, took the Trademan's Cup with a new speed record of eighty-three kilometers per hour. For Britain, the only performance of note was that of Colonel Samuel F. Cody with a biplane so big it was dubbed the 'tramcar.' An American by birth, Cody became a British subject at a public ceremony in the midst of the meeting" (Looping the Loop, pp. 50-51).
Est: $5,000-$6,000.

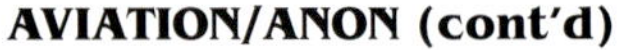

45

AVIATION/ANON (cont'd)

45. Aerodrome de la Crau. ca. 1910.
$77^3/_4$ x $54^1/_8$ in./197.5 x 137.5 cm
M. Teissier, Nimes
Cond A–/Slight tears and stains, largely at seam.
"The popularity of various forms of entertainment—the theatre, the cinema, the circus—has waxed and waned over the years, but one form of spectacular show has continued to increase its appeal . . . This is the air show, display, pageant, call it what you will . . . By 1910 flying had become a popular sport for sightseers, and at any field where experimental flying went on large crowds would assemble whenever possible" (*History of Aviation*, by John W. R. Taylor & Kenneth Munson). And though this particular 2-sheet design isn't for an air show per se—it's for an air field near Marseilles that was open to the public and apparently had a constant influx of flying machines—it does secure the viewer's attention with a sky filled with the most cutting-edge technology of its day: Blériot, Wright, Voisin and Farman craft, as well as a dirigible tossed-in for good measure. *Rare!*
Est: $8,000-$10,000.

ANONYMOUS

46. USAAF. 1945.
$38^1/_4$ x $59^1/_8$ in./97 x 150 cm
Havas (Agency), Paris
Cond A.
The United States Army Air Forces was a part of the U.S. Army during World War II, the direct precursor to the U.S. Air Force, existing between 1941 and 1947. For an exposition of American aeronautic supremacy being held at the Eiffel Tower immediately following the end of the Second World War, an anonymous posterist keeps the iconography direct and the message straightforward with the Tower being supported by the insignia of the ASAAF as formation flights fill the sky.
Est: $1,200-$1,500.

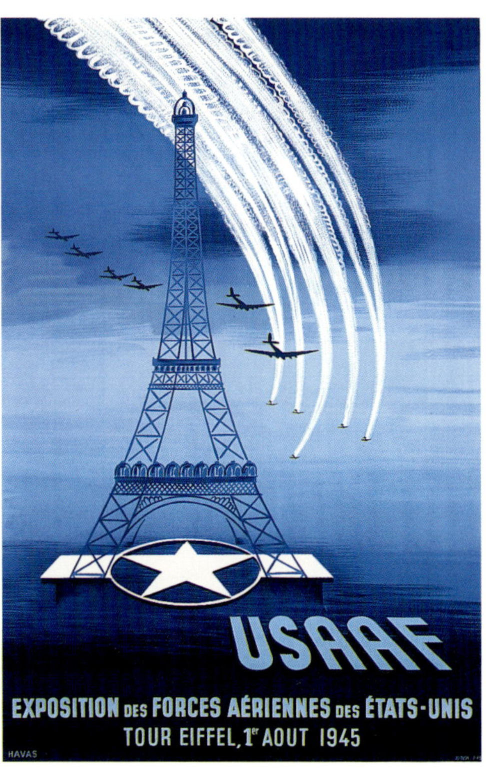

46

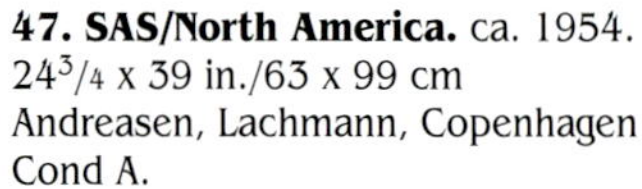

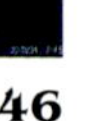

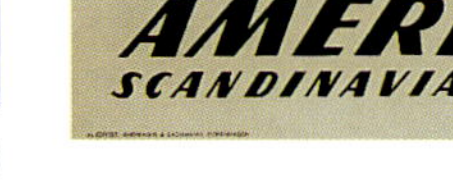

47

47. SAS/North America. ca. 1954.
$24^3/_4$ x 39 in./63 x 99 cm
Andreasen, Lachmann, Copenhagen
Cond A.
Founded on August 1, 1946, as a partnership between the state airlines of Denmark, Sweden and Norway to handle intercontinental traffic to Scandinavia, SAS rapidly became the leading carrier in the Nordic countries.

In 1954, SAS became the first airline in the world to operate a transpolar route, flying nonstop from Copenhagen to Los Angeles. Almost immediately the route became the air travel option of choice with Hollywood celebrities and production people when traveling to Europe, which conversely became a publicity coup for the airline. Though SAS was enormously popular with American tourists in the 1950s, this particular pro-

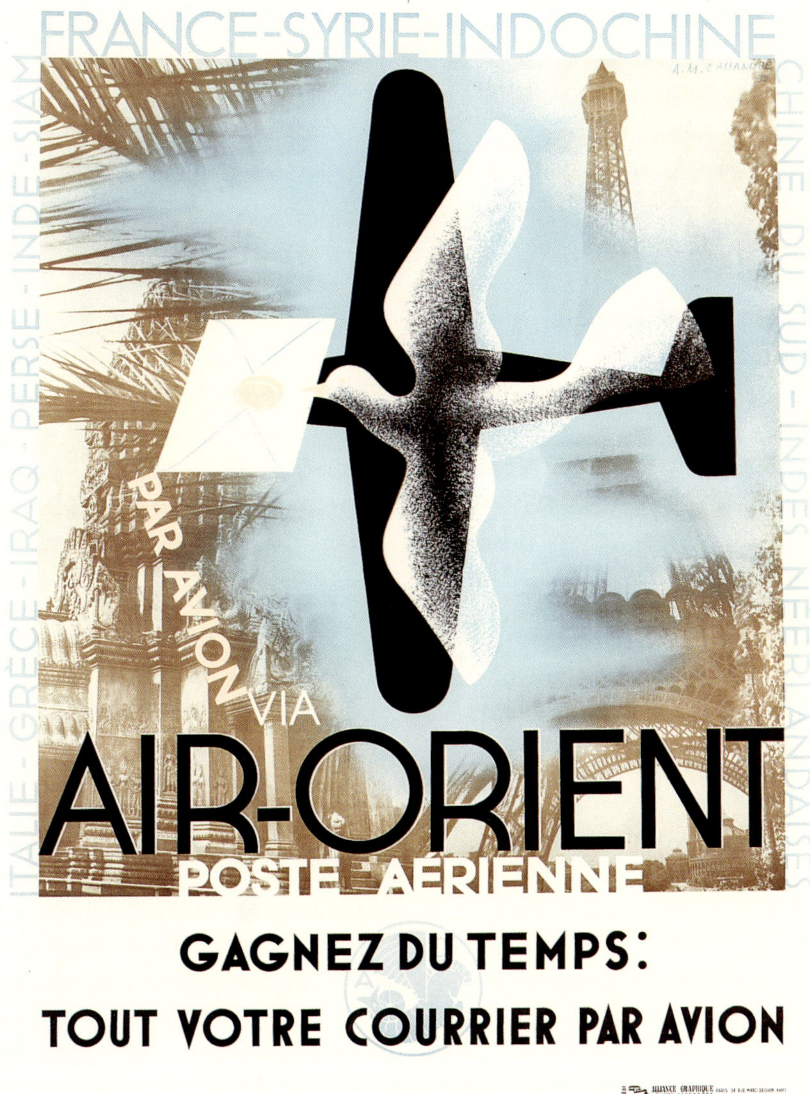

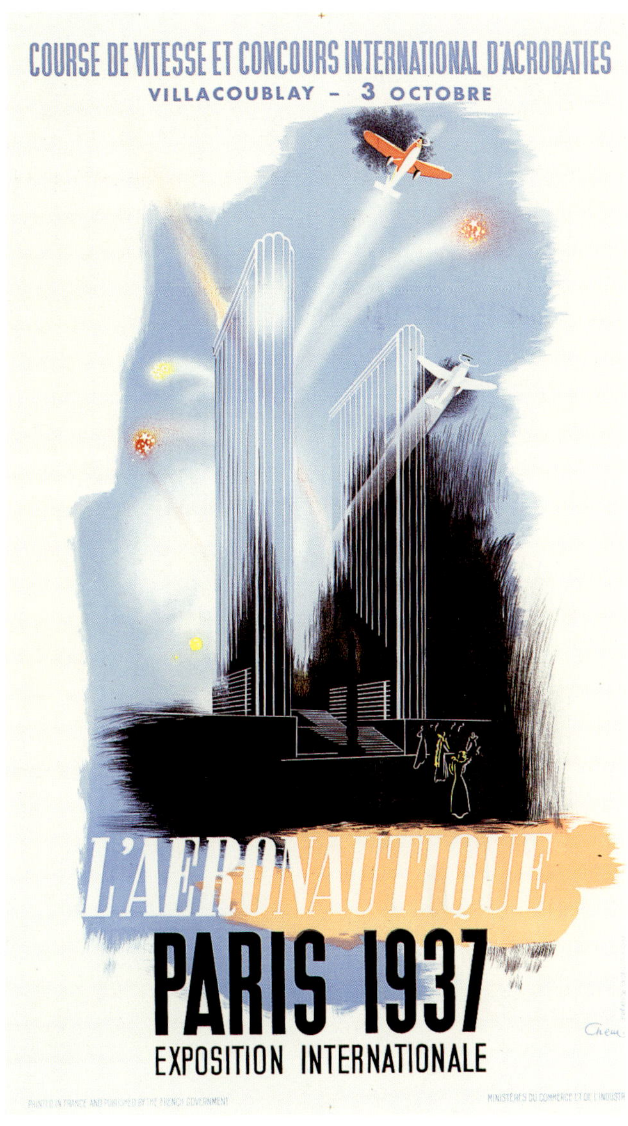

48

49

50

motion encourages travel to the United States, calling upon the resonant—if not altogether as-abundant-as-pictured—icon of the American Bison as its calling card with the unobtrusive silhouette of an SAS aircraft appearing in the poster's upswept skies. Though a glyph appears in the prairie next to the foreground buffalo (with the initials "O.N."), no positive identification of the artist could be made.
Est: $1,000-$1,200.

A. M. CASSANDRE
(Adolphe Mouron, 1901-1968)
For other works by Cassandre, see Nos. TK

48. Air-Orient. 1932.
$23^3/_4$ x $31^5/_8$ in./60.3 x 80.3 cm
Alliance Graphique, Paris
Cond A.
Ref: Cassandre/Weill, p. 61; Cassandre/BN, 65;
    Mouron, ill. 144; Cassandre Suntory, 57;
    PAI-XXXI, 166
Superimposed images are a Cassandre specialty, and here the technique works exceptionally well. Unusual for him, however, is the use of photography—seen here as a background—yet he handles it with equal mastery. Air Orient was formed in 1930 by a merger of two smaller airlines; three years later it became one of the components of Air France.
Est: $12,000-$15,000.

CHEM

49. L'Aéronautique/Paris 1937.
$22^7/_8$ x $39^1/_4$ in./58.1 x 99.6 cm
Crèation Lavarde-Chem
Cond A–/Unobtrusive tears at folds.
Ref: PAI-XXVIII, 226
This poster announcing an air show, planned in conjunction with the Paris World's Fair of 1937 and held at Orly airport, shows planes flying above, around and through two imaginary skyscrapers.
Est: $2,000-$2,500.

PAUL COLIN (1892-1986)
For other works by Colin, see Nos. 11, 281-288.

50. 18eme Salon Internationale de l'Aviation. 1949.
$15^3/_4$ x $23^5/_8$ in./40 x 60 cm
Imp. Bedos, Paris
Cond A.
Ref: Colin Affichiste, 144; PAI-XL, 316
Three years after his excellent design for the 1946 event, Colin conceived another brilliant work for the 18th Parisian International Air Show. Once again emphasizing the worldwide nature of the show, he places a jet repeatedly circling the golden globe through a break in the clouds. Another fine example of uncluttered brevity.
Est: $1,200-$1,500.

AVIATION POSTERS (cont'd)

A. FORTERRE

51. Grand Meeting d'Aviation/Issy-les-Moulineaux.
1909.
46$^1/_8$ x 31 in./117.2 x 78.8 cm
Affiches Forterre, Paris
Cond B+/Slight tears at folds and edges.
Everything that takes to the sky—Antoinette, Blériot,
Voisin and Wright flying machines, as well as an airship
and a representative bird—calls our attention to the
golden promise of a future in flight. The air show, which
took place over 1909's Halloween weekend, was held
in Issy-les-Moulineaux, a commune in the southwest-
ern suburbs of Paris, located approximately four miles
from the center of the French capital. *Rare!*
Est: $4,500-$5,500.

ABRAM GAMES (1914-1996)

52. British Europen Airways.
24 x 39$^1/_2$ in./61 x 100. 3cm
Baynard Press, London
Cond A–/Slight tears at edges.
Games' personal philosophy of "maximum meaning,
minimum means" gave all his works a distinctive conceptual and visual quality. In the case of his poster
for British European Airways, he applies this maxim
by keeping the land masses less distinct than the far-
reaching winged embodiment of the airline (even though
it isn't the airline's logo; that winged key appears unobtrusively at the bottom). Interestingly, even though
"Europe's principal cities" are pin-spotted, they aren't
identified—all the better to allow the traveler to make
the decision on their own without alienating a single
potential flyer. Formed in 1946 by an Act of Parliament,
BEA was the sister airline of British Airways Limited,
created to handle the heavy demand for transatlantic
flights. BEA ceased operations in 1974 when it was
merged with the British Overseas Airways Corporation
to form British Airways. The son of a professional
photographer, Games was taught rudimentary design
skills by his father, and later went to art school at night.
At the age of eighteen, he found a job as a "lettering
artist" at a publicity studio; in due course he went
freelance, working mostly for the London Transport,
the Post Office and Shell-Mex. In 1958, he was named
officer of the Order of the British Empire for his distinguished graphic work, and earned the title of Royal
Designer for Industry.
Est: $1,000-$1,200.

JEOFFROY

53. Fêtes Artistiques de Rodez. 1910.
31$^7/_8$ x 20$^1/_2$ in./81.1 x 52 cm
Cond A–/Unobtrusive tears at folds.
With the city's eighty-meter tall cathedral serving as
the poster's centerpiece, Jeoffroy generates public
interest in the summertime artistic festival being held
in Rodez, the southern French city situated in the
Aveyron *département*. Of course, not all things artistic
can be found in museums or galleries. The artistry of
man conquering the air, for example. And so the city's
festival included a day of aviation, the participants of
which are represented here by the ever-popular Blériot.
Est: $1,700-$2,000.

LOUIS LESSIEUX (1848-1925) & CARREY

54. Prix d'Aviation/Angers. 1912.
45$^1/_4$ x 61$^3/_8$ in./115 x 155.7 cm
Les Editions Nationales, Paris
Cond B+/Slight tears at folds and edges.
Ref: Sport à l'Affiche, 182; Looping the Loop, 55;
   PAI-XXVII, 89
Under the withering glances of other pilots and military
bigwigs, Roland Garros raises his hand in victory,
bringing his Deperdussin racer to a halt with the five
struggling members of the ground crew acting as the
aircraft's brakes—since early planes were built without
them—the sole competitor to complete the Angers Circuit of the French Aéro-Club's 1st Grand Prize for Aviation. "The first contest to show the extent to which the
aeroplane could be depended upon as an instrument
of war was held over a one hundred fifty-seven kilome-
ter course between the towns of Anger, Choloet, and
Saumur in the region of Anjou in western France. A

surprising total of thirty-five constructors entered their
machines and practically all the famous pilots of
Europe were on hand. Most of the military attaches
accredited to Paris were present—keenly interested in
the potentialities of different monoplanes and biplanes"
(Looping the Loop, p. 83). The mid-June event was
scheduled for its favorable weather conditions, perfect
for filling the skies with the "crates" and their hardy
pilots. But instead, the 1912 test of skill took place
under dark skies, the aircraft buffeted by battering rain
and immobilizing winds. Just before the event was
postponed due to the squalls, Garros landed, taking
the event, surely to the chagrin of the other contestants.
"'It was a moving, at times agonizing, demonstration,'
reported *Le Matin*. 'The most marvelous show of valor
in aviation,' chimed in writer Jacques Mortane. The
exploit of Garros against a fierce wind had placed him
ahead of all the pilots in the world" (p.83). *This is the
larger format.*
Est: $7,000-$9,000.

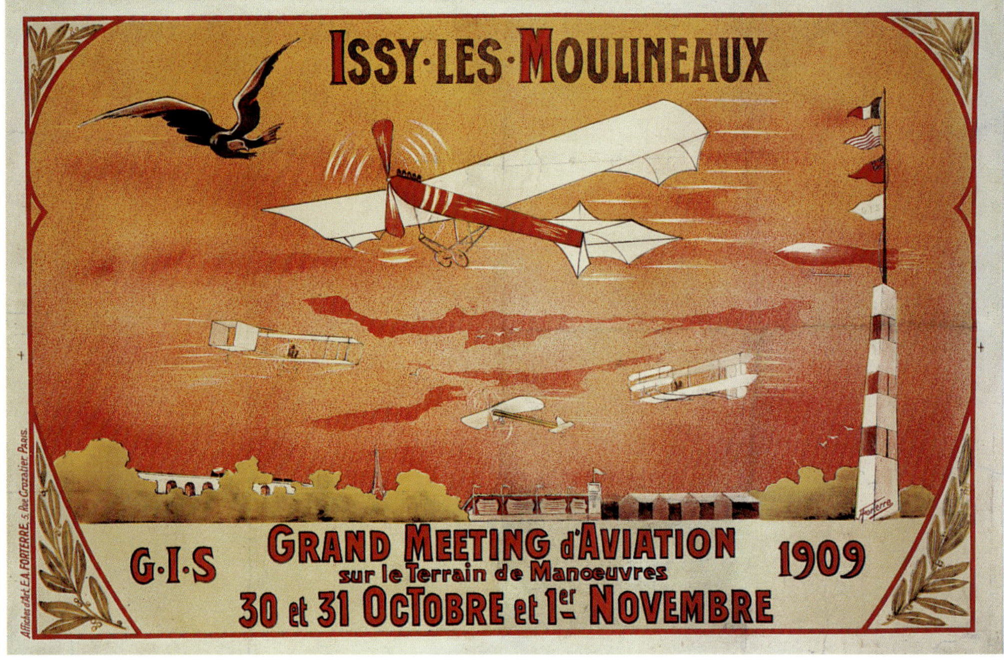

51

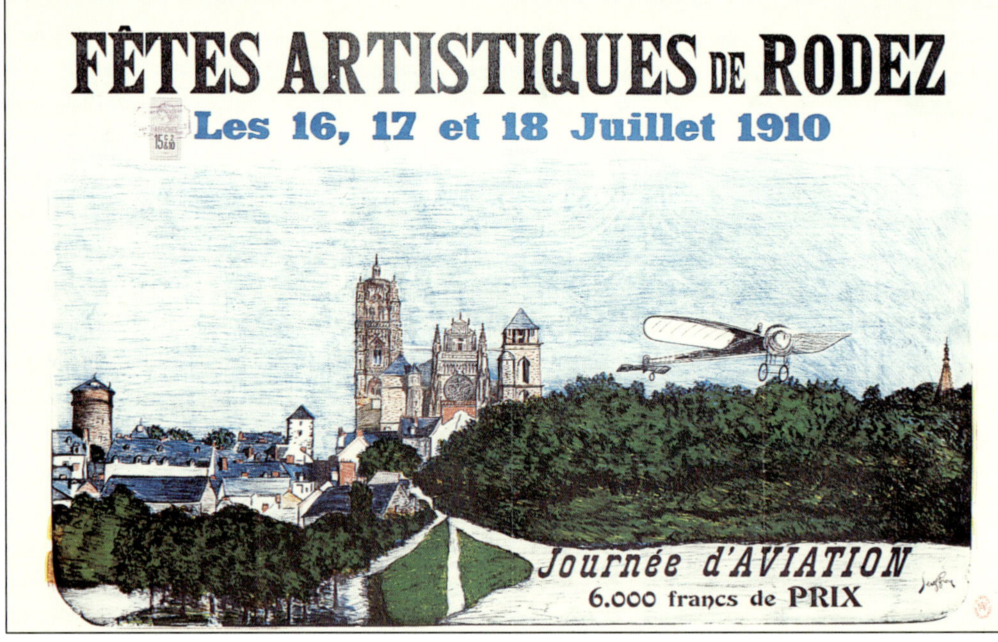

53

AUGUST FRITZ PFUHLE (1878-1969)

55. Danziger Fest u Flugwoche. 1911.
23$^1/_8$ x 35$^1/_4$ in./58.8 x 89.5 cm
Hollerbaum & Schmidt, Berlin
Cond B+/Restored tears at paper edges.
Ref: DFP-III, 2541
In spite of the turbulent timeframe during which it
was produced, a solemn serenity pervades this Pfuhle
poster for a summertime festival and flight week taking
place in Danzig, which at this point was the provincial
capital of West Prussia. Though the colors of the city
and the German realm fill the skies, there's nothing
overtly jingoistic about the design; rather it seems an
open invitation to explore the future—courtesy of the
Farman biplane—without neglecting to appreciate the
past—the city's Marienkirche dominates the skyline,
even though in the not-too-distant future the structure
would be completely destroyed during World War II.
Today, Danzig is known as Gdansk, capital of Poland's
northern Pomorskie province. It is one of the chief Polish ports on the Baltic Sea and serves as a leading
industrial and communications center.
Est: $2,700-$3,000.

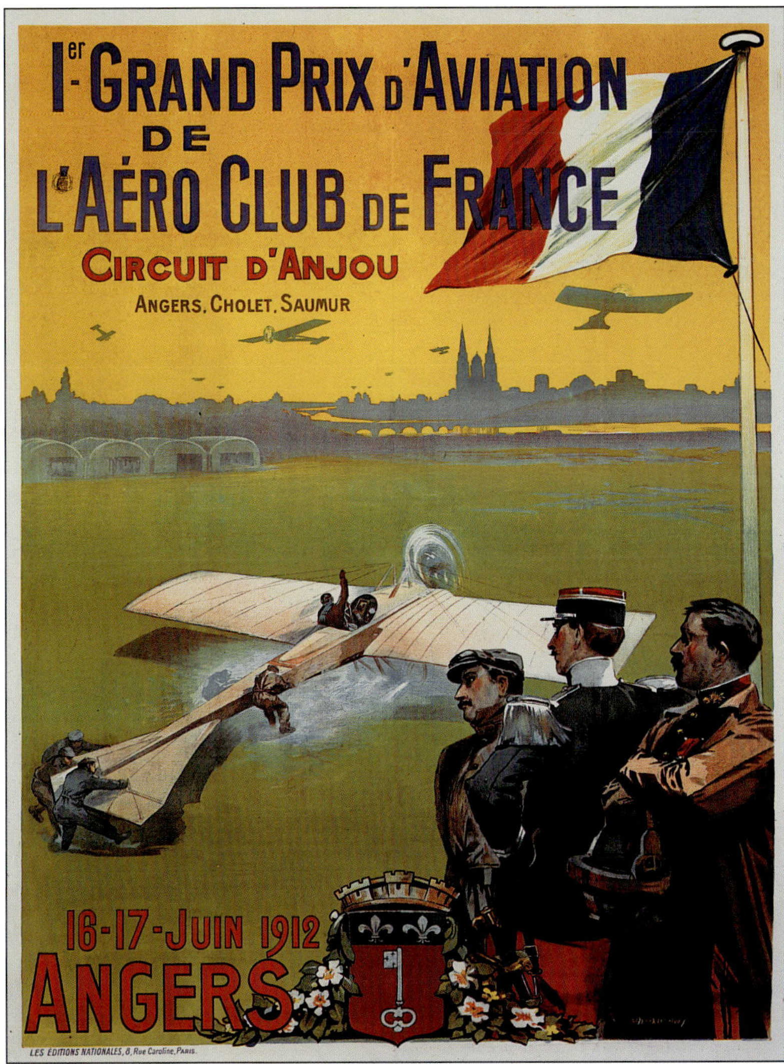

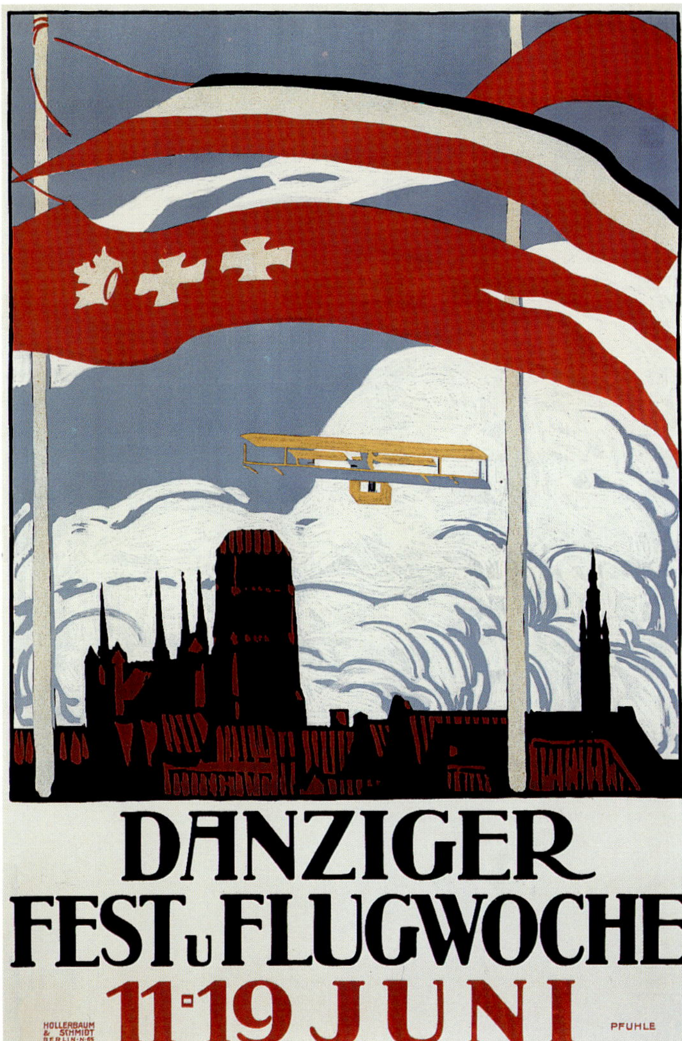

54

55

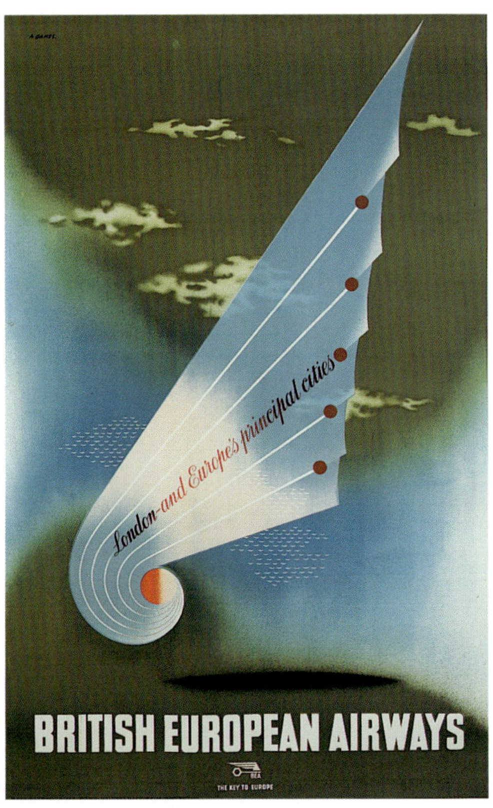

52

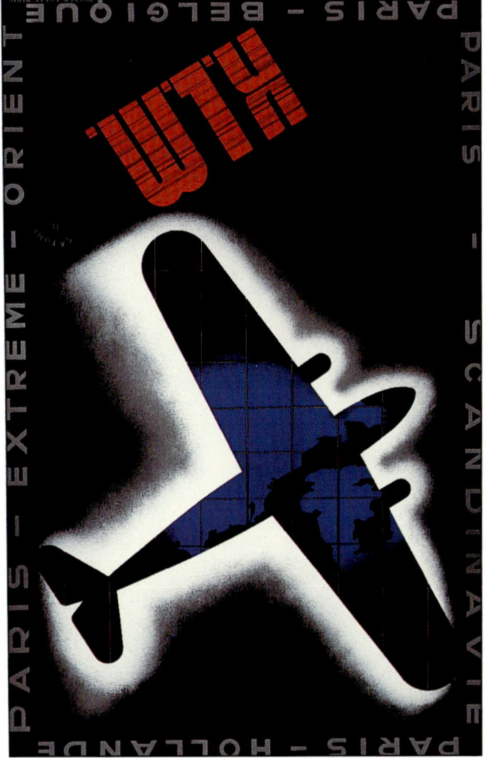

56

pictorial representation and the lettering into near-pure graphic design. Upon viewing his poster for KLM, it's immediately clear why those comparisons are made. With the sparest graphic means necessary and without tonal excess we're instantly made aware of the airline's global reach, with encircling text included for specificity's sake. KLM Royal Dutch Airlines was founded on October 7, 1919, and has continued to operate under the same name to this day—though today it's a subsidiary of Air France—making it the oldest scheduled airline in the world with a continuous history. **Est: $4,000-$5,000.**

ROGER DE VALERIO (1896-1951)

57. Jeune Français/Pilotes. ca. 1940.
$23^1/8$ x $31^3/8$ in./58.6 x 79.8 cm
Devambez, Paris
Cond A–/Tears at folds.
Ref: Toujours Plus Haut, p. 39
The French Ministry of War in charge of Military Aviation asks the youth of France this simple question: "How will you become pilots without it costing you anything while profiting from numerous advantages?" It's a good bet that they can find out the answer by sending away to the address given. De Valerio's recruitment poster succeeds simply by not trying too hard, presenting a trio of planes that compose the French tricolors and an heroic bust of an aviator in profile. With those essentials provided, the rest of the message falls into place.
Est: $2,000-$2,500.

MUNETSUGU SATOMI (1900-1995)

56. KLM. 1933.
$24^3/8$ x 39 in./62 x 99 cm
Poster Novia, Paris

Cond A.
Satomi could be called—quite unpatronizingly, indeed in high praise—the Japanese Cassandre; both excelled in distilling a subject down to its essence, blending its

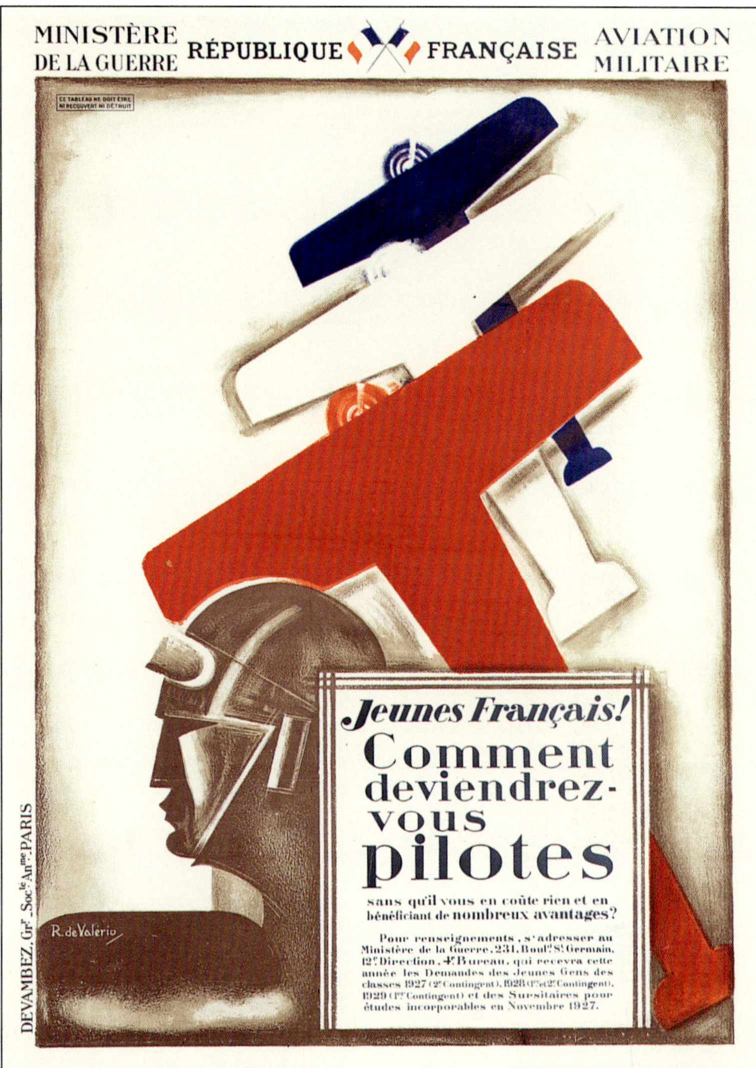

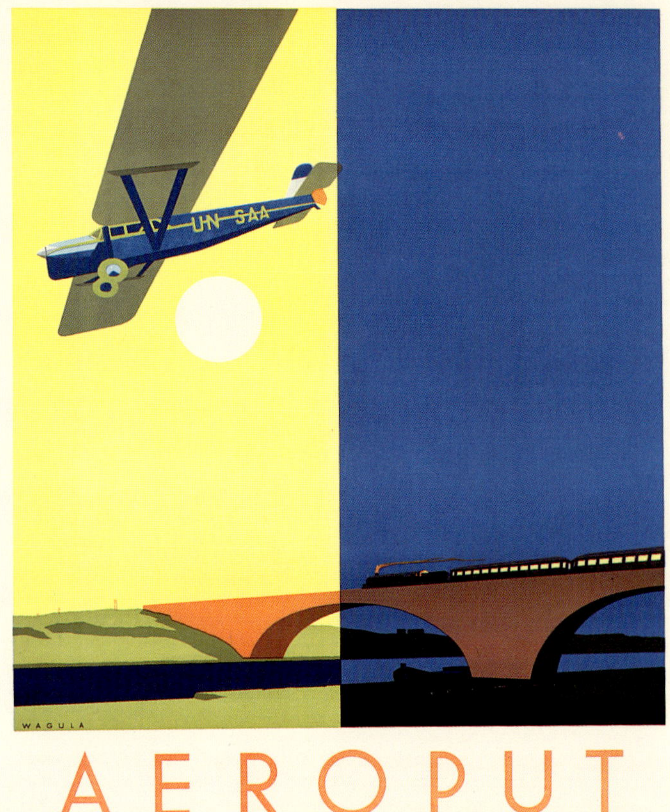

57

60

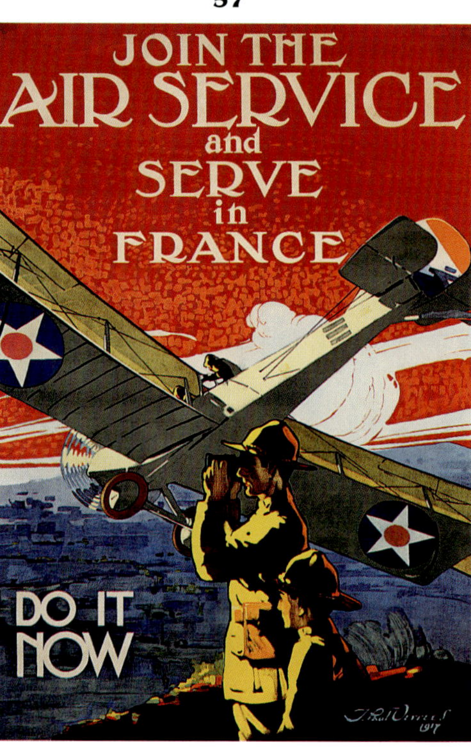

58

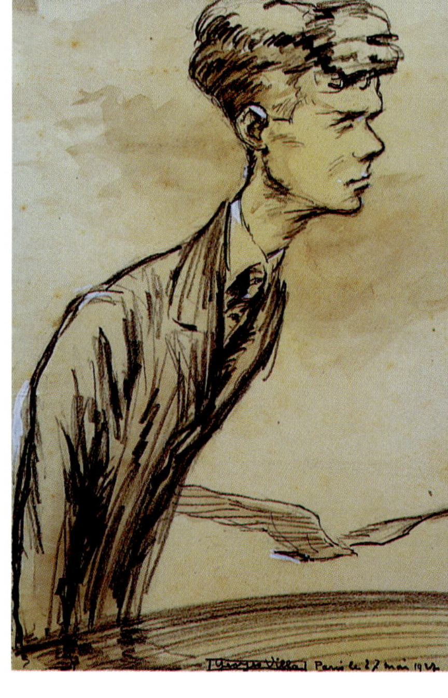

59

AVIATION POSTERS (cont'd)

J. PAUL VERREES (1889-1942)

58. Join the Air Service. 1917.
$24^3/4$ x $36^3/4$ in./62.9 x 93.5 cm
Cond B–/Restored losses at top corners.
Ref: Looping the Loop, 71; Rawls, p. 179;
      PAI-XXXVI, 557
An imaginative recruiting poster for pilots in World War I, with a very good representation of the flimsy biplanes they were expected to fly. Verrees was born in Belgium and came to the U.S. in 1909; this poster was considered one of his finest, and one of the best aviation posters ever designed anywhere.
Est: $1,500-$1,800.

GEORGES VILLA (1883-?)

59. Charles Lindbergh. 1927.
$7^7/8$ x $10^5/8$ in./19.8 x 27 cm
Hand-signed crayon and gouache drawing. Framed.
Charles Augustus Lindbergh, Jr. (1902-1974) was a pioneering American aviator who became a cultural icon and an indelible part of popular history as the first person in history to successful pilot a nonstop flight across the Atlantic Ocean aboard "The Spirit of St. Louis." Known as "Lucky Lindy" and "The Lone Eagle," Lindbergh would endure tragedy (the much-publicized kidnapping and murder of his infant son) and controversy (his leadership in the movement to keep the United States out of World War II would earn him a reputation as a Nazi sympathizer), both of which would only add to his legendary status. This Villa caricature comes from shortly after he completed his flight from Roosevelt Airfield in New York to Paris on May 21, 1927. Though not altogether flattering, Lindbergh's determination and focus come through loud and clear.
Est: $1,200-$1,500.

HANNS WAGULA (1894-1964)

60. Aeroput Yugoslavia (Air Travel Yugoslavia).
$23^7/8$ x 37 in./60.6 x 94 cm
Tipografica, Zagreb
Cond A.
Ref: PAI-XXI, 458
The headline that accompanies this day-and-night image loses some of its Slavic snap in translation, but you'll get the idea: "Train travel leaves you tired; air travel leaves you rested." (And yet, with its windows lit against the dark, the image of the train possesses an undeniable romantic allure.) The artist, who has been praised for his color sense, executes the design in handsome primaries.
Est: $1,700-$2,000.

BRITISH RAILWAYS

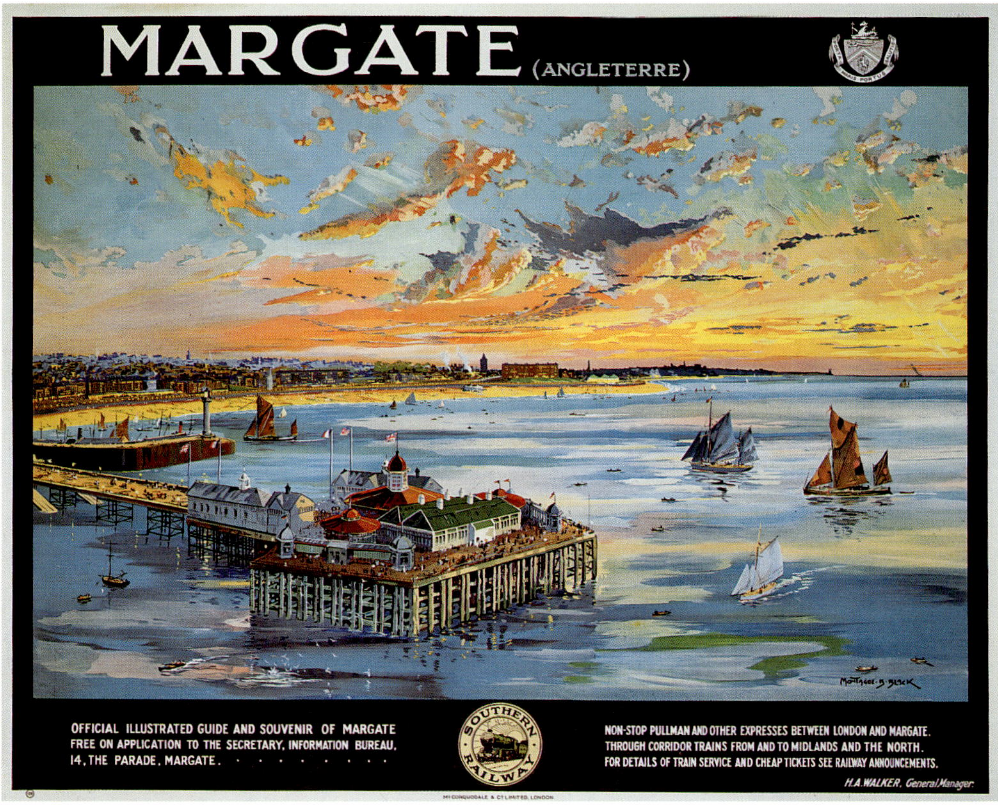

61

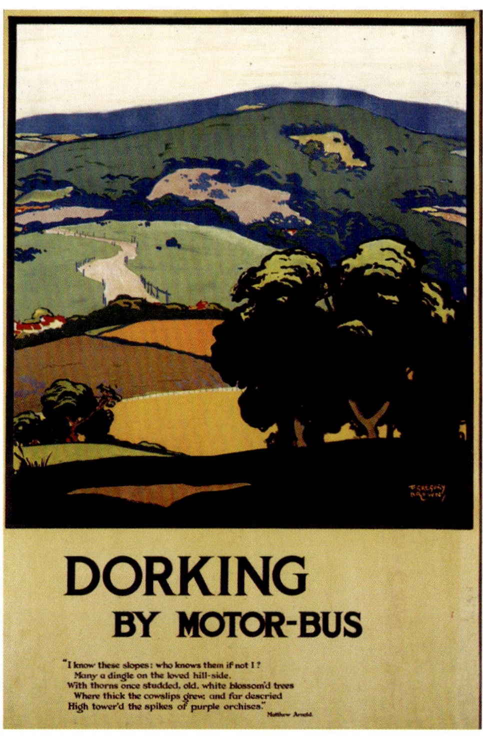

62

Innsbruck via Harwich poster:

63

MONTAGUE BIRREL BLACK (1884-?)

61. Southern Railway/Margate.
49^1/$_2$ x 39^3/$_4$ in./125.6 x 101 cm
McCorquodale & Co., London
Cond A.
Margate, located in Kent, England, has the proud heritage of being one of Britain's first seaside resorts. It was the first one to offer donkey rides and the first to introduce deck chairs as a part of its amenities. Black's poster for the town—whose dramatic sky alone makes a visit to the area seem worthwhile—is a sunny panorama featuring two long-gone points of interest: the Margate Jetty—destroyed by a storm in 1978—and the Stone Pier's lighthouse—which collapsed into the sea after its foundations were undermined during the Great Storm of February 1st, 1953. Born in Stockwell, North London, Black specialized in military and naval artwork. In addition to his maritime designs, he also executed posters for the British LNER, LMS and SR lines.
Est: $4,000-$5,000.

F. GREGORY BROWN (1887-1941)

62. Dorking by Motor-Bus. 1920.
19^3/$_4$ x 30 in./50 x 76.2 cm
Dangerfield, London
Cond A-/Slight stains, largely at paper edges. Framed.
Reviewing an exhibit of his posters, the *Observer* noted, "Mr. Gregory Brown has helped as much as any man to raise the tone of the 'poor man's picture gallery' . . . Mr. Brown always keeps the pictorial part of his designs quite distinct from the lettering which, though both are harmoniously adjusted in the complete poster, could be cut away without impairing the balance of the picture . . . (He) knows how to get surprisingly rich and varied effects in three or four printings. His flat tints form their pattern without the help of . . . a black outline, the effect being rather like that of stencil work" (Sparrow, 1924, p. 118). This description fits Brown's promotion for bus service to southeast England's Dorking to a tee—by focusing on the Surrey Hills (one of the first areas in England to be designated an "Area of Outstanding Natural Beauty") that wrap around the town, the bottom verse by Matthew Arnold serves as a lovely accompaniment rather than extraneous enticement. An unforced destination poster *par excellence*.
Est: $1,000-$1,200.

AUSTIN COOPER (1890-1964)

63. LNER/Innsbruck via Harwich.
50 x 40^1/$_8$ in./127 x 102 cm
Hermann Sontag, Munich
Cond A-/Unobtrusive folds.
Sometimes using British railways was only the jumping-off point for a much larger journey, such as this Cooper poster promoting travel between a town in Essex and the Austrian capital of the federal state of Tyrol. The mountain vista alone should have been sufficient enticement to pack the twice-daily trains. Cooper grew up in Manitoba on the Canadian prairie. At thirteen, he was sent to Cardiff, Wales, to study art. He returned to Canada and began his career as a commercial artist in Montreal, went back to Britain as a soldier during World War I and settled permanently in London in 1922 where he would go on to produce over the next two decades a multitude of fine posters for British railways.
Est: $2,500-$3,000.

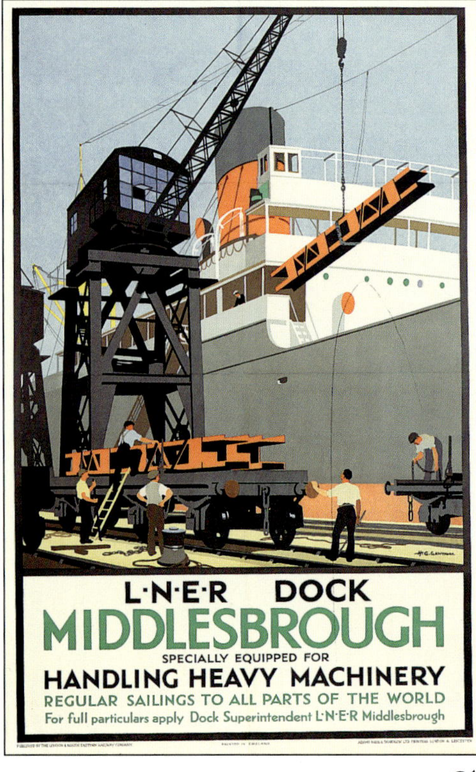

64

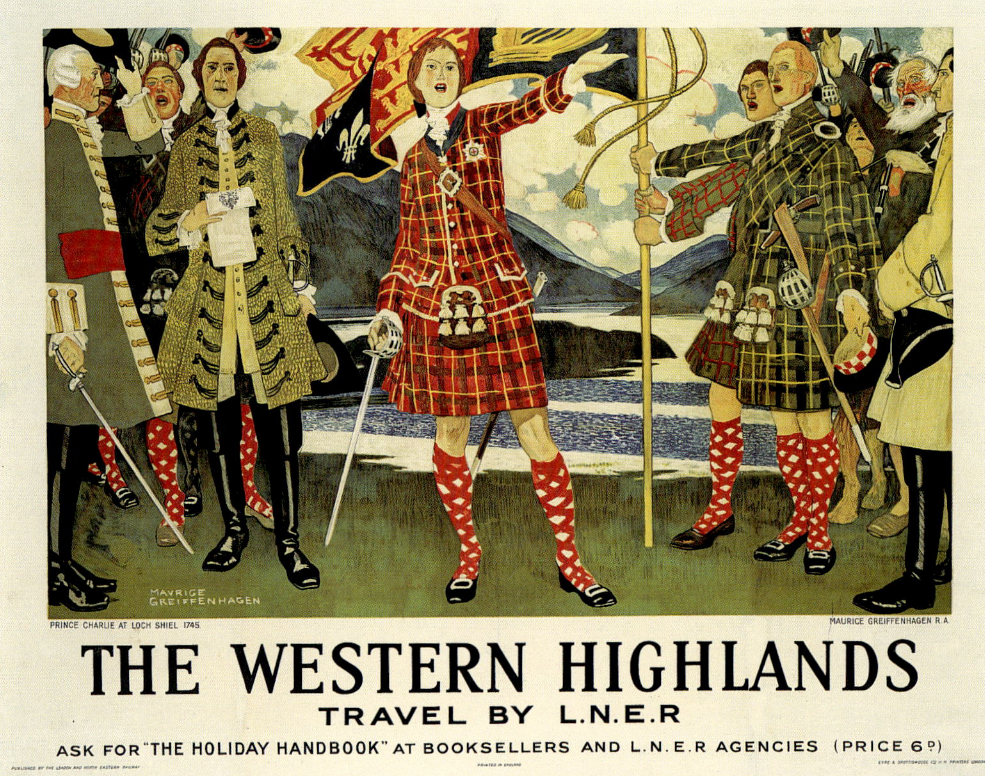

65

BRITISH RAILWAYS (cont'd)

HENRY GEORGE GAWTHORN (1879-1941)

64. LNER/Middlesborough.
25 x 39⅝ in./63.5 x 100.6 cm
Adams Bros. & Shardlow, London
Cond B+/Slight tears at folds.
Of course, the LNER wasn't just the tool of the tourist community. It was also an industrial stalwart capable of taking on any challenge that came its way. Hence this impressive Gawthorn Art Deco design that shows a crane loading metal beams onto a vessel from the LNER dock in Middlesborough, a large town in northeast England, "specially equipped for Handling Heavy Machinery." "Born in Northampton, (Gawthorn) studied at Regent Street Polytechnic. He began his career as an architect but later turned to pictorial art. He wrote several books on poster design and publicity and produced posters for the LNER. His self-portrait can be spotted in many of his posters, complete with pince-nez and a Panama hat" (Railway Posters, p. 155).
Est: $2,500-$3,000.

MAURICE GREIFFENHAGEN (1862-1931)

65. The Western Highlands/L.N.E.R.
49¼ x 39⅛ in./125 x 99.4 cm
Eyre & Spottiswoode, London
Cond B+/Unobtrusive folds.
Loch Shiel is a twenty-five kilometer-long freshwater loch situated in the Scottish Western Highlands' Lochaber district. The nature of the loch changes considerably along its length, being deep and enclosed by mountains in the northeast and shallow—surrounded by bog and rough pasture—in the southwest. In 1745, Bonnie Prince Charlie—the son of James Francis Edward Stuart and the exiled claimant to the thrones of England, Scotland and Ireland—was rowed the length of the loch in order to raise his standard at Glenfinnan and begin a campaign that would culminate in him reclaiming the throne. And it's this scene, full of hope and the promise of a new day that Grieffenhagen reproduces in his poster for the LNER. Sadly, the campaign failed, but that's no excuse not to journey to the Western Highlands aboard the LNER, now is it?
Est: $1,700-$2,000.

GREIWIRTH

66. The Flying Scotsman/LNER. 1928.
25 x 40 in./63.5 x 101.6 cm
Vincent Brooks, Day & Son, London
Cond B+/Slight tears at folds.
To advertise the LNER's London-Edinburgh express service, Greiwirth has his locomotive literally—and explosively—taking to the sky from its departure point at King's Cross. *Rare & impressive!*
Est: $4,000-$5,000.

67. Hornsea/LNER.
25 x 39¾ in./63.5 x 101 cm
T. Haynes Chorley & Co., Manchester & London
Cond B+/Slight tears at folds.

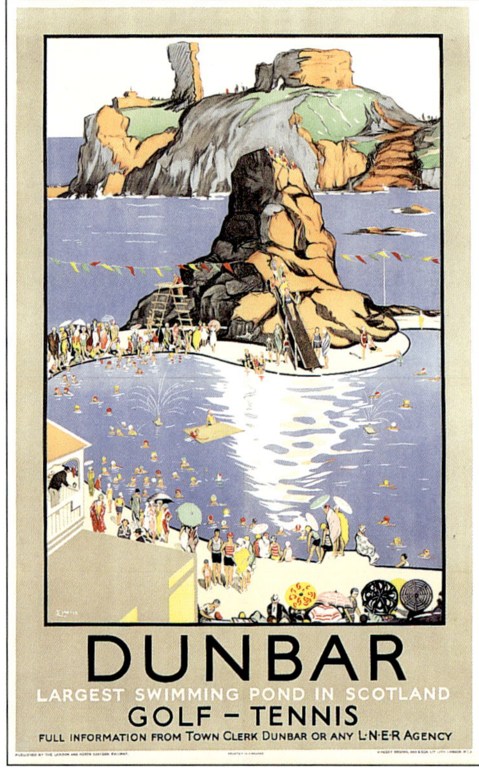

68

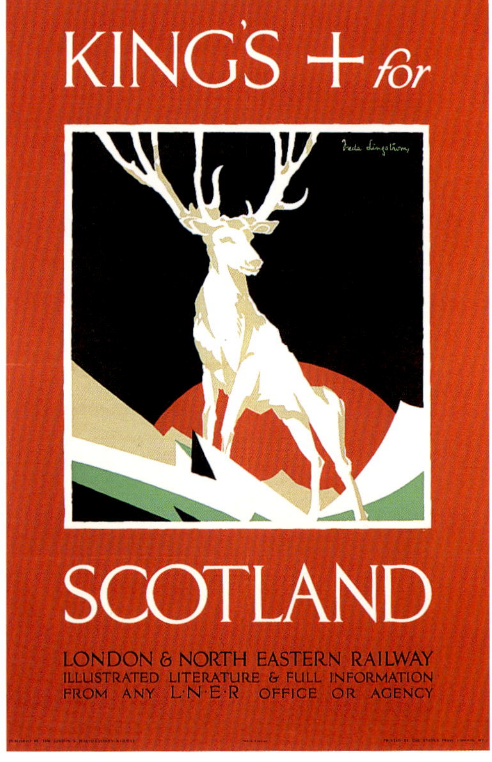

69

Ref: PAI-XXXVII, 42
Hornsea is a small picturesque holiday center located between the sandy beaches of the North Sea and Hornsea Mere, the largest freshwater lake in Yorkshire. Of all the attractions Hornsea has to offer, The Mere is one of the most beautiful. Situated on the western side of the town, the lake not only offers activities all year round, but also houses 250 different species of birds on its sanctuary. This, however, is not the face of Hornsea that Greiwirth has chosen to put forth for the LNER, opting instead for a teeming familial beach scene with an inbound liner that puts a twin-funnel exclamation mark onto the peachy-sky tableau.
Est: $2,000-$2,500.

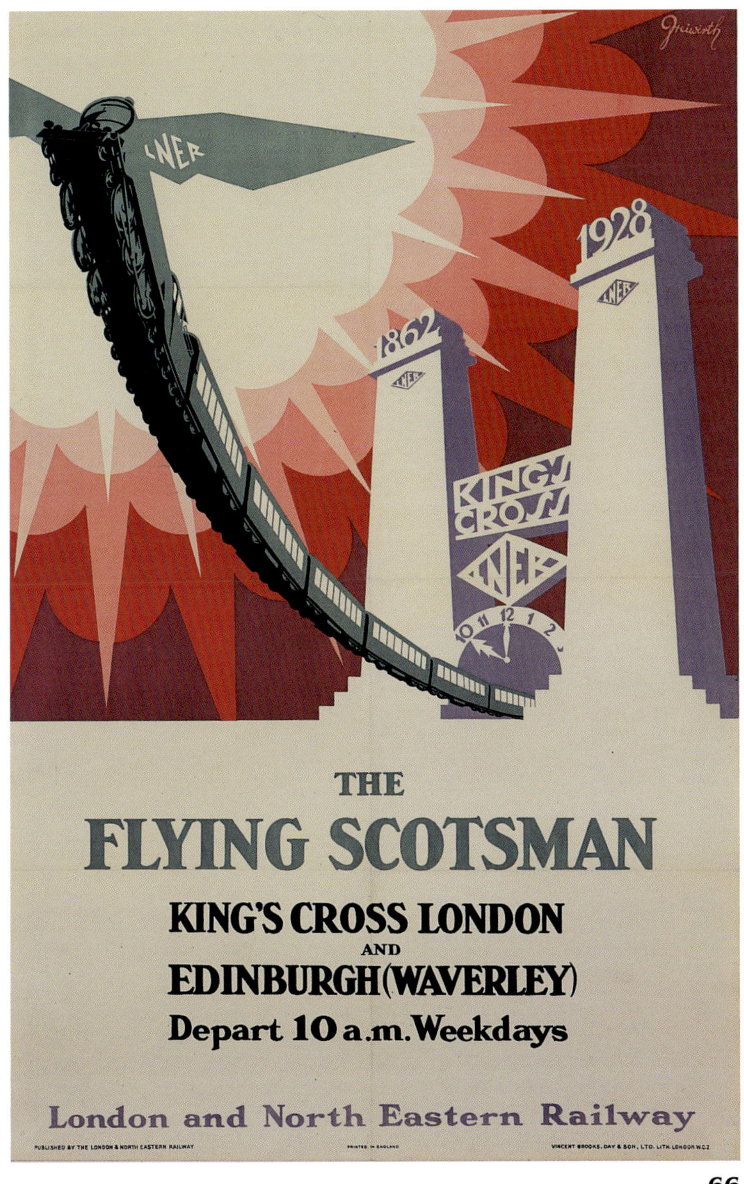

66

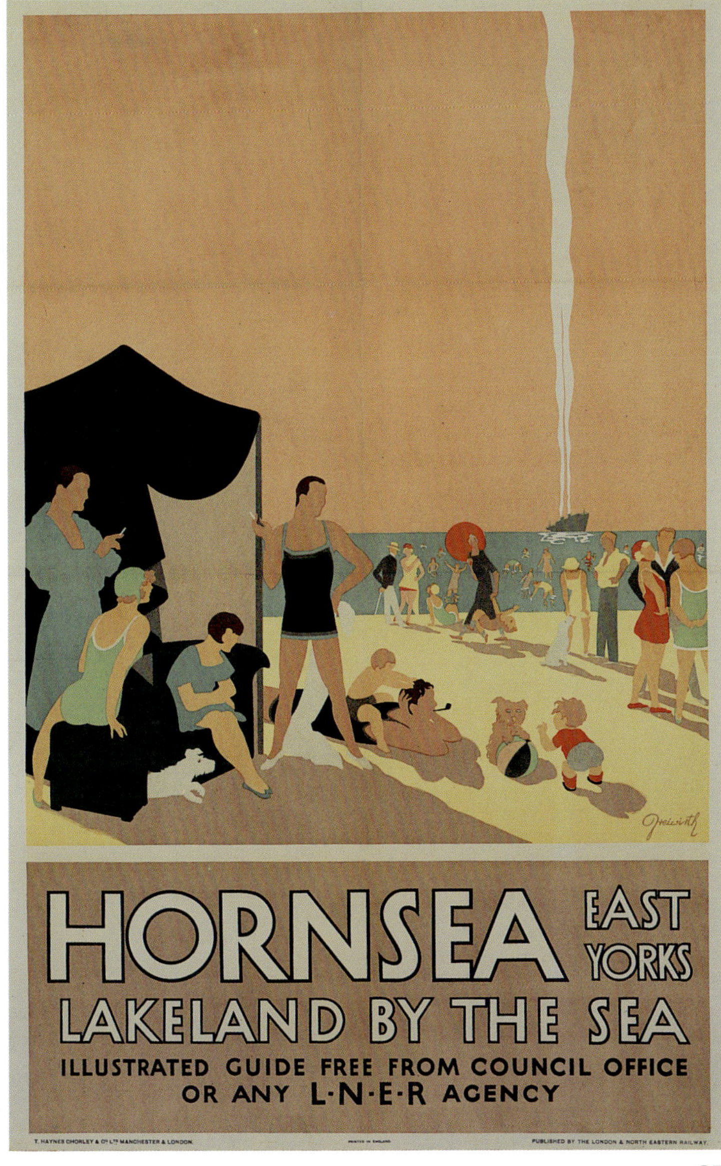

67

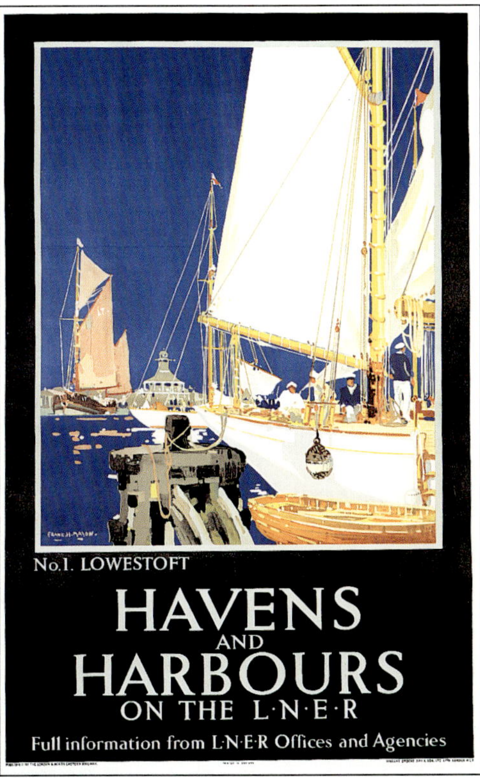

70

E. LANDER

68. Dunbar/LNER.
25 x 39³/₄ in./63.3 x 101 cm
Vincent Brooks, Day & Son, London
Cond A–/Unobtrusive folds.
The Royal Burgh of Dunbar is located on the southeast coast of Scotland, approximately thirty miles east of Edinburgh. It gained a reputation as a seaside holiday and golfing resort in the 19th century, the "Bright and Breezy Burgh" famous for its bracing air. And though the poster makes mention of the fact that both tennis and golf are viable options for the visiting sportsperson, Lander focuses solely on the "Largest Swimming Pond in Scotland" and its tony bathers, backed by the ruins of the city's castle that was deliberately destroyed in 1568.
Est: $2,000-$2,500.

FREDA LINGSTROM (1893-?)

69. Scotland/LNER.
25 x 40 in./63.5 x 101.5 cm
The Avenue Press, London
Cond B+/Slight tears at folds.
Since every informed traveler in the British Isles knows that King's Cross is the jumping-off point for LNER excursions to Scotland, Lingstrom settles upon an impressively regal reindeer (an unexpected, but accurate member of the Scottish fauna) to lure people north. "After studying at the central School of Arts and Crafts and Heatherleys, (Lingstrom) was commissioned by the Norwegian and Swedish governments to do Scandinavian drawings for English travel propaganda. She designed posters and booklet covers for the LNER and was known for her landscape paintings" (Railway Posters, p. 156).
Est: $1,700-$2,000.

FRANK H. MASON (1876-1965)
70. Havens and Harbours/LNER.
25 x 40 in./63.6 x 101.5 cm
Vincent, Brooks, Day & Son, London
Cond A–/Unobtrusive folds.
Mason served in the Royal Navy before launching himself as a marine painter. His services were in great demand by shipping lines and the British Rail, as well as engineering and shipbuilding firms. Here, in the first of a series that celebrated destinations on the LNER route that were known for their bays and sheltered inlets, he turns his talents to the harbor at Lowestoft, with a pair of schooners highlighting the resort's North Sea nautical magnificence.
Est: $2,000-$2,500.

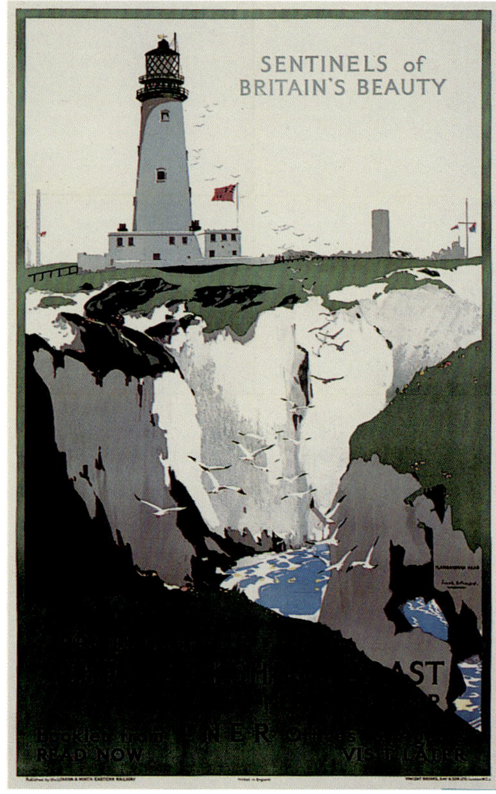

71

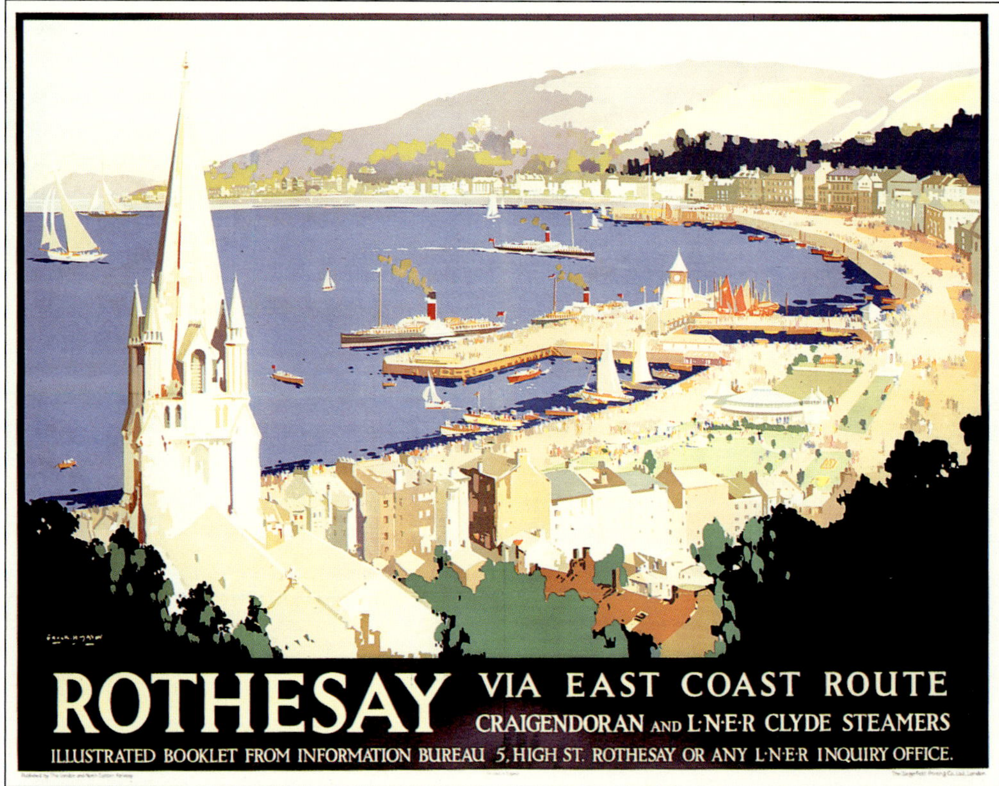

72

BRITISH RAILWAYS/MASON (cont'd)

71. Yorkshire Coats/LNER.
25 x 39$^3/_8$ in./63.5 x 101.3 cm
Vincent, Brooks, Day & Son, London
Cond B+/Slight tears at folds.
Flamborough Head is a seven mile-long chalk headland promontory on the Yorkshire Coast of England, between the Filey and Bridlington bays of the North Sea. Seen hazily in the far background of this Mason design we can just make out a rectangle jutting upwards. This is actually a chalk tower built in 1674, which is the oldest surviving complete lighthouse in England. Together with its more contemporary cousin of the foreground, they serve as the "Sentinels of Britain's Beauty" and Mason's wonderfully direct artwork for the LNER makes it easy to "Remember the Yorkshire Coast" as an alternative for next summer's getaway.
Est: $2,000-$2,500.

72. Rothesay/LNER.
50 x 40 in./127 x 101.5 cm
The Dangerfield Printing Co., London
Cond B+/Slight tears at folds.
Mason gives us a bird's-eye view of Rothesay, the principal town on the east coast of the Isle of Bute, Scotland. With its fine examples of Victorian architecture peppered throughout Rothesay, its expansive beach, its esplanade and bustling wooden pier serviced by numerous LNER steamers sailing from Wemyss, its quite easy to see why the town has been a popular tourist resort for the past two centuries for Glaswegians going "doon the watter." Interestingly enough, Mason didn't include Rothesay's most historically significant site: the ruins of Rothesay Castle, the ancestral home of the Stuart Kings, built in the early-Twelfth Century.
Est: $2,500-$3,000.

ARTHUR C. MICHAEL

73. Scarborough/LNER.
24$^7/_8$ x 39$^7/_8$ in./63 x 101.3 cm
R. H. Perry, London
Cond A.
While much of Europe's railroad advertising focused on the glamour or modernity of the ride itself, the British rail always emphasized the destination. Here, the LNER invites travelers to experience one of the very best places in Britain in which to savor the atmosphere of the Victorian seaside. Michael's expansively tiered panorama gives every attraction its due: promenades,

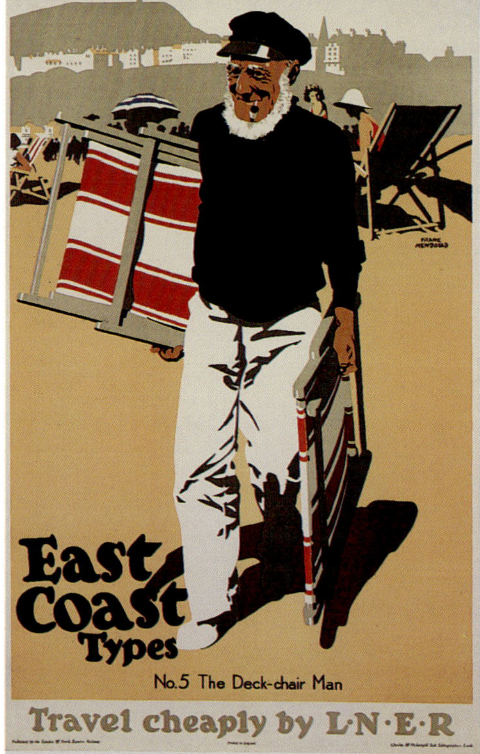

75

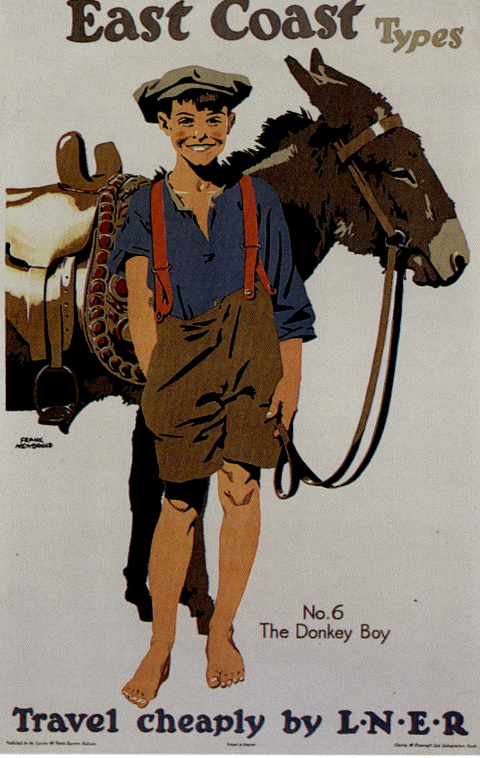

76

pavilions, cafes, chalets, pretty little shelters, the elegant bulk of the Spa, the ruins of the 12th-century castle built around a Roman signal station in the distance and the popular sandy beaches of the South Bay, all located a stone's throw from the North Sea. Michael was a painter and etcher, who in addition to designing posters for the LNER, illustrated books and periodicals.
Est: $2,500-$3,000.

FRANK NEWBOULD (1887-1950)

74. East Coast Frolics. 1933.
25$^1/_4$ x 39$^5/_8$ in./64 x 100.6 cm
Chorley & Pickersgill, Leeds
Cond A–/Unobtrusive folds.

Ref: Railway Posters, p. 146, No. 2
"A set of six (Newbould) posters (were) exhibited in the 1933 LNER Poster Exhibition at the New Burlington Galleries in London. These simple posters use humour to entice the viewer to the east-coast resorts" (Railway Posters, p. 146). With an array of indigenous, fish, foul and amphibians, the artist created "humanized" reasons to come to "The Drier Side" of the island; in this case, a sky-gazing crustacean holds a telescope up to his little lobster eye and declares it to be "Another perfect day." And by calling him a "shellback" we're not only informed that he's a marine decapod, but that he's a seasoned veteran sailor as well.
Est: $1,700-$2,000.

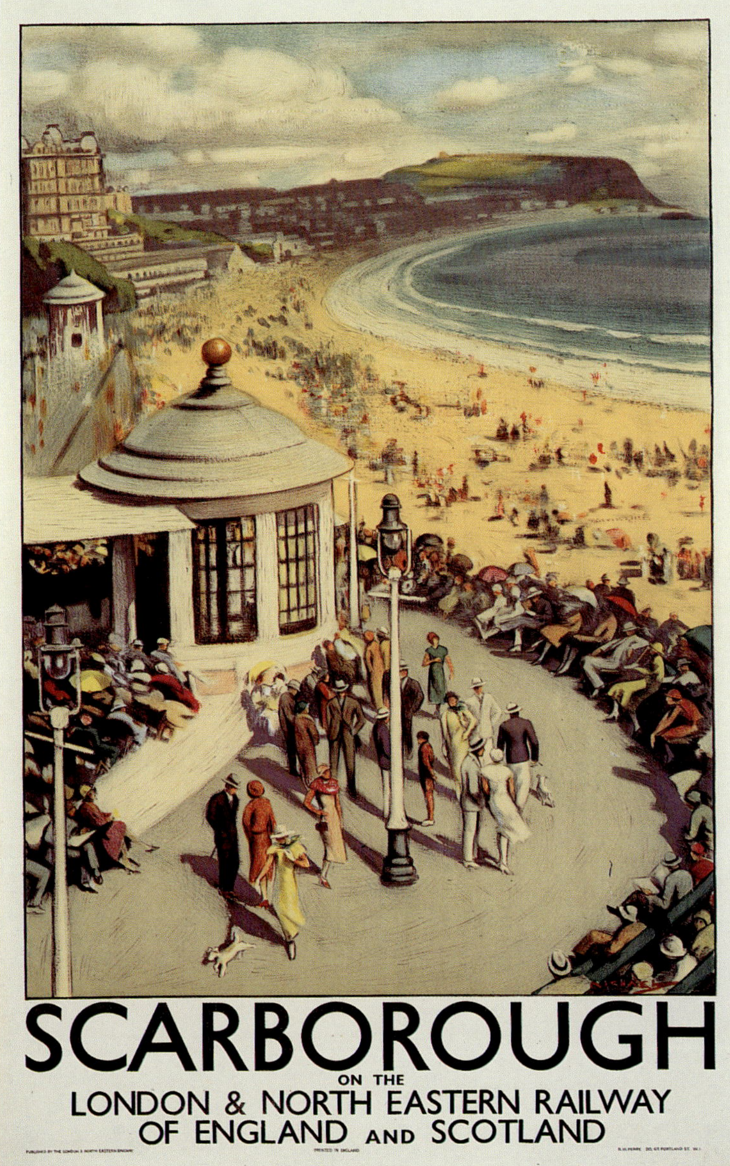

73

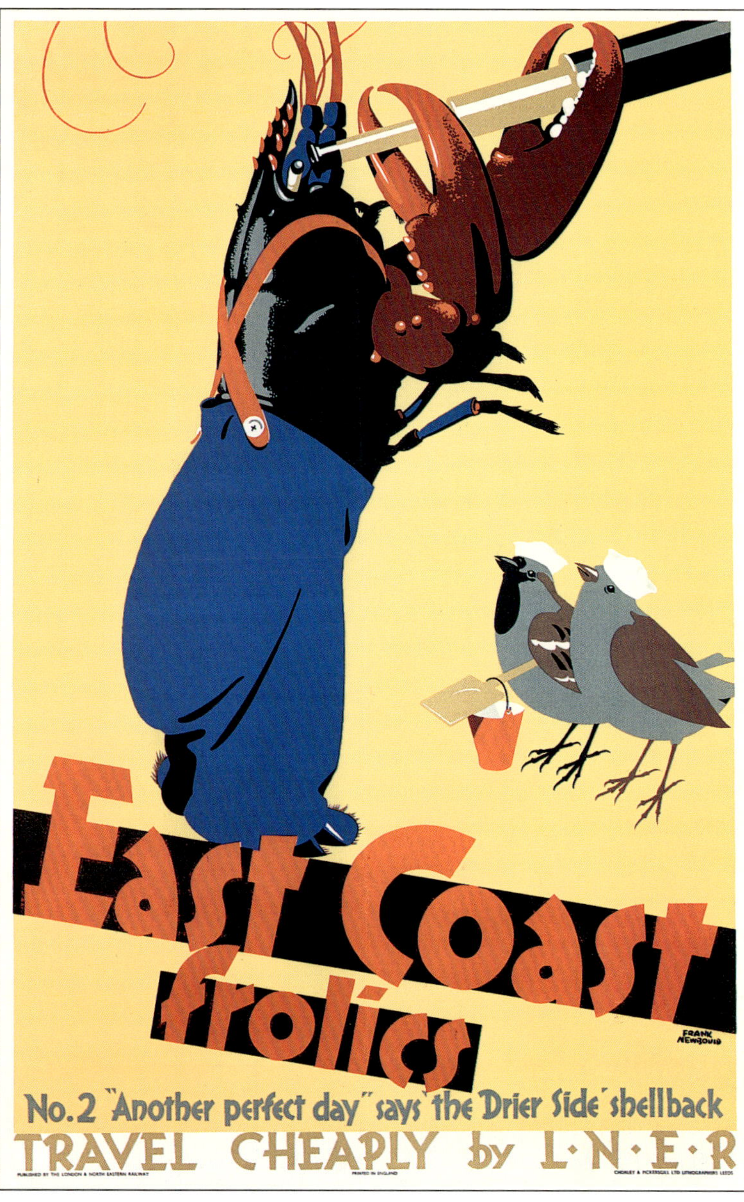

74

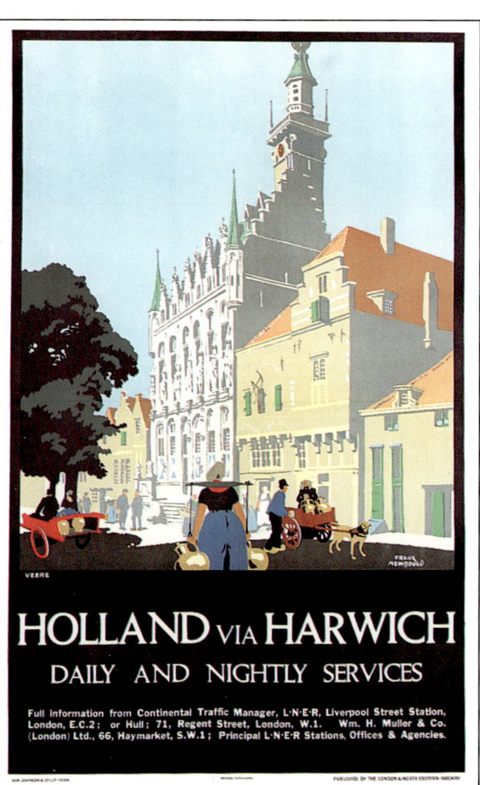

77

75. East Coast Types/LNER. ca. 1923.
25 x 39⁵/₈ in./63.3 x 100.7 cm
Chorley & Pickersgill, Ltd. Lith., Leeds
Cond A–/Unobtrusive folds.
Ref: Golden Age of Travel, 120
The "'East Coast Types' series by Frank Newbould (was) issued by the LNER to promote the holiday areas the company had taken over from the North Eastern and Great Eastern Railways after the grouping in 1923" (Golden Age, p. 102). And here we see "Type" Number 5, "The Deck-chair Man," a salty dog who's apparently given up his life at sea in favor of the less-perilous adventures of the service industry. Even though lugging canvas chairs about for tourists isn't the most glamorous job, Newbould fills his subject with such a sly, welcoming nature that the viewer can't help but be won over by his mischievous air. Newbould started the landscape school of English poster design and achieved great impact through his use of flat, solid colors. He was one of the few artists working on British railway posters who was also a fine lithographer. Calling him "one of our best-known designers," Austin Cooper described his works as characterized by "simplified realism, a masterly use of harmonious color, an irreproachable sense of values, a ruthless elimination of unnecessary detail" (Cooper, p. 89).
Est: $1,700-$2,000.

76. East Coast Types/LNER. ca. 1923.
24⁷/₈ x 39³/₄ in./63.2 x 100.8 cm
Charley & Pickersgill, Leeds
Cond B+/Slight tears at folds and paper edges.
So, if you get tired of just sitting around and taking in the view from your canvas chair of the previous poster, you can move on to "Type" No. 6, "The Donkey Boy," whose fresh-faced regard lets you know right up front that he'd be more than happy to take you for a ride along the beach on his faithful and friendly domestic ass.
Est: $1,700-$2,000.

77. Holland via Harwich/LNER.
25 x 40 in./63.5 x 101.7 cm
Ben Johnson, York
Cond A–/Unobtrusive folds.
While Austin Cooper reminded us that a trip to Austria could all begin by hopping aboard an LNER train and heading for Harwich (see No. 63), Newbould brings up a possibility a little closer to home (if you live in England): Veere, Holland. During the Seventeenth and Eighteenth Centuries, the small city located on the Veerse Meer was a prosperous trading area. Approximately 750 houses could be found inside the city walls then, compared to about 300 now. These days, Veere's primary industry is tourism. Newbould makes his pitch for travel to Veere with subtlety, concentrating on its low-key charm and the architectural superiority of Veere's town hall.
Est: $2,000-$2,500.

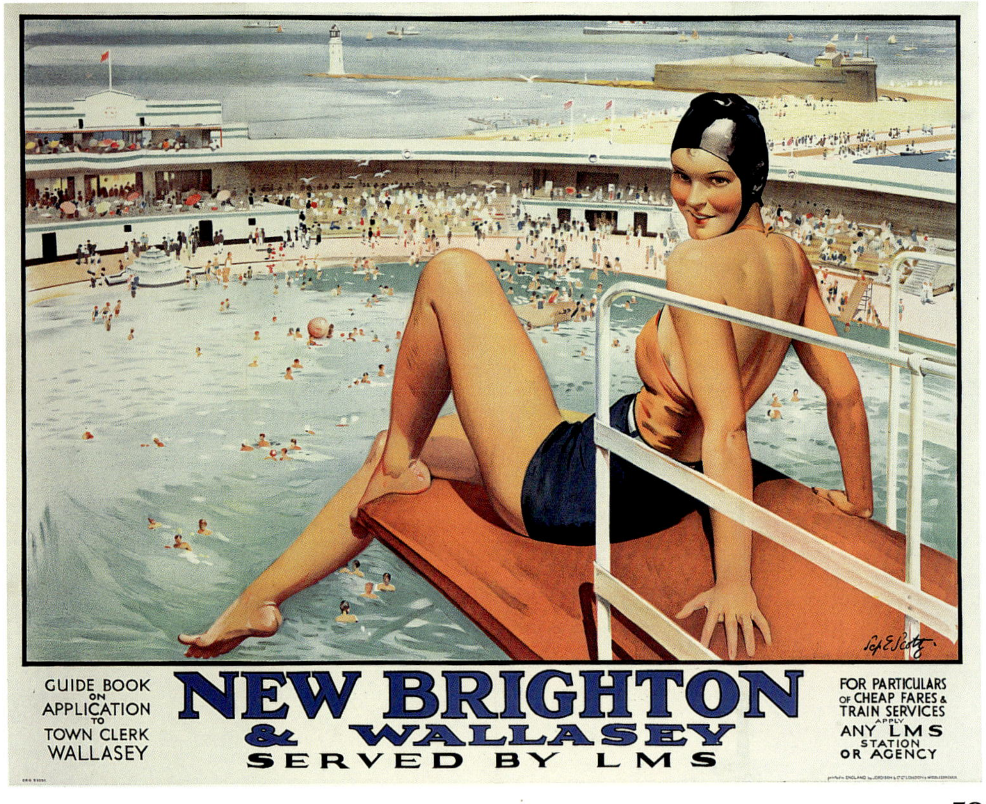

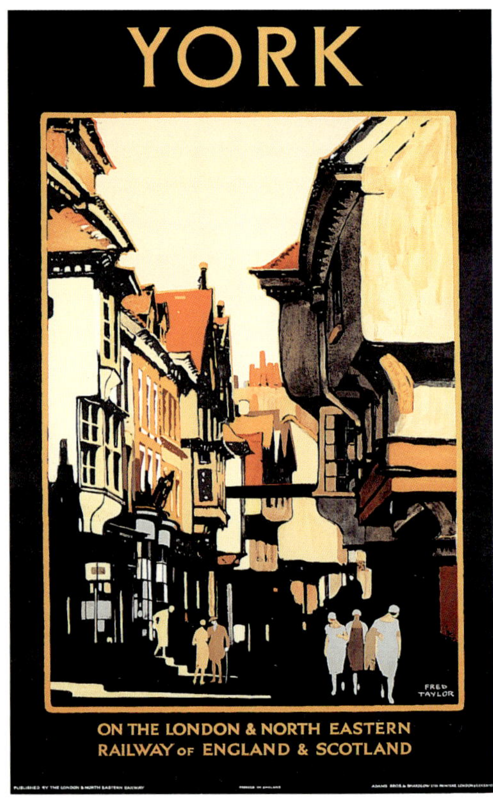

78   79

BRITISH RAILWAYS (cont'd)

SEPTIMUS E. SCOTT (1879-?)

78. New Brighton & Wallasey/LMS. ca. 1930.
50 x 40 in./127 x 101.5 cm
Jordison, London
Cond A–/Unobtrusive folds.
Ref: Railway Posters, p. 110; PAI-III, 400
Well, hello there! This coy sunbather invitingly posed on a high dive certainly makes a compelling argument for a seaside getaway aboard the LMS Railway. A lively beach scene is taking place behind her, but make no mistake about it—flirtation is the name of the game in this sexy Scott promotion. Scott was a landscape painter and graphic designer who created several noteworthy images for the Canadian Pacific and British railways.
Est: $3,000-$4,000.

FRED TAYLOR (1875-1963)

79. York/London & Northeastern Railway.
24$^1/_8$ x 39$^1/_2$ in./61.5 x 100.4 cm
Adams Bros. & Shardlow, London
Cond A–/Unobtrusive tears in top and bottom text areas.
York is a compact walled riverside city, situated at the confluence of the Ouse and Foss rivers. And even though York is home to the largest Gothic cathedral in England, Taylor sets his eye on one of the city's unique secular attractions: The Shambles, perhaps York's a majority of its iconic street. Formerly the lamb-butchers district, it retains most of its feel from around four hundred years ago; however, now instead of meat venders, The Shambles is crammed with gift and craft shops and several cafes. Known for his prolific works for the rail and shipping clients, Taylor is also considered one of the principal, and finest, designers for the London Underground.
Est: $1,700-$2,000.

MISTINGUETT
(1873-1956)

For longevity and popular appeal, few French performers can match Mistinguett. From the time that she made her debut as a nightclub singer at the age of seventeen until she stopped touring in 1948 at a well-preserved seventy-five, Mistinguett was the French music-hall incarnate—delicious and dazzling.

No less a critic than Colette agreed. In reviewing Mistinguett's 1933 revue "Folies en folie" for *Le Matin*, she concluded, "She is a national property . . . her pupils the color of the chicory flower, her long legs, her cheerful smile and her sentimental expressions" (Folies-Bergère, p. 12). All of this is apparent in the posters that follow. Our selection shows The Miss early and late in her career, clothed and unclothed, raffish and refined.

How Mistinguett got her name is retold by Alain Weill: "Her friends from Enghien nicknamed the youthful Jeanne Bougeois, Helyette, the heroine of an opera by Audran, whom they claimed she resembled. Inventing a play on words based on a popular refrain 'La Vertinguette,' the Miss hummed, 'It's la Vertin, Miss Helyette, it's a Vertin . . . It's Mistinguette.' The songwriter Saint-Marcel who was at her side told her, 'If you ever appear on stage, my little girl, call yourself Mistinguette,' and that's what she did!" (Folies-Bergère, p. 13). The final "e" disappeared before the century was over.

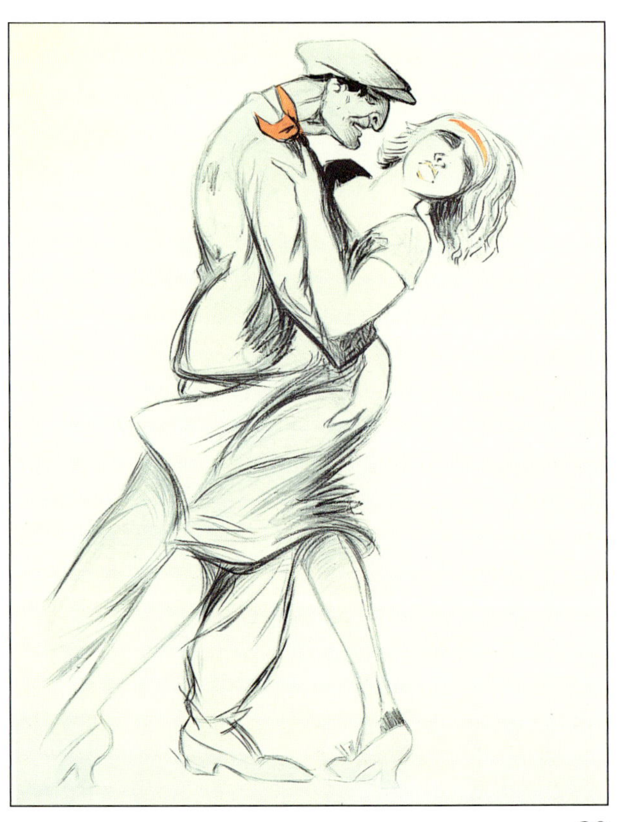

80

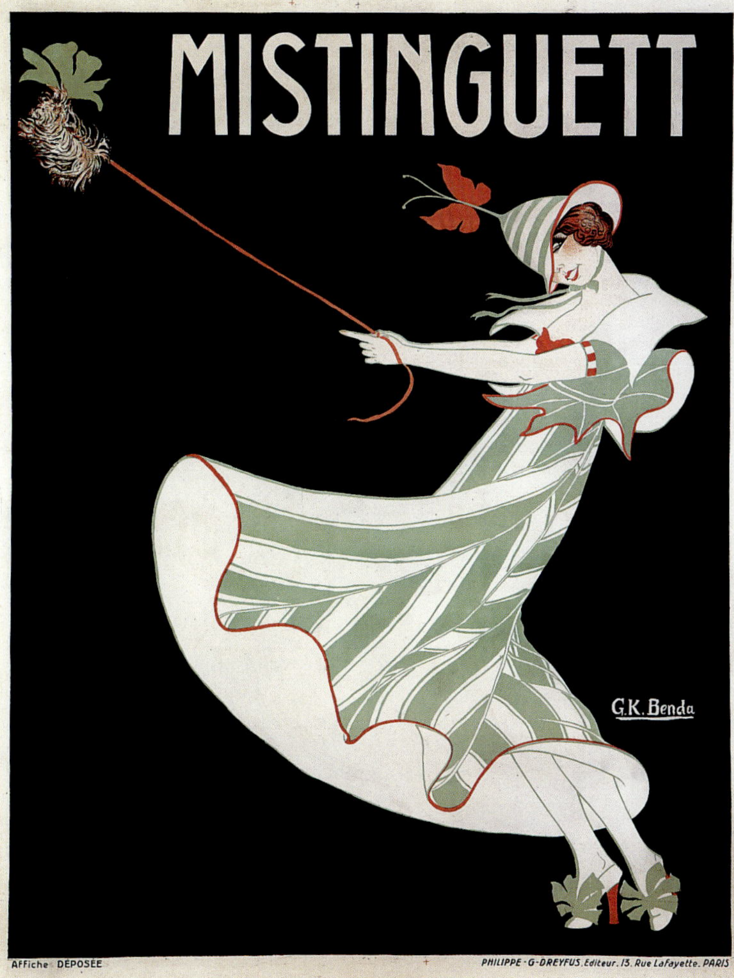

81

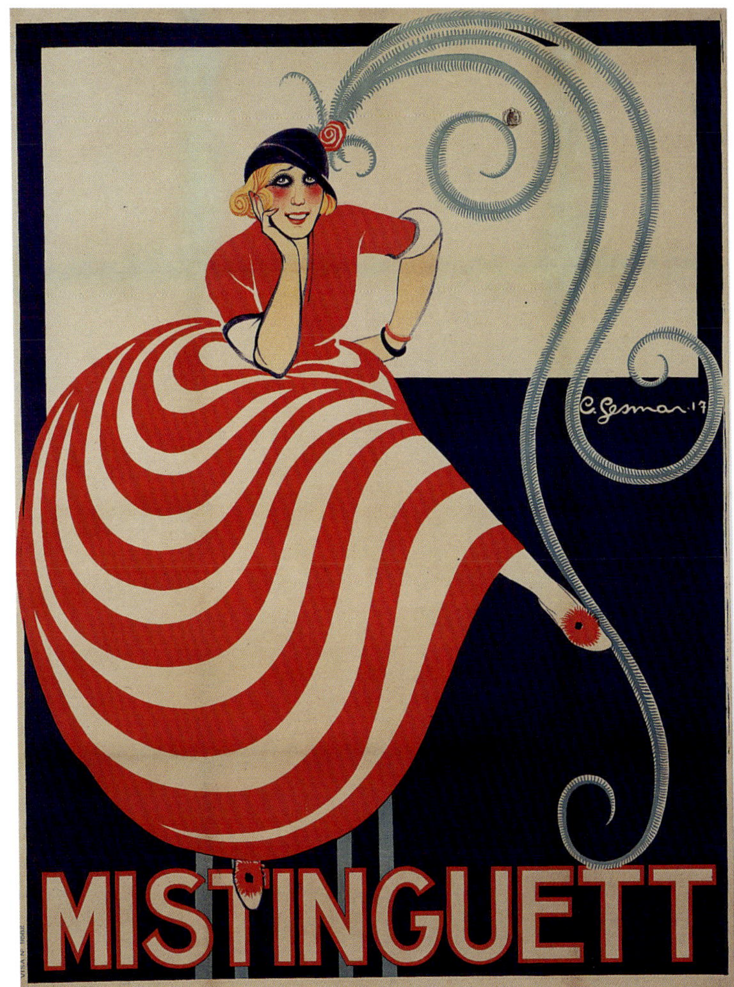

82

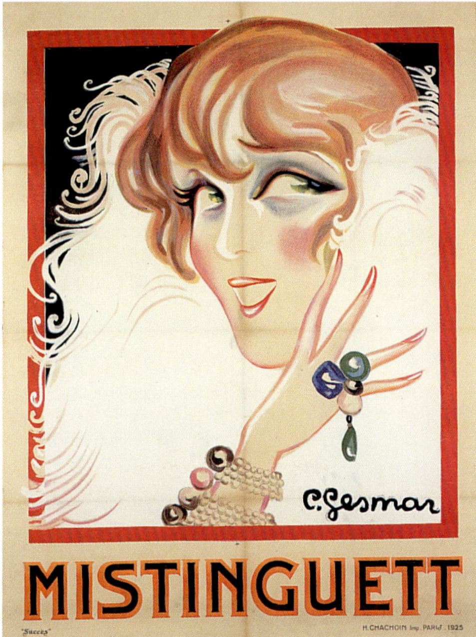

83

ADRIEN BARRÈRE (1877-1931)

80. Apache Dance.
$46^7/_8$ x $62^3/_4$ in./119 x 159.5 cm
Cond B+/Slight tears at folds and edges.
When you combine a sneering lowlife and a compro-
mised woman you don't typically expect to find such an
undercurrent of balanced form and uneasy sensuality.
Of course it wouldn't seem that outside-the-norm if
you were familiar with the so-called "apache dance,"
because that's what we're being treated to here. The
faux-Native American label found its way into popular
French slang via Western dime novels and short films
with the term "apache" coming to denote a streetwise

Parisian tough guy. The dance craze that ensued consisted basically of one of these "thugs" "roughing-up"
his partner. Barrère blends threat and grace in perfectly
balanced proportions, presenting danger and desire
in just the manner that the public craved at the time.
The actual poster changes the pose of the dancers and
was produced for Mistinguett's first film role in 1908's
"L'Empreinte," with Max Dearly (*see PAI-XII, 80*).
Est: $2,500-$3,000.

G. K. BENDA (Georges Kugelmann)

81. Mistinguett. ca. 1913.
$45^7/_8$ x $60^3/_4$ in./ 119 x 154.3 cm
Philippe Dreyfus, Paris
Cond B+/Unobtrusive tear in left ankle and collar of
     dress.
Ref: PAI-XLI, 406
Benda is the pseudonym of a painter and graphic artist
who resided in Paris a good many years, as there are
records of his having exhibited paintings in various
salons between 1907 and 1921. He produced only a
handful of posters, with this Mistinguett design being
especially memorable. Catching her in this whirling
moment breezily communicates that she was a breath
of fresh air, a fact to which all of those who were fortunate enough to see her perform uniformly agree.
Est: $3,000-$3,500.

CHARLES GESMAR (1900-1928)
For other works of Gesmar, see Nos. 339-347.

82. Mistinguett. 1917.
$45^3/_4$ x $63^1/_4$ in./116.3 x 160.5 cm
Imp. Minot, Paris
Cond A–/Unobtrusive tears at folds and edges.

Ref: PAI-XXXIV, 386
Mistinguett was Gesmar's chief client and close friend
from the time he was seventeen until his untimely
death eleven years later, and he created dozens of
designs for her in that comparatively brief time. Here,
in one of the earliest, the visual impact emanates from
sheer graphic brio—an almost dizzying repetition of
curlicues and swirls, growing in magnitude from the
small rosette on her hat through the swooping ostrich
plumes to the stripes on her voluminous skirt. *Rare!*
Est: $5,000-$6,000.

83. Mistinguett. 1925.
47 x $63^1/_8$ in./119.5 x 160.4 cm
Imp. H. Chachoin, Paris
Cond B/Usual stains at folds.
Ref: PAI-XLI, 405
The fluff of the white ostrich feathers is a perfect foil
for the famous music-hall star's irresistibly flirty quality.
Even the sparkling jewels that give the poster its infor-
mal name can't outdazzle her green eyes and winning
smile. In his short life, Gesmar created more than fifty
posters, all filled with zest and colors; he designed
posters and costumes for Mistinguett from about 1917
until his death.
Est: $1,700-$2,000.

84. Mistinguett/Casino de Paris. 1922.
$44^7/_8$ x $61^1/_2$ in./114 x 156 cm
Cond B+/Slight tears at folds and paper edges.
Ref: Deco Affiches, p. 17; PAI-XXIII, 48
Perched on a stool in a black cocktail dress, showing
plenty of elegant slender leg, Mistinguett flashes a
vivacious smile as she chats with a green parrot.
Est: $5,000-$6,000.

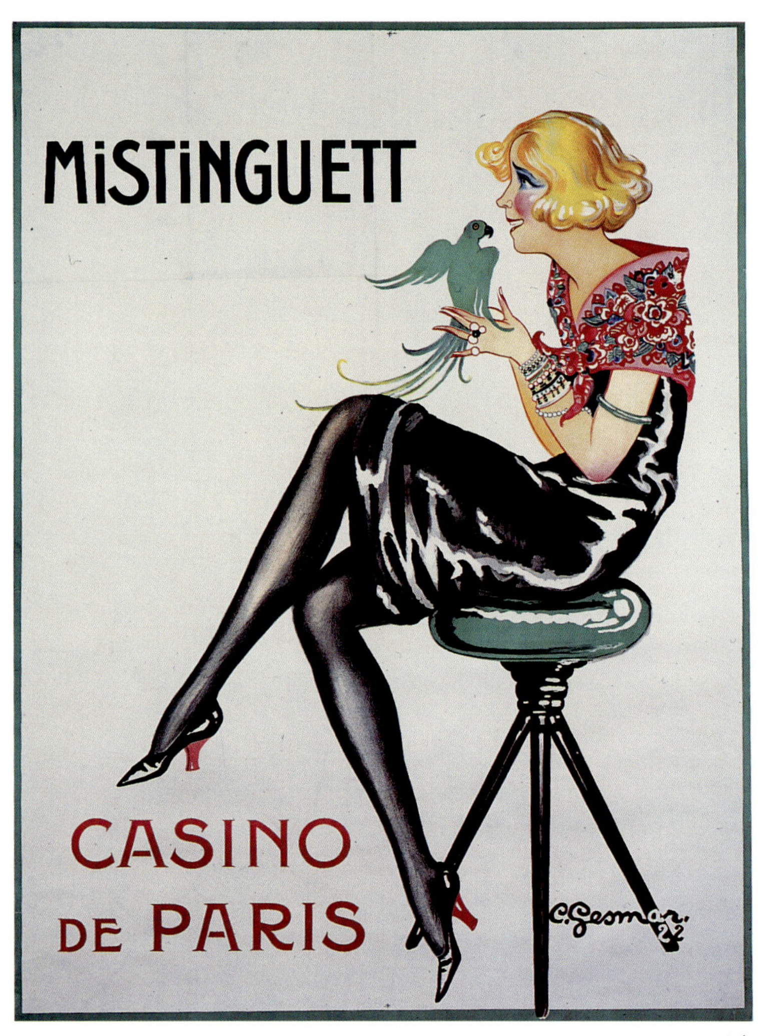

MISTINGUETT
CASINO
DE PARIS

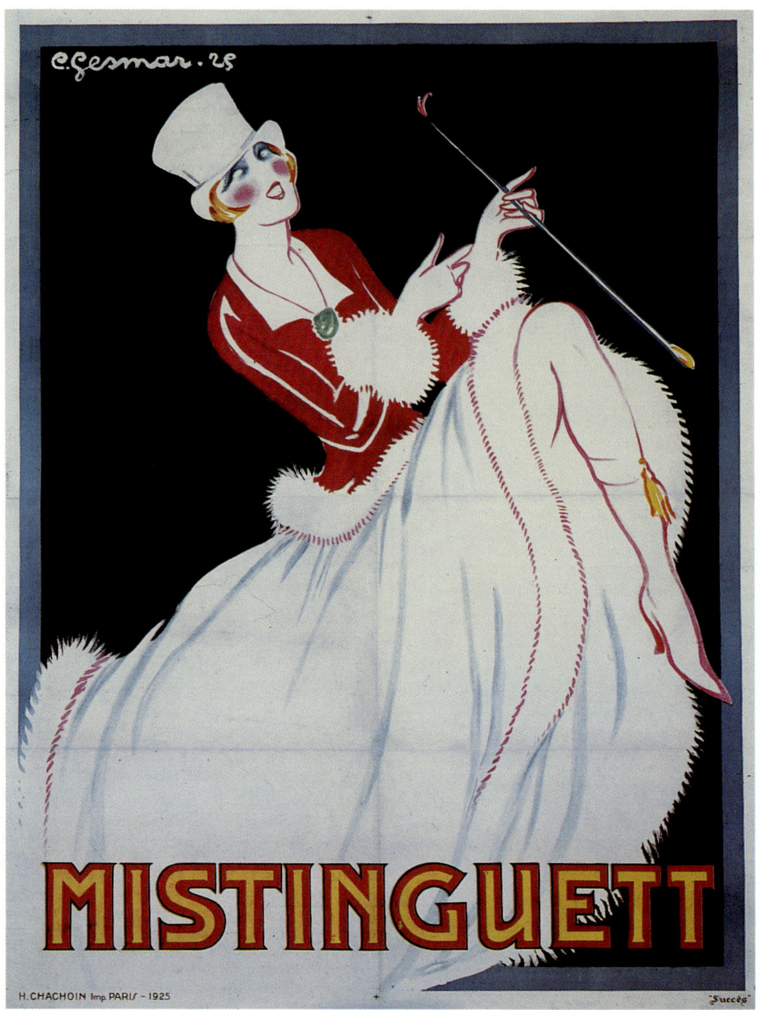

MISTINGUETT
H.CHACHOIN Imp. PARIS - 1925

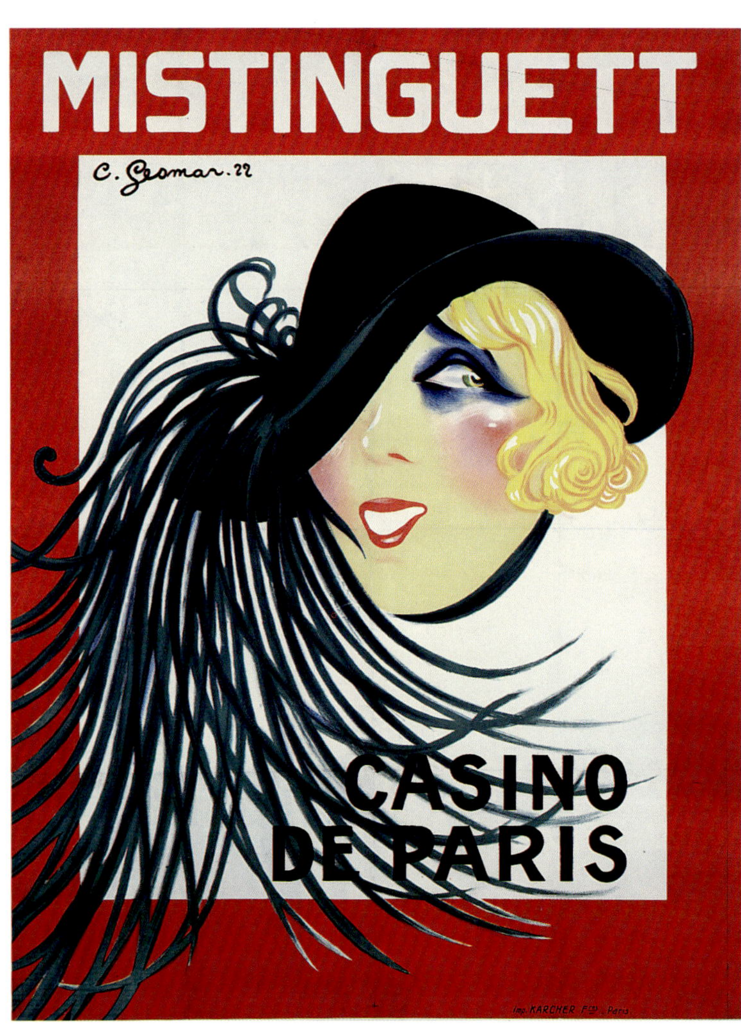

MISTINGUETT
CASINO
DE PARIS

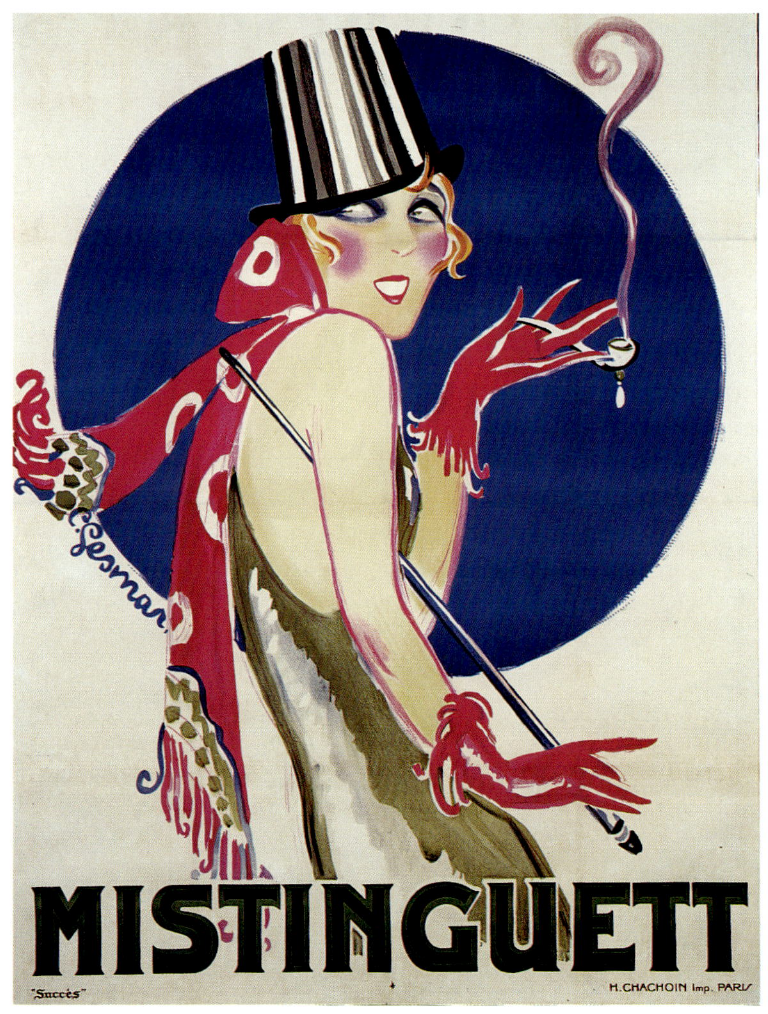

MISTINGUETT
H.CHACHOIN imp. PARIS

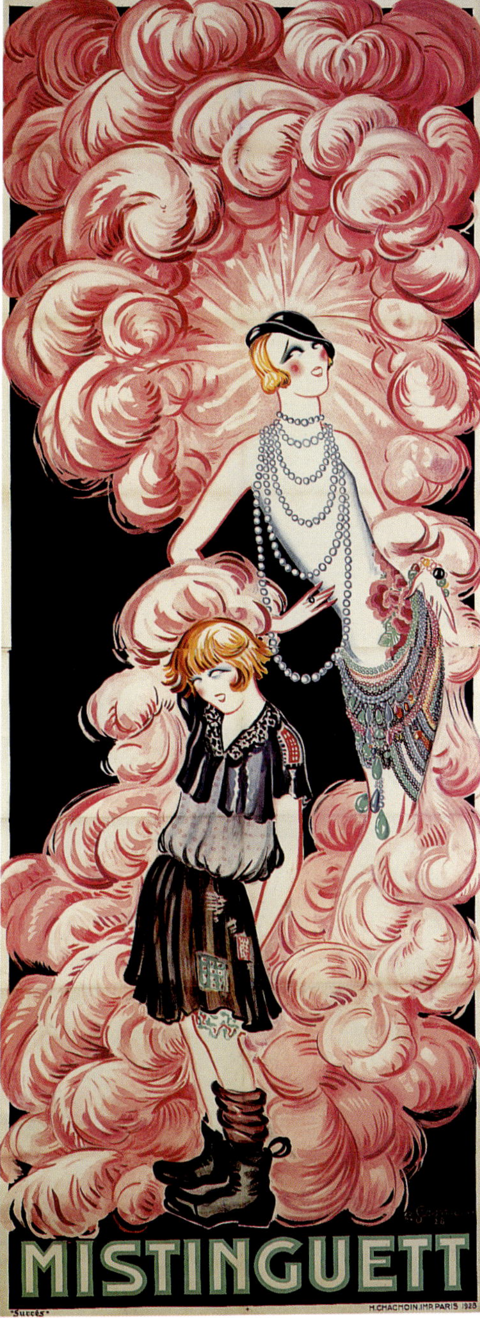

88

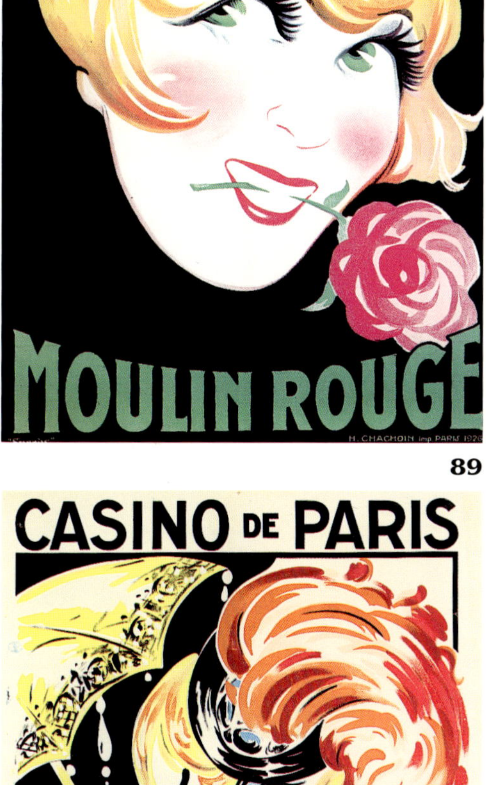

89

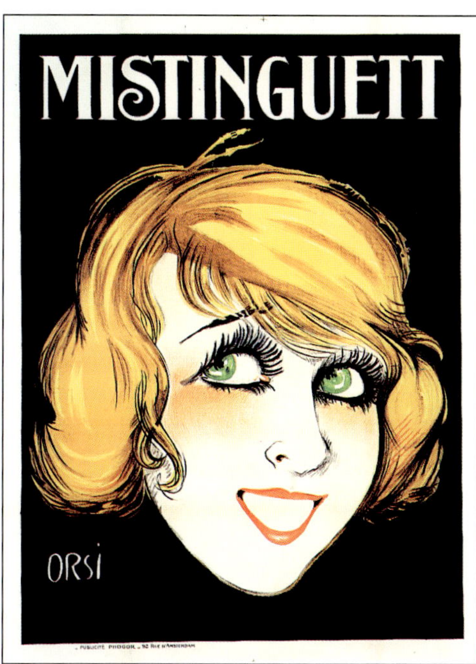

90

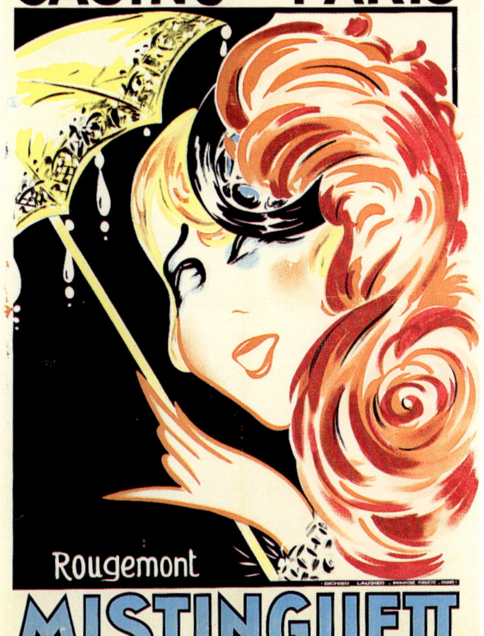

91

MISTINGUETT/GESMAR (cont'd)

85. Mistinguett. 1925.
47 x 63^1/$_8$ in./119.4 x 160.2 cm
Imp. H. Chachoin, Paris
Cond B+/Slight tears at folds.
Ref: PAI-VI, 100
One of the most smashing and rare of all of Gesmar's designs for the Miss, with the music hall legend high-stepping in a white top hat and a fur lined skirt. The matching riding crop not only serves as an ideal accessory, it also adds just the right amount of sass.
Est: $5,000-$6,000.

86. Mistinguett/Casino de Paris. ca. 1926.
45^1/$_2$ x 61 in./115.8 x 155.6 cm
Imp. Karcher, Paris
Cond B+/Slight tears at folds.
Ref: PAI-XXXIX, 57
Forever fashionable, the all-knowing eye of Mistinguett's crowd-pleasing savvy peers out from beneath a floppy black hat adorned with cascading aquamarine feathers. Judging from the headgear we've seen along the way, the Miss was apparently partial to being adorned with blue-green plumage. Apart from confirming that trend, Gesmar shows his typical admirable restraint, aware of the fact that when one has the good fortune to be designing promotional material for the face of

the Parisian music hall, all one has to do to capture the public's attention is to put that vivacious face forward. *Rare!*
Est: $4,000-$5,000.

87. Mistinguett.
45^5/$_8$ x 61^1/$_8$ in./116 x 155.3 cm
H. Chachoin, Paris
Cond B/Slight tears at folds.
Ref: PAI-XLI, 401
A magnificent design from Gesmar, flaunting the jewel in the crown of the French music-hall in all her flirtatious glory. The picture of elegance, from the teardrop-pearl setting on her pipe to her top hat and cane, Mistinguett is in the spotlight. She's slim, stylish and stepping out, ready to take on all the good things that life is just waiting to offer her. Although never shy of throwing a few masculine touches into her wardrobe choices (*see* PAI-XXXVII, 492 & PAI-XXXVI, 556), she simply radiates an alluring air of feminine poise and sensuality.
Est: $10,000-$12,000.

88. Mistinguett. 1928.
45 x 123 in./114.2 x 312.5 cm
Imp. H. Chachoin, Paris
Cond B/Slight tears and stains at folds.
Ref: Theaterplakate, 155; PAI-XXXVIII, 349
In this spectacular two-sheet poster, Gesmar showed the two distinct stage personae affected by Mistinguett: the flamboyant showgirl and the Parisian street urchin. She was equally effective and popular in both guises. The poster is usually referred to as "Rags to Riches."
Est: $7,000-$9,000.

89. Mistinguett/Moulin Rouge. 1926.
30^1/$_2$ x 47^1/$_8$ in./77.5 x 119.7 cm
Imp. H. Chachoin, Paris
Cond B/Slight tears and stains along folds.
Ref: Folies-Bergère, 63; Hillier, p. 249;
      Theaterplakate, 155; PAI-XXXIX, 58
Mistinguett achieved her greatest success at the Moulin Rouge, where this 1926 revue was simply called "Mistinguett." Weill indicates: "It is one of Gesmar's most beautiful posters: without jewels or fancy dress, it's the Miss, child of Paris, which he shows us here . . . alluring, tender, and roguish with the rose between her lips which we would like to pluck." (Folies-Bergère, p. 11).
Est: $2,000-$2,500.

ORSI (1889-1947)

90. Mistinguett.
45^3/$_4$ x 61^1/$_4$ in./116.2 x 155.5 cm
Publicité Phogor, Paris
Cond B+/Slight tears at folds.
Ref: PAI-XXXIX, 59
While other posterists may give us the Miss costumed, jeweled, posed and propped, Orsi shines his spotlight on her face alone: Big green eyes, red hair, pointed chin and unforgettable saucy smile. This prolific posterist—whose life is a complete mystery—produced a quantity of posters, mostly theatrical and all with strong, eye-catching graphics.
Est: $2,500-$3,000.

ROUGEMONT

91. Mistinguett/Casino de Paris. ca. 1939.
30^5/$_8$ x 47 in./77.8 x 119.3 cm
Richier Laugier, Paris
Cond B/Slight tears at folds and edges.
Ref: PAI-XXXIX, 459
With a nod to the great Gesmar, Rougemont gives us a dazzling close-up of Mistinguett, full of the sparkle and flamboyance that she always projected on stage.
Est: $2,000-$2,500.

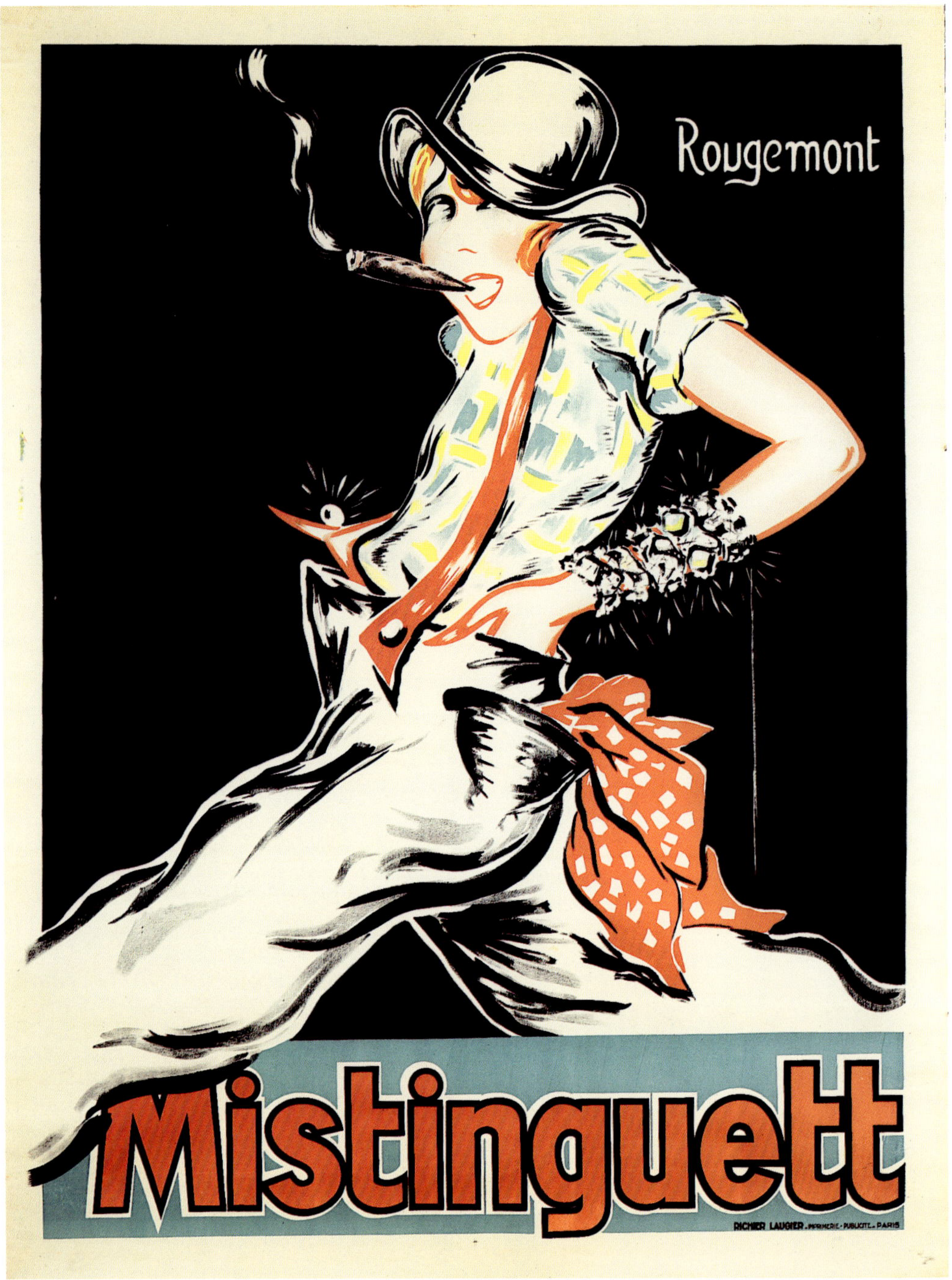

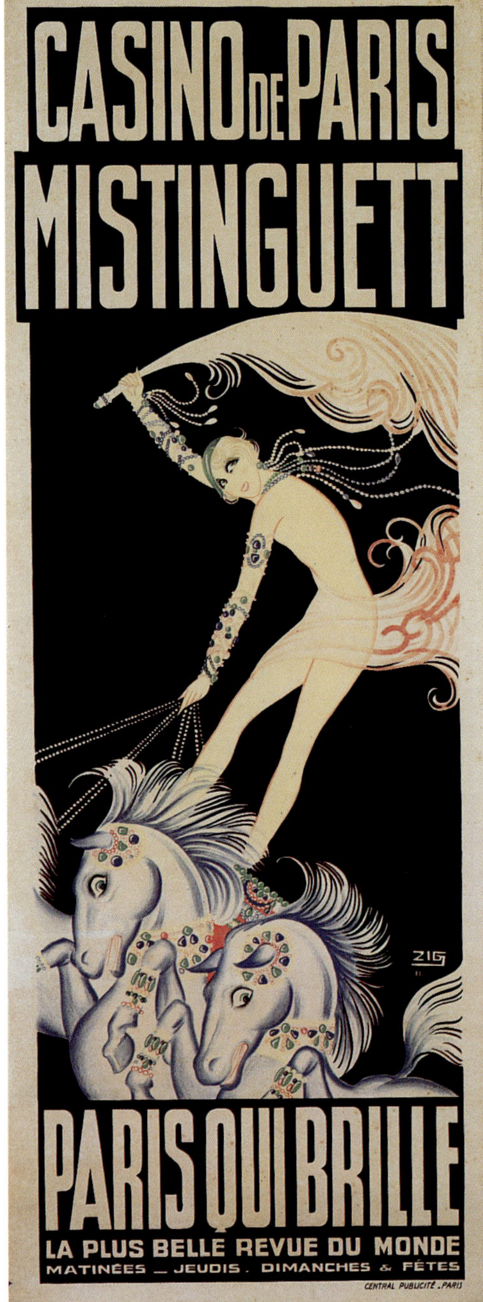

95

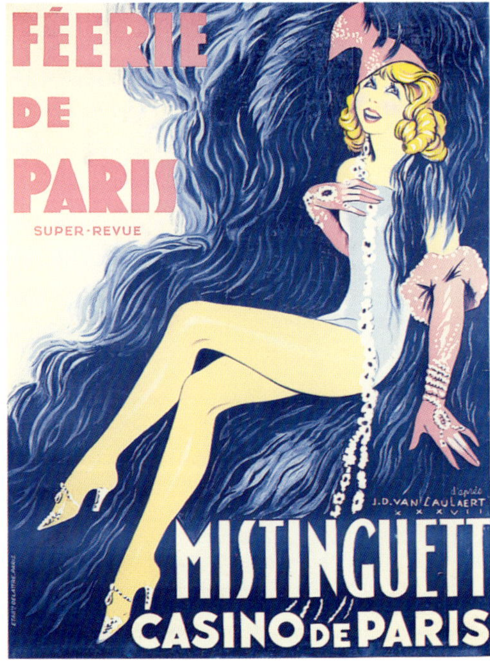

94

MISTINGUETT/ROUGEMONT (cont'd)

92. Mistinguett.
$47^1/_8$ x 63 in./119.7 x 160 cm
Richier-Laugier, Paris
Cond B+/Unobtrusive folds.
Ref: PAI-XXXVII, 492
The famous entertainer in an adorably bumptious pose
with a rakish derby, red suspenders and cigar. This is
surely one of the most unusual and endearing of the
Mistinguett posters. Who else could—or would—carry
off armloads of jewels worn with a hobo air?
Est: $10,000-$12,000.

PAUL SELTEN (Seltenhammer)

93. Folies en Folie/Mistinguett. 1933.
$46^5/_8$ x $123^7/_8$ in./118.5 x 314.5 cm
Impressions France/Pierre Havez, Paris
Cond B–/Slight tears and stains.
Ref: Folies-Bergère, 71; PAI-XXII, 503
"It was in this revue, 'Folies en Folies,' that Mistinguett
created her most famous song, 'C'est vrai' (It's true)
. . . Selten . . . a regular collaborator of the Folies-
Bergère . . . was given the honor of producing the poster
for the show. He did a fine job. Two rows of boys
shaded from grey to black surround the Miss. Three
hands (two black and one grey, a skillful color scheme)

try to hold her. She—frail but delighted—smiles. Her
arms are covered with the usual bracelets, her famous
legs (at the time insured for the price of a private house
on the Champs-Elysées) are barely hidden by a veil'"
(Folies-Bergère, p. 12). Against all the somber tuxedos
in this two-sheet design, Mistinguett shines.
Est: $6,000-$8,000.

JEAN-DOMINIQUE VAN CAULAERT (1897-1979)

94. Mistinguett/Féerie de Paris/Casino de Paris.
1937.
$45^3/_4$ x $62^7/_8$ in./116.2 x 159.7 cm
Imp. Delattre, Paris
Cond B/Slight tears and stains, largely at folds and edges.
Ref: Folies-Bergère, 79; PAI-XXXII, 544
"Féerie de Paris" was such a hit that the box office of
the Casino de Paris had to be enlarged. The theme of the
revue was a tour of Paris monuments, led by Mistinguett
wearing a six-foot high Eiffel Tower of a costume. Van
Caulaert could only fit part of it into this design—a great
cascade of blue plumes, against which Mistinguett's
accessories and, well, other accessories stand out. The
poster certainly doesn't give away the star's age at the
time—sixty-two. Van Caulaert's specialty was portraits.

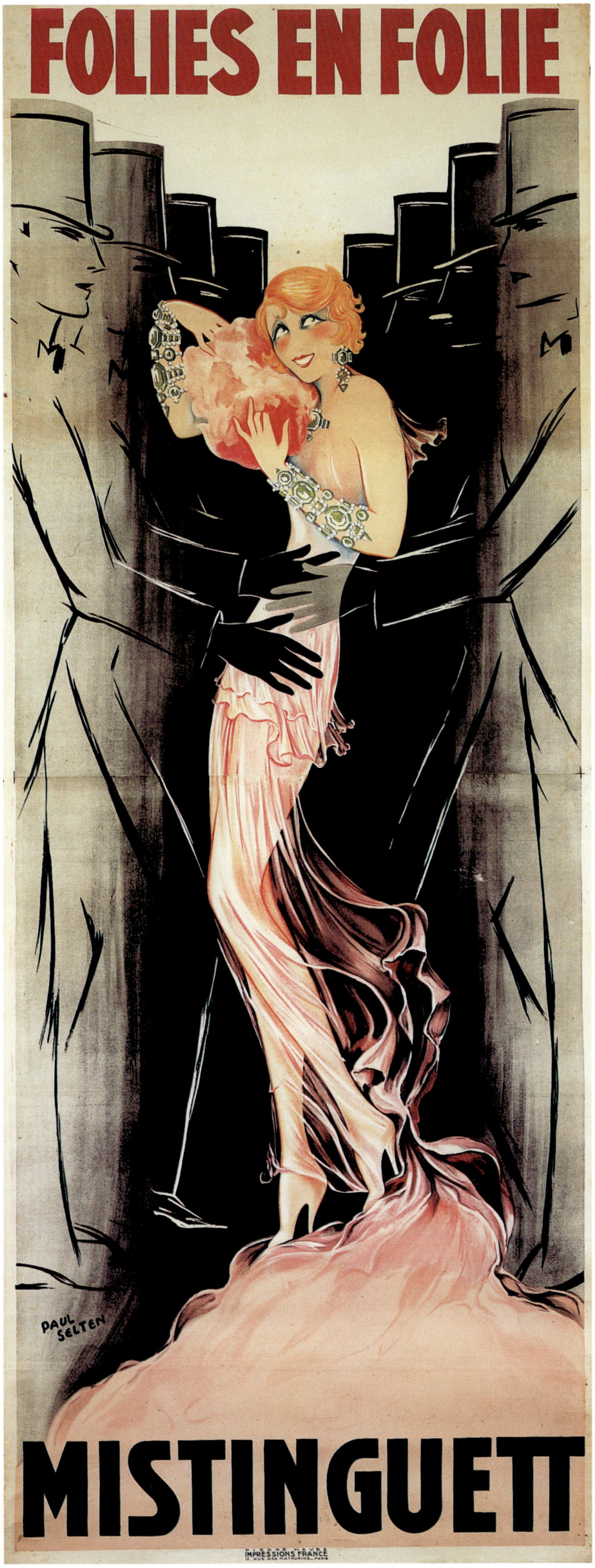

93

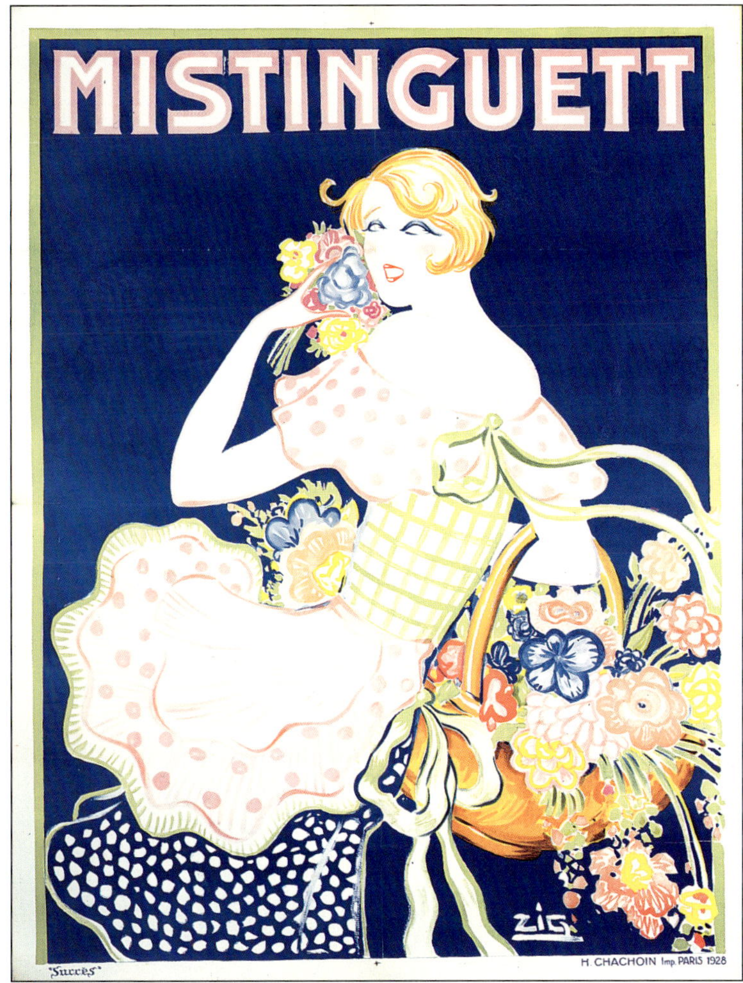

96

He painted all the luminaries of his time and brought that skill to bear in his posters as well. He became the official painter of the French war department in the 1930s and his poster portraits include all the music hall and recording greats of France, such as Josephine Baker, Cécile Sorel, Rina Ketty and, of course, Mistinguett. *This is the larger format.*
Est: $2,000-$2,500.

ZIG (Louis Gaudin, ?-1936)

95. Casino de Paris/Mistinguett/Paris Qui Brille. 1931.
$31^1/_2$ x $86^5/_8$ in./80 x 220 cm
Centrale Publicité, Paris
Cond B/Slight tears and stains at folds and edges.
Ref: PAI-XLI, 411A
Zig's poster for Mistinguett's "Paris Dazzles" revue more than lives up to its designation: a bejeweled Mistinguett, pink-tinged feather in one hand, reins of her playful team of blue horses in the other, spotlit against a black background. *This is the largest format.*
Est: $2,500-$3,000.

96. Mistinguett. 1928.
$47^3/_8$ x 63 in./120.5 x 160 cm
Imp. H. Chachoin, Paris
Cond B+/Slight tears at folds.
Ref: PAI-XXXVI, 576
Mistinguett, queen of the French music-hall, had a way of outliving her designers. After her favorite, Gesmar, died in 1928, she switched to Zig. The artist had been a habitué of Montmartre cabarets where he sang and recited at the drop of a beret. Both of them affected a flamboyantly showy style, which exactly suited the Miss persona, and after he proved himself with set and costume designs, she ultimately trusted him with the design of her posters. Here, Zig gives us Mistinguett as a country girl complete with a basket of flowers. Beyond its graphic flair, it's Zig juxtaposing the star's saucy sexiness with *naïf* trappings—like Brigitte Bardot in her gingham bikini—that makes the image so effective.
Est: $4,000-$5,000.

MISTINGUETT/Zig (cont'd)

97. Mistinguett. 1932.
62$^{1}/_2$ x 46$^{3}/_4$ in./158.5 x 118.7 cm
Imp. H. Chachoin, Paris
Cond B/Restored tears.
Ref: PAI-XXXV, 398
Zig poses Mistinguett coquettishly in a bare-back swim-suit, sporting an enormous black cartwheel hat that serves to halo her face. Mistinguett gives us proof that at fifty-nine she is still as attractive as ever.
Est: $4,000-$5,000.

98. Bal de Marins.
24$^{5}/_8$ x 18$^{7}/_8$ in./62.6 x 48 cm
Gouache, ink and crayon maquette.
Sleaze ahoy! Looking at this maquette for a Sailors Ball presided over by "la vraie de vraie" Mistinguett, I'm reminded that these days, at least in the United States, people take themselves far too seriously. Imagine a public event held today that encouraged people to dress-up like scoundrels and prostitutes! Well, by gum, that certainly would undermine every last family value and unravel every last moral fiber! Fortunately, we have mementos such as this to remind us that life should consist of more than useless "terror alert" levels and shampoo being confiscated at airport security checkpoints. Of course, all the playful debauchery is classic Zig and Mistinguett, from the "Unstable Hotel" to the announcement that mercy will be taken upon "fille de joie" who arrive without invitations And speaking thematically, it's hard to beat the statement that Mistinguett "makes hearts and ships keel over."
Est: $2,500-$3,000.

ANONYMOUS

99. Cycles Gladiator. ca. 1895.
53 x 38$^{3}/_4$ in./134.5 x 98.4 cm
Imp. G. Massais, Paris
Cond A–/Restored bottom border. Framed.
Ref: Bicycle Posters, 42; Petite Reine, 47; Ailes, p. 11;
    Musée d'Affiche, 22; Reims, 154; PAI-XXXVI, 117
This is, without question, one of the most sensational designs for a bicycle ever created, yet the artist hid his name—the outlines of his initials can barely be seen in the lower right corner. Even Alexandre Henriot, the great collector who organized the huge 1896 poster show at Reims, was unable to credit him. Many of the Gladiator posters proclaimed the bike to be "Sans Egale"—without equal. The same can be said when comparing this design to the thousands of other bicycle posters of the period.
Est: $20,000-$25,000.

100. Veilchen "Kaiser Wilhelm II".
14$^{1}/_2$ x 37 in./18$^{1}/_4$ x 46.3 cm
Hollerbaum & Schmidt, Berlin
Cond B/Tears, largely near edges; recreated top and
    bottom margins.
Apparently, less than one-hundred years ago, being the leader of a major world power was enough to get a perfume named in your honor. And even though it's unlikely that we're going to see "Lavender 'George W. Bush'" on the shelves anytime soon, that would be a fairly approximate equivalent to the product being promoted here: Violet "Kaiser Wilhelm II." Thankfully the last German Emperor and King of Prussia doesn't make an appearance in the design. Rather, we're treated to bewitching Art Nouveau tendrils of the fragrance emanating off of representative flowers, transporting this woman somewhere far from her otherwise drab existence.
Est: $1,400-$1,700.

101. Cuisine au Gaz.
37$^{7}/_8$ x 50$^{3}/_8$ in./96.2 x 128 cm
Affiches Camis, Paris
Cond B/Slight tears at folds.
Cleanliness, speed and economy. Who could ask for anything more when it comes to setting up one's kitchen? And even though this housewife may be a bit overdressed to be preparing a meal, she's clearly more than satisfied with the results she's getting from cooking with gas. It's not clear if this was an institutional ad for the gas industry or whether a manufacturer's name was to have been imprinted at the bottom.
Est: $2,000-$2,500.

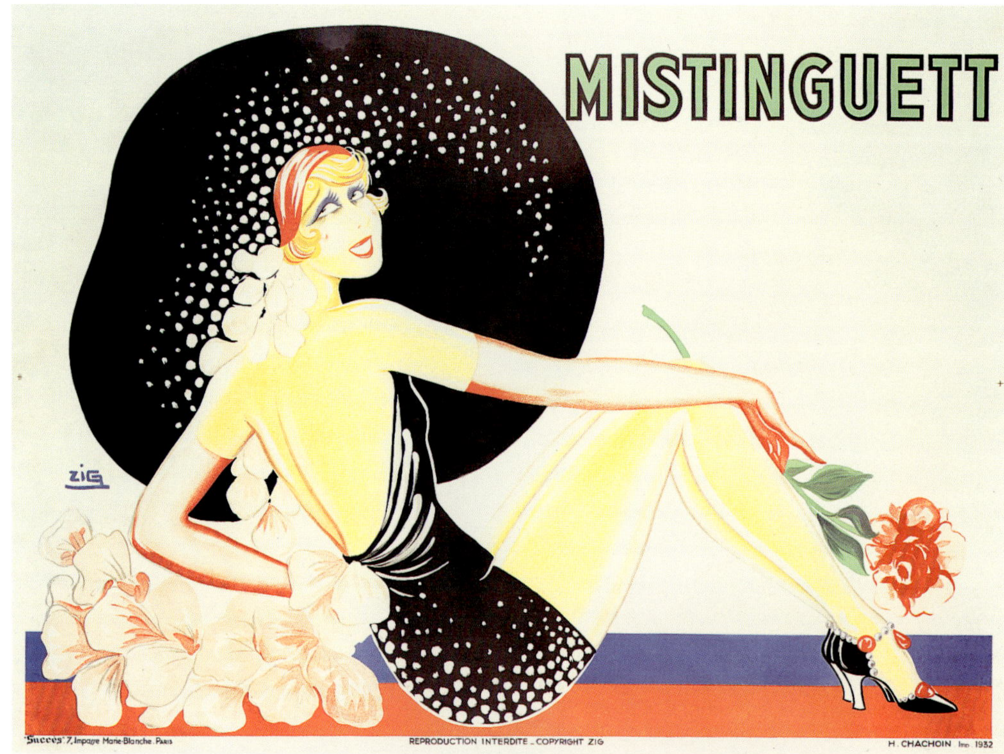

97

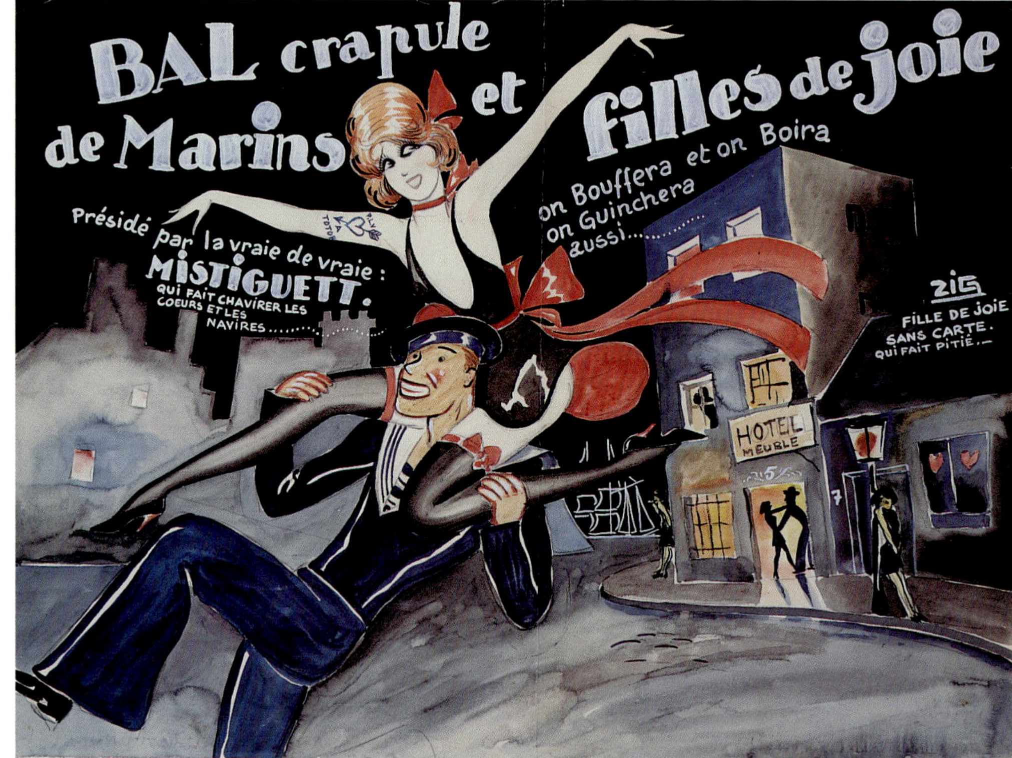

98

102. Salamonski/Fantaisie Serpantine. ca. 1899.
25 x 38$^{3}/_8$ in./63.3 x 97.4 cm
Affiches Louis Galices, Paris
Cond A–/Slight tears and stains at edges.
With its peculiar blend of horsemanship and illuminated diaphony, Salamonski surely has to be the wildest Loïe Fuller-inspired spoof to ever come our way. Sadly, no record appears to have been kept as to the specifics of Eugen Marrder's "Serpentine Fantasy" beyond what's given in this anonymous promotion, which is truly a shame seeing as it would be interesting to find out exactly what came of merging the "Dance of the Seven Veils" with some good old-fashioned equestrian know-how.
Est: $1,400-$1,700.

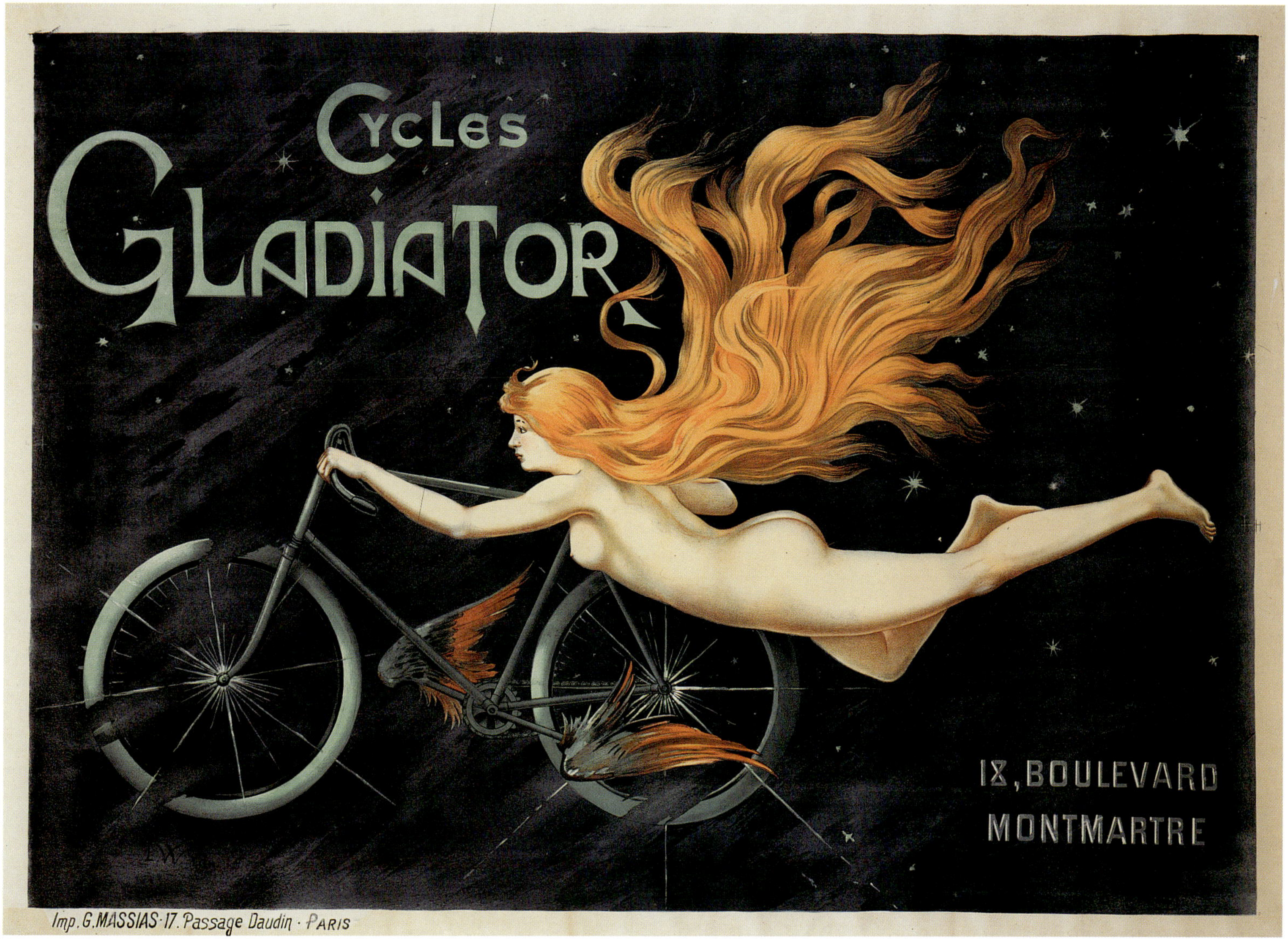

99

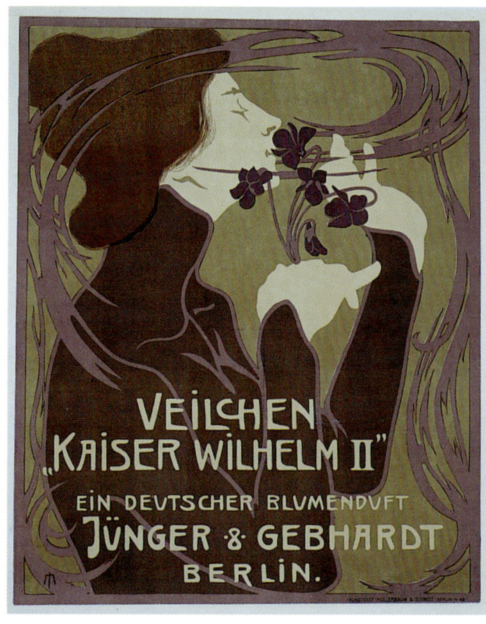

100

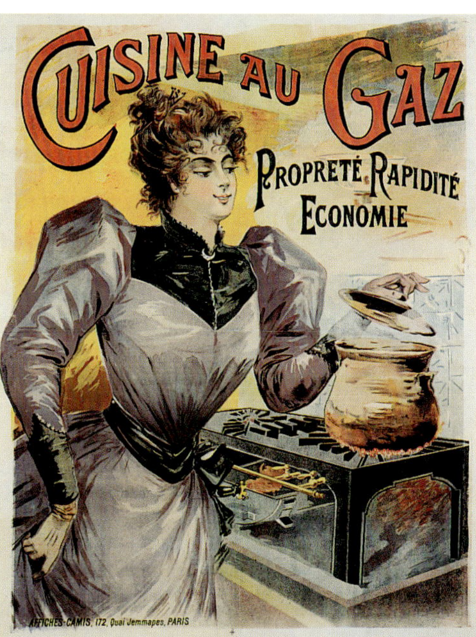

101

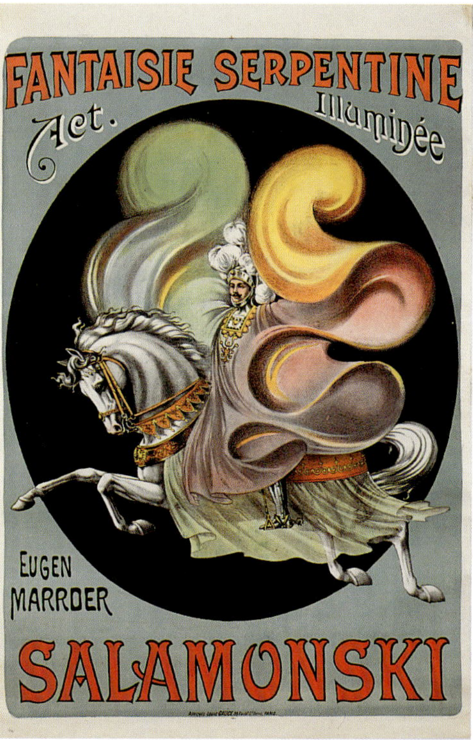

102

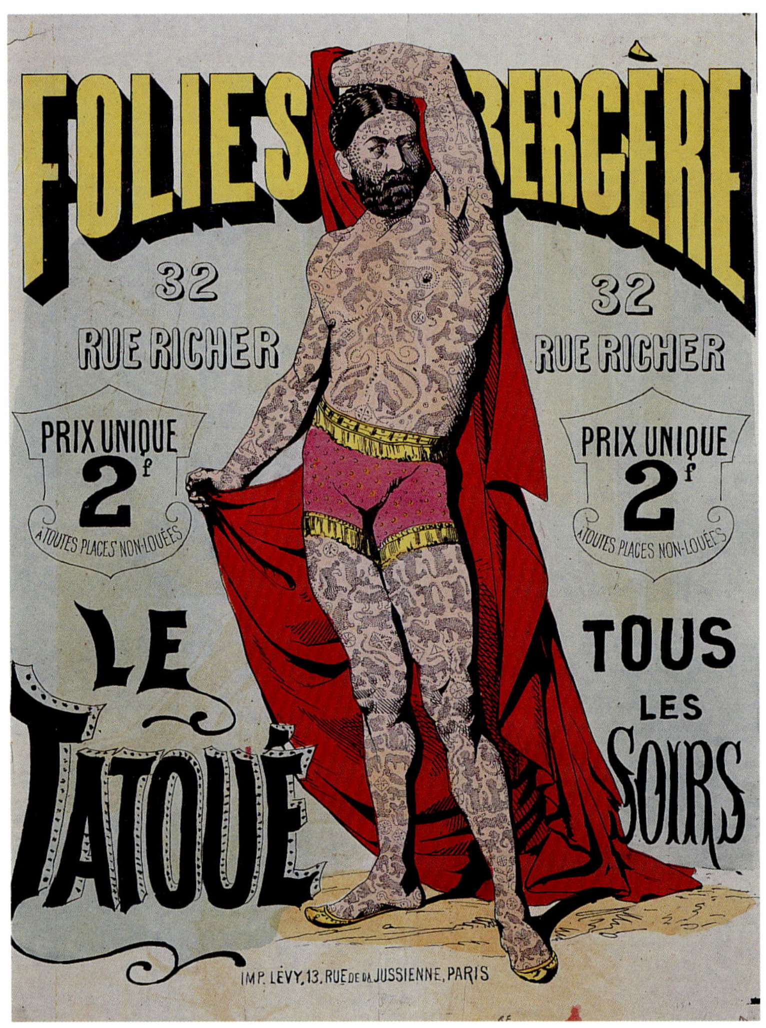

103

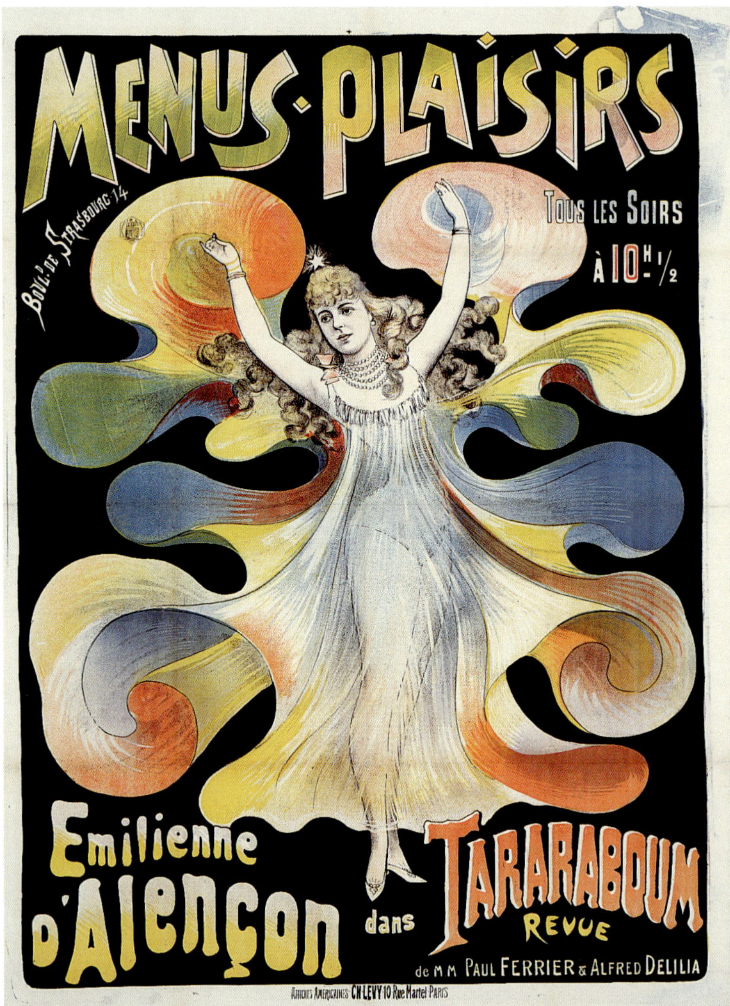

104

ANONYMOUS (cont'd)

103. Folies-Bergère/Le Tatoué. 1874.
17$^1/_4$ x 23$^3/_4$ in./43.7 x 60.4 cm
Imp. Lévy, Paris
Cond B+/Tears and creasing at edges/P.
Ref: Spectacle, 1051
Even in an age where body art is fairly commonplace,
the sight of this illustrated man is enough to make you
stop and take notice. The difference between then and
now is that back in 1874 having a body covered with
tattoos was enough to get you a headlining gig at the
Folies-Bergère; now it might be enough to get you into
a band. Maybe. *Of special interest: a handwritten
certificate from Emile Lévy appears verso, certifying
that on September 24, 1874, he printed 500 copies
of this poster.*
Est: $3,000-$4,000.

104. Menus-Plaisirs/Emilienne d'Alençon. ca. 1896.
35 x 48$^5/_8$ in./89 x 123.6 cm
Ch. Levy, Paris
Cond B+/Slight tears at folds.
Emilienne d'Alençon was one of the desirable women
of the French Belle Epoque stage that came to be
known as the *Grand Trois*—a trio of famous courte-
sans that included Liane de Pougy and La Belle Otero.
Though she studied acting at the Conservatoire for a
relatively brief period of time, she became a sensation
for an act that she developed at the Cirque d'Eté that
she later reprised at the Folies-Bergère to great acclaim
that essentially amounted to a languid ballet performed
in an entirely pink ensemble in the company of a warren
of pink-dyed rabbits. Here, however, for an appearance
in the Menus-Plaisirs' "Tararaboum Revue," she appears
to have traded one form of froth for another and taken
a turn for the Loïe Fuller, which just goes to show that
no matter how popular a performer may be, it certainly
doesn't hurt to augment that notoriety with the *sensation du jour.*
Est: $2,000-$2,500.

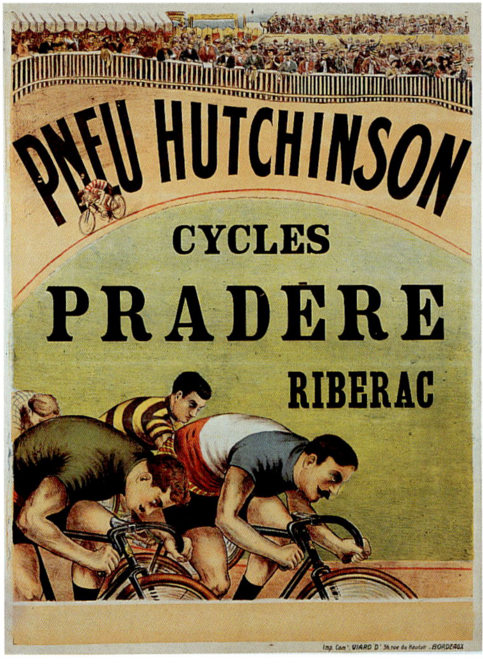

105

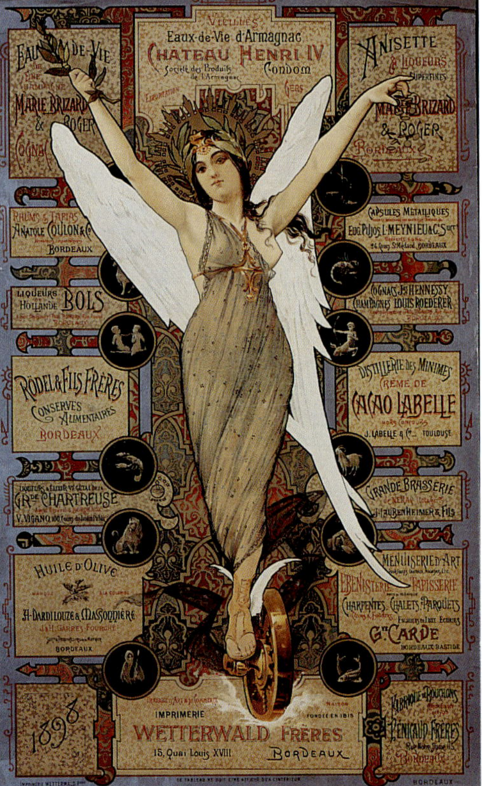

106

105. Pneu Hutchinson/Cycles Pradère.
45$^3/_4$ x 62$^1/_2$ in./116.2 x 158.7 cm
Imp. Com. Viard, Bordeaux
Cond A.
The situation is thoroughly velodramatic as these neck-
and-neck racers head towards the Finish Line—except
for the guy in the red-and-white striped shirt, who doesn't
stand a snowball's chance in Hades of garnering any
glory this day. Of course, one suspects that the competitor in the French tricolored jersey will in short order
break away from the pack, no doubt because he's riding a Pradère bicycle outfitted with Hutchinson tires,
which receive almost equal billing in this uncredited
design. Though this isn't pointed out with any sort of
lithographic overindulgence, the association is clear.
Est: $2,000-$3,000.

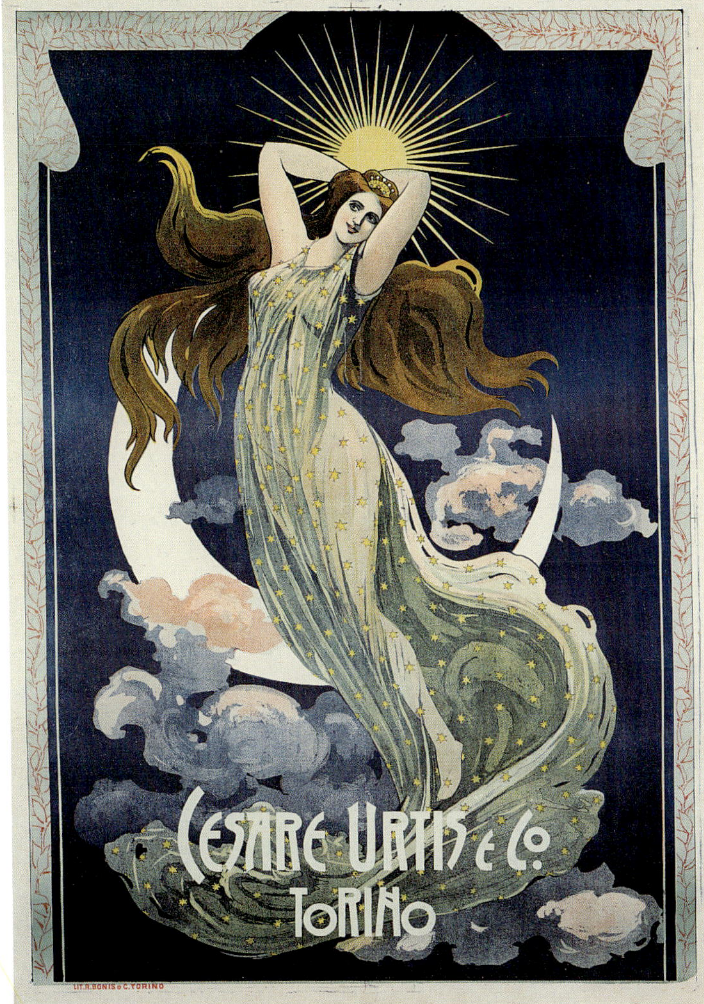

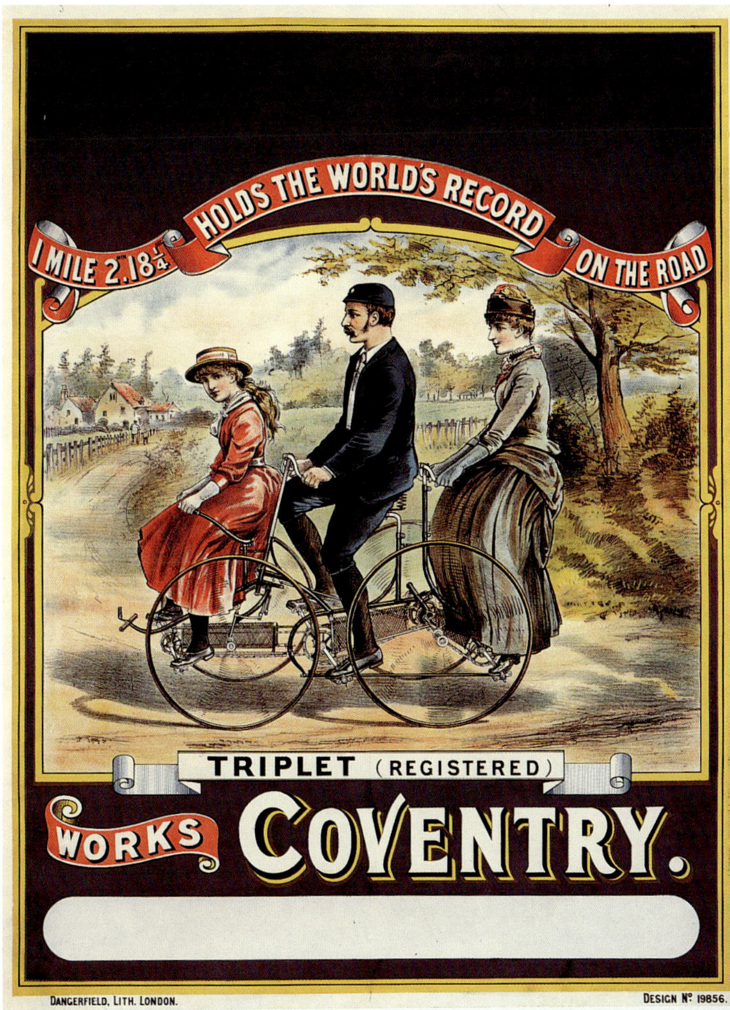

107

108

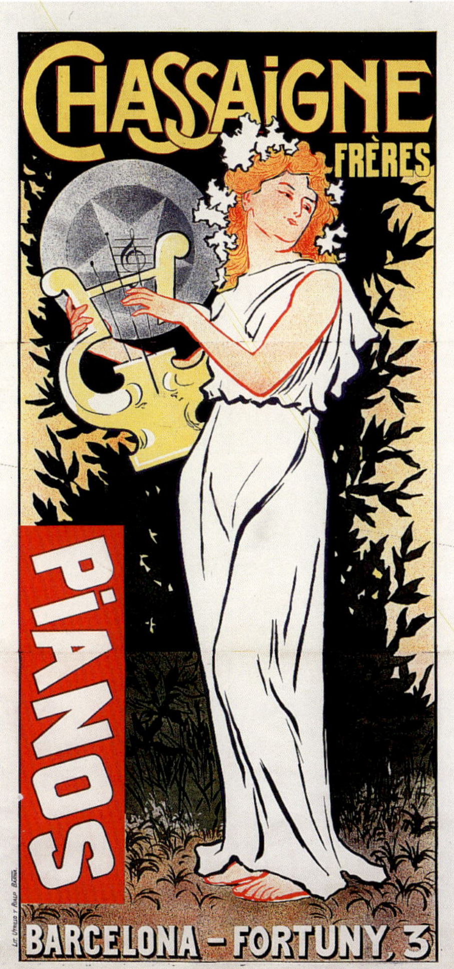

109

106. Wetterwald Frères. 1898.
17¹/₈ x 29 in./43.5 x 73.6 cm
Imp. Wetterwald Frères, Bordeaux
Cond B+/Slight cresing and tears in margins/P.
A most interesting design by a printing firm that spe-cializes in labels for almost any and all industries, from confections to rugs to beverages. A lot of credits in a small space, but yet so ingeniously displayed that they don't seem cumbersome. And all this abetted, of course, by a curvaceously mercurial angel of heaven-sent com-merce. Because, honestly, what advertisement, no matter how expertly created, isn't made better with the inclusion of allegorical suggestiveness?
Est: $2,000-$2,500.

107. Cesare Urtis & Co./Torino. ca. 1890.
26⁷/₈ x 39 in./68.3 x 99 cm
Lit. R. Bonis, Torino
Cond B+/Unobtrusive folds.
Without an electrical apparatus or light bulb in sight, an anonymous posterist produces an unforgettable image for Torino's Cesare Urtis & Company, one of the city's first purveyors of electric lighting. And who needs the tools of the trade when a diaphonously-draped goddess of illumination can provide adequate persuasion on her own, her barely-concealed charms backlit by a midnight sun that cuts through the evening fantasia. Simple in conception, magnificent in execution.
Est: $2,000-$2,500.

108. Rudge Cycle/Coventry Triplet. ca. 1890.
37¹/₄ x 50¹/₂ in./94.5 x 128 cm
Dangerfield Litho., London
Cond B–/Recreated top area.
Ref: Dodge, p. 77 (var)
"The (Rudge Cycle Company's) Triplet first appeared in 1888 and won the Grande Medaille d'Or at the Exposition Universelle in Paris, 1889. 'This machine is, without doubt, the fastest and safest tandem ever built, and in the latter part of 1888 several sensation-ally fast performances were accomplished on the road on it . . . The secret of success of the machine lies in the way it adjusts itself to the inequalities of the road, and is self-balancing . . . The foremost rider, who may be a lady, has regular Whatton handles . . . Steering is entirely under the control of the central rider, and the machine is very obedient, and can be guided with great exactness and ease'" (Dodge, p. 77). Making the quad-cycle the perfect choice for a mother/father/daughter frolic down country lanes.
Est: $2,000-$2,500.

109. Chassaigne Frères Pianos.
37¹/₄ x 75³/₄ in./94.7 x 192.3 cm
Lit. Utrillo y Rialp, Barcelona
Cond A–/Slight tears at folds and edges.
Towering over the consumer with 3-sheet Art Nouveau grandeur, this muse of stringed percussion instruments creates instant credibility for Chassaigne Pianos with-out an upright or a grand needing to be lithographically recreated. The Barcelona-based firm produced pianos and player pianos in between 1864 and 1967.
Est: $1,500-$1,800.

110. Exposition d'Affiches/Galerie Praubert. 1889.
45¹/₂ x 16¹/₂ in./115.8 x 42 cm
Jules Pequignot, Paris
Cond B+/Unobtrusive tears and stains at seam.
Ref: Affichomanie, 18; Chaumont/Expossons, p. 9;
     Weill, 78; Reims, 161; PAI-XXVIII, 93
The text above this frieze of townsfolk racing through the street asks, "Where are they running to?" The letter-ing below answers the question: to a poster exhibition. The show, at a local gallery in Nantes, was one of the earliest poster exhibitions ever held and was organized by poster collector Boucard. In addition to be-ing of historical value—every serious poster collector should strive to have this image—the poster offers the pleasures of superb design and acute social observation. The six figures, of every age and station, represent the human comedy with great affection.
Est: $3,000-$3,500.

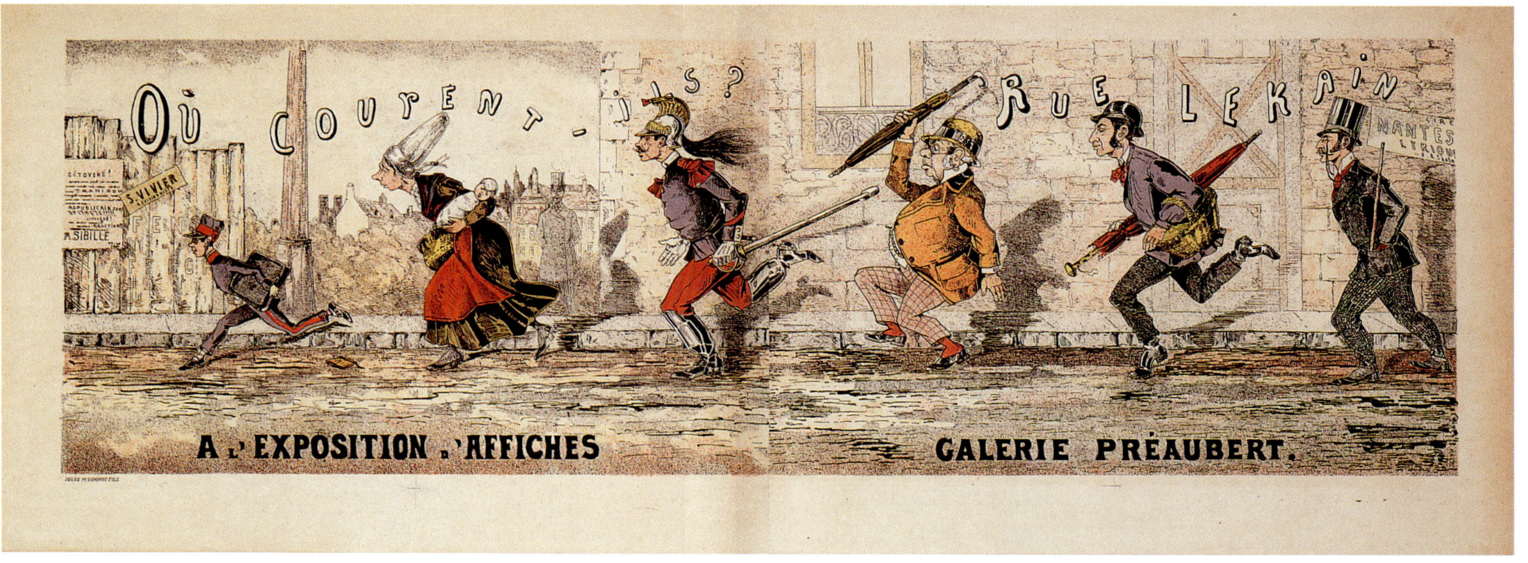

110

111. Le Matin/Loterie du Siècle. 1897.
58³/₈ x 43¹/₈ in./148.3 x 109.5 cm
Imp. Lemercier, Paris
Cond B/Slight tears at folds.
In its own hyper-greedy way, this promotion for *Le Matin*
is actually rather refreshing. Because apart from the
bottom text line that encourages us to read today's
edition of the newspaper, this anonymous creation is
all about one thing: free money. And the tastefully-
draped allegorical bringer of easy riches nicely compli-
ments the text line that labels the *Matin* drawing the
"Prettiest Lottery of the Century."
Est: $2,200-$2,600.

112. The Dazzler.
39¹/₂ in./26³/₈ in./100.2 x 67 cm
J. Morgan, Cleveland
Cond B/Restored tears, largely in margins.
Typically, when one hears mention of a "horseless carriage," thoughts turn to the early days of automotive
infatuation. However, that wouldn't be the case in this
poster for Cosgrove and Grant's Comedians production
of "The Dazzler," which features a carriage being pulled
by an octet of lovely ladies instead of the more cus-
tomarily seen equine team. No doubt, feminists will
object to the women-as-draft-animals association made
here, and who can blame them? However, regardless
of the plot connivance that justified this harnessing—
which sadly doesn't appear to have been recorded for
posterity—the anonymous designer reproduces turn-
of-the-twentieth-century couture with dazzling panache.
Est: $1,000-$1,200.

113. Rose Melville/"Sis Hopkins".
26⁵/₈ x 37 in./67.2 x 94 cm
H. A. Thomas & Wylie, N.Y.
Cond B+/Restored tears at paper edges.
Even though the "Sis Hopkins" character might not ring
any bells in the minds of today's movie buffs, Rose
Melville (1873-1946) created a character that made
her one of America's elite stage and screen celebrities
during the first two decades of the Twentieth Century.
In 1879, Rose's sisters—Josephine, Ida and Maud—
founded "The Melville Sisters Stock Company," a troupe
that Rose would join a decade later. After the company
amicably separated, Rose and her sister, Ida, remained
together, touring in *Zeb*, a comedy about a southern
Indiana hillbilly family. Among the characters created
in *Zeb* was "Sis Hopkins," an unsophisticated teenager
played by Rose. In 1900, Carroll Flemming wrote a
three-act musical comedy, *Sis Hopkins*, which became
a Broadway hit. Sis's lament, "There ain't no sense in
doin' nuthin' for nobody what won't do nuthin' for you,"
was among the most quoted stage lines for a decade.
At least two humor magazines, *Sis Hopkins* and *Foolish
Humor*, capitalized on its popularity and a novel was
written based upon the play. The Sis Hopkins doll, with
wired braided pigtails, became a collectible. In 1914,
Melville brought Sis to the Silver Screen and over the
course of the following two years portrayed her in no

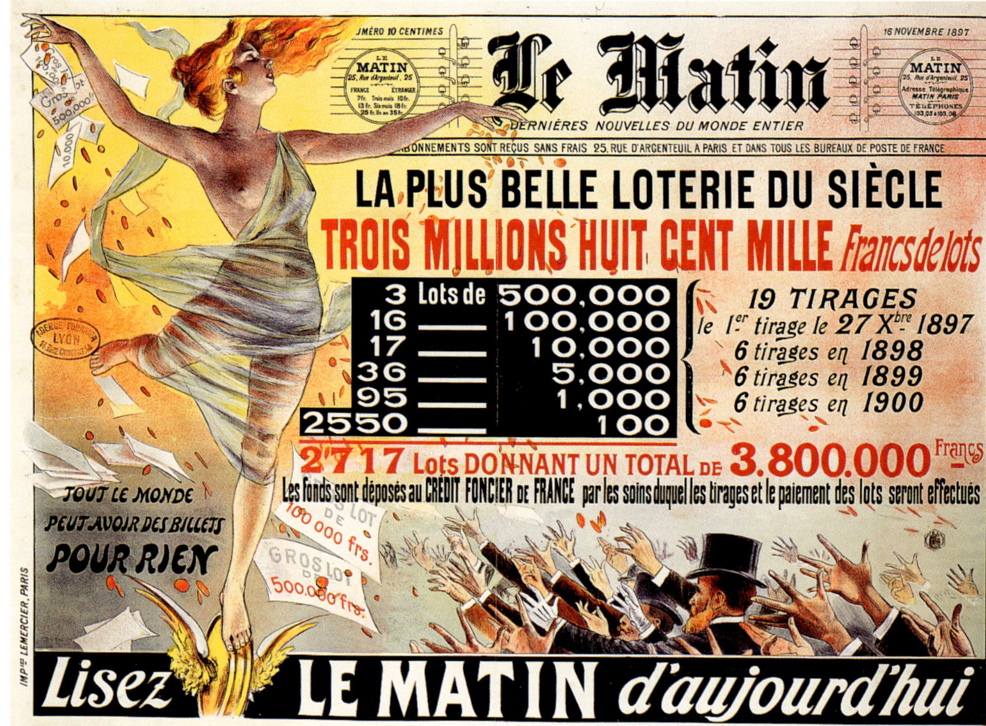

111

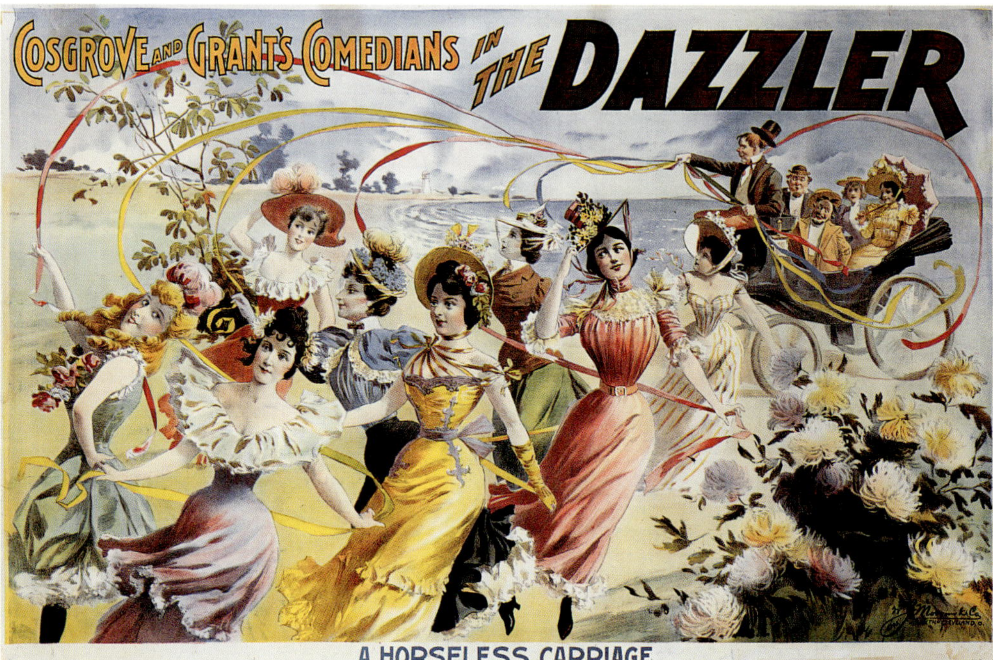

112

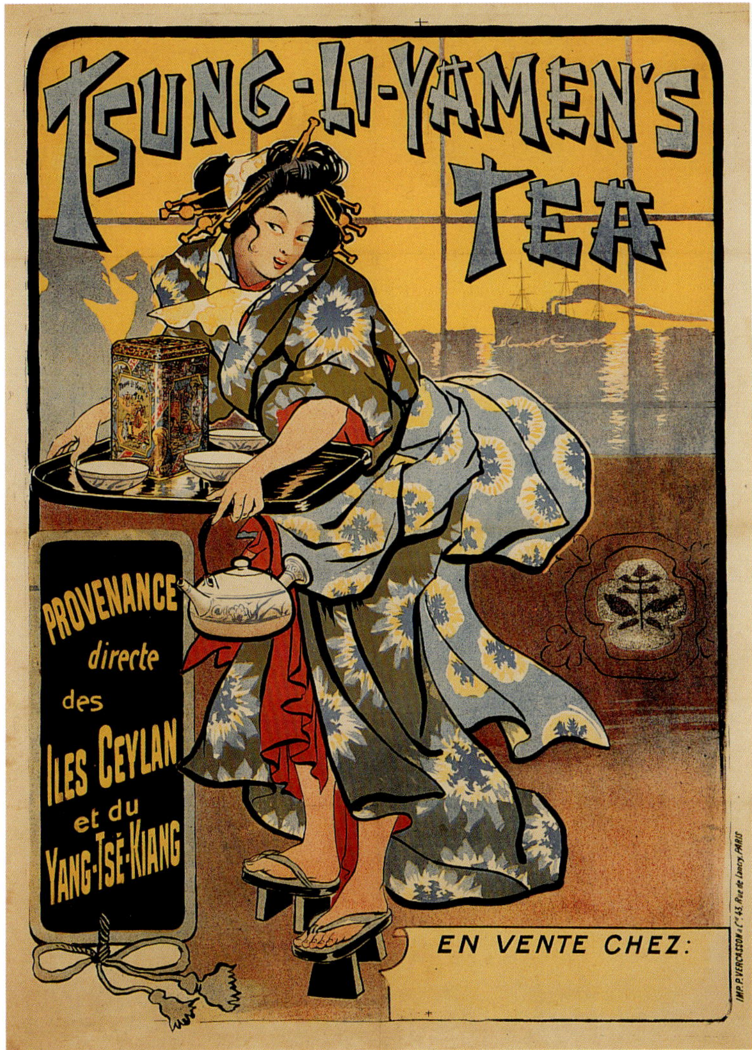

114

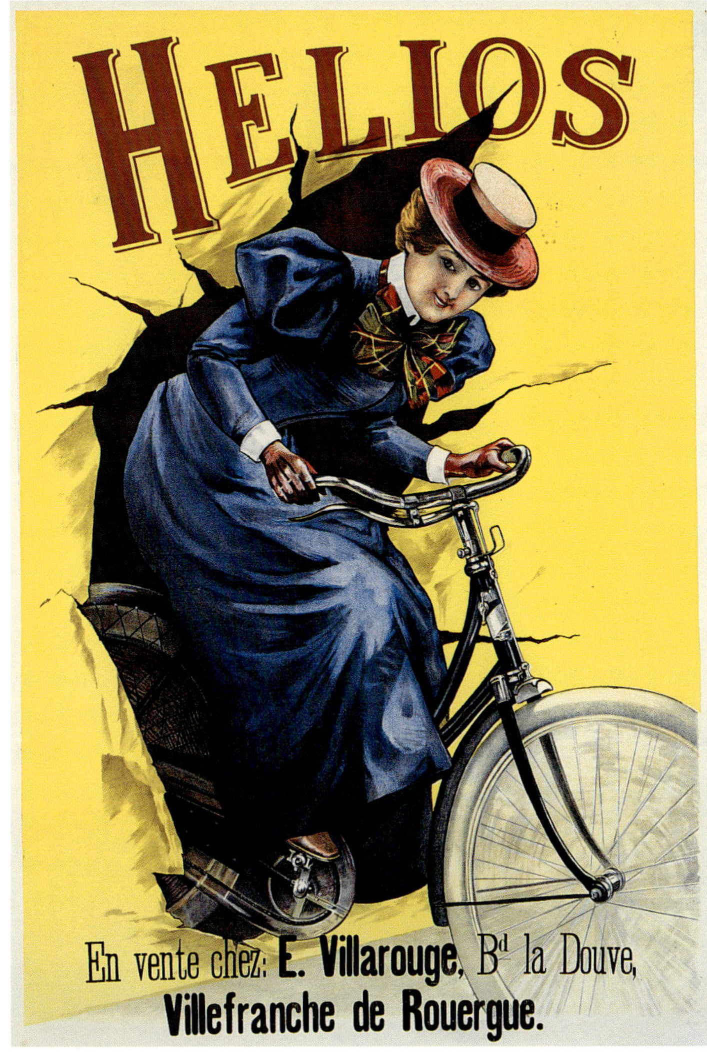

115

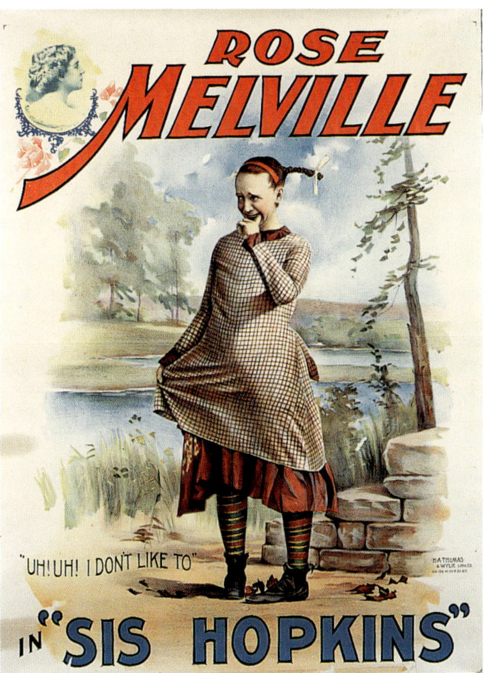

113

116

That this brand of tea actually bears the name of that agency would seem to indicate that these importers were operating with the blessing of the Chinese government, even though the tea they're importing appears to be a blend of leaves obtained from both China and the Indian peninsula. The anonymous posterist has created a wondrous hodgepodge, more an artistically-licensed Chinoise or Japonism than an accurate depiction. Its vibrant colors, though lovely, are unlikely to have been worn locally during the period, though the concubine's *geta* certainly are accurate enough.
Est: $1,500-$1,800.

115. Helios.
$29^5/8$ x $44^3/8$ in./75.5 x 112.5 cm
Cond B+/Restored tear at lower right corner.
As she bursts onto the scene on her brand new bicycle, this well-covered rider looks as if she has absolutely no idea what to expect now that she's on the other side. It's amusing, but it truly reinforces the fact that the bicycle was instrumental in expanding the horizons of many a woman during the Belle Epoque whose world previously began and ended with her front door.
Est: $2,000-$2,500.

116. Squelette des Oiseaux. ca. 1899.
$40^7/8$ x $60^7/8$ in./103.8 x 154.6 cm
Imp. F. Champenois, Paris
Cond A.
Not a poster that reflects one's expected vision of beauty, this institutional design simply—and accurately—titled "Bird Skeletons" possess an eerie, austere appeal. This assemblage of bones—a "Rooster Skeleton" and a "Penguin Leg"—obviously was originally issued with a sheet or accompanying poster that corresponded to the numbers on display for identification purposes. Sadly, we cannot make the same offer, and all skeletal identification will be left to the osteologist fortunate enough to obtain this poster.
Est: $1,000-$1,200.

fewer than twenty black-and-white silent shorts. The popularity of the character inspired *Motion Picture* magazine to feature Rose on its May 1916 cover. The following year she retired, having appeared in the same role more than an estimated 5,000 times before more than five million people. It's a record that's still unmatched.
Est: $800-$1,000.

114. Tsung-Li-Yamen's Tea. ca. 1900.
$35^1/2$ x 50 in./90.2 x 127 cm
Imp. P. Vercasson, Paris
Cond B+/Slight tears at folds and edges.
The Tsungli Yamen was a foreign trade bureau created by the Chinese Empire in 1861 following the Convention of Peking in order to promote trade with the West.

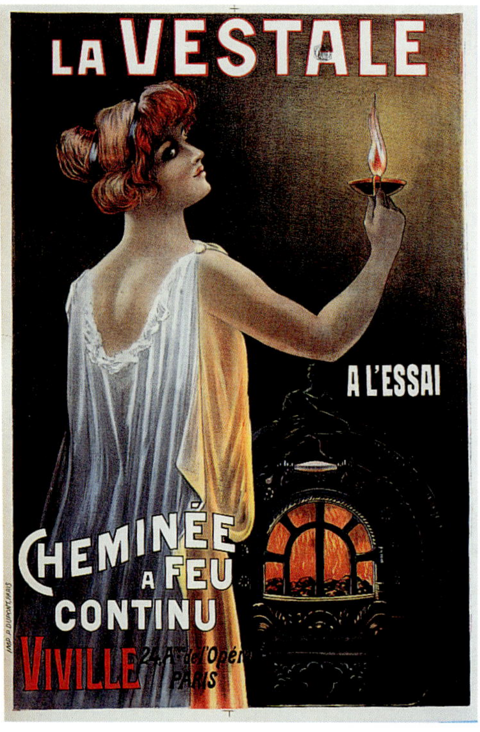

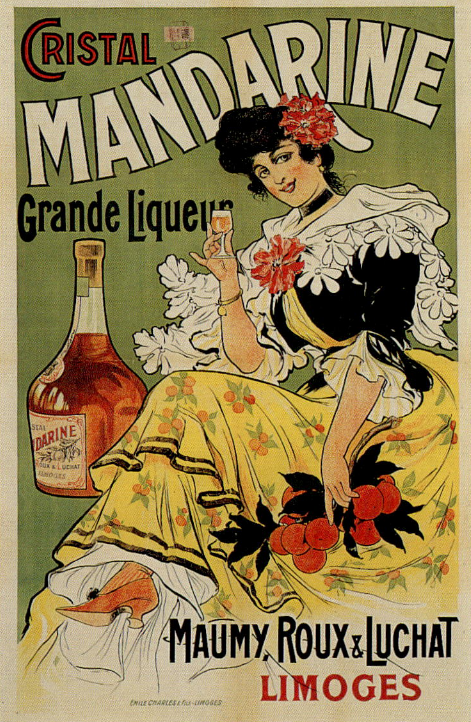

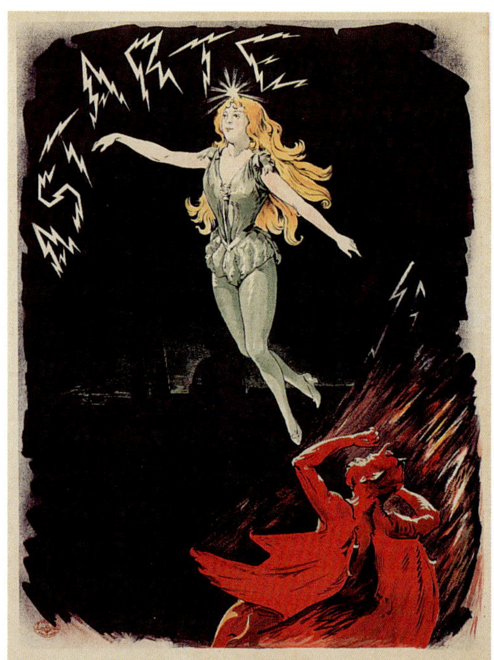

117

118

119

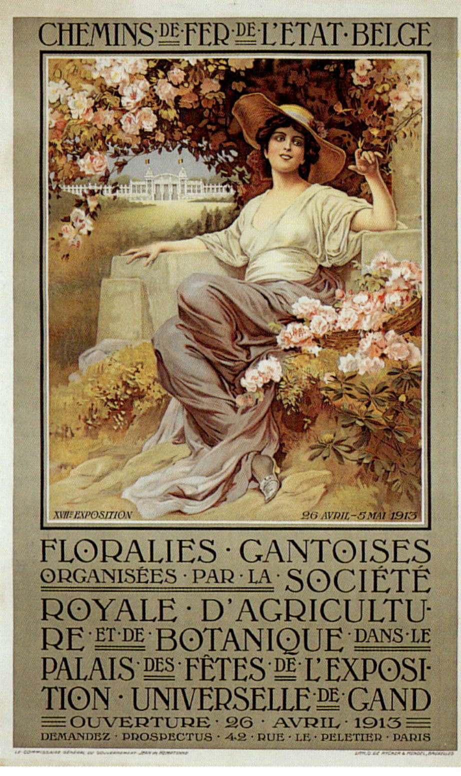

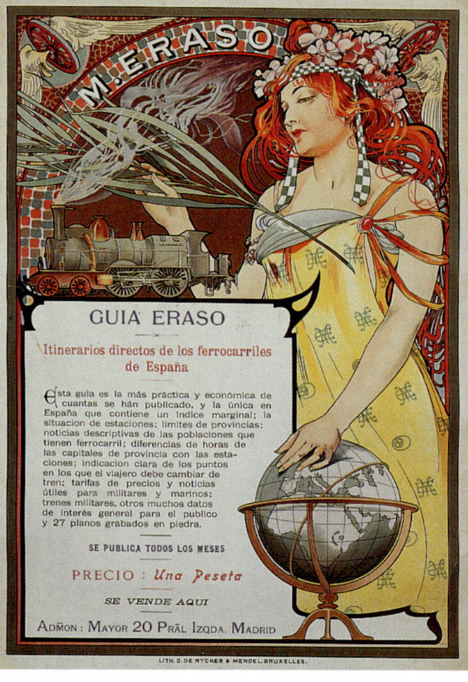

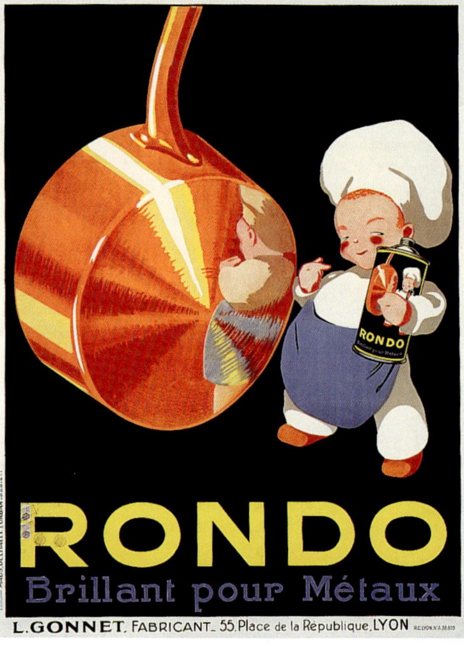

120

121

122

ANONYMOUS (cont'd)

117. La Vestale.
$31^5/_8$ x $47^3/_4$ in./80.4 x 121.2 cm
Imp. P. Dupont, Paris
Cond A.
For the most part, people are aware that a vestal—or vestal virgin as they are more commonly referenced—is a pure and chaste woman. But were you aware that the term also connotes a virgin consecrated to the Roman goddess Vesta and to the service of watching the sacred fire perpetually kept burning upon her altar? It's surely the latter of these two signifiers that the makers of the tested Vestale fireplace wish to associate themselves, a fact reflected in the sancro-sensual artwork of this anonymous designer.
Est: $1,500-$1,800.

118. Cristal Mandarine. 1906.
$33^1/_8$ x $50^7/_8$ in./84.2 x 129.2 cm
Emile Charles, Limoge
Cond B/Slight tears at folds.
The municipality of Limoges in France's Limousin region is known worldwide for many things—its medieval enamels on copper, its nineteenth century porcelain, its oak barrels used in the production of cognac. However, one of its overlooked—and now unavailable—treasures may very well have been Cristal Mandarine, a tangerine-infused liqueur of the finest quality. And their dainty spokesmodel appears to be completely devoted to the citrus-meets-spirits cause, from the tone of her stockings and shoes to the print of her skirt to the bunch she casually dangles as she toasts the viewer with a knowing smile.
Est: $1,700-$2,000.

119. Astarte.
$27^5/_8$ x $37^1/_2$ in./70.2 x 95.4 cm
Pionier, Berlin
Cond A–/Unobtrusive folds.
What a very Pagan creation for a common household item! Well, at least we have to assume that this is a promotion for the Astarte light bulb even though there's no actual rendering of the illumination source in the poster. But with its name emblazoned in lightning bolts and Satan being banished by both the brilliance of the name and the goddess that places said name in the heavens, it seems like a fairly safe supposition. And what a name it is—Astarte is a major northern Semitic goddess, connected with fertility, sexuality and war, worshiped by the Greeks as Aphrodite and whose name very well might have inspired the designation of Easter in an attempt to adapt certain Pagan festivals into Christianity. Now there's a pedigree!
Est: $1,200-$1,500.

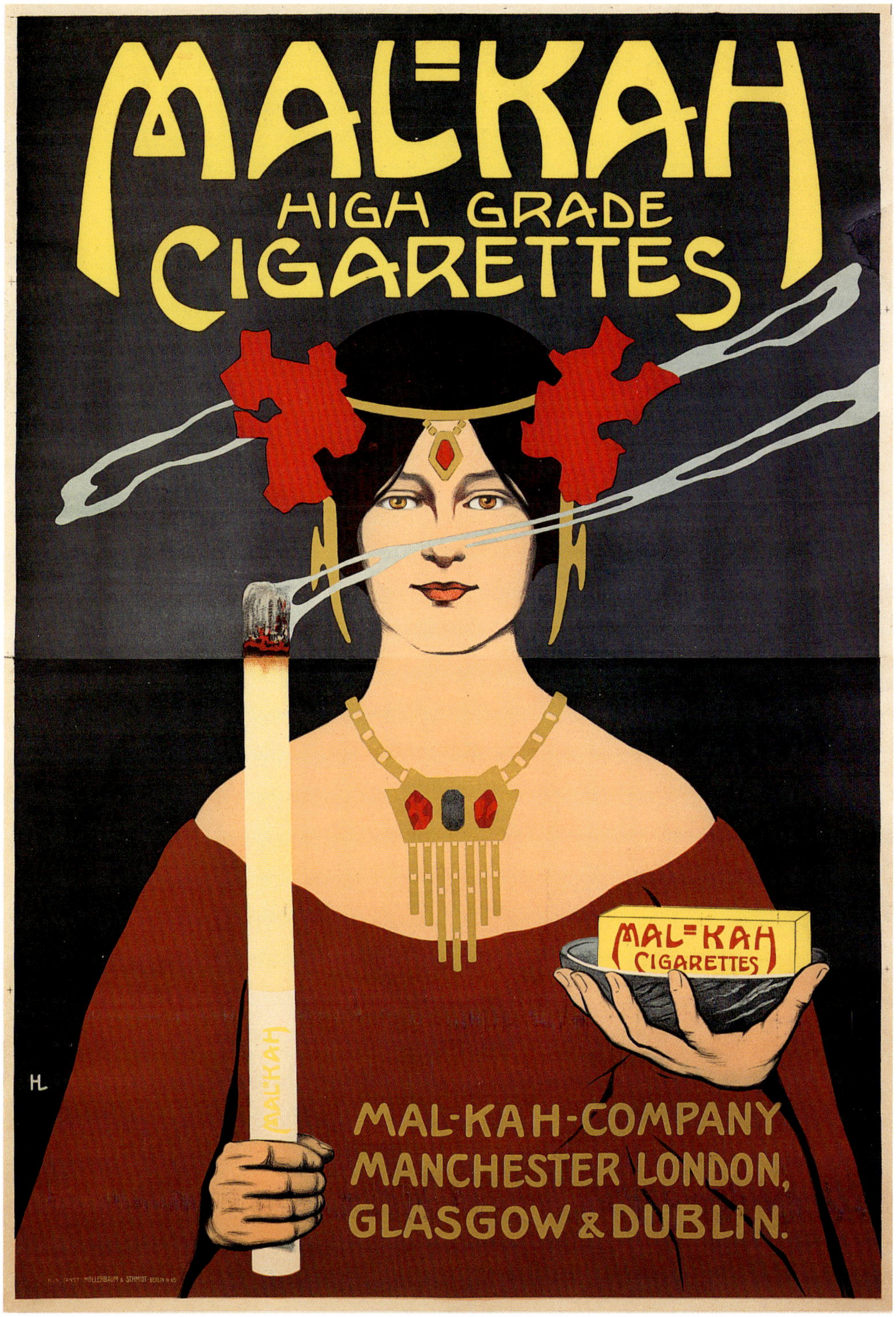

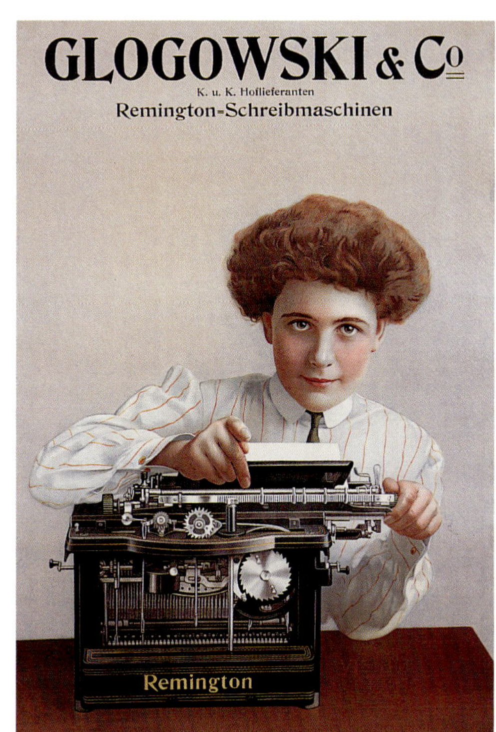

124

123

120. Floralies Gantoises. 1913.
$25 \times 39^{7}/_{8}$ in./63.4 x 101.2 cm
Lith. O. de Rycker & Mendel, Bruxelles
Cond A–/Slight tear in border.
What began back in 1809 as a modest Belgian exhibition of fifty plants based on the English model of proper gardening technique has steadily grown into a spectacular exhibition without equal. Every five years, for ten days in April—which for all intents and purposes makes the event the Olympics of floral competitions—*Les Floralies Gantoises* is a huge event with entries from around the globe. For the 1913 Ghent Flower Show (the only time the exhibit was canceled was during World War II), an unnamed posterist calls upon peonies and pulchritude to make their promotional point, with laid-back sensuality and ease of travel—provided by the Belgian State Railway—sealing the deal. The 2005 edition of the Flower show included an international competition with more than 750 different classes, with entries from participating gardeners judged by a jury from twenty-four countries.
Est: $1,200-$1,500.

121. M. Eraso. 1900.
$13^{3}/_{4} \times 19^{1}/_{2}$ in./35 x 49.5 cm
O. de Rycker & Mendel, Bruxelles
Cond A–/Slight tears and stains at edges.
Ref: España, 1078; PAI-XXXV, 136
There's an inclination here to declare that this lovely Art Nouveau design—whose uncredited creator clearly spent a few moments thumbing through the Mucha handbook—is a stock poster, available to any advertiser wise enough to replace the words in the text panel. There are, however, a tad too many details for this to be the case: the well-rendered locomotive, the initials of the monthly Spanish rail guide repeated in the soft yellow frock and the wheels-in-flight motif of the upper corners. The textual praise and explanation of the tourist publication is truly superfluous. The undisputed star here is the lovely, light-as-air Art Nouveau eye-candy—deliriously floral coif, understated diaphony et al.
Est: $1,200-$1,500.

122. Rondo.
$46^{1}/_{4} \times 62^{1}/_{2}$ in./117.5 x 157.9 cm
Imp. Maus. Delhalle & Urban, Paris
Cond A.
"Brilliant" doesn't only apply to the job done by Rondo metal polish, but also to the work done by an anonymous posterist, who artfully recreates the product's logo on a grander scale. It's a fairly standard promotional concept, but its execution is positively masterful.
Est: $1,400-$1,700.

123. Mal-Kah Cigarettes.
$37 \times 54^{1}/_{2}$ in./94 x 138.3 cm
Hollerbaum & Schmidt, Berlin
Cond A.
With a cigarette the size of a torch more suited to spelunking than smoking, the initially-identified "H.L." calls our attention to the big tobacco satisfaction of Mal-Kah cigarettes with a 2-sheet Byzantine priestess more than adequately prepared to worship at the altar of nicotine. The British Isles tobacco company also used this image as the artwork on their "No. 3" brand tin-lid packaging. Actually, princess might be a more accurate way of describing this woman rather than priestess, seeing as "mal-kah" is the Hebrew word for "queen."
Est: $2,500-$3,000.

124. Remington/Glogowski & Co. ca. 1910.
$26^{3}/_{8} \times 39^{5}/_{8}$ in./67 x 100.7 cm
Cond B+/Slight tears and creases at bottom edge.
It's apparent that this secretary—or executive assistant if you prefer a more politically correct appellation—is a rather serious-minded individual who wouldn't use anything but the finest office equipment available to perform her duties. And even though she appears to be mid-letter, she takes a moment to directly point out to the viewer that Remington typewriters are the machine of choice. A wonderful anonymous creation that presents both technical specificity and compelling humanity.
Est: $1,500-$1,800.

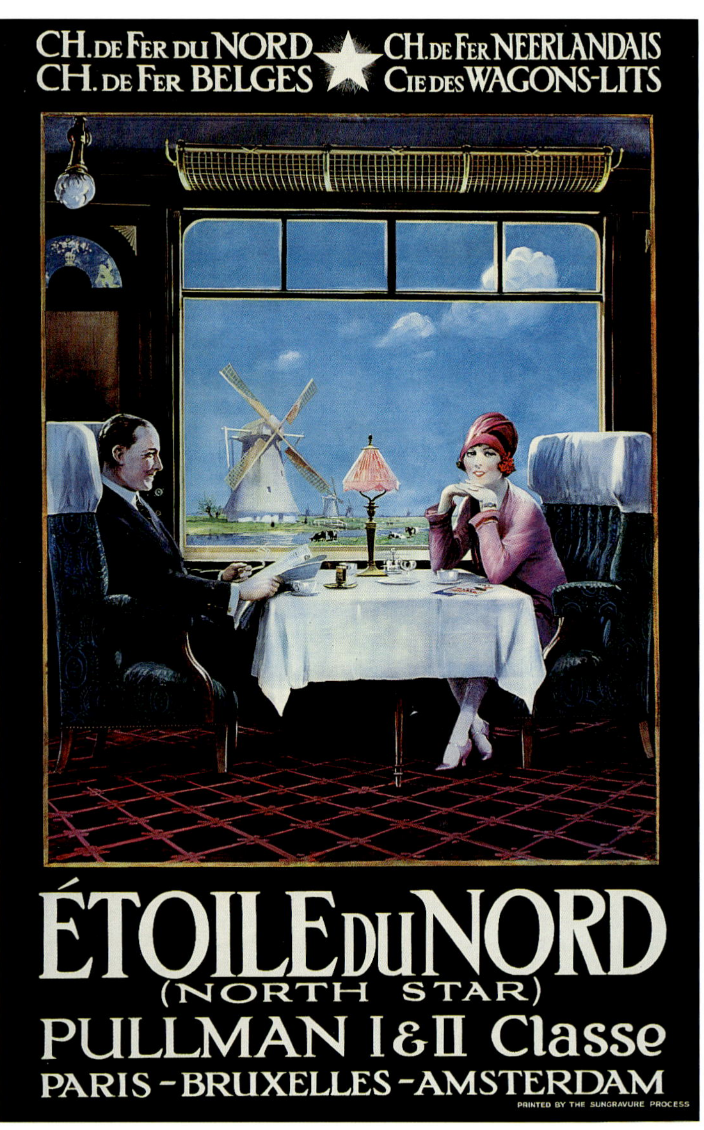

125

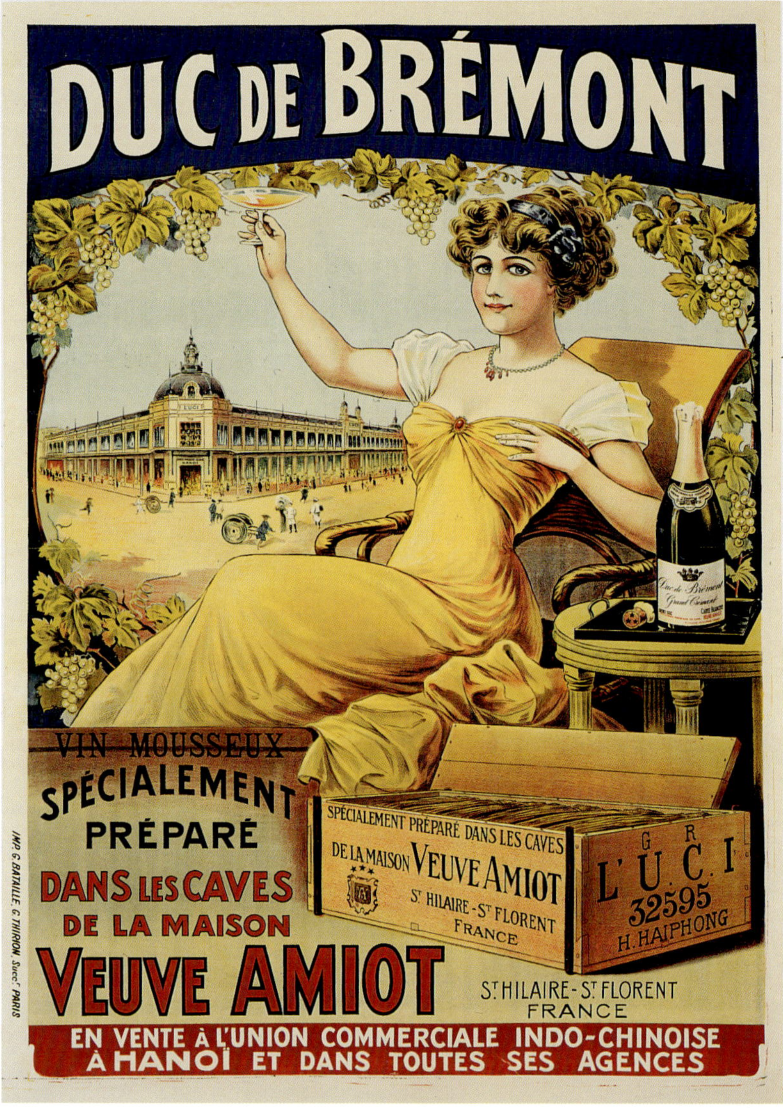

126

ANONYMOUS (cont'd)

125. Étoile du Nord. 1927.
$25^1/8$ x $39^3/8$ in./64 x 100 cm
Printed by The Sungravure Process
Cond A.
Ref: Wagons-Lits, 188; Wagons-Lits II, 215
Because they were executed during the same calendar year, it's interesting to compare just how stylistically different this poster for the "North Star" service between Paris and Amsterdam is from Cassandre's design (*see* PAI-XLII, 179) for the same route. Whereas the better-known design relies on sleek Art Deco sensibilities and a geometric construct, this anonymous creation appeals to the senses—most dramatically to our sense of class. Two very different approaches, both as effective as they are diverse.
Est: $2,000-$2,500.

126. Duc de Brémont.
$38^3/8$ x $54^3/4$ in./97.5 x 139.2 cm
Imp. G. Bataille, G. Thirion, Paris
Cond A–/Unobtrusive folds.
Simply because one's responsibilities takes one far afield doesn't necessarily mean that all of the creature comforts of hearth-and-home need be denied. For example, take Duc de Brémont sparkling wine for example—even if you find yourself in the capital of French Indochina, the product of the Veuve Amiot cellars is still happily within your reach. The uncredited poster is rather aglow with the portent of colonial optimism thanks to the golden lass that dominates the design, a woman who serves as both a deliciously pale embodiment of the beverage in question and of the opportunistic consumer whom the company hopes to entice.
Est: $2,000-$2,500.

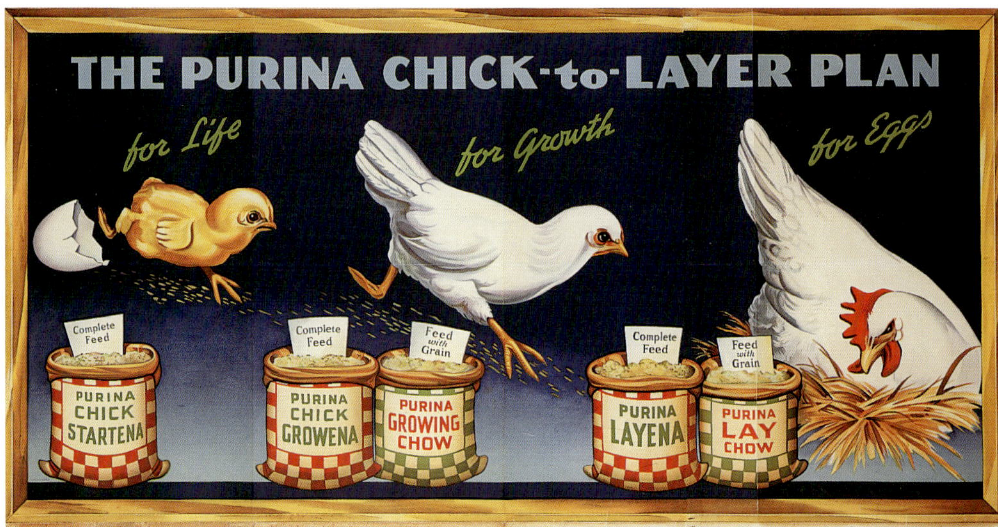

127

127. The Purina Chick-to-Layer Plan.
43 x $82^3/4$ in./109.1 x 210 cm
Cond B–/Slight tears at folds and borders; recreated margins.
From chick to pullet to hen, Purina has the feeds that formulate the perfect "Chick-to-Layer Plan" for this White Leghorn. As adorably and accurately rendered as the ad is, the "for Life, for Growth, for Eggs" credo certainly adds a simple, earthy authenticity to the promotion as well. Remarkably enough, the Layena feed is still being offered by Purina Mills and is touted on their website as a "16%-protein high-calcium ration formulated for top-producing laying birds once they reach 18 weeks of age." Founded in 1894 by William H. Danforth, Purina Mills has grown to become the largest animal nutrition producer and distributor in the United States.
Est: $2,000-$2,500.

128. Cunard White Star.
$25^1/4$ x $37^5/8$ in./64.1 x 95.5 cm
The British Color Printing Co., London
Cond B+/Unobtrusive tears near edges; excellent colors.
An uncredited posterist divides our attention in equal

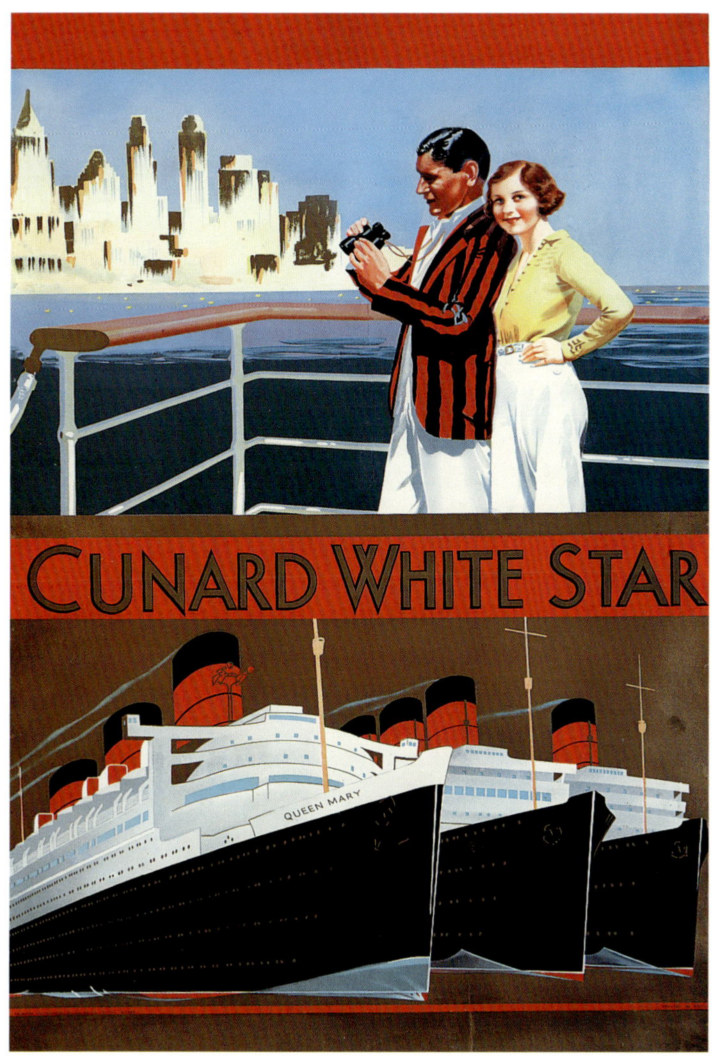

128

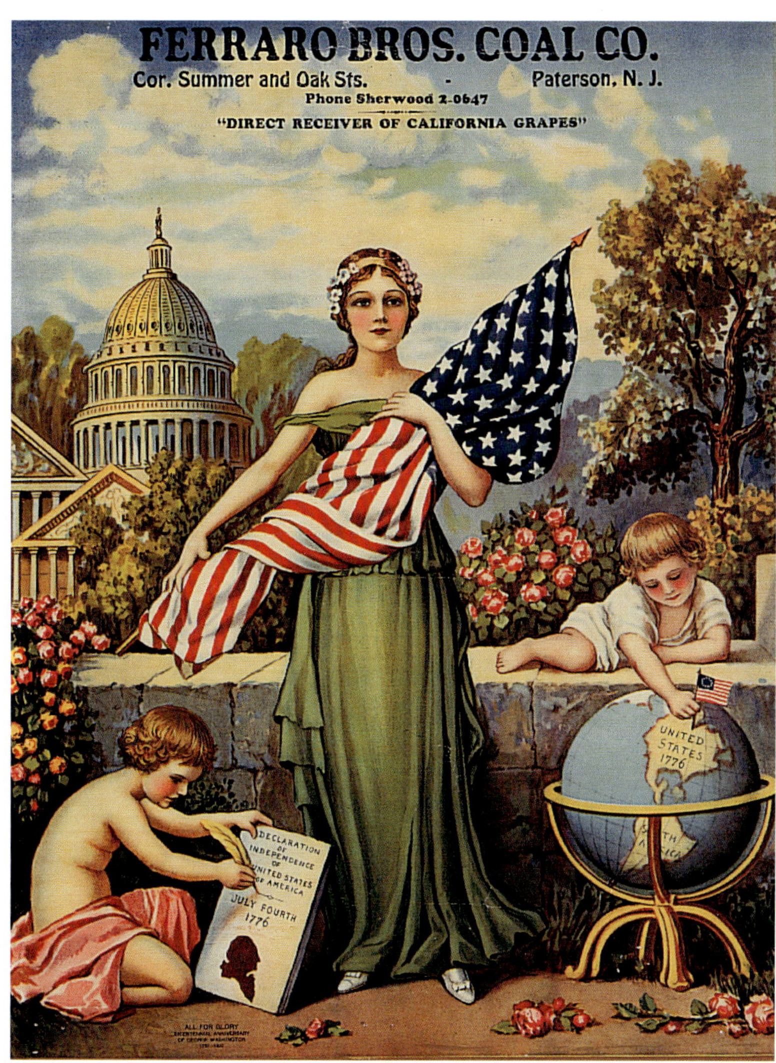

129

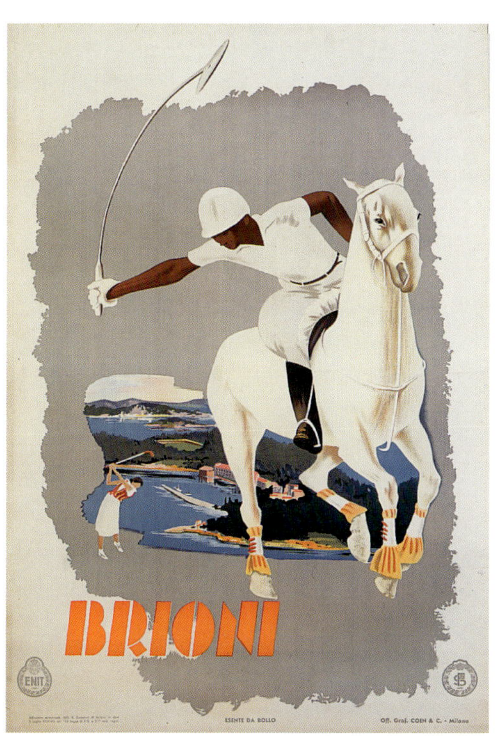

130

parts for the White Star Line: one part dedicated to the traveler and the destination (with a gentleman not afraid to make a bold fashion choice set against a confectionary skyline), with the other half devoted to the ships that can get you there in style. The only word fit to describe the *Queen Mary*—seen here with two other unnamed Cunard liners—is impressive. From her 750-foot long promenade deck to her anchors that weighed sixteen-tons apiece to her aft funnel that rose seventy-eight feet above the boat deck. The *Queen Mary* made one-thousand voyages for Cunard before being sold to the city of Long Beach, California, for $3,450,000, where she serves as an aesthetic reminder of a bygone, more luxurious era. It's interesting to note that when it came time to christen this ship, Lord Roydon, Cunard's director, asked King George V if he had any objections to the ship being named after "the most illustrious queen of England." The King replied, "That is the greatest compliment that has ever been made to me or my wife." And that is how a ship intended to be named "Queen Victoria" became the *Queen Mary*.
Est: $2,000-$2,500.

129. Ferraro Bros. Coal Co. 1932.
$14^3/8$ x $19^1/4$ in./36.5 x 48.8 cm
Cond B+/Slight tears at edges. Framed.
Published on the occasion of the Bicentennial Anniversary of George Washington's Birthday (February 22, 1732), this wondrous slice of idyllic Americana from the Ferraro Brothers of Paterson, New Jersey, combines robust allegory and structural permanence to celebrate the legacy of the first president of the United States. From the capitol building for which he laid the corner-

stone to the Constitutional Congress that he championed to the country he helped to place on the map, the historical significance of the only person ever to be elected president unanimously is commemorated with robust clarity. Not so clear, however, is why a New Jersey purveyor of fossil fuels would also tout themselves as a "Direct Receiver of California Grapes."
Est: $1,700-$2,000.

130. Brioni.
$26^3/8$ x $38^3/4$ in./67 x 98.3 cm
Off. Graf. Coen, Milano
Cond A–/Slight stains at paper edges.
Though today "Brioni" is most widely-known as a high-fashion clothing company, this anonymous poster was done to promote travel to the island-chain resort on the coast of the Adriatic Sea for which it was named. In 1893, Viennese business magnate Paul Kupelwieser bought the whole archipelago—which had formerly served as a naval base for the Austro-Hungarian Navy—and created an exclusive beach resort with first class hotels, restaurants, a casino, a sailing regatta, a golf course and a yacht harbor, quickly becoming a focal point in the social life on the Austrian Riviera. Famous for its scenic beauty, Brioni became part of Italy after World War I, eventually being acquired entirely by the Italian state in 1930. In 1945, Brioni became part of Yugoslavia, and after it gained independence in 1991, Croatia gained control of the area. As seen in the poster, polo was a focal sport during the heyday of the resort; the International Polo Tournament that dated back to the Kupelwieser era was reintroduced in 2004.
Est: $1,200-$1,500.

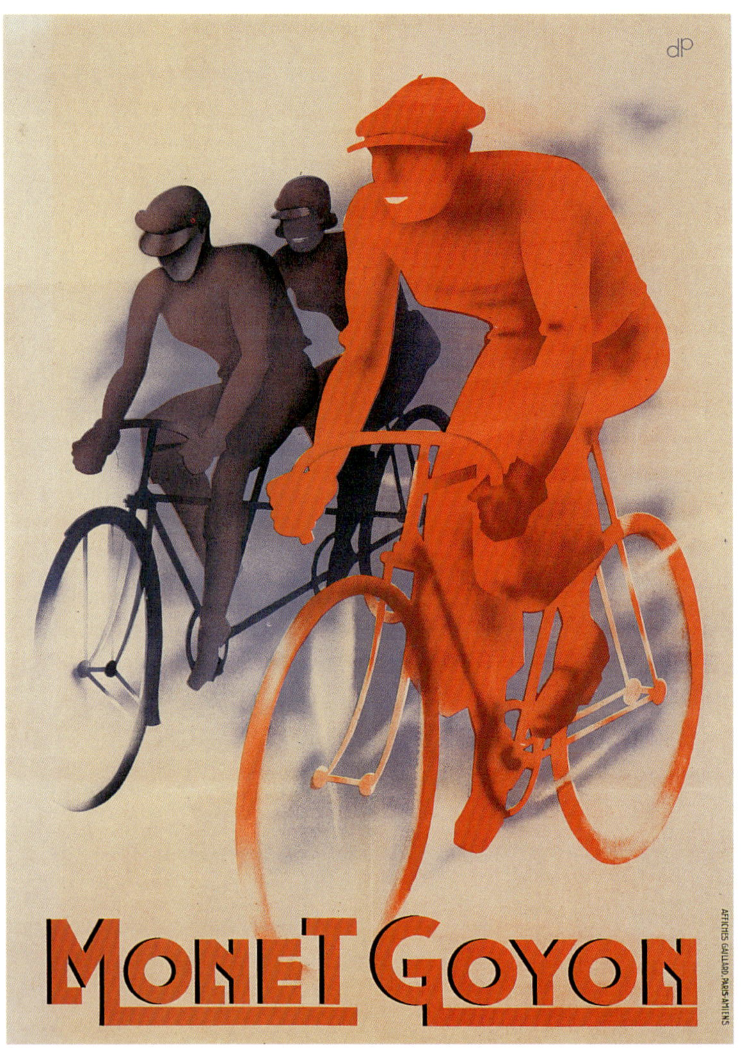

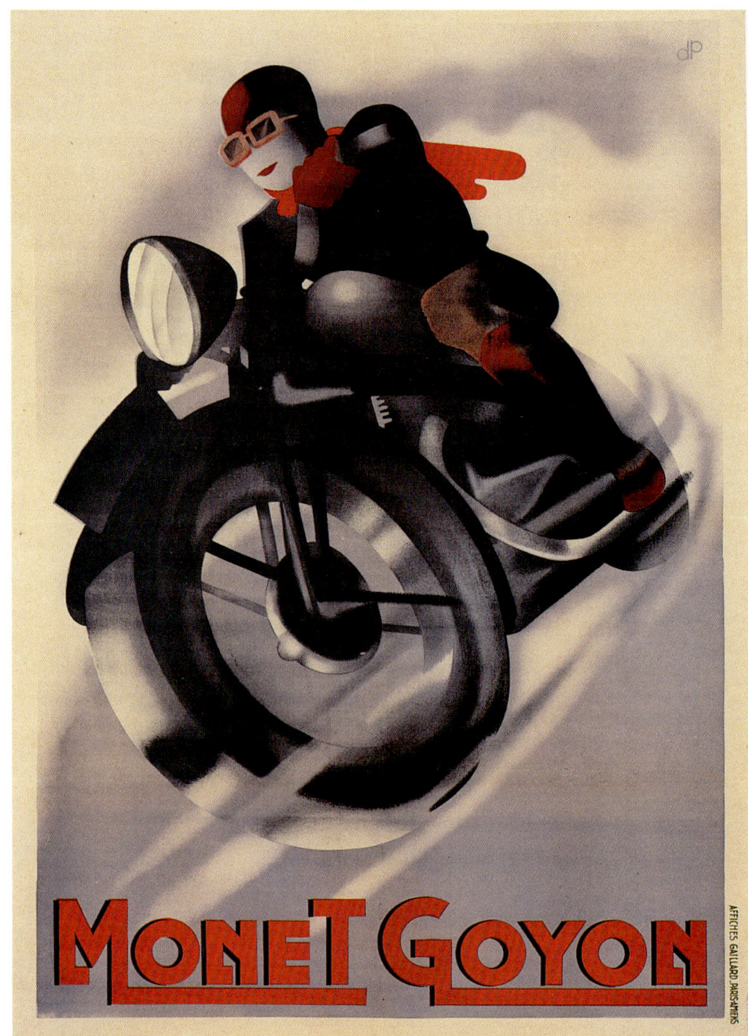

131

132

ANONYMOUS (cont'd)

131. Monet Goyon.
$31^1/_4$ x $44^1/_4$ in./79.5 x 112.3 cm
Affiches Gaillard, Paris-Amiens
Cond B+/Slight creases.
In 1916, during WWI, Joseph Monet and Adrien Goyon began manufacturing non-motorized vehicles in order to provide handicapped people with a means of recovering mobility. They quickly branched out into the production of bicycles and, as the following poster shows, motorcycles and motorized bikes. Here, an artist who identifies himself with the initials "d.p." provides us with a simplified, color-coded promotion for Monet Goyon bikes—red for single passenger, blue for tandem, which with the drop-out white of the rider's satisfied smile nicely incorporates the French origin of the pedal-powered machines without forcing the issue.
Est: $2,000-$2,500.

132. Monet Goyon.
$31^1/_2$ x $44^3/_8$ in./80 x 112.7 cm
Affiches Gaillard, Paris-Amiens
Cond A-/Unobtrusive folds.
The French-made Monet & Goyon cycles were a very popular make during their time of production. Between 1919 and 1959, they were as popular with the amateurs as they were with the road-and-track pros. Once again, "d.p." keeps things streamlined and effortlessly focused, setting a female enthusiast to the open road with such unbridled freedom that she may as well be navigating the rarefied air of a carefree partly cloudy sky as the commonplace expanse of a dusty stretch of highway.
Est: $2,500-$3,000.

133. Let's Go Skiing This Winter.
21 x $31^1/_4$ in./53.3 x 79.5 cm
Cond B+/Restored tears near paper edges.
In Japanese woodblock art, a flattened perspective allows the viewer to place themselves wherever they so choose within the represented landscape. In this anonymous promotion for winter sport fun (the signa-

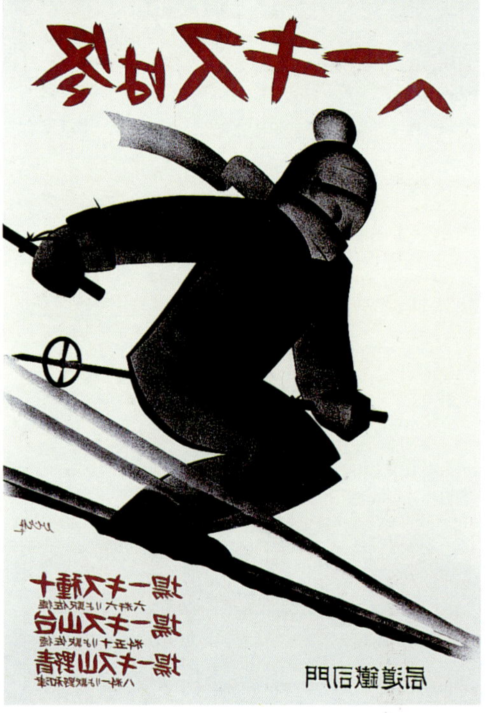

133

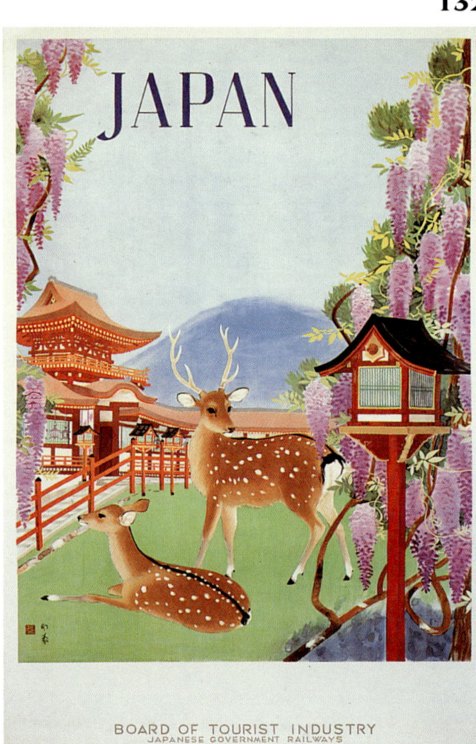

134

ture that appears beneath the skier is executed in such personalized *kanji* that no translation could be made), executed in shades of charcoal and drop-out white leaves no question as to where the viewer should be placing themselves: on the slopes. The poster's text informs us that the Moji Railroad Corporation services three resorts in the Yamaguchi Prefecture—

the southernmost prefecture on the island of Honshu—perfect for a downhill getaway: Tokusa, Daisan and Aonoyama, all located just minutes from their stations. The poster's right-to-left text indicates that it's likely a pre-World War II creation.
Est: $1,000-$1,200.

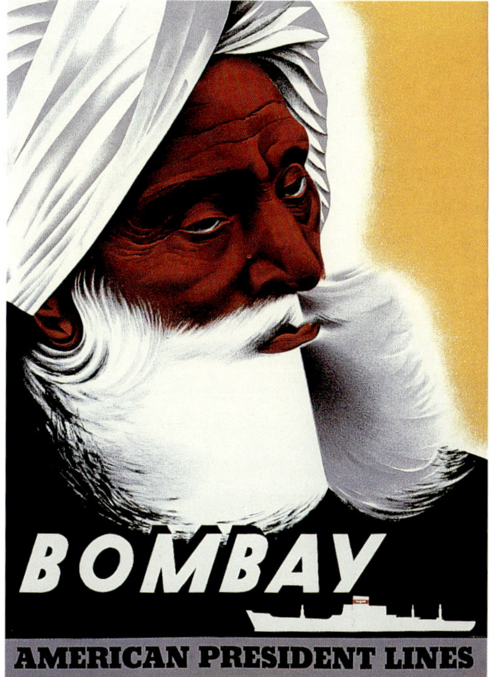

135

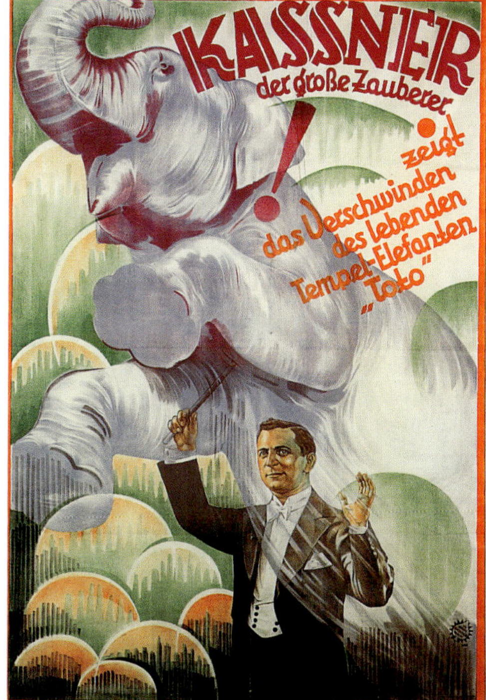

136

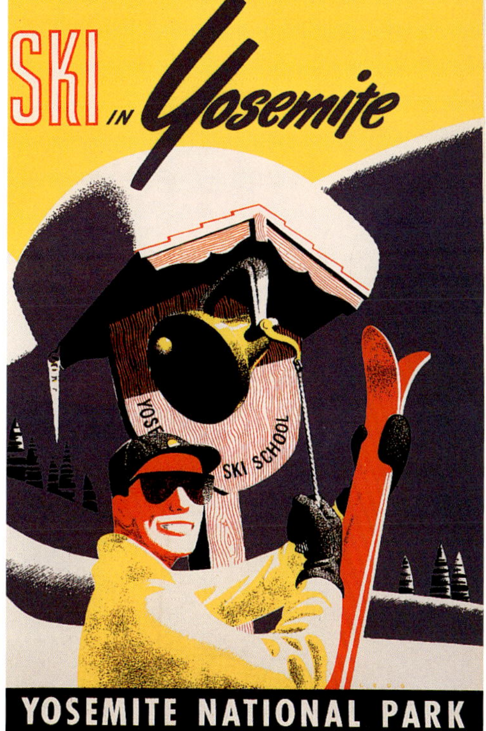

137

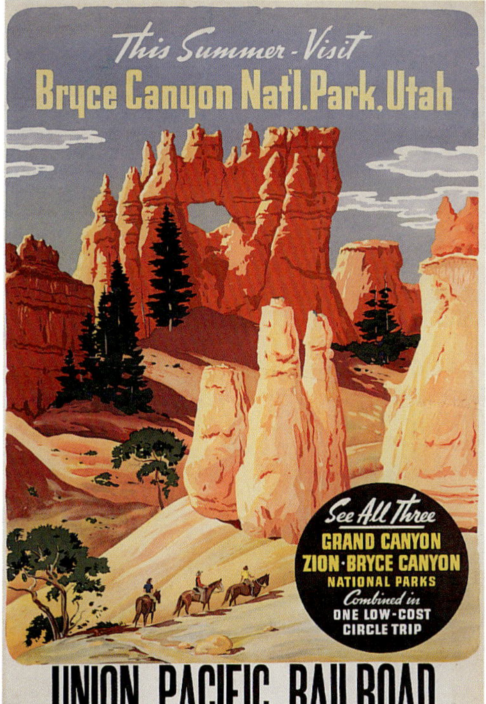

138

139

136. Kassner/Der Grosse Zauberer. 1930.
$34^7/8$ x $52^1/4$ in./88.6 x 132.7 cm
Adolph Friedlander, Hamburg
Cond B/Slight tears and creases at folds. Framed.
Ref: Magic Posters, 91; PAI-XXXVIII, 155
"In the twenty years before World War II, Alois Kassner
(1887-1970) was Germany's major illusionist. The
Krassner extravaganza was a magic show in the style of
Thurston's in the United States. The show carried tons
of equipment and twenty people and was transported
in two railway cars. Among Kassner's big features was
The Vanishing Elephant" (Magic Posters, p. 14). Which,
if you judge from the poster, was achieved with the
mere wave of a wand and soon thereafter, a rapidly
dissolving pachyderm.
Est: $1,200-$1,500.

137. Ski in Yosemite.
$22^1/2$ x $34^7/8$ in./57 x 88.6 cm
Cond A–/Slight tears at paper edges.
Set aside as a national park in 1890, California's
Yosemite embraces a spectacular tract of scenery in
the Sierra Nevada range, encompassing both mountain
and valley terrain. The park contains a grand collection
of waterfalls, meadows, and forests that include groves
of giant sequoias, the world's largest living things. This
poster, however, eschews ancient redwoods in favor of
chillier pleasures, its hearty bell-ringer making it clear
to even the rookie downhiller that Yosemite Ski School
is definitely in session. Though not singled out textu-
ally, the sunnily-recreated vista is most likely the Bad-
ger Pass ski area, California's original ski resort, which
opened to the public in 1935.
Est: $1,000-$1,200.

138. Union Pacific Railroad/Bryce Canyon.
$27^1/2$ x $41^3/8$ in./69.8 x 105.1 cm
Cond B/Tears, largely in top text area.
Ref: PAI-XXXIX, 103
To encourage Americans to spend their summer vaca-
tions visiting the national parks of the great Southwest
by rail, Union Pacific created a "circle trip" that included
stops at the Grand Canyon, Zion and Bryce Canyon for
a single price. This fine landscape creation was one of
the posters used to promote that route. In this view of
Bryce Canyon, stone arches and striking formations in
sandy-yellow and flaming burnt sienna contrast sharply
with the turquoise sky and deep green vegetation, the
grandeur of it utterly dwarfing the horseback riders
passing through at the base of the canyon.
Est: $1,000-$1,200.

134. Japan.
25 x $38^1/8$ in./63.5 x 97 cm
Kyoto Printing, Tokyo
Cond A.
Although deer are more commonly associated with Kyoto's neighbor Nara (famous for the deer they keep in
their parks where tourists can buy deer crackers from
vending machines to feed them), it's Kyoto's Heian Jingu
Shrine—the nation's spiritual center and one of the most
famous tourist sites in Japan—that's being used here
as tourist bait by the Japanese Government Railway. It's
interesting to take note of the design's use of *fujihana*,
or wisteria, which is a symbol almost as synonymous
with Japan as the cherry blossom, often used in the
arts to symbolize love or the female aspect of things
(as opposed to a pine tree for male). Though a signature does appear in the design's lower-left corner, the
kanji being used is so archaic that it eludes translation.
Est: $1,200-$1,500.

135. American President Lines/Bombay.
$28^1/8$ x $39^3/4$ in./71.5 x 101 cm
Cond A.

Originally an archipelago of seven islands, Bombay—or
Mumbai as it's known today—was named *Bom Baia* by
Portuguese settlers in 1534, translating as "good bay"
in their native tongue. Ceded to Charles II of England
in 1661 as part of the dowry for Catherine de Braganza,
these islands were in turn leased to the British East
India Company in 1668. In time, Bombay became the
capital of the state of Maharashtra and the most popu-
lous city of India. American President Lines advertises
their service to the city with a heavy-lidded *Sikh*, rele-
gating the silhouette of their vessel and its spread eagle
logo to a somewhat miniature status. In 1938, the United
States Government took over management of the Dollar
Steamship Company, which was in financial distress,
and transferred their assets to the newly formed American President Line. The company operated transpacific
and round-the-world services, but the war in Europe
disrupted them. After the war, APL returned to the
high seas and continued passenger service until 1973.
Today, they still trade as a cargo company.
Est: $1,000-$1,200.

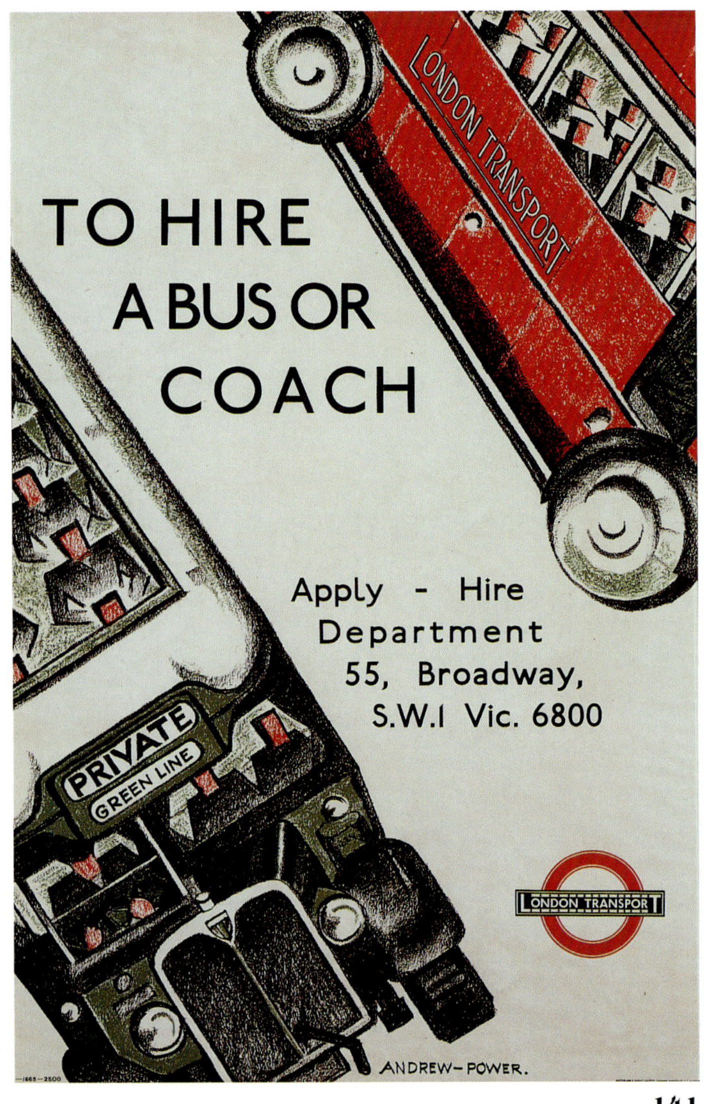

141

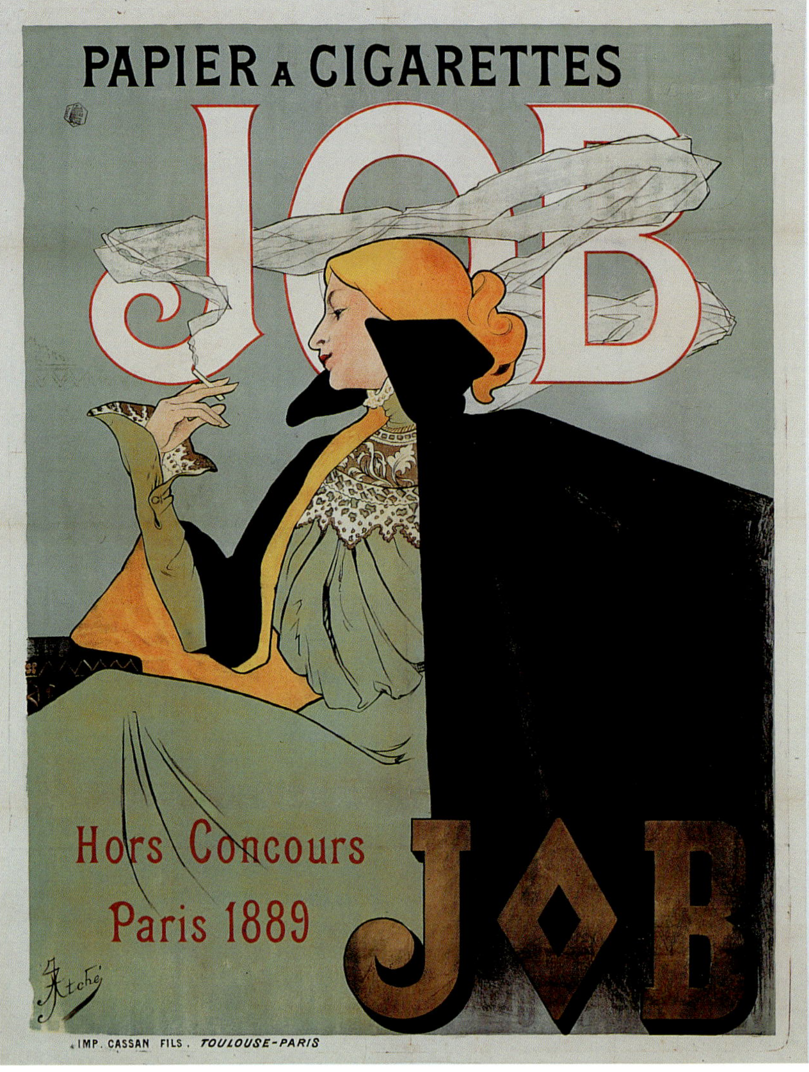

144

ANONYMOUS (cont'd)

139. World's Fair of 1940/New York.
20 x 30 in./50.8 x 76.1 cm
Polygraphic Company of America, NYC
Cond B+/Vertical tear through the "F" in "Fair."
Ref: PAI-XXXVII, 442
Does a fifty-cent admission price exist for anything anymore? Well, for four
bits, the happy spectator could gain entrance to the pageant of "Peace and
Freedom" known as the New York World's Fair. Among all the iconic pomp,
wonder and displays of the "World of Tomorrow," one figure appears to stand
out beyond the others: George Washington. Originally intended to mark the
150th celebration of his inauguration, his statue, designed by James Earle
Fraser, stood at one end of the Court of Peace, looking down Constitution
Mall to the Theme Center. There's a certain irony that among all of the
fair's visionary symbols and images, Washington seems peculiarly out of
place. The World of Tomorrow ostensibly had nothing to do with Washington or his world; his statue was encased in the Time Capsule and buried,
ready only to meet the world again—in whatever state it may exist—in
6939 AD. *For a different look at the New York World's Fair by Joseph
Binder, see No. 170.*
Est: $1,200-$1,500.

IB ANDERSEN (1907-1969)

140. Politiken. 1965.
$24^1/4$ x 68 in./61.5 x 172.7 cm
Henrik Sandbergs Stentrykkeri, København
Cond A.
Ref: PAI-XXXIV, 235
What this 2-sheet collage represents is hard to determine—perhaps the
multifaceted nature of today's world as reported by one of Copenhagen's
daily papers. However the graphic design is excellent, as is always the case
with Andersen. His two dozen or so posters show the strong influence of
Cubism and the Bauhaus. He also came by his talent naturally—as the son
of Denmark's preeminent posterist, Valdemar Andersen.
Est: $1,500-$1,800.

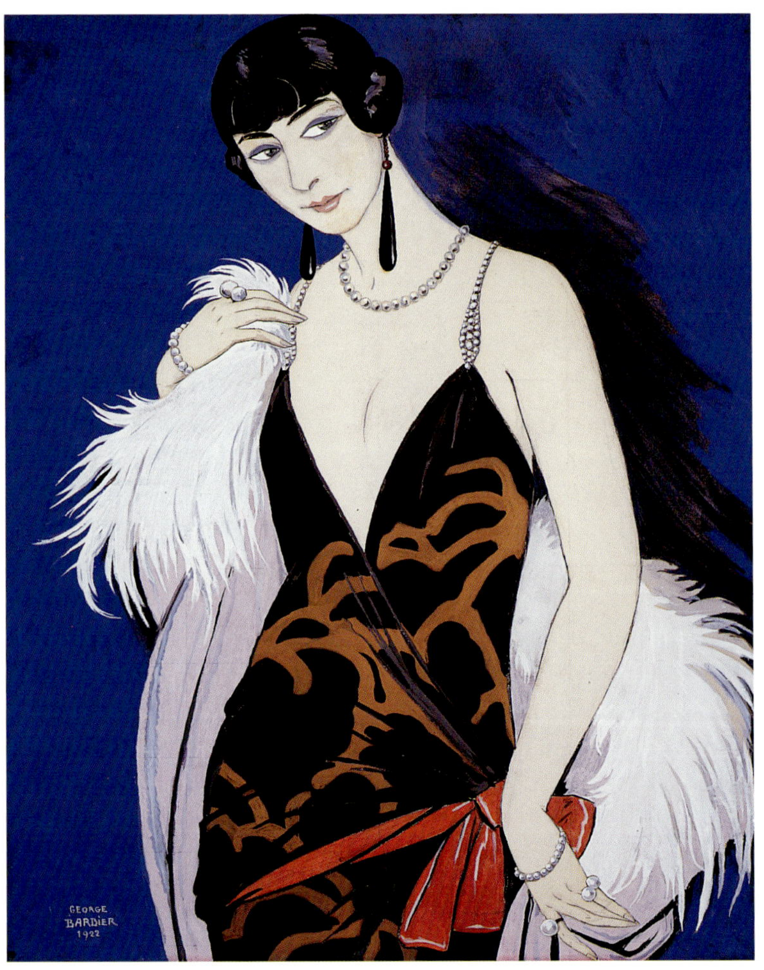

146

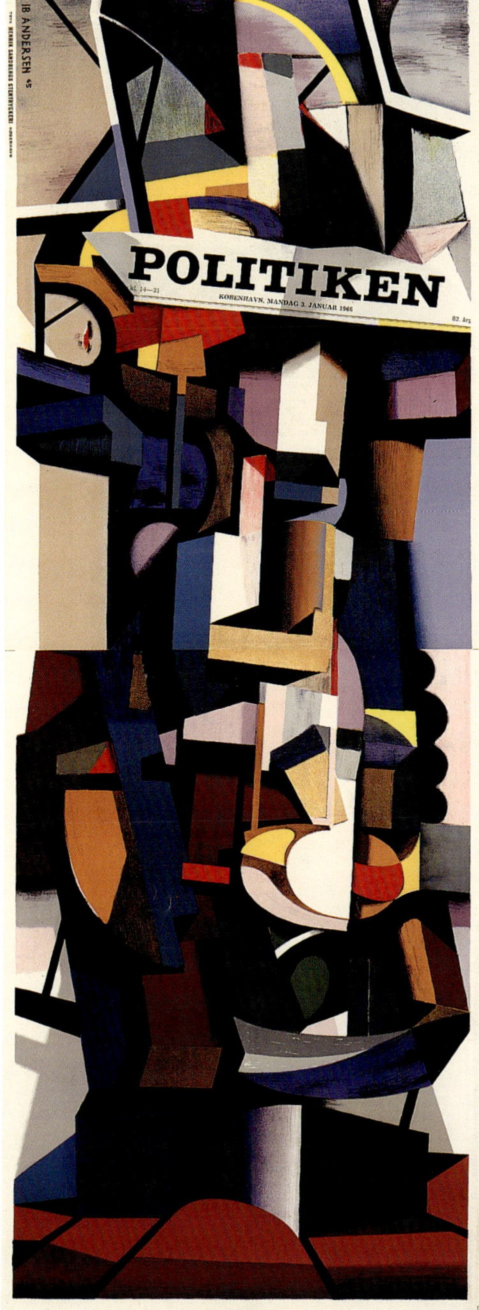

140

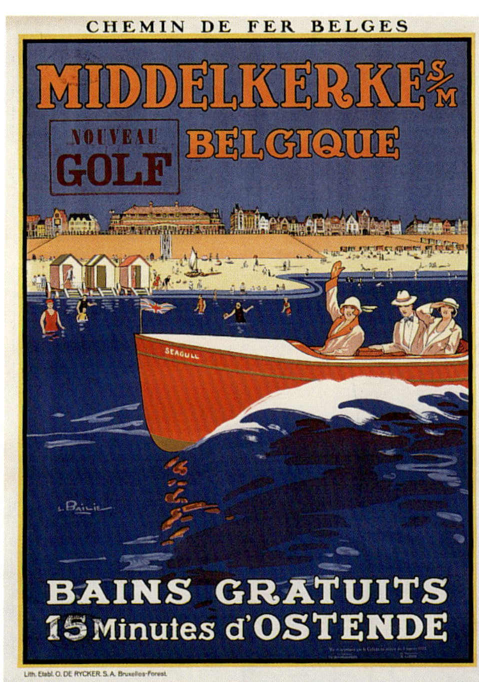

145

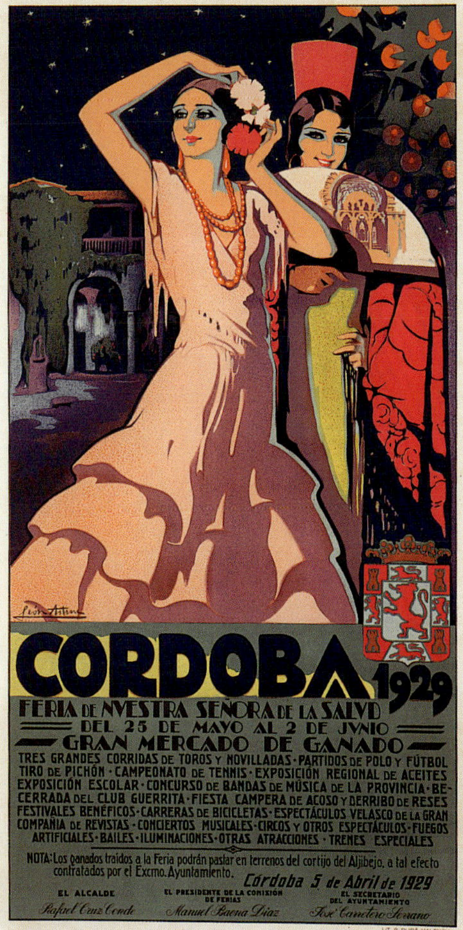

143

ANDREW-POWER (Sybil Andrews, 1898-1992 & Cyril Power, 1872-1951)

141. London Transport/To Hire a Bus or Coach. 1934.
$19^1/4$ x $29^3/4$ in./49 x 75.6 cm
Waterlow, London
Cond A. Framed.
"Andrew-Porter" was the signature of the joint studio of Sybil Andrews and Cyril Power, in which Power got the orders and Andrews created the designs. They had met at the Grosvenor School of Modern Art in London, where Power was a teacher and Andrews a pupil. Under the influence of Claude Flight, another teacher there, they adopted an avant-garde Futurist style whose hallmark was the depiction of movement and speed. Though no specific destination is singled out, this poster urges interested groups to travel in chartered comfort with busses and coaches rented from the London Transport's Hire Department, with an emphasis clearly placed on efficient, well-ordered directness.
Est: $1,700-$2,000.

ARTIS

142. Magasins Réunis.
$25^1/8$ x $38^3/4$ in./63.8 x 98.5 cm
Imp. Maurice Dupuy, Paris
Cond A–/Slight stains at paper edges.
Magnolias meet mod, striking the perfect promotional contrast in this superb Artis Art Deco promotion for the Magasins Réunis department store's summer spectacular.
Est: $1,400-$1,700.

MANUEL LEON ASTRUC

143. Cordoba. 1929.
16 x $31^1/2$ in./40.5 x 80.2 cm
Lit. S. Durá, Valencia
Cond A.
Founded in ancient Roman times, Córdoba shares a name with the Andalusian province to which she serves as a capital. By the 10th Century, Córdoba was the largest city in Europe, filled with palaces and mosques. Though today it's more modest in size, modern Córdoba's streets and buildings still evoke its Moorish heritage—as does the fan of one of the two stunning señoritas that grace this Astranne advertisement for the

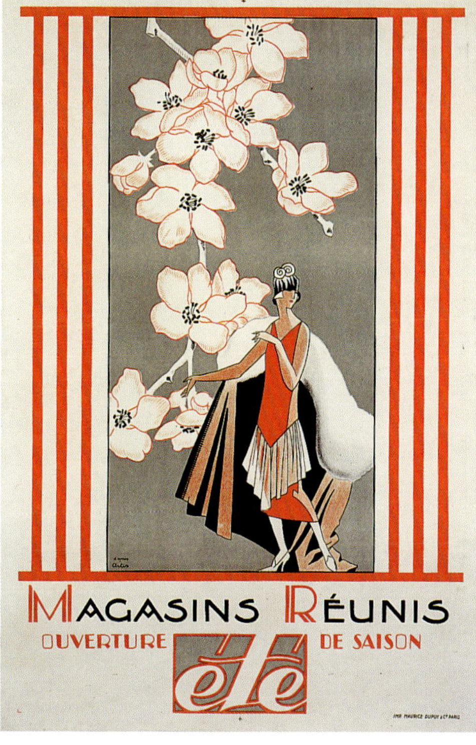

142

city's Feast of Our Lady of Health. Although dedicated to one of the most revered of Catholic icons, the Virgin Mary, the fair is hardly a reserved affair, known for its spirited abandon and 24-hour-a-day revelry.
Est: $800-$1,000.

JANE ATCHÉ (1880-?)

144. Job. 1896.
$42^1/2$ x $56^1/2$ in./108 x 143.4 cm
Imp. Cassan Fils, Toulouse
Cond B+/Slight tears and stains at fold and edges; excellent colors.
Ref: DFP-II, 24; Reims, 208; Abdy, p. 149; Wine Spectator, 101; PAI-XXXVIII, 165
"We know just enough about Jane Atché to be intrigued. She was born in Toulouse, worked in lithographic prints—at first in black and white only, later in color—and earned an honorable mention at the Salon of the Société des Artistes Français in 1902. Her scarce posters all disclose that Mucha was obviously (a strong influence)" (Wine Spectator, 101). Abdy, in fact, considers Atché one of Mucha's two best followers in France (p. 100). Of her half dozen known posters, this one for the cigarette paper firm is her most spectacular. We get the lyricism of Art Nouveau in the handling of the green dress and the smoke, combined with a compelling Lautrecesque management of the solid black cape as it slashes through the design. On all levels, it succeeds completely.
Est: $10,000-$12,000.

SAMUEL COLVILLE BAILIE (1879-1926)

145. Middelkerke. 1923.
$29^3/8$ x 41 in./74.6 x 104 cm
O. de Rycker, Bruxelles
Cond A–/Unobtrusive folds.
Ref: Côte Belge, 113
The de Rycker printing firm was the frequent choice of Belgian beach resorts for creating and printing their posters. The firm had its own design studio along with access to many talented artists including the painter Fernand Toussaint, a personal friend of de Rycker himself, and the English designer S. C. Bailie. This destination poster for the Belgian railway is only one of several Bailie/de Rycker collaborations. For the coastal resort of Middelkerke, Bailie places us at sea—the North Sea —looking in at the beautiful no-fee beach and casino located fifteen minutes from Ostende. We're apparently arriving at the same time as another motorboat, the noble *Seagull*, whose party, judging from the fore flag, has made its way across the Channel and is spending some time cruising the Belgian coast. The overall impression of the poster is friendly and welcoming, which is precisely the attitude one ought to find in a destination design.
Est: $2,000-$2,500.

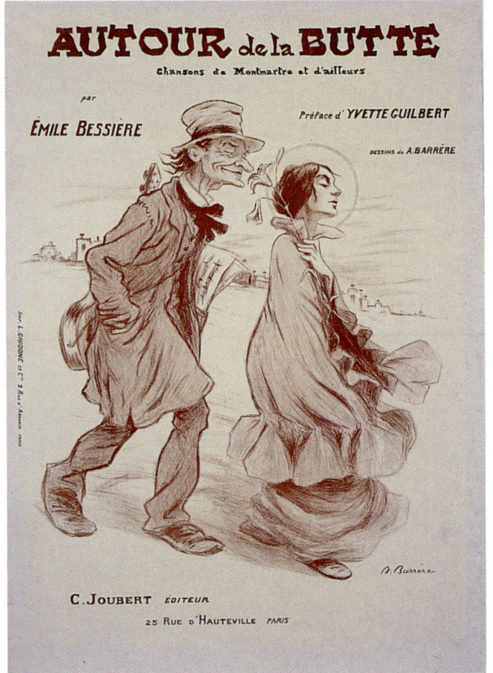

147

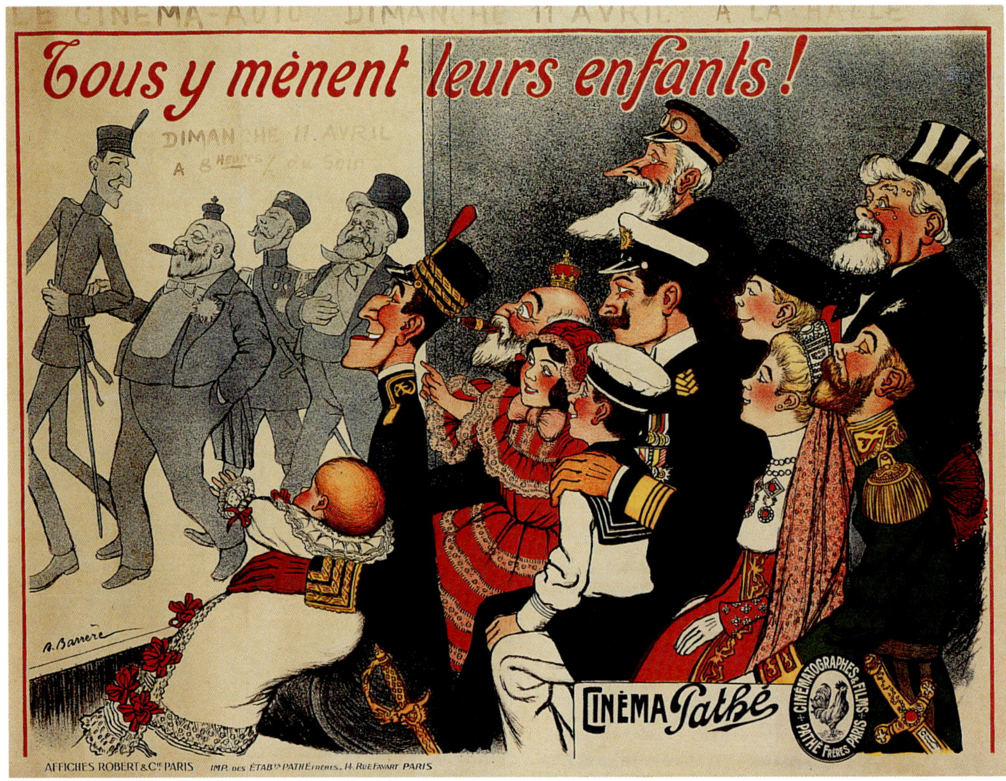

148

GEORGES BARBIER (1882-1932)

146. Bal des Petits Lits Blancs. ca. 1922.
31 x 39³/4 in./78.7 x 101 cm
Hand-signed goache and ink drawing on paper.
Framed.
Ref (All Var but PAI): Timeless Images, 120;
    Modes & Publicité, 16; Affiche Réclame, 39;
    PAI-XXI, 50

An academically trained painter and illustrator, Barbier
worked primarily for the fashion magazines of Paris,
contributing not only drawings, but articles, too. This
is a preliminary study for his poster promoting a modish
charitable affair in January 1923. That same month,
he penned the following withering description of the
event for *la Gazette du bon ton*: "The dowagers sit next
to actresses and ageless, unidentifiable crones, em-
balmed by their lotions and potions, wearing their
pearls like a disease . . . The beautiful people lean on
their elbows with their patrician faces and sigh . . . In
the balconies, showgirls dressed in pink and blue put
on innocent airs as if they were little shepherdesses
. . . Forget the polite trappings of the cotillion; hands
wave in the air with the crazy joy that madmen bring
to their pleasures" (Affiche Réclame, p. 68). For all his
barbed words, Barbier's image of an idealized Art Deco
woman—short hair, plucked eyebrows, dangling earrings
and plunging neckline—must have inspired at least as
many ticket buyers as the deluxe raffle offerings.
Est: $7,000-$9,000.

ADRIEN BARRÈRE (1877-1931)

147. Autour de la Butte. 1899.
26 x 37 in./66 x 94 cm
Imp. L. Guidhone, Paris
Cond B+/Slight tears at fold and edges.
Ref: PAI-XXXIII, 194

This lovely poster is for a Montmartre songbook aptly
titled "Around The Hill." The book boasts quite a distinguished collaboration—edited by Émile Bressière,
illustrated by Barrère, with a preface written by none
other than café-concert sensation, Yvette Guilbert. And
the image couldn't be more ideal—a willowy muse,
sanctified by the rising of the full moon, leading a bohemian troubadour willingly into the night. No wonder
that *L'Estampe et l'Affiche*, when announcing its publication, described it as an "Amusante affichette, très
joliment dessinée."
Est: $1,500-$1,800.

148. Cinéma Pathé. ca. 1909.
59¹/2 x 46 in./151.2 x 117 cm
Affiches Robert, Paris
Cond B/Slight tears at fold; traces of hand-written site
    information.
Ref: Célébrités, 151; PAI-XLII, 116

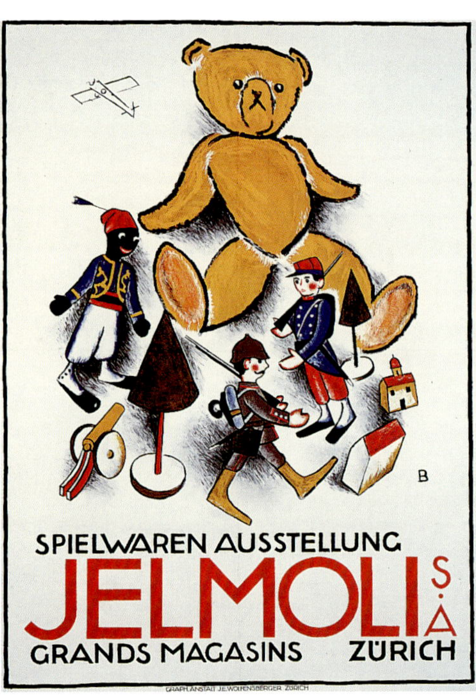

151

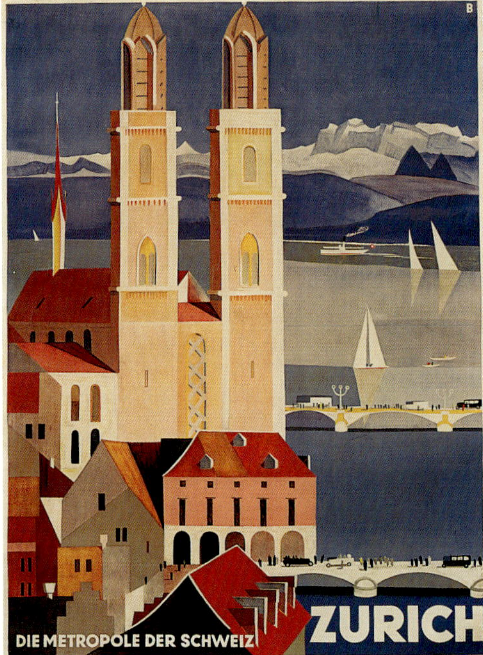

152

One of the first—and possibly most important—film
posters ever done. "The sovereigns all bring their children to the 'Pathé' cinema to see the first news reels
that will turn them into stars. In the room, one recog-
nizes Alphonse XIII and his son, Edouard VII, Léopold II,
Fallièrs, Victor-Emmanuel III and his children Umberto
and Yolande, Nicolas II with his wife Alexandra and
their son Alexis" (Célébrités, p. 95). *The following
hand-written text appears at the top of this poster
and on the illustrated screen: "Le Cinema-Auto
Dimanche 11 Avril a la Halle A 8 heures¹/2 du Soir."*

"I didn't invent films; I industrialized them," stated
Charles Pathé (1863-1957), the man who became the
first international cinema mogul. Something of an adventurer, this son of a butcher from Vincennes traveled
around the world for a while, but returned home broke
in 1894, just in time to see a demonstration of Edison's
peephole machine, the Kinetescope. Interested, he
raised enough money to rent one and for the first time
in his life realized a profit. He then joined-up with a
mechanically-minded friend and the two of them devised
their own projector and camera equipment. In 1896,
he persuaded his three brothers—Emile, Théophile
and Jacques—to join him in the founding of Pathé
Frères. At first they made only the equipment, but in
1898 they expanded into film production. Soon, the
Pathé insignia of the Gallic rooster became known and
instantly recognizable throughout Europe. From their
inception as a moviemaking entity through World War
I, Pathé produced by far more film footage than all
other European and American producers combined.
Est: $12,000-$15,000.

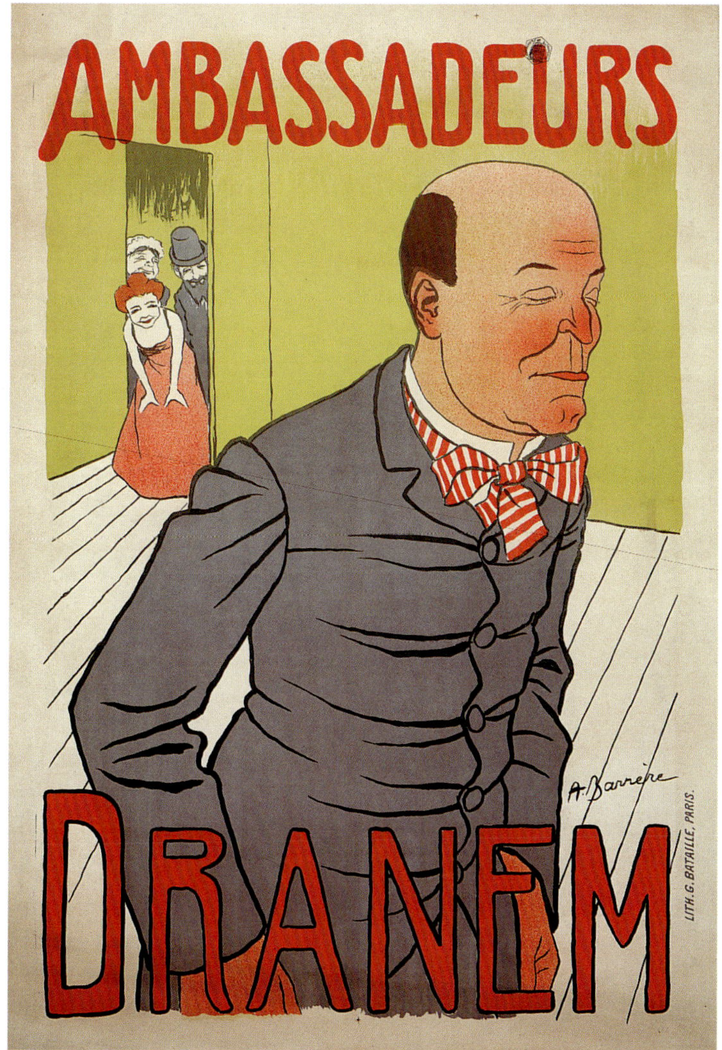

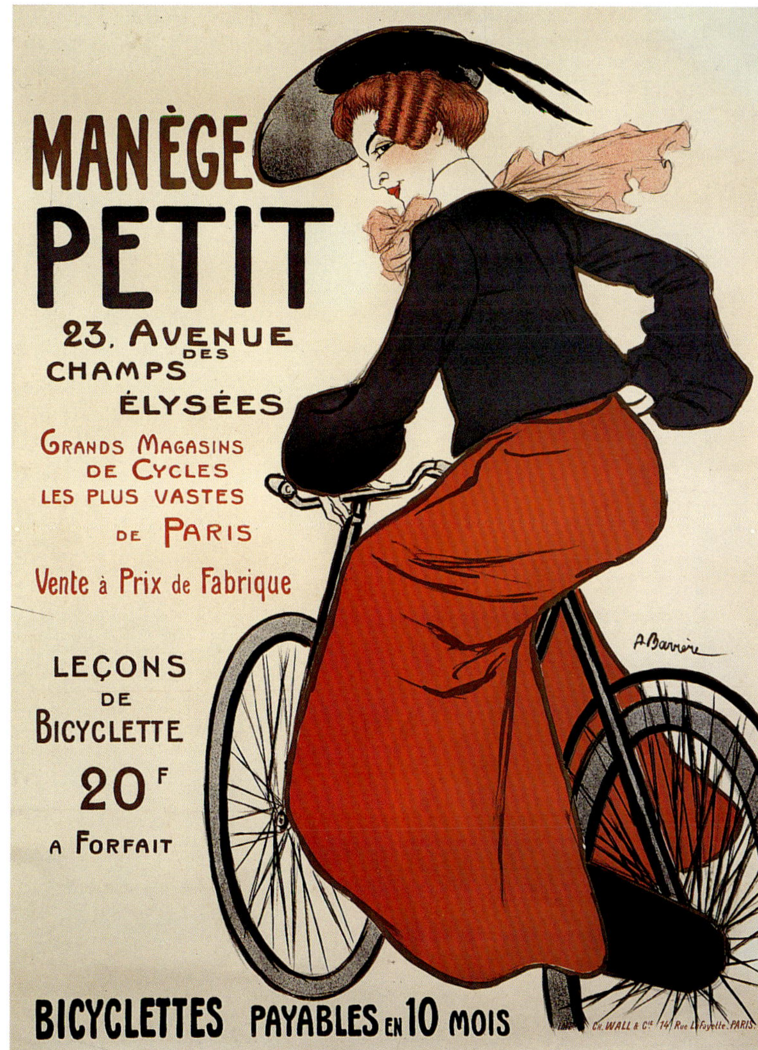

149

150

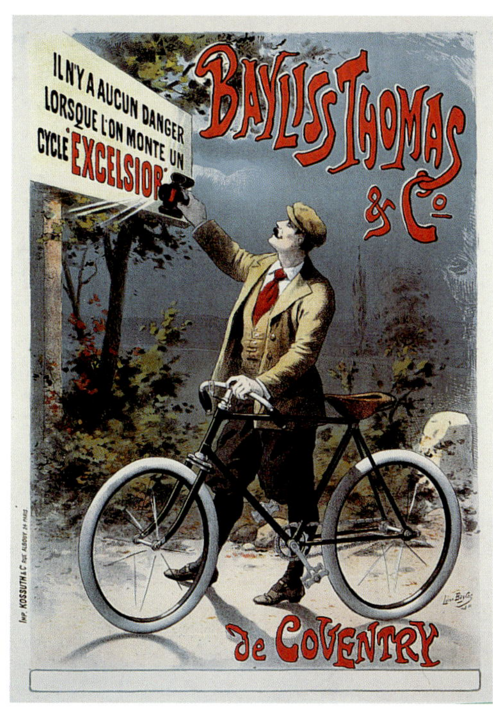

153

what homely face and affected a burlesque hick appearance, singing his nonsense songs with his eyes closed. He appeared in all the major music-halls of the day, even starring in nine films. The color, composition, movement and sympathetic treatment make this one of the best of Barrère's works.
Est: $3,000-$4,000.

150. Manège Petit.
$39^3/8$ x $54^3/8$ in./100 x 138 cm
Imp. Ch. Wall, Paris
Cond A–/Unobtrusive tears at paper edges.
Ref: PAI-XLI, 11
The brunette in the red skirt casts a coy glance backward as if to seek our approval of her assumably newly-acquired bike riding skills. The poster—something of a departure for Barrère, who is better known for his broad caricatures—is an advertisement for riding lessons, as well as bicycles for sale, which according to the design is the largest selection in all of Paris.
Est: $3,000-$4,000.

OTTO BAUMBERGER (1889-1961)

151. Jelmoli/Spielwaren Ausstellung. 1915.
$35^3/4$ x $50^1/4$ in./90.7 x 127.5 cm
J. E. Wolfensberger, Zürich
Cond B+/Unobtrusive tears at folds.
Ref: Baumberger, 23; PAI-XXII, 23
This charming poster in fresh-paint colors for a toy exhibition (with amusements for girls sadly underrepresented) is one of several designs that Baumberger created for the Zurich branch of this Swiss department store chain.
Est: $1,700-$2,000.

152. Zurich. 1929.
$36^3/8$ x $50^1/2$ in./92.5 x 128.3 cm
Wolfsberg, Zürich
Cond B/Slight tears and creases.
Ref: Baumberger, 155; Wobmann, 86; PAI-XXI, 54
A lovely design with the buildings in sunset colors standing out warmly against the clear icy blue of Lake Zurich. *This is the larger format.* A smaller format stacks the city name and description into a two-line panel below the illustration; a third version omits the descriptive text altogether. A native of Zurich, Baumberger regarded himself primarily as a painter, creating posters merely to generate some income. Nonetheless, he produced a magnificent body of more than 200 posters, distinguished not by a style, but by stylistic diversity—each perfectly suited to the clients' needs.
Est: $1,700-$2,000.

LUCIEN BAYLAC (1851-1913)

153. Cycle 'Excelsior'/Bayliss Thomas. 1896.
$35^7/8$ x $51^1/4$ in./91.2 x 130 cm
Imp. Kossuth, Paris
Cond A.
"There isn't any danger when one rides an Excelsior bicycle." Of course you have to assume that someone shrewd enough to take along a sufficiently bright light in order to read this sign during the course of their nighttime ride was already making his way atop a Bayliss Thomas of Coventry machine. So in many ways Baylac's advertisement is somewhat guilty of preaching to the choir; however, the concept that Excelsior is the bike for the serious rider comes across with steadfast resolve.
Est: $1,700-$2,000.

149. Dranem/Ambassadeurs. ca. 1905.
32 x $47^1/2$ in./81.3 x 121.5 cm
Lith. G. Bataille, Paris
Cond A.
Ref: DFP-II, 42 (var); Café-Concert, 47; Caradec/Weill, p. 128; PAI-XV, 113
A familiar comic figure of the French stage, Dranem (Armand Menard, 1869-1935) capitalized on a some-

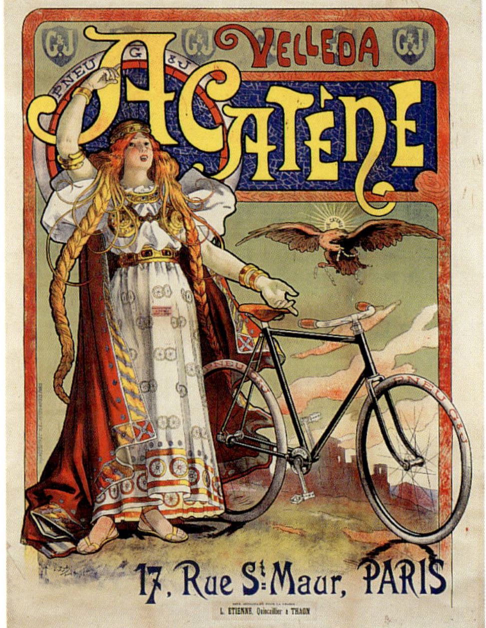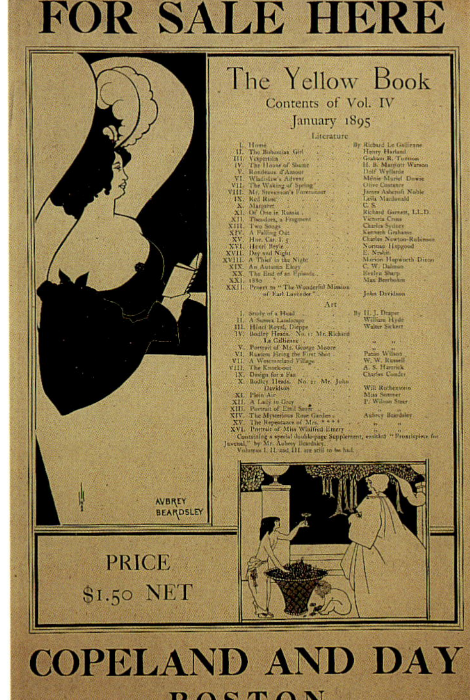

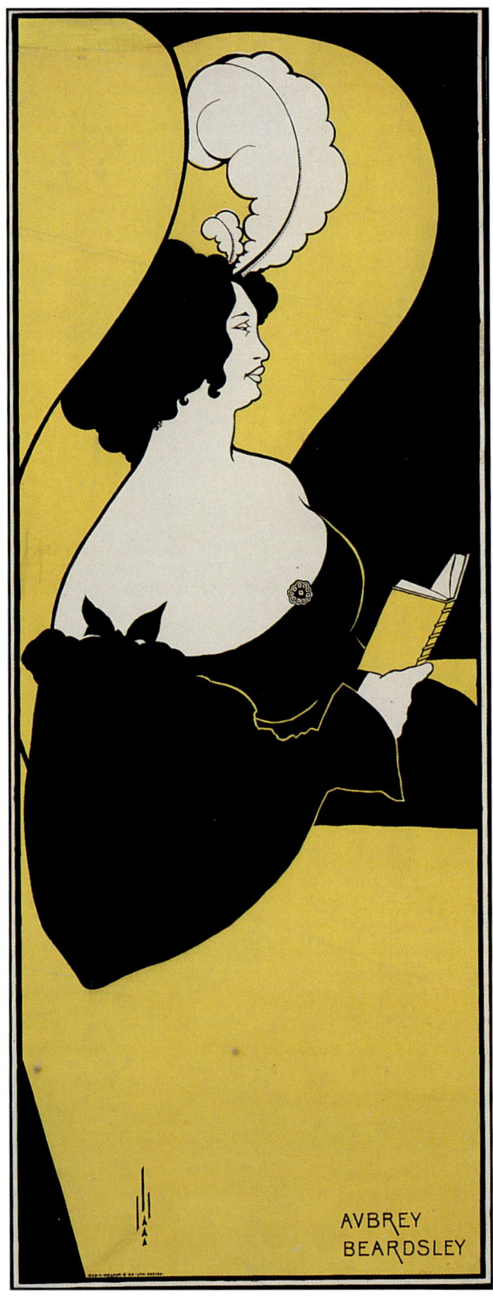

154

155

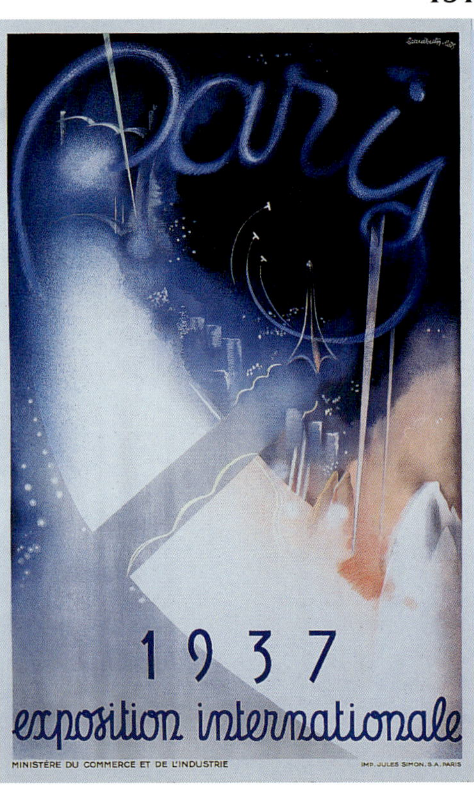

157

158

156

154. Acatène Velleda. ca. 1894.
$47^1/_8$ x $62^1/_8$ in./119.6 x 157.7 cm
Imp. Kossuth, Paris
Cond B/Slight tears and stains at edges and folds.
This proclamatory valkyrie would appear to be none
other than Velleda, the Germanic priestess who was
one of the leaders of the Batavian uprising against the
Romans. Here, however, rather than taking on an entire
empire, she lends her name to a brand of bicycle determined to crush the tyranny of chain-driven models
with their chainless ride: the Acatène Métropole. Adding further melodrama to the proceedings is the background's chain-rending raptor, a bird of prey supplied
with its own Latin motto that translates as "Woe to
Chains." As is typically the case in posters for the
Acatène Métropole bicycle, it's made perfectly clear
that their product was outfitted with American-made
G & J tires. Baylac worked under Jules Chéret and the
Master's influence is clearly evident in his designs. Other
than that fact, the artist remains a bit of an enigma,
known to us solely from the ten posters he produced
during the span of one year between 1894 and 1895.
Est: $1,700-$2,000.

AUBREY BEARDSLEY (1872-1898)

155. The Yellow Book/Copeland and Day. 1894.
$12^1/_4$ x$18^3/_4$ in./31 x 47.5 cm
Cond A–/Slight stains, largely at edges.
Ref: DFP-I, 9; Beardsley, 335; PAI-XXIX, 217
This is the second use of the design for publisher's
Unwin of London (*see* PAI-XIII, 93), originally used to
advertise a line of children's books. Here it announces
the January 1895 issue of their magazine *The Yellow
Book* and includes a table of contents as well as an
additional drawing by Beardsley. The magazine was
founded by Beardsley and American writer, Henry
Harland, in London on January 1, 1894. Brian Reade
notes: "Such winged chairs were known as grandfather's
chairs, and Beardsley may have intended to represent
a grandmother sitting in an appropriate chair and reading to her grandchildren from one of the books . . .

The gown with its leg-of-mutton sleeves is of the Nineties,
but the feather is in the mode of the late eighteenth or
early nineteenth century. Instead of age and maturity
therefore Beardsley has formulated a disturbing sensuality in the features of the woman. This was the kind
of negligent irony which repelled so many of his own
generation" (Beardsley, p. 343).
Est: $2,000-$2,500.

156. The Yellow Book/Copeland and Day. 1894.
$8^3/_4$ x $23^1/_4$ in./22.3 x 59 cm
Geo. H. Walker, Boston
Cond B–/Restored tears, largely at corners. Framed.
Ref: PAI-XXXV, 181 (var)
This is the image-only version of the previous design.
Est: $2,000-$2,500.

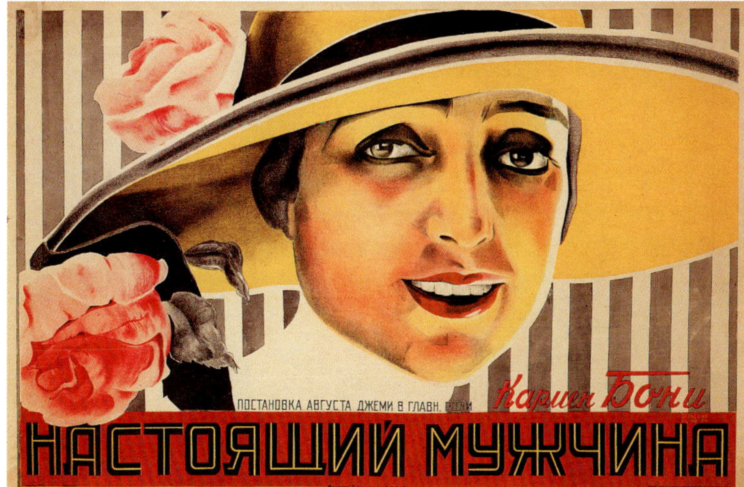

159

EUGENE BEAUDOIN (1898-?) &
MARCEL LODS (1891-1978)

157. Paris 1937/Exposition Internationale. 1936.
$24^3/_8$ x $39^1/_8$ in./62 x 99.5 cm
Imp. Jules Simon, Paris
Cond A.
Ref: Purvis, p. 84; PAI-XXXIII, 200
The skywriting, the night scene, the hint of futurism, all contribute to the sense of romance and excitement in this most effective design. The milky azure image with its shimmering pink and white flashes of light won first prize in a poster competition held by the French Ministry of Commerce for the Paris 1937 World's Fair. Its co-creators were architects who were involved in several construction projects together around Paris, including the overall design for the upcoming 1937 World's Fair; they entered the competition on a whim, and regrettably, never produced another poster. After a partnership that extended from 1925 to 1940, Beaudoin left to become director of architectural studies at a school in Geneva, while Lods stayed in private practice in Paris. *This is the medium format.*
Est: $1,700-$2,000.

JOSE BELON (1861-1927)

158. L'Intransigeant.
$43^1/_8$ x $58^3/_4$ in./109.6 x 149.3 cm
Imp. Paul Dupont, Paris
Cond B+/Slight tears at folds.
Certainly not all newspapers in turn-of-the-twentieth-century France had an anti-Semitic bent, but *L'Intransigeant* (*The Hard-Line*) certainly appears to have had tendencies leaning in that direction. At the very least they didn't think very highly of Alfred Dreyfus, the highest-ranking Jewish artillery officer in the French army at the time, who had been wrongfully convicted— and later pardoned—of treason. This isn't terribly surprising seeing as its editor, Henri Rochefort's, extreme nationalism led him to take a strong stand against Dreyfus during the Dreyfus Affair. As proof we offer this Belon design that promises a satiric cartoon focusing on current events in every issue of the paper that just so happens to feature a caricatured Dreyfus being released from Devil's Island, casting a decidedly Satanic shadow as he goes. Belon was a painter whose designs, often in a humorous vein, were regularly exhibited in various French galleries between 1910 and the year of his death, 1927. His posters are not numerous, but always interesting.
Est: $1,500-$2,000.

ANATOLY BELSKY (1896-1970)

159. A Modern-Day Hero. 1930.
$42^1/_8$ x 28 in./107 x 71.3 cm
Cond A-/Slight tears at edges.
If someone asked you to guess which movie this poster advertised, is there any chance in a million that you would guess "Little Lord Fauntleroy?" And even though it's the sunny visage of Carmen Boni that dominates this Belsky design, an Italian version of "Fauntleroy" being released in the Soviet Union is precisely what's being promoted here. Of course, invoking a title associated with British aristocracy never would have flown with the Communist party higher-ups at the time, so the more socialist-friendly "Modern-Day Hero" was chosen. The novel by Frances Hodgson Burnett became

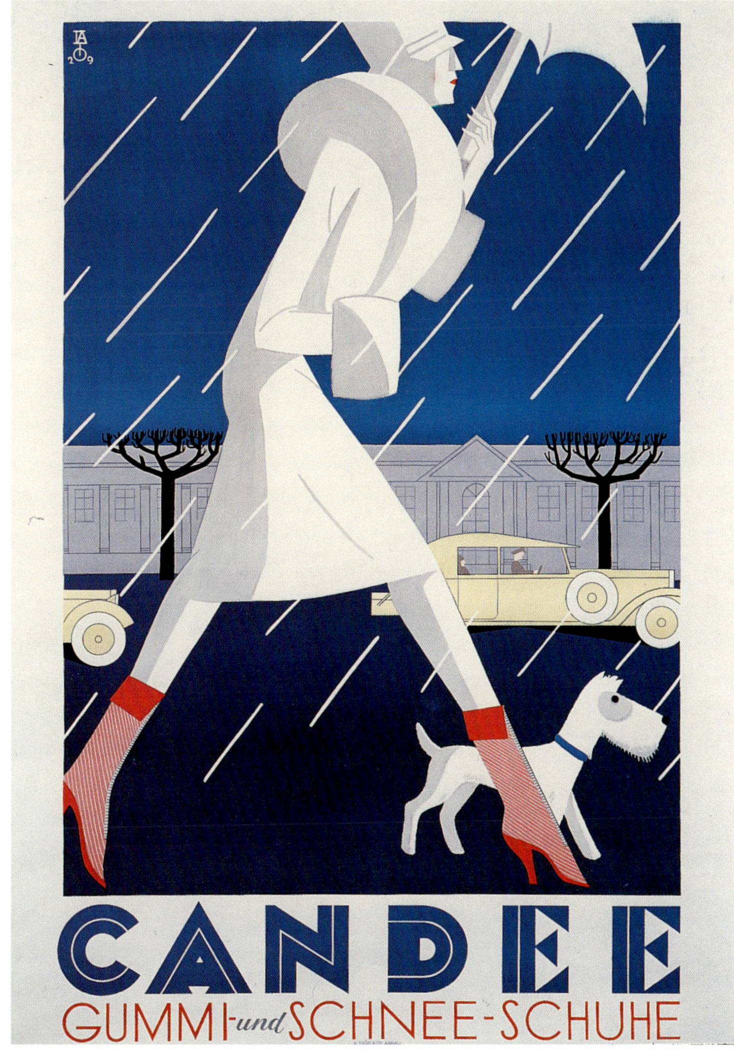

160

such a huge success that Hollywood couldn't wait to film it. That version (starring a twenty-eight year-old Mary Pickford as the lord from Brooklyn, no less) was such a smash that no less than a dozen versions in various countries were done. So why isn't a little boy on the poster instead of Boni? The answer lies in box office potential: Carmen Boni, who played the lad's mother, was a big name in Italian romance films, so the studio decided put the movie's financial fate in the image of a star rather than an unknown child. Incidentally, Fauntleroy was played by a real American boy (imported for authenticity, which is slightly peculiar seeing as it was a silent film) named Arnold Kent who in turn was given the Italian-sounding screen name "Manetti." Moscow-born Belsky was a set designer before he turned to creating film posters in the late 1920s. His style often involved concentrating on a single character. "Belsky also designed propaganda decorations and exhibitions, including the Soviet Exhibition at the 1928 Philadelphia exhibition" (Russian Films, p. 301).
Est: $2,000-$2,500.

EDUARDO GARCIA BENITO (1891-1961)

160. Candee. 1929.
$35^3/_8$ x 51 in./89.8 x 129.5 cm
A. Trüb, Aarau
Cond A.
Ref: Femme s'Affiche, 203; Art Deco, p. 182; PAI-XXIX, 218
An image from the high point of the '20s, just before "The Crash"—perhaps the rain beginning to cascade from the sky is the artist's premonition. At any rate, it reminds us of bad weather ahead and the need for Candée snow boots. Unlike in olden days—only a decade before—when a glimpse of stocking was looked on as something shocking, the boots now have to look good all the way up. And they do, thanks to the great fashion illustrator Benito. His cool background colors make certain that the red boots stand out, and his high 1920s style evokes glamorous New York (indeed, the New Yorker) far more than benign, bland Switzerland. *This is the German-language version.*
Est: $5,000-$6,000.

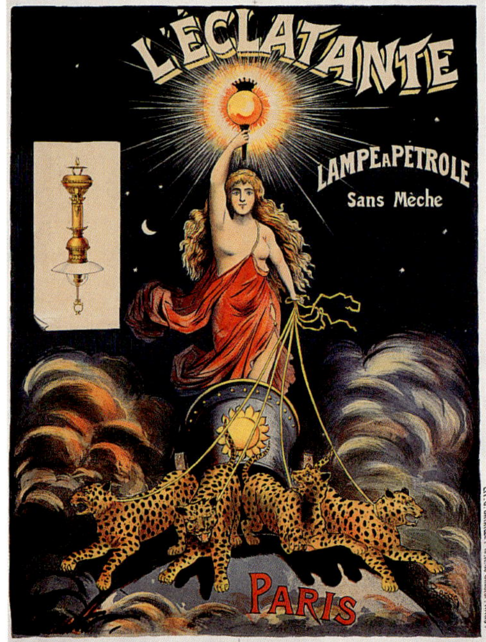

161

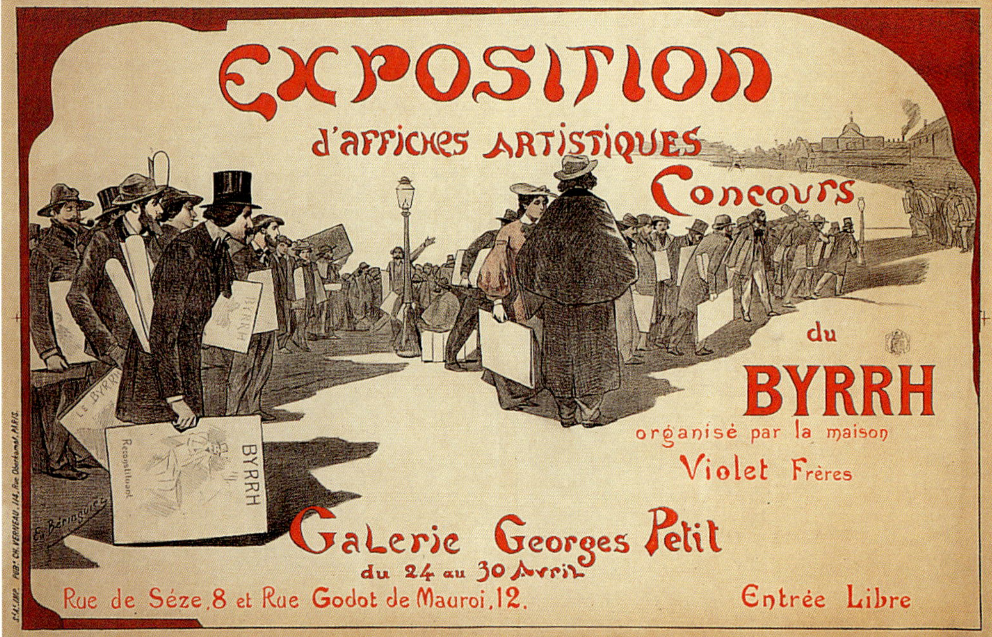

162

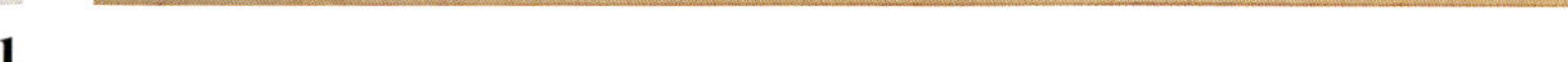

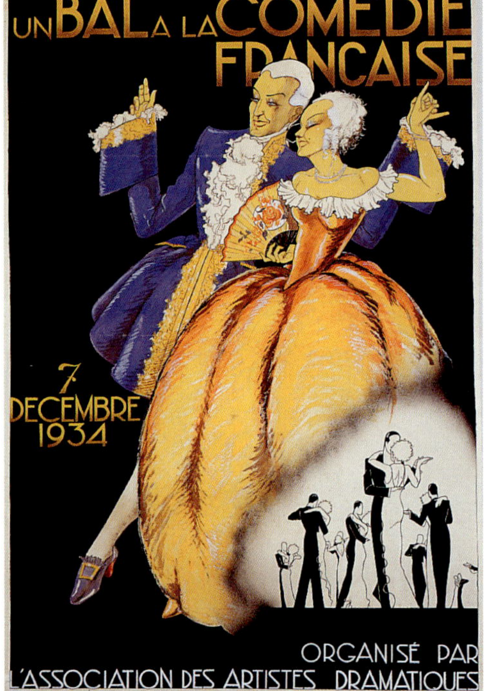

163

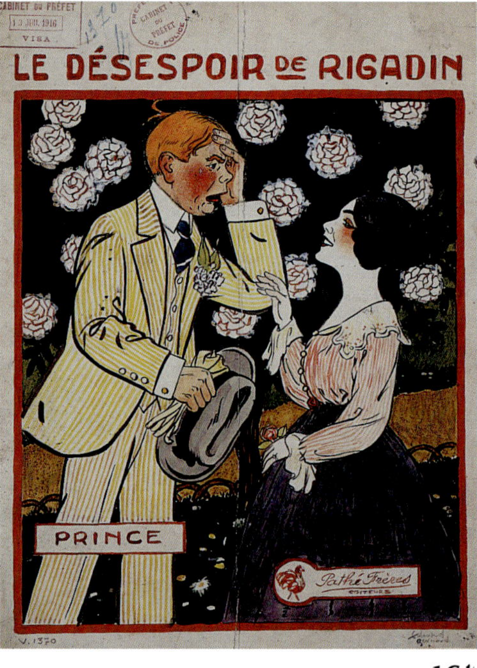

164

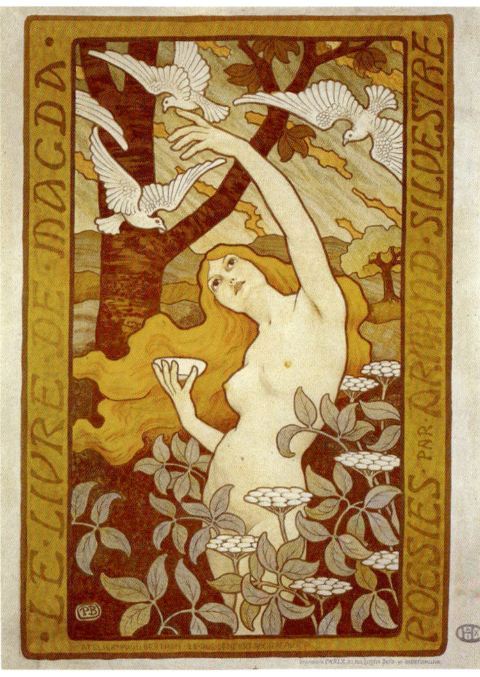

167

LOUIS BERGÈ

161. L'Éclatante.
23¹/2 x 31³/4 in./59.7 x 80.8 cm
Lit. G. Bataille, Paris
Cond A.
Tastefully uneroticized but still packing ferocious promotional punch thanks in large part to the team of
snarling cheetahs that pulls her chariot through the
heavens, this Promethean torch bearer brings illumination to mankind via L'Éclatante, the oil lamp that lights
without the assistance of a match. Mythic, yet altogether convincingly persuasive advertising.
Est: $1,400-$1,700.

EUGENE BÉRINGUIER

162. Exposition d'Affiches Artistiques/Byrrh.
47 x 31 in./119.5 x 78.7 cm
Ch. Verneau, Paris
Cond A–/Restored tears in margin.
Give artists an opportunity to vie for glory—not to
mention cash prizes, one has to assume—and chances
are that they're going to show up in droves. And that's
precisely the notion that Béringuier puts forth to the
public in this promotion for an artistic poster exhibition
and competition sponsored by the makers of Byrrh
aperitif being held at the Georges Petit gallery. And with
such a multitude of talent, logic dictates that more than
a few exceptional posters are bound to be on display.
Est: $2,000-$2,500.

ANDRÉ BERMOND (1903-1983)

163. Bal a la Comedie Francaise. 1934.
31¹/2 x 46⁵/8 in./80 x 118.6 cm
Gouache maquette.
Bermond's proposed artwork for the publicity of a
highly prestigious charity ball benefiting an actors'
retirement home celebrates the tradition of a glorious
theatrical past while opening a portal into a very
soignée, Art Deco black-and-white present.
Est: $1,700-$2,000.

EDOUARD ALEXANDRE BERNARD
(1879-1950)

164. Le Désespoir de Rigadin. 1911.
10 x 13¹/4 in./25.4 x 33.7 cm
Gouache and ink maquette. Framed.
This celluloid royalty can best be described as three
celebrities in one. Around 1908, French filmmakers
discovered that most financially successful one-reelers
gave the audience a well-defined, familiar character—
and an avalanche of series came into being. And though
perhaps the best-known of these were the "Nick Carter"

and "Zigomar" series, there were literally dozens of
these identifiable personas cranking out comedies. The
most prolific of these characters was Rigadin, a character created by music-hall star, Charles Petidemange,
who also performed as Charles Seigneur, and adopted
a third name for his work in film: Prince. Between 1909
and 1917, Prince's "lovable bumbler" appeared in an
incredible total of close to 300 films. Rigadin (known
in the States and in England as "Whiffles") was essentially a white-collar type, perennially chasing women of
questionable virtue and being tyrannized by females
in general—his girlfriend, her mother or chaperone,
assorted mothers-in-law and so on. The basic idea was
to parody the overly-melodramatic stage plays of the
day. And it's not much of stretch to conclude that the
headache Rigadin appears to be in the throes of in this
Bernard maquette for "Rigadin's Despair" may very
well have been caused by the perky lass with whom he
shares the artwork, though truth be told she certainly
appears pleasant enough.
Est: $1,700-$2,000.

165. Les Exploits d'Elaine. 1914.
13 x 17 in./33 x 43.2 cm
Gouache and ink maquette. Framed.
A bevy of damsel-in-distress exploits alliteratively filled
the screens of movie houses during the early-Twentieth
Century, from *Dolly of the Dailies* to the *Perils of*

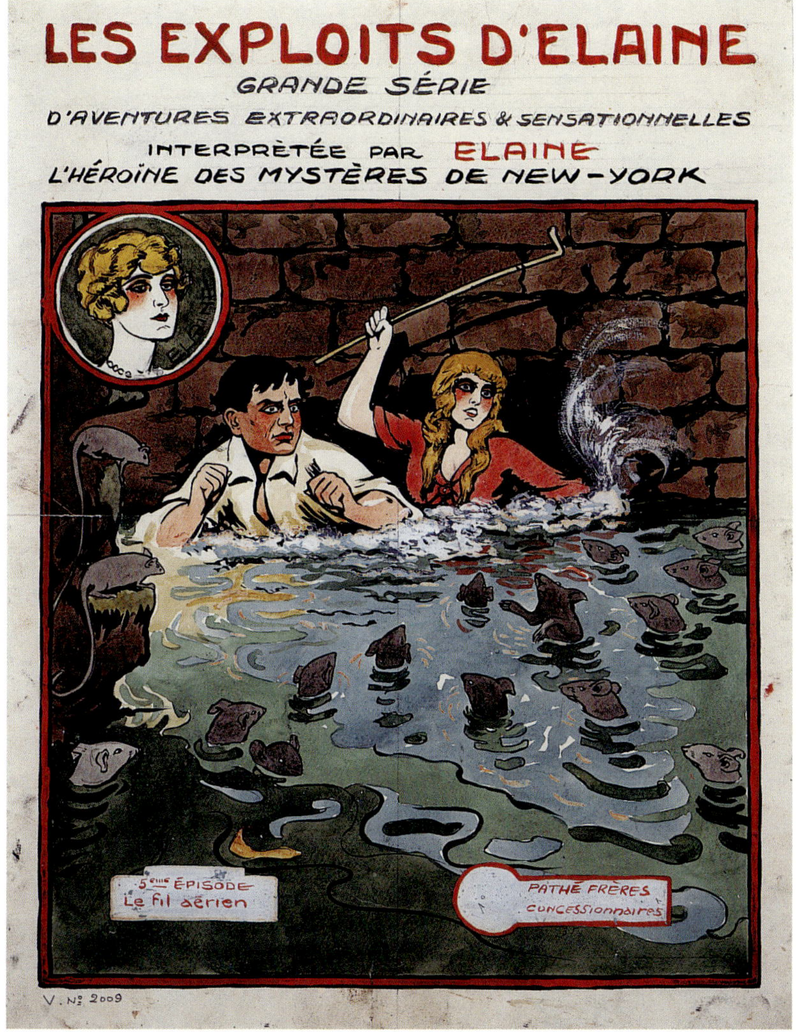

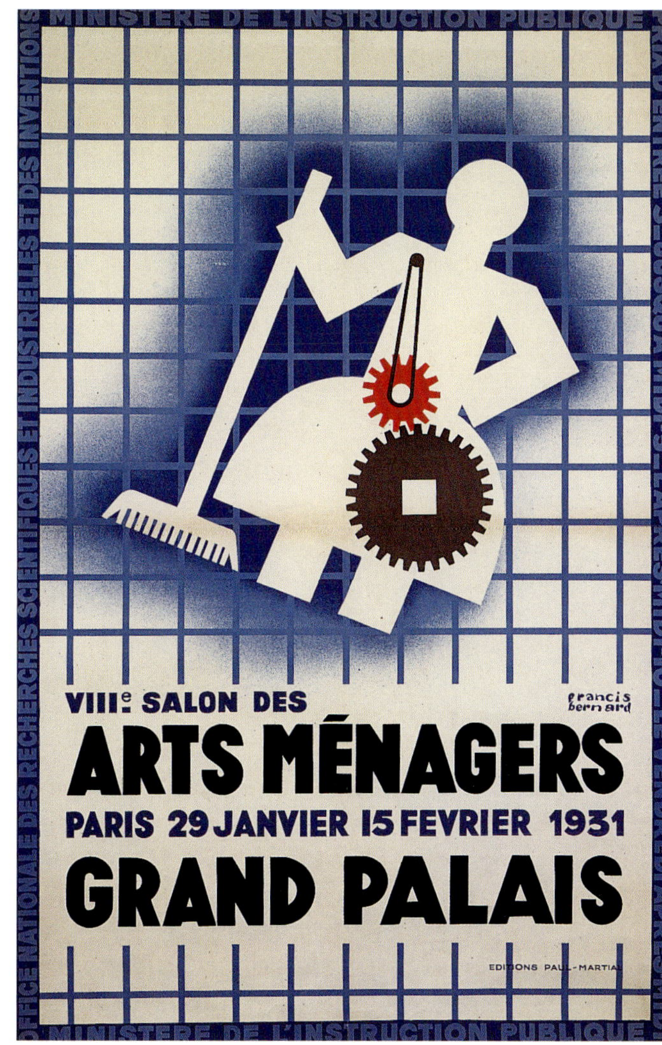

165

166

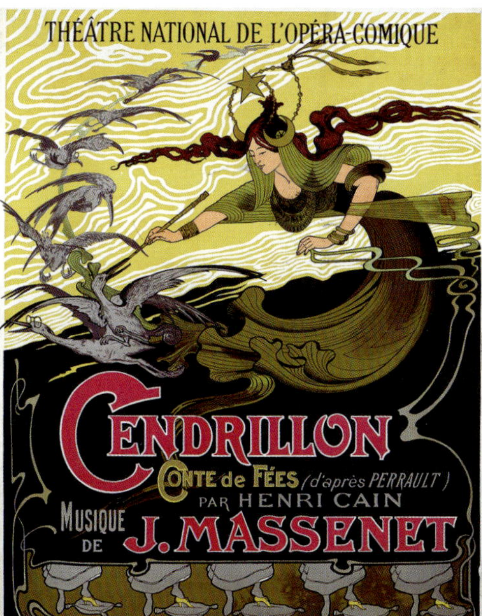

168

Pauline to the *Hazards of Helen* to *The Fates and Flora Fourflush*. And though Pauline may be the most remembered of these serials, it was the *Exploits of Elaine* that was actually the superior product, with better production values and more imaginative story lines. *Elaine* also added a new element to serial lore: the "scientific" villain, who in turn needed to be vanquished by a "scientific" detective, which led to the now-commonplace use of gimmicky weapons and sci-fi gadgets. *The Exploits of Elaine* came into being when newspaper magnate Randolph Hearst, after convincing Pathé to put out the *Perils of Pauline*, decided that he didn't want to be left behind when the popularity of serials took off and con-

vinced them to do another one. Both *Pauline* and *Elaine* starred Pearl White in the heroine roles, with Arnold Daly playing Detective Craig Kennedy, her "scientific" detective sidekick "inspired" by Sherlock Holmes. The premise of the serial was that Elaine's father was done in by a sinister malefactor known as "Clutching Hand," with Elaine tracking down the mysterious murderer with the help of Detective Craig. Chapter Five, promoted here by Bernard with verminated glee, was entitled "The Poisoned Room," a description of a chamber created by the dastardly villain that was decorated with wallpaper impregnated with "arseniuretted hydrogen," a tasteful embellishment that emitted a gas guaranteed to poison everyone in the room once water was introduced. **Est: $2,000-$2,500.**

FRANCIS BERNARD (1900-1979)

166. Arts Ménagers. 1931.
$24^3/_8$ x $38^1/_2$ in./62 x 97.6 cm
Editions Paul Martial, Paris
Cond B+/Slight tears at paper edges; unobtrusive folds.
Ref: Affiche Réclame, 21
"'The Ideal Home Exhibition was born in 1923 in the form of a home appliance competition organized on the initiative of Jules-Louis Breton, former Undersecretary of State for inventions during the war of 1914-1918, originator and first director of the National Office of Scientific and Industrial Research and Inventions . . . Created at first to reward inventors for the best home appliances, the Salon very quickly saw a great diversification of activities, including everything that contributed to the comforts of a home. Among the topics of the sometimes transitory or quasi-permanent sections of the Salon, one finds dwellings (displays of architecture and design), furnishings, home economics, gastronomy, etc.' Beginning in 1930, Francis Bernard became the poster artist who attracted attention to the Salon. He created a 'Mechanical Maid' symbolizing modern techniques at the service of a traditional cleaning lady that he that he would go back to unceasingly again and again until the 1960s, much like Loupot did

with his Saint-Raphaël personages" (Affiche Réclame, p. 49). Originally a caricaturist, Bernard began working exclusively as a designer for Paul Martial around 1927. The association gave him the opportunity to become a first-class graphic designer.
Est: $1,700-$2,000.

PAUL BERTHON (1872-1909)

167. Le Livre de Magda. 1898.
$16^3/_4$ x $23^1/_4$ in./42.6 x 59 cm
Imp. Chaix, Paris
Cond A–/Slight tears and stains at edges.
Ref: DFP-II, 66; Berthon & Grasset, p. 97;
    Timeless Images, 29; PAI-XXXVIII, 239
An advertisement for a book of poetry by Armand Silvestre. One may doubt whether the poems themselves were as lyrically lovely as Berthon's ethereal, Art Nouveau illustration of a nude forest nymph, who seems—her hair especially—to be a part of the landscape. "Berthon's small but characteristic body of work . . . epitomizes the Art Nouveau style on paper" (Berthon & Grasset, p. 8).
Est: $1,700-$2,000.

EMILE BERTRAND

168. Cendrillon/J. Massenet. 1899.
$23^1/_4$ x $31^3/_8$ in./59 x 79.7 cm
Imp. Devambez, Paris
Cond A–/Horizontal fold.
Ref: French Opera, 35; Theaterplakat, 48;
    Spectacle, 649; Gold, 155; PAI-XXXVIII, 187
"For Massenet's musical version of Cinderella, Bertrand evokes an eerily haunting twilight mood, animated by a fairy directing a flock of geese. Art-Nouveau ornamentation throughout the design brings the elements of this admirable composition together in a memorable image" (Gold, p. 109). Active primarily around the turn of the century, Bertrand, a member of the Société des Artistes Français, was an engraver and painter who exhibited his works at several of their Salons.
Est: $1,000-$1,200.

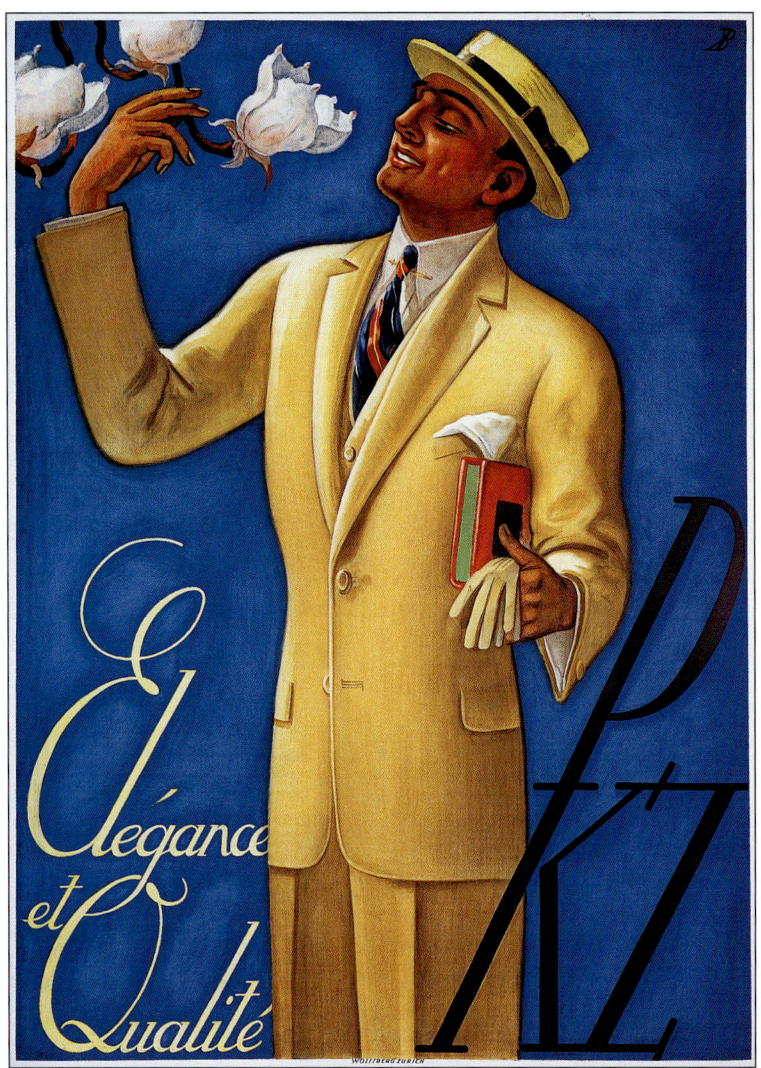

169

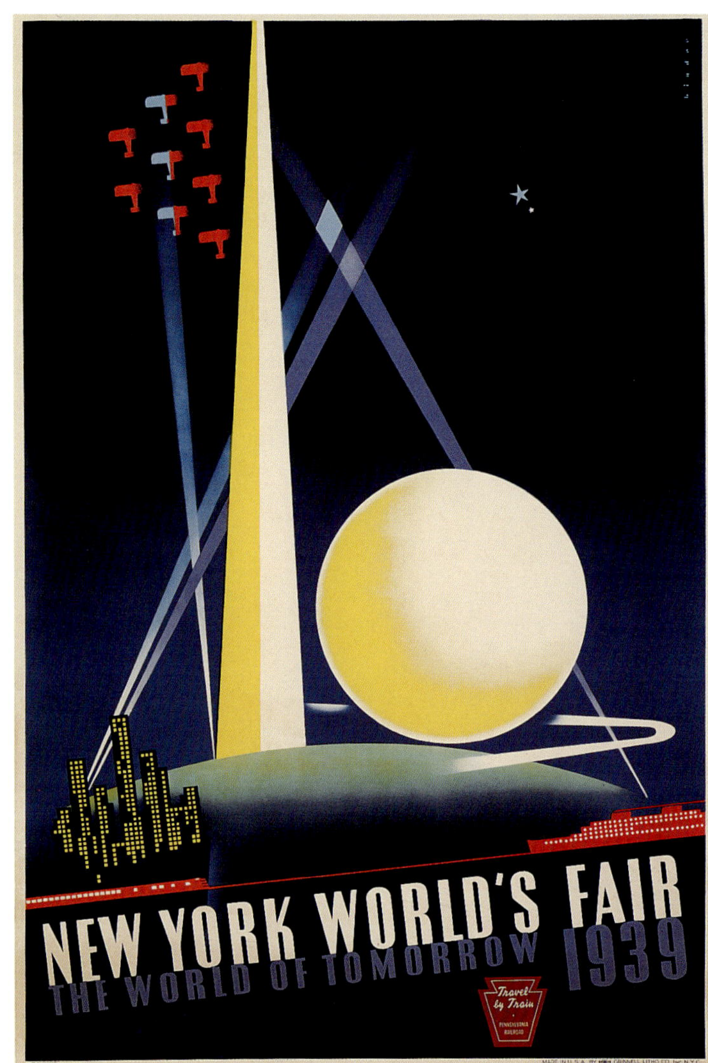

170

KARL BICKEL (1886-1982)

169. PKZ/Elegancé et Qualité. 1928.
35$^7/_8$ x 50$^1/_2$ in./91.2 x 128.3 cm
Wolfsberg, Zürich
Cond A/Exceedingly fresh colors.
Ref: PAI-XX, 387
Bickel produced fashionable posters for all the leading Swiss merchants, notably Greider of Zurich and Chausseures Scheuer of Geneva. This poster for PKZ shows the reason for his popularity: a flair for classy images that compliment the fashions that they promote. The gentleman sniffing a magnolia is in rich yellow against a Prussian-blue background. The text in this version is French; it was also printed in German.
Est: $4,000-$5,000.

JOSEPH BINDER (1898-1972)

170. New York World's Fair/World of Tomorrow. 1939.
20 x 30$^1/_2$ in./50.6 x 77.5 cm
Grinnell Litho., N. Y. C.
Cond A.
Ref: Art Deco, p. 113; Weill, 427; PAI-XXXVII, 439
The Trylon and Perisphere, ubiquitous symbols of the Fair, glow like celestial objects against a night sky. Airplanes, searchlights, skyscrapers and an ocean liner provide other signs of modernity in this design, first-prize winner of the poster contest organized by the Fair's sponsors. Binder was born in Vienna and trained there and in Munich. After a term as professor at the Municipal Institute in Frankfurt, he returned to Vienna to teach at the Academy. On the eve of World War II, he joined the exodus of talented, politically incorrect Germans and Austrians to America where he became a leading designer of posters for the war effort. He also won acclaim for his historical paintings and portraits.
Est: $2,500-$3,000.

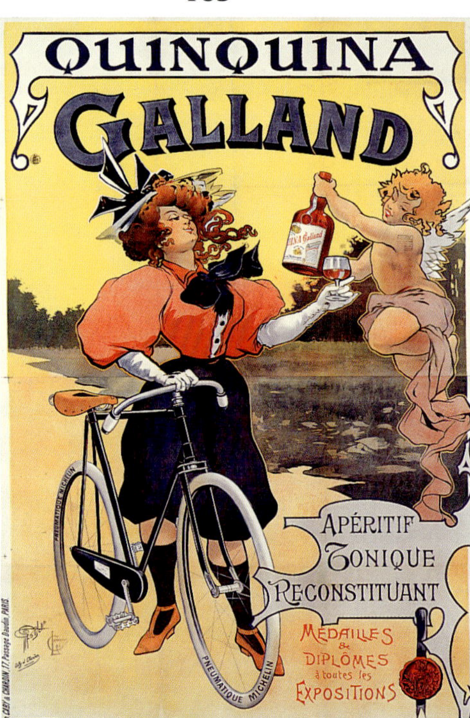

171

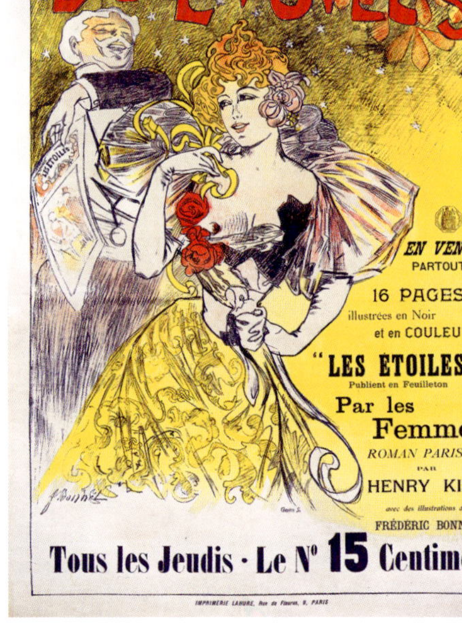

173

GEORGES BLOTT

171. Quinquina Galland.
53$^5/_8$ x 80$^1/_2$ in./136 x 204.6 cm
Imp. Caby & Chardin, Paris
Cond B/Slight tears at folds and seam.
It's a good rule of thumb that if a cherub appears at the side of the road with a bottle of liqueur while you're taking a bike ride that it might be an appropriate time to take a break. Plus, chances are pretty good that since this angelic emissary has picked Galland Quinquina—winner of many medals and commendations—as the *tipple du jour* that the experience is going to be downright heavenly. And remember: if you have to drink and bicycle, please remember to do so responsibly—and on Michelin tires.
Est: $2,500-$3,000.

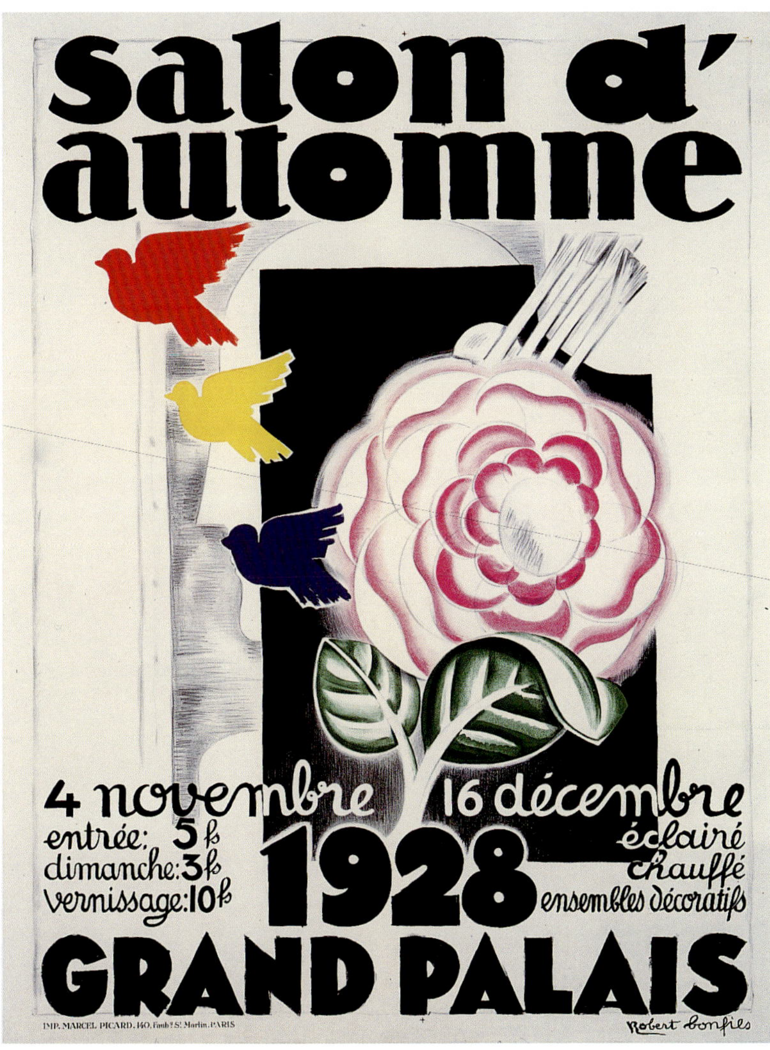

172

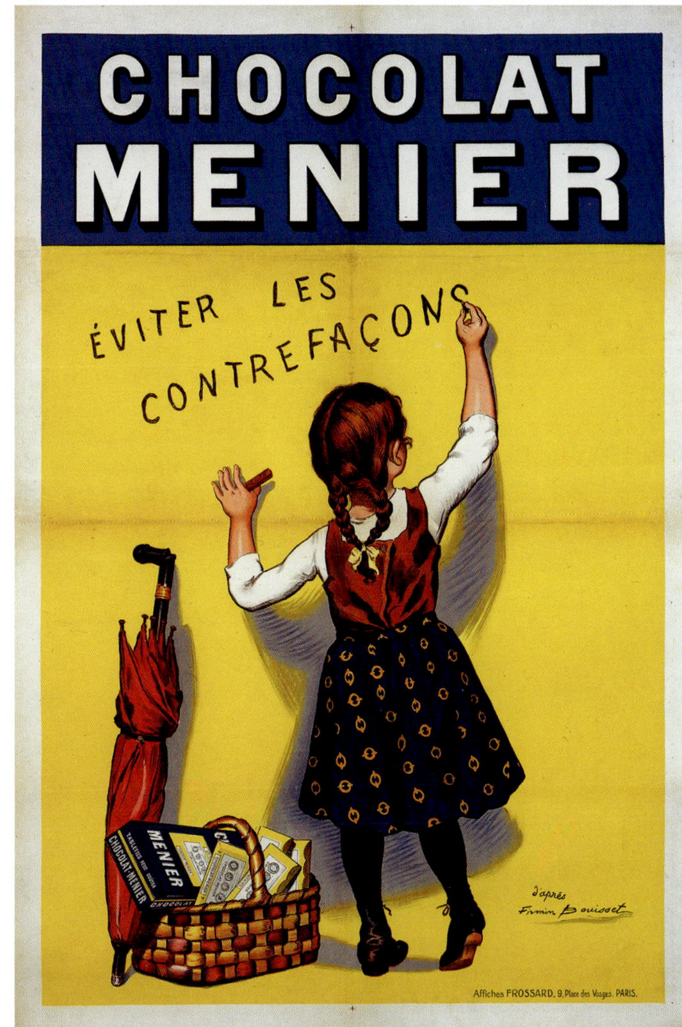

174

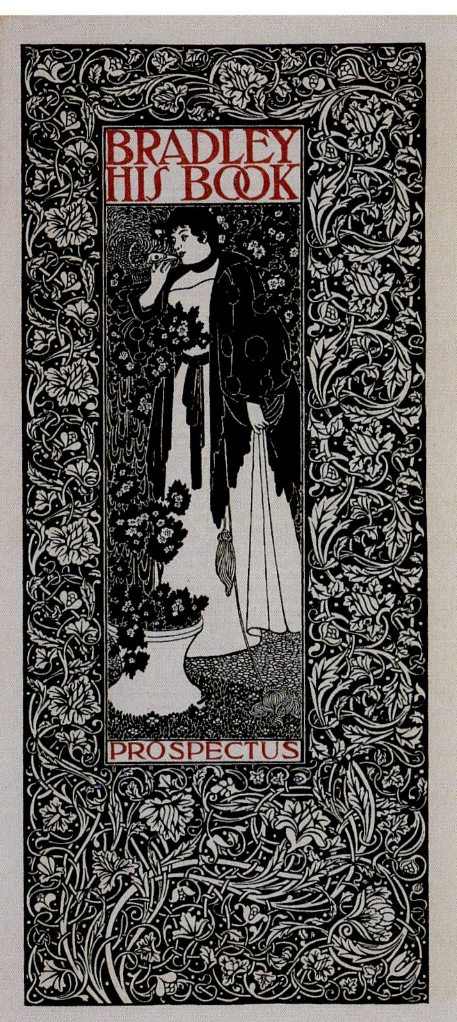

175

ROBERT BONFILS (1886-1972)

172. Salon d'Automne. 1928.
47 x 63^1/$_8$ in./119.8 x 160.3 cm
Imp. Marcel Picard, Paris
Cond A.
Ref: PAI-XVI, 145
Salon d'Automne refers not just to the time of the year of this annual art exhibition, but also to the group of artists who exhibited their work there. One of their ranks gives us graphic assurance that we will see the flowering of fine art at the 1928 show. Bonfils was a decorator and printmaker who contributed regularly to *Gazette du Bon Ton*.
Est: $4,000-$5,000

FRÉDÉRIC BONNET

173. Les Etoiles.
22^7/$_8$ x 31^1/$_4$ in./58.2 x 79.5 cm
Imp. Lahure, Paris
Cond A.
With a Bonnet design that's as frilly, fanciful and girlie as can be, *Les Etoiles*—a sixteen-page women's maga-zine illustrated in both black-and-white and color—announces the serialized publication of a *Roman Parisien* of the same name, with illustrations provided by the artist of this poster. In other words, an ideal match of subject matter to artistic execution.
Est: $1,200-$1,500.

FIRMIN BOUISSET (1859-1925)

174. Chocolat Menier/Eviter les Contrefacons.
ca. 1895.
31^1/$_8$ x 46^3/$_4$ in./79 x 118.7 cm
Affiches Frossard, Paris
Cond B/Slight tears and stains at folds.
Ref (All Var): DFP-II, 85; Reims, 237; Maindron, p. 42;
  Musée d'Affiche, 49; Weill, 75; Masters 1900, 75;
  Chocolate Posters, Cover & p. 20; Karcher, p. 75;
  PAI-XL, 240

In this lesser-seen, later version of the design, the young girl is writing "Eviter les Contrefacons" ("Avoid Substitutes"). Regardless of version, the seductive charm of the composition remains, making it one of the most appealing posters by this artist who frequently used children as his theme. *This is a later "d'après" printing of the poster, done in a smaller format and printed by Frossard.*
Est: $2,500-$3,000.

WILLIAM H. BRADLEY (1868-1962)

175. Bradley/His Book/Prospectus. 1895.
5 x 10 in./12.5 x 25.4 cm
Cond A. Framed.
Ref: PAI-XL, 241
In 1895, Bradley moved from Chicago to Springfield, Massachusetts where he established The Wayside Press, a publishing and graphic arts venture whose main product was *Bradley: His Book*, an art magazine appearing monthly. Although no direct proof exists, we can assume that this design may have been used by Bradley to introduce his new magazine at the exhibi-tion organized by the Boston Society of Arts and Crafts, held in 1896; it is known that he was anxious to make a good impression on his peers and contrib-uted "two or three cases of Wayside Press printing" to the exhibition (Hillier, p. 152). It's interesting to note that part of the text included within this prospectus points out "That there will be a Poster for each num-ber of the Magazine. The first will be 22 x 60 inches, and lithographed in four colors; these can be placed at one dollar each. Subscribers, however, can obtain them, while the edition lasts, at 50 cents a copy."
Est: $1,400-$1,700.

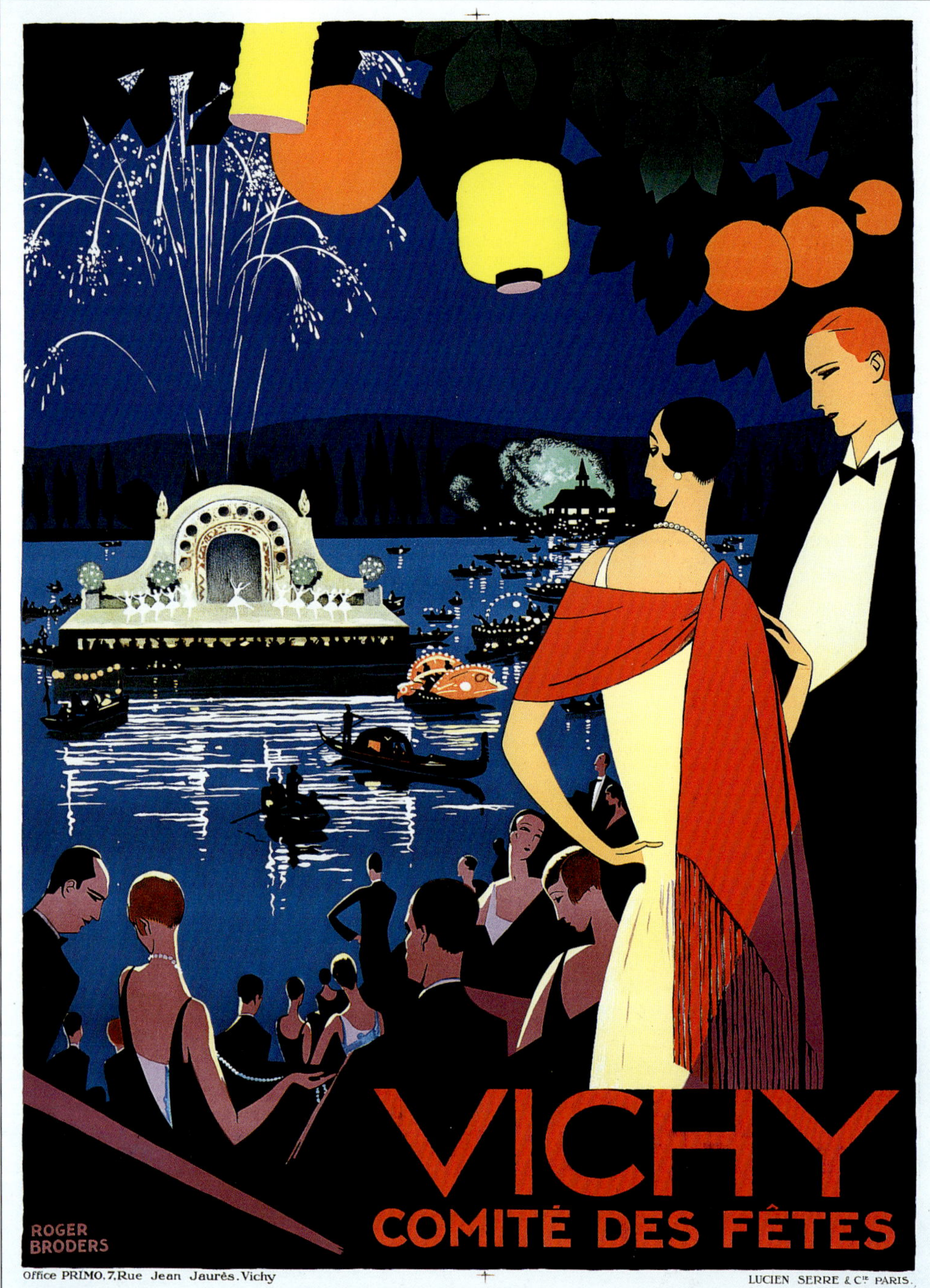

178

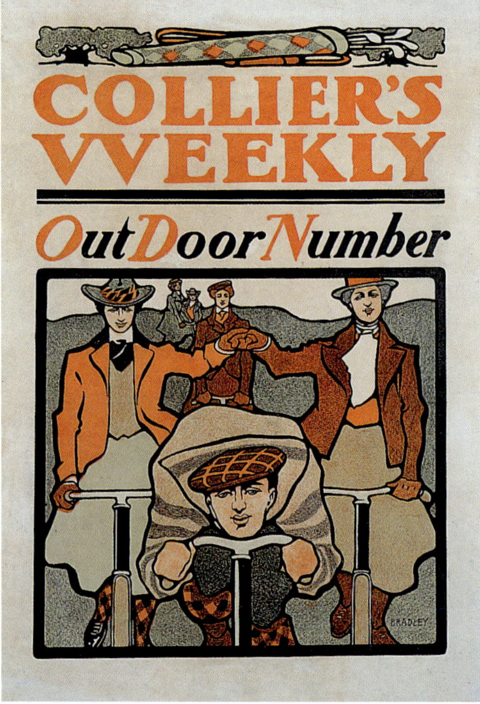

176

177

BRADLEY (cont'd)

176. Collier's Weekly/Out Door Number. 1900.
$11^1/_8$ x $16^1/_2$ in./28.3 x 42 cm
Cond A–/Unobtrusive tears at edges.
In his advertisement for the "Out Door Number" of *Collier's Weekly*, Bradley sets down a bit of cyclic horseplay, demonstrating in the process one of the best reasons to get out of the house and get some exercise—because it's fun. *Rare!*
Est: $1,700-$2,000.

FRANK BRANGWYN (1867-1956)

177. The Studio. 1899.
$21^1/_4$ x $32^3/_4$ in./54 x 80.6 cm
Cond B/Restored tears, largely in bottom text area.
Ref: DFP-I, 23; PAI-XXVII, 303
Born in Bruges, Belgium, painter, etcher, lithographer and muralist Frank Brangwyn studied under the tutelage of William Morris at age fifteen before leaving art behind to answer the call of the sea. Eventually, the urge to create bested maritime exploits and he returned to design, including being called upon by Siegfried Bing, the Paris dealer who christened the international arts style he championed as "Art Nouveau," to create the facade of Bing's gallery. The flowing lines of the art lovers fronting an industrial landscape was one of

Brangwyn's efforts for *The Studio*, a monthly publication, which according to the promotional text had "the largest circulation in the world of any magazine devoted to the Arts." It's interesting to note that Art Nouveau was sometimes referred to as "Studio style" during this period, making it quite probably the focal design issue of the monthly, which featured its first article on poster collecting in 1897.
Est: $1,500-$1,800.

ROGER BRODERS (1883-1953)

178. Vichy/Comité des Fêtes. ca. 1926.
$30^3/_4$ x $42^1/_4$ in./78 x 107.4 cm
Lucien Serre, Paris
Cond A+
Ref: Broders, p. 55; Broders/Travel, p. 55;
    Deco Affiches, p. 93; PAI-XIX, 236A
A nighttime scene on the shores of a lake—with a floating stage on which a ballet is in progress, glittering boats on the water and a land-based audience in evening dress beneath colorful lanterns—makes a strong case for attending the Vichy Festival. As always, Broders places us at just the right vantage point to catch all the action. *Without a doubt, one of the rarest and most spectacular of all Broders posters.*
Est: $17,000-$20,000.

179. Menton. 1923.
$30^1/_8$ x $42^5/_8$ in./76.4 x 108.2 cm
Cornille & Serre, Paris
Cond B/Restored tears, largely at paper edges.
Ref: Broders, p. 94; Broders/Travel, p. 19;
    Affiches Riviera, 115; PAI-XXXVIII, 207
Menton is at the eastern end of the French Riviera, right on the Italian border (to step back to this vantage point, Broders might have had to show his passport). It had been best known as the "citrus city," before a British physician in the late 19th century discovered it had the mildest climate on the French Riviera and sent home raving reviews of its lovely, unspoiled setting. Word spread, convalescents came from all over Europe and the citrus city boomed as a health resort. We view its pastel buildings across the bluest of water, through some vivid-orange trunked pines.
Est: $1,500-$1,800.

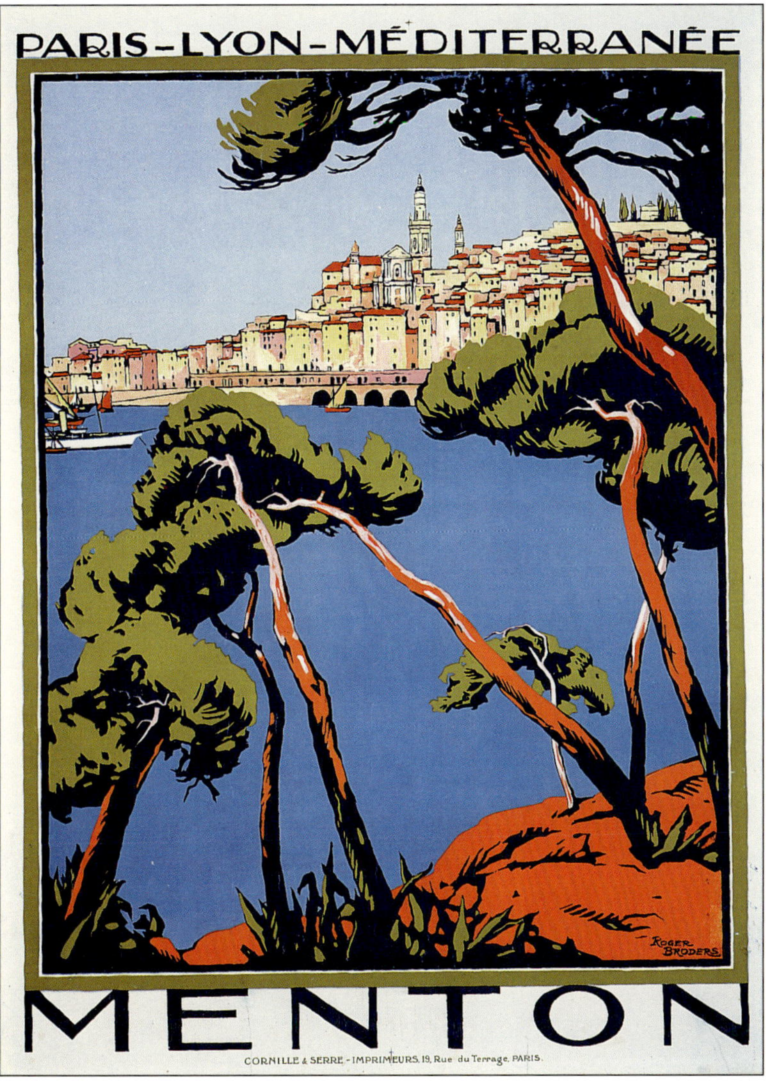

179

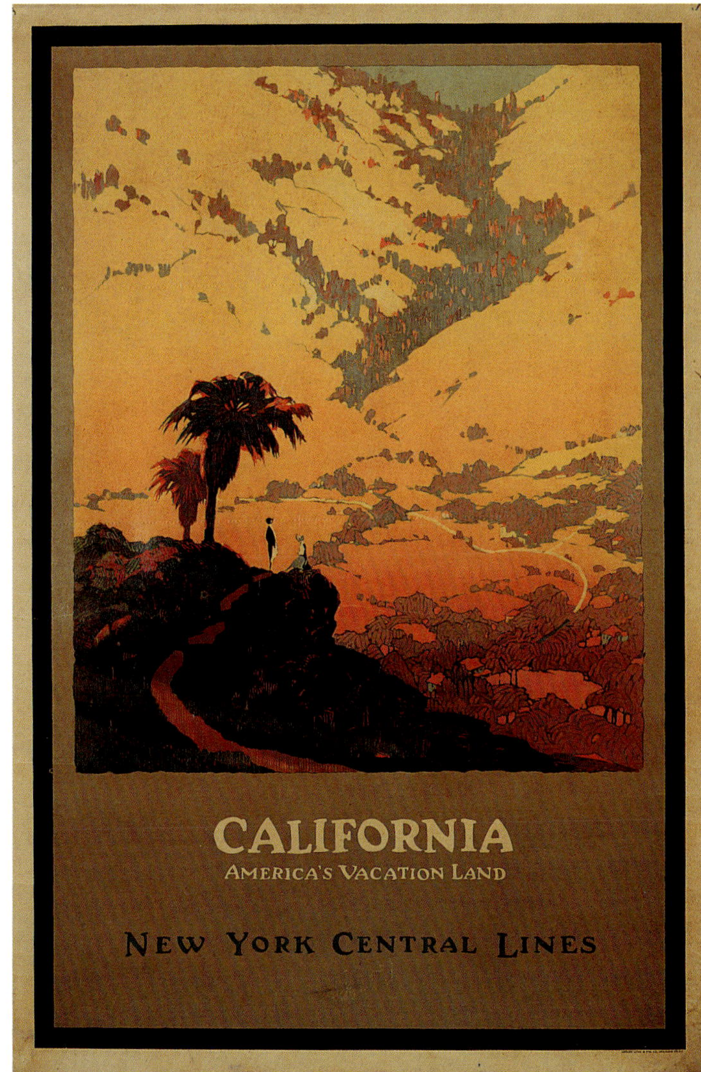

180

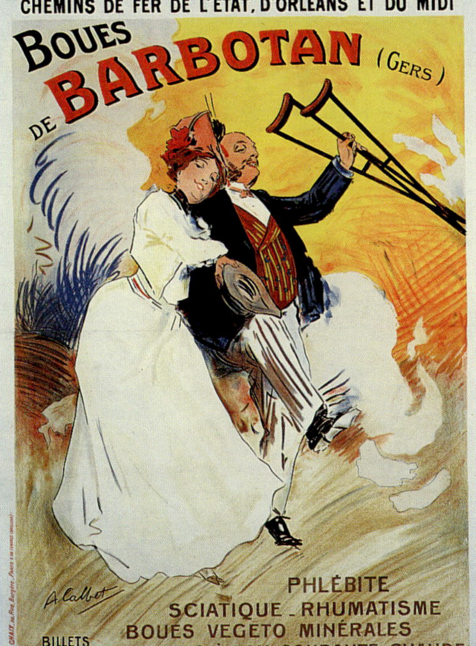

181

182

known for his interpretation of California subjects, his work was often included in the New York Art Directors Club's annual exhibition. *California* proved to be the most popular and remunerative of the series, setting the campaign's success" (American Railroad, p. 68). **Est: $2,000-$2,500.**

ANTONIN CALBERT (1860-?)

181. Boues de Barbotan. 1906.
29 x 41⁷/₈ in./73.6 x 106.5 cm
Imp. Chaix, Paris
Cond B/Slight tears at folds and paper edges.
Barbotan-les-Termes is a beautiful floral spa, a village situated in the mid-Pyrenees where a curative tradition of healing waters and clays coexist with the distillation of fine armagnac. And thanks to these restorative mud baths, this portly *bon vivant*—who undoubtedly arrived at the resort via the State, Orleans or Central Railways —appears to be ready to cast off his crutches and gambol headlong back into the good life. And his wife couldn't be happier. An optimistically unforced promotion by an artist best known for his aquarelles and colorful drawings.
Est: $1,500-$1,800.

GASPAR CAMPS (1874-1931)

182. Jaramago Valadia.
15¹/₂ x 21¹/₂ in./39.4 x 54.6 cm
Cond A–/Slight staining in margins only.
When it comes to creating sensual tobacciana, there was hardly a posterist alive who could compare to Camps. Take the nicotinic señorita featured in this printer's proof for Jaramago Valadia rolling papers for example—luxuriantly robed, an ornate bauble with flawless skin and expertly-applied cosmetic excess. Transported as she is by her preferred addiction, she fairly oozes drowsy sensuality.
Est: $1,200-$1,500.

JON O. BRUBAKER (1875-?)

180. California/New York Central Lines. 1926.
26³/₄ x 40⁷/₈ in./68 x 103.7 cm
Latham Litho, Long Island City, N.Y.
Cond B/Slight creasing and tears in margins and below the bottom text area.
Ref: American Railroad, 87
New York "Central's first poster (July 1925) commem-orated the commissioning of its massive high-level Hudson River Bridge in Castleton, New York . . . Central produced its second poster nearly a year later, in July 1926. Jon O. Brubaker's *California, America's Vacation Land*, a powerfully evocative depiction of California's distinctive golden hills aglow in sunset hues, sold 'western wanderlust' . . . Brubaker . . . whom Central's publicist's termed 'one of the foremost poster artists of the country,' was well known for his 'color harmony and tone quality.' A California resident who was best

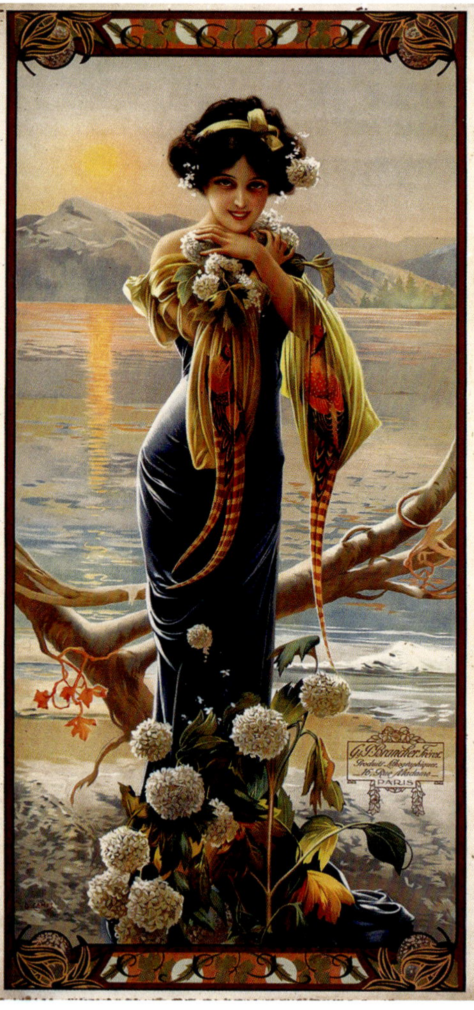

183

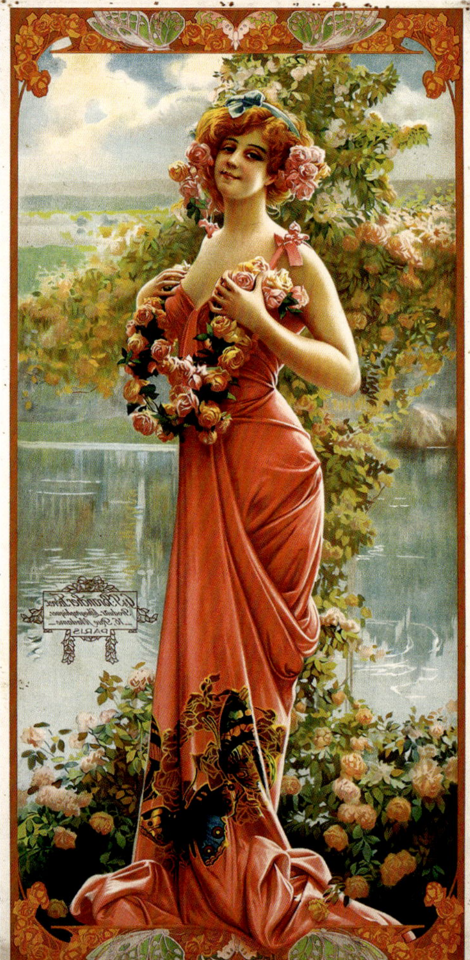

184

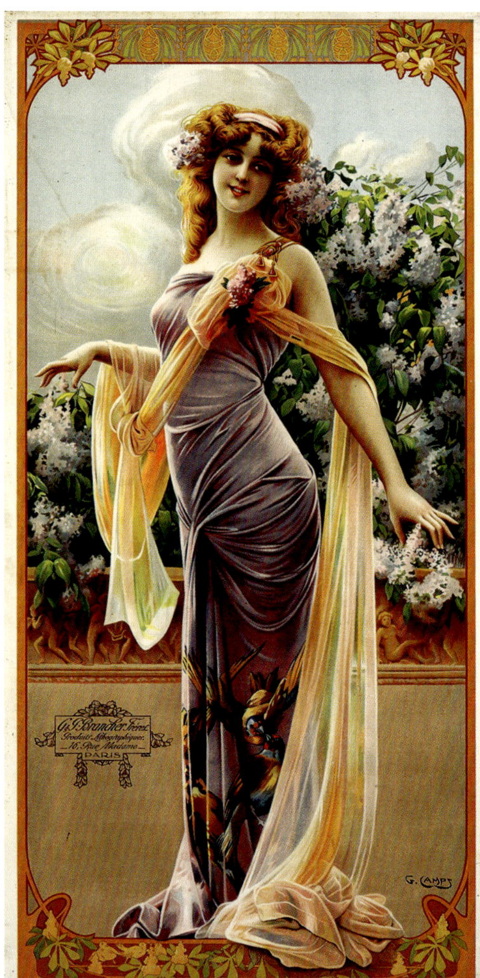

185

CAMPS (cont'd)

183. Evening Hydrangea. ca. 1904.
$13^3/_4$ x $28^1/_8$ in./34.8 x 71.5 cm
G & P Brancher, Paris
Cond A/Usual rod stains at top and bottom edges.
Ref: PAI-XXXIII, 245 (var)
Camps, a Spaniard who spent most of his career in France, was one of a number of artists hired by the Champenois printing house to fill the void when Mucha left for America in 1904. Creating both advertising and decorative works, Camps eventually found his own groove—less graphic than Mucha and more akin to oil painting, marked by soft edges and shadings, as well as loads of sentiment. This exquisite Art Nouveau celebration of beauty—female and natural—are executed with meticulous workmanship and lithographic skill. The raven-tressed beauty in teal with a pheasant-motif shawl admires white hydrangeas on the shore of a mountain lake at sunset.
Est: $2,000-$2,500.

184. Enraptured Rose. ca. 1904.
$13^7/_8$ x $28^1/_8$ in./35 x 71.5 cm
G & P Brancher, Paris
Cond A/Usual rod stains at top and bottom edges.
Ref: PAI-XXXIII, 246 (var)
The statuesque auburn-haired woman standing lakeside clasps a garland of pink roses against her flushed gown adorned with a flurry of fantastic butterflies as flowers flow to the horizon's vanishing point. Nice words, to be sure, but they fall disappointingly short of capturing the subtle seduction of sharing a moment in person with this Camps beauty. Though previously-seen versions of this decorative panel were executed for the F. Champenois printing firm (*see* PAI-XXXIII, 246), this one—as well as the other two Camps' designs—was executed by one of his affiliated firms, the Brancher Frères, also of Paris.
Est: $2,000-$2,500.

185. Lilac Allure. ca. 1904.
$13^1/_2$ x $28^1/_8$ in./35 x 71.5 cm
G & P Brancher, Paris
Cond A/Usual rod stains at top and bottom edges.
Ref: PAI-XXXVIII, 215 (var)

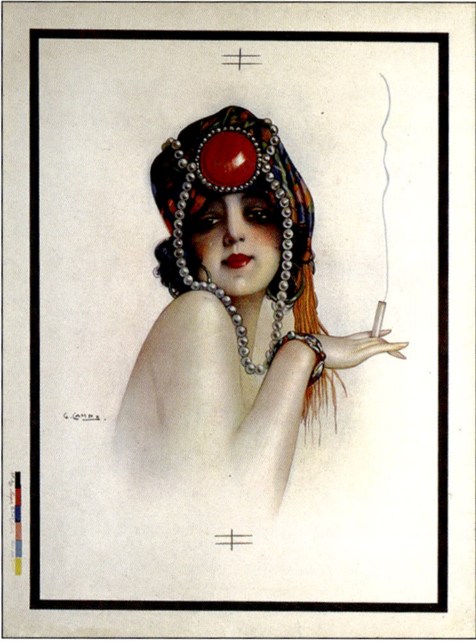

A blonde sylph draped in lavender diaphany—though stock-still, given the illusion of imminent flight grace of a flock of kaleidoscopic fowl posed flittingly about her gown's skirt—poses prettily in front of a carved wall lush with lilacs. A strong argument for the necessity of beauty for beauty's sake.
Est: $2,000-$2,500.

186. Flappers Deluxe: Two Panels.
Each: $16^1/_4$ x $22^3/_8$ in./41.3 x 57 cm
Cond A.
In spite of their luxurious attire, Camps' women seem altogether corporeal, non-allegorical entities that aren't likely to dissipate if a strong breeze would happen to come along. Take for example this pair of bejeweled flappers, who, though sumptuously decked-out and clearly accustomed to the finer things that life has to

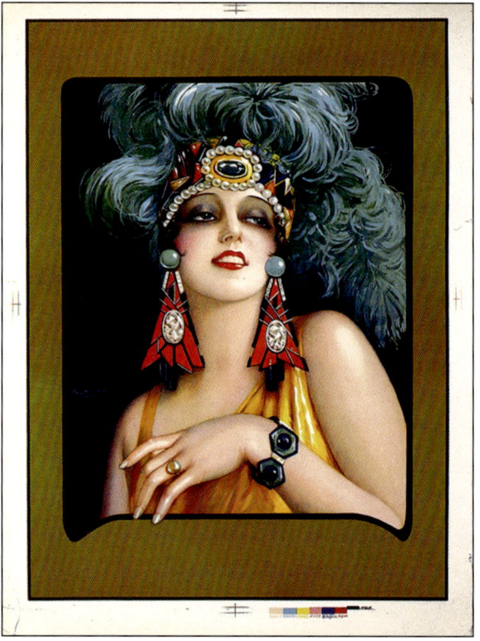

186

offer, are imbued with an easy playfulness and natural beauty sorely lacking in some of Camps' contemporaries.
Est: $2,500-$3,000. (2)

ANTONIO CAÑAVATE GOMEZ

187. S.E. el generalismo. 1937.
$31^1/_2$ x $43^3/_4$ in./80 x 111 cm
Rivadenyra, Madrid
Cond B/Restored losses.
Ref: Guerra Civil, 771
In his poster in support of the Republicans during the Spanish Civil War, Cañavate Gomez has chosen General Francisco Franco, leader of Nationalist Spain, as his main target, portraying him as the *Caballo de Bastos* (Knight of Clubs) from a deck of Spanish playing cards. The club he carries, while key to the caricature, is also a

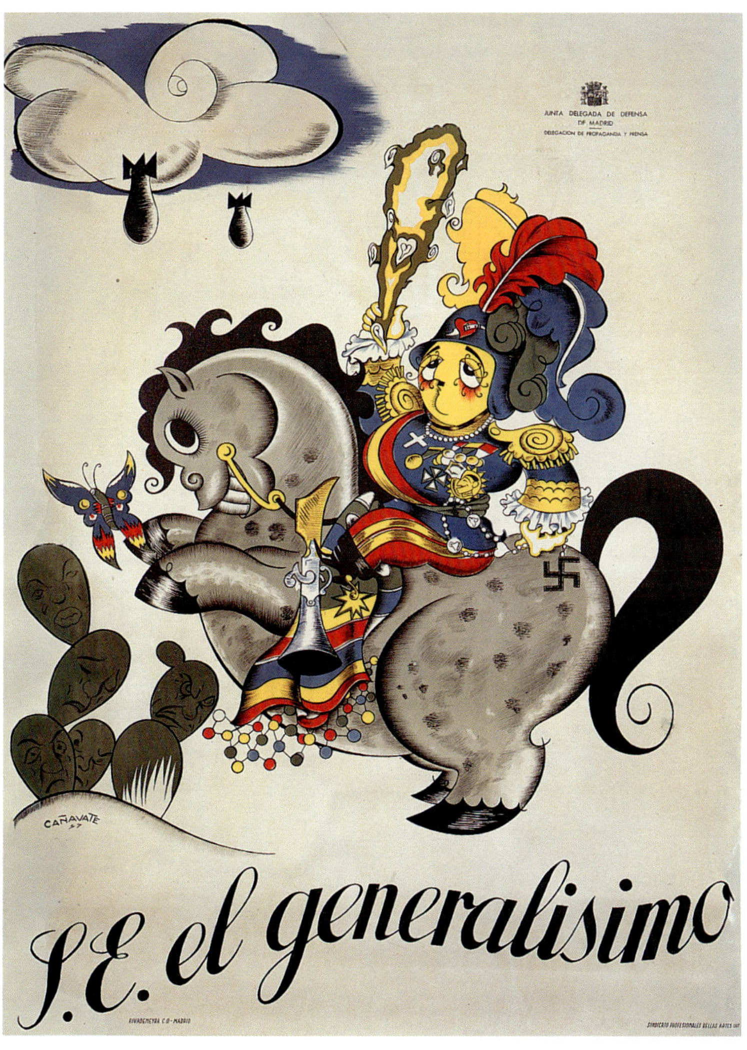

187

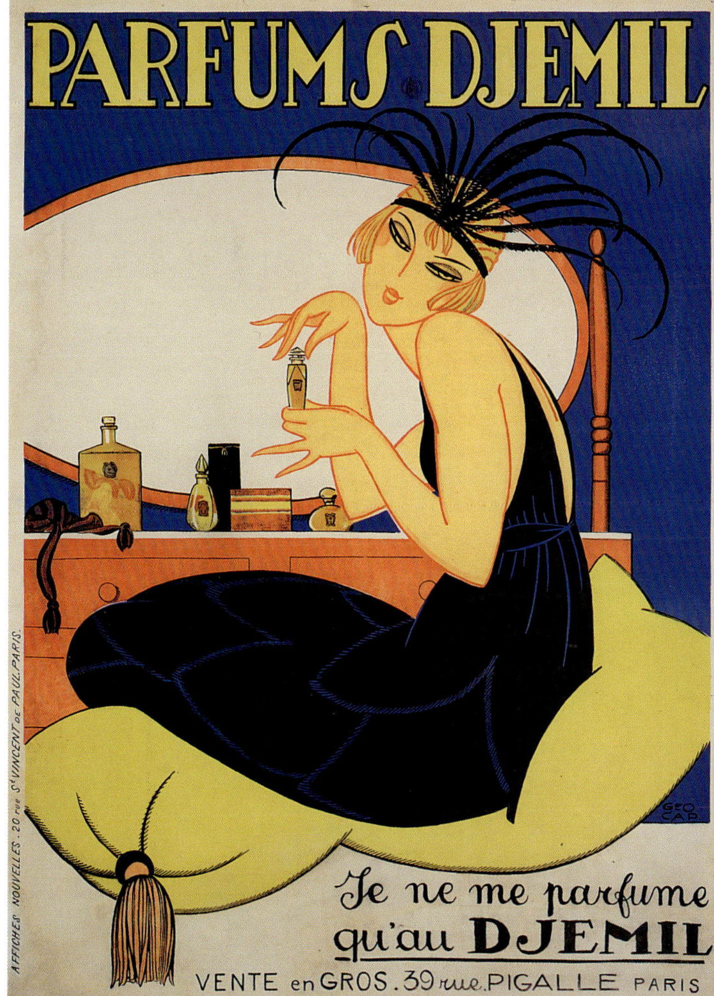

188

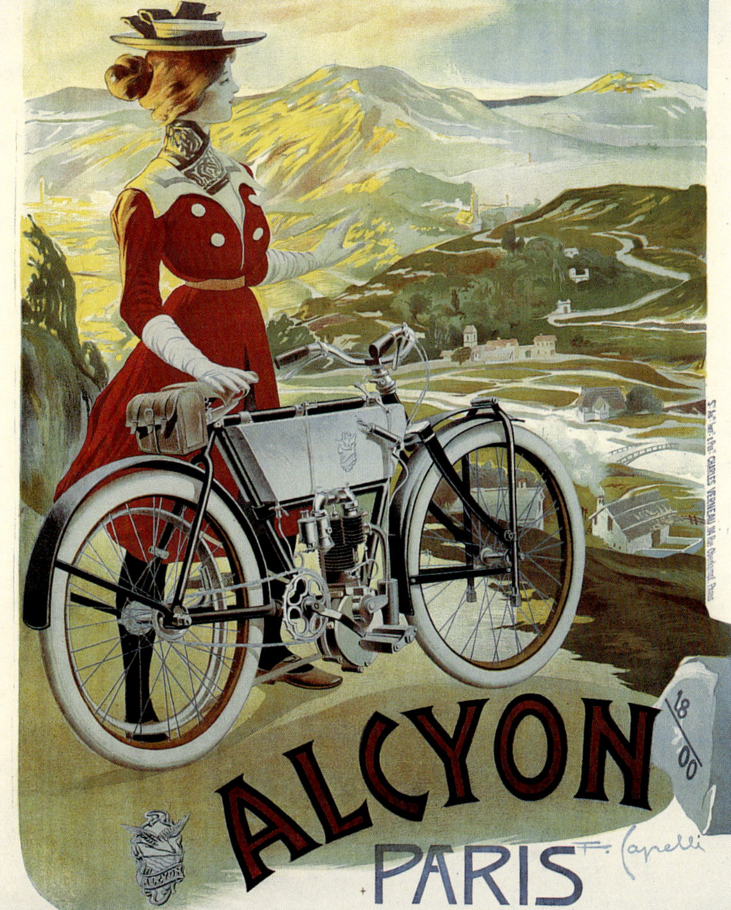

189

symbol of the violent and repressive nature of Franco's leadership. The artistic trope of having a horse mimic or reflect the characteristics of the rider frequently called upon by Spanish artists is also used by Cañavate Gomez. Franco's body type—short and round—is echoed in his rotund steed, whose exaggerated smile—cruel, not friendly—marks him as an active participant in the atrocities as he rears-up to crush the anthropomorphic cacti without losing his leer. And as to Franco himself, it would certainly appear as if the artist is deliberately inverting the images of strength and masculinity typically associated with the propaganda seen from the Spanish Civil War, portraying "El Generalisimo" as extravagantly effeminate. The artwork may even be going so far as to accuse Franco of being secretly homosexual: the rider and horse appear to be chasing a butterfly, and the Spanish word for butterfly, *mariposa*, is slang in certain dialects for a gay man. Of course, the Nazi association included in the design needs no explanation. *Rare!*
Est: $1,700-$2,000.

GEORGES CAP

188. Parfums Djemil.
$37^3/_4$ x $53^1/_2$ in./96 x 136 cm
Affiches Nouvelles, Paris
Cond B/Tears and stains, largely near edges.
Ref: PAI-XIII, 121
On a soft green pillow, a flapper in a midnight-blue dress strikes a pose backed by an array of scents displayed on her vanity, coquettishly professing, "I only perfume myself with Djemil." Who would even want to question such fashionable flirtation?
Est: $2,000-$2,500.

F. CAPELLI

189. Alcyon.
$40^1/_2$ x $54^3/_4$ in./102.7 x 139 cm
Charles Verneau, Paris
Cond A–/Unobtrusive tears at folds.
As opposed to the unrest seen in Gautier's poster for the same brand of bicycle (*see* No. 18), this satisfied rider appears placidly content to have arrived at the peaceful vista that she's observing from her hilltop vantage point, a point-of-view she was able to attain thanks to her motorized Alcyon ride.
Est: $2,500-$3,000.

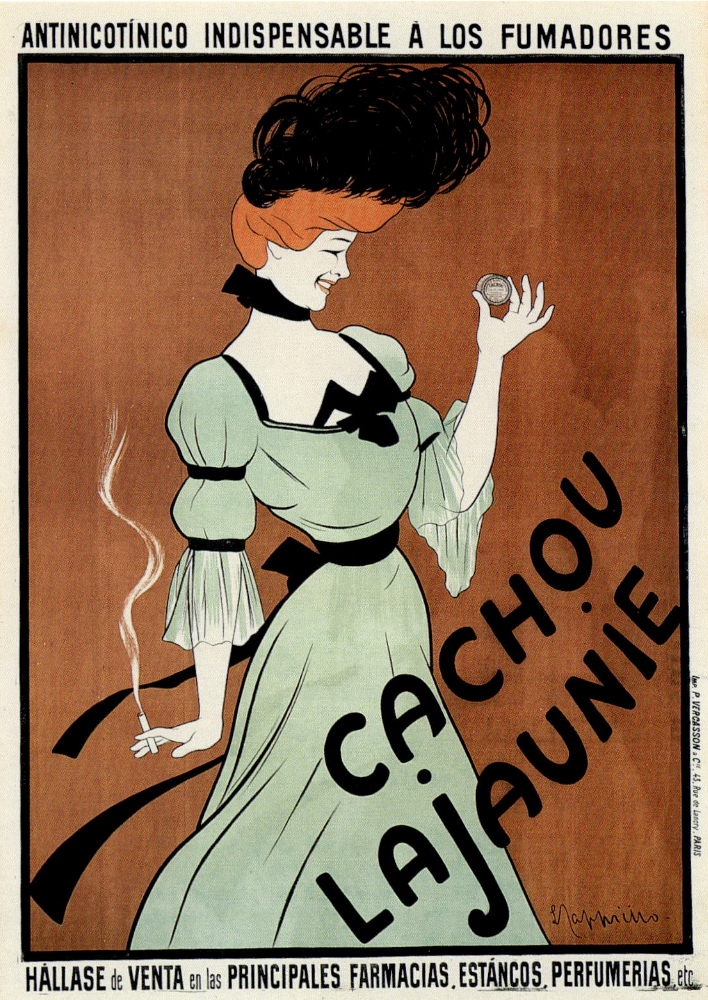

190

191

LEONETTO CAPPIELLO (1875-1942)
For another work of Cappiello, see No. 10.

190. Cachou Lajaunie. 1900.
39 x 54³/₄ in./99 x 139 cm
Imp. Vercasson, Paris
Cond B+/Slight tears at folds and edges; image and colors excellent.
Ref (All Var but PAI): Cappiello/Rennert, 6; Cappiello, 231;
   Cappiello/St. Vincent, 4.10; Wine Spectator, 202; PAI-XL, 247
"This is Cappiello's first poster for the Lajaunie breath freshening candies
that are 'indispensable to smokers' . . . His emerging style of bright colors
and flat planes is already evident in the woman's red hair, green dress and
the brown background" (Cappiello/Rennert, p. 43). "The pharmacist, Léon
Lajaunie, set up his pharmacy in Toulouse. After developing several invig-
orating elixirs,
he turned to cachou, as an aromatic for perfuming the breath whose
strong flavor covered smoker's breath" (Health Posters, p. 169). *This is the
Spanish-language version.*
Est: $4,000-$5,000.

191. Corset Le Furet. 1901.
39¹/₂ x 54¹/₈ in./100.5 x 137.3 cm
Imp. Vercasson, Paris
Cond B/Unobtrusive restored tears along folds.
Ref: Cappiello/Rennert, 20; Cappiello, 238; Cappiello/St. Vincent, 4.8;
Menegazzi-I, 465; PAI-XXXIX, 165
"A somewhat daring design by 1901 standards: This corset, which 'stays
firm but doesn't restrain,' promises to give its wearer 'the suppleness of the
Orient with the charm of France.' In yet another of the lavish testimonials
in his 1903 self-promotion, Vercasson quotes the director of the Bordeaux
company, who, full of admiration and appreciation for this image, indicates
that it 'exceeds our expectations" and "contributed to the popularization
of our trademark' (Cappiello, p. 117)" (Cappiello/Rennert, p. 51).
Est: $3,000-$4,000.

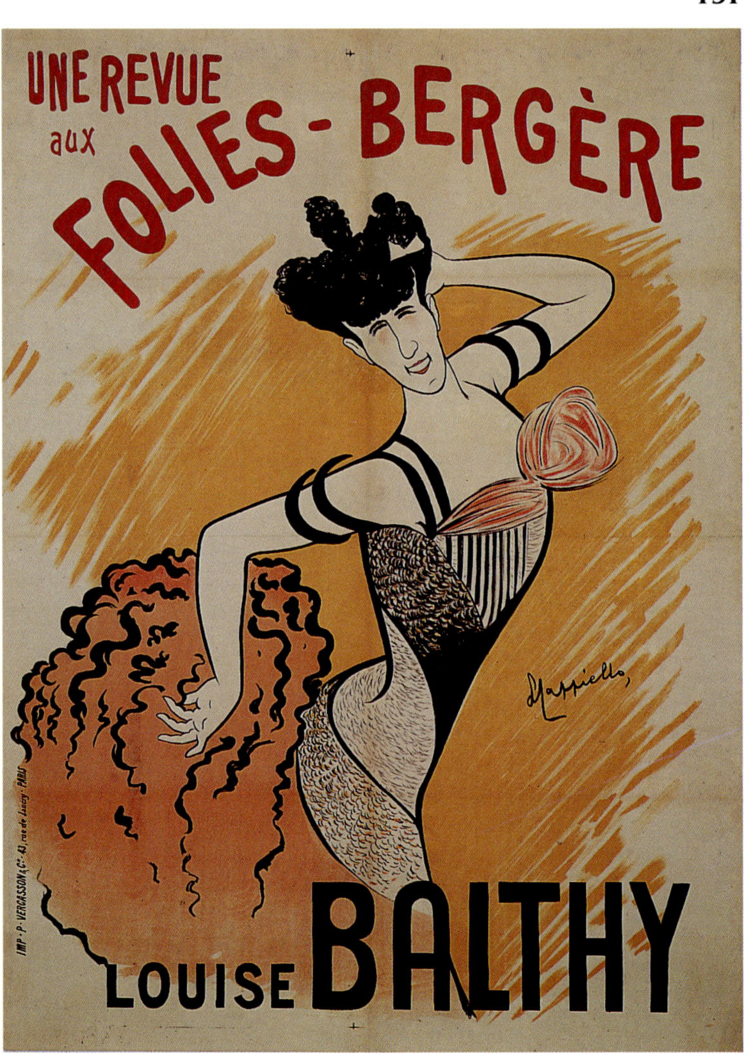

192

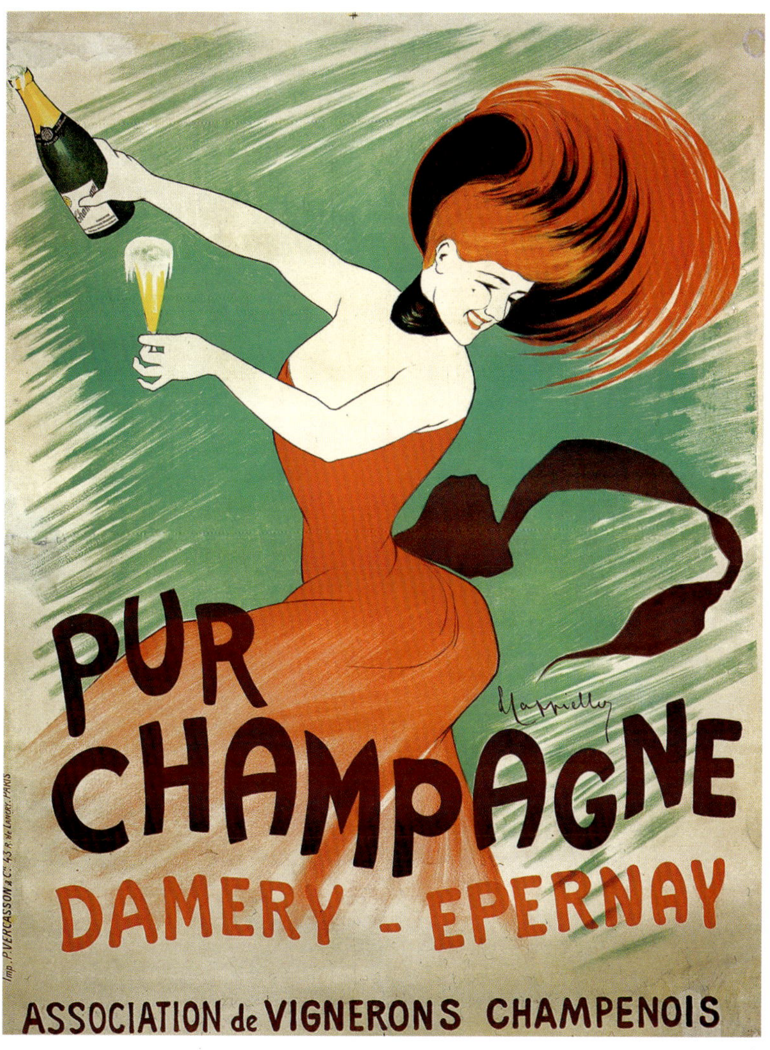

194

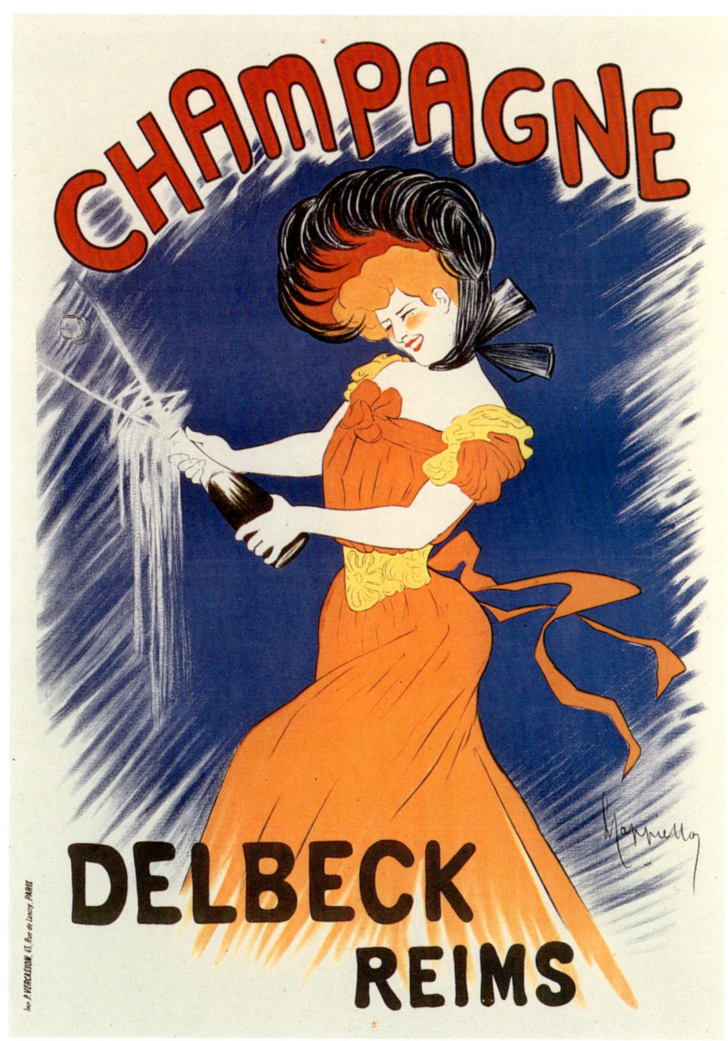

195

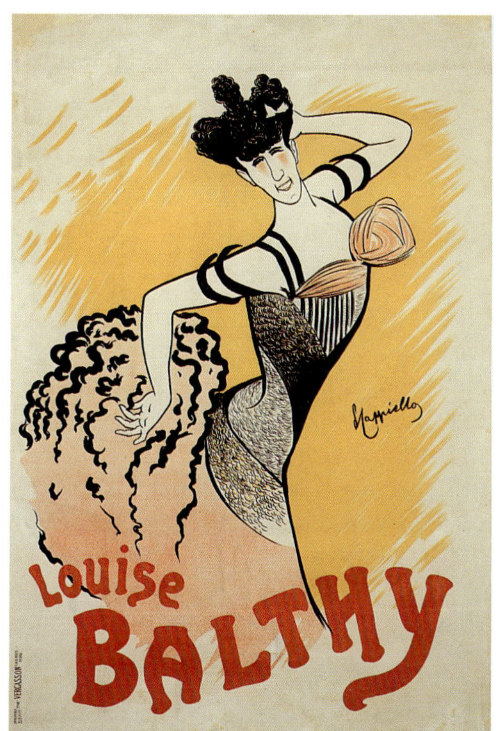

193

CAPPIELLO IN "BOOKS AND PERIODICALS"

Note that Cappiello's masterful illustrations in a deluxe edition of *La Princesse de Babylone*
and his numerous, delightful caricatures in the periodical *Le Rire*
are featured in the section at the end of this sale.

---

192. Louise Balthy/Folies-Bergère. 1902.
39^1/$_2$ x 55 in./100.3 x 139.6 cm
Imp. Vercasson, Paris
Cond B+/Slight tears at folds.
Ref: Cappiello/Rennert, 31; Cappiello, 215;
    Cappiello/St. Vincent, 4.2; Wine Spectator, 182;
    PAI-XXXVI, 199
"Louise Balthy (1869-1926), like Réjane, got off to a precocious start, being hired by the Eldorado at 17, and getting favorable notices in the revue 'Taraboum' in 1892. She became best known for comic songs that she delivered while maintaining a somewhat stern demeanor. However, her talents also included parodying various styles of dancing, impersonating other actresses (most notably Sarah Bernhardt), and playing a mean xylophone. A native of Bayonne near the Spanish border, she sometimes affected the occasional Spanish mannerism, a fact that Cappiello makes clear in this design for the revue's opening at the Folies-Bergère on March 8, 1902" (Cappiello/Rennert, p. 57).
Est: $3,000-$4,000.

193. Louise Balthy/Folies-Bergère. 1902.
31 x 47^1/$_2$ in./78.7 x 120.6 cm
Imp. Vercasson, Paris
Cond B–/Restored tears and paper loss at top and
    bottom edges.
Ref: Cappiello/Rennert, 31b; PAI-XXIX, 244
This is the smaller version of the previous poster, issued without top text and with Balthy's name only at the bottom.
Est: $2,500-$3,000.

194. Pur Champagne/Damery-Epernay. 1902.
38^7/$_8$ x 52^5/$_8$ in./98.7 x 133.6 cm
Imp. Vercasson, Paris
Cond B–/Restored tears at folds and edges.
Ref: Cappiello/Rennert, 32; Cappiello, 246;
    Wine Spectator, 160; PAI-XLI, 134

"Cappiello's first design for this drink was titled 'Elixir Peruvien' (*see* Wine Spectator, 159), but that product most probably never reached the marketing stage. Never one to waste a good design, Vercasson then sold it to the champagne producers of the Damery-Epernay region. In yet another of the promotional letters that Vercasson used in 1903, the director of the champagne association indicated that this poster is 'perfect' in that it 'clearly conveys the joyful spirit' of someone drinking champagne from the Champenois region" (Cappiello/Rennert, p. 58).
Est: $2,000-$2,500.

195. Champagne Delbeck/Reims. 1902.
38^1/$_2$ x 55 in./98 x 139.6 cm
Imp. P. Vercasson, Paris
Cond A.
Ref: Cappiello/Rennert, 33; Wine Spectator, 158;
    Cappiello, 259; Femme s'Affiche, 27; PAI-XLI, 133
"In a typically exuberant Cappiello moment, this stunning charmer winces prettily as she pops the cork of a Champagne Delbeck bottle. The business was started in 1832 by the scion of a Flemish banking family, Frédéric-Désiré Delbeck. The business remains in the family today (a rarity in the world of champagne) and the company remains very art conscious in its promotions. In the late 19th century, some of the artists the company hired to design its labels, advertisements and posters included Klimt, Mucha, Gallé, Ergé, Andreis, Chalon and Tristan Bernard" (Cappiello/Rennert, p. 58).
Est: $5,000-$6,000.

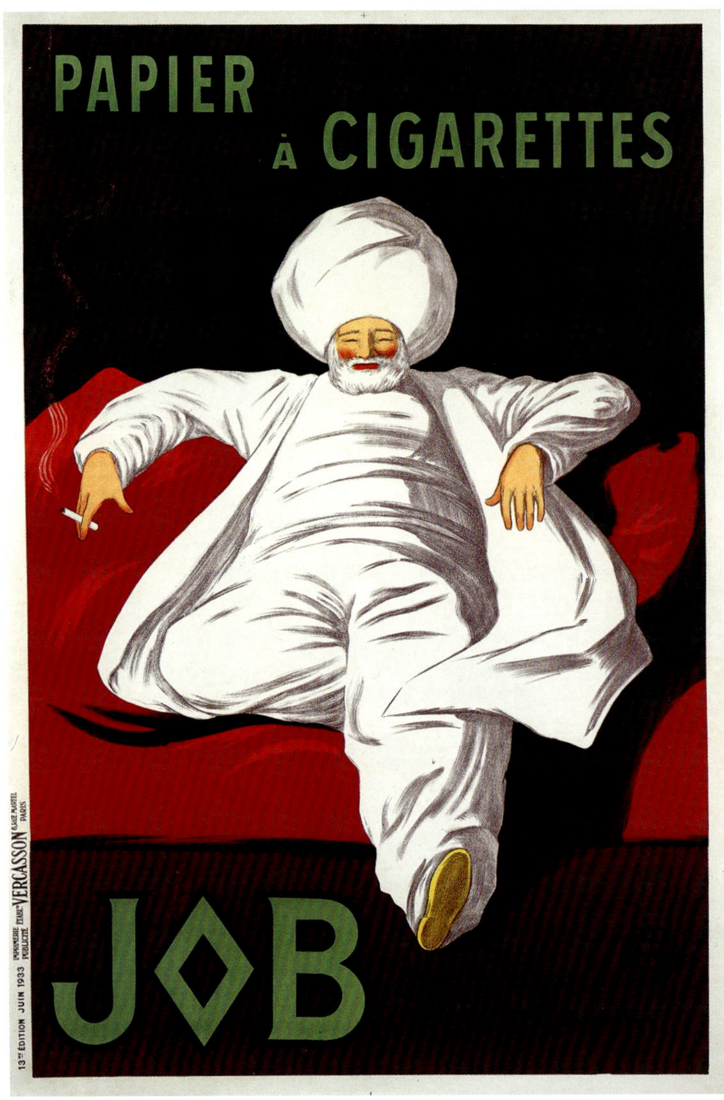

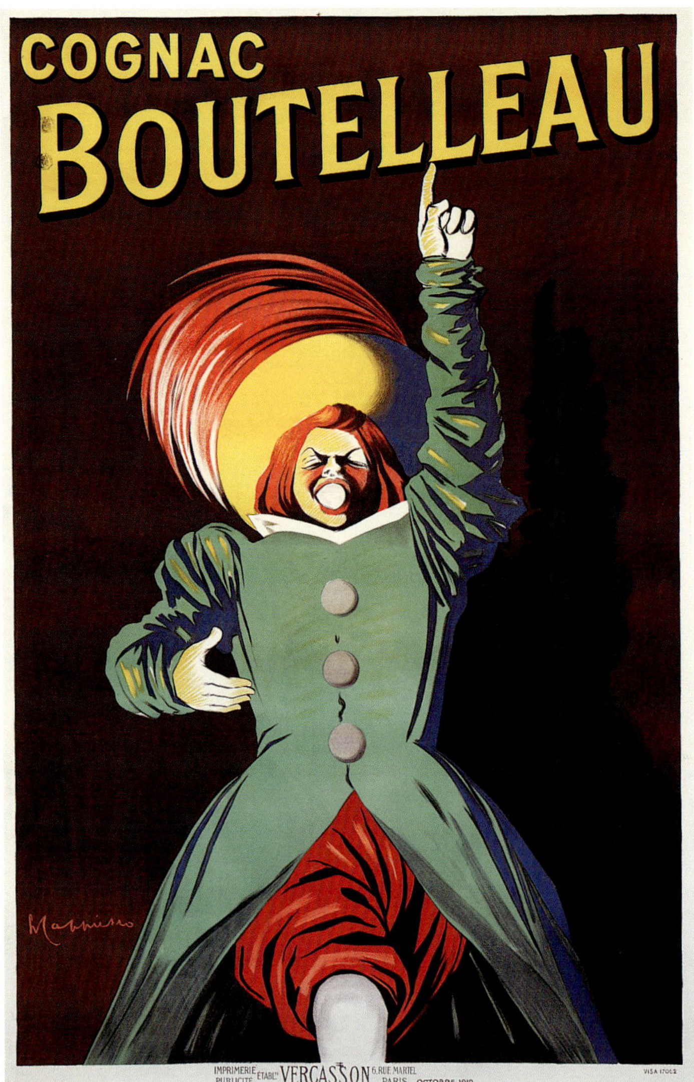

198

199

CAPPIELLO (cont'd)

196. Angelus Liqueur. 1907.
$26^3/8$ x $38^5/8$ in./67.7 x 98 cm
Imp. P. Vercasson, Paris
Cond B/Slight tears at folds.
Ref: Cappiello/Rennert, 120; Cappiello, 276; Cappiello/St. Vincent, 4.27; PAI-XXXIII, 250
One of Cappiello's early successes in the exaggeration department was the little bell ringer holding on for dear life to the clapper of an enormous bell to toll out the word for Angelus liqueur. It's the artist's literal interpretation of the word "angelus," which is the ringing of the bells inviting the faithful to prayer. But for all of the extravagant overstatement one associates with Cappiello, it's the sense of motion that the designer brings to his designs that turns a liquor ad into a visual playground. Critic Marcel Fromenteau couldn't have agreed more: "What characterizes an M. Cappiello poster is the 'movement' of the people he places in the scene. Movement that carries you away, unbridled, very often joyous movement; leaping like one crazed, if I may and if I dare say. And it's not only his people that he animates, naturally; but also animals and objects, and always with the same immoderate comic allure and irresistibility" (Cappiello, p. 131). *This is the medium format.*
Est: $1,400-$1,700.

197. Le Cacao Poulain. ca. 1911.
$47^1/8$ x 63 in./119.6 x 160 cm
Imp. Vercasson, Paris
Cond A–/Slight tears at edges and folds.
Ref: Cappiello/Rennert, 173; Chocolate Posters, p. 30; PAI-XL, 265
"Cacao Poulain boasts that it is 'inundating the world,'

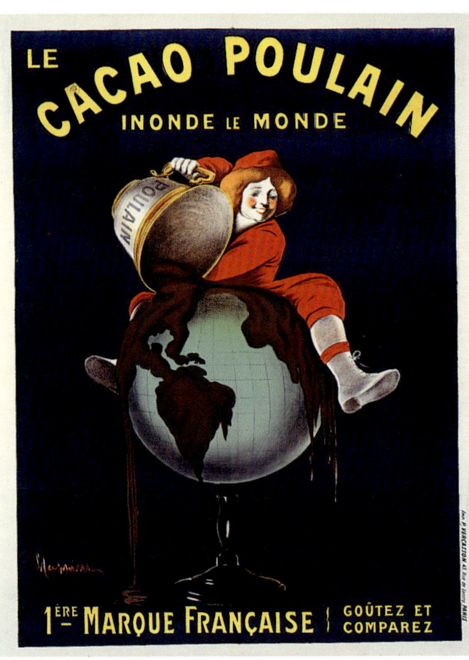

196

197

a statement that inspired the artist to produce a winsome image of a kid gleefully doing just that . . . August Poulain started to learn about cocoa products at age 13, when he entered an apprenticeship at a Paris confectionary. He started his own business ten years later in 1848, at a time when chocolate was still regarded as an exotic delicacy. The firm stayed in the family and is still in business, making more than 30,000 tons of cocoa products annually" (Cappiello/Rennert, p. 127).
Est: $2,000-$2,500.

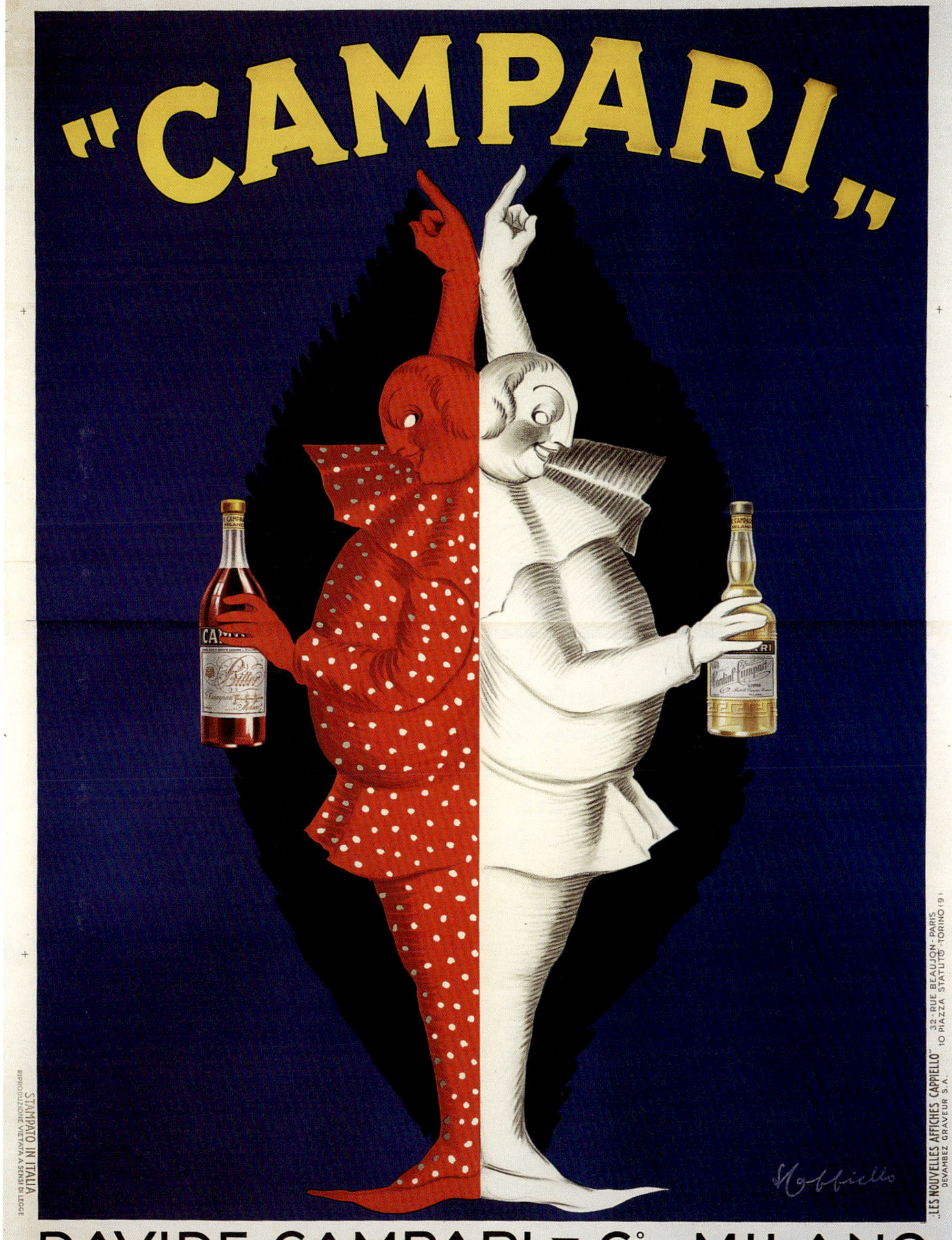

201

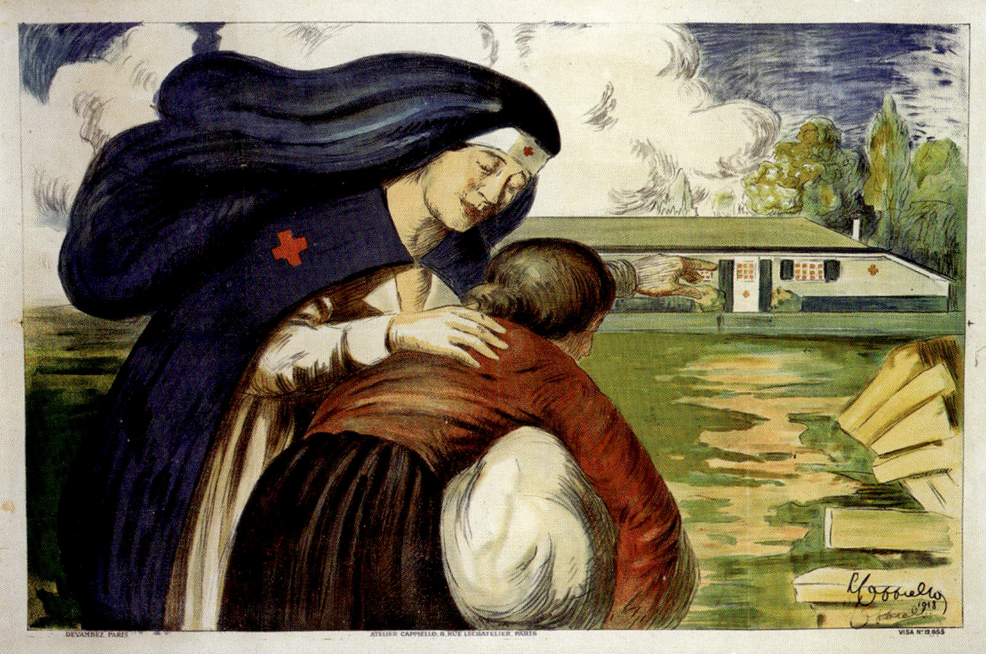

200

198. Job/Papier à Cigarettes. 1933.
22⅞ x 34⅝ in./58 x 88 cm
Imp. Vercasson, Paris
Cond A.
Ref (All Var but PAI): Cappiello/Rennert, 228;
    DFP-II, 124; Wine Spectator, 205; PAI-XXXIX, 199
"Cappiello showed the pleasure of smoking by project-
ing an image of a hedonistic Middle-Eastern potentate
luxuriating with a self-rolled cigarette. In fact, the im-
perious pasha floats on his couch like a fat white cloud
—an incongruous and therefore memorable image"
(Cappiello/Rennert, p. 156). An impressive design, seen
here in its thirteenth printing—some sixteen years *after*
Cappiello's departure from the Vercasson fold.
Est: $2,500-$3,000.

199. Cognac Boutelleau. 1919.
49¼ x 77⅝ in./125 x 197.2 cm
Imp. Vercasson, Paris
Cond A–/Unobtrusive tears at top edge.
Ref: Cappiello/Rennert, 274; PAI-XXXIX, 192
"It stands to reason that someone might get a little upset if they had their heart set on a particular nip after a
hard day's travails, but Cappiello's worked-up courtier
looks as if he just might blow his top if he doesn't
get his hands on some Cognac Boutelleau very soon!
Edmond Boutelleau gave his name to a brand of cognac
he started distilling in 1849; it has been in the hands
of Cognac Tiffon since 1990, but the original name has
been retained on the label. The poster is dated October
1919, but the fact that Cappiello was no longer under
contract to Vercasson on that date and that the Visa
Number still appears there all indicate that this poster
was probably designed in 1917 and production started
a bit later. Wars certainly have a way of disrupting the
best-laid plans" (Cappiello/Rennert, p. 183).
Est: $3,000-$4,000.

200. Red Cross. 1918.
47 x 31¼ in./119.3 x 79.5 cm
Imp. Devambez, Paris
Cond B/Slight tears at folds.
Ref: Cappiello/Rennert, 285; PAI-XL, 269
"In a wartime institutional poster without text, a Red
Cross nurse comes to the assistance of a person in distress, most likely a refugee from the devastated areas
of eastern France where trench warfare had stalled for
four long years. The Red Cross was originally established by Swiss humanitarian, Henri Dunant, after a particularly bloody clash between the French and Austrians
in 1859, to impartially care for those wounded regardless of their allegiance. Cappiello depicts the mission
of the Red Cross with delicacy and tenderness" (Cap-
piello/Rennert, p. 190).
Est: $1,000-$1,200.

201. "Campari". 1921.
79 x 108 in./200.8 x 274.5 cm
Imp. Devambez, Paris/Torino
Cond A–/Unobtrusive folds.
Ref: Cappiello/Rennert, 331
"Campari comes in two versions, the red Bitter and
the white Cordial; here's Cappiello's graphic solution
to promoting separate yet equal cocktail refreshment"
(Cappiello/Rennert, p. 215). *This is the 2-sheet format
of this rare and wonderful design.*
Est: $17,000-$20,000.

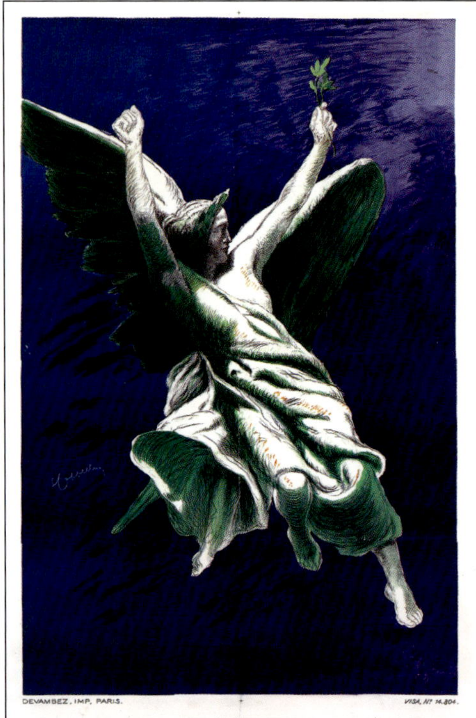

204

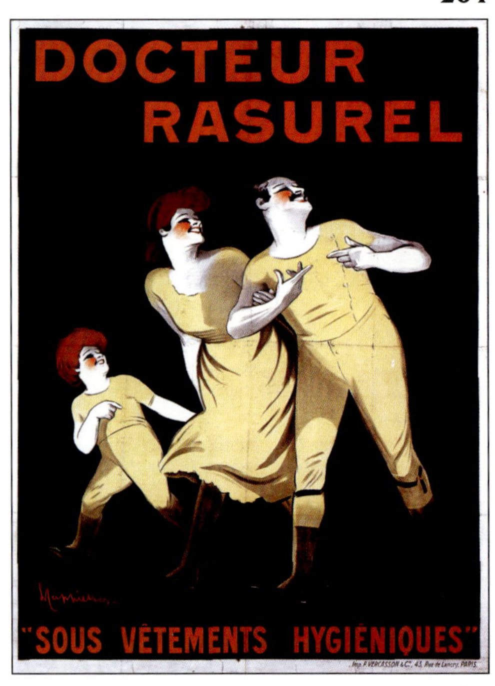

205

202

CAPPIELLO (cont'd)

202. Cordial Campari. 1921.
54$^{1}/_{4}$ x 77$^{7}/_{8}$ in./138 x 197.8 cm
Devambez, Paris/Torino
Cond B+/A few restored tears, largely at edges.
Ref: Cappiello/Rennert, 332
"Obviously, Cordial Campari not only will make you
feel like the cock of the walk—it'll also make you feel
like riding one. That is, if there is one handy" (Cappiello/
Rennert, p. 215). *Rare!*
Est: $8,000-$10,000.

203. Cordial Campari. 1921.
52$^{1}/_{2}$ in./77$^{3}/_{8}$ in./133.3 x 196.5 cm
"Maga," Paris (Printed in Italy)
Cond A.
Ref: Campari, Vol. 3, p. 94
Although Cappiello executed several posters for this
company. and this unsigned, stupendous creation has
all the hallmarks of the master, I didn't include it in
my catalogue raisonné as I could find no confirmation
of its authorship. However, as archives of the Campari
company now clearly indicate that it is by Cappiello,
we'll gladly credit it to him as well. What we are shown
is an eerily footlight illuminated harlequin as he begins

the process that we suspect will end in the draining of
his bottle of Cordial Campari. "The story of this world-
famous brand name started in 1860 in the little Italian
town of Novara, where Gaspar Campari opened his small
wine shop. Within two years, he earned enough to open
a cafe on a busy street corner in Milan. Annoyed that
his competitors were able to sell everything that he did,
he determined to produce his own distinctive liqueur
in order to serve something unique; to this end, he developed a recipe for a type of bitters and made a sam-
ple batch. His timing was impeccable: bitters . . . were
just coming into vogue at the time, and the Campari
bitter was an instant success. The enterprise grew, and
by the time of Gaspar's death in 1882, the product was
selling throughout the world. His son, Davide (1887-
1936), expanded the family business even more, and
in 1892, added a second successful beverage, Cordial
Campari" (Cappiello/ Rennert, p. 214). *Rare!*
Est: $12,000-$15,000.

204. La Victoire Exposition. 1919.
31$^{3}/_{8}$ x 47 in./80 x 119.5 cm
Imp. Devambez, Paris
Cond B/Slight tears at folds.

Ref (Both Var): Cappiello/Rennert, 290; PAI-XXXII, 227
"A winged female figure—nearly appearing to be a statue
that has been freed from gravity's shackles—raises her
hands in victory, a sprig of laurel grasped firmly in her
right hand, in order to gather the masses for a cele-
bratory exhibition of Devambez poster artists at the
agency's gallery to commemorate La Victoire, the conclusion of the First World War. Benefiting the National
Committee for Physical and Sports Education and
Social Hygiene, Cappiello's promotion is nothing short
of triumphant" (Cappiello/Rennert, p. 192). *This is the
version of the poster before the addition of letters.*
Est: $2,500-$3,000.

205. Docteur Rasurel/Sous Vêtements.
45 x 61$^{1}/_{8}$ in./114.2 x 155.3 cm
Imp. P. Devambez, Paris
Cond C+/Restored tears at folds and edges. Framed.
Ref: Cappiello/Rennert, 353; PAI-XXXIV, 288
"Doctor Rasurel was a trademark for a line of thermal
underwear, union suits and other textile products for
the home . . . There's a certain dubious quality to the
supposed medical professional standing behind the
mannequin torso in order to best display his name-

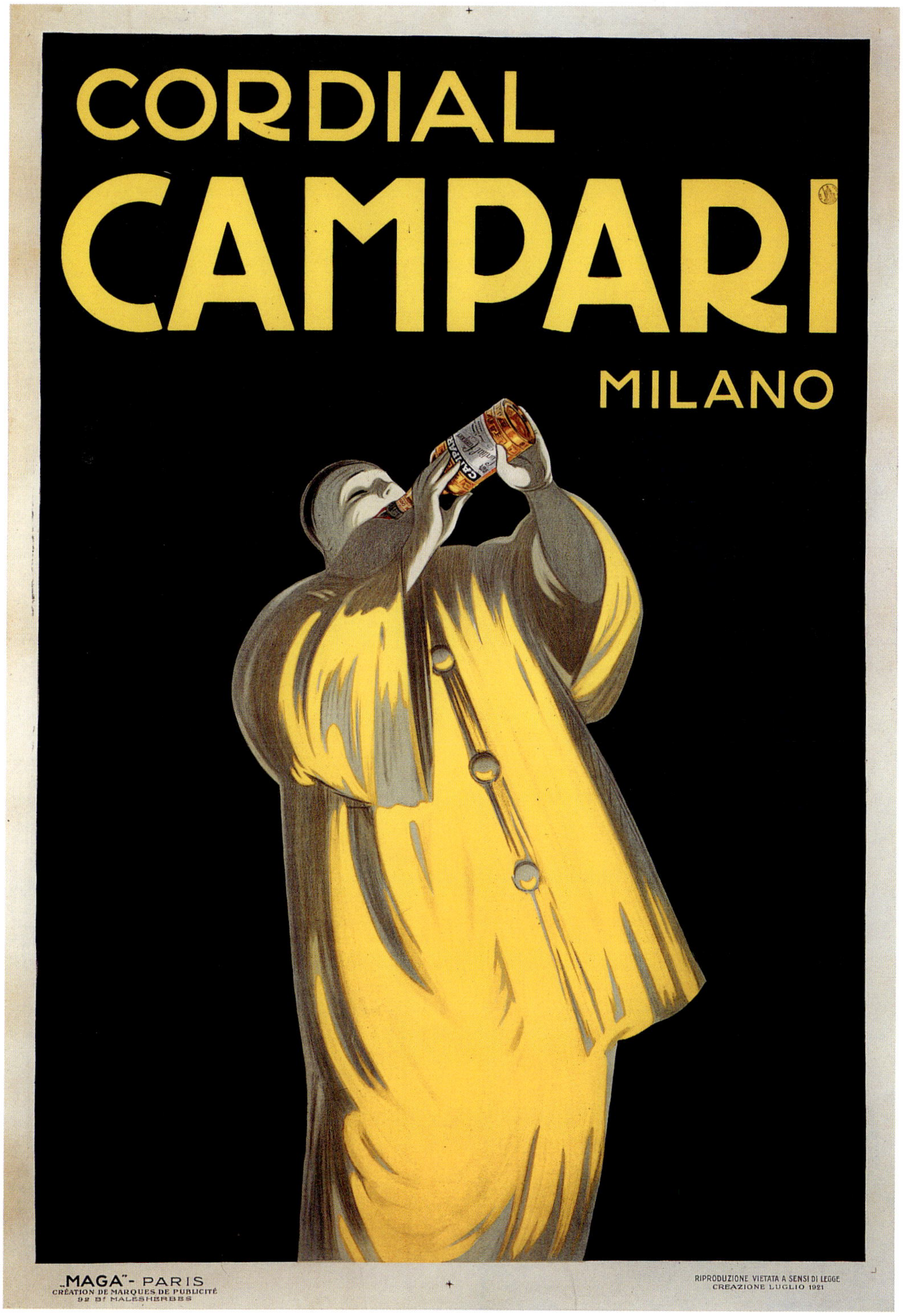

203

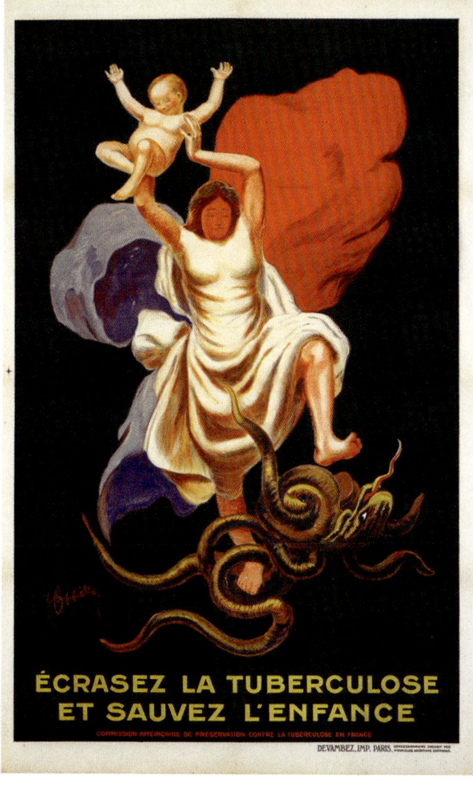

206

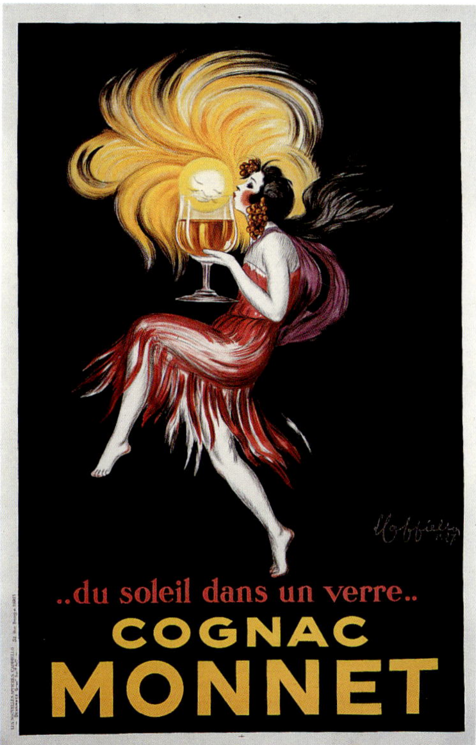

207

sake thermal undershirt, something of a charlatan's smirk gracing his face that confesses to the fact that he may not be a real doctor—which, in fact, was true, as the name derived from a clever marketing scheme rather than an accredited professional. That grin, however, is more than offset by the mannequin, whose face shows signs of Pinocchioish vitality, obviously having been warmed to real boyhood by his Rasurel undershirt" (Cappiello/Rennert, p. 227).
Est: $2,000-$2,500.

206. Écrasez la Tuberculose. ca. 1922.
$19^3/_8$ x $49^1/_2$ in./49 x 80 cm
Imp. Devambez, Paris
Cond B+/Unobtrusive fold.
Ref: Cappiello/Rennert, 359; Karcher, 472; PAI-XXXI, 347
"An institutional effort far from Cappiello's usual joyousness, but no less memorable. Holding an infant aloft, the spirit of France stamps out the menace of tuberculosis (*Écrasez la Tuberculose*), which in the

1920s was a serious health problem throughout most of Europe. With her white robes cinched with a giant red and blue bow, she resembles a triumphant patriotic angel in stark contrast to the ugly serpentine shape of the disease" (Cappiello/Rennert, p. 229).
Est: $1,200-$1,500.

207. Cognac Monnet. 1927.
$50^3/_4$ x $78^7/_8$ in./128.8 x 200 cm
Imp. Devambez, Paris
Cond A.
Ref: Cappiello/Rennert, 443; PAI-XLI, 149
"'Sunshine in a glass' is the company slogan of Cognac Monnet, and Cappiello, with a charming literal-mindedness, depicts exactly that—and, of course, the pure black background makes it stand out prominently. The cognac firm was founded in 1905 by Jean Gabriel Monnet, and is today part of the Hennessy Corporation" (Cappiello/Rennert, p. 275).
Est: $5,000-$6,000.

208. Dentrifices des Bénédictins. 1922.
47 x $63^1/_8$ in./119.4 x 160.2 cm
Imp. Devambez, Paris
Cond B+/Slight tears at folds.
Ref: Cappiello/Rennert, 363
"The monastery that developed the Dentifrices des Bénédictins formula is located on a mountain in the old town of Soulac, a small village on the coast near Bordeaux. The monks actually made the product at one time, but in 1880, a decree forbade religious orders from most commercial activities, so a pharmaceutical firm took over the production. To keep this tradition alive, Cappiello shows a dandy from another era admiring his shiny teeth in a hand mirror" (Cappiello/Rennert, p. 231).
Est: $4,000-$5,000.

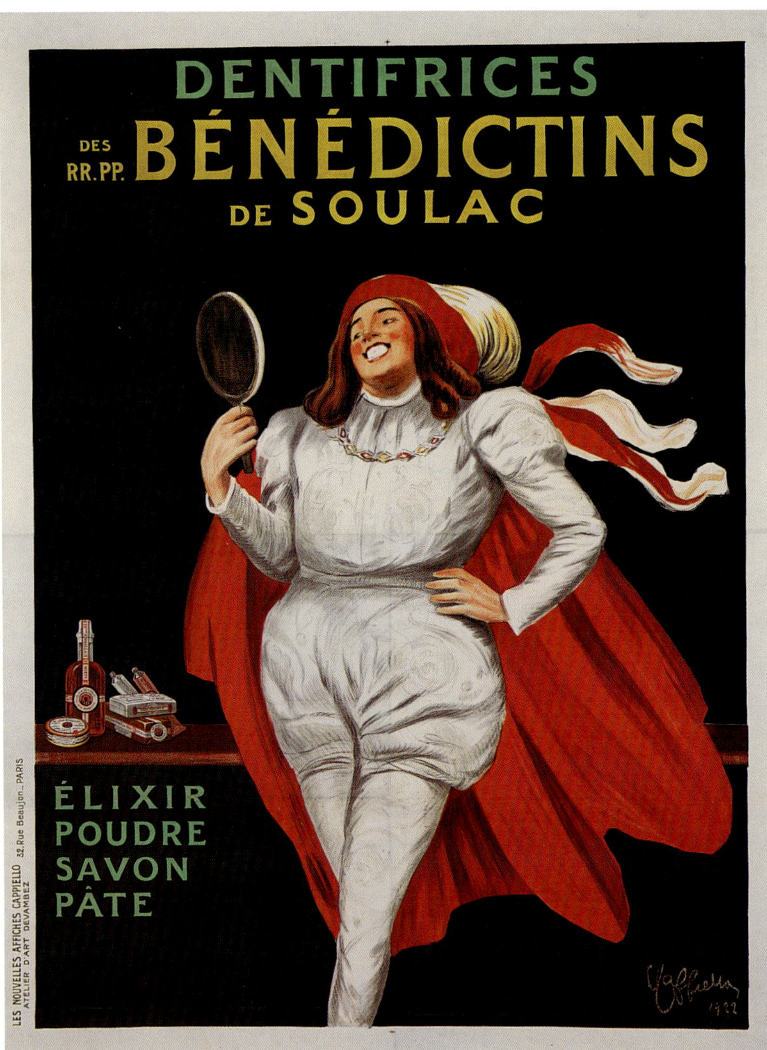

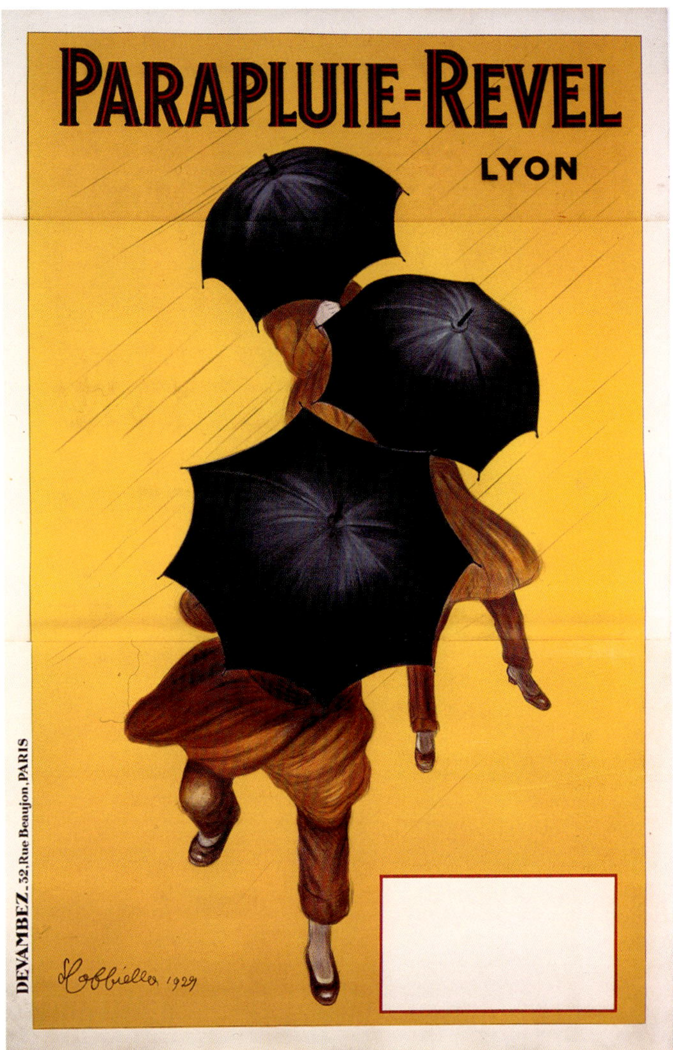

208

209

CAPPIELLO (cont'd)

209. Parapluie-Revel. 1929.
78³/₄ x 124¹/₂ in./200 x 316 cm
Imp. Devambez, Paris
Cond B+/Horizontal nineteen-inch tear at lower left edge.
Ref (All Var but PAI): Cappiello/Rennert, 373;
    Karcher, 245; Cappiello/St. Vincent, 4.68;
    PAI-XLI, 153
"For the Revel company of Lyon, Cappiello produced
one of his most masterful works, a design at once simple and effective that immediately focuses attention
on the product: the Parapluie-Revel, the umbrellas
braving the storm like black ships' sails. All the elements of fine poster design are here: bold shapes,
strong contrasts (the background is a surprising sunny
yellow), tight yet lively composition, unusual perspective—and no more detail than necessary. Who needs
faces? The wind-blown coats describe the weather elo-
quently. Mr. Revel founded the company in Lyon in
1851; at the time of this poster, umbrellas were made
of both cotton and silk" (Cappiello/ Rennert, p. 236).
One of Cappiello's most popular designs, it went
through several variants over the span of its graphic
lifetime; *this is the 3-sheet version.*
Est: $3,000-$4,000.

210. Frankreich. 1937.
23³/₄ x 38³/₄ in./60.2 x 98.4 cm
Editions Nouvelles Cappiello, Paris
Cond A.
Ref (Both Var): Cappiello/Rennert, 500; PAI-XXX, 439
Paris hosted a World's Fair in 1937 and "this is one of
a number of general posters created for that occasion,
one that specifically promotes travel to France. But in
contrast to practically all posters attempting to attract
the population of a foreign country to travel to your
home turf, Cappiello shows the remarkable, classic
restraint customary in his later posters. The allegorical
statuary of Marianne atop a patriotic French relief relays
a dignified call to travel that one can appreciate for its
simple beauty as much as for the unmistakable mes-

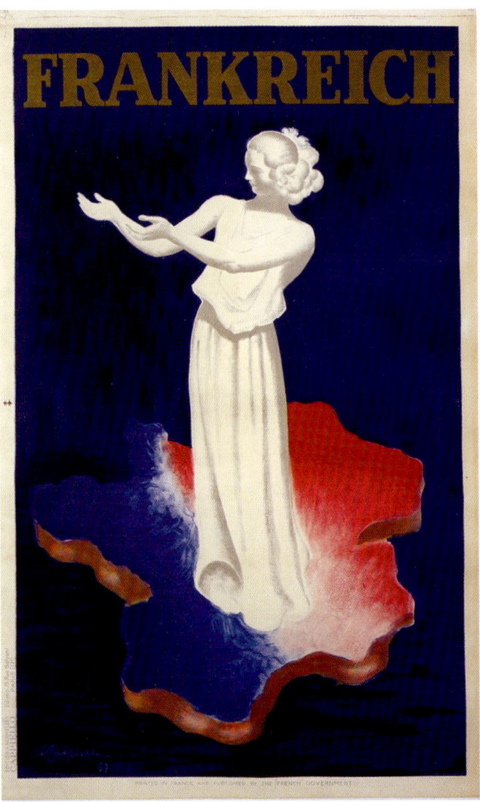

210

sage it sends" (Cappiello/Rennert, p. 323). *This is the
German-language version.*
Est: $1,200-$1,500.

211. Nitrolian. 1929.
47³/₈ x 63¹/₈ in./120.4 x 160.2 cm
Imp. Devambez, Paris

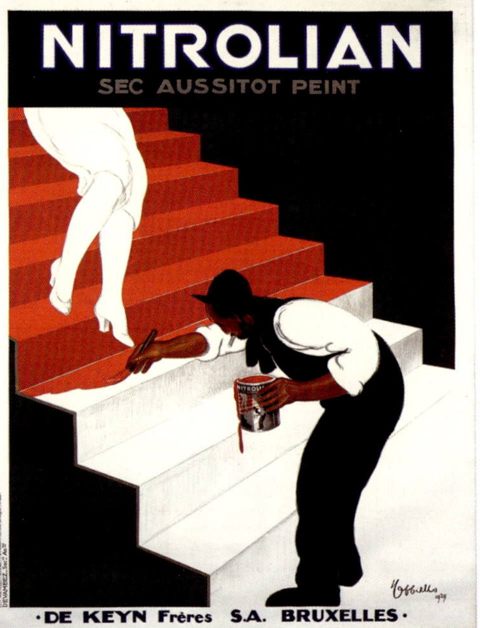

211

Cond A.
Ref: Cappiello/Rennert, 470; PAI-XLII, 168
"Watching paint dry" may epitomize unbearable bore-
dom; but with his image of crimson paint being applied
a mere step ahead of advancing feet, Cappiello makes
it clear in a flash that Nitrolian paint is dry in a flash
and ready for business.
Est: $2,500-$3,000.

212. Veuve Amiot/Crémant du Roi. 1922.
47¹/₈ x 63¹/₈ in./119.8 x 160.4 cm
Imp. Devambez, Paris
Cond A.

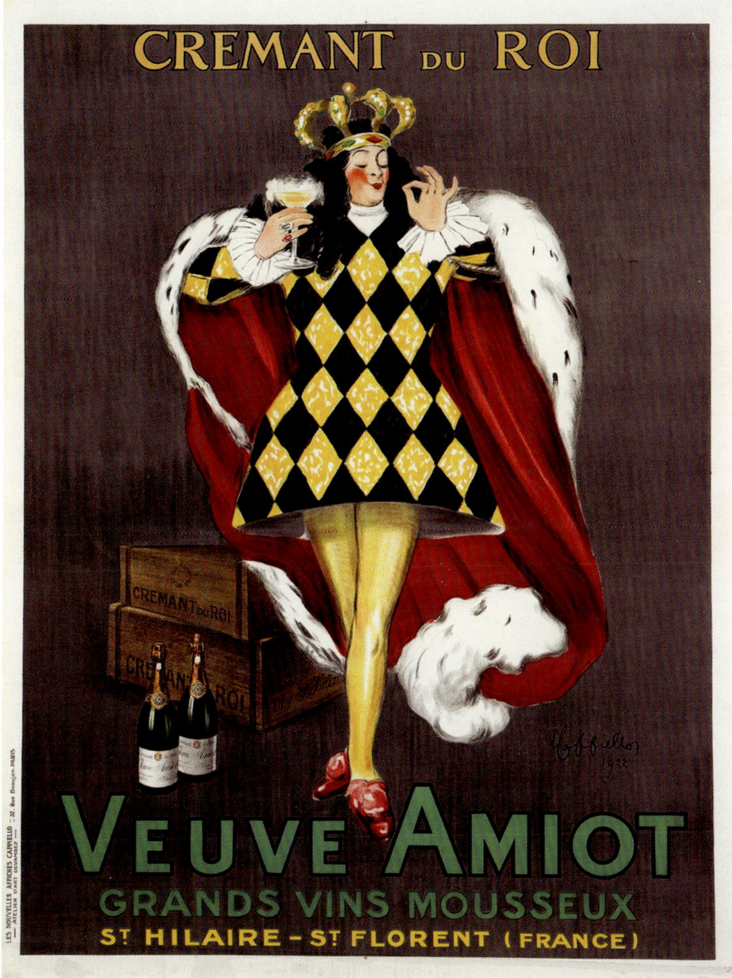

212

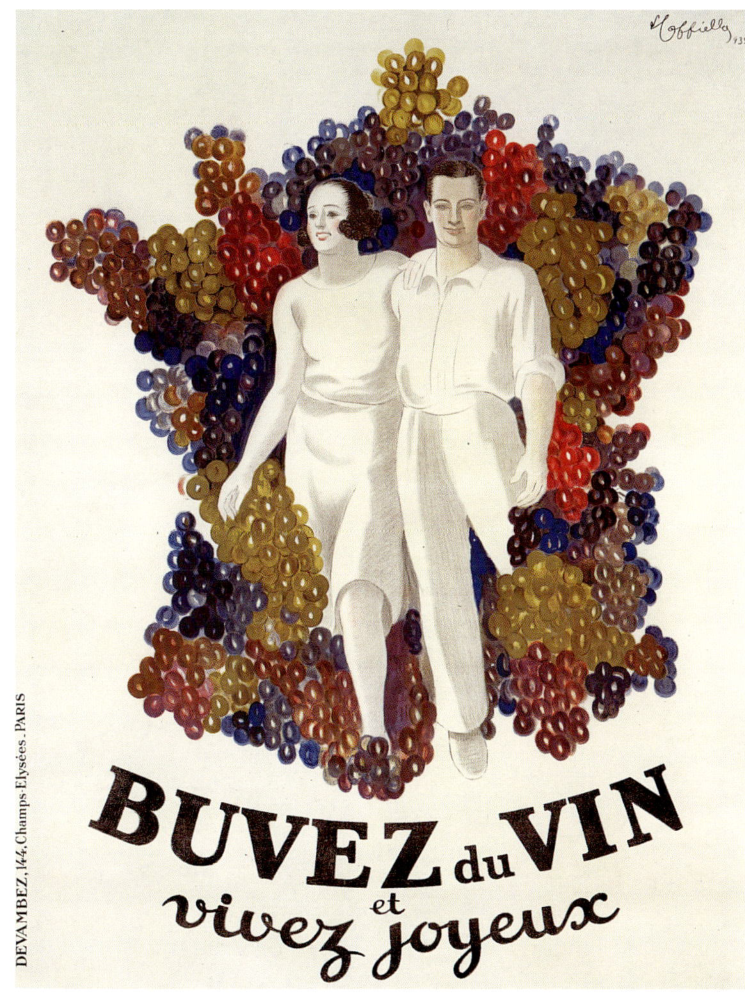

213

214

215

---

them anyhow. (Another version of the poster—*see* PAI-IX, 107—adds the notion of the happiness that comes from drinking wine with fish.) And, indeed, we see happiness—in human form—emerging from a France-shaped mass of grapes. With at least 100 posters for wines and spirits to his credit, Cappiello was the logical choice for this commission—and the right choice as his brilliant solution proves. *This is the larger format.* **Est: $5,000-$6,000.**

214. 26eme Salon des Humoristes. 1933.
$15^5/8$ x $23^1/4$ in./39.6 x 59 cm
Imp. Devambez, Paris
Cond A.
Ref (Both Var): Cappiello/Rennert, 501; PAI-XXXIX, 203
Laugh and the world laughs with you. Cappiello had designed the poster for the 1922 Salon (*see* PAI-XXXIX, 195) and "now, twenty-five years after his first poster for the occasion, he was commissioned to create the graphic promotion for the event for a third time. Keeping things simple, we're shown a few of the many faces of comedy, the pink bow of this duplicitous joker tying everything up nicely, while at the same time, providing the sole color present in the design" (Cappiello/Rennert, p. 310). *This is the smaller format.*
Est: $1,700-$2,000.

215. Bally. 1934.
$76^7/8$ x $117^3/4$ in./220.2 x 299.1 cm
Imp. Devambez, Paris
Cond A.
Ref: Cappiello/Rennert, 515 (var); Cappiello, 341; PAI-XL, 274C
A year after Cappiello created this slick poster for Bally, a contemporary critic used it as an example of the artist's mastery in giving utilitarian objects special treatment: "Even for Bally, where two different shoes are pictured, Cappiello can't limit himself to a strict interpretation. His subtle imagination doesn't give us the shoes on feet; with unequaled elegance, he places the man's oxford on a silken palm and holds the narrow heel of the woman's pump in his fingers as if it were a work of art" (Pierre Guéguin, in *Cappiello*, pp. 154-5). *This is the largest, 3-sheet format.*
Est: $2,500-$3,000.

Ref: Cappiello/Rennert, 377; PAI-XLII, 165
"It appears as if we've come across this rouged monarch draped in his royal robes (*Cremant du Roi*) during a transcendent moment, carried away on the exquisite proboscis-tickling bubbles of Veuve Amiot sparkling wine. A convincing design of infinite charm that effortlessly persuades without sacrificing one jot of intimate amusement. In 1884, Elisa Amiot suddenly found herself a widow (*veuve*) with four children to raise. As she lived in the Saumur region, an area whose sparkling wines had become all the rage, she went into the distilling business. She proved to have a flare for

so effectively promoting both herself and her bubbly that her firm prospered right from the start" (Cappiello/Rennert, p. 240).
Est: $2,500-$3,000.

213. Buvez du Vin. 1933.
$44^7/8$ x $59^1/8$ in./114 x 150.3 cm
Imp. Devambez, Paris
Cond A–/Unobtrusive folds; slight tears at paper edges; mage and colors excellent.
Ref: Cappiello/Rennert, 508; PAI-XLI, 154
The French hardly need to be told to "drink wine and live happily," but here the French wine industry reminds

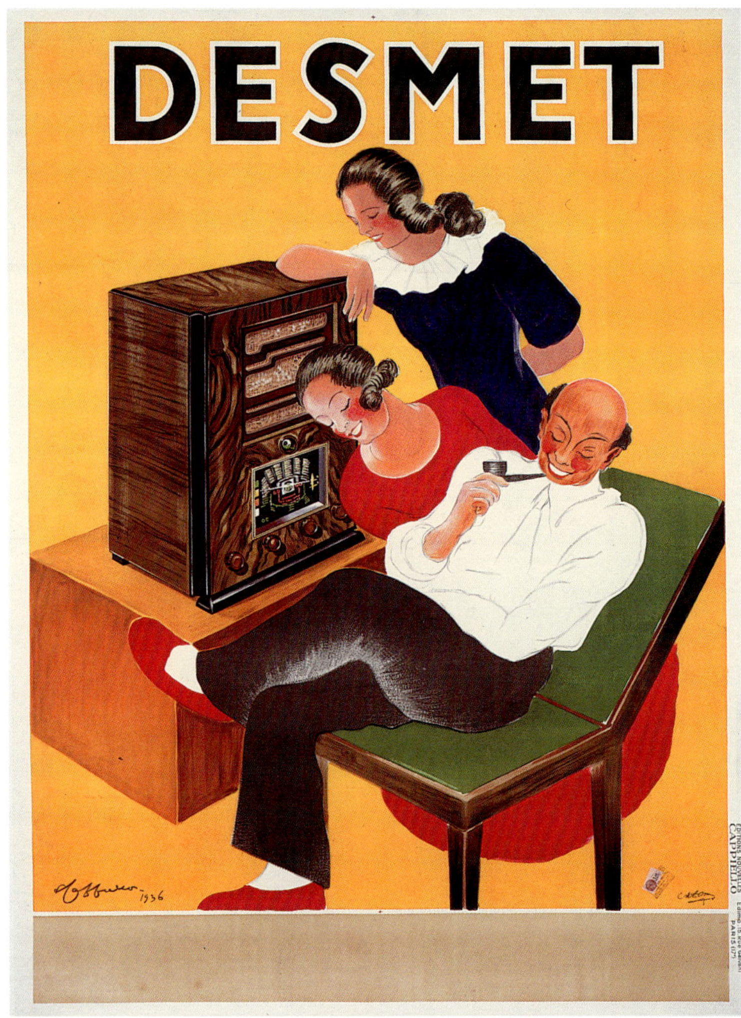

216

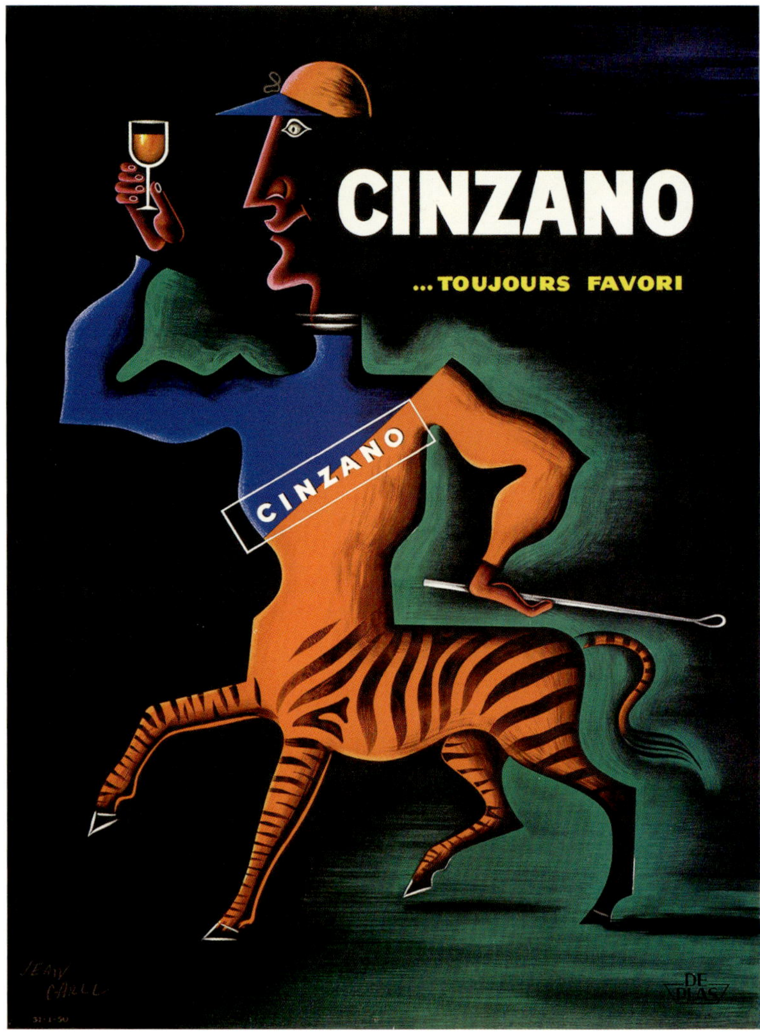

218

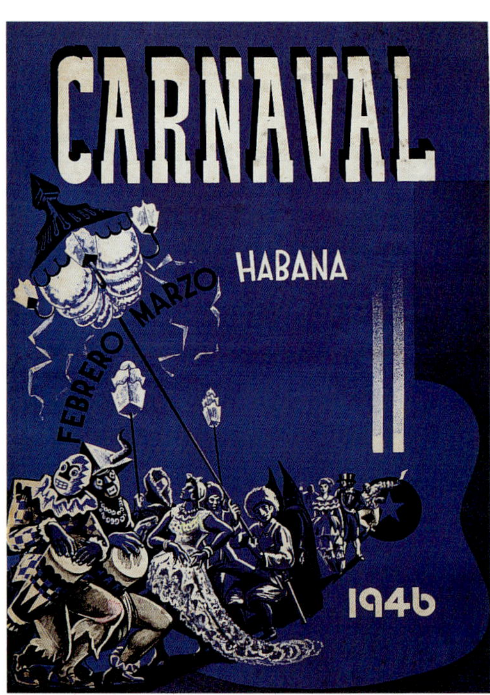

217

CAPPIELLO (cont'd)

216. Desmet. 1936.
46 x 63 in./117 x 160 cm
Editions Nouvelles Cappiello/Edimo, Paris
Cond A.
Ref: Cappiello/Rennert, 521; PAI-XL, 274
"Again, we're presented with a domestic scene: This time a family, subtly clad in French tricolors, enjoys the programming coming across the airwaves on their Desmet radio. The bright contrasting colors against the rich orange background add to the overall warmth of the scene" (Cappiello/Rennert, p. 320). *Rare!*
Est: $5,000-$6,000.

ENRIQUE CARAVIA MONTENEGRO (1905-1992)

217. Carnaval/Habana. 1946.
13^1/$_2$ x 19 in./34.3 x 48.3 cm
Cond B/Slight tears at stains.
The festivities are in full swing and where better to celebrate a Caribbean pre-Lenten festival season than Cuba's capital. This poster places all of its boisterous focus on the "Comparsa," the shortened name for the "conga de comparsa," which is the band that plays the conga during a Cuban Carnival celebration consisting of a large group of dancers performing on and traveling along the streets. Though not pictured in the poster, traditionally these dancers are followed by a *carrosa* (carriage) where the musicians play. Born in Havana, Caravia studied drawing and painting at both the School of Villate and San Alejandro Academy. In 1924, he moved to the United States to study commercial art, after which he furthered his artistic education in Europe —primarily in Rome in Madrid—as well as in Mexico,

where he studied engraving and printmaking at the School of Free Arts. A truly multifaceted and talented artist—a landscape and portrait painter, a muralist who also created mosaics and interior decorative paintings —who in time became a director at San Alejandro Academy, Caravia is also known as the father of poster art in Cuba. *Rare!*
Est: $1,700-$2,000.

JEAN CARLU (1900-1997)

218. Cinzano. 1950.
46^1/$_4$ x 63 in./117.5 x 160 cm
De Plas, Paris
Cond A–/Slight creases at edges.
Ref: Carlu, 76; PAI-XXXV, 221
The old aristocratic Cinzano family always used top talent for their commercial designs. Carlu—along with Charles Loupot, A. M. Cassandre and Paul Colin—was one of the "gang of four" who led French advertising art between the wars, distinguishing themselves and their medium with almost everything they created. Here, Carlu comes up with a startling centaur to create an image of distinction for the vermouth. Best known in France for his posters for Monsavon (*see* No. 219) and Air France, firms for which he also served as art director, and remembered in the United States for his war mobilization posters, Carlu was honored in 1981 with a retrospective at the Museé de l'Affiche in Paris.
Est: $6,000-$7,000.

219. Mon Savon c'est Monsavon. 1925.
46 x 62^1/$_4$ in./116.7 x 158.2 cm
Editions d'Art Robert Lang, Paris
Cond A–/Slight tears at paper edges.

Ref: Carlu, 10; PAI-XIII, 131
One of Carlu's most inspired creations and the one that launched his career: the triangular shape of the well-tanned brawny bather virtually leads our attention to the blue soap in his hand. The design, which shows the cubist influence on the artist, was reproduced in nearly every magazine dealing with graphic arts, garnering much praise at the time. It still works flawlessly.
Est: $4,000-$5,000.

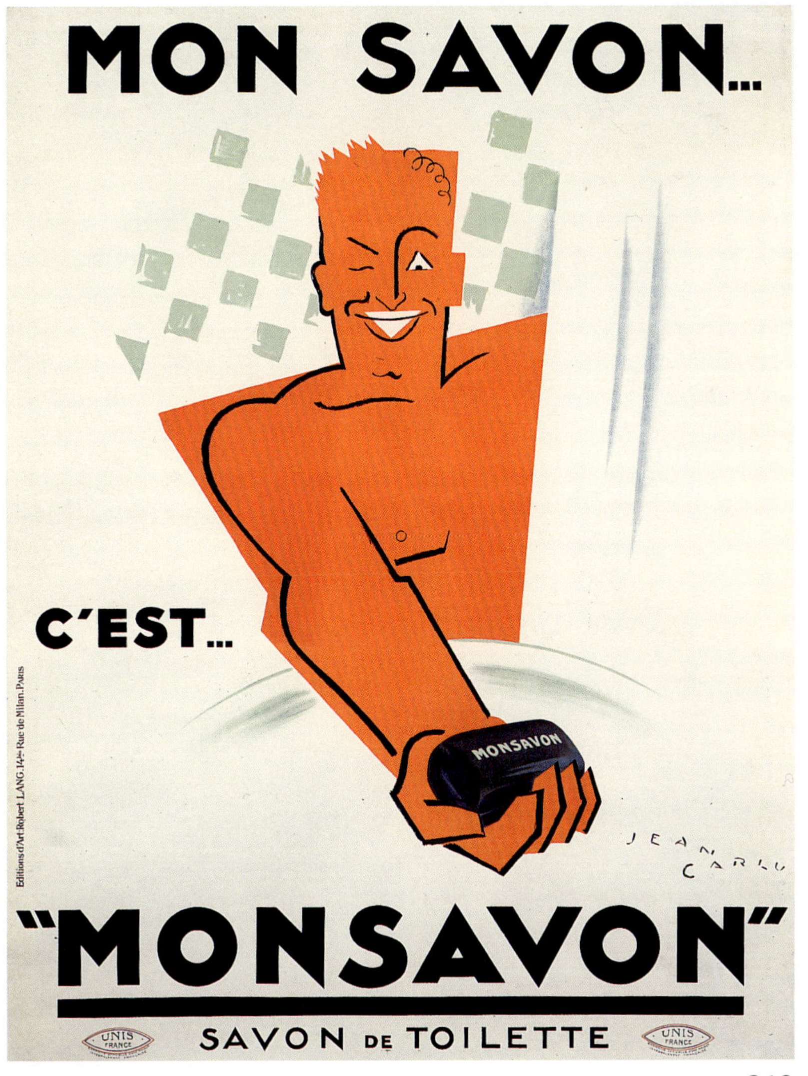

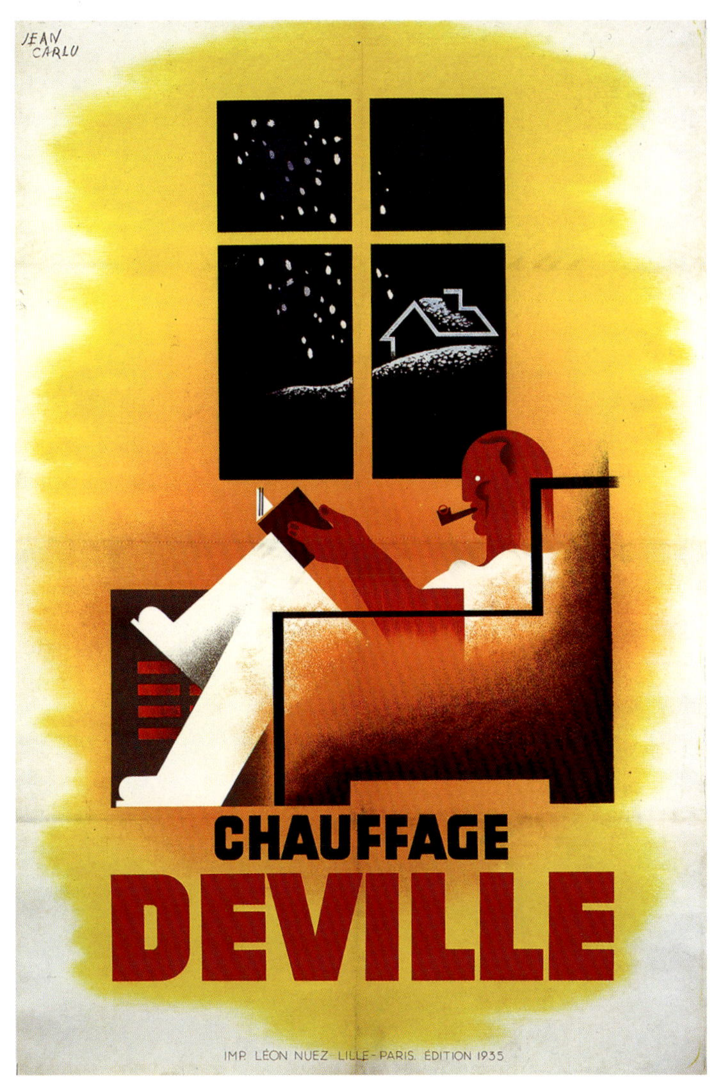

219

220

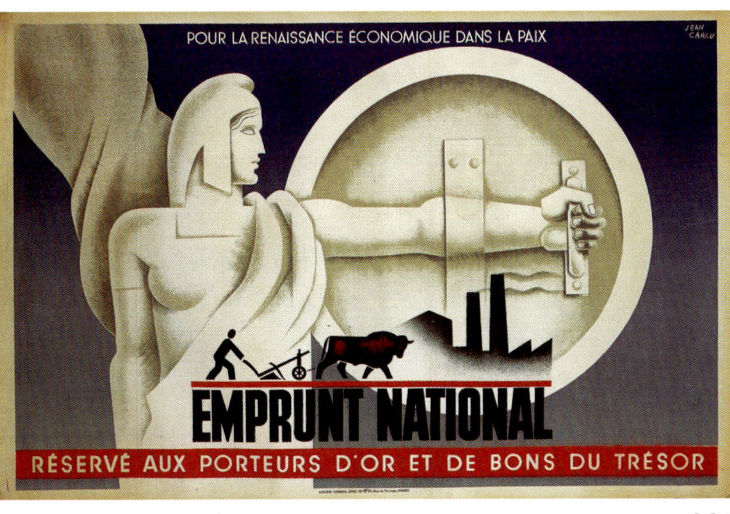

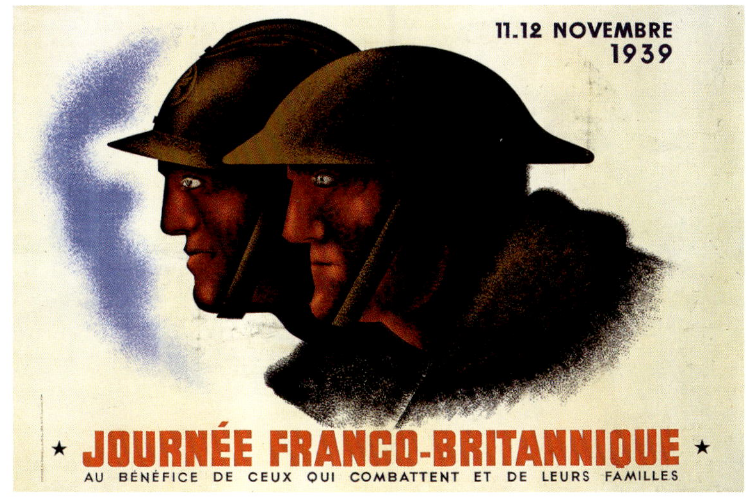

221

222

220. Chauffage Deville. 1935.
30⁷/₈ x 47 in./78.2 x 119.5 cm
Imp. Leon Nuez, Lille
Cond B/Slight tears at folds.
Ref: Carlu, 46; PAI-XXXVI, 208
Carlu creates a hieroglyph of stunning efficiency to promote Deville heaters. Combining a completely flattened perspective with stringent geometry and deeply imbued tonal evocation, the artist places us immediately on the toasty side of an environmental duality. The Deville company is alive and well today; established in 1896, they now enter a third century as purveyors of functional, stylish comfort.
Est: $2,500-$3,000.

221. Emprunt National. 1938.
47¹/₂ x 31⁵/₈ in./120 x 80.2 cm
Imp. Lucien Serre, Paris
Cond A–/Slight tears and stains at edges.
Ref: PAI-XVI, 177
In red, blue and white—naturally—this homage to commerce was executed for a national bond drive "for economic recovery"—evidently the last public borrowing before World War II. Quite impressive, this was one of Carlu's last designs in France before his departure for the United States, where he would remain for the duration of the war.
Est: $1,200-$1,500.

222. Journée Franco-Britannique. 1939.
47¹/₄ x 31 in./120 x 78.7 cm
Cond B/SLight tears and stains at folds.
Ref: Carlu, 48; PAI-XXXV, 222
This is the smaller of the two formats of this design, one of the last made by Carlu in France before departing for the U.S. where he was sent to work on the 1939 World's Fair and then remained stranded for the duration of World War II. The profiles of a French and a British soldier commemorate the 21st anniversary of Armistice Day and the end of World War I. The poster was most obviously intended to inspire those thrown into the fray of a new European conflagration.
Est: $1,000-$1,200.

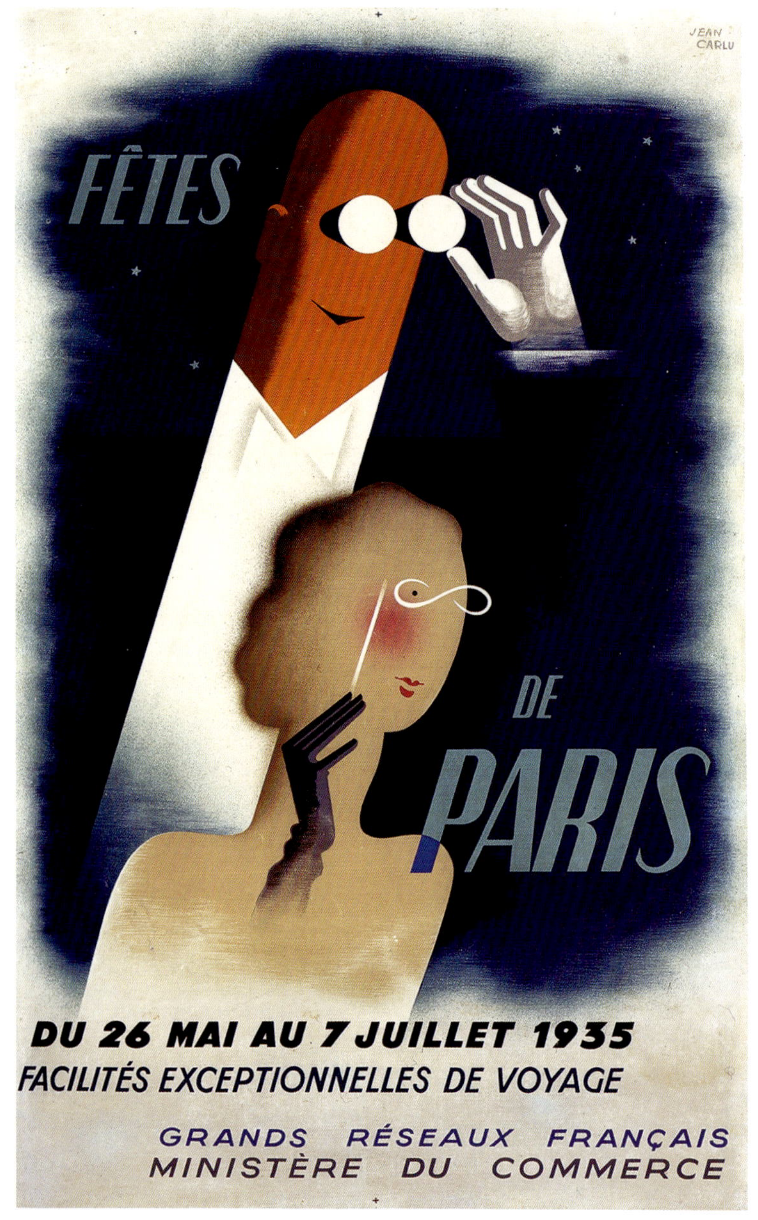

223

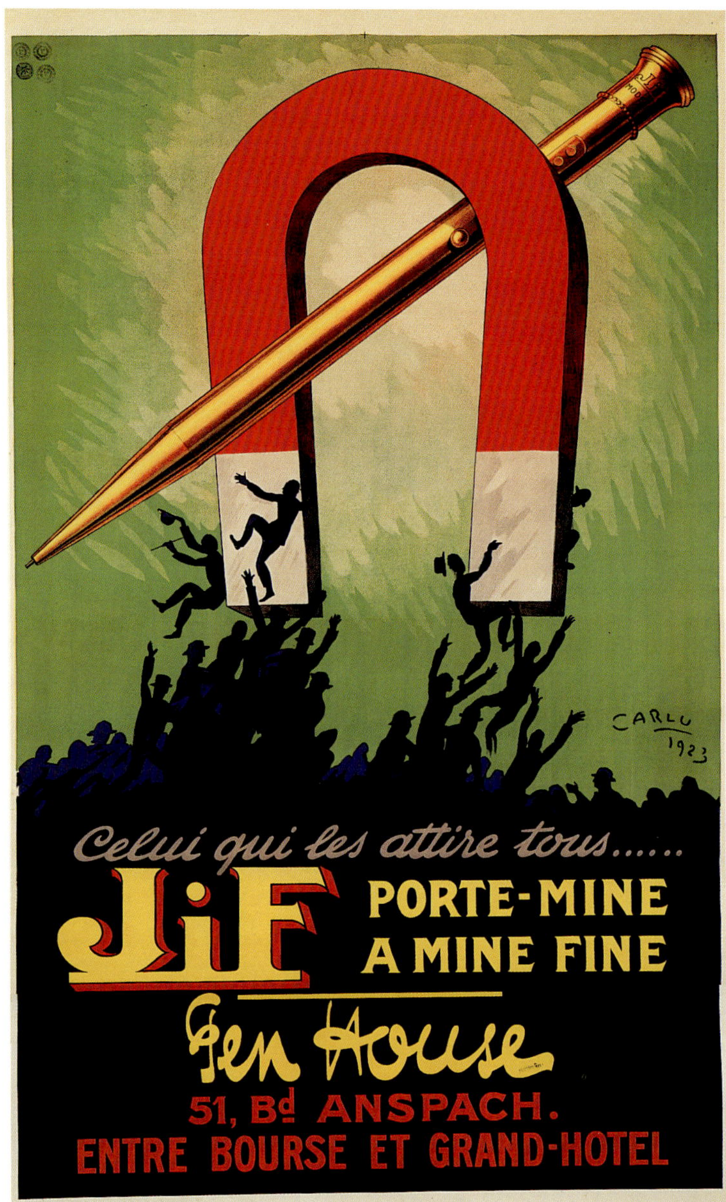

224

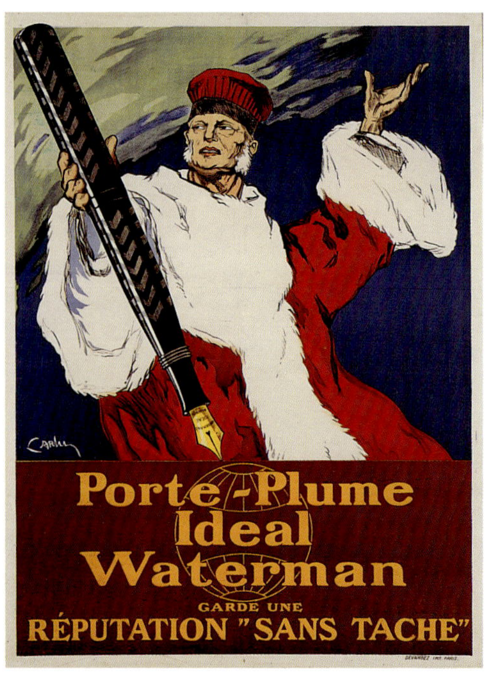

225

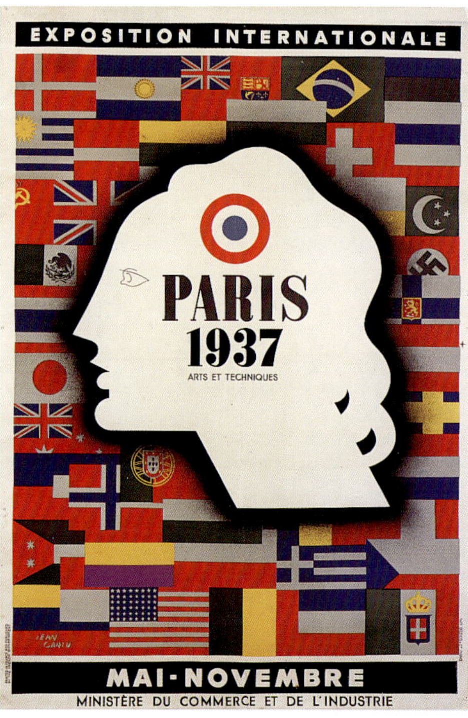

226

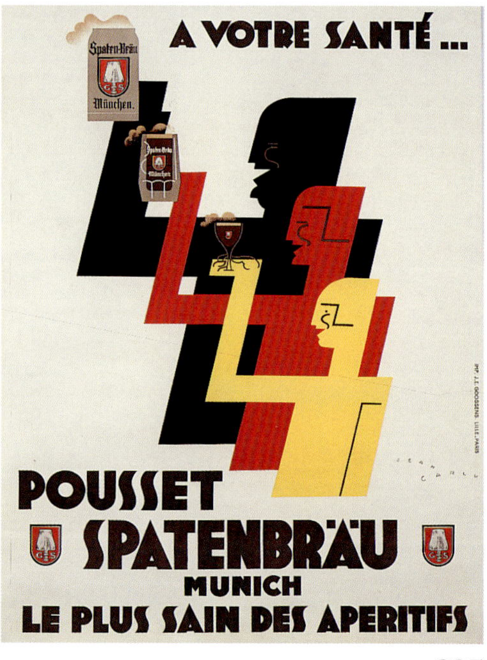

227

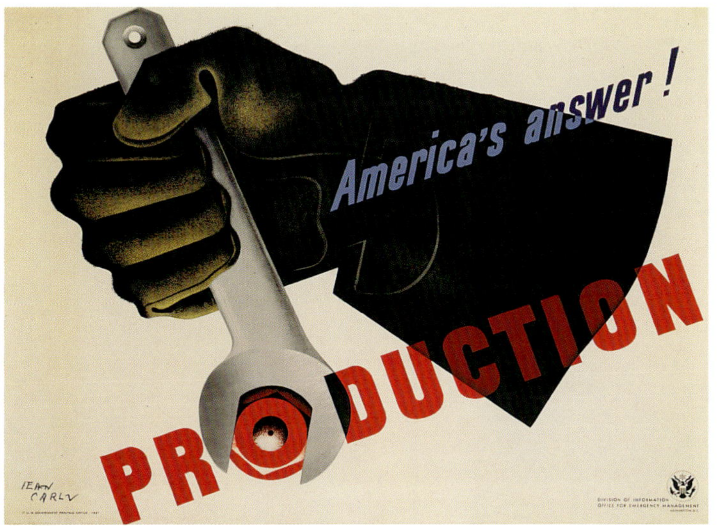

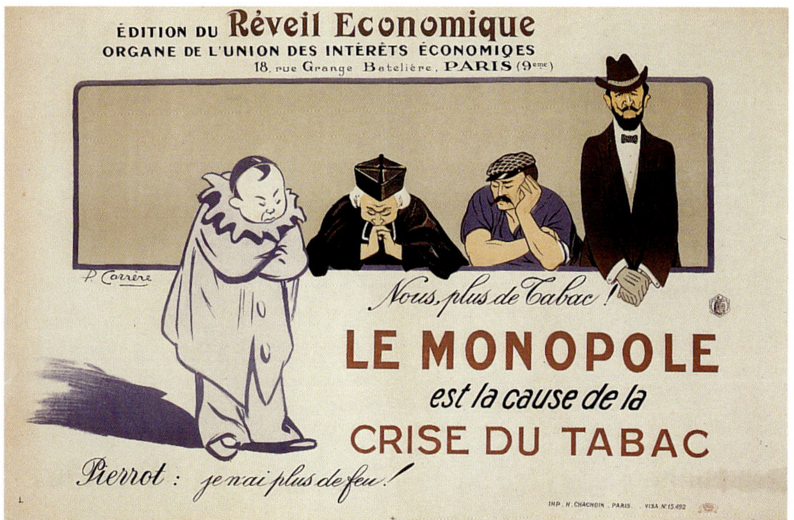

228

230

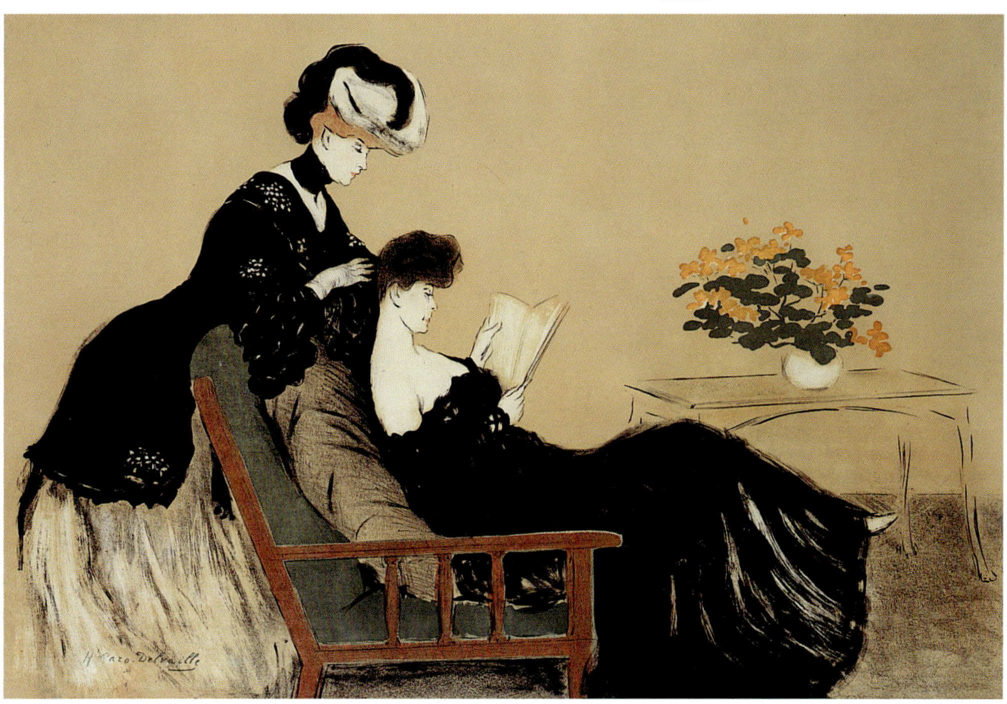

229

"the healthiest of aperitifs," so well-being is amply reinforced in terms of hoisting a Spatenbräu. And Carlu's stylized trio of health-conscious whistle wetters reminds us that there's the perfect-sized Spaten for every concerned party.
Est: $1,200-$1,500.

228. Production. 1942.
40 x 29³/₄ in./101.4 x 75.6 cm
U. S. Government Printing Office, Washington, D.C.
Cond A.
Ref: Carlu, 49; Modern Poster, 197; PAI-XXXVIII, 236
Arguably America's most substantive role in World War II was supplying the sheer material preponderance that eventually overwhelmed the much more aggressive and better trained German and Japanese forces. This is one of the first posters that mobilized Americans and made them aware of the one way they could help to end the bloodshed. Carlu worked in the United States from 1939 to 1952. When he first submitted this design, in the pre-Pearl Harbor summer of 1941, it was a mobilization poster; it became a war poster when it was reissued in 1942.
Est: $1,700-$2,000.

HENRY CARO-DELVAILLE (1876-1926)

229. L'Art Décoratif.
50¹/₄ x 34¹/₂ in./127.5 x 87.5 cm
Cond A.
Ref: PAI-XLII, 176
Caro-Delvaille's paintings of elegant Parisian interiors —and the women who inhabit them—won him many Salon prizes. This restrained yet intimate moment in a sitting room—an interpretation bordering on the voyeuristic—is a ravishing example of his vision let loose on lithography. The text on the completed version of the poster describes *L'Art Décoratif* as "a monthly review of modern art."
Est: $4,000-$5,000.

P. CARRÈRE

230. Le Monopole/Crise du Tabac. ca. 1915.
45⁵/₈ x 30³/₈ in./115.8 x 77 cm
Imp. H. Chachoin, Paris
Cond B/Restored tears.
Actually, World War I may have had a little more to do with the tobacco shortage mentioned in this Carrère design than the machinations of the French tobacco monopoly (better known as Seita, the makers of the classic Gauloise and Gitanes brands). However, the "Economic Awakening," the mouthpiece of the Union of Economic Interests obviously felt differently. To that end, they demonstrate their displeasure with the monopoly by showing iconic figures in the throes of tobacco deprivation, from Pierrot—who poutingly proclaims that he has no more fire—to the prayerful clergy to the representative of the middle class—who completes Pierrot's sentiment by informing us that even if the performer could provide some spark, the public at large wouldn't have anything to light-up anyway. Cleverly confrontational.
Est: $1,200-$1,500.

JEAN CARLU (cont'd)

223. Fêtes de Paris. 1935.
23³/₄ x 39 in./60.5 x 99 cm
Cond A–/Slight tears and stains at edges.
Ref: Carlu, 37; PAI-XV, 187
For the 1935 Paris summer fair, Carlu creates a stylized couple in Art Deco fashion, attending a formal cultural event under the stars. One of the most impressive designs in Carlu's impressive body of work. *This is the smaller format.*
Est: $5,000-$6,000.

224. Jif. 1923.
42⁷/₈ x 73³/₄ in./109 x 187.2 cm
Cond A–/Unobtrusive folds.
"That which attracts them all . . . . . ." A peculiar notion to put forward seeing as lead is a nonmagnetic metal. But like a magnet to steel, the public is drawn to the Jif writing instrument, the "Propelling Pencil with the Fine Point" (the wordplay is actually far more charming in the original French), available at Paris' Pen House. A droll design, playfully enormous and incongruously irresistible. *Rare!*
Est: $2,500-$3,000.

225. Waterman/Porte-Plume Ideal. ca. 1925.
28¹/₂ x 39³/₈ in./72.3 x 97.5 cm
Imp. Devambez, Paris
Cond B+/Slight tears at folds. Framed.
Ref: Crayons, 51; PAI-XXXII, 239
One of the earliest and rarest of all Carlu designs. With a stoic judge staking his reputation to testify on the behalf of the spotless reputation of the pen in question, thereby placing the authority of the courts firmly behind the writing instrument, could there be any further question that the Waterman product was anything less than "Ideal"?
Est: $2,000-$2,500.

226. Paris 1937.
31⁷/₈ x 46³/₈ in./80.7 x 118 cm
Imp. Bedos, Paris
Cond B+/Slight tears at edges.
Ref: Carlu, 43; PAI-XXXV, 223 (var)
Carlu was in charge of the Graphic Arts Pavilion at the Paris World Fair of 1937. In addition to commissioning images from Colin and Cappiello, he created this poster himself: the head of Marianne, symbol of the French republic, silhouetted against a montage of flags from the many participating nations. The design was printed in several sizes. *This is the smaller format with text in French.*
Est: $1,200-$1,500.

227. Spatenbräu. 1927.
23³/₄ x 31⁵/₈ in./60.2 x 80 cm
Imp. J. E. Goosens, Paris
Cond A.
Ref: Carlu, 18; Litfass-Bier, 229
"To your health." It's a benevolent enough sentiment, but one that's become—through time and repetition— fairly easy to ignore. However, the brewers of Spatenbräu beer are quick to remind us that their beverage is

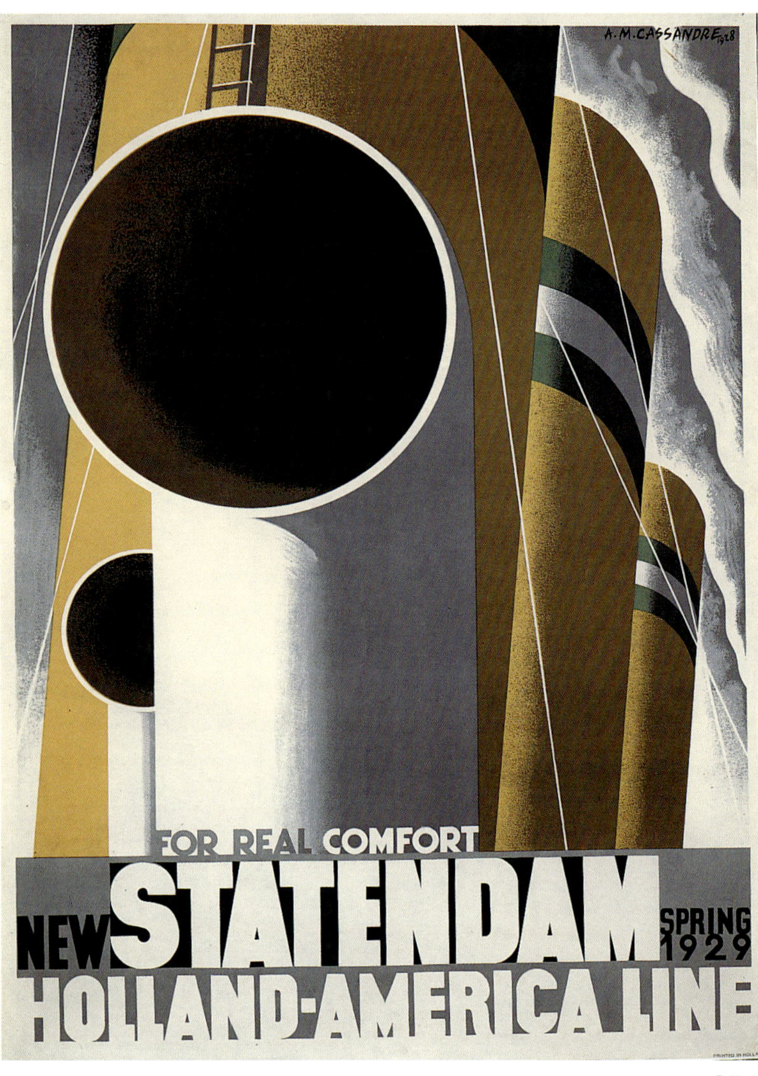

231

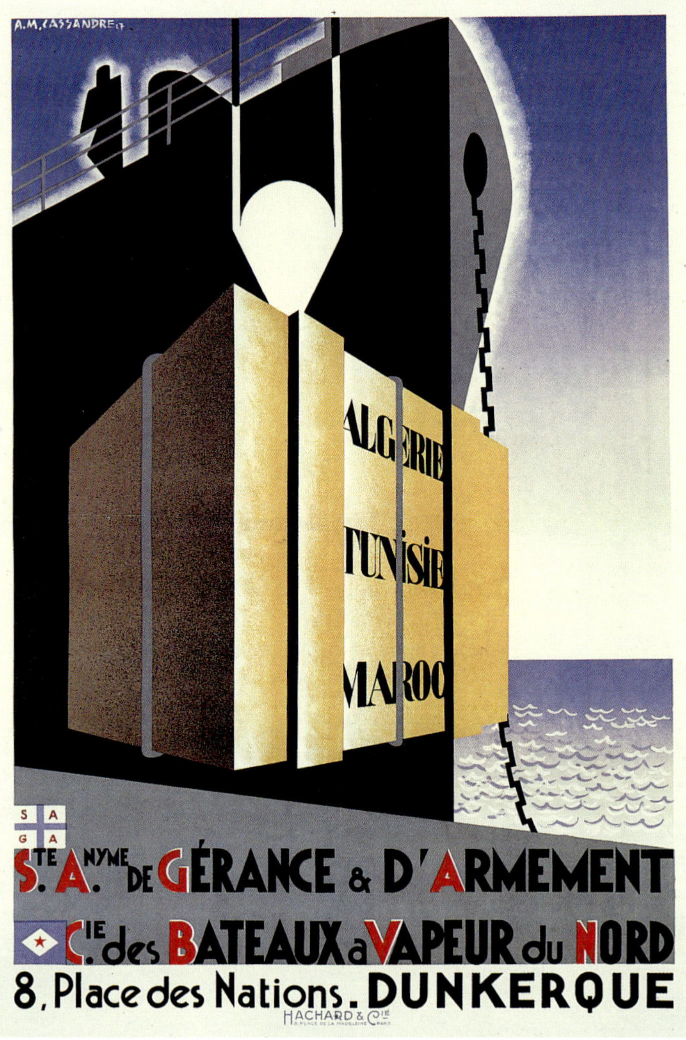

232

A. M. CASSANDRE
(Adolphe Mouron, 1901-1968)

For another work of Cassandre, see No. 48.

231. Statendam. 1928.
$25^3/_4$ x $35^1/_2$ in./65.4 x 90.2 cm
Hijgh & Van Ditmar, Rotterdam (not shown)
Cond A–/Unobtrusive tears at paper edges.
Ref: Cassandre/Weill, p. 23; Cassandre/BN, 18 (var);
    Mouron, 104, Pl. 13; Brown & Reinhold, Pl. 12;
    Cassandre/Suntory, 20; PAI-XXX, 319
A dramatic arrangement of ventilation cowlings and
funnels creates a a powerful impact. In contrast with
the rigid geometry of the ship's lines, the wavy trail of
smoke provides the feeling of three-dimensional plas-
ticity. A masterly poster by any standard, which is also
sometimes seen with a wide brown border surrounding the central image (*see* PAI-XLII, 181).
Est: $12,000-$15,000.

232. S.A.G.A. 1927.
30 x 44 in./76.1 x 101.8 cm
Hachard & Cie., Paris
Cond A–/Unobtrusive tears at folds.
Ref: Cassandre/BN, 15; Mouron, Pl. 8;
    Brown & Reinhold, 26 & Pl. 8;
    Cassandre/Suntory, 68; PAI-XLII, 180
A stylized composition of a crate being unloaded from
a liner. Brown & Reinhold note that "this poster marks
the beginning of Cassandre's most consistent and
dynamic period of postermaking . . . he begins playing
with the notion of perspective in a Cubist fashion . . .
resorts to a prominent distortion of scale" and we see
"his first use of gradation in rendering the sky" (p. 13).
Est: $7,000-$8,000.

233. L'Atlantique. 1931.
$25^5/_8$ x $38^7/_8$ in./60 x 98.8 cm
Alliance Graphique, Paris
Cond A.

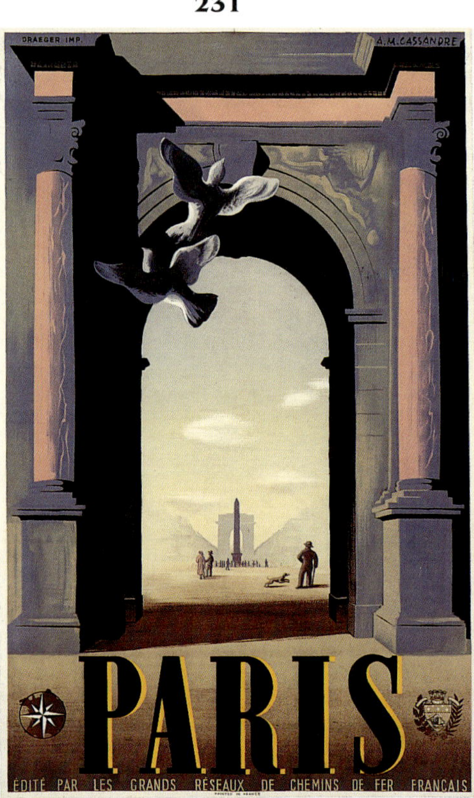

235

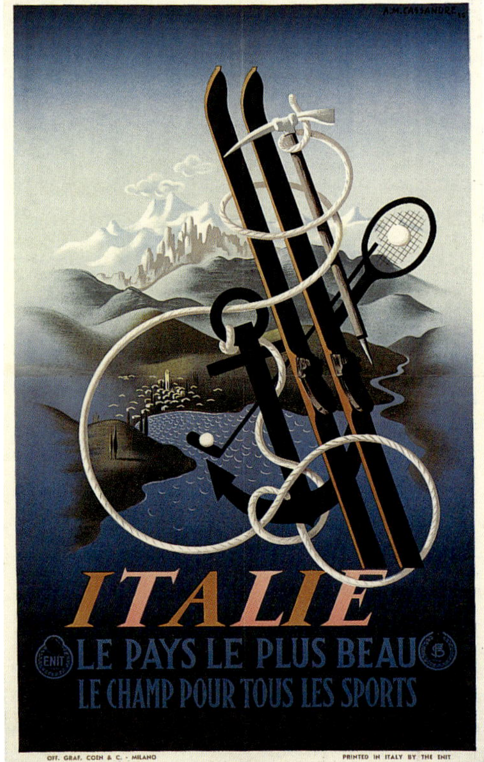

236

Ref: Cassandre/Weill, p. 48; Cassandre/BN, 55;
    Mouron, Pl. 34; Brown & Reinhold, 67 & Pl. 31;
    Cassandre/Suntory, 66; Moderno Francés, p. 172;
    Timeless Images, 107; Avant Garde, p. 161;
    PAI-XLII, 186
There is hardly any purer example of Cassandre's finding formal beauty in the creations of the machine age
than this. His game here is to render the ship as nearly

to a perfect rectangle as possible, centered on the
sheet—this simplicity is all the more striking because
unlike the "Normandie" (*see* No. 234), the ship is not
seen head on, but at an angle. "Instead of a sleek
oceangoing vessel," as Brown & Reinhold note, "Cassandre's rendition becomes a mammoth wall of steel
that towers in fantastic and unreal fashion over a
minuscule tugboat." Yet there's an almost humorous

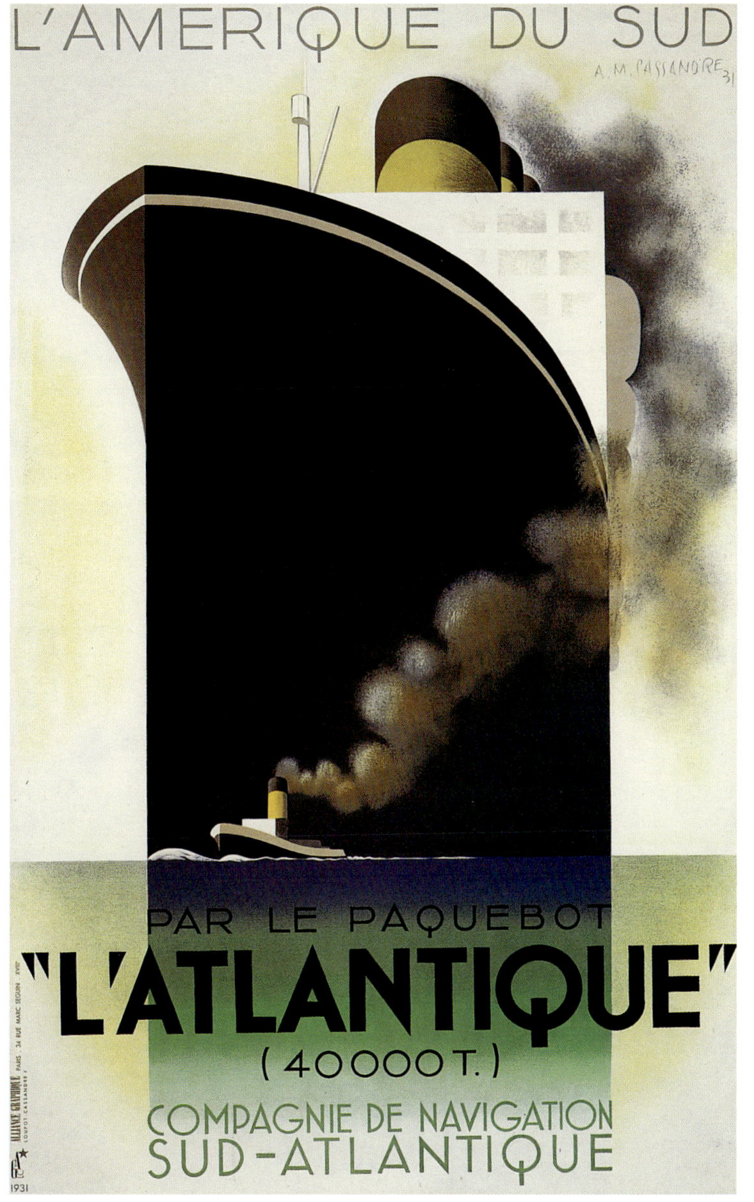

233

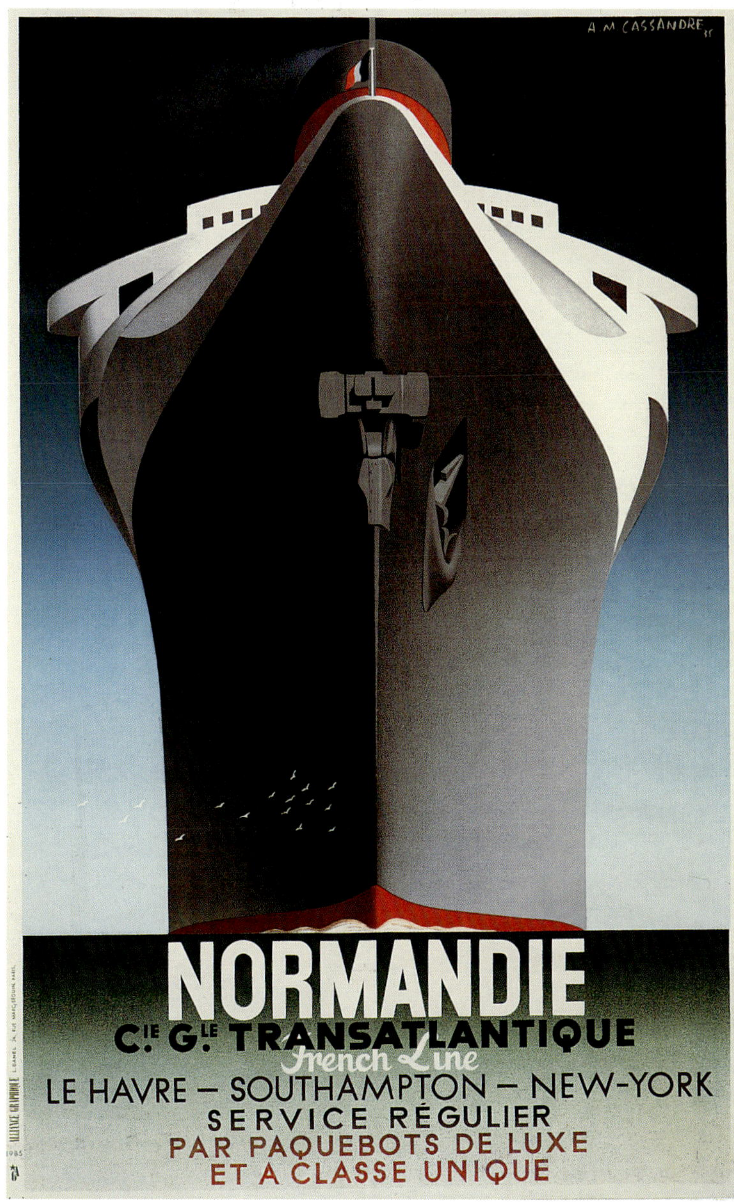

234

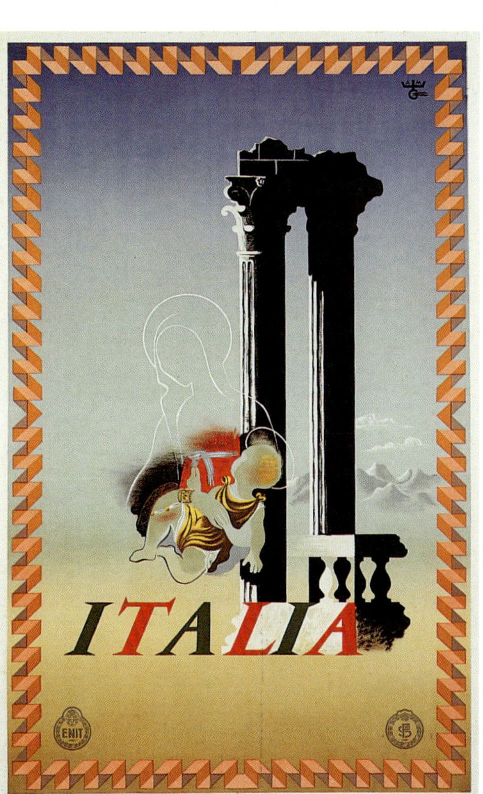

237

touch in the way the little tug is turned to "imitate" its huge companion's exact angle, as though aspiring to be its equal. *This is the smaller format and the finest specimen we have ever seen!*
Est: $30,000-$40,000.

234. Normandie/Voyage Inaugural. 1935.
24¹/₄ x 39 in./61.5 x 99cm
lliance Graphique L. Danel, Paris
Cond A–/Folds show.
Ref (All Var but PAI): Cassandre/Weill, p. 91;
    Cassandre/BN, 89; Mouron, 56;
    Brown & Reinhold, 53; Cassandre/Suntory, p. 91;
    Weill, 345; Deco Affiches, p. 33;
    Musée d'Affiches, p. 65; PAI-XLII, 196
An advertisement for the *Normandie* and her "First Arrival in New York City on June 3 (1935)" touted that "The arrival in New York Harbor of the gigantic super-liner *Normandie* will inaugurate a new era of transatlantic travel. She will set new standards of luxury and speed, steadiness comfort and safety . . . not merely the largest liner afloat (79,280 tons) . . . but in almost every respect *a new kind of liner!*" And in almost every respect, this Cassandre masterpiece was a new way of selling the glamour and excitement of ocean liner travel. A deceptively simple, but impressive design with the ship towering above us, a flight of small birds at bottom giving the image as much scale and strength as the imposing hull itself.
Est: $10,000-$12,000.

235. Paris. 1935.
24³/₈ x 39¹/₂ in./61.8 x 100.3 cm
Imp. Draeger, Paris
Cond A–/Slight tears at edges.

Ref: Cassandre/Weill, p. 58; Cassandre/BN, 99;
    Mouron, Pl. 53; Brown & Reinhold, 102 & Pl. 54;
    Cassandre/Suntory, 62; Affiche Réclame, 99;
    Voyage, p. 141; PAI-XXXVII, 188
Eight years after his great geometric successes for rail travel, Cassandre was working in a more poetic vein. Roman arches, with columns tinged pink by the early morning sun, and a tall obelisk at the Place Concorde link the Louvre to the Arc de Triomphe and combine to create a dreamy vista of Paris as a tourist destination steeped in history.
Est: $2,000-$2,500.

236. Italie. 1936.
24¹/₄ x 39¹/₂ in./61.8 x 100.2 cm
Off. Graf. Coen, Milano
Cond B/Slight tears at folds.
Ref (All Var but PAI & Cassandre/BN): Cassandre/Weill,
    p. 15; Cassandre/BN, 103; Mouron, 192;
    Brown & Reinhold, 58; Alpes, Pl. 10;
    Cassandre/Suntory, 63A; PAI-XIII, 146
Cassandre designed this and two other Italian tourism posters during a working summer holiday on the shore of Lake Maggiore in northern Italy. The Mussolini regime had passed a law banning Italian companies from commissioning French artists; to get around it, Cassandre's future publisher in Italy, Augusto Coen, invited him to work in Italy. Though the style was a dead giveaway, Cassandre had to play along with the charade and use the monogram "A.M.C." to conceal his French name. This particular creation centers on a montage of sports and recreational objects against a panorama of Italian topography. *This is the rare French-language version of the poster.*
Est: $2,000-$2,500.

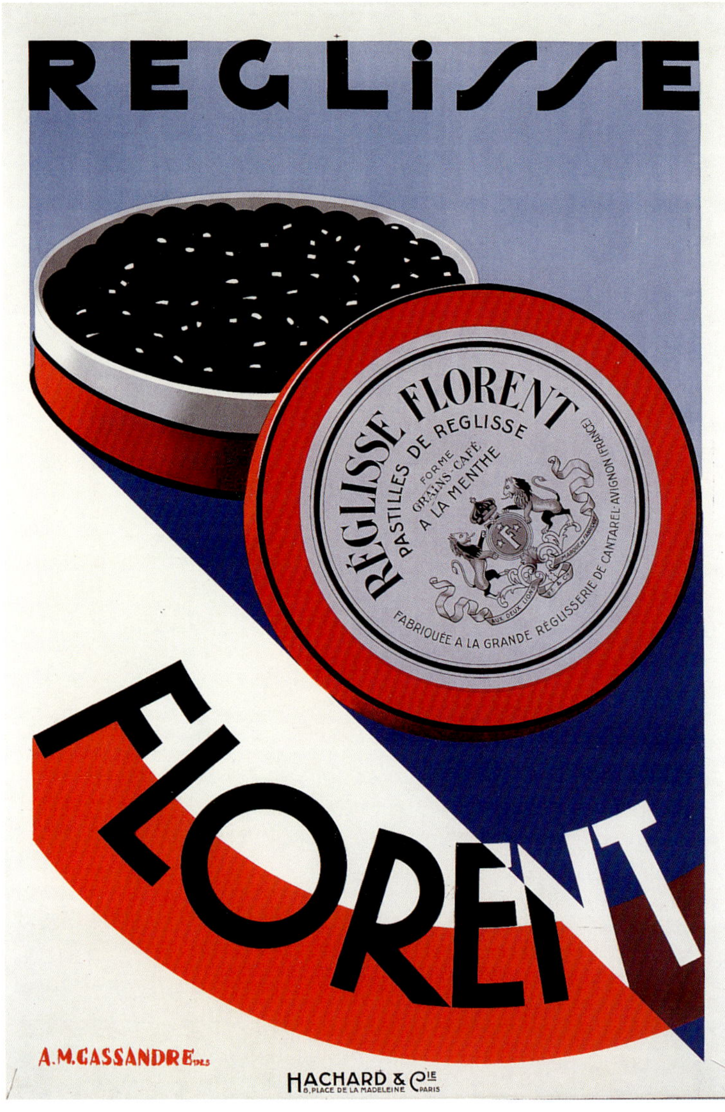

238

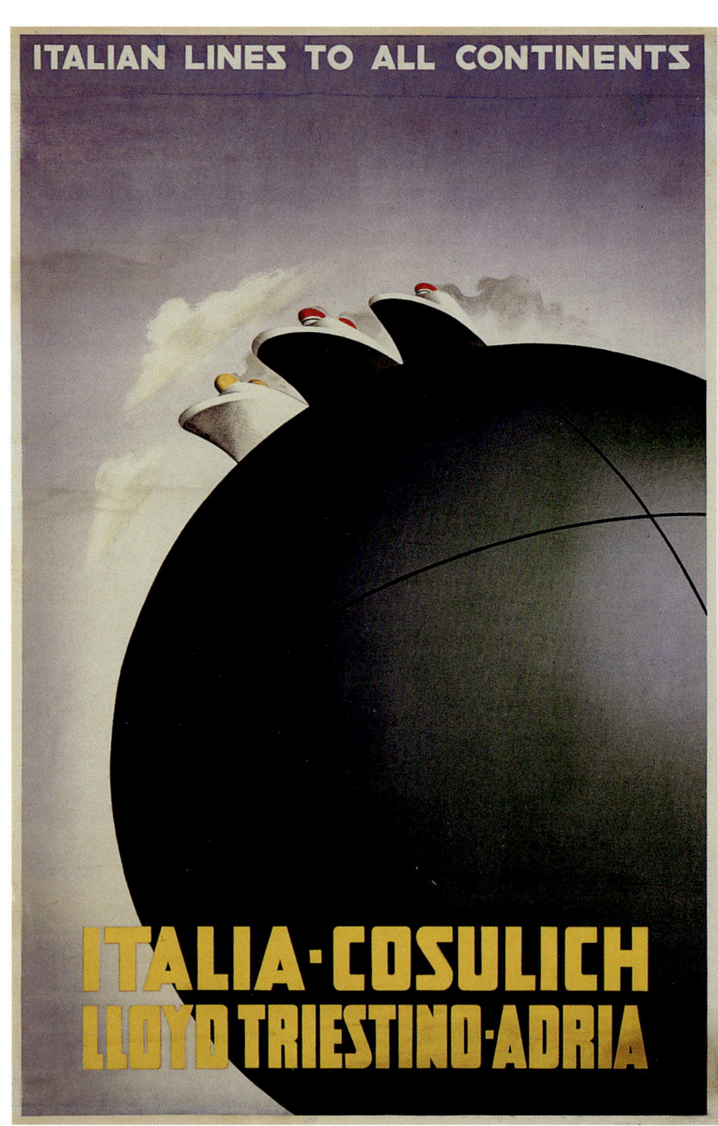

239

A. M. CASSANDRE (cont'd)

237. Italia. 1936.
$24^3/8$ x $39^1/4$ in./62 x 99.7 cm
Off. Graf. Coen, Milano
Cond A.
Ref: Cassandre/BN, 102; Mouron, Pl. 61;
  Brown & Reinhold, 58; Cassandre/Suntory, p. 179;
  PAI-XXXVII, 189
And here we see one of the other two creations that
Cassandre produced to generate Italian tourism during
that summer of 1936, this one centering on art and
culture, merely hinting at a mountainous landscape in
the background. Instead, the focus is on the instantly
recognizable subjects of the fore.
Est: $1,400-$1,700.

238. Réglisse Florent. 1925.
$39^1/4$ x $59^1/4$ in./99.7 x 150.5 cm
Hachard & Cie., Paris
Cond A. Framed.
Ref: Cassandre/Weill, p. 8; Cassandre/BN, 6;
  Mouron, Pl. 5; Brown & Reinhold, 4;
  Cassandre/Suntory, 10; Moderno Francés, p. 154;
  PAI-XLII, 198
To advertise a licorice pastille, Cassandre turns to
the "object poster," the new rage from Germany and
Switzerland. A big close-up of the product helps lodge
the label in the consumer's mind and produces a
simple, strong circle-based design.
Est: $4,000-$5,000.

239. Italia-Cosulich. 1936.
$23^3/4$ x $37^3/8$ in./60.6 x 95 cm
Cond B–/Restored tears, largely near edges.
Ref: Mouron, III.100 (var); PAI-XLI, 163
The boast of the Trieste-based shipping line Cosulich

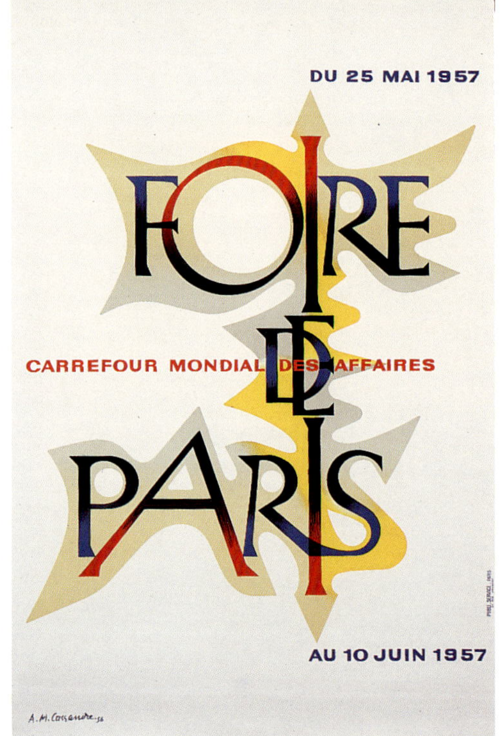

241

242

to cover the entire world and Cassandre's love of pure
geometric form come together perfectly in the image
of a trio of liners steaming in unison around the globe.
And the incongruity of the three somewhat-oversized

ships precariously placed atop the globe—an artistic
statement that speaks to perspective on more than
one level—adds eye-catching impact to the design.
Est: $6,000-$8,000.

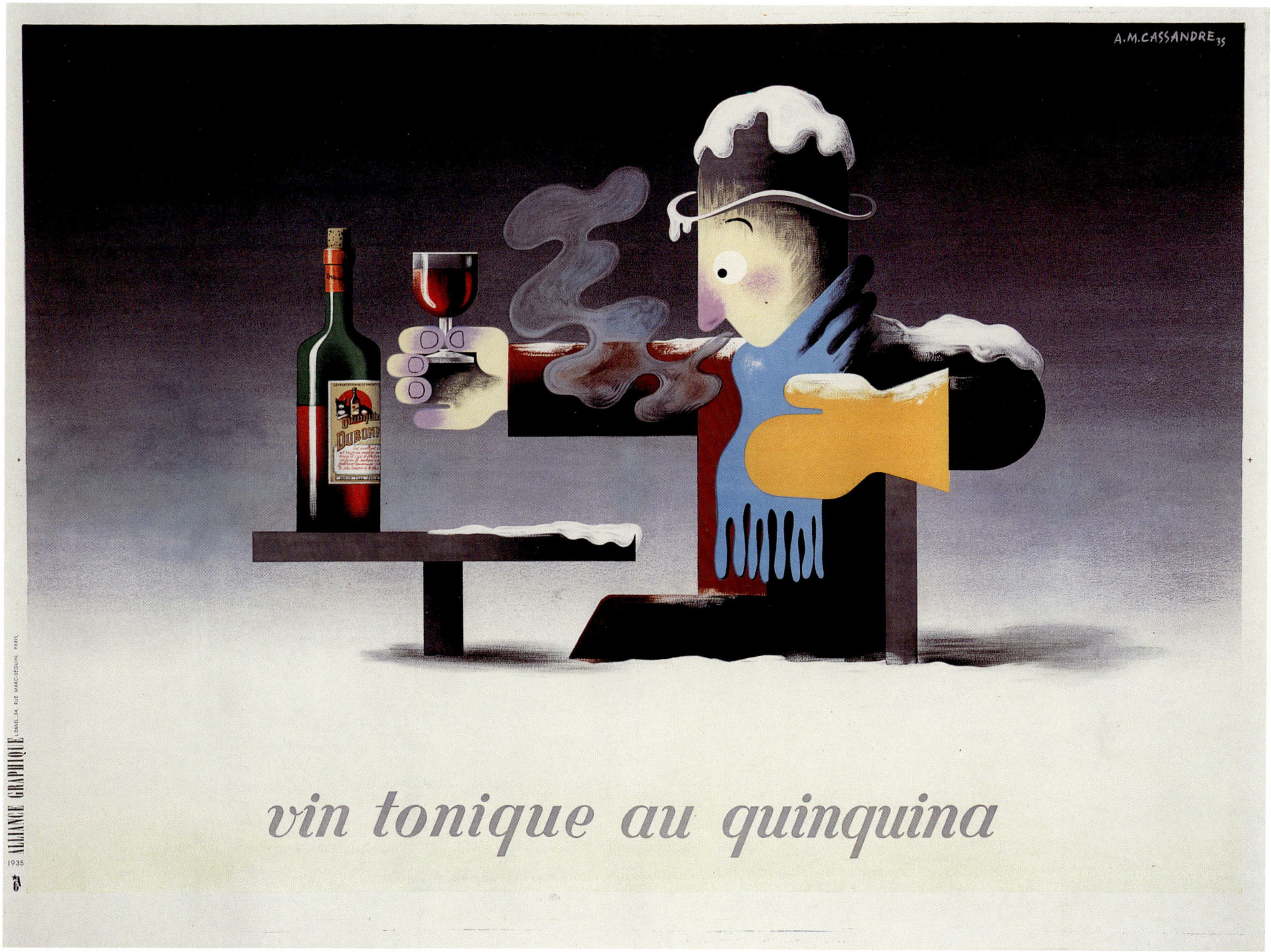

240

aperitif (*see* PAI-XLI, 164) was used on huge billboards and tiny menu cards as well as every size and format in between, and the public never seemed to tire of it. The image owes a great deal of its long life to graphic flair and conceptual wit. But what Cassandre probably didn't realize at the start was that the seated character's silhouette and gestures would lend themselves to the kind of variations that give an advertising campaign "legs." Here, we see to what great lengths—or shall we say depths—the drinker will go to get his favorite tipple. Then one warming sip and he won't mind the cold at all. Mouron indicates that while "Cassandre personally designed numerous projects showing the figure of the drinker from the 1932 triptych in a variety of situations" (46b), only two were published as posters. One was the summer scene, showing the benefit of adding a bit of cassis or lemon to the drink, and the other was this one—the winter image. *Rare!*
Est: $40,000-$50,000.

241. Venezia. 1951.
24³/₄ x 39³/₈ in./62.7 x 100 cm
Calcografia & Cartevalori, Milano
Cond A–/Unobtrusive tears.
Ref: Mouron, P. 16 (var); Cassandre/Suntory, 65;
  PAI-XL, 283
Cassandre originally created this atmospheric design—with a block of text at the bottom—for the Venice Graphic Design Conference in 1951. For several years afterwards the image was used annually, and the Italian Government Tourist Bureau liked it so much they employed it in the form seen here as a destination poster for Venice.
Est: $2,000-$2,500.

242. Foire de Paris. 1957.
24¹/₂ x 39¹/₈ in./62 x 99.4 cm
Publi-Service, Paris
Cond A.
Ref: Mouron, Pl. 70; Cassandre/Suntory, 185;
  PAI-XXIV, 218
This very late Cassandre design contains elements of abstract art, yet retains the clarity and easy legibility that were his lifelong hallmarks. It advertises a trade fair at the "business crossroads of the world"—Paris. *This is the medium format.*
Est: $1,500-$1,800.

243. Bonal. 1935.
47¹/₄ x 63¹/₈ in./120 x 160.4 cm
Imp. L. Danel, Paris
Cond A.
Ref: Cassandre/Weill, p. 72; Cassandre/BN, 91;
  Mouron, Pl. 63; Moderno Francés, p. 189;
  PAI-XLII, 274
In this version of the image, printed two years after the original (*see* No. 244), the background has been changed to yellow and sienna, but the intoxicating stars remain pink. Additionally, an extra line of text appears at bottom pinpointing the liqueur's origin. "In *Bonal*, an eye-catching white figure silhouetted against its black shadow seems to balance a realistically rendered bottle of Bonal against a vibrant warm background of luminous yellows. The vigorous graphic treatment of the bottle spilling its stream of pink stars is in sharp contrast to the abstractness of the figure poised like a tightrope walker on the brand name at the bottom of the poster" (Mouron, pp. 54-55).
Est: $2,500-$3,000.

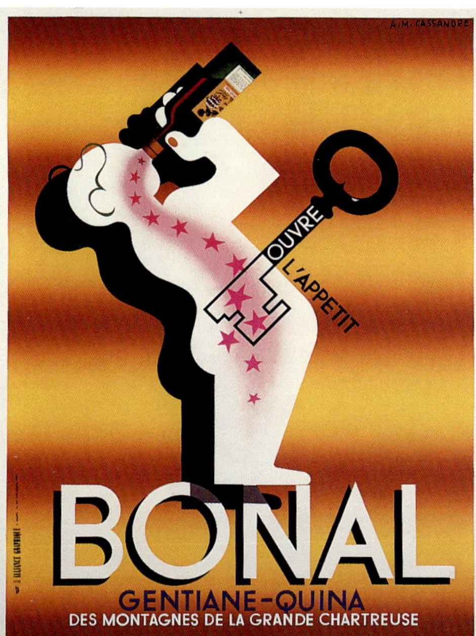

243

240. Dubonnet/vin tonique au quinquina. 1935.
78¹/₂ x 59 in./199.5 x 150 cm
Alliance Graphique, Paris
Cond A–/Unobtrusive tears at folds and edges.
Ref: Cassandre/Weill, p. 85; Cassandre/BN, 92;
  Mouron, Pl. 46b; Cassandre/Suntory, 33;
  PAI-XXII, 250
Cassandre's immortal triptych design for this French

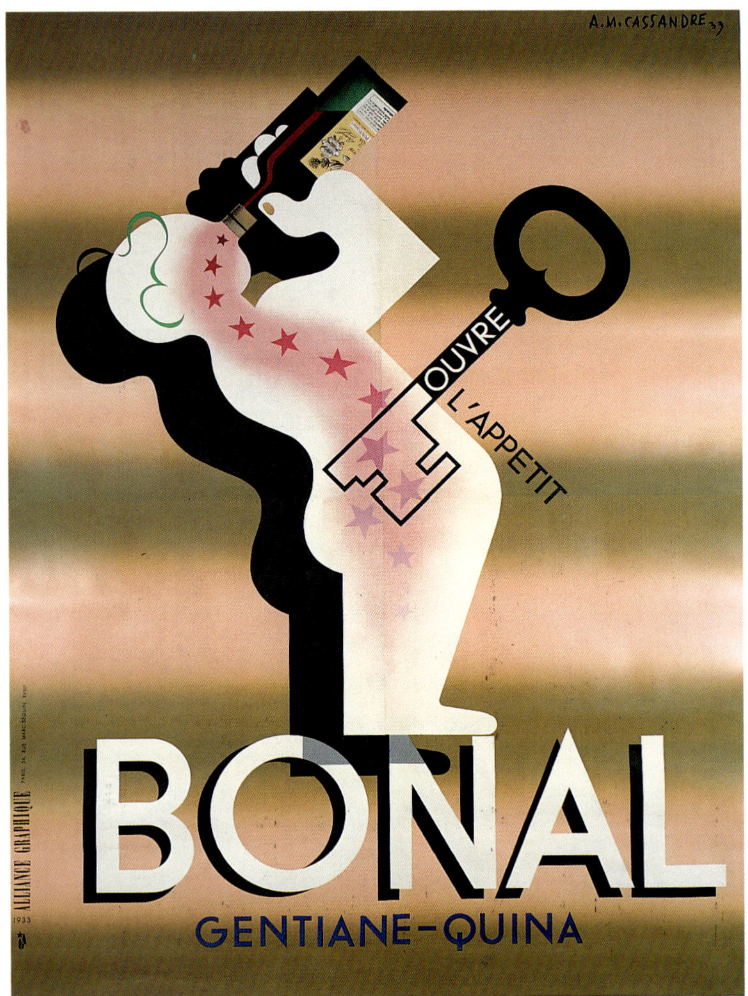

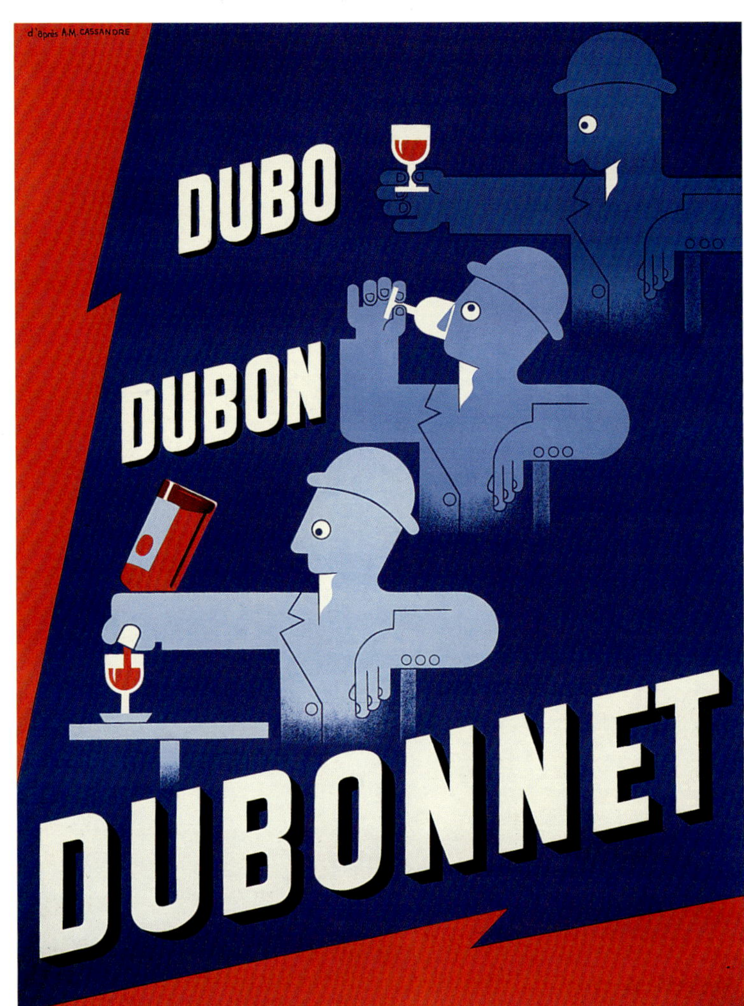

244

245

A. M. CASSANDRE (cont'd)

244. Bonal. 1933.
91^1/$_2$ x 121^3/$_4$ in./232.3 x 309 cm
Alliance Graphique, Paris
Cond A.
Ref: Mouron, III.63 (var); PAI-XXVIII, 211
This is the large four-sheet format of Cassandre's
design for Bonal aperitif through which he makes it
graphically clear that Bonal is the key that will "open
your appetite."
Est: $4,000-$5,000.

245. Dubo-Dubon-Dubonnet. ca. 1948.
44^3/$_4$ x 61 in./113.6 x 155 cm
Imp. Bedos, Paris
Cond B+/Slight tears at folds and edges.
Ref: PAI-XXXIII, 275
"One is so enchanted by the immediately grasped idea
—'Dubious—It's good—The name of the wine'—that
the subtleties of the conception may go unnoticed. But
it is precisely the rolling eye (simply rendered as a disc
within a circle), the warm color suffusing the drinker by
stages as the word fills with color, and the immobility
of the body in contrast to the shifts in position of hand,
head and eye that bear the imprint of Cassandre's genius
as a poster designer" (Word & Image, p. 60). *This later
version of the famous 1935 poster, in red, white
and blue, based on his design ("d'après Cassandre")
is in all likelihood a post-World War II edition.*
Est: $3,000-$3,500.

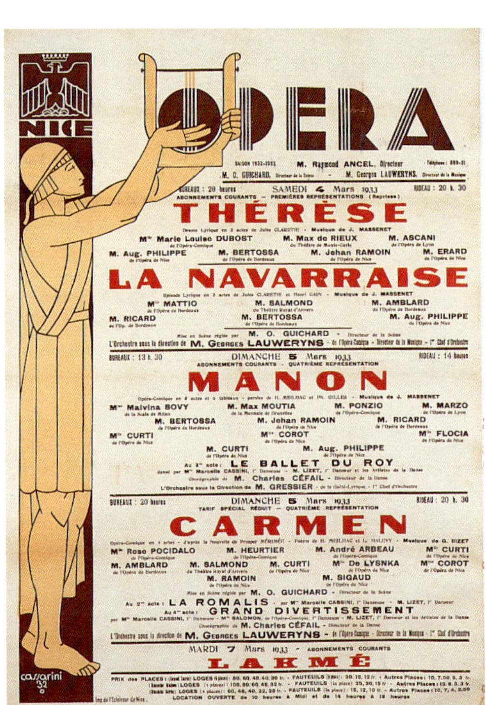

246

JEAN CASSARINI (1910-)

246. Opera/Nice. 1933.
33^1/$_4$ x 48^7/$_8$ in./84.3 x 124.3 cm
Imp. de l'Eclaireur de Nice
Cond B+/Slight stains, largely at edges.
Three days in the life of the 1932-33 Nice Opera season
(three Massenet operas and Bizet's "Carmen" all within
a four-day span, no less) are brought to the attention
of the aria-loving French public with the assistance of

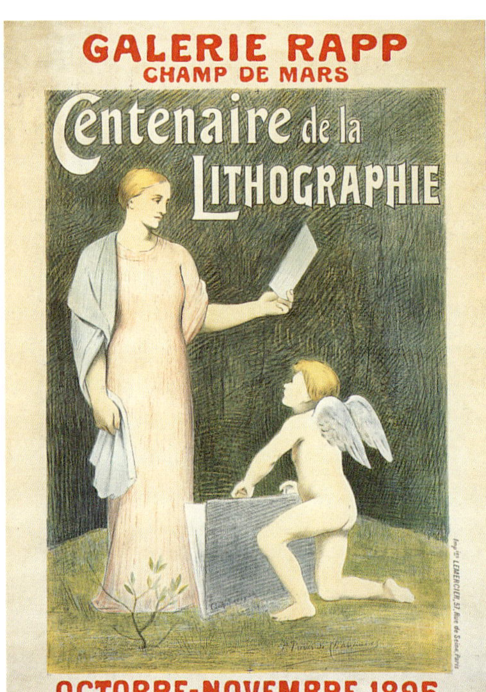

248

Apollo, who among his other duties in Greek and
Roman mythology, served as the lyre-bearing god of
music. Cassarini, a native of Nice, tended to work primarily in a Cubist style. He displayed at all the traditional Salons, including the Salon des Peintres Témoins
de leur Temps. In 2005, he was commissioned by the
Nice Opera to recreate one of his tableau from the
opera "Chu" as a mosaic frieze.
Est: $1,400-$1,700.

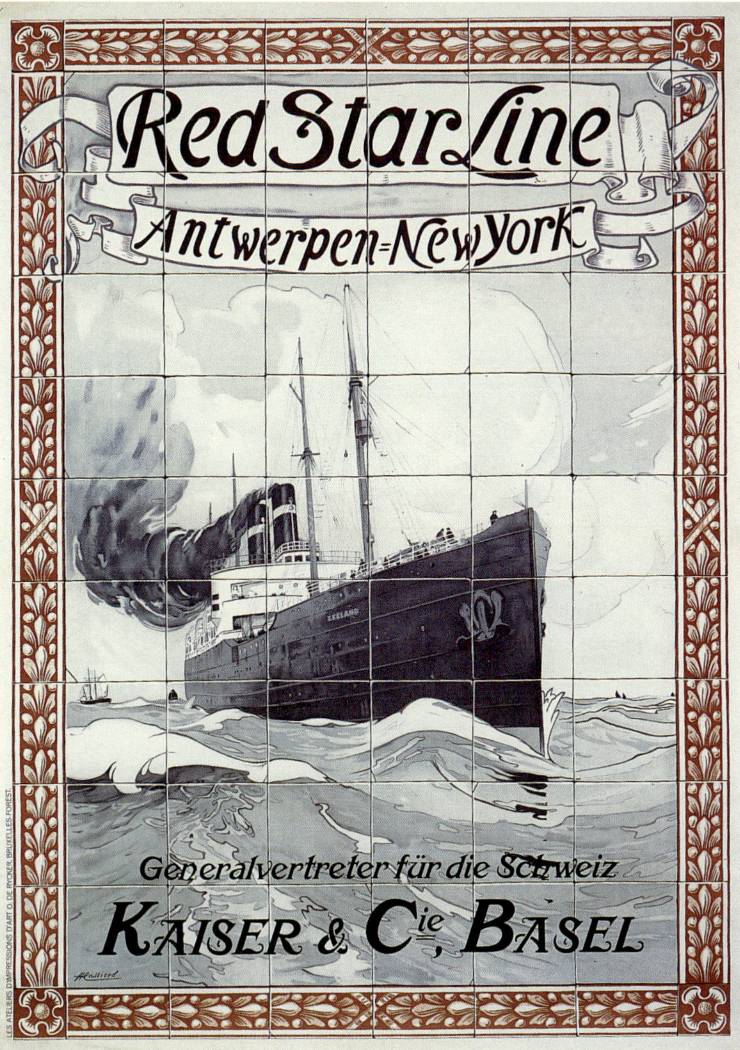

247

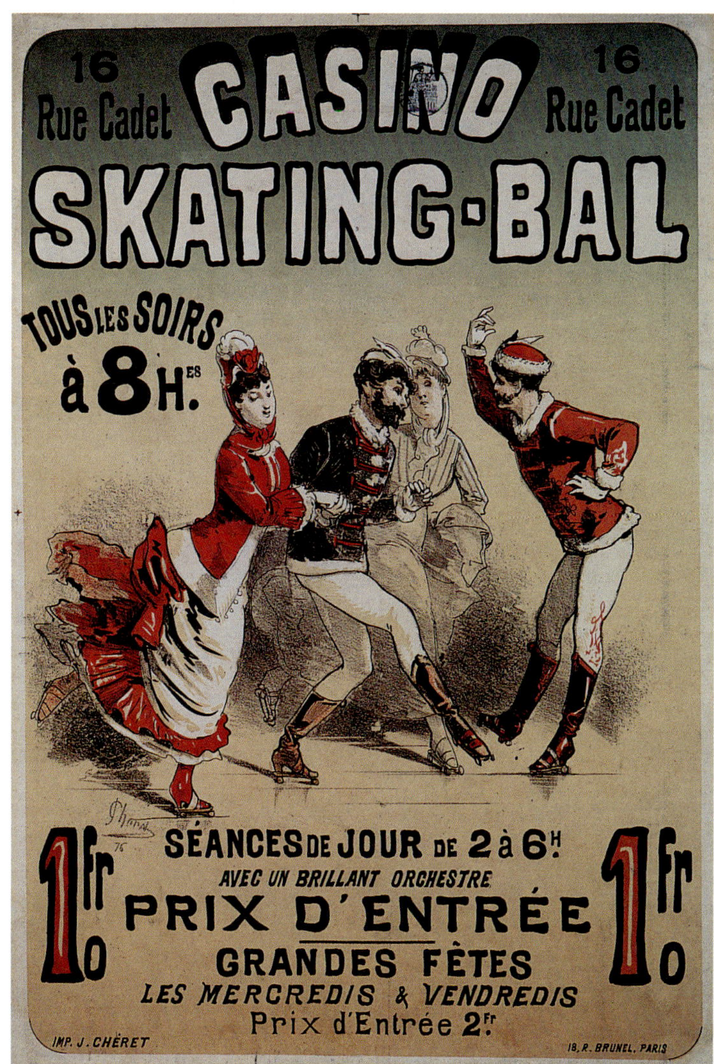

249

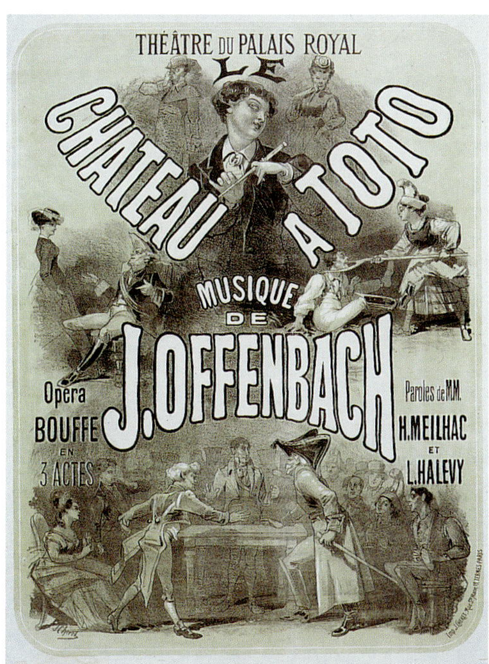

250

HENRI CASSIERS (1858-1944)

247. Red Star Line/Antwerpen-New York. 1901.
$43^3/_8$ x $60^1/_2$ in./110.2 x 153.7 cm
O. De Rycker & Mendel, Bruxelles
Cond A–/Slight tears and stains in borders; image excellent.
Ref (Both Var): DFP-II, 1003; PAI-XXXI, 133
Cassiers depicts the "Zeeland" on a delft blue tile wall, with navy blue text on unfurled banners up top and the name of a shipping concern at bottom, with everything enclosed within a decorative sepia border. This is an inspired device that only augments the marvelously detailed rendering of the ship, with its figures visible on deck. A distinguished Belgian painter and magazine reporter/illustrator turned posterist, Cassiers became an aquarellist of note at an early age, placing his work at many exhibitions and earning various kudos. In the 1890s, he traveled as a roving magazine contributor. In poster work, he stays with his painterly style, most frequently depicting a folksy scene to which text is added.
Est: $4,000-$5,000.

PIERRE PUVIS DE CHAVANNES (1824-1898)

248. Centenaire de la Lithographie. 1895.
$40^3/_8$ x $58^1/_8$ in./102.6 x 147.7 cm
Imp. Lemercier, Paris
Cond B+/Slight tears and stains at paper edges.
Ref: Gold, 182; PAI-XLI, 176
"In the hands of this traditional painter, a design for a hundredth-anniversary exhibit of lithography becomes an allegorical scene in which this somewhat austere female figure represents the printing industry and the little cherub symbolizes the artists who labor in the lithography field. The use of mythological beings, predominantly female, was characteristic among the classically inclined designers" (Gold, p. 126). When recovery from an illness detoured Puvis de Chavannes in Italy, he abandoned his dreams of becoming an engineer in favor of studying classical art. Mostly self-taught, he created few posters, but attained a great measure of popularity and was consigned at one point to create the murals for the Paris Pantheon, a project which consumed five years of his artistic life.
Est: $1,500-$1,700.

JULES CHÉRET (1836-1932)

We remind our readers that posters produced by Chéret at his own printing plant (Imp. Jules Chéret) before its 1881 merger with Chaix are especially rare and most collectable. This statement applies to the first five offerings by the artist seen here.

249. Casino Skating-Bal. 1876.
$15^1/_2$ x $23^1/_8$ in./39.5 x 58.7 cm
Imp. J. Chéret, Paris
Cond B+/Slight tears at edges.
Ref: Broido, 354; Maindron, 286; PAI-XXXVIII, 258
With a quadrille of skaters that appear to be prepared to break into a *pas de quatre* at a moment's notice, Chéret promotes a roller-skating rink on the Rue Cadet. The entire scenario is so theatrical—most-especially in the balletic bent of the gentlemen skater's quasi-militaristic outfits—that one almost has to believe there was an unadvertised roller-dance presentation that went along with the advertised "brillant orchestre." *Rare!*
Est: $1,500-$1,800.

250. Le Chateau à Toto. 1868.
$21^5/_8$ x $29^1/_4$ in./55 x 74.3 cm
Imp. J. Chéret, Paris
Cond B+/Slight water stains at paper edges.
Ref: Broido, 27; Maindron, 20; French Opera, 16; PAI-XLI, 182
On sea-green tinted paper, Chéret utilizes black and white as his only colors in this episodic design for frequent collaborator J. Offenbach's comic opera, "Le Chateau à Toto." "Offenbach, the son of the cantor of the Cologne synagogue, came to Paris as a youth. He played in the orchestra of the Opera-Comique, managed several theaters and wrote more than 100 theatrical works, with which he established the tradition of French operetta . . . This is one of the earliest color lithograph posters in existence today" (French Opera, p. xix.).
Est: $1,200-$1,500.

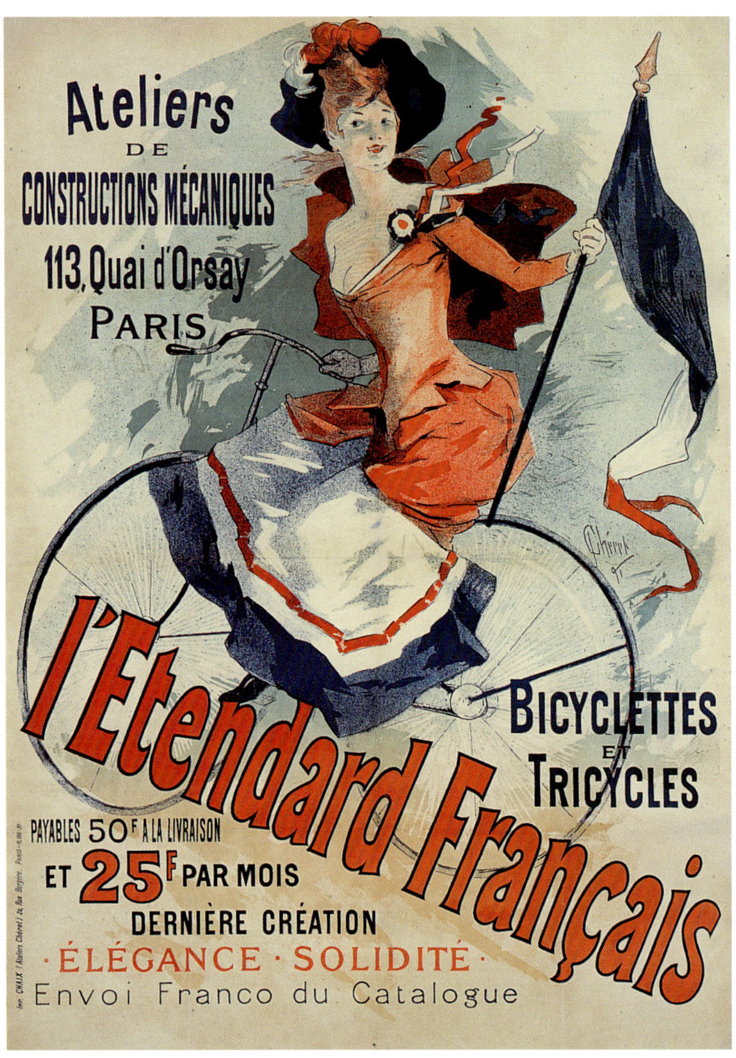

254

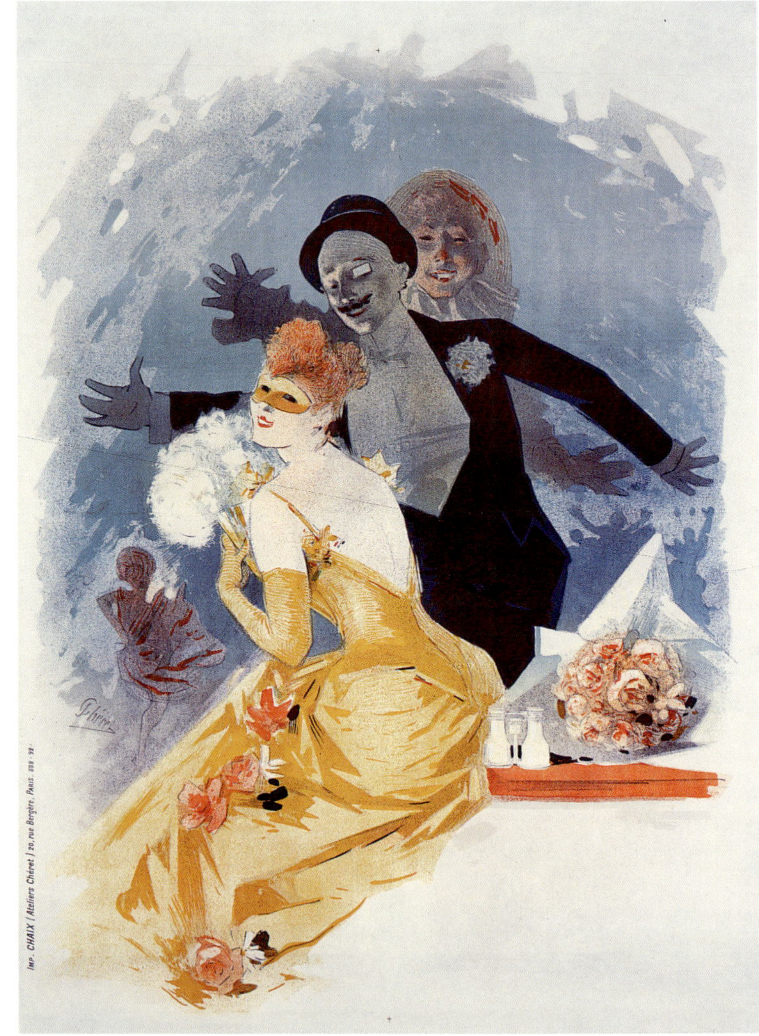

255

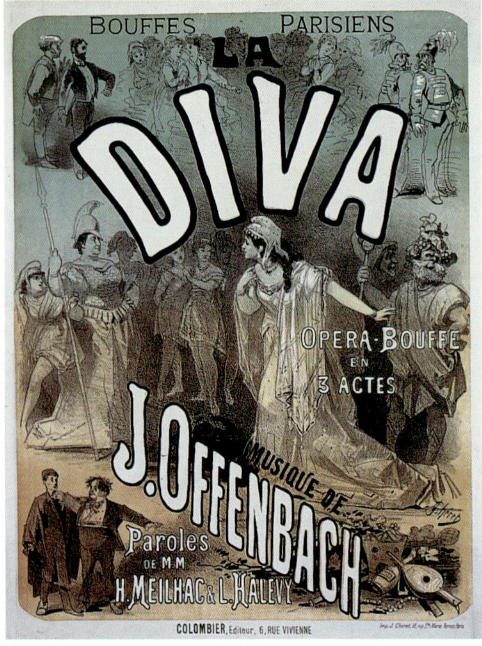

251

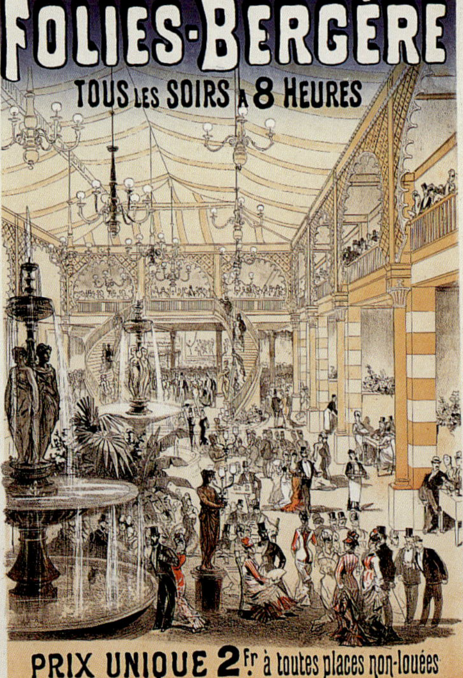

252

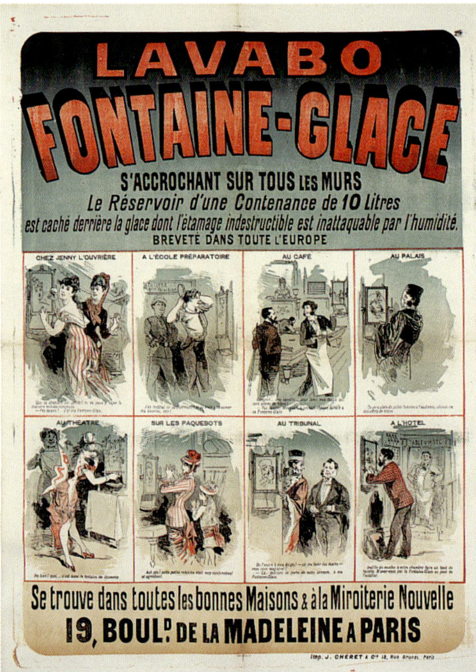

253

JULES CHÉRET (cont'd)

251. La Diva. 1868.
21³/₈ x 29³/₈ in./54.3 x 74.6 cm
Imp. J. Chéret, Paris
Cond B+/Slight tears at folds and edges.
Ref: Broido, 30; Maindron, 26; Theaterplakate, 12;
 PAI-XXXV, 239
What's in a name? In this case, virtually everything.
"La Diva" is "the Mailhuc/Halévy/Offenbach homage to
Hortense Schneider, a thinly veiled musical autobiog-
raphy of the actress with new songs" (Operetta, p. 64).
Chéret's duo-tone potpourri gives the viewer an excel-
lent theatrical sweep, presenting a goodly amount of
what's in store for them. It should be noted that many
of Chéret's earliest posters, in the 1860s, were created
for the Offenbach operettas.
Est: $1,500-$1,800.

252. Folies-Bergère/Tous les Soirs. 1878.
15⁷/₈ x 23³/₄ in./40.5 x 60.2 cm
Imp. Jules Chéret, Paris
Cond A.
Ref: Broido, 98; Maindron, 93; Folies-Bergère, 34 (var)
"This poster by Chéret depicts a view of the Folies-
Bergère after the director, Sari, had bought the adjoin-
ing bedding store in 1875 and laid out the garden and
the covered promenade . . . In *Les Croquis Parisiens* .
. . the great writer J. K. Huysmans accurately described
the Folies-Bergère . . . "What is truly admirable, truly
unique, is the outdoor character of this theater. It is
ugly and it is superb, it is of an outrageous yet exquisite
taste. The garden with its upper galleries, its arcades
cut out like coarse wooden lace, with its full diamond
and its hollow trefoil, tinted in red and gold ochre, the
garnet-red and tawny striped ceiling made of cloth with
ornamental tufts and tassels, its imitation Louvois
fountains with three women back-to-back between two
enormous imitation bronze saucers, planted in the

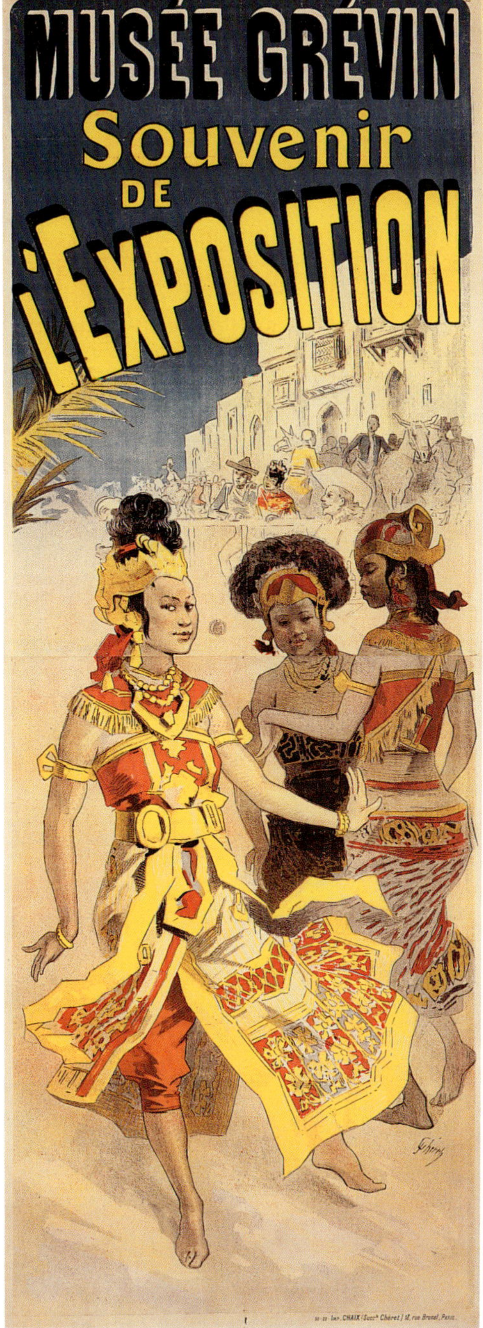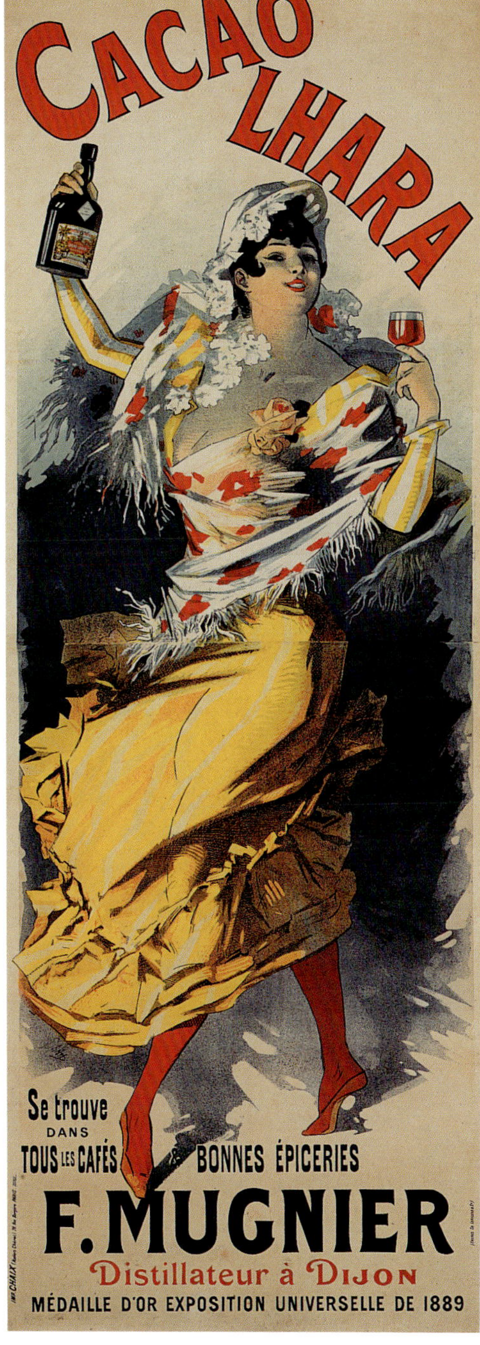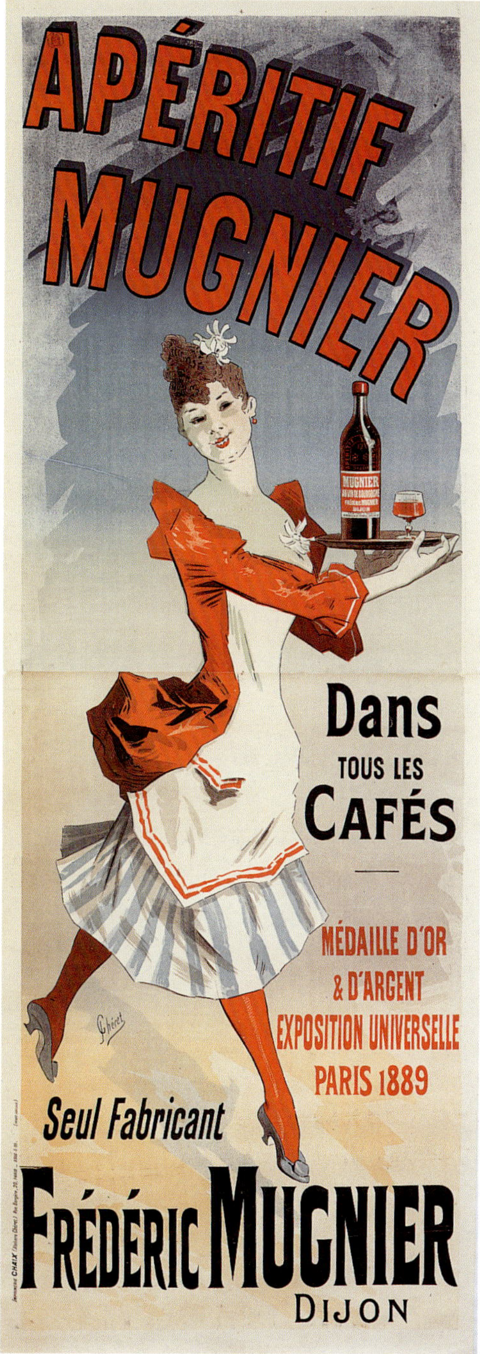

256 **257** **258**

midst of green tufts, its walks covered with tables, rattan couches, chairs and counters staffed with fiercely rouged women, resembles at the same time the rush of the rue Montesquieu and an Algerian or Turkish bazaar . . . Alhambra-Poret, Duvel-Moorish with, in addition, a vague odor of old suburban outdoor saloons, embellished with Oriental colonnades and mirrors, this theater, with a playhouse whose faded red and dirty gold clashes with the spanking new luxury of the sham garden, is the only place in Paris which reeks as exquisitely of the make-up of paid love and the bark of the wearied corruptions" (Folies-Bergère, p. 8).
Est: $1,200-$1,500.

253. Lavabo/Fontaine-Glace. 1879.
35 x 49³/4 in./89 x 126.3 cm
Imp. J. Chéret, Paris
Cond B/Slight tears and stains at folds.
Ref: Broido, 1025; Maindron, 848
Mirror, mirror on the wall, what's the fairest washbasin/ mirror combo of them all? The answer is surprisingly crystal clear—Fontaine-Glace, the brand with a ten-liter reservoir hidden behind the silvering to stave off the ravages of humidity. Though a single panel would surely have served the purpose of promoting the product's utility, Chéret presents eight charming situations where the quality mirror set comes in handy, ranging from a judge's chambers to a steamship stateroom and almost everywhere in-between. *Rare!*
Est: $2,000-$2,500.

254. L'Etendard Français. 1891.
33⁷/8 x 48¹/2 in./86 x 123 cm
Imp. Chaix, Paris
Cond B+/Unobtrusive tears at folds.
Ref: Broido, 998; Maindron, 820; Reims, 345;
    DFP-II, 219; Bicycle Posters, 52; PAI-XL, 21
The bicyclist—appropriately in blue, white and red— holds the banner of the bicycle firm whose name means "banner" as well as "standard," both obviously implied in the design. The company offers a payment plan of fifty francs down and twenty-five per month thereafter —but we're not told for how many months! It is somewhat surprising that Chéret prepared only two bicycle posters during a fifty-year career that encompassed the cycling craze.
Est: $3,000-$4,000.

255. Théâtre de l'Opéra/Carnaval 1892.
34¹/2 x 48¹/2 in./87.6 x 123.3 cm
Imp. Chaix, Paris
Cond B+/Slight tears at folds.
Ref (All Var): Broido, 286; Maindron, 244; DFP-II, 228;
    Reims, 294; PAI-XLII, 224
On the first Saturday evening in 1892, the Théâtre National de l'Opéra sponsored a masked ball. The event proved to be understandably popular, and the theater repeated it twice more in February and then again in March, using this same image all four times. The focus of Chéret's poster is an exhilarated couple —he in full-tilt boogie, she perched precariously on

the balcony: The better to see and be seen, my dear. *Before the addition of letters. Rare!*
Est: $5,000-$6,000.

256. Musée Grevin/Souvenir de l'Exposition. 1890.
33³/4 x 94¹/2 in./85.6 x 240 cm
Imp. Chaix, Paris
Cond B+/Slight tears at folds.
Ref: Broido, 466; Maindron, 379; PAI-XLI, 191
The poster advertises a presentation at the Musée Grevin, which made a point of mounting attractions on topical subjects. This entertainment was a retrospective of the 1889 World's Fair in Paris and shows three Javanese women in colorful native dress.
Est: $1,500-$1,800.

257. Cacao Lhara/F. Mugnier. 1893.
33³/4 x 96 in./85.7 x 244 cm
Imp. Chaix, Paris
Cond B+/Slight tears and stains at folds and edges.
Ref: Broido, 864; Maindron, 730; DFP-II, 241;
    PAI-XXXVI, 251
Mugnier's success bottling a cherry-flavored liqueur called Bigarreau (*see* PAI-XXXVI, 251) eventually enabled him to expand until he had the largest distillery in the Dijon area. In this two-sheet design, the drink being advertised is a chocolate-flavored one in Mugnier's prize-winning line, and Chéret offers it to us from the hand of a dark-haired temptress in a mantilla and shawl.
Est: $2,500-$3,000.

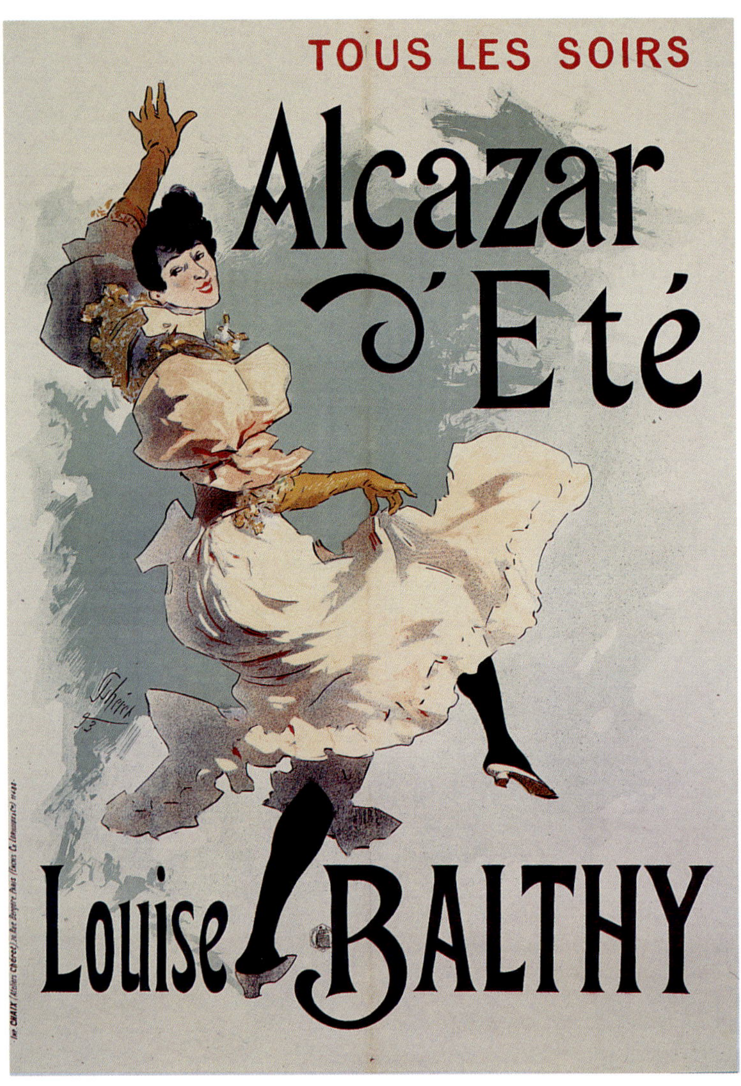

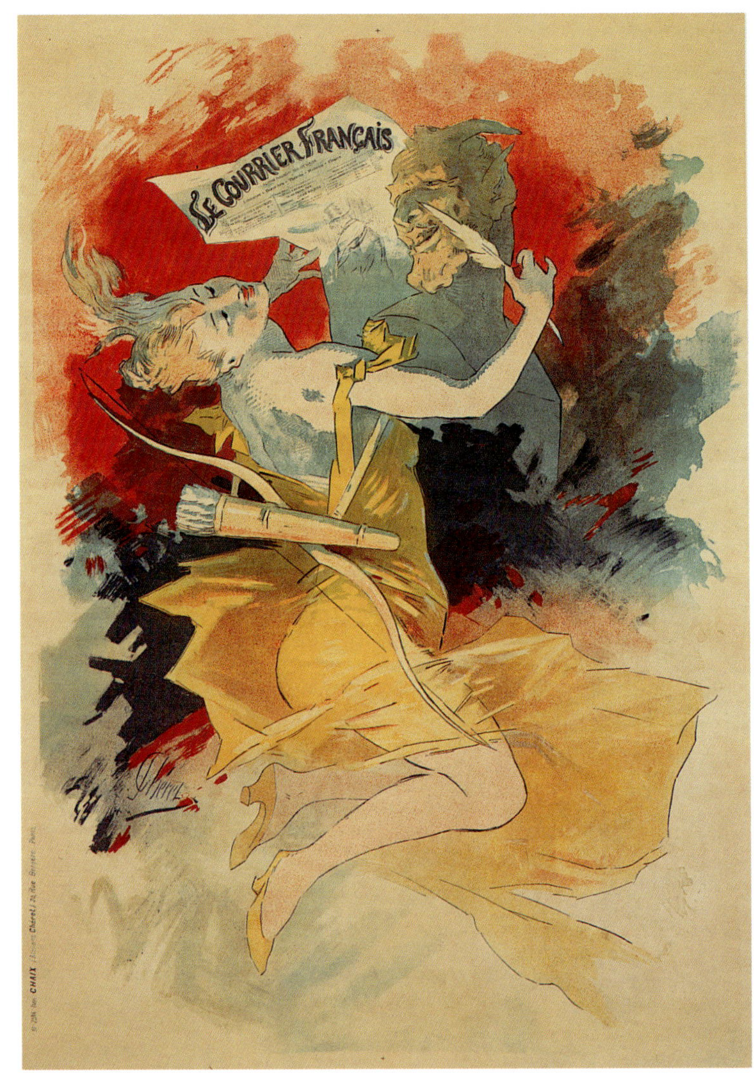

259

260

JULES CHÉRET (cont'd)

258. Apéritif Mugnier. 1895.
34^1/$_2$ x 97^1/$_4$ in./87.5 x 247 cm
Imp. Chaix, Paris
Cond B+/Unobtrusive folds.
Ref: Broido, 861; Maindron, 727; PAI-XLII, 234
The pert, sweet-faced waitress alone is enough to convince us of the merits of the beverage, and Chéret appears to be aware of it, as he leaves out all background in this 2-sheet design other than shaded blue. The client was a company started in 1863 by Frédéric Mugnier, who prepared a potion from a wine base flavored with blackberries and cherries. *This is a rare version of the design printed seven years prior to the more-commonly seen version of the poster that advertises the beverage as Quinquina Mugnier.*
Est: $2,500-$3,000.

259. Alcazar d'Eté/Louise Balthy. 1893.
33^3/$_4$ x 48^1/$_2$ in./85.7 x 123.2 cm
Imp. Chaix, Paris
Cond A–/Slight stains at folds.
Ref: Broido, 173; Maindron, 153; Spectacle, 828;
   PAI-XXXVI, 253
Looking over her shoulder, the performer executes a nimble step. The pointy-chinned Balthy (1869-1925) was a well-known interpreter of humorous songs who had already become a headliner at the Eldorado at the age of seventeen; later she worked at other cabarets, including the Scala, the Bodinière and, here, at the Alcazar d'Eté. Cappiello showed her almost ten years later, at the Folies-Bérgère (*see* No. 192).
Est: $2,500-$3,000.

260. Le Courrier Français. 1891.
32^3/$_8$ x 47^1/$_8$ in./72.2 x 119.7 cm
Imp. Chaix, Paris
Cond B+/A few restored tears.
Ref: Broido, 580; Maindron, 470; Maitres, 49;
   DFP-II, 216; Fit to Print, 112; PAI-IX, 224
This charming design with a centered shapely fairy was

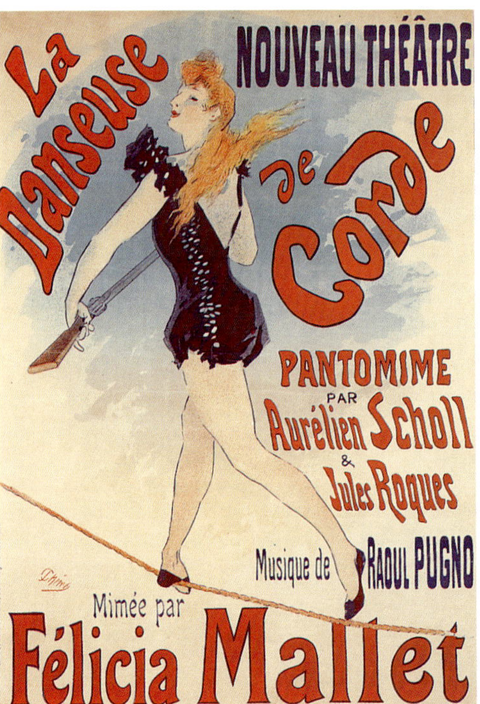

261

used in several ways. The well-traveled sprite was used to advertise two art exhibitions arranged by *Le Courrier Français*, it was used as a circulation promotion for the newspaper without the appearance of text (this is the version seen here), it was sold in several editions as artwork for the home, and lastly, in a reduced format it was used as a supplement to the magazine's March 28 issue.
Est: $2,500-$3,000.

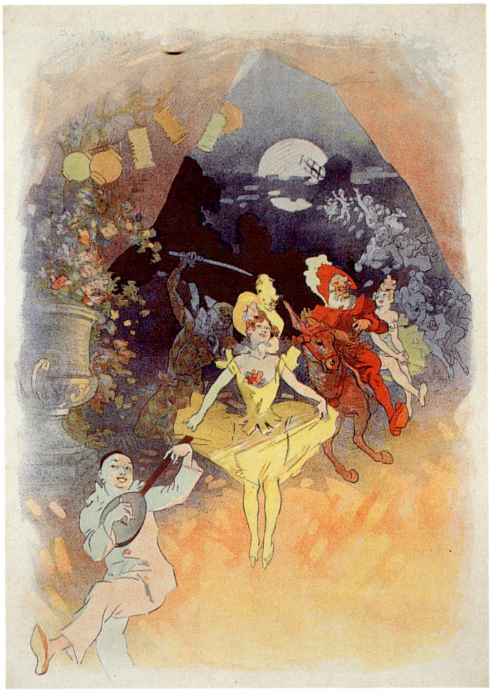

262

261. Nouveau Théâtre/La Danseuse de Corde. 1891.
33^1/$_2$ x 48^1/$_8$ in./85 x 122.2 cm
Imp. Chaix, Paris
Cond B–/Slight tears at folds and edges. Framed.
Ref: Broido, 244; Maindron, 208; Reims, 324;
   PAI-XXXVII, 247
Both the inaugural ("Scaramouche") and this second offering starred Félicia Mallet—and both posters were designed by Chéret. Clearly she was as accomplished an acrobat as she was a mime. Chéret shows her in a spangly costume, navigating the slack wire with a rifle

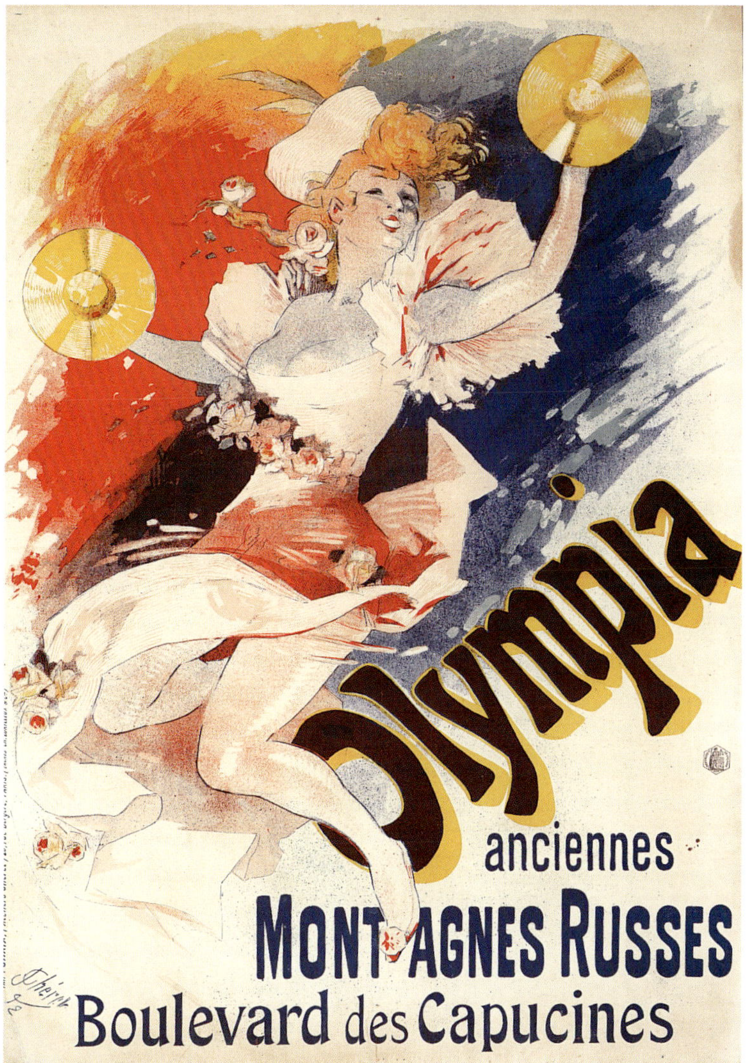

263

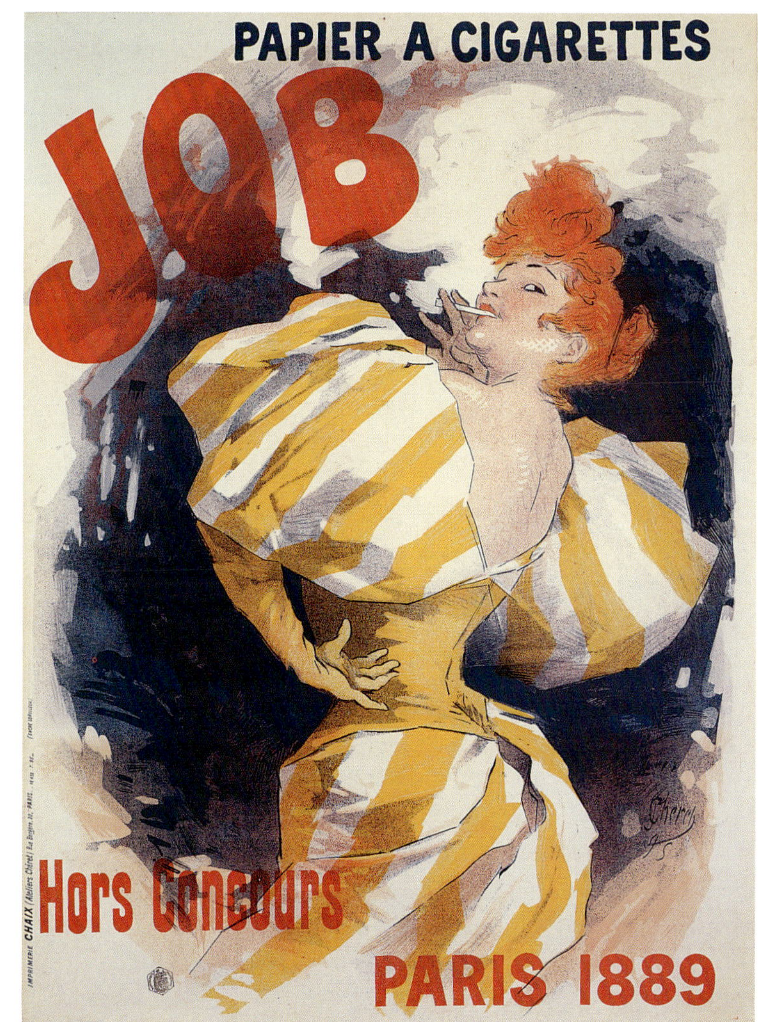

264

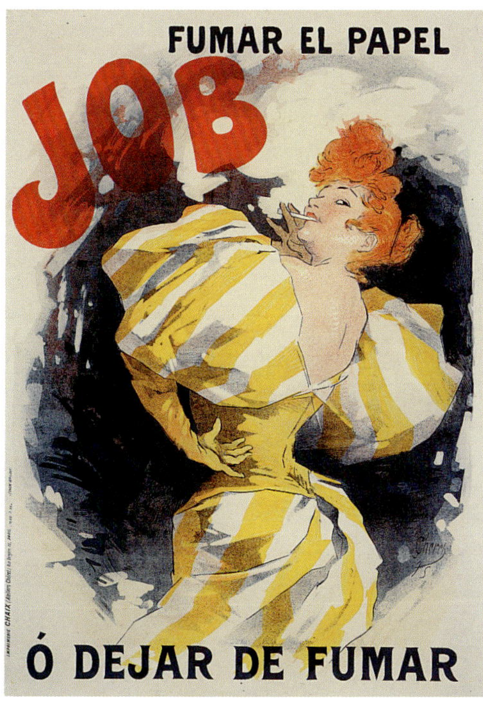

265

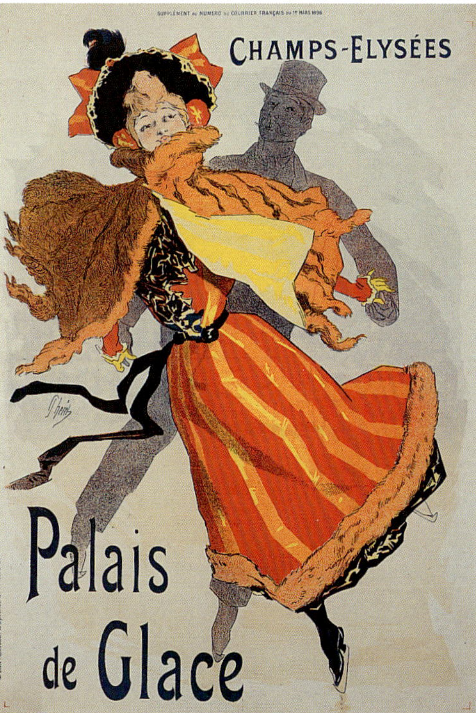

266

263. Olympia/Anciennes Montagnes Russes. 1893.
33 x 47$^1/_2$ in./83.8 x 120.6 cm
Imp. Chaix, Paris
Cond B/Unobtrusive folds; water stain at right edge.
   Framed.
Ref: Broido, 345; Maindron, 278; Gold, 146;
   Maitres, 133; DFP-II, 225; Folies Bergère, 28;
   Masters 1900, p. 12; PAI-XLII, 231
With éclat and élan, to say nothing of a pair of cymbals, the ebullient, unabashedly hedonistic sprite calls us to the Olympia to enjoy the "Russian mountains"—French term for the rollercoaster. The poster was used for the opening of this new establishment, in April of 1893; it was one of the first places in Paris that called itself a "music-hall," borrowing a word from British show business. There was a bumpy ride as an added attraction to the usual stage spectacles, but to call it a rollercoaster was probably somewhat euphemistic. *This is the larger format.*
Est: $3,500-$4,000.

264. Job/Papier à Cigarettes. 1895.
33$^7/_8$ x 46$^5/_8$ in./86 x 118.5 cm
Imp. Chaix, Paris
Cond A–/Slight tears at paper edges; very fresh colors.
Ref: Broido, 1028; Maindron, 850; Maitres, 1; DFP-II, 255;
   Reims, 465; Wine Spectator, 6; PAI-XLI, 214
The defiant gesture of an emancipated woman daring to flout conventional manners is caught with perfection; the fact that it happened over a century ago adds to its piquancy. One of Chéret's best and most famous designs.
Est: $5,000-$6,000.

265. Job/Fumar el Papel. ca. 1895.
34$^1/_8$ x 48$^1/_2$ in./86.8 x 123 cm
Imp. Chaix, Paris
Cond A.
Ref: Broido, 1030
This is the rare Spanish-language version of the previous design.
Est: $5,000-$6,000.

in hand, leaving one to question if perhaps a well-balanced display of marksmanship wasn't an uncredited portion of the evening's festivities as well.
Est: $1,400-$1,700.

262. Musée Grévin/Fantoches de John Hewelt. 1900.
34$^1/_4$ x 48$^1/_2$ in./87.2 x 123.4 cm
Imp. Chaix, Paris (not shown)
Cond A–/Slight tears and stains at edges.
Ref: Broido, 471; DFP-II, 267; PAI-XLII, 237
This is the before-lettering version of Chéret's charming poster for *Les Fantoches*, a puppet-show extravaganza staged at the theater of the Musée Grevin, a frequent Chéret client—in fact, the design was so eye-catching that it was also used to announce a *Fête des Artistes* at the venue (*see* PAI-XV, 222). Some versions of the image show the printer's name, while others, such as this, have no text at all. With text or word-free, Chéret's fine sense of composition and great lithographic skill shine.
Est: $2,000-$2,500.

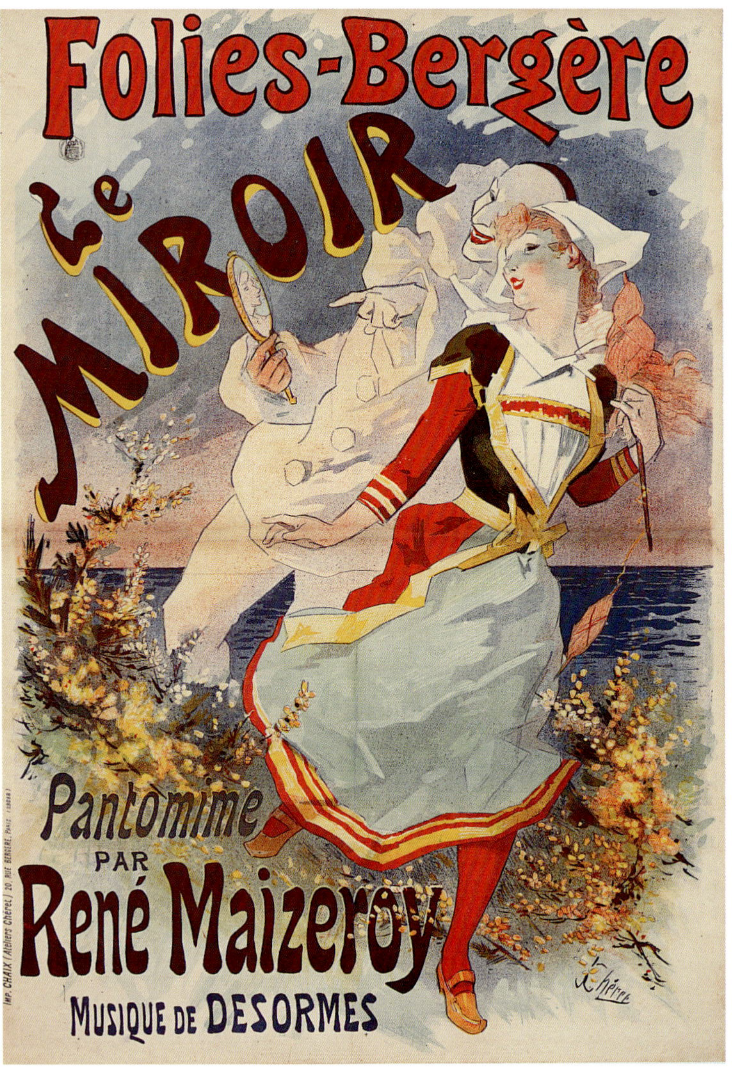

267

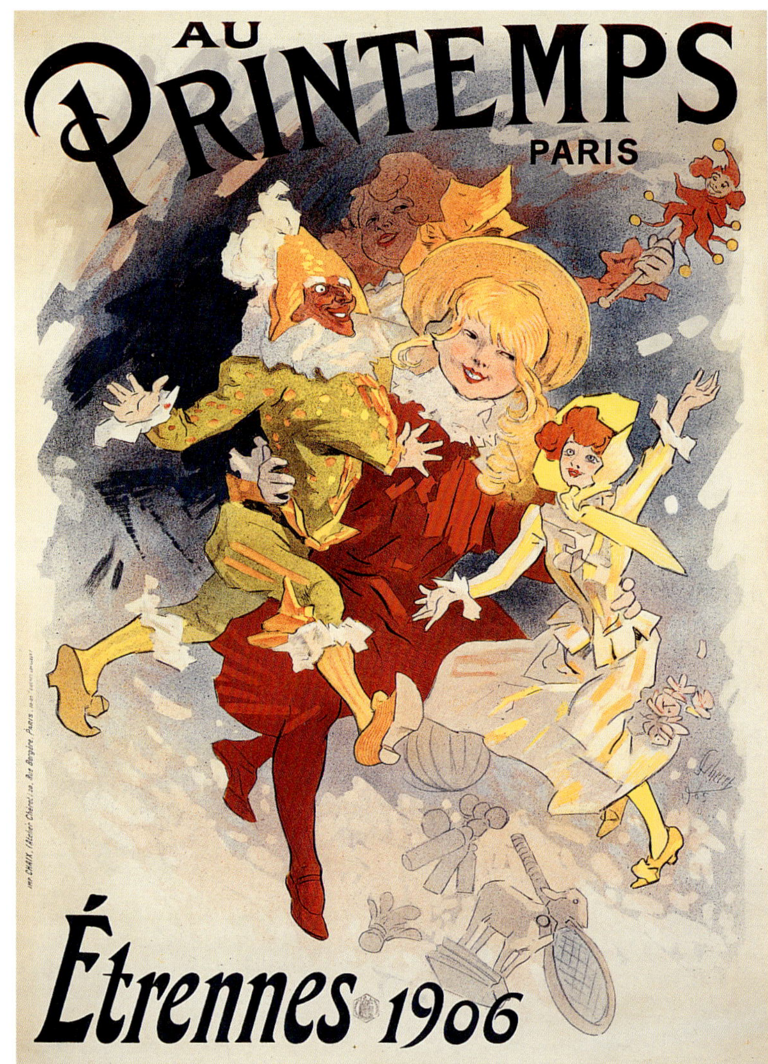

268

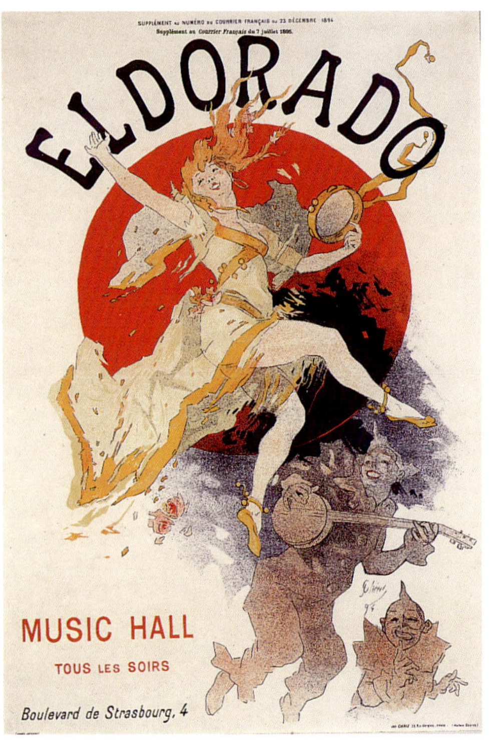

269

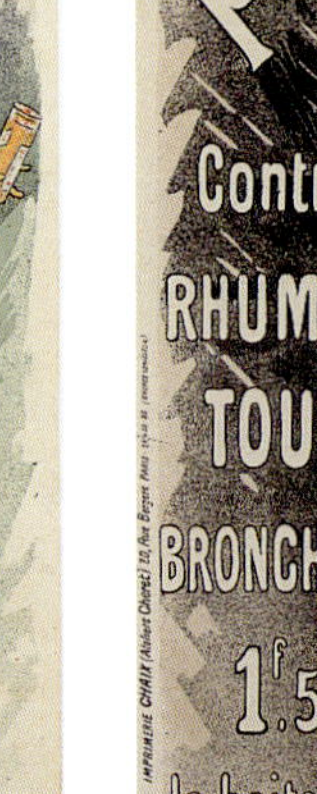

270

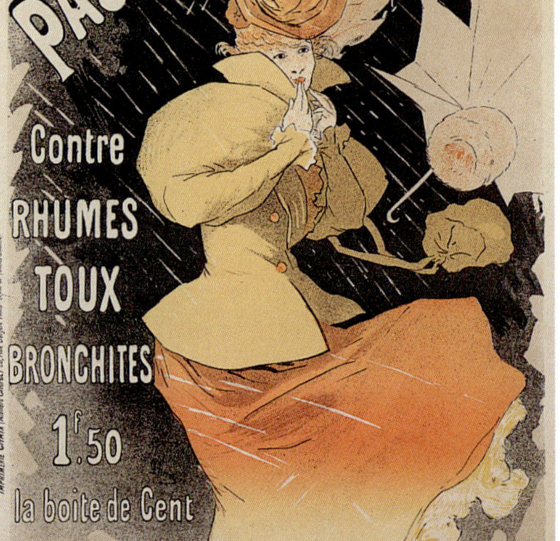

271

JULES CHERET (cont'd)

266. Palais de Glace. 1896.
$15^{1}/_{4}$ x $22^{1}/_{2}$ in./38.7 x 57 cm
Imp. Chaix, Paris
Cond A.
Ref: Broido, 371; PAI-XXIX, 305
The skater in the red-and-yellow striped skirt is one of the loveliest of the several designs—always with a shadowy top-hatted male figure in the background—that Chéret created for the Paris ice-skating rink between

1893 and 1900. *This is the Courrier Français version.*
Est: $2,700-$3,000.

267. Folies-Bergère/Le Miroir. 1892.
$33^{1}/_{4}$ x $48^{3}/_{8}$ in./84.4 x 122.8 cm
Imp. Chaix, Paris
Cond B–/Restored tears at folds.
Ref: Broido, 122; Maindron, 110; Maitres, 157;
  DFP-II, 224; PAI-XLI, 199
In this charming poster for a musical pantomime at the Folies-Bergère, Chéret shows actress René Maizeroy in

Dutch costume, complete with wooden shoes, cavorting alongside the sea. Her companion, a lightly sketched Pierrot, holds up the mirror mentioned in the entertainment's title.
Est: $2,000-$2,500.

268. Au Printemps/Etrennes. 1905.
$34^{1}/_{2}$ x $48^{3}/_{4}$ in./87.7 x 123.9 cm
Imp. Chaix, Paris
Cond A–/Restored tears; vibrant colors.
Ref: Broido, 695; PAI-VIII, 83

For the toy department of the Printemps department store, Chéret drew a grinning little girl carrying dolls nearly her own size—a highly engaging scene. Chéret's first design for the store was carried out in 1880; twenty-five years later, he executed his last one for this—or any other—store and he displays that he clearly hasn't lost his touch. It is, in fact, his very best design in the series. *Rare!*
Est: $5,000-$6,000.

269. Eldorado/Courrier Français. 1894.
$14^3/_8$ x $21^1/_8$ in./36.5 x 53.6 cm
Imp. Chaix, Paris
Cond A. Framed.
Ref: Broido, 218; PAI-XLII, 225
The dancer is boundless joy personified, and the red spotlight on her adds to the impact of this vivacious work. This version is from the series Chéret contributed to the *Courrier Français*, a lively 12-page weekly magazine, started in 1894, which championed the work of many leading posterists. But this isn't the design's first appearance in that newspaper; that version hails from some six-and-a-half months prior. Apparently this airborne gypsy was popular enough to bring back for a return engagement with slightly altered text down-left.
Est: $2,000-$2,500.

270. Pastilles Géraudel. 1896.
$15^1/_8$ x $22^1/_4$ in./38.5 x 56.5 cm
Imp. Chaix, Paris
Cond A–/Slight tears at folds and paper edges; usual horizontal fold; colors excellent.
Ref: Broido, 911; PAI-XLI, 208
Prancing through a blizzard as if she were two-stepping through falling cherry blossoms, this blithe figure is courting a cough that only Géraudel lozenges could fend off. Which makes perfect sense since their common sense slogan, "'If you cough, take Géraudel Pastilles' appears like a leitmotiv in all the publicity campaigns for the product, whether in France, or as far abroad as China . . . This is one of the most striking examples of the work by Jules Chéret . . . The clarity of the color is astonishing and denotes the influence of Impressionist painting" (Health Posters, p. 14). *This is the Courrier Français version.*
Est: $2,500-$3,000.

271. Pastilles Poncelet. 1896.
$15^1/_4$ x $27^1/_2$ in./38.8 x 57.2 cm
Imp. Chaix, Paris
Cond B+/Slight stains at folds and edges.
Ref: DFP-II, 260 (var); Broido, 911;
        Health Posters, 29 (var); Gold, 33; PAI-XL, 306
"With consummate mastery, this poster does credit to the artist as both illustrator and poster designer . . . Its dynamic hinges on the opposition between the violence of the storm and the serene resistance of the young girl . . . This symbolism is engaged to support the message of the publicity slogan ('For Colds—Coughs—Bronchitis'). Pastilles Poncelet were made from tar, licorice, ipecac, codeine and potassium chlorate" (Health Posters, p. 31). *This is the Courrier Français format.*
Est: $1,000-$1,200.

272. Femme brunne au bonnet.
$13^1/_2$ x $15^1/_2$ in./33.7 x 39.4 cm
Hand-signed oil painting on canvas. Framed.
Provenance: Collection A. Astre (noted verso)
Exhibited: "Exposition-Retrospective Jules Chéret," Grand Palais, Paris, November 1933 (Cat #1963)
No disrespect to the cavalcade of *Chérettes* that have pranced their way through countless graphic works by the artist over the years, but this russet-haired beauty in oil has something that they simply don't possess: a personality that is all her own. Though at times it would seem that the majority of those lithographic cuties were patterned after the same model, it's abundantly clear that they weren't modeled after *this* woman: disheveled, perhaps a drink or two into the evening and deliciously lickerish, she looks like a woman on the prowl. Especially since she's something that we don't typically see from Chéret—an overtly-sexual female—this gorgeous woman comes across as an immediate standout. As if you couldn't see that for yourself.
Est: $12,000-$15,000.

273. Portrait de Mlle S. Guyot.
$12^1/_4$ x $16^1/_2$ in./31 x 42 cm
Hand-signed oil painting on canvas. Framed.
Provenance: Collection A. Astre.
Exhibited: "Exposition-Retrospective Jules Chéret," Grand Palais, Paris, November 1933 (Cat #1964)
Far more respectable than her auburn-tressed counterpart (*see* No. 272) this bonneted, apple-cheeked brunette is nonetheless a fine example of the depths of the artist's non-lithographic capacity and artistic sensitivity. "Chéret's success as a poster artist overshadowed his work in drawings, pastels and oils. Since he neither showed at the Salons nor placed his fine art with a gallery (he sold directly to interested clients), his paintings were not seen by the general public until 1912. In that year, a large exhibition of his original works was held at the Louvre's Pavillon de Marsan. Visitors for whom Chéret's posters were a part of the daily life of Paris were astonished by his ability as a fine artist" (Broido, p. xiii).
Est: $12,000-$15,000.

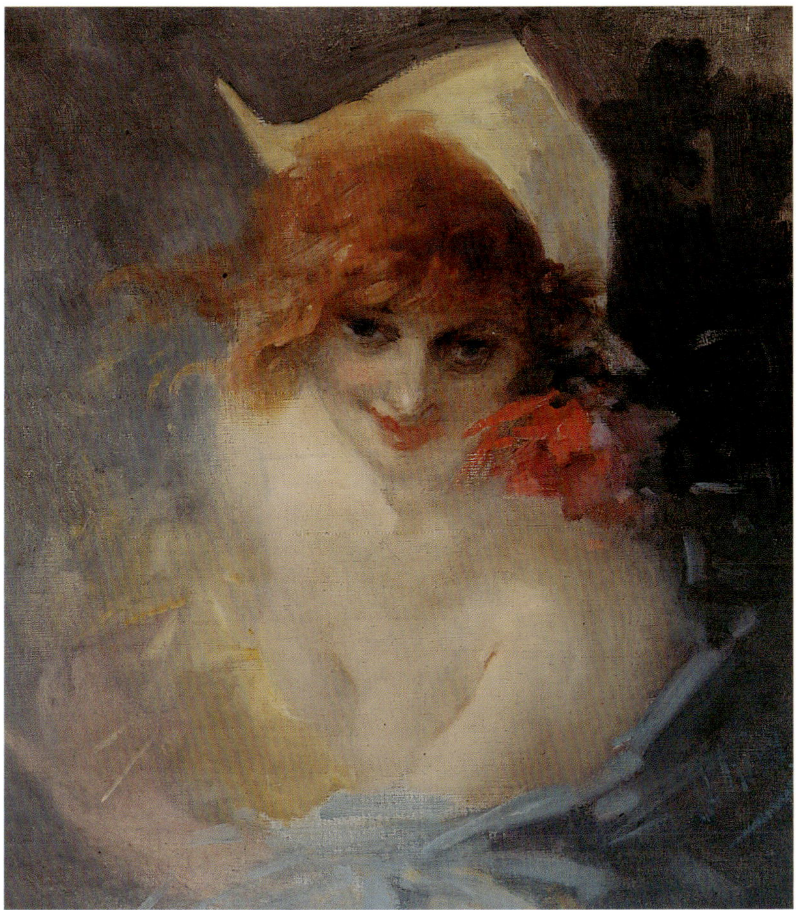

272

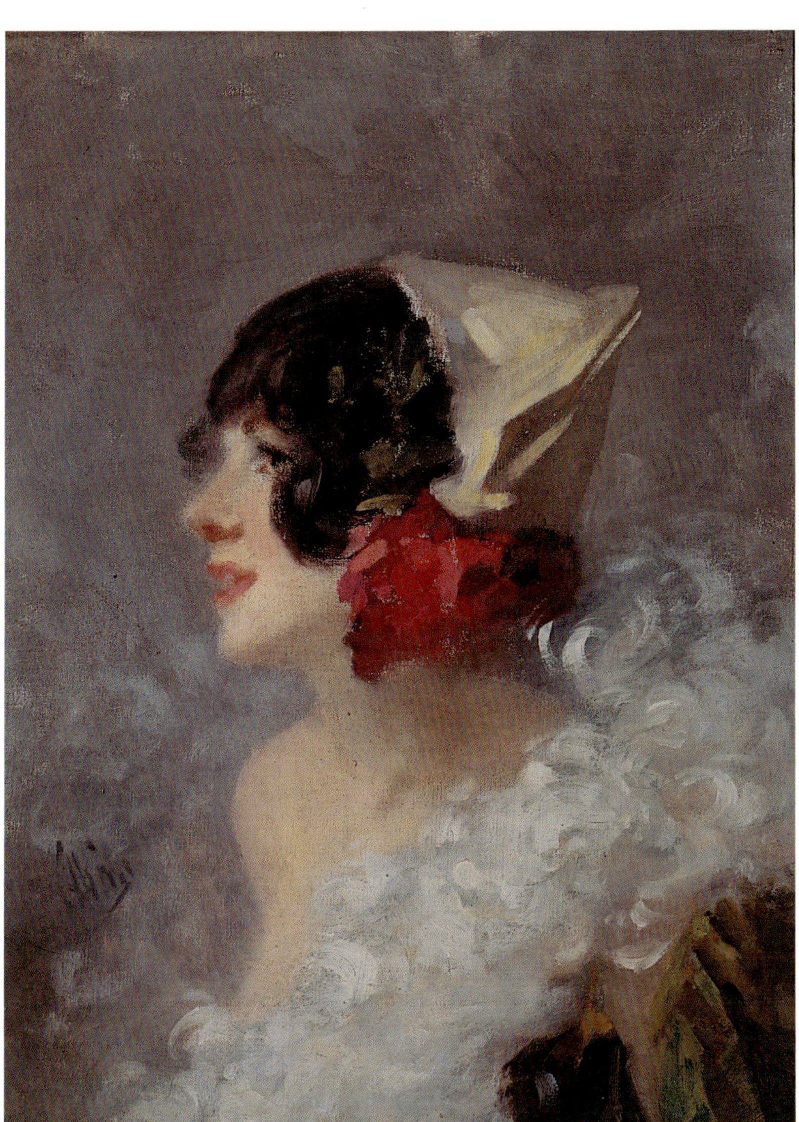

273

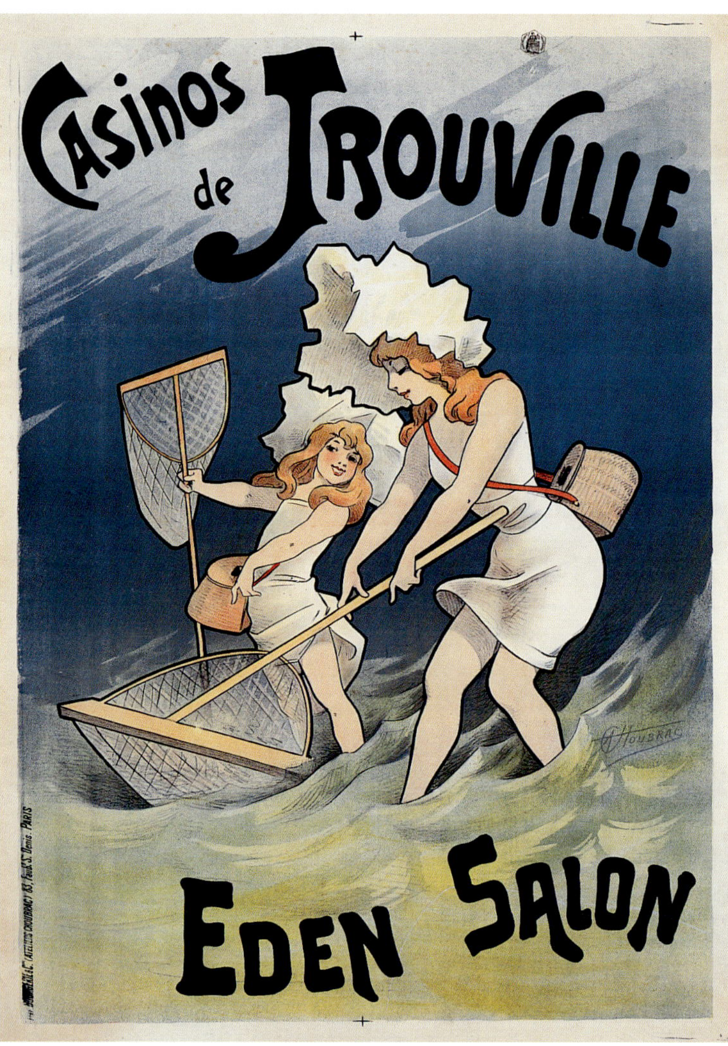

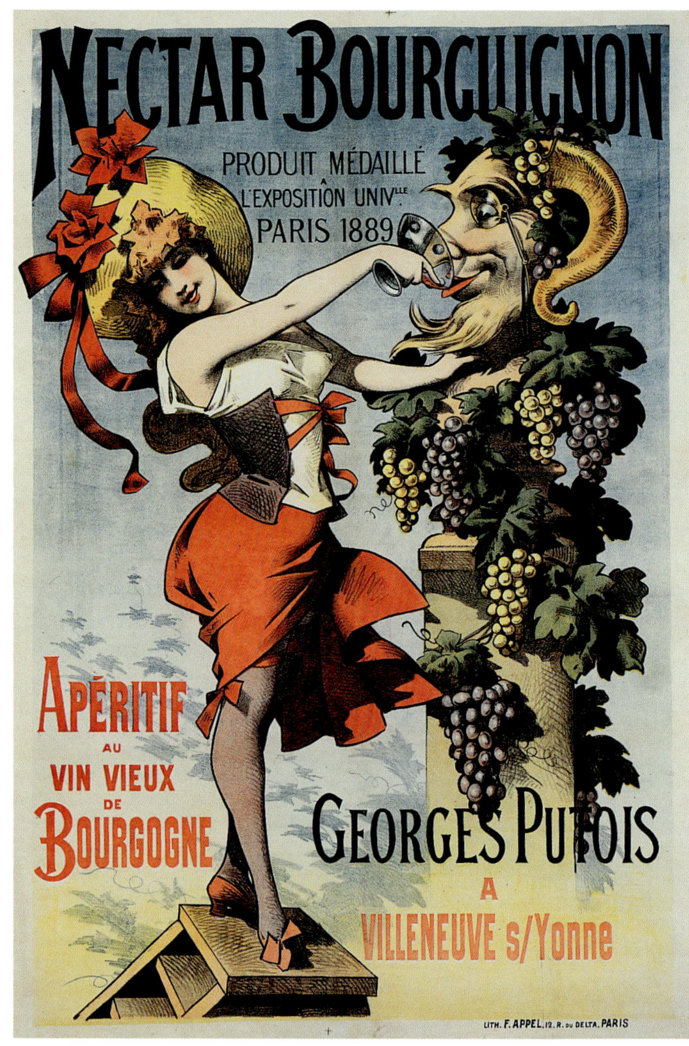

274

275

ALFRED CHOUBRAC (1853-1902)

274. Casinos de Trouville. ca. 1897.
35⅝ x 49¾ in./90.5 x 126.3 cm
Imp. Bourgerie, Paris
Cond A–/Unobtrusive folds.
Ref: PAI-XXVII, 374
It's questionable what these two lovely young ladies hope to catch in the surf, but their smart sense of fashion and sunny dispositions are sure to ensnare the attention of the style savvy beach-goers sharing the strand of the Trouville resort. Choubrac, as always, is clever enough to put the feel of the message above cluttering detail. The artist was one of the pioneers of French poster art; in 1884, when Maindron published his first article on posters, he listed only nine active posterists known to him, and included the three poster artists whose work made up the first poster exhibition, held that same year in the Passage Vivienne in Paris: Alfred and Léon Choubrac, and Jules Chéret.
Est: $2,000-$2,500.

275. Nectar Bourguignon. 1891.
38⅜ x 58⅞ in./97.5 x 149.6 cm
Lith. F. Appel, Paris
Cond A–/Unobtrusive folds.
Ref: Reims, 567; DFP-II, 273; Maindron, p. 53; PAI-XXVII, 373
She's so winsome and the aperitif made from aged burgundy is so delicious that a bust of Bacchus himself comes alive to drink it down. Another testament to the tipple's excellence: its medal at the 1889 Paris World's Fair. The poster is unsigned, but the 1896 Reims catalogue as well as Maindron, both clearly indicate that the image is Choubrac's work. It's done in the slightly caricaturistic style he developed at the beginning of his career when he worked for several journals. Sagot immediately put this poster in his 1891 catalogue, offered it for three francs and declared it to be a "très jolie pièce." The following year, Choubrac produced the largest billboard to date—eight sheets—for the same drink, again featuring the figure of Bacchus, but this time surrounded by frolicking villagers. *Rare!*
Est: $3,500-$4,000.

276. Cycles Humber.
38 x 58¾ in./96.7 x 149.2 cm
F. Appel, Paris
Cond A–/Slight tears and stains at paper edges.
Ref: PAI-XXXIX, 239
The importance of the bicycle to women's emancipation is undeniable. The potential for unchaperoned freedom that the transportation afforded is a contribution that is all but incomprehensible to most contemporary women. However, in this promotion for the British-manufactured Humber bicycle, this voluptuous rider in canary chiffon not only seems perilously-dressed in terms of operating a chain-driven vehicle, but a bit astonished as well to be so gloriously on her own; hopefully the effects will wear off for safety's sake. But, in this bedazzled moment, one can't help but be won over by her winsome visage.
Est: $1,700-$2,000.

277. Folies-Bergère/Les Sisters Barrison. 1896.
31½ x 23¾ in./80 x 60.3 cm
Ateliers Choubrac, à la Seine
Cond A–/Unobtrusive folds.
Ref: Folies-Bergère, 82
"Jacques Charles indicates that the five Barrison girls were in fact not 'sisters' at all, that this was solely the imagination and promotion of Marchand, the director of the Folies-Bergère, who put together the first appearance on a Parisian stage of a troupe of chorus girls: Lona . . . Sophia, Inger, Olga and Gertrude helped to make the 90's the finest days of the Folies-Bergère. A. Brisson in his magazine *la Revue Illustrée* described them as follows in 1896: 'Their gallant exercises performed each evening at the Folies-Bergère attract the crowd. What do people like most about them? The pale gold of their hair, the litheness of their bodies, the whiteness of their teeth, the carmine of their smile, the slightly acid freshness of their voices, their mechanical toy waddle, the gracefulness of their slender legs, the sensuous seething of their frilly and beribboned underwear—this kind of charm cannot be explained—it must be experienced' . . . Alfred Choubrac

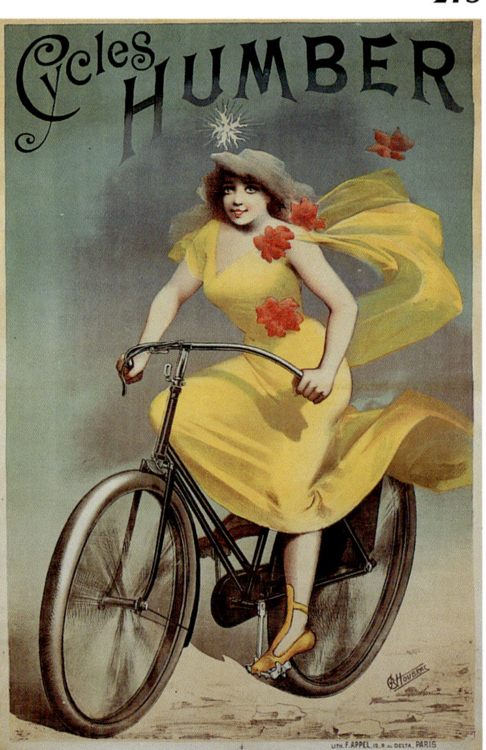

276

. . . depicts them seated in a childish yet perverse pose, smoking cigarettes. Smoking, for a woman, at a time when feminine emancipation was at its very beginning, was shocking, provocative, and something thought poorly of by the bourgeoisie. Their childish appearance adds even more to the scandal except—and the posterist is well-aware of this—when it concerns women which one comes to ogle stealthily in a music hall" (Folies-Bergère, p. 13).
Est: $1,400-$1,700.

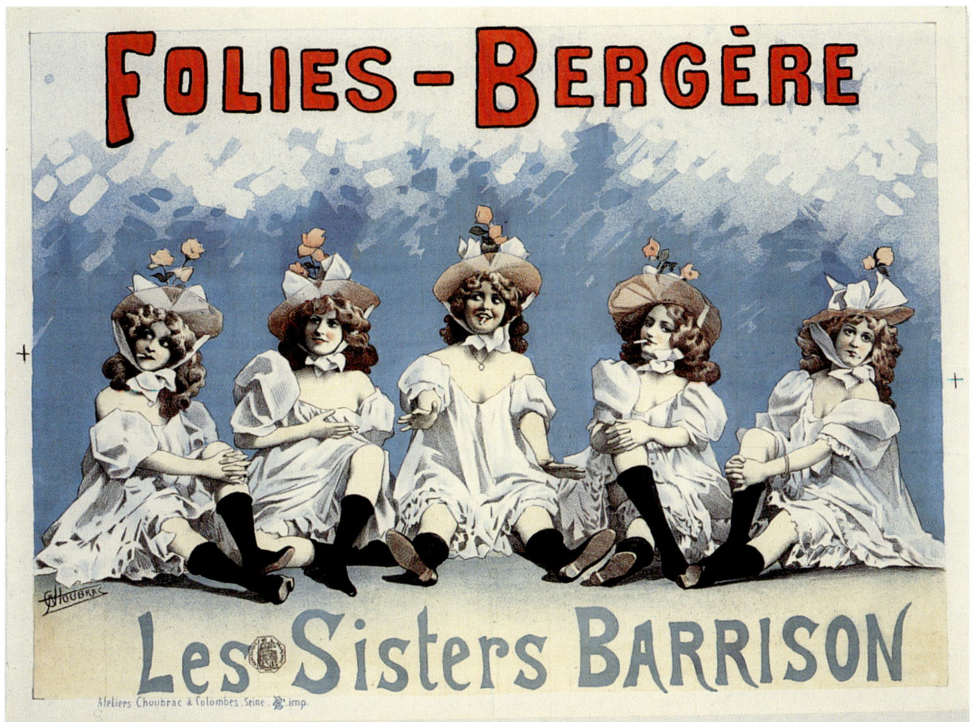

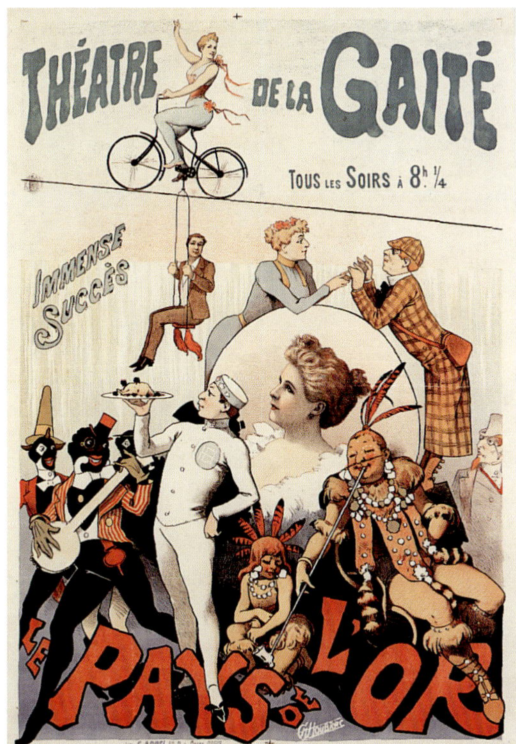

277

278

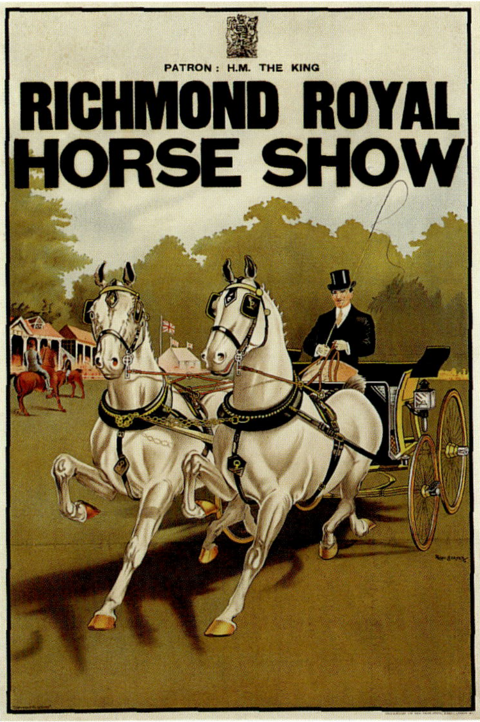

279

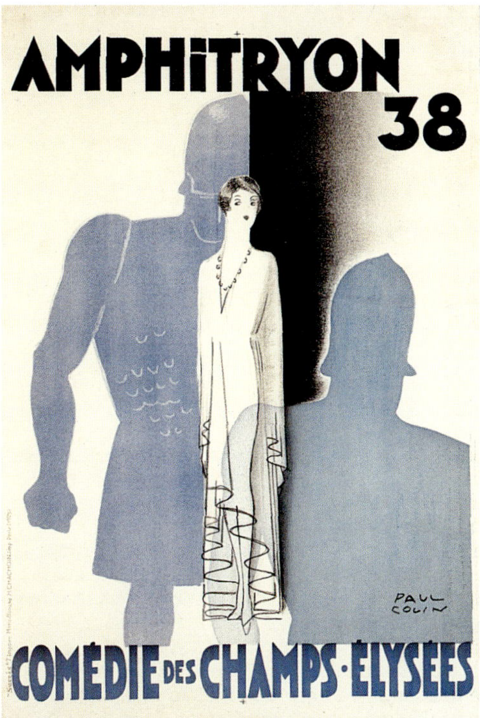

280

281

278. Théâtre de la Gaité/Le Pays de l'Or. ca. 1894.
$32^1/8$ x $47^1/8$ in./81.8 x 119.8 cm
Lith. F. Appel, Paris
Cond B/Slight tears at folds and edges.
Ref: Reims, 573; PAI-XL, 309
Given the time of its production and a few key graphic elements—the trio of minstrels and the peace pipe smoking Native Americans at right—one has to imagine that the "Immense Success" playing at one of Paris' oldest theaters titled "Gold Country" had something to do with the Gold Rush in the western United States. Just precisely how that framework supported the other spectacular elements of the production is somewhat vague seeing as the diversion appears to have had as much impact as theatrical pyrite despite its initial popularity.
Est: $1,400-$1,700.

J. VINCENZ CIZZARZ (1873-1942)

279. Theod. Beyer Lithograph. ca. 1905.
$20^3/8$ x $28^1/2$ in./51.7 x 72.4 cm
Theod. Beyer, Dresden
Cond B+/Slight tears at horizontal folds and edges.
With Art Nouveau reverence, Cizzarz composes this promotion for Dresden's Beyer lithographic firm. It's difficult to tell whether the ebon-clad woman is a benevolent patron of the arts or an angelic muse for

the poster's reverential artist. But in the end it matters very little precisely which function she fulfills in this poster-within-a-poster seeing as the results are refined and sublime regardless of interpretation.
Est: $1,700-$2,000.

RALPH CLEAVER

280. Richmond Royal Horse Show. 1906.
39 x $58^3/4$ in./99.2 x 149.2 cm
Gale & Polden, London
Cond B+/Slight tears at folds.
Under the patronage of His Majesty the King (Edward VII at this point in time) and promoted by a regal team of Arabians, how could anyone believe that the Richmond Royal Horse Show could be anything other than a majestic event. The Richmond Royal Horse Show was started in 1892 by Richmond Park veterinarian W. J. Hatton and grew into a major equestrian event. It became part of the South of England show in 1967, but was revived in the 1990s by local residents, returning to its traditional Old Deer Park venue with the Crown Estates permission. The show has been instrumental in the success of some of Britain's greatest riders.
Est: $1,700-$2,000.

PAUL COLIN (1892-1986)

281. Amphitryon 38. 1929.
$15^1/2$ x $23^1/4$ in./39.3 x 59.1 cm
Imp. H. Chachoin, Paris
Cond B+/Slight tears at paper edges.
Ref: Colin, 37 (var); Colin Affichiste, 12 (var);
    PAI-XLI, 233
The original *Amphitryon* was an ancient Roman comedy by Plautus retelling the myth of Alcmene, a Greek heroine torn between conjugal love for her soldier husband and adulterous lust for the god Jupiter. Playwright Jean Giraudoux updated the story and called it "version 38" to bring attention to the fact that he was not the only one to plagiarize the great classic—others had done so many times before him in various guises. Jean Renoir, not yet the famed film director he was to become, played the role of the Greek soldier Amphitryon. The heroine's conflict is graphically portrayed by Colin: her two temptations are drawn alike, varying only in shades of blue, while she is shown in black and draped in indecision. *This is the smaller format.*
Est: $1,700-$2,000.

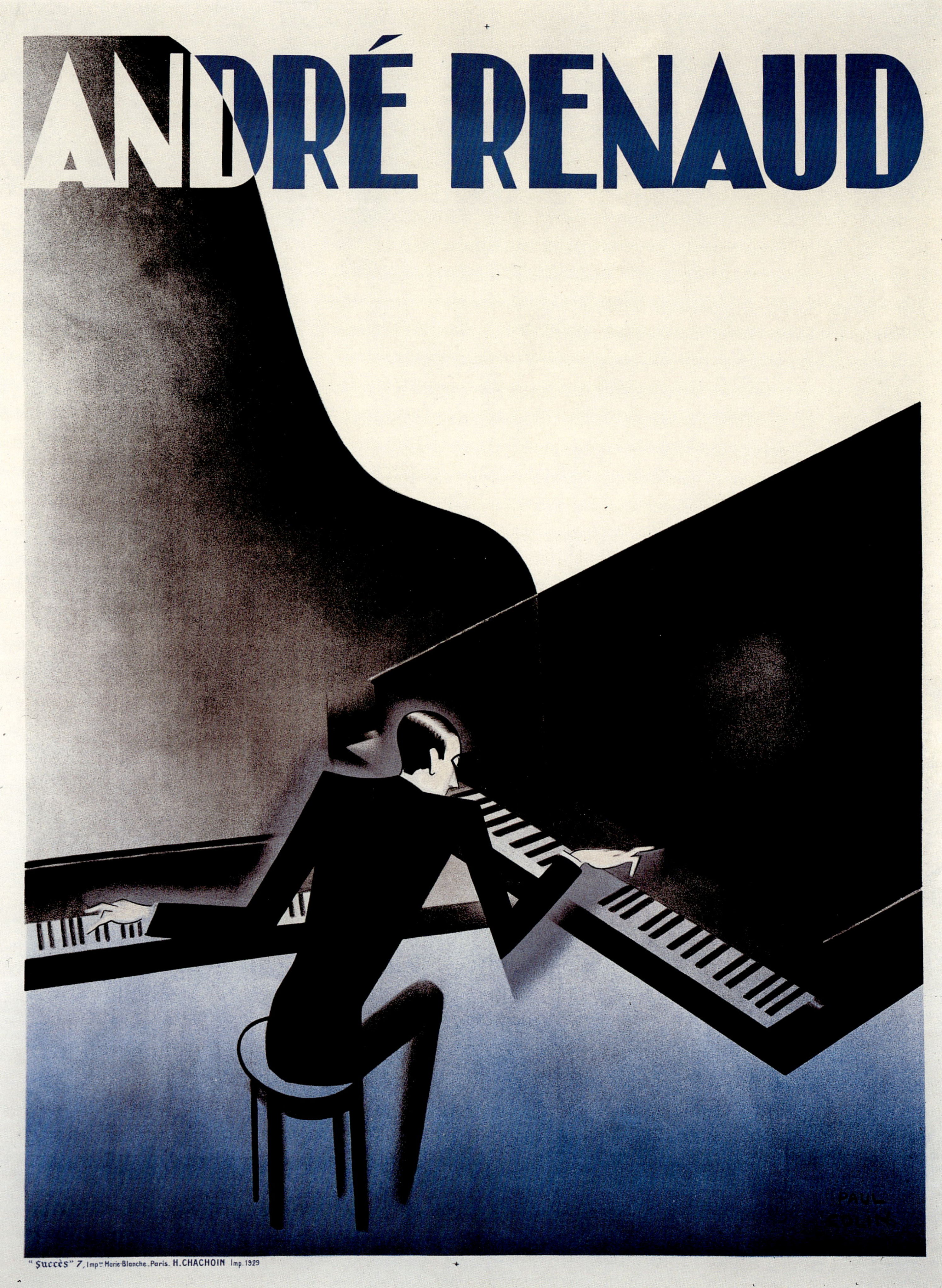

ANDRÉ RENAUD
PAUL COLIN
"Succès" 7, Imp.ᵉ Marie-Blanche.-Paris. H.CHACHOIN Imp.1929

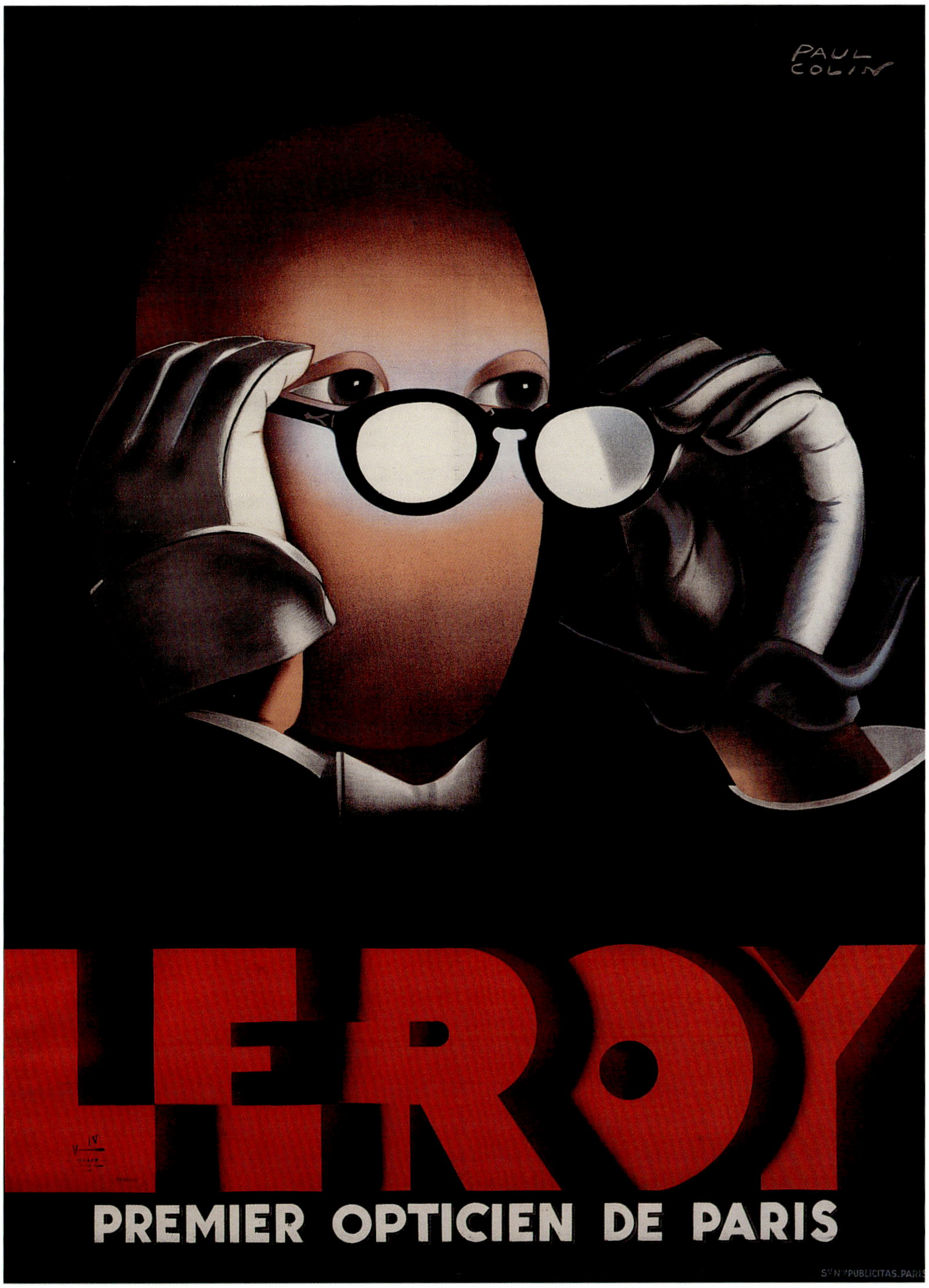

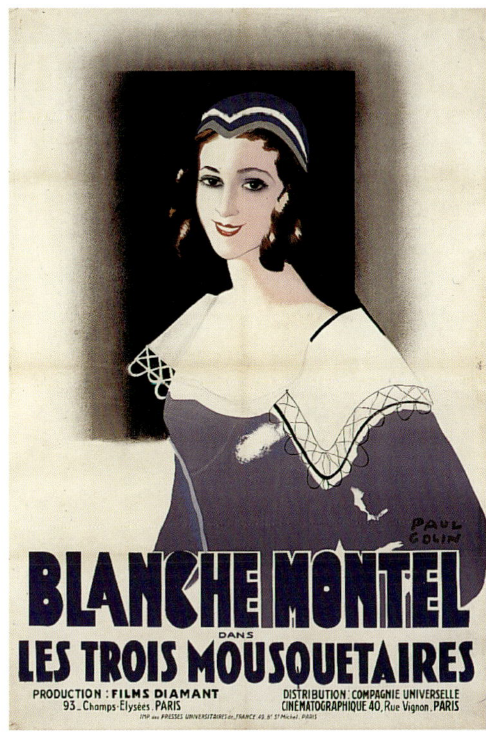

284

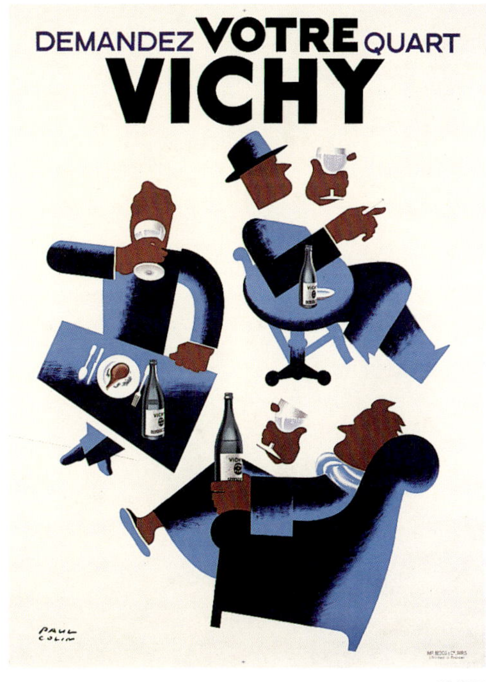

285

283

PAUL COLIN (cont'd)

282. André Renaud. 1929.
$46^1/2$ x $62^5/8$ in./118 x 159 cm
Imp. H. Chachoin, Paris
Cond A–/Slight tears at paper edges.
Ref: Colin, 39; Colin Affichiste, 74; Art Deco, p. 99;
    PAI-XXXVIII, 292
The two pianos that André Renaud simultaneously
played look like a double exposure, but, like all the
geometric "tricks" of Colin, they are deliberately drawn
for maximum effect. And the effect that Colin seeks
here—to overwhelm us with the wizardry of Renaud—
is achieved by the sheer mass of the combined pianos.
Est: $25,000-$30,000.

283. Leroy/Premier Opticien de Paris. 1938.
$45^1/4$ x $62^1/2$ in./115 x 158.7 cm
Publicitas, Paris
Cond A–/Unobtrusive folds. Framed.
Ref: Colin, 92; Colin Affichiste, 178;
    Deco Affiches, p. 59; Timeless Images, 115 (var);
    PAI-XXXIII, 300
"As Colin devoted himself mostly to show business, his
commercial designs are rare. Among these, *l'opticien*

Leroy, done for one of his friends, is one of the best.
Featureless but for the eyes, a man's face stands out
on a dark background. Is he at the theater, as his dress
suggests? With his gloved hands he puts on his glasses.
A halo around his eyes, done with airbrush, helps further to magically draw our eyes to his. At the bottom,
in big red Art Deco letters in relief, the optician's name
—and that's all. In its succinctness, a perfect illustration of Colin's theory that a poster must be 'a telegram
addressed to the awareness'" (Deco Affiches, p. 113).
Leroy remains the premier optician in Paris to this day;
Colin likely deserves some of the credit. *This is the
1-sheet format. Also, take note of the World War II
censorship stamp in the lower left corner.*
Est: $12,000-$15,000.

284. Les Trois Mousquetaires/Blanche Montel. 1932.
$31^1/4$ x $46^7/8$ in./79.3 x 119 cm
Imp. des Presses Universitaires de France, Paris
Cond B/Slight tears and stains at folds.
Ref: Colin Affichiste, 42
Colin dispenses with his more typical multifaceted pro-
motional style in order to deliver this straightforward

portrait of Blanche Montel (1902-1998) as Constance
Bonacieux, a role that she would assume in both of
the French-released "Three Musketeer" films of 1932.
Colin executed several posters for the film, which was
the first sound version of the Alexandre Dumas swash-
buckling classic.
Est: $1,400-$1,700.

285. Vichy/Demandez Votre Quart. 1948.
$45^3/4$ x $62^7/8$ in./116 x 159.7 cm
Imp. Bedos, Paris
Cond A.
Ref: Colin, 106; PAI-XL, 318
A bottle of Vichy mineral water at every occasion is
clearly the message. The green bottles are the only
element rendered realistically here; everything else is
stylized in form and color.
Est: $1,700-$2,000.

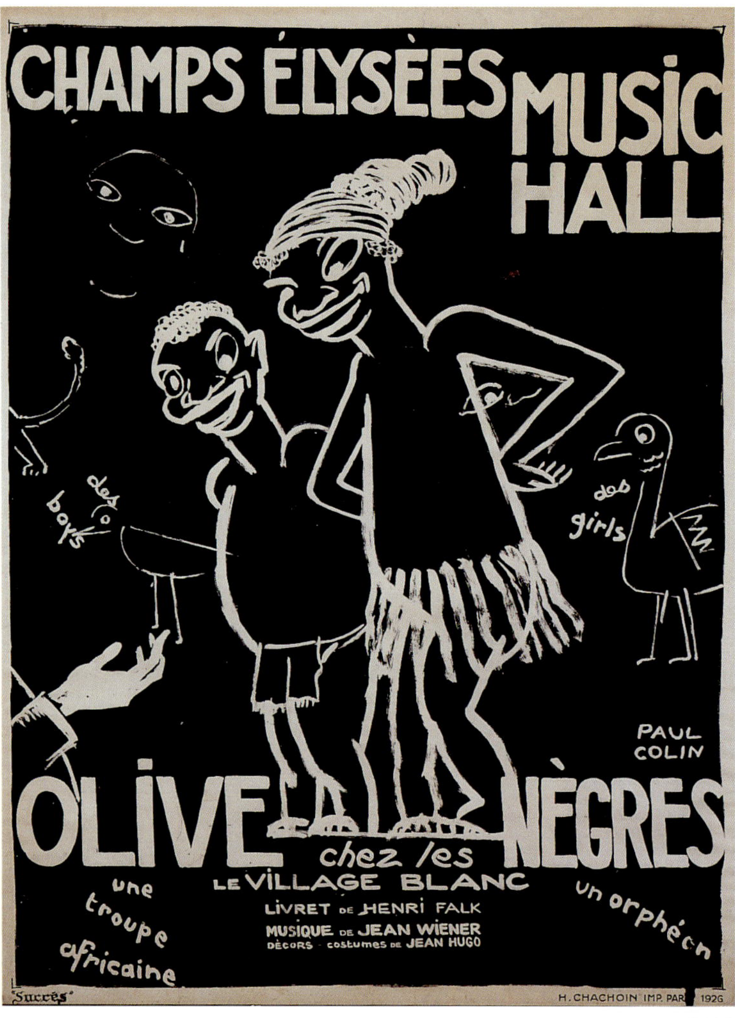

286

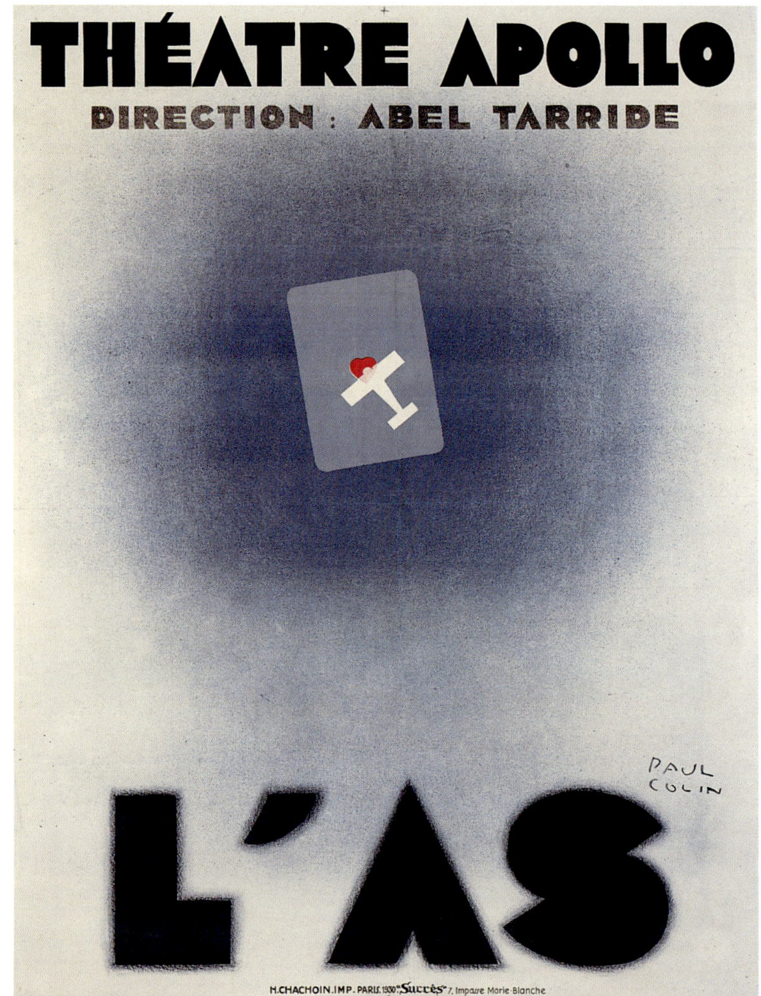

287

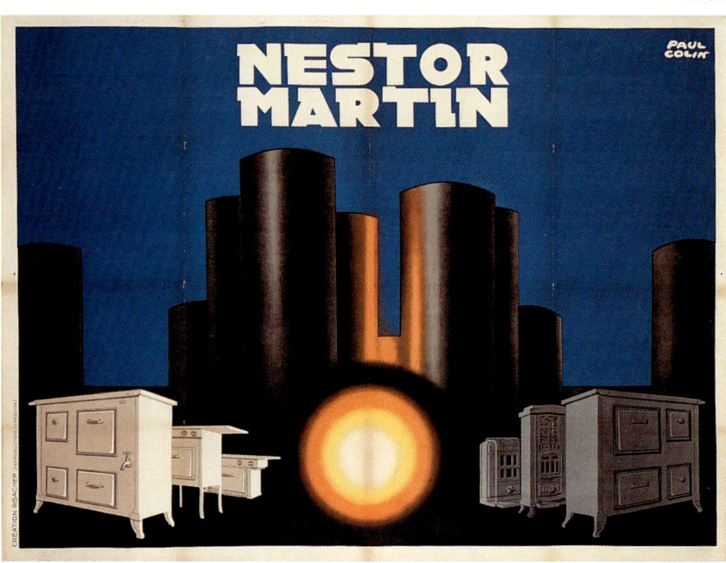

288

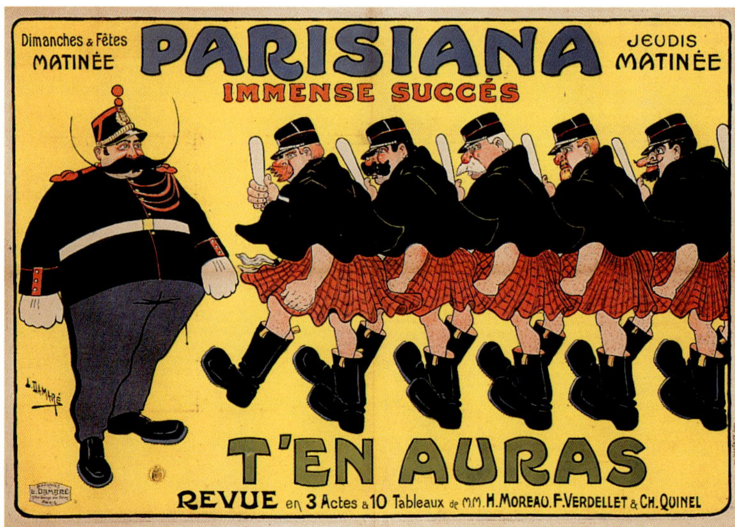

292

PAUL COLIN (cont'd)

286. Olive chez les Nègres. 1926.
$45^5/_8$ x $61^1/_2$ in./115.8 x 156.3 cm
Imp. H. Chachoin, Paris
Cond A–/Slight tears. Framed.
Ref: Colin, 16; PAI-XI, 186
"This unusual poster—the only other black-and-white poster of Colin which I have ever seen is that of Madika (*see* Colin, 42)—celebrates an equally unusual, and now somewhat obscure, sketch at the Théatre des Champs-Élysées. Colin himself does not recall it but we can surmise that 'Olive Nègres' was a sketch meant as a parody of the colonial exhibits which were being organized all over France at that time. A couple of Africans are shown visiting the French in 'Le Village Blanc.' The caricature was as much of the hosts as of the visitors. The primitive look, enforced in its black-and-white simplicity, is further abetted by the hand-drawn lettering. The book for this sketch was by Henri Falk, music was by Jean Wiener . . . and decors and costumes by the great painter, Jean Hugo, great-grandson of Victor Hugo" (Colin, p. 7).
Est: $2,500-$3,000.

287. Théatre Apollo/L'As. 1930.
46 x $62^1/_4$ in./117 x 158 cm
imp. H. Chachoin, Paris
Cond B+/Slight tears at folds and edges.
"During the 1930's Colin did a great deal of the advertising art for the Théatre de l'Apollo, then situated next to the Casino de Paris, and his prodigious output for it included dozens of programs and posters" (Colin, p. 9). One such design is this superlative poster for "The Ace," a soaring theatricality being presented at the Apollo. Though no specifics could be unearthed regarding the story line, Colin's promotional work is subtle and stunning: he places a tiny aircraft within a hazy indigo expanse that in turn is ensconced within a blue-grey rectangle with a heart at its focal point. In doing so, Colin masterfully informs the viewer that not only is the namesake pilot of the piece a devil-may-care fly-boy, but an "Ace of Hearts" as well. *Rare!*
Est: $4,000-$5,000.

288. Nestor Martin.
63 x $47^1/_2$ in./160 x 120.2 cm
Création Rischer, Paris
Cond B/Slight tears and stains at folds.
Ref: Karcher, 176 (var); PAI-XX, 217
Here, Colin gives us a striking image for the Nestor Martin factory. A radiant ball of fire casts its glow on the stylized steel furnaces that take on the appearance of factory towers—symbols of the company's solidity as well as the heat-producing stoves and radiators that come off the production line.
Est: $2,000-$2,500.

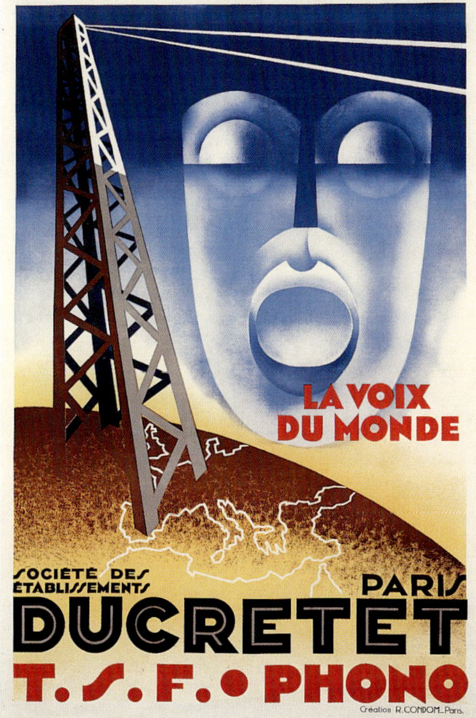

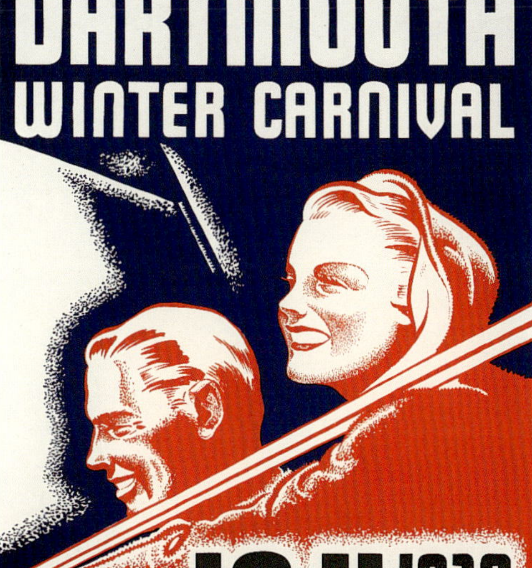

293

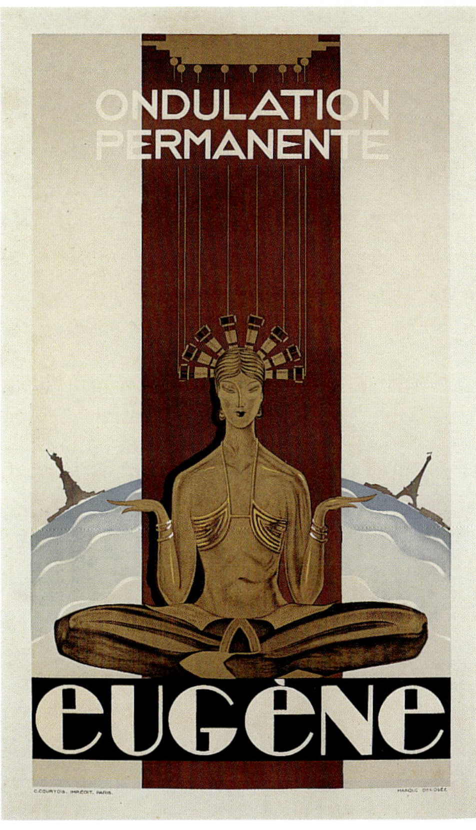

290

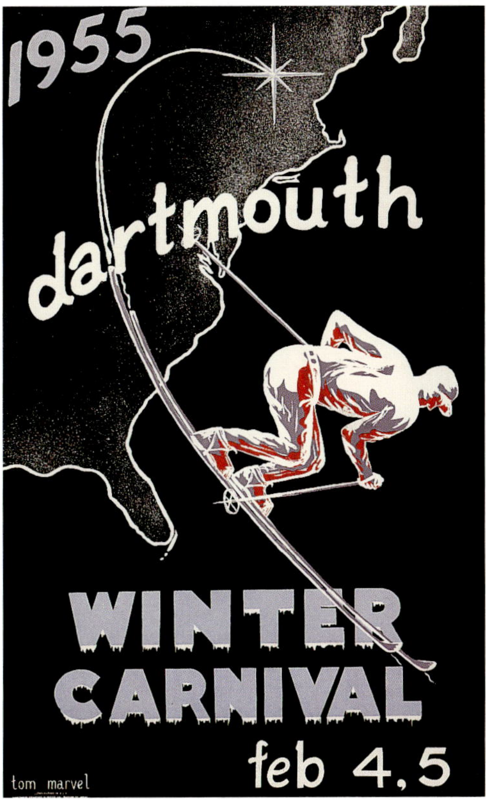

294

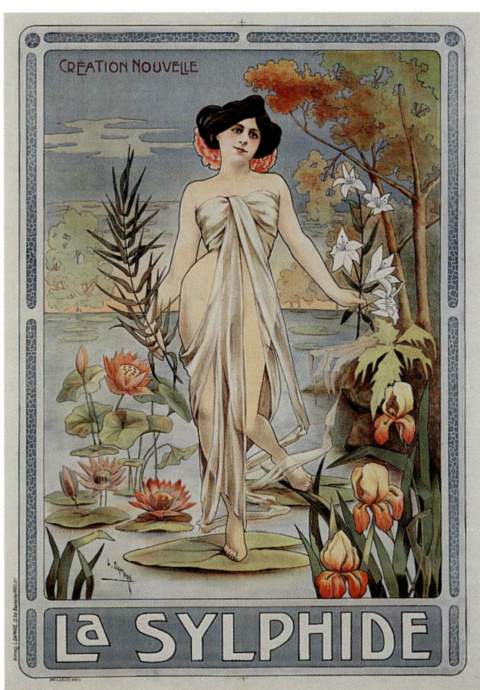

291

R. CONDOM

289. Ducretet.

$30^3/4$ x 47 in./78 x 119.5 cm
Création R. Condom, Paris
Cond A.
With a monolithic tower firmly planted in Europe and the visage of a robotic announcer blaring out its message, Ducretet radio, "The Voice of the World," advertises its product with stunning futuristic, near-science fictional grandeur. Though not as well known as some of his contemporaries, Eugène Ducretet (1844-1915) is nonetheless a key figure in the development of wireless broadcasting—in 1897, one year after Guglielmo Marconi's experiments in transmission, French radio pioneer Ducretet began trial broadcasts from a mast on the third level of the Eiffel Tower and France's wireless age was born.
Est: $1,500-$1,800.

C. COURTOIS

290. Eugène. ca. 1928.

$21^1/8$ x $35^3/4$ in./53.8 x 90.8 cm
Imp. Édit, Paris
Cond A–/Slight stains in borders.
Ref: PAI-IX, 160 (var)
Perfect Art Deco symmetry marks this poster for a permanent-wave product. This particular version of the Courtois design turns the central model into a golden idol of cosmetology, with a uniformly undulating sea gently roiling between New York and Paris in order to reinforce the universal appeal and efficacy of the product. *Rare and impressive!*
Est: $2,500-$3,000.

L. DAMARÉ (?-1927)

291. La Sylphide.

$35^1/8$ x 50 in./89.2 x 127 cm
Imp. L. Galice, Paris
Cond A.

Draped in sheer and flora-friendly, this graceful brunette sylph tiptoes her way across the lily-pads. But for what or for whom is she doing this? It's stated that this belle embodies a "new creation," but all other textual assistance has been left off this specimen of the Damaré design. It seems more likely than not that she's commercially bound to some cosmetic product judging from her surroundings. But when it comes to Art Nouveau advertising, a subject's environs hardly provide concrete evidence for the product they're promoting. In the end, the mystery that surrounds her only serves to deepen our appreciation of the loveliness that she brings to the commercial realm in spite of a lack of trade specificity.
Est: $1,000-$1,200.

292. Parisiana/T'en Auras. 1903.

$48^1/2$ x $34^5/8$ in./123.2 x 88 cm
Imp. Louis Galice, Paris
Cond B/Slight tears and stains at folds.
Ref: PAI-XXXIII, 308
It's hard to imagine that Damaré's dimwitted platoon of Empiric generals made much of an impact in the manner of crowd control. So it's fairly safe to assume that the "it" in the title of the "You're Gonna Get It!" revue playing at the Parisiana could only be referring to an evening of high jinks and hilarity. No biographical data for Damaré is available, yet he (or she) worked for the Folies-Bergère, the Olympia and other top music halls for years, always coming up with humorous, attention-getting designs of this sort.
Est: $1,200-$1,500.

DARTMOUTH WINTER CARNIVAL

293. Dartmouth Winter Carnival/Feb. 10-11 1939.

Artist: **Dom Lupo**
$21^7/8$ x $34^1/8$ in./55.5 x 86.7 cm
Child-Walker School, Boston
Cond A.
Ref: PAI-XXXVI, 291
The flush of thrilling wintertime socializing pervades Lupo's poster for the 1939 Winter Carnival. The social scene of this particular Dartmouth weekend is chronicled in *Winter Carnival,* a fictional filmed account of the celebration. The plot follows the matinee-contrived romance between a Dartmouth professor and his old flame, a divorced duchess who had held the crown of Winter Carnival Queen in her younger days. Regardless of the saccharine contrivances, the film is an entertaining look at Winter Carnivals of yesteryear, one that not only shows students meeting their dates at the train station, but also footage of athletic events and black-tie fraternity dances. Incidentally, *Winter Carnival* was named "one of the five objectionable pictures of 1939" by the Catholic Legion of Decency—a distinction shared by *Gone With the Wind* and *Of Human Bondage.*
Est: $1,000-$1,200.

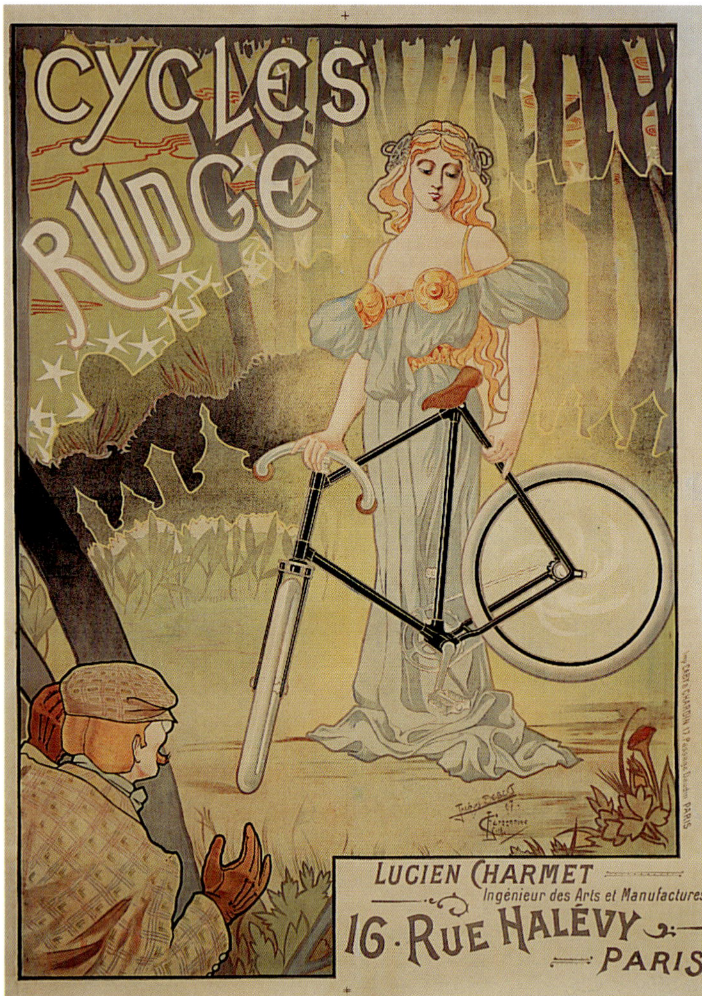

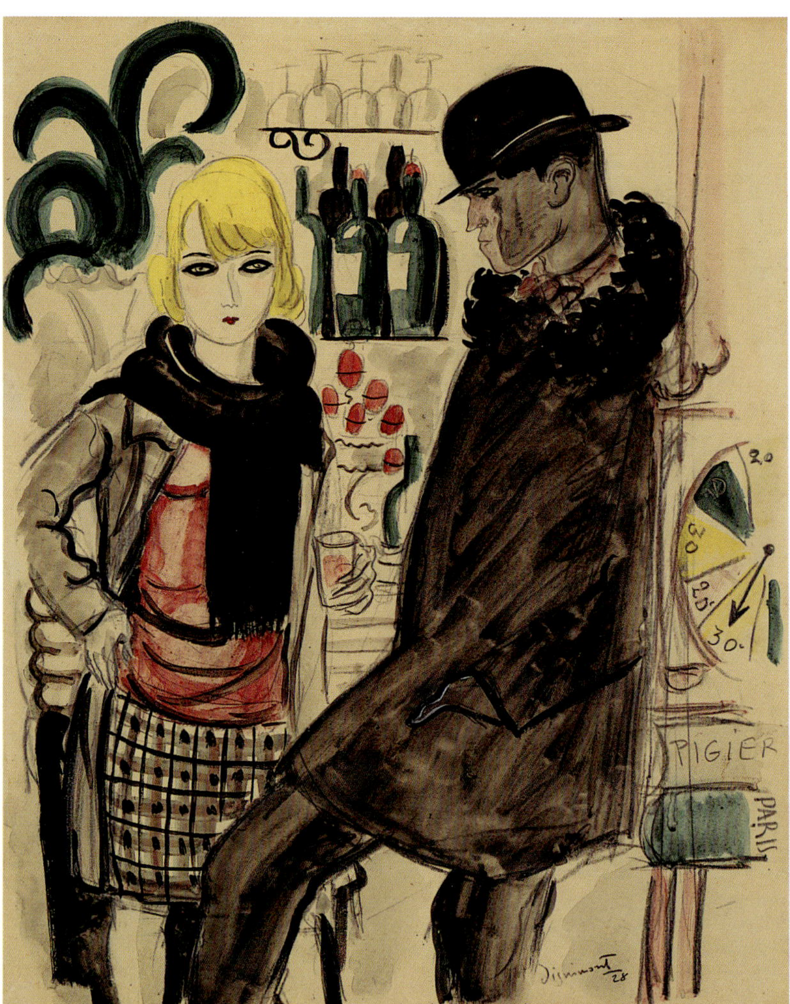

295

301

DARTMOUTH CARNIVAL (cont'd)

294. Dartmouth Winter Carnival. 1955.
Artist: **Tom Marvel**
20⁵/₈ x 33³/₄ in./52.3 x 85.8 cm
Winthrop, Boston, MA
Cond B/Slight tears at folds and edges.
Dubbed in 1919 as "the Mardi Gras of the North" by *National Geographic* magazine, the Dartmouth Winter Carnival is the oldest collegiate winter festival in the United States. Founded in 1910 by members of the Dartmouth Outing Club who wished to promote the then-fledgling pastime of recreational skiing, participants from nearby colleges trekked to Hanover, New Hampshire, attempting to defeat Dartmouth men at skiing and snow-shoeing events. It didn't take long for the Dartmouth event to develop into the most celebrated college weekend in the nation. And as this Marvel poster clearly shows, Dartmouth was one of the jumping-off points from which skiing would become a widespread national pastime.
Est: $1,000-$1,200.

JACQUES DEBUT

295. Cycles Rudge. 1897.
43¹/₄ x 60⁵/₈ in./109.8 x 154 cm
Imp. Caby & Chardin, Paris
Cond B+/Slight tears at folds.
Ref: Petite Reine, 43; PAI-XXVII, 10
Debut, an artist born in the second half of the 19th century and primarily known for his work as a painter, created, at the very least, one design as a posterist for Rudge in this lithograph brimming with magical implications. The mere mortal who stumbled upon this clearing was not prepared to discover the otherworldly scene of a heavenly creature, manifesting the total repose of a goddess, as she placidly inspects her Rudge bicycle. Being in unfamiliar territory and unsure of his next move, the enamored gent can only gaze on with secret admiration. Rudge was a British make, manufactured by Dan Rudge of Wolverhampton, but sold and advertised extensively in France.
Est: $1,400-$1,700.

FRANCIS DELAMARE (1895-1972)

296. Mercedes-Duurt. ca. 1936.
24¹/₈ x 39¹/₈ in./61 x 99.5 cm
Studio Francis Delmare, Bruxelles
Cond B+/Four-inch tear at lower paper edge.
Ref: PAI-XXI, 155
Comparing the latest model of a typewriter with a streamlined locomotive communicates that the office machine is the most modern, up-to-date design available. So, even though Delamare's design lets the consumer know that this Mercedes is as powerful as a speeding locomotive, whether or not it's faster than a speeding bullet really depends on just how super one's typing skills are.
Est: $1,200-$1,500.

CHARLES DELAUNAY (1911-1988)

297. Jo Bouillon/Columbia. 1938.
30³/₈ x 45³/₈ in./77 x 115.2 cm
Imp. H. Chachoin, Paris
Cond B+/Slight tears at folds.
History may remember him best as Josephine Baker's fourth husband—with whom she would adopt a dozen children from around the world that were known as the "Rainbow Tribe"—but Frenchman Jo Bouillon was quite the musician in his own right, "a prodigy in a family of prodigies. He had won first prize in violin at the Paris Conservatory, but fell in love with jazz, turning from classical music to show business" (Josephine, p. 265). And to promote his recordings with his orchestra on Columbia Records some nine years before his marriage to Baker, Delaunay places a cameo portrait of Bouillon front and center, with his line-drawn orchestra caught up in the prismatic whirlpool of carefree swing behind him.
Est: $1,700-$2,000.

DANIEL DE LOSQUES
(David Thoroude, 1880-1915)

298. Thé Chinbara. ca. 1910.
25¹/₄ x 68¹/₄ in./64 x 173.3 cm
Affiches Devambez, Paris

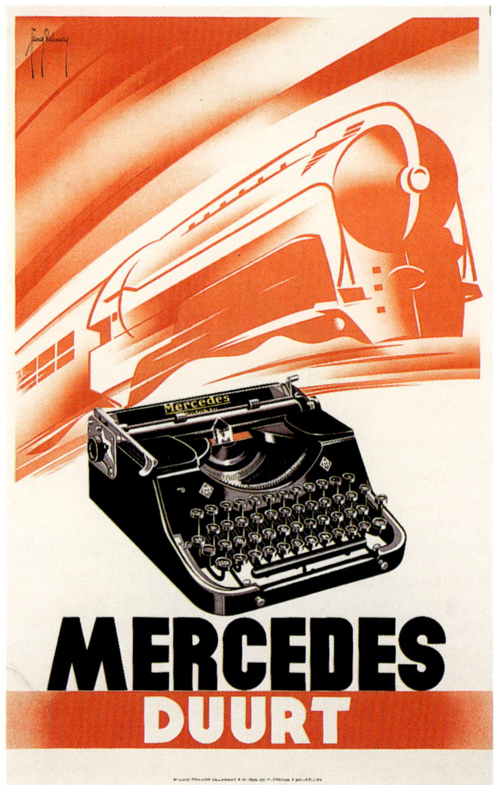

296

Cond B+/Slight tears, largely at folds.
In another de Losques poster for Chinbara tea that focuses on a product imported from Sri Lanka (*see* PAI-XXXVIII, 409), the artist uses a swayback ethnic waiter as his central attention-getter. In this poster for Chinbara, one that promotes the "Best Chinese Black Tea," not only does he switch the ethnicity, posture and garb

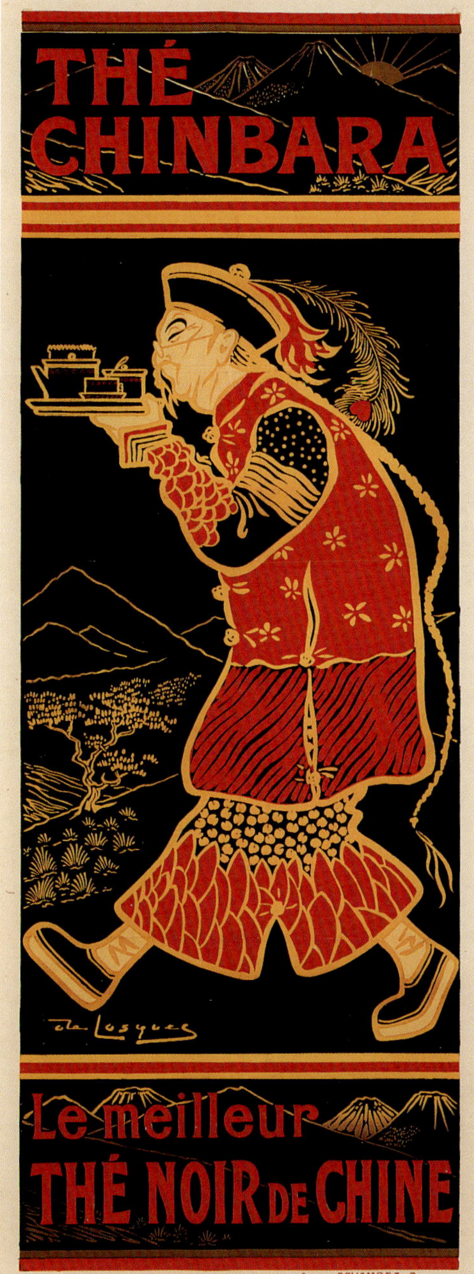

298

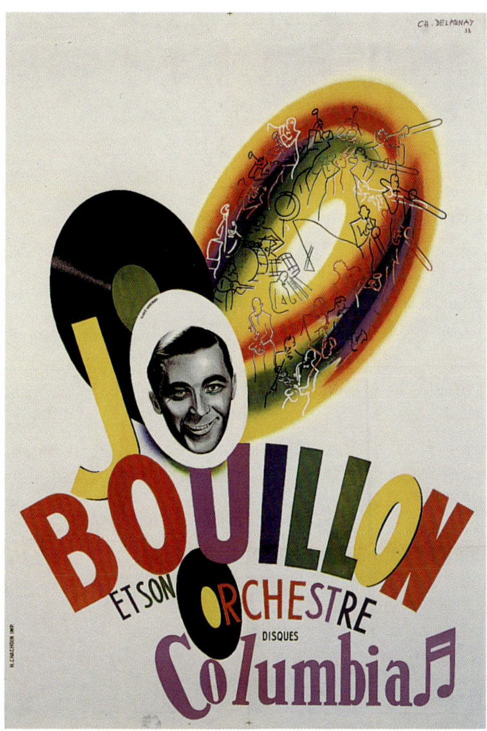

297

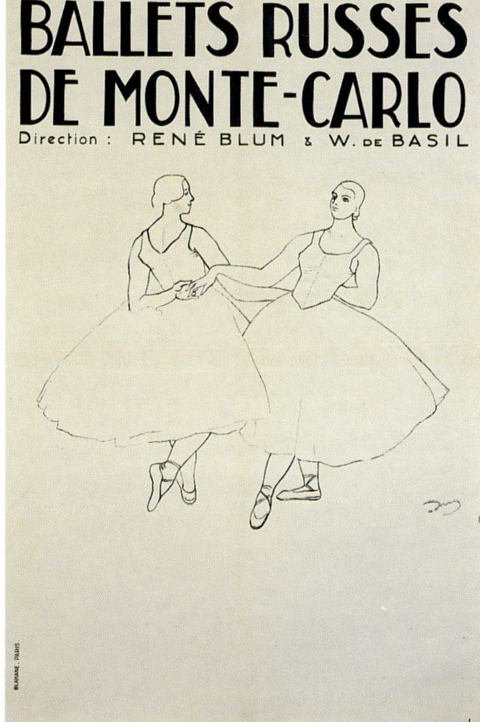

299

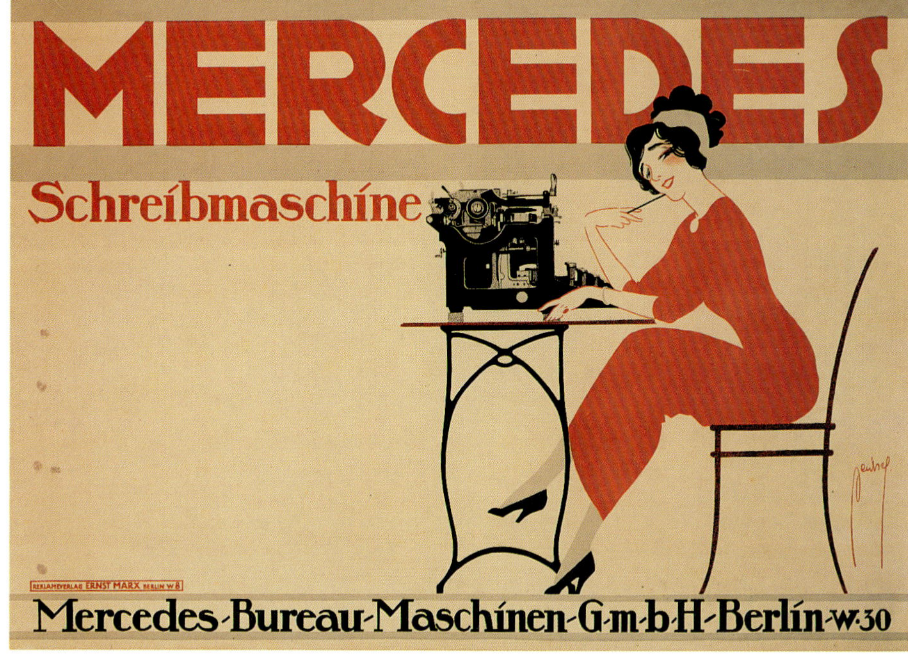

300

of the singular server, he adjusts the decorative background landscapes to better reflect the indigenous artwork of the country from where the tea is exported. De Losques was the pseudonym of David Thoroude, who studied law and started out as a law firm employee before switching to art. This is one of the many theatrical and commercial designs he created, along with magazine illustrations and caricatures during the period 1904-1914. His career was cut short by his death in aerial combat during World War I.
Est: $1,700-$2,000.

ANDRE DERAIN (1880-1954)

299. Ballets Russes de Monte-Carlo. 1932.
$33^3/4$ x $46^3/4$ in./78 x 119 cm
Blahane, Paris
Cond A.
Ref: PAI-XXXIIII, 44
The celebrated French painter, designer, illustrator and sculptor André Derain was intimately associated with the ballet, having designed sets and costumes for Massine, Fokine and other leading choreographers of the period. When the Ballet Russes de Monte Carlo was founded in 1932 under the direction of René Blum and Wassili de Basil, Derain created the costumes for its first production, Balanchine's pantomime *Concurrence*. It is for that first season that Derain designed this poster.
Est: $1,500-$1,800.

ERNST DEUTSCH (1883-1938)

300. Mercedes. 1911.
$37^3/8$ x $27^3/4$ in./94.8 x 70.5 cm
Ernst Marx, Berlin
Cond B+/Restored tears, largely at left paper edges.
Ref: DFP-III, 518; Wember, 205; Takashimaya, 87; Dryden, p. 32; Femme s'Affiche, 167;
PAI-XXVII, 150
The typist and the lettering are all red, the typewriter black—and the rest is just blank paper, so that our eye is focused, willy-nilly, on the subject of the poster. There are two versions of this image: one printed by Berlin's J. Bargou and this one by Ernst Marx. Deutsch was a fashion designer born in Vienna and active also in Berlin and Paris. In 1933, he moved to Hollywood and became a set and costume designer, signing his works "Dryden."
Est: $2,000-$2,500.

ANDRE DIGNIMONT

301. Massard's Bar. 1928.
$18^1/2$ x $23^1/4$ in./47 x 59 cm
Hand-signed gouache and crayon artwork. Framed.
Ref: Affiche Réclame, 72 (var)
The fashionable sleaze virtually seeps off of this Dignimont maquette for the grand opening of Paris' Massard's Bar. The bar just so happened to be a frequent haunt of Josephine Baker, due in part to its proximity to the Théatre Champs-Elysées. "The theme of this poster is hardly surprising. In fact, Dignimont specialized in the evocation of the haunts of bad boys and women of little virtue. Francis Carco, for whom he illustrated several literary works such as *l'Equipe*, *l'Homme traque*, *Nuits de Paris*, *Perversité*, enthusiastically greeted art so closely connected to his own way of thinking. In 1936, Jean Renoir solicited the artist to execute the poster of his film *la Partie de campagne*. It was to be his only contribution to this type of publicity" (Affiche Réclame, p. 100). *An extremely rare creation—so rare in fact that only one known copy of the completed poster exists, and that copy is housed at the Musée des Arts Décoratifs.*
Est: $10,000-$12,000.

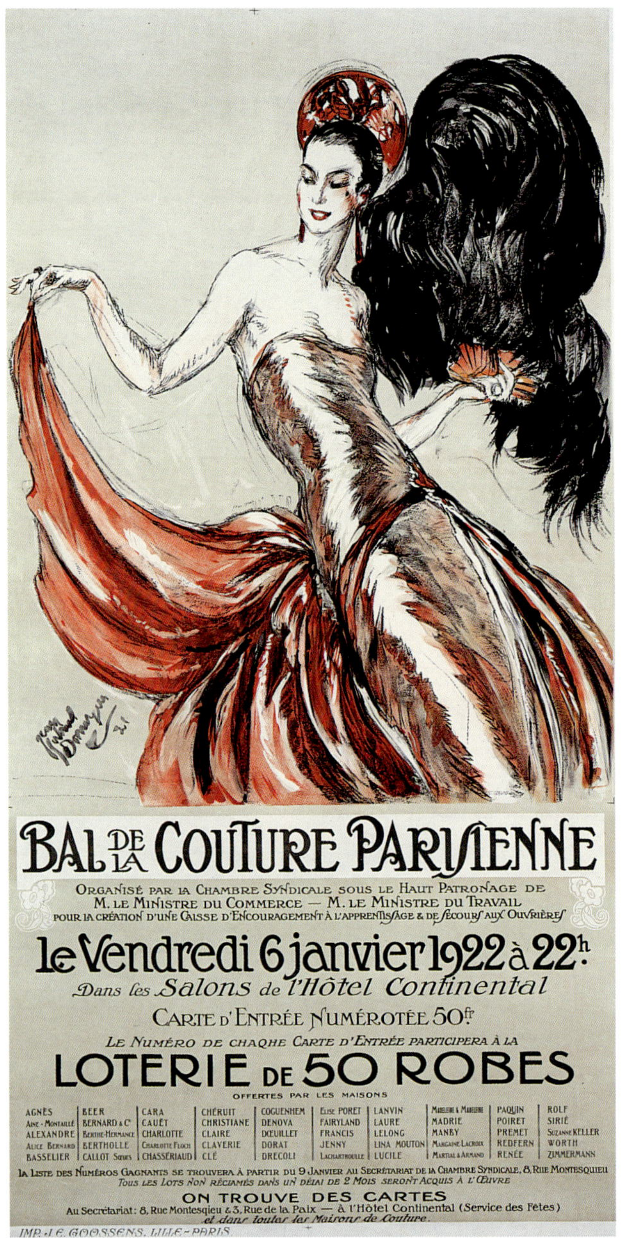

305

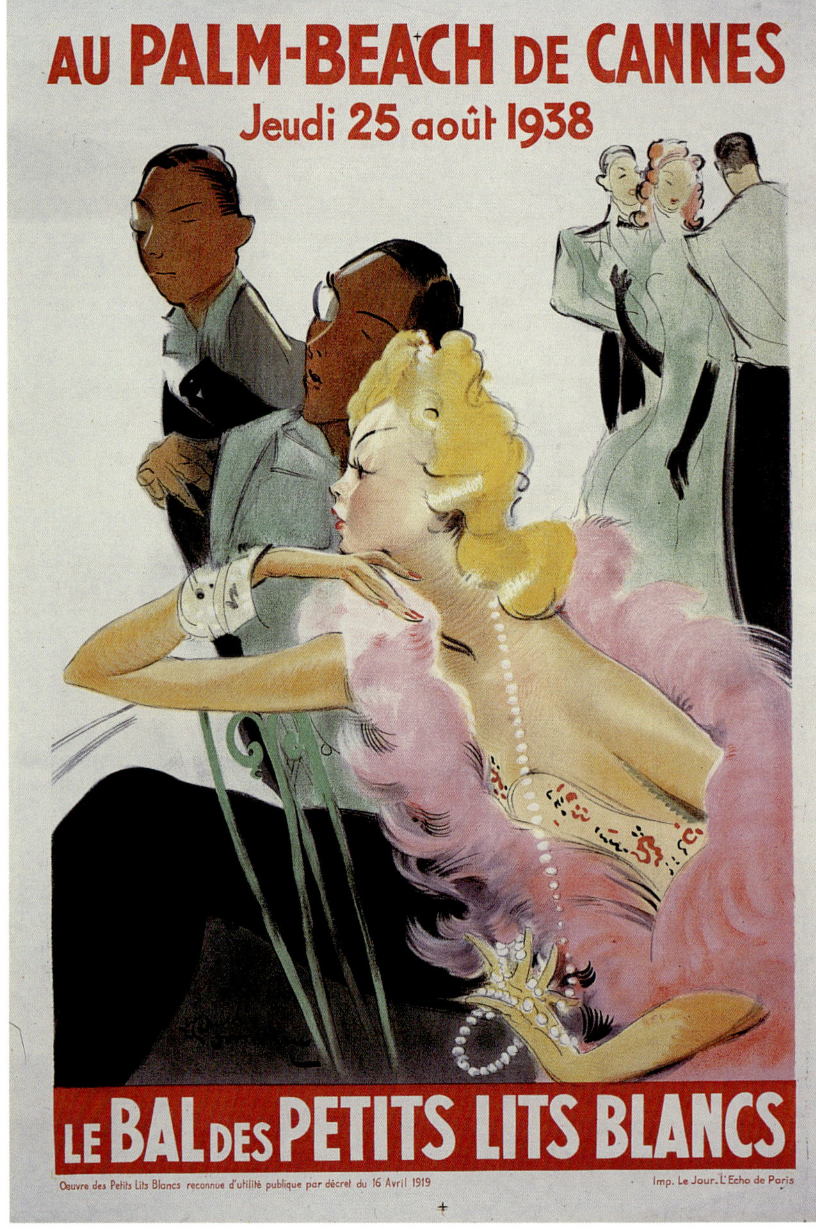

306

GEORGES DOLA
(Edmond Vernier, 1872-1950)

302. La Comtesse Maritza. 1930.
31$^1/_2$ x 47$^1/_4$ in./80 x 120 cm
Atelier Dola, Paris
Cond A–/Unobtrusive folds.
In Dola's promotion for a French production of Hungarian composer Emmerich Kálmán's fluffy operetta, men are but common playthings for the beautiful, spirited Countess Maritza. In actuality, the lighthearted romp revolves around Maritza's reluctance to give up her freedom in the name of tradition, but romance rules the day as true love arrives in the form of—what else—a disguised nobleman serving as her bailiff. Taking his pseudonym from the town of Dôle in the province of Jura where he was born, this painter and lithographer earned a reputation for numerous music covers and portraits of performing artists, as well as posters for the stage. He lectured as professor of the Cercle International des Arts.
Est: $1,000-$1,200.

303. Qu'en Pensez-Vous? 1929.
30$^1/_8$ x 46$^1/_2$ in./76.5 x 118 cm
Edition Max Esching, Paris
Cond A.
"What Do You Think About It?" Well, if the "It" we're talking about is this Dola Art Deco set of "It" triplets, we think they're rather lovely. Unfortunately, the details concerning this obscure seaside operetta remain a mystery beyond from what we've been given here. However, judging from the Dola details, it must have been a breezy affair, indeed.
Est: $1,500-$1,800.

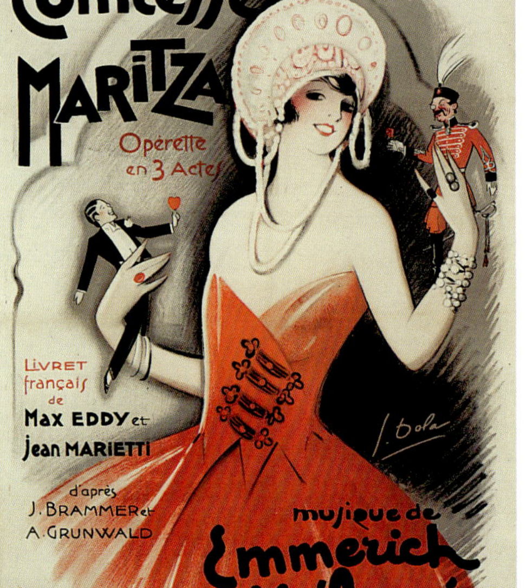

302

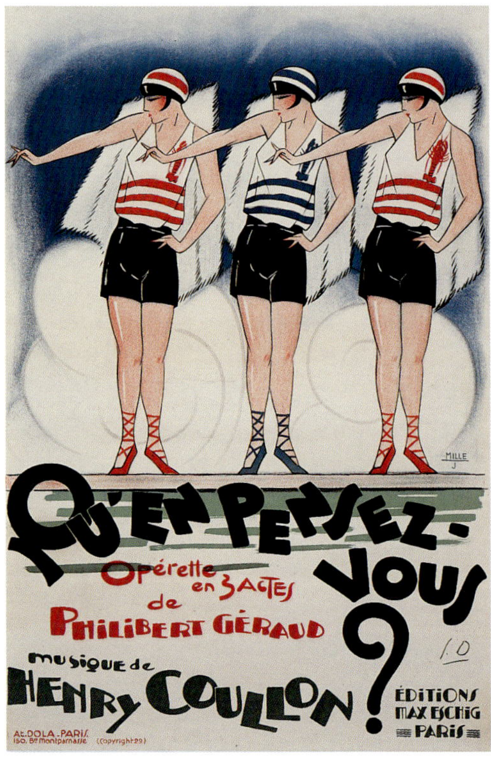

303

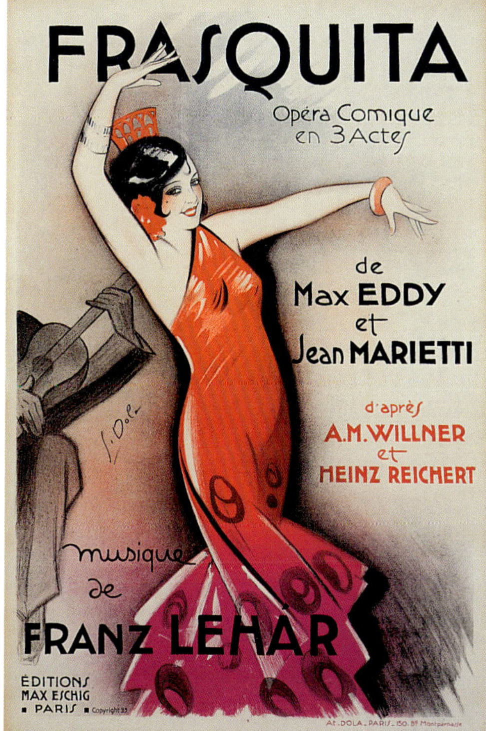

304

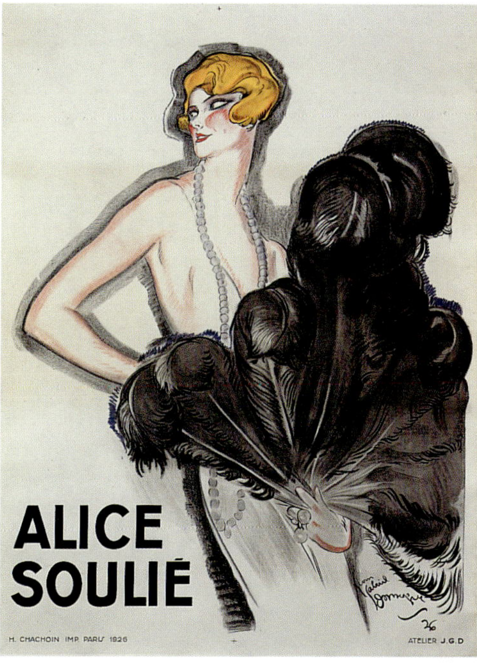

307

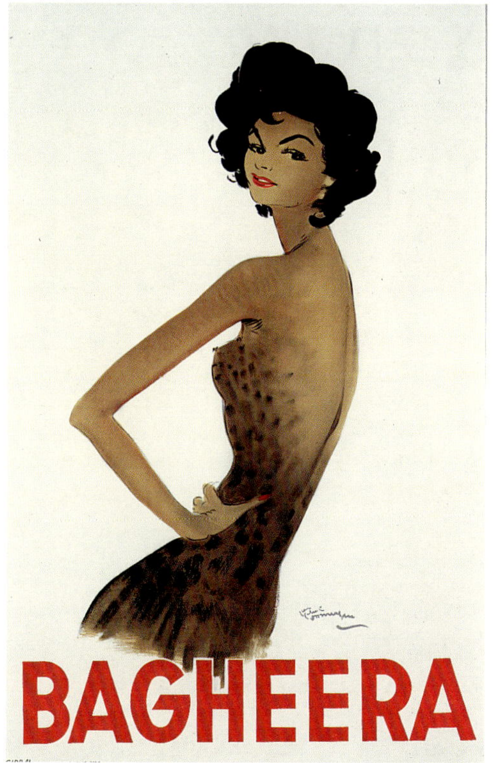

BAGHEERA

308

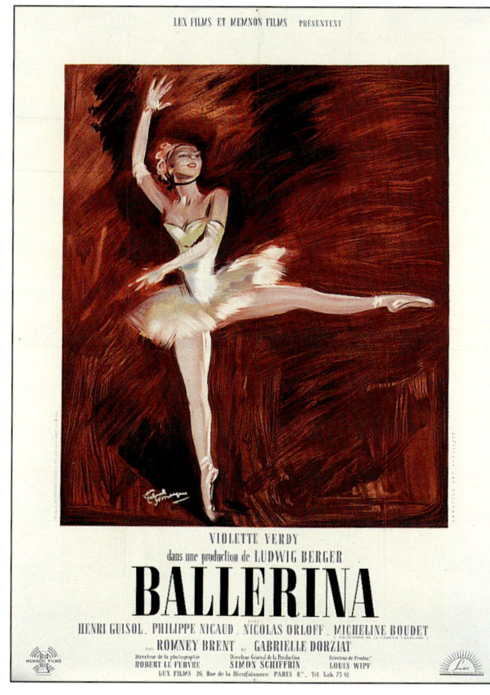

309

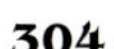

310

JEAN-GABRIEL DOMERGUE (1889-1962)

305. Bal de la Couture Parisienne. 1921.
$31^1/2$ x $63^1/8$ in./80 x 160.2 cm
Imp. J. E. Goosens, Lille
Cond B+/Slight tears at paper edges.
Ref: PAI-X, 214
A charity ball sponsored by the Parisian fashion trade
is advertised with lithe, sophisticated elegance. Fifty
major design firms are listed as sponsors.
Est: $3,000-$4,000.

**306. Le Bal des Petits Lits Blancs au Palm-Beach
de Cannes.** 1938.
$15^1/2$ x $23^3/4$ in./40 x 60.5 cm
Imp. Le Jour-Echo de Paris
Cond A–/Unobtrusive folds.
Here's a Domergue curio: a poster where the men out-
number the women. But with women as lissome and
mondaine as the Domergue archetype, these gentleman
probably don't mind that the odds aren't precisely in
their favor in terms of finding a companion for the evening. Besides, everyone is pretty in the artist's world, so
how upset can you get? This swank Cannes charity gala
was held to aid a children's hospital.
Est: $1,700-$2,000.

307. Alice Soulié. 1926.
46 x $62^1/4$ in./116.8 x 158 cm
Imp. H. Chachoin, Paris
Cond A–/Slight stains at edges.
Ref: PAI-XXXVI, 297
Domergue was a painter known for his high-style fashion drawings. His women are always sleek, elegant and
smart. Blond cabaret performer—and rumored trans-
vestite—Alice Soulié is no exception, with her rope of
oversized pearls and sumptuous black feather fan.
Est: $1,400-$1,700.

308. Bagheera.
30 x 46 in./76.2 x 117 cm
Girbal, Paris
Cond A. Framed.
Ref: PAI-VIII, 337
An alluring kittenish brunette in a sequined gown. Apart
from the fact that this maneater *chanteuse* drew inspi-
ration from the black panther in Rudyard Kipling's *The
Jungle Book* in her choice of stage names, nothing is
known.
Est: $2,500-$3,000.

309. Ballerina. 1950.
44 x $62^1/4$ in./111.6 x 158 cm
Imp. de la Cinématographie Français, Paris
Cond B–/Tears and stains at folds.
Ref: PAI-VIII, 338
A rare Domergue film poster, featuring an *en pointe*
portrait of featured dancer Violette Verdy against a
maroon background. Verdy—nee Nelly Guillerm—was
one of the premier ballet dancers of the 20th Century.
Born in Pont-L'Abbe, France, she made her debut with
Les Ballets de Champs-Elysées in 1945 and, after
performing with several other companies throughout
Europe and the United States, became the principal
ballerina for the New York City Ballet from 1958 to
1977. She is currently a professor at Indiana University.
Est: $1,400-$1,700.

310. Can-Can.
$30^5/8$ x $46^1/2$ in./77.8 x 118.2 cm
Imp. Robaudy, Cannes
Cond B/Slight tears, largely near paper edges.
Ref: Phillips II, 214
It's unclear as for whom Domergue designed this scin-
tillating poster as all previously seen copies appear
before the addition of text. But that's not to say that
he doesn't deliver on the peek-a-boo promise of one
of the greatest dance crazes of all time with a wink of
an eye, a flash of flesh and the dazzle of petticoats.
Est: $2,000-$2,500.

304. Frasquita. 1933.
$30^3/4$ x $47^3/8$ in./78 x 120.2 cm
Edition Max Esching, Paris
Cond A.
The flamenco machinations of a shapely raven-haired
beauty draws the viewer's eye to this Dola poster like a
moth to a flame for the featherweight Lehar musical
indulgence, *Frasquita*. The frothy plot unspools as
follows: Armand Mirabeau, a wealthy young Parisian,
arrives at a Spanish seaport with his friend Hippolyt in
order to meet his fiancée, Dolly Girot. By complete
chance, Armand encounters a gypsy named Frasquita.
She ensnares him with her charms and then spurns him
in revenge for his having accused her of stealing his
cigarette case. Meanwhile, back in Paris, Dolly, deeply
offended by Armand's fickle behavior, marries Hippolyt
and Frasquita, who has realized that she truly loves
Armand, pursues, and is reunited with her only true
love. Not surprisingly, everyone lives happily ever after.
Est: $1,000-$1,200.

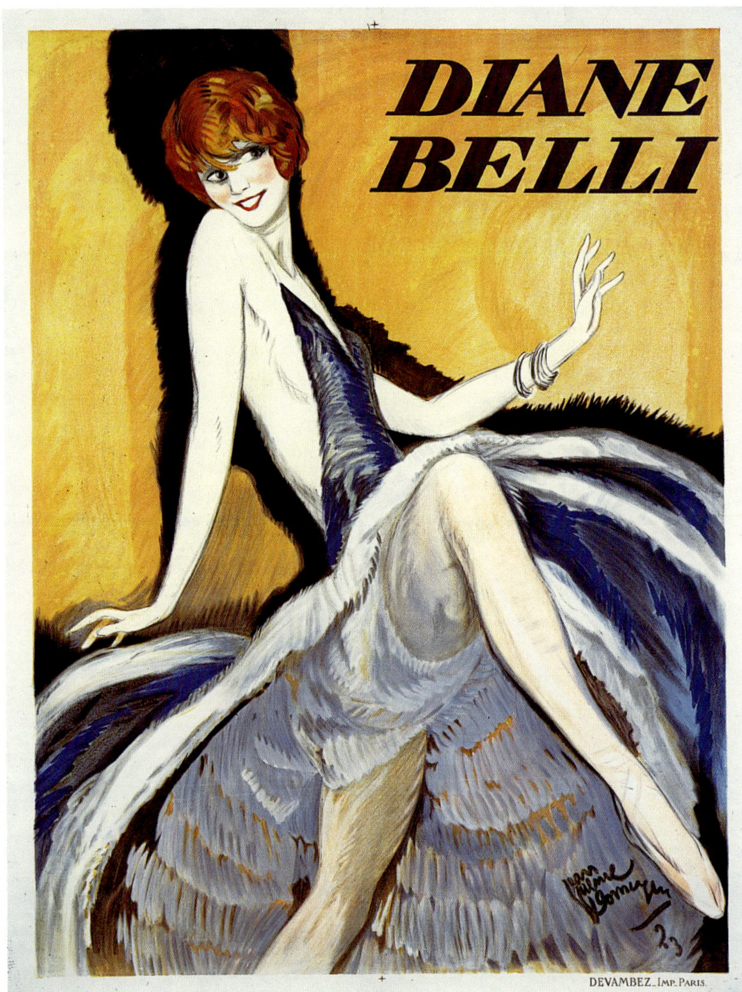

311

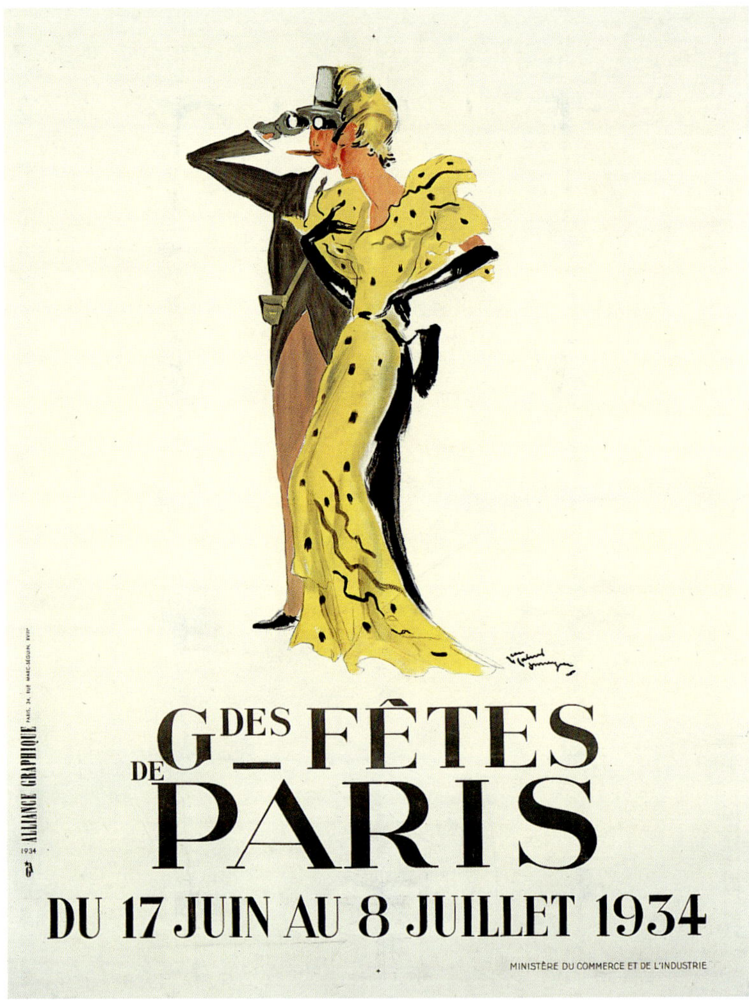

312

DOMERGUE (cont'd)

311. Diane Belli. 1923.
$47^1/_4$ x 63 in./120 x 160 cm
Imp. Devambez, Paris
Cond B+/Slight tears at folds.
Ref: PAI-XXV, 293
Showing off a shapely leg and her most seductive smile, the performer is caught, as all of Domergue's beauties are, at her very best. *Rare!*
Est: $5,000-$6,000.

312. Gdes Fêtes de Paris. 1934.
$47^1/_4$ x $63^7/_8$ in./120 x 161 cm
Alliance Graphique, Paris
Cond B+/Slight tears and stains.
Ref: PAI-VIII, 330
You don't need to show any Paris landmarks in the background or anything at all for that matter, reasoned Domergue: the ultrachic couple will amply suffice to affirm the splendor of the event. And so they do—in little more than shades of yellow, beige and green.
Est: $3,000-$4,000.

313. Monte-Carlo. 1937.
$24^5/_8$ x $38^3/_4$ in./62.5 x 98.2 cm
Imp. Nationale, Monaco
Cond A.
Ref: PAI-XLII, 266
Very little information is given and very little is needed with such a comely invitation perched atop a diving board to lure anyone with an appreciation for the female form to Monte Carlo. Domergue's posters are populated with beautiful women in glowing colors, portrayed with chivalrous flattery at their seductive best by someone to whom beauty was an inexhaustible well of inspiration. Domergue lived a life nearly predisposed to that kind of attitude: his home was Monte Carlo and the Cote d'Azur where Europe's most glamorous women were frequently seen, with Domergue himself a member of the smart set he so often portrayed.
Est: $2,000-$2,500.

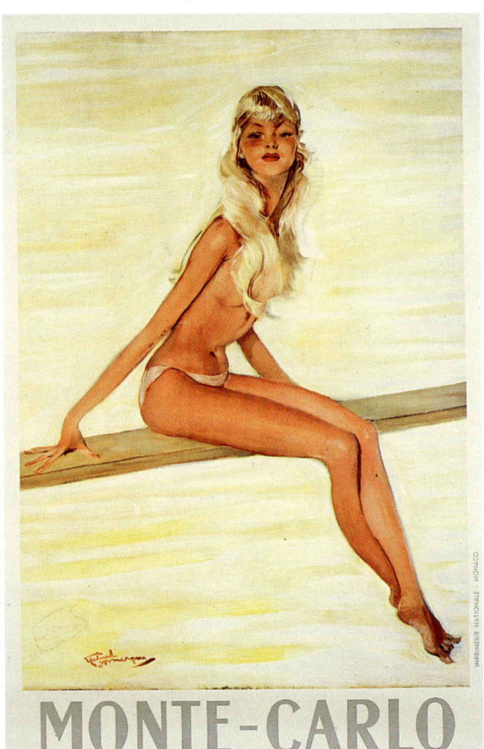

313

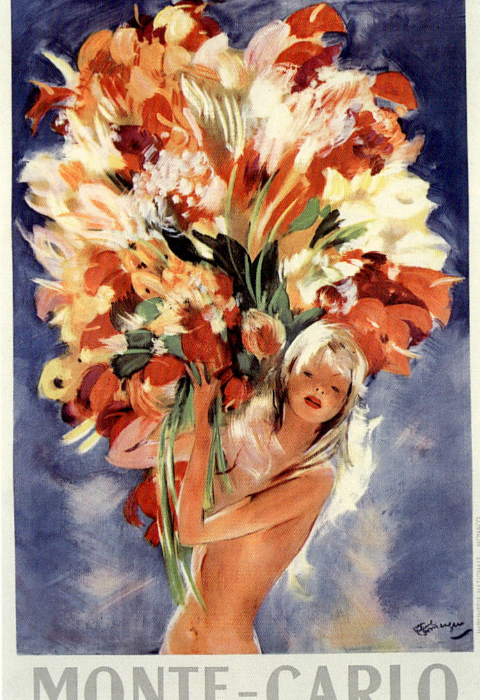

314

314. Monte-Carlo. ca. 1937.
$24^1/_2$ x $38^1/_2$ in./62.2 x 97.8 cm
Imp. Nationale, Monaco
Cond A.
Ref: PAI-XXXIII, 317
And once again Domergue reels us into the sunny world of Monte Carlo with this temptingly tanned willow wisp—quite probably the blonde from the previous poster having descended from her perch. With a spectacular pyrotechnic display of indigenous flora thrown in for good measure.
Est: $2,000-$2,500.

315. Parisiennes.
33 x $45^3/_4$ in./83.8 x 116.2 cm
Cond A–/Unobtrusive folds.
A fine filtered cigarette made from Maryland tobacco, much like a beautiful woman, is something that never goes out of style. Even though the cigarette part of that

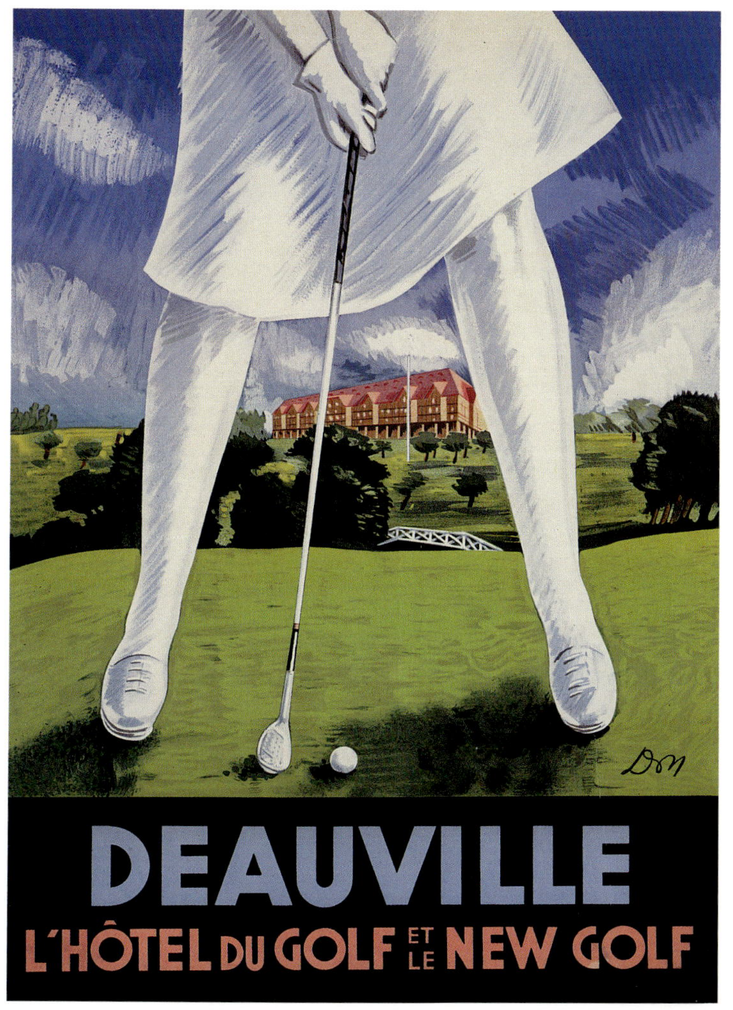

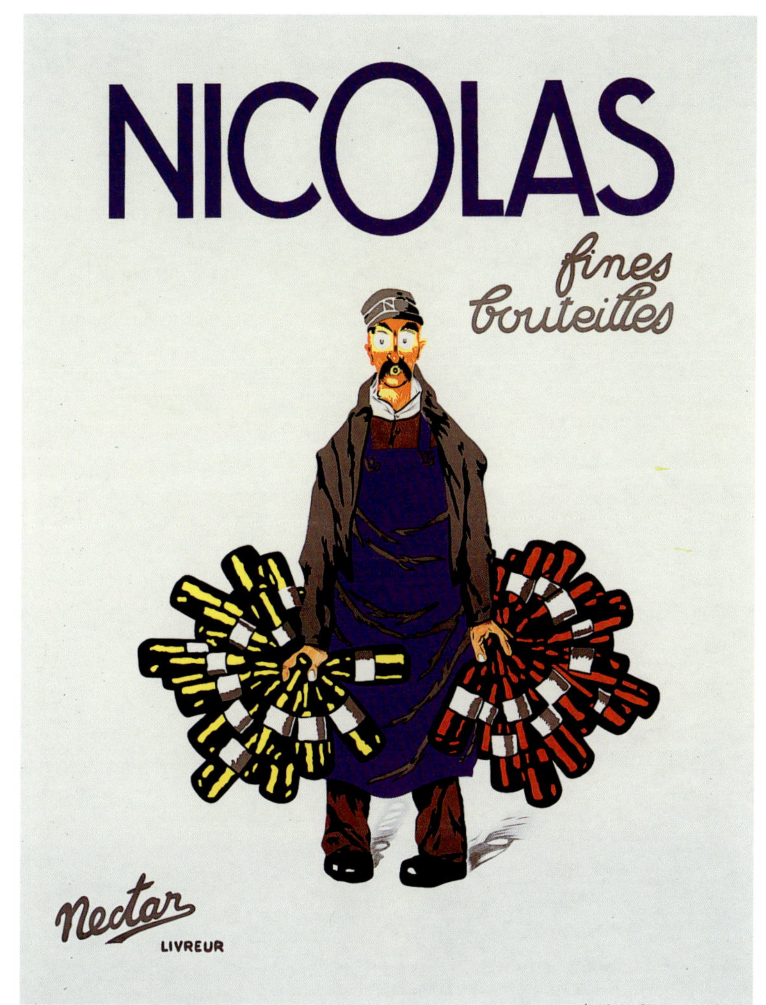

316

318

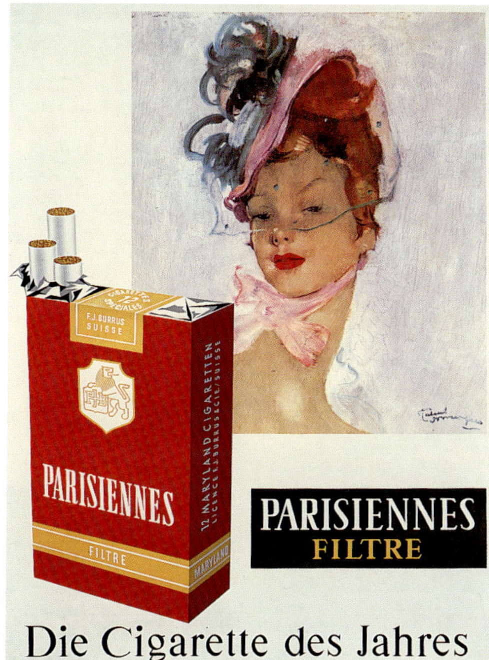

315

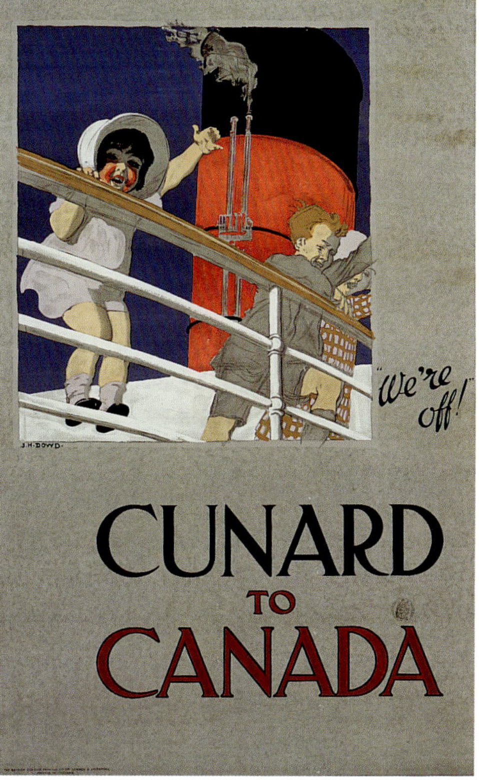

317

the Hôtel du Golf and the New Golf peeping through the stance" (Golf, p. 35).
Est: $2,500-$3,000.

J. H. DOWD

317. Cunard to Canada.
24 x 39 in./61 x 99 cm
British Colour Printing Co., London
Cond A–/Slight stains at paper edges.
Let's face the facts: adults enjoy travel immensely, but going on a trip away from their day-to-day lives drives children over the edge. Dowd captures this unbridled joy in his poster for the Cunard Line's service to Canada, nailing the pure excitement of the journey's first moments with a hearty "We're off!" But with the way these moppets are hanging off the ship's railing, let's hope that their parents aren't too far out of the picture.
Est: $1,400-$1,700.

DRANSY (Jules Isnard, 1883–ca. 1945)

318. Nicolas/Fines Bouteilles. 1930.
47 x 63$^1/_2$ in./119.4 x 161.2 cm
Editions H. Perrier, Paris
Cond A.
Ref: Nectar/Nicolas, 2; Gourmand, p. 38; Karcher, 96 ;
   PAI-XXXVIII, 316
Nicolas was—and is—one of the major wine dealers/distributors in France, and in 1922, the head of the family firm, Etienne Nicolas, asked Dransy to design a poster to show that the company delivers directly to your home. The delivery man, given the name Nectar, became one of the most popular, instantly recognizable images on the walls of France, and was used in dozens of variations. The image was the inspiration for later posters by Iribe, Loupot and Cassandre, among others. This however, is based on the original image of Dransy's, which the Poyet Frères agency supplied with the name in blue on top and a different color (yellow) for the left side bottles; hence the subscript "d'après Dransy."
Est: $3,000-$4,000.

supposition may be somewhat faulty, that's the graphic equation put forth by the artist. Much like Pal before him, there wasn't a commission that Domergue received that he felt couldn't be spruced up with the addition of a beautiful woman. How very fortunate for us.
Est: $1,700-$2,000.

JEAN DON (1900-1985)

316. Deauville. 1929.
21$^5/_8$ x 30$^1/_4$ in./55 x 76.9 cm
Cond B+/Tears, largely near paper edges.
Ref: Golf, p. 35

Don was a prolific illustrator whose specialty was portraits and posters of celebrities of stage and film; otherwise, little is known of him. This is more or less a complete stylistic departure for the artist—and a superbly imaginative departure at that. "The first Deauville golf club was founded in 1899. The new one, designed by Tom Simpson was built in 1929. An original composition by Don . . . with a plunging perspective showing

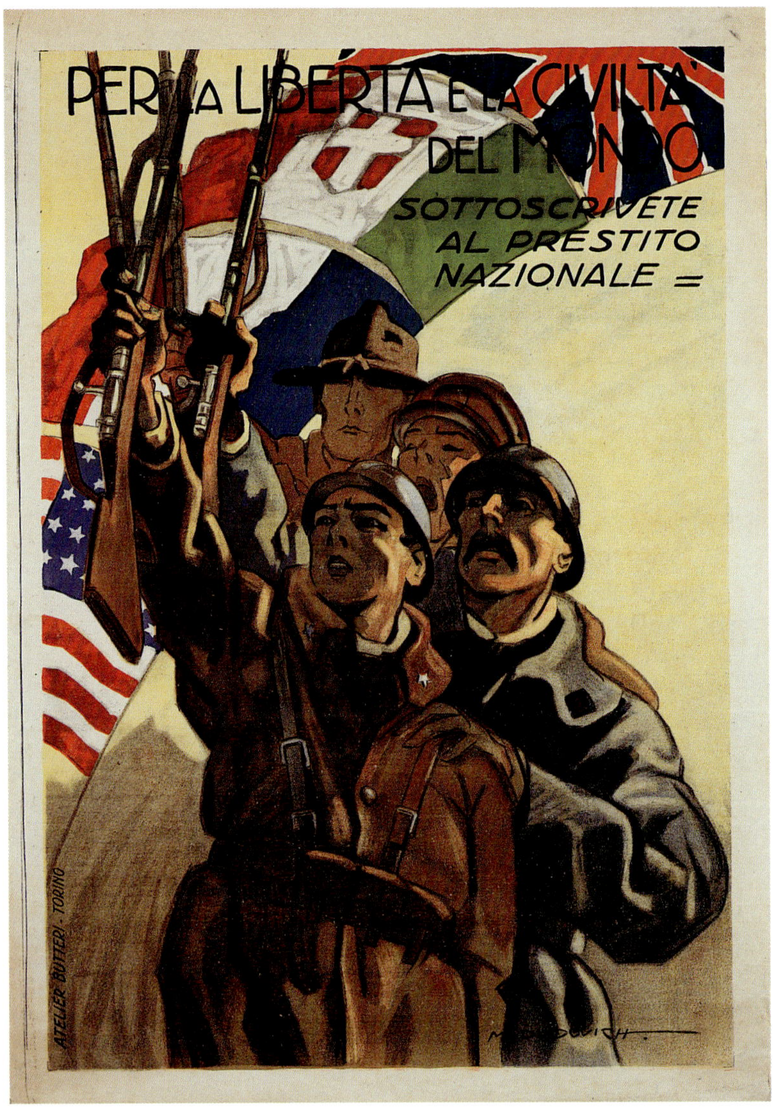

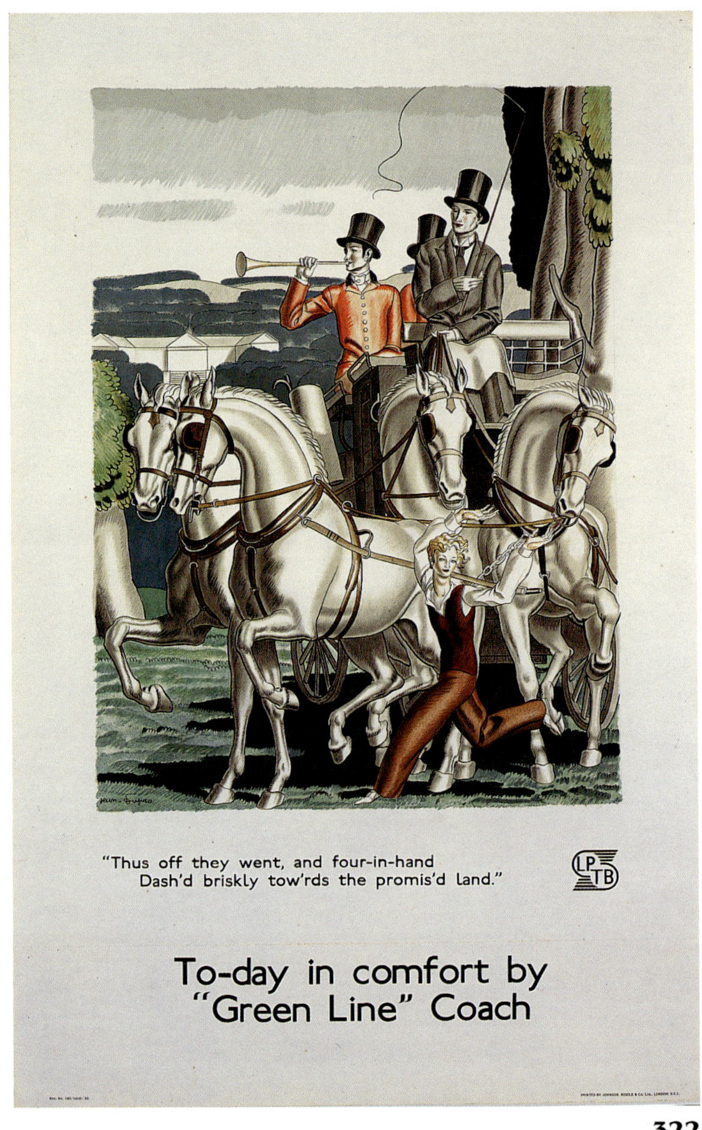

320

322

ALBERT DUBOUT (1905-1976)

319. Le Schpountz/Fernandel. 1952.
46$^1/_8$ x 61$^1/_4$ in./117 x 155.6 cm
Imp. Monégasque, Monte-Carlo
Cond A–/Slight tears at stains and edges.
Ref: Dubout, p. 43; PAI-XXXI, 433
This toothsome rube loaded down with what would appear to be an estate's worth of accouterments expertly
sums up with graphic shorthand the story line of *Le
Schpountz*, Pagnol's comic tale starring Fernandel as
a humble grocery clerk who envisions himself as the
perfect actor to portray great tragic heroes on film.
However, when he finally tries to break into the industry, his bumbling efforts at acting make him instead an
instant success as a knockabout comedian. Virtually
all of Pagnol's films were issued throughout the world
with great success; this is the notable exception which
was never shown outside France, as it is a send-up
of France's own film industry with too many in-jokes to
make it—in the opinions of the experts of the time—
universally hilarious. Fernandel was one of the Pagnol's
favorite character actors. He started out in show biz
as Fernand Contadin, but when he started pursuing a
young lady whose mother didn't care for him and
referred to him as "Fernand d'elle" ("That Fernand of
hers"), he decided to make the slight his stage name.
Est: $1,200-$1,500.

MARCELLO DUDOVICH (1878-1962)

320. Per la Liberta. ca. 1918.
27$^1/_2$ x 39$^3/_8$ in./70 x 100 cm
Atelier Butteri, Torino
Cond A–/Slight tears and stains at paper edges.
Ref: Dudovich, cat. no. 112, fig. 98
Four soldiers, four flags, four firearms raised in soli-
darity "For the Freedom and Civilization of the World."
Simple and powerful, these American, French, Italian
and British symbols make for a powerful lithographic
inducement to participate in a late-World War I Italian

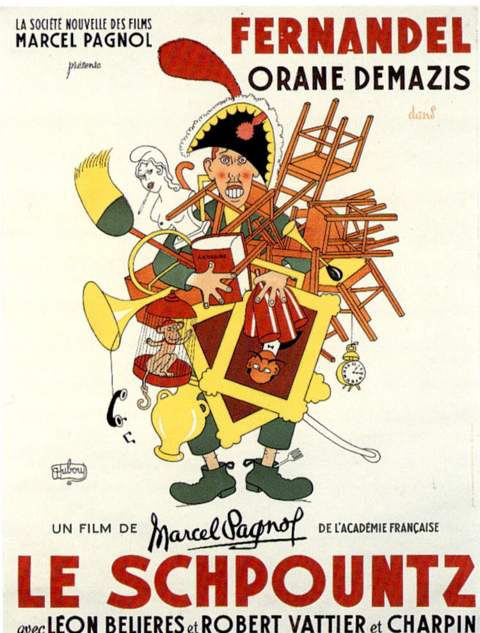

319

bond drive. At the age of nineteen, Dudovich arrived
in Italy from his native Trieste. After an initial stint at
Ricordi, he was hired at Chappuis in Bologna. He was
there form 1899 to 1905 before rejoining Ricordi, where
he established himself as Italy's premier posterist.
Est: $1,400-$1,700.

MAURICE DUFRENE (1876-1955)

321. Rayon des Soieries. 1930.
31 x 46$^3/_4$ in./78.7 x 118.7 cm
Imp. Chaix, Paris

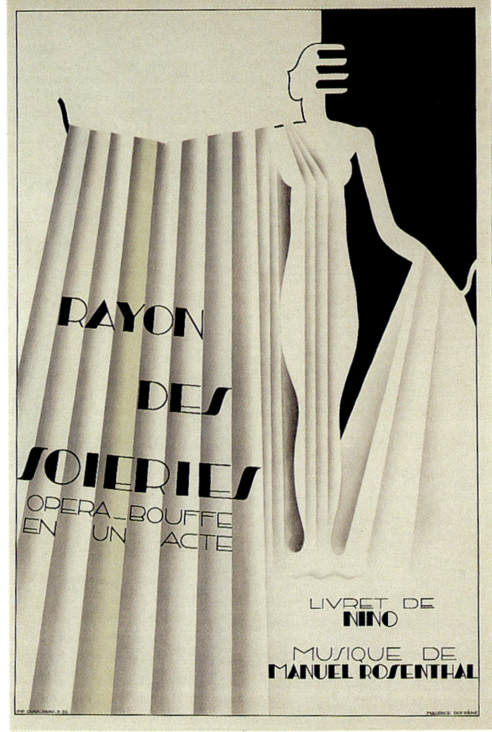

321

Cond A–/Slight stains, largely at edges. Framed.
Ref: French Opera, 17; Timeless Images, 116;
    Femme s'Affiche, 196; Theaterplakate, 166;
    PAI-XLII, 271
This spectacular yet restrained Art Deco poster was
created for the 1930 opening of an operetta by Manuel
Rosenthal involving intrigues in the silk department of
a department store. Most of the design is black and

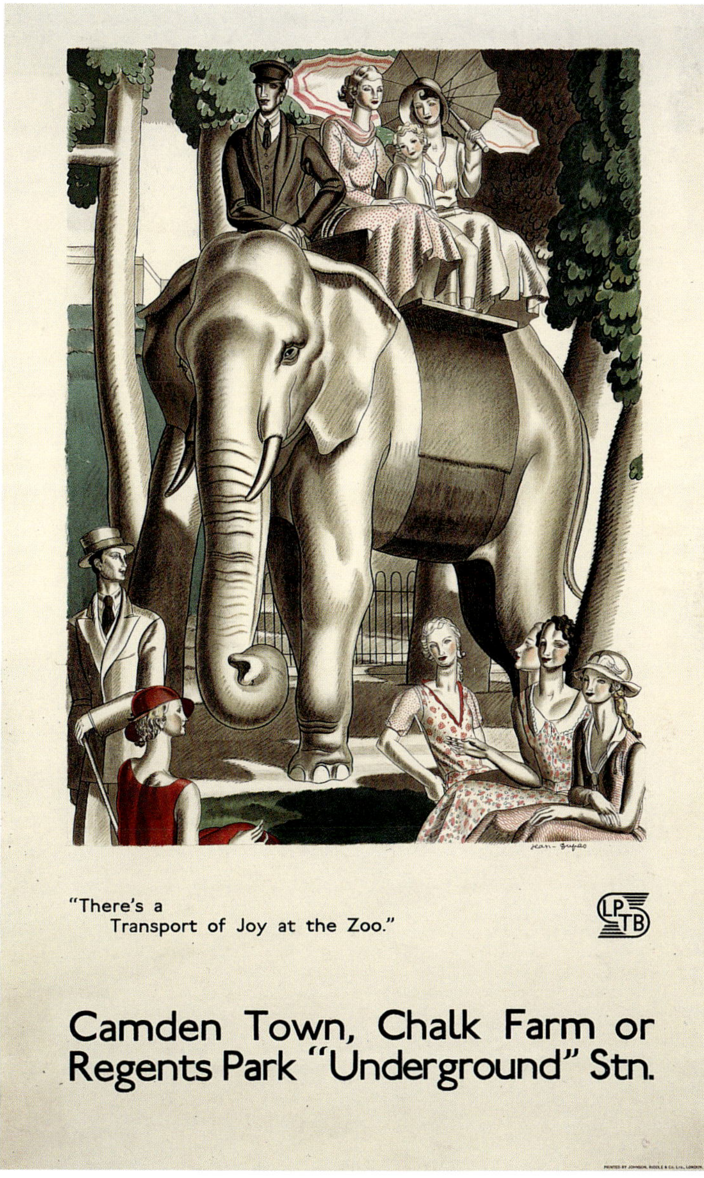

323

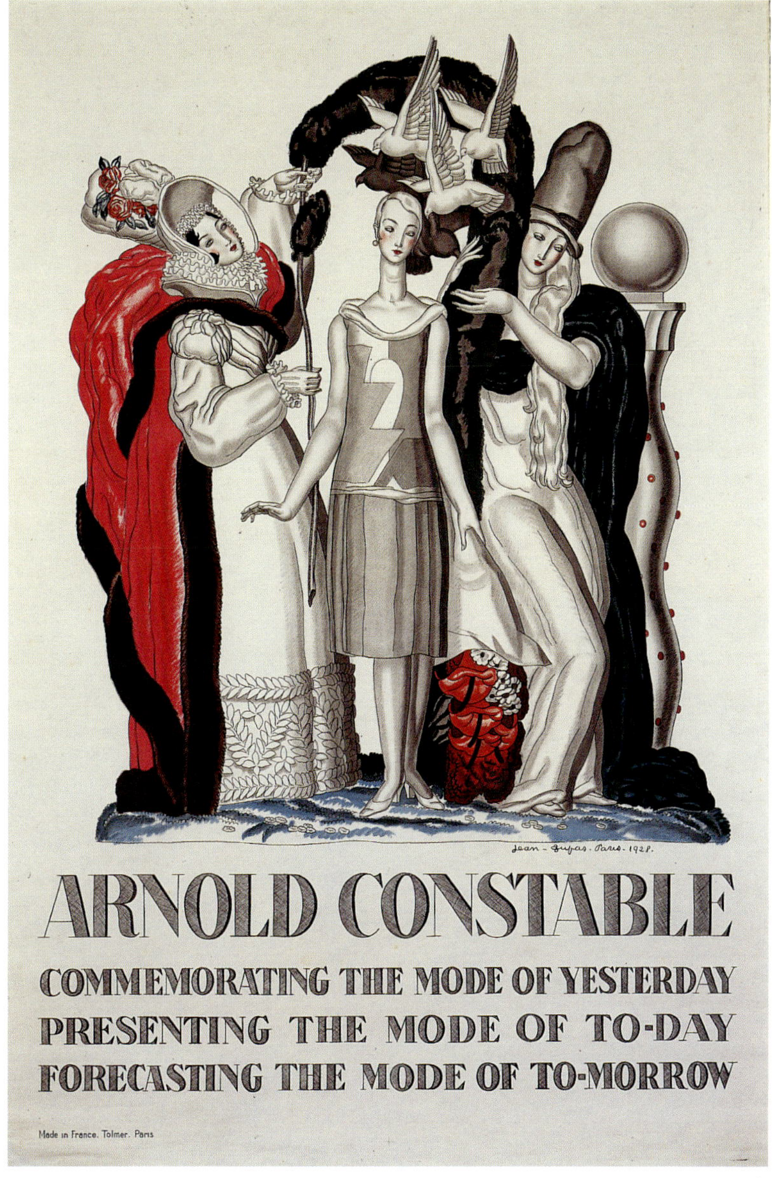

324

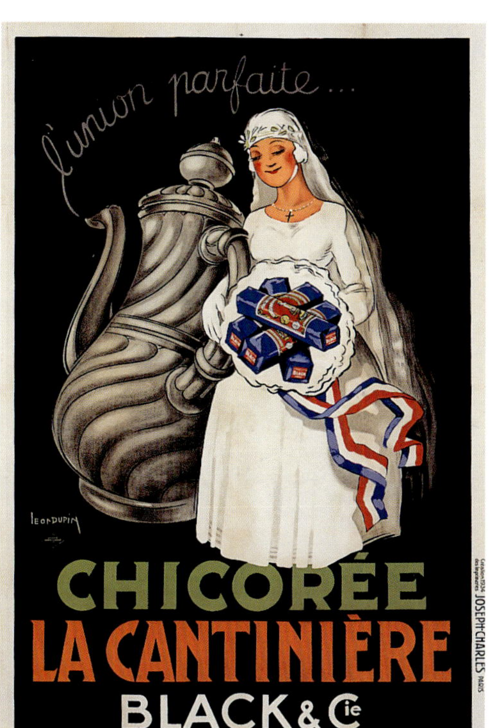

325

JEAN DUPAS (1882-1964)

322. "Green Line" Coach. 1933.
25 x 30^1/$_8$ in./63.5 x 102 cm
Johnson, Riddle, London
Cond A–/Horizontal fold in bottom text area.
Ref: PAI-XXIV, 373
A genteel scene, so typical of Dupas, for Green Line
Coach, one of the bus companies incorporated, along
with the Underground, into London Transport in 1933.
After Dupas won the gold medal at the 1922 Salon
des Artistes Français, he began to acquire a prestigious international clientele including the Sèvres
porcelain works, Saks department store in New York
and the London Underground, for which he designed
six posters between 1930 and 1933.
Est: $3,000-$4,000.

323. Camden Town, Chalk Farm or Regents Park.
1933.
23^3/$_8$ x 38^5/$_8$ in./59.3 x 98 cm
Johnson, RIddle & Company Ltd., London
Cond B+/Slight tears and stains at edges; image and
colors excellent.
Ref: Weill, 398; PAI-X, 221
In his invitation to hop aboard London Transport, Dupas
populates his design with the genteel, fashionable
people from the very fringes of our imagination, occu-
pants of the realm that exists in the split second before
true wakefulness alchemizes into peaceful slumber,
gorgeous quasi-humans with Modigliani necks in idealized settings. Only this time, he throws an elephant in
for good measure. And the results are startling, phan-
tasmagoric and utterly unforgettable.
Est: $3,000-$4,000.

324. Arnold Constable. 1928.
31 x 47^1/$_4$ in./78.7 x 120 cm
Tolmer, Paris
Cond A.
Ref: Tolmer, p. 79; PAI-XXX, 491
In all of his posters, Dupas presented highly stylized,
very fashionable people in idealized and extravagant
settings. Here, he gives us a look at the past, present
and future fashions of Arnold Constable.
Est: $4,000-$5,000.

LEON DUPIN

325. Chicorée la Cantinière. 1934.
38^3/$_4$ x 58^3/$_4$ in./98.5 x 149.3 cm
Joseph-Charles, Paris
Cond B+/Slight tears at folds.
Here comes the bride, all dressed in white and toting
a surprisingly nationalistic bouquet of Black & Company's Cantinière chicory instead of the usual bunch
of flowers. The oversized coffee pot declares it a "Perfect Union" and Dupin's newlywed appears sweetly
inclined to agree. Clearly, this woman (whose lily-white
ensemble leads us to believe that she must be a virgin
when it comes to taking caffeinated chances) loves her
coffee and certainly isn't about to add anything to the
mix that would lessen that relationship. Though not
hugely popular in the United States, chicory is a commonplace additive to—or even a substitute for—coffee
throughout Europe. Little is known of Dupin. He was
born about 1900; his poster output is slight but distinguished, most of it having been done at the Joseph-
Charles plant from about 1929 through 1936.
Est: $1,400-$1,700.

white, but some of the lengths of fabric hanging from
the figure's arm are tinged the most exquisitely pale
shades of pink and green. Dufrène also created the
operetta's sets and costumes.
Est: $2,000-$2,500.

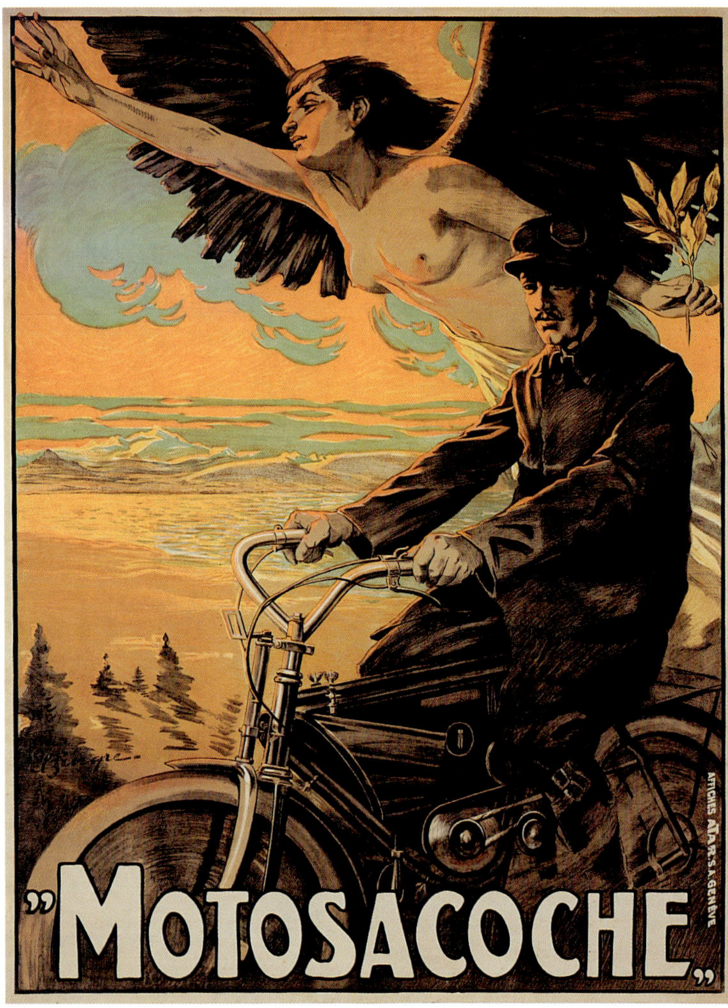

327

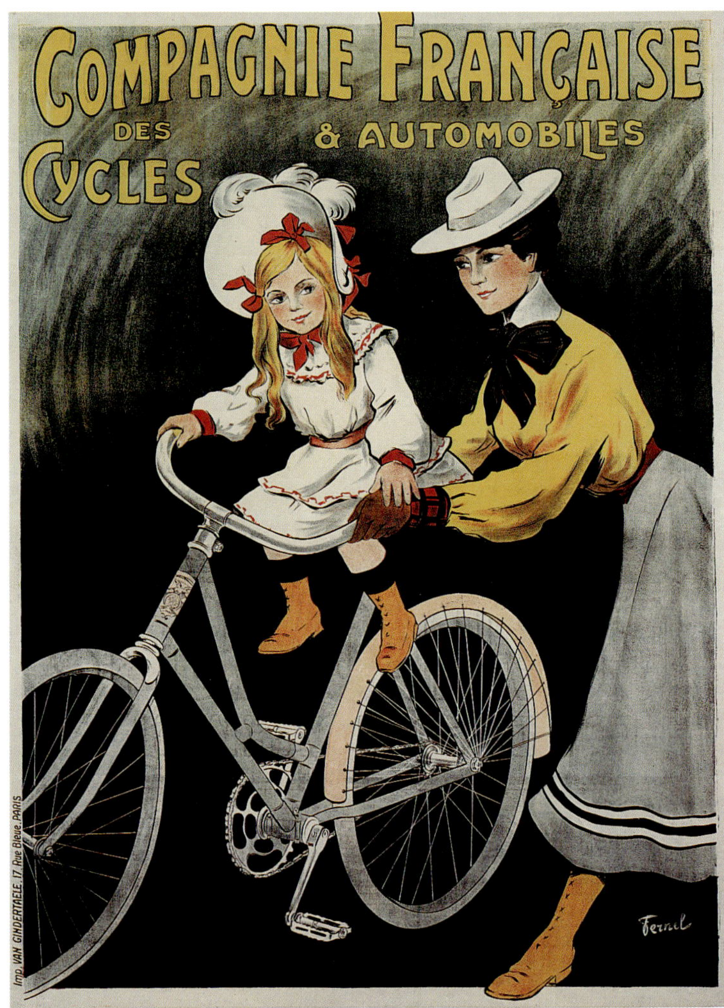

329

LEONIDA EDEL (1864-1940)

326. Grande Albergo Ardesio. 1905.
39^1/4 x 77^1/4 in./99.7 x 196.3 cm
D'Arte Grafiche, Bergamo
Cond A–/Slight tears at paper edges.
Ref: Bolaffi, p. 86; PAI-XXXIV, 217
The meticulously executed composition sends a clear message that you can rest and recuperate in this Alpine resort, even without the Italian textual explanation. And the vivid colors used throughout the poster only help to imbue the design with healthful portent.
Est: $2,500-$3,000.

EDOUARD ELZINGRE (1880-1966)

327. "Motosacoche".
42^1/2 x 57^1/8 in./108 x 146 cm
Affiches ATAR, Genève
Cond A–/Slight tears in upper left margin.
"Switzerland had some twenty motorcycle manufacturing companies, starting in 1899, the year in which Motosacoche was founded. Henri and Armand Dufaux started out producing small engines for bicycles, but devoted themselves almost immediately to the production of motorcycles and engines of 250 cc to 1000 cc, under the MAG trademark" (*One Hundred Years of Motorcycles*, Massimo Clarke, editor, p. 190). Elzingre's poster for the motorcycle borders on the sacrosanct, with the bare-breasted emissary hovering over the focused rider coming across as more of a guardian angel than any embodiment of the company's excellence. The serious nature of the design demonstrates beyond a shadow of a doubt that Motosacoche was wholeheartedly dedicated to not only manufacturing the most powerful bike on the market, but also the safest ride available.
Est: $4,000-$5,000.

CANDIDO ARAGONESE DE FARIA (1849-1911)

328. Ando Genjiro/Jongleur Japonais.
30^1/2 x 48^5/8 in./77.5 x 123.4 cm
Imp. Formstecher, Paris
Cond B/Slight tears and stains at folds.

Ando Genjiro, Japanese Juggler. Said like that, it almost sounds as if that title might be the name of a "Saturday Night Live" sketch or Rob Schneider's latest "comedy." But this Faria poster is no laughing matter, demonstrating with a central portrait and eight performance cameos that Mr. Genjiro took his juggling and balancing very seriously. And the lowest central inset shows a prop table set up with a reverence more closely associated with an altar than a variety act. Too bad that no record of his time on-stage appears to have been kept.
Est: $1,200-$1,500.

FERNAND FERNEL (1872-1934)

329. Compagnie Française des Cycles & Automobiles.
39^1/4 x 54^5/8 in./99.8 x 139 cm
Imp. Van Gindertaele, Paris
Cond B+/Slight tears at folds.
Ref: PAI-VI, 116
No doubt some day soon, this little wannabe cyclist will be able to ride away of her own volition, exploring horizons of which she can only dream today. But seeing as of this moment she can't quite reach the pedals, her mother helps her to get a taste of what hitting the open road is all about atop her Compagnie Française bicycle. A charmingly naive Fernel creation.
Est: $2,500-$3,000.

FELDTMANN

330. Norddeutscher Lloyd Bremen. ca. 1937.
23^7/8 x 32^3/4 in./60.7 x 83.3 cm
Wilh. Jontzen, Bremen
Cond B/Slight tears and creases at edges.
Everything seems as bright and optimistic as possible in this Feldtmann poster for the Norddeutscher Llloyd Bremen Line, what with the ornamental birds perched atop the foreground spray of bamboo and three single-stack ships—the *Gneisenau*, the *Potsdam* and the *Scharnhorst*—setting sail for the Far East atop golden seas. It is, however, a bit difficult not to notice the Nazi flags flying on the stern of all three vessels and not be taken somewhat aback. The North German Lloyd Company was founded in 1857 by the amalga-

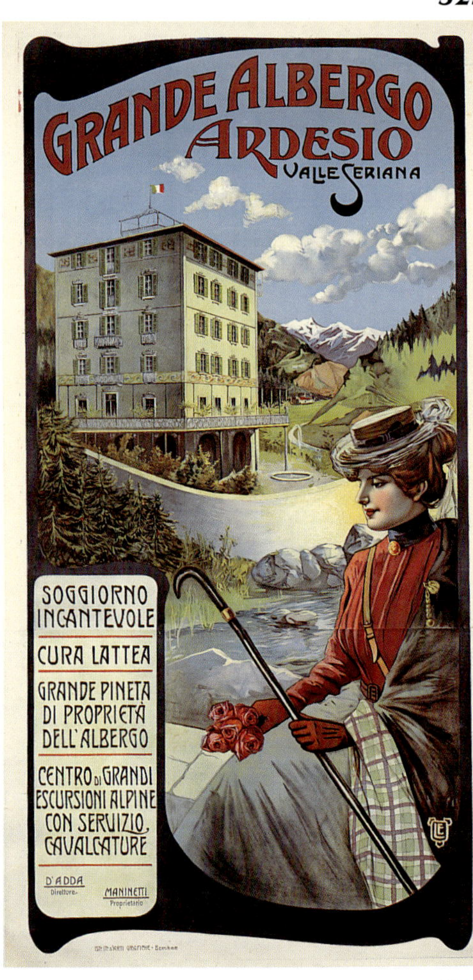

326

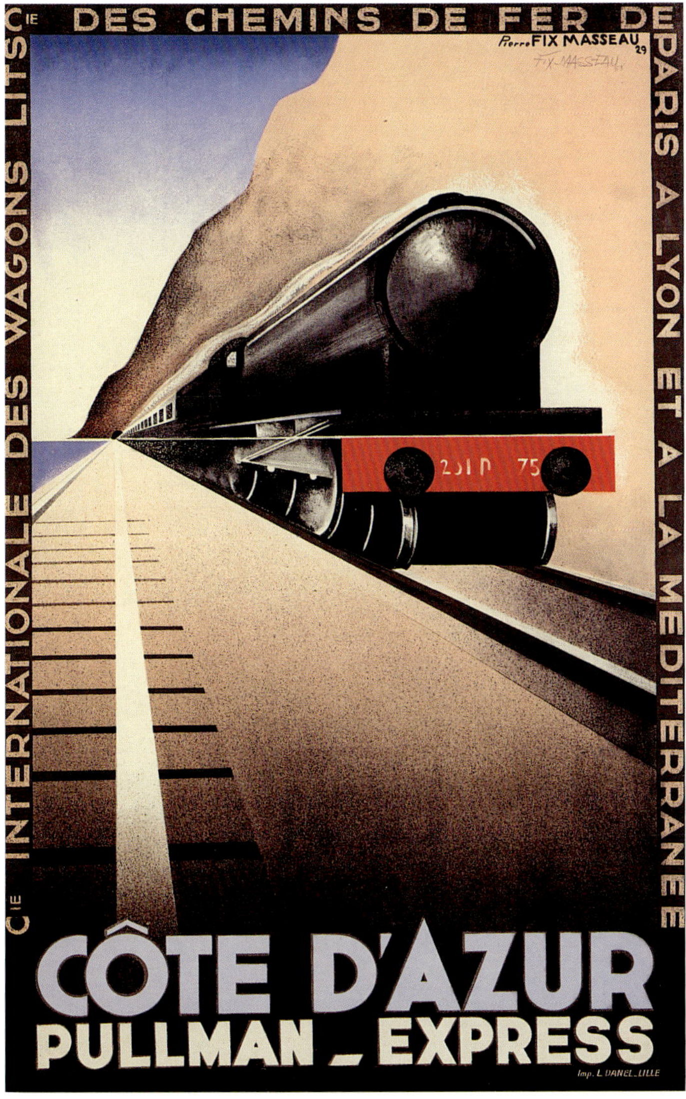

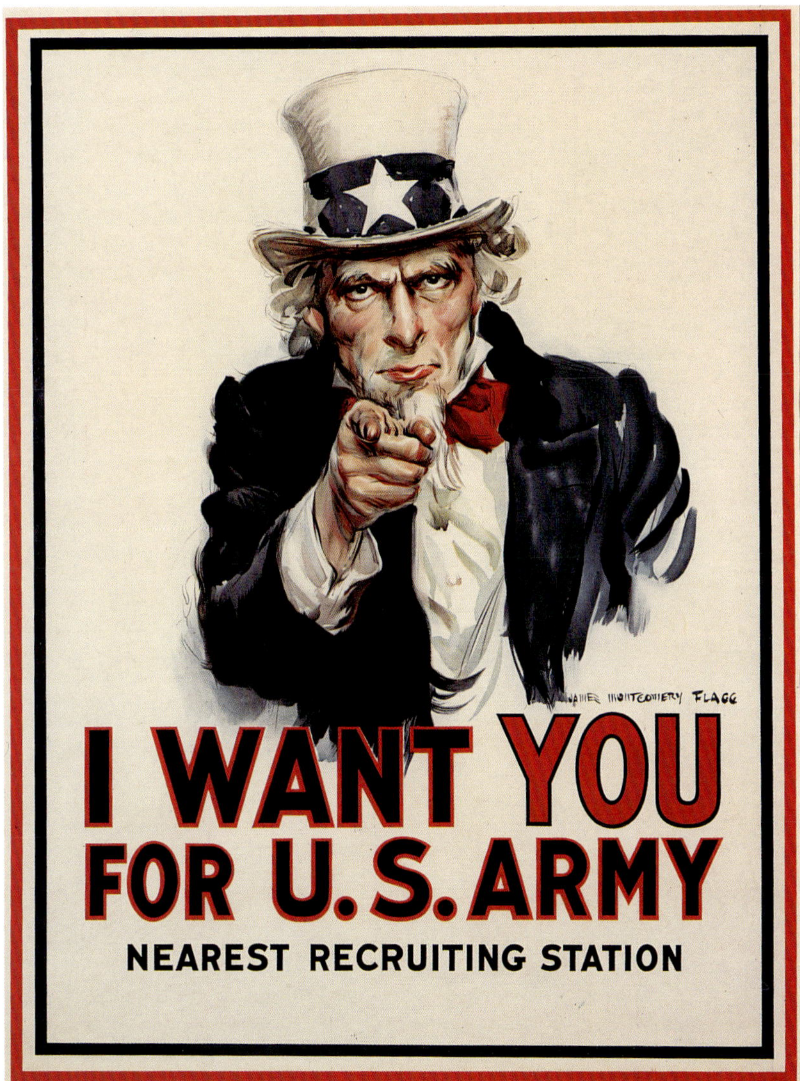

331

332

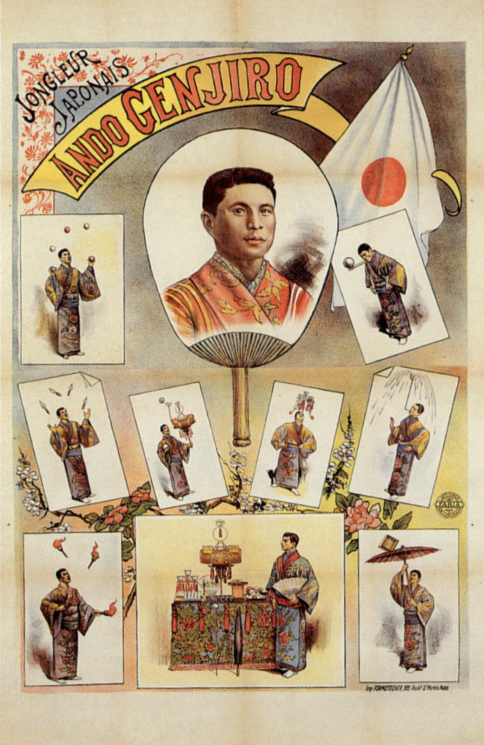

328

330

PIERRE FIX-MASSEAU (1905-1994)

331. Côte d'Azur/Pullman Express. 1929.
24 1/8 x 39 in./61.2 x 99 cm
Imp. L. Danel, Paris
Cond A.
Ref: Fix-Masseau, p. 5; Chemins de Fer, 113;
  Railway Posters, 132; Train à l'Affiche, 268;
  Affiches Azur, 14; Affiches Riviera, 8;
  PAI-XXXVIII, 336
"Fix-Masseau seemed particularly adept at putting the
speed and power of locomotives to good effect in his
graphic designs. This 1929 poster for the luxury Côte
d'Azur Pullman trains of the PLM adopts a track-level
viewpoint to emphasize the streamlined 'windcutter'
profile of the train engine" (Railway Posters, p. 112).
Est: $8,000-$10,000.

JAMES MONTGOMERY FLAGG (1870–1960)

332. I Want You for U.S. Army. 1917.
28 7/8 x 40 1/4 in./75.8 x 102.2 cm
Leslie-Judge Co., N.Y.
Cond A. Framed.
Ref: Rawls, p. 13; Theofiles, 11; Darracott, p. 13;
  PAI-XX, 503
Although Flagg was a successful and prolific magazine
illustrator by the time World War I started, Theofiles
points out that this poster was to become "his greatest
public triumph." According to him, Flagg posed for it
himself and his "rendering was originally used on a
Leslie's Magazine cover in late 1916, and was quickly
adopted by the Army when the war broke out. All told
nearly 5 million were printed in both world wars." In
spite of this, Theofiles correctly indicates that "specimens (of this original version) are still scarce" (pp. 9
& 24). Uncle Sam became a motif in many other Flagg
posters in both wars, including one in 1941 with Uncle
Sam admonishing. "I Want YOU, F.D.R.—Stay and finish
the job (*see* PAI-XL, 328)!"
Est: $1,700-$2,000.

mation of four smaller companies. The line gained
nearly instant success, which only grew over the years,
servicing New York, London, Baltimore, New Orleans,
Brazil, the Far East and Australia. At the outbreak of
World War I, many of their ships took refuge in United
States ports. These liners were seized by American
authorities in 1917 and after the Armistice, the company lost every worthwhile ocean going steamer as war
reparations. In 1920, NDL chartered ships from the
United States Shipping Board to resume services, gra-
dually rebuilding their fleet. But, during World War II,
they again lost almost their entire fleet and once more
were forced to operate with chartered ships. In 1970,
the company joined forces with the Hamburg America
Line to become HAPAG-Lloyd.
Est: $1,000-$1,200.

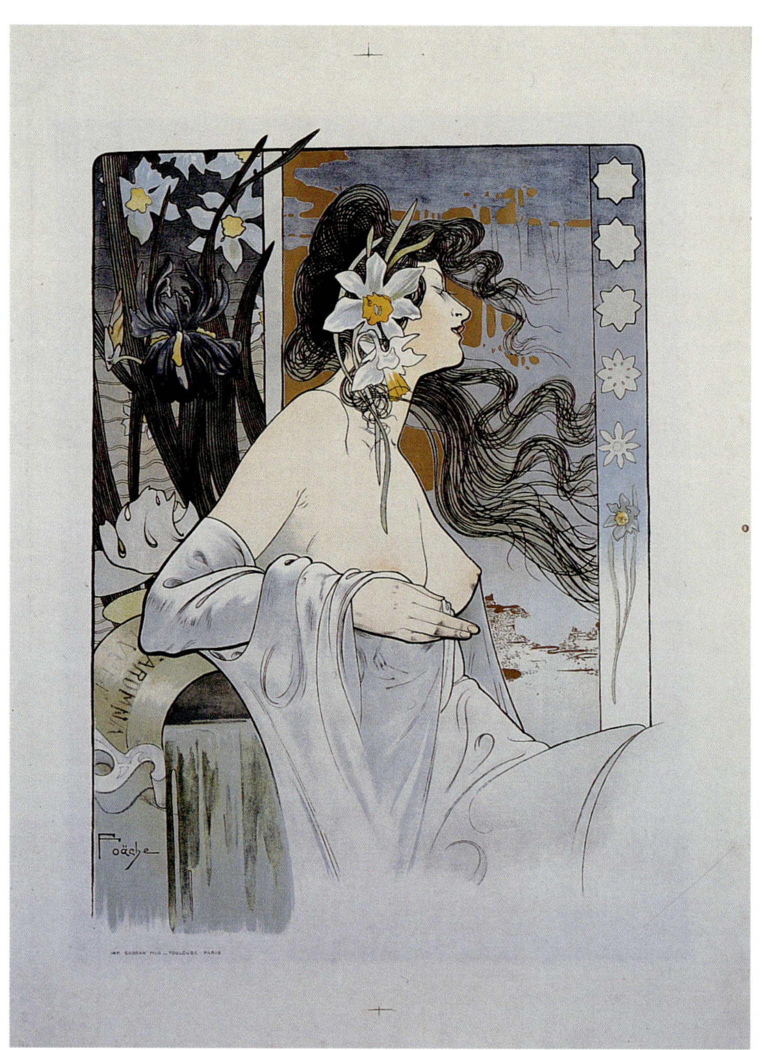

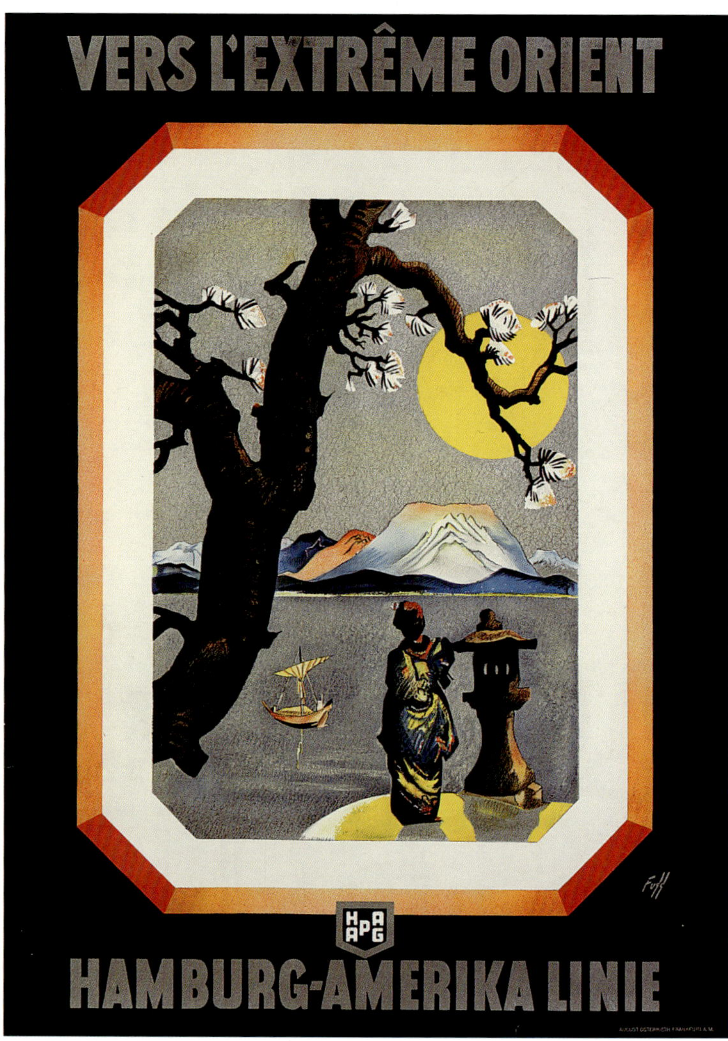

333

335

ARTHUR FOACHE (1871-1967)

333. La Garonne. 1898.
$20^3/_4$ x $28^1/_4$ in./52.7 x 71.7 cm
Imp. Cassan Fils, Toulouse
Cond A/P.
Ref: DFP-II, 359 (var); Abdy, p. 148; PAI-XXXI, 452
In this rare, before letters version, it was a limited-edition print offered by Cassan Fils printers to its valued clients; in another edition, it was a full-fledged poster for the printer, with his name in large type at the bottom of the design. "Foâche was an artist from the south of France, who worked in Toulouse. His poster for 'La Garonne' has close affinities with Mucha's second 'Salon des Cent' poster, yet it has independent merit. As befits the portrayal of a water goddess, the coloring is aqueous, pale blue, and pale green. The sky in the background is streaked with gold. On the panel on the right he combines two favorite symbols by gently transforming a star into a narcissus" (Abdy, p. 149). *The widest margins that we have ever seen on this image!*
Est: $3,500-$4,000.

DOMINIQUE CHARLES FOUQUERAY (1872-1956)

334. Théatre National de l'Opera/Gala de la Marine. 1936.
16 x 24 in./40.5 x 60.7 cm
L'Atlantique, Paris
Cond A.
A charity gala benefiting French sailors—held at the Théatre National de l'Opera and organized by an association of former Naval Academy students—is promoted with stately command by Fouqueray. Although the history of the French Navy goes back to the Middle Ages, it did not become a consistent instrument of national power until the seventeenth century with Louis XIV. Fouqueray acknowledges this in his artwork, not simply with frigate and battleship, but with then-and-now examples of admirals and the sophisticated women with whom they consort.
Est: $1,400-$1,700.

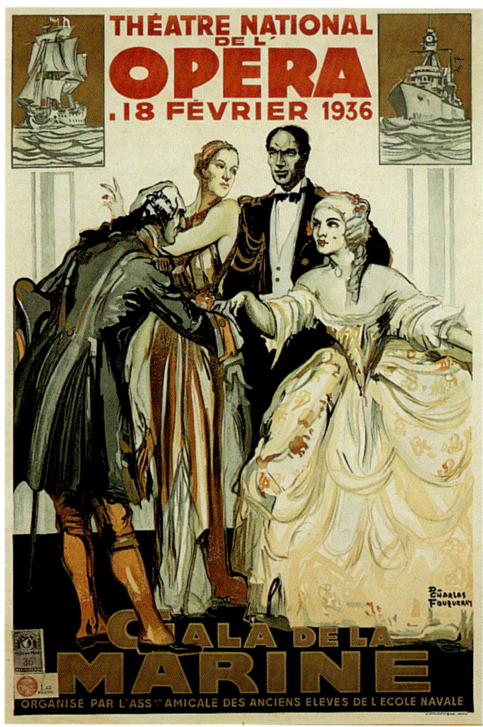

334

ALBERT FUSS (1889-1969)

335. Hamburg-Amerika Linie/Vers l'Extrême Orient.
$23^1/_4$ x 33 in./59 x 84 cm
August Olsterrieth, Frankfurt
Cond A–/Slight tears at edges.
Fuss throws open a *mado* into a world of Far Eastern exoticism with a Japanese woodblock art-influenced promotion for the Hamburg-Amerika Line—made all the more lustrous with the addition of metallic silver ink. Though the view might be a bit stylized, the allure of

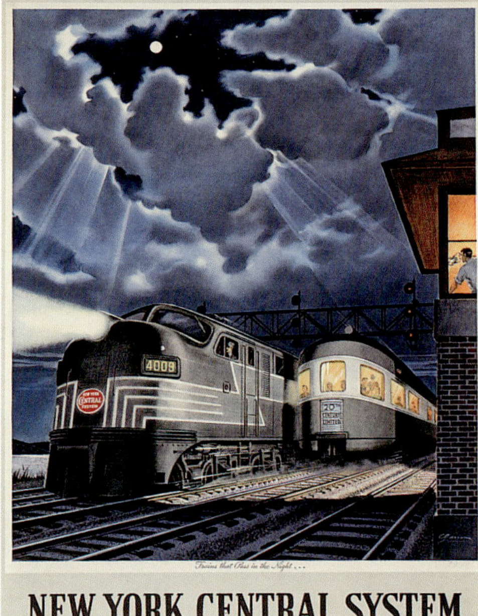

336

the unfamiliar is powerfully enticing. Perhaps the artist's most interesting inclusion in his panoply of assorted details may very well be the *ishi doro*, or stone lantern to the right of the awaiting geisha. Seen all over Japan —at shrines, temples, graveyards and private gardens —*ishi doro* all have a hollowed out top piece, which lead many people, including contemporary Japanese, to think that they might have originally been used for illumination. Today, however, they are simply ornamental for the most part, decorative pieces carved from granite or syenite.
Est: $1,200-$1,500.

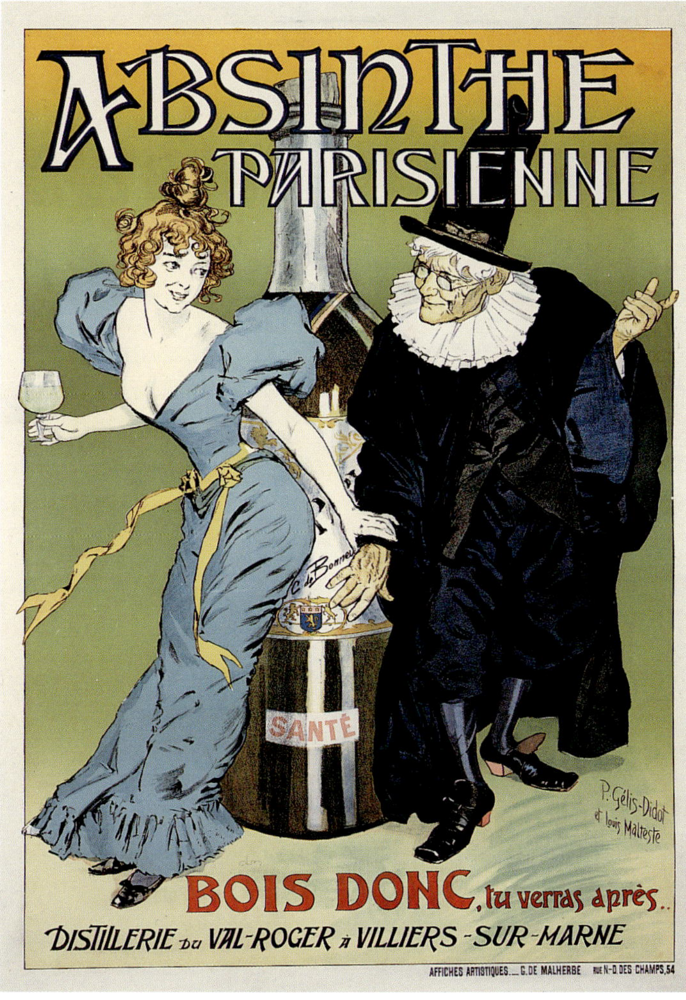

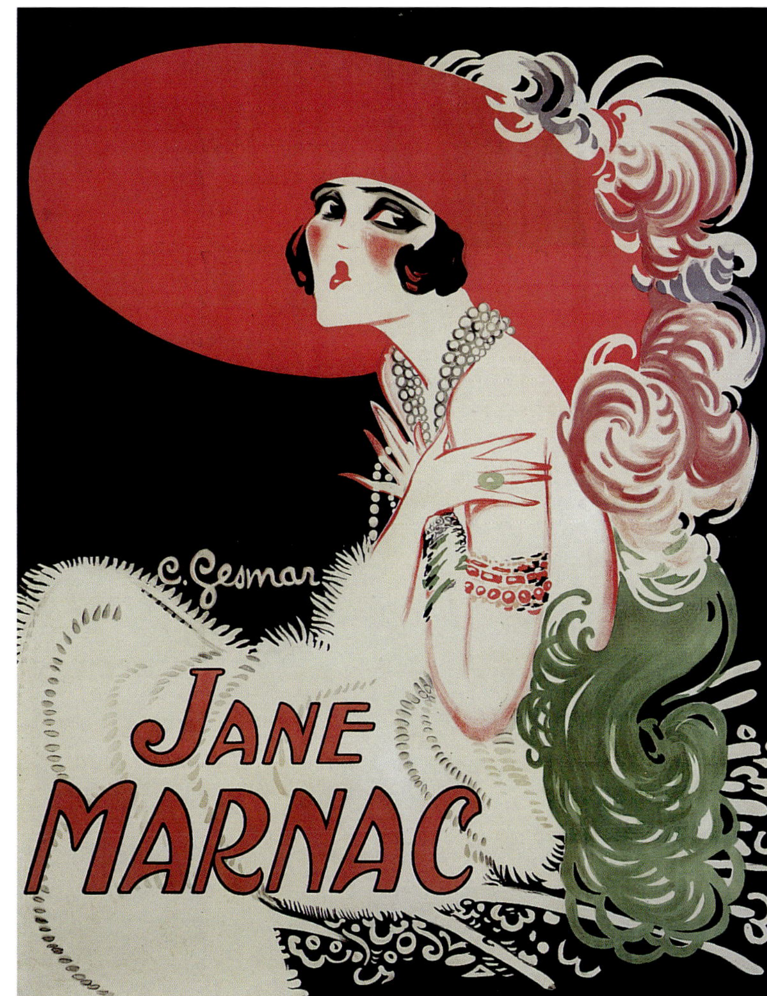

338

339

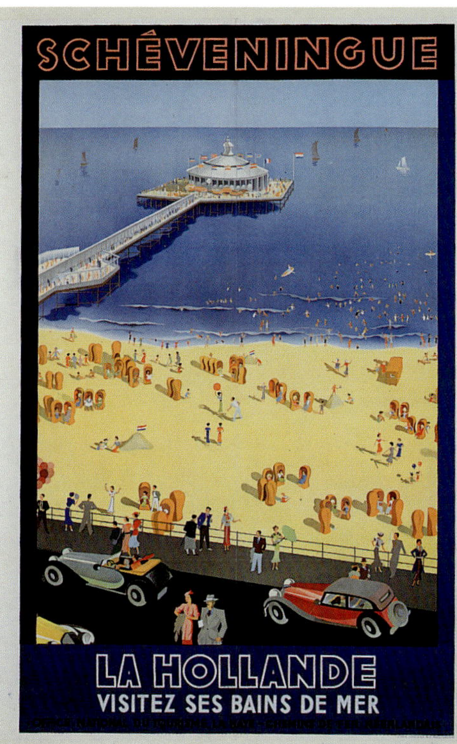

337

GACSON

336. New York Central System/Trains that Pass in the Night. ca. 1948.
15^1/$_2$ x 21^1/$_4$ in./40 x 54 cm
Cond A.
Most of the crack trains in the New York Central's "Great Steel Fleet" spent their time hurrying coddled passengers overnight between New York City and Chicago,

presenting a challenge to the poster artists engaged to convey all that night time activity in pictures. This scene displays an especially creative use of light to dispel the darkness. The modern diesel's headlight stabs through the night ahead; signal lights stand sentinel on the four-track mainline; a towerman flashes an "all clear" to the passing trains, illuminated by a flood light behind the building; the warm glow of the observation car tells us the passengers on the famous 20th Century Limited are having a high old time. Above all the action, a full moon peaks through the clouds and is reflected on the Hudson River below. If that's not enough, the classic paint scheme on the Central's diesel locomotives was always known as the "lightning stripe."
Est: $1,400-$1,700.

EMMANUEL GAILLARD

337. La Hollande/Schéveninque.
27^1/$_4$ x 39^1/$_2$ in./69.2 x 100.3 cm
L. Van Leer, Amsterdam
Cond B+/Slight tears at folds.
Ref: PAI-XXXVIII, 344 (var)
Though the popular beach resort of Schevinengen is an entity in and of itself, it's also considered to be a part of The Hague, located just to the northwest of its center city. Comprised of the Zuiderstrand and Noorderstrand (South and North beaches), Schevinengen is a Dutch sun lover's paradise, offering all the seaside fun one could ever want, while at the same time providing access to all of the trendiest amenities. Gaillard extends an idyllic invitation to the French-speaking beachgoer with this uncompromisingly lovely scene, complete with an abundance of beach chairs that dot the strand like sun-shielding sarcophagi.
Est: $1,700-$2,000.

PIERRE-HENRI GELIS-DIDOT (1853-?) & LOUIS MALTESTE (1862-1928)

338. Absinthe Parisienne. 1896.
33^1/$_4$ x 47^1/$_2$ in./84.5 x 120.7 cm
G. DeMalherbe, Paris
Cond A.
Ref: Reims, 659; Boissons, 287; Absinthe, p. 110;
   Absinthe Affiches, p. 75; PAI-XXIII, 236
Molière's medical fool, Diafoirus, and a young woman join forces to promote the effects of this brand of absinthe. "Drink it and see," they urge. The author of the Reims catalogue terms the deeply decolletaged dress as being blue, but it seems clear to us that this young woman with her copper hair swept up in a topknot is a fresh-looking version of *la féerie verte*, the "green fairy" who was the Parisians' personification of this potent, and eventually outlawed, drink. Reims describes Gelis-Didot as freelance art director and author of many works, including *Le Peinture décorative en France*; about his partner Malteste, we have discovered nothing.
Est: $2,500-$3,000.

CHARLES GESMAR (1900-1928)

For other works by Gesmar, see Nos. 82-89.

339. Jane Marnac.
46^3/$_8$ x 60^3/$_8$ in./118 x 153.3 cm
Cond B+/Slight tears at folds and edges.
She has been called the most Parisian of all stage stars and in her ninety active years (1886-1976) Jane Marnac played hundreds of theatrical roles and sang in numerous operettas, most notably in the French version of Noel Coward's "Waltz Time." And though the venue for which this poster was executed remains unspecified, Marnac gets the full Gesmar treatment—ropes of pearls, blanketing furs, an extravagantly-plumed hat that could almost be the star of its own review and an expression that piques the viewer's interest to such a degree that attendance becomes mandatory. *Excruciatingly rare!*
Est: $8,000-$10,000.

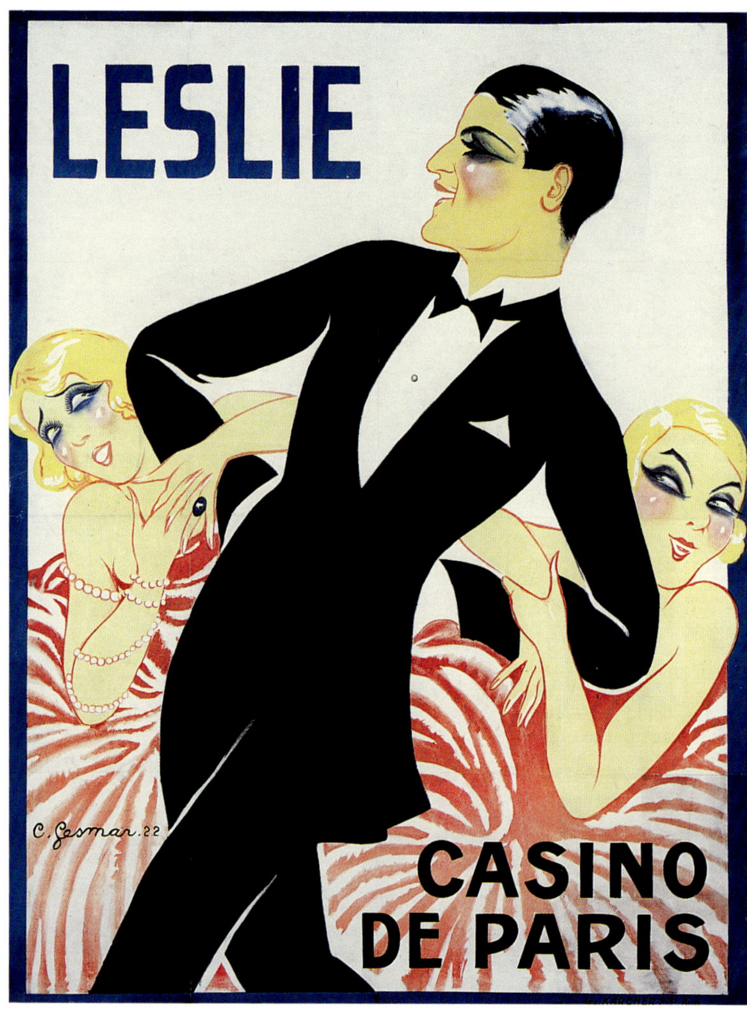

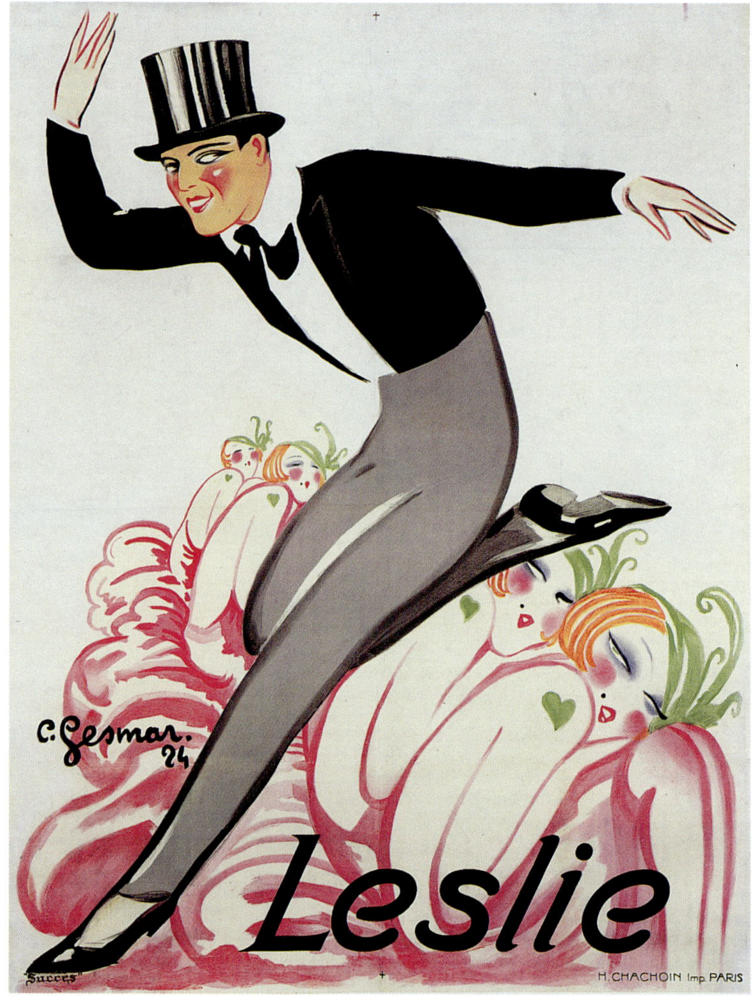

340   341

CHARLES GESMAR (cont'd)

340. Leslie/Casino de Paris. 1922.
45⁵/₈ x 61 in./116 x 155 cm
Imp. Karcher, Paris
Cond B–/Slight tears at folds and edges.
Ref: PAI-XLII, 293
Though this well-heeled ladies' man is identified with a singular moniker, it's fairly safe to assume that we're looking at Earl Leslie, the younger American dancer who became Mistinguett's partner—both on and offstage—after her breakup with Maurice Chevalier. By the time of this poster's production, their romance had begun to cool, so Mistinguett probably wasn't much affected by his lithographic canoodling with a pair of moony-eyed chorines for an appearance at the Casino de Paris.
Est: $5,000-$6,000.

341. Leslie. 1924.
46¹/₈ x 62³/₈ in./118 x 158.4 cm
Imp. H. Chachoin, Paris
Cond B/Slight tears at folds and edges.
Which sophisticated hoofer is able to leap a gaggle of chorus girls in a single bound? Leslie, that's who! Much as we saw in the previous poster, Gesmar makes it clear with panache to spare that Leslie was without a doubt a favorite with the ladies. *Exceedingly rare!*
Est: $8,000-$10,000.

342. Guy Sarlin. 1925.
46 x 62 in./117 x 157.6 cm
Imp. H. Chachoin, Paris
Cond A–/Slight tears, largely near paper edges.
Ref: PAI-XIV, 265
Often flamboyant in his unabashedly adoring posters for Mistinguett, Gesmar here uses restraint—and only one color, cinnabar red, other than black—letting the dynamism of the dancer speak for itself.
Est: $2,000-$2,500.

343. Doriane. ca. 1926.
45¹/₄ x 60³/₄ in./115 x 154.3 cm
Imp. Kaplan, Paris
Cond A.
Ref: PAI-XXIX, 368
A rare work by Gesmar for a relatively obscure per-former: the singer Doriane (Paule Dorian). Gesmar dazzles us with the opulence of her costume and the strands of pearls, intrigues us with the mystery of her dark eyes and places her against a black background that gives her a spotlit look. Although the poster is undated, the bobbed hair, which became popular in 1926, pinpoints it fairly accurately. Doriane was appear-ing that season and the next at La Cigale; this was probably the high point of her career, which seems to have started at La Mesange in the early 1920s and ended toward the end of the decade at L'Olympia.
Est: $5,000-$6,000.

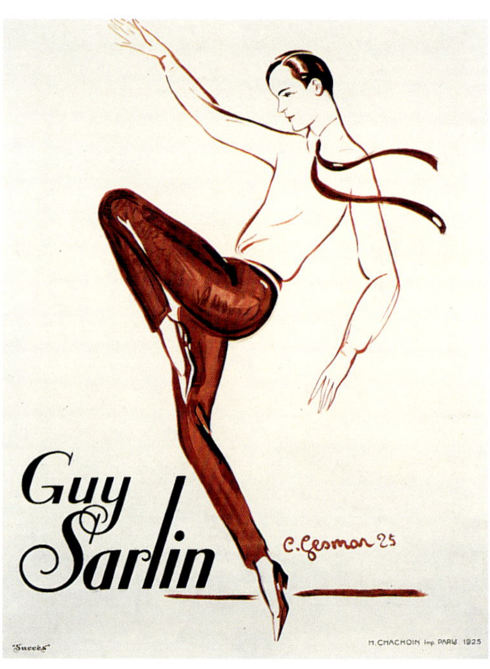

342

<table>
<tr><td>

</td><td>

INCREMENTS

Bidding at our auction will be strictly by the following increments:

To $2,000	by $100
$2,000–$5,000	by $200
$5,000–$10,000	by $500
$10,000–$20,000	by $1,000
$20,000–$50,000	by $2,000
$50,000–$100,000	by $5,000
$100,000–over	by $10,000

</td></tr>
</table>

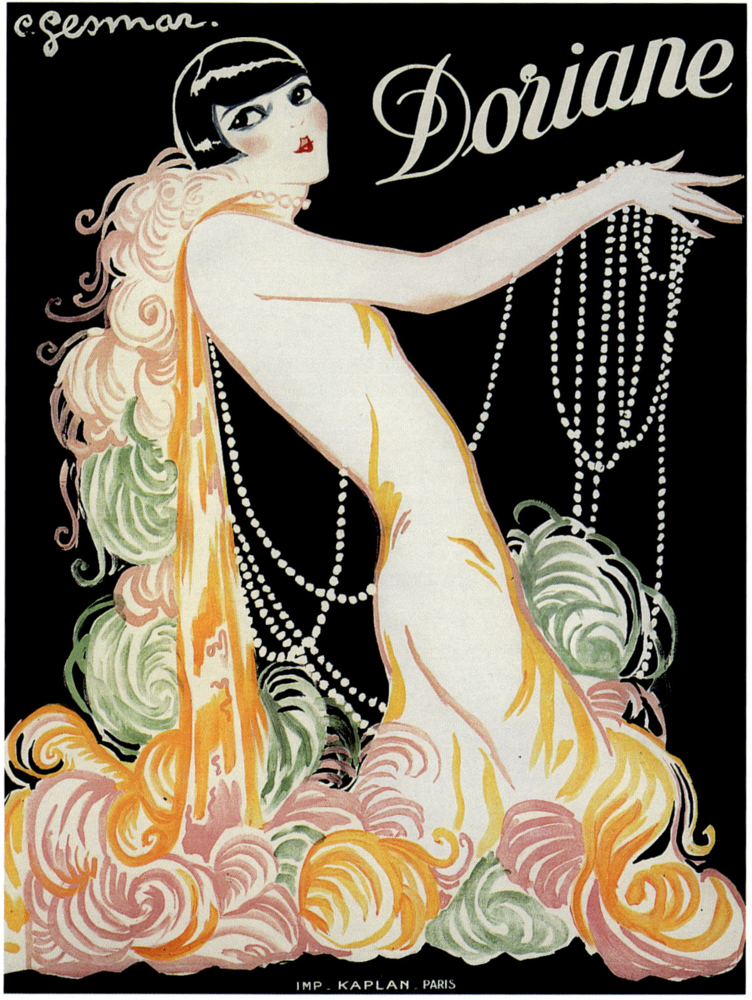

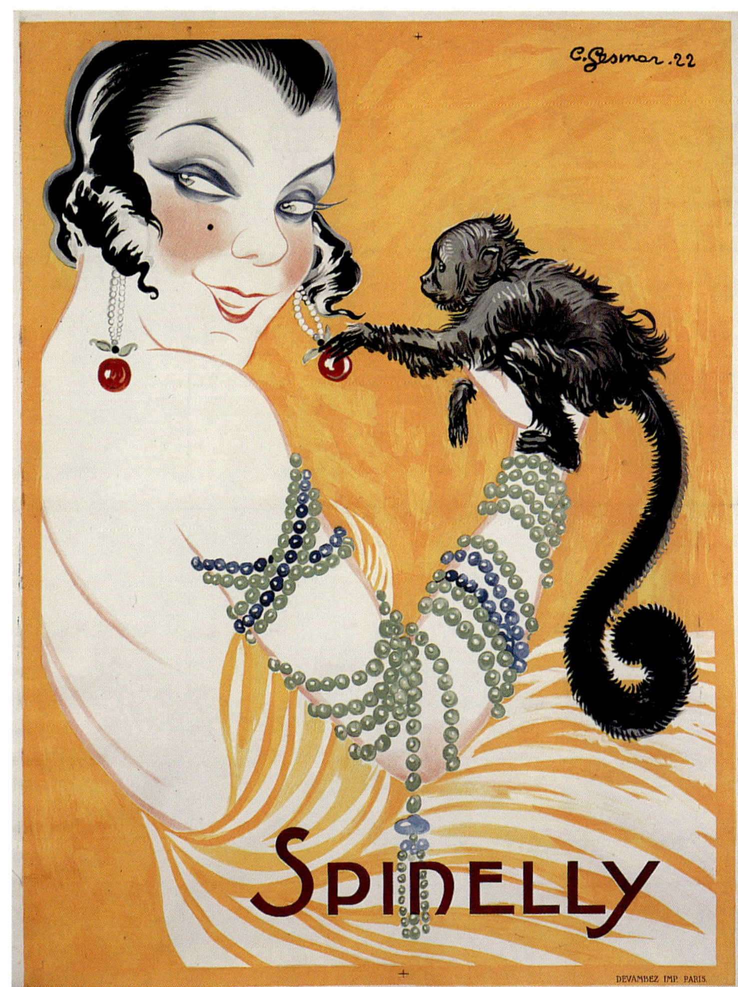

is said that it was Spinelly who discovered Gesmar a year earlier. It is not clear what the relevance of the monkey in this design is or whether he had a role in her revue; it is clear he has a large part in attracting our attention to this rare poster.
Est: $5,000-$6,000.

345. Bal des Petits Lits Blancs à L'Opéra. 1928.
$15^3/_4$ x $31^5/_8$ in./40 x 80.3 cm
Imp. Françaises Réunies, Paris
Cond B+/Unobtrusive folds.
Ref: PAI-XII, 228 (var)
In one of Gesmar's most dazzling—and elusive—designs, this beauty dressed seemingly in nothing but beads invites us most tantalizingly to a charity ball at the Opera, sponsored by the newspaper, *L'Intransigent*. As is hinted at by the abed tikes below, this famous annual event benefited a children's hospital. *Rare!*
Est: $1,700-$2,000.

346. Harry Baur. 1928.
47 x $62^7/_8$ in./119.2 x 159.7 cm
Imp H. Chachoin, Paris
Cond B+/Slight tears at folds and edges.
Ref: PAI-XXXI, 62
A marvelously incisive character study of one of France's premier stage and film personalities. Harry Baur (1880-1943) was one of the giants of the French performing arts. Trained in stagecraft from an early age, he was at his best portraying powerful characters, both fictional and historical; in that regard, he was the Paul Muni of the French cinema in the 1930s. He essayed Jean Valjean in "Les Misérables" (1934); Emperor Rudolph II in "Le Golem" (1936); Beethoven in "Un Grand Amour de Beethoven" (1936); Rasputin in "La Tragedie Imperiale" (1938); and he was both "Rothschild" (1934) and "Volpone" (1939). During the Nazi occupation, the German authorities somehow got wind of the fact that Baur's wife was Jewish and they promptly arrested her; Baur refused to comply meekly and so he, too, was taken and subjected to torture as a suspected Allied agent. A few days later, he tragically died from internal injuries sustained during his interrogation.
Est: $2,500-$3,000.

345

346

344. Spinelly. 1922.
$46^3/_8$ x 62 in./117.7 x 157.6 cm
Imp. Devambez, Paris
Cond A–/Unobtrusive folds.
Ref: PAI-XXX, 509
Andrée Spinelly was born in Paris in 1890. After appearing in all the major music halls in Paris, as well as in Cochran's Revue of 1926 in London and Ziegfeld's *Midnight Frolic* in New York in 1927 among others, she began a career in radio and recording in the late 1920s and moved onto films in the 1930s. She played a spy in two of her early films and became typecast in such roles. Although Gesmar's career is closely associated with that of Mistinguett, his very first poster, dating to 1916 at the age of sixteen, was, in fact, for Spinelly. It

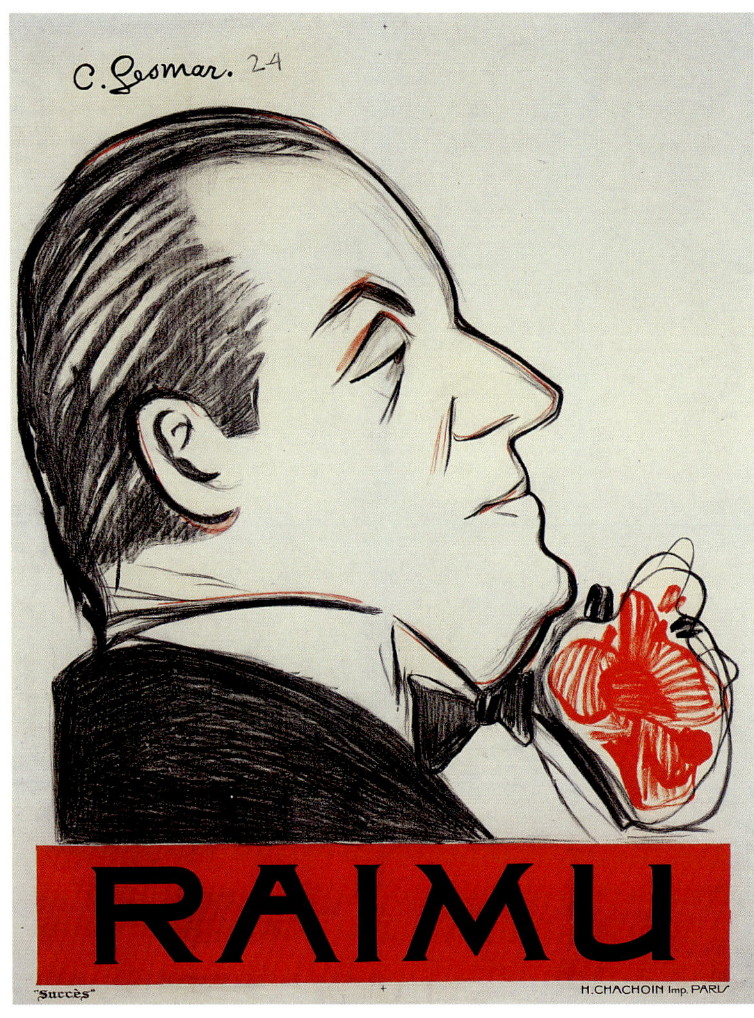

347

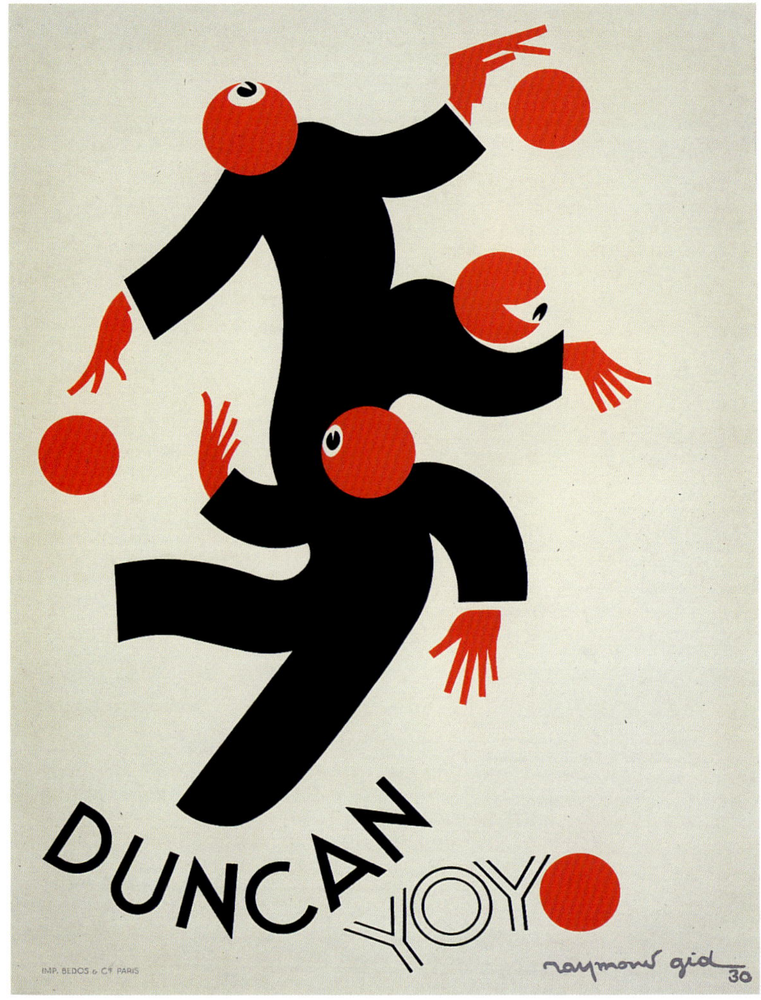

348

CHARLES GESMAR (cont'd)

347. Raimu. 1924.
$47^3/8$ x 63 in./120.5 x 160 cm
Imp. Chachoin, Paris
Cond B+/Slight tears at folds and edges.
Born Jules Auguste Muraire (1883-1946), this native of Toulon would adopt the stage name Raimu and take to the boards of Paris after coming to the attention of music hall star Félix Mayol, who was also a Toulon native. Though already a leading actor, Raimu gained wide acclaim in 1929 for his starring role in the stage production of the Marcel Pagnol play *Marius*, a role he would reprise to international acclaim in the film version of the play some two years later. By his late forties, Raimu had become one of his country's most respected actors and considered the ultimate actor by luminaries such as Alec Guinness, Marlene Dietrich and Orson Welles. Gesmar's poster portrait of the actor captures him in profile, filled with the depth and dignified gravitas that one would expect to find in a performer of such respected renown. *Rare!*
Est: $3,000-$4,000.

RAYMOND GID (1905-2000)

348. Duncan Yoyo. 1930.
$23^3/4$ x $31^1/4$ in./60.4 x 79.4 cm
Imp. Bedos, Paris
Cond A.
Ref: Gid, Checklist #24
Trained as an architect, Gid became a graphic journeyman, creating corporate logos, typography and posters for a number of major clients. His stripped-down, elliptical style with economic traces of color is evident in this amazing poster for Duncan yo-yos, a fantastic lithographic pictograph where it's impossible to discern where one yo-yo starts and another begins—with no strings attached, mind you. Though the oldest surviving terra cotta yo-yos decorated with paintings of mythological figures have been traced to 500 BC, the yo-yo craze genuinely took-off the year of this poster's production when Donald F. Duncan bought out Pedro Flores' Santa Barbara yo-yo factory. Duncan would team-up with Hearst newspapers during the 1930s to promote yo-yo contests, initiating a fad that would ride a wave of popularity until the 1960s and make the maple wood toy a pop culture icon.
Est: $4,000-$5,000.

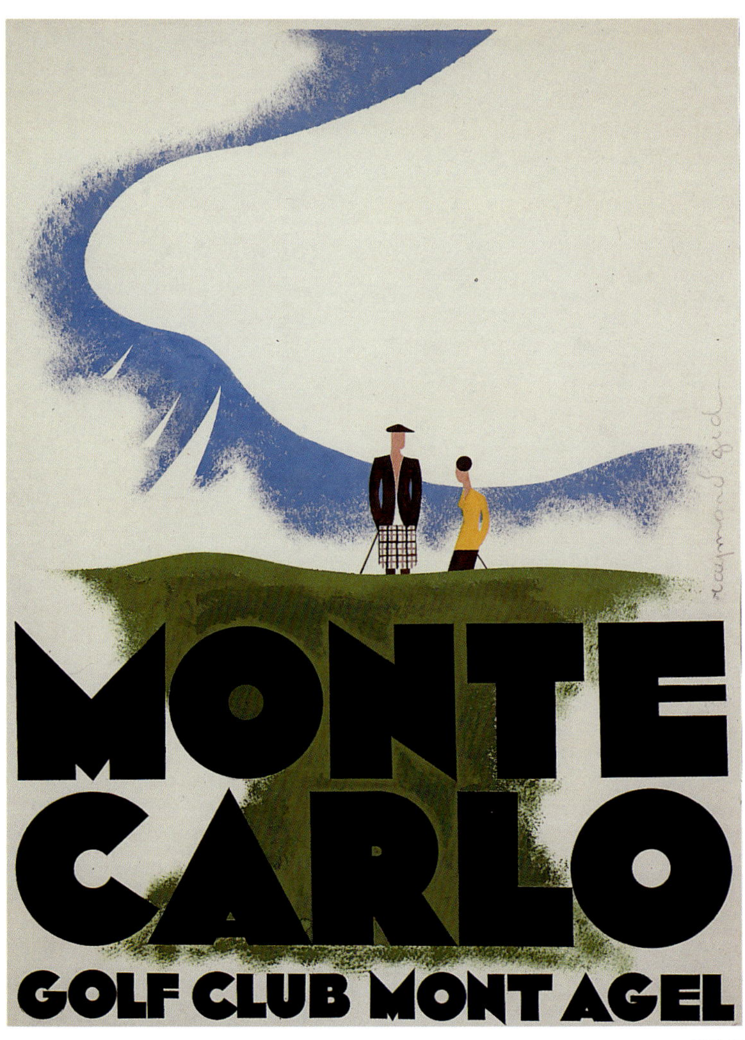

349

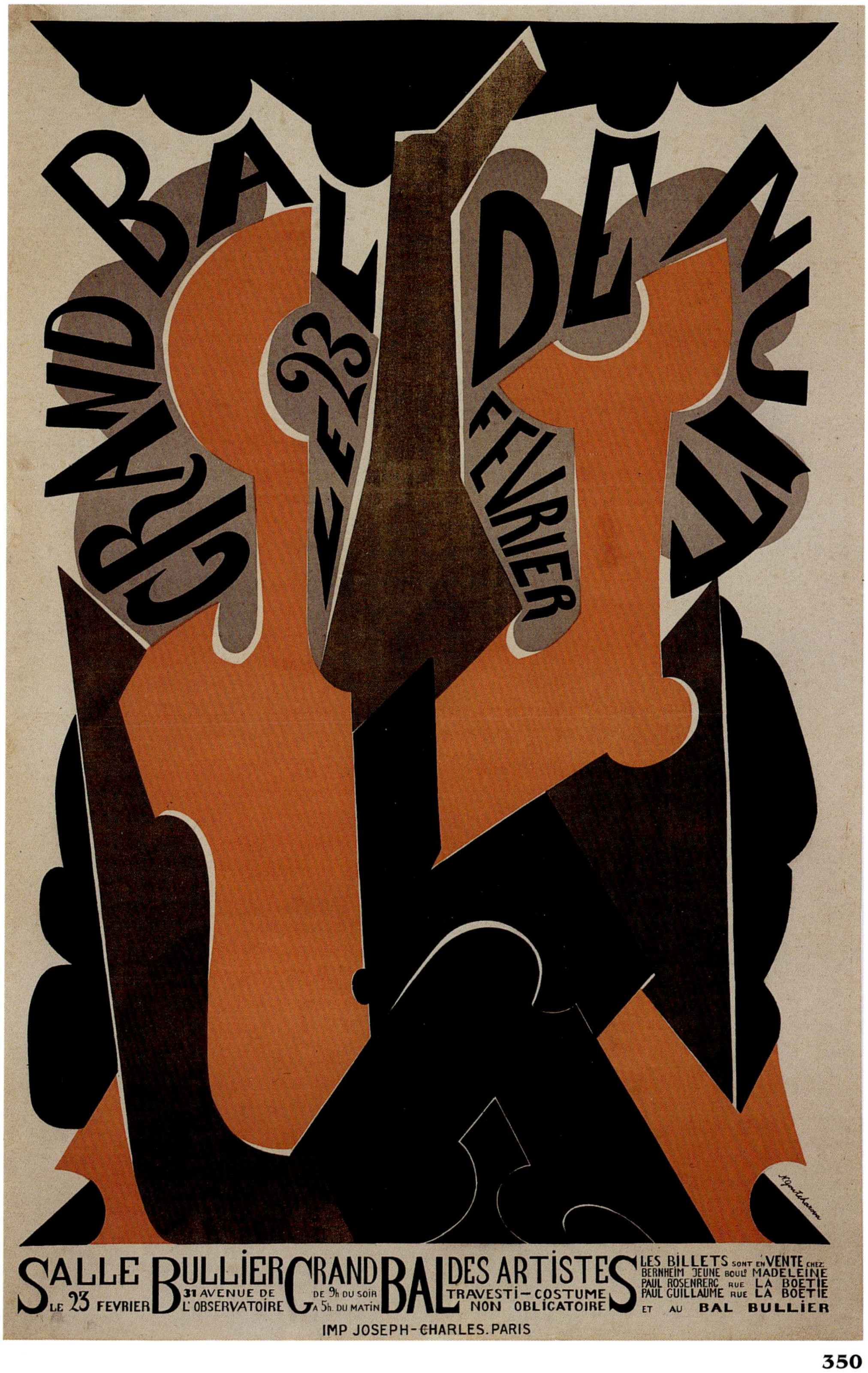

349. Monte Carlo/Golf Club Mont Agel. 1932.
23 x 31^5/8 in./58.9 x 80.4 cm
Gouache and ink maquette on board. Framed
Ref (All Var): Gid, 99; Golf, p. 40; Affiches Riviera, 213
Though the size of the completed poster was somewhat larger (32^1/4 x 48^7/8 in./82 x 124 cm), the artistic integrity of the artwork remained intact in lithographic form: the sweeping sky, the twosome cresting a rise in the fairway, the lettering that couldn't be any more specific without latitude and longitude. "This elegant poster focuses more on perfect graphics than people's outfits: just a few lines portray the atmosphere" (Golf, p. 40). In other words, quintessential Gid.
Est: $6,000-$7,000.

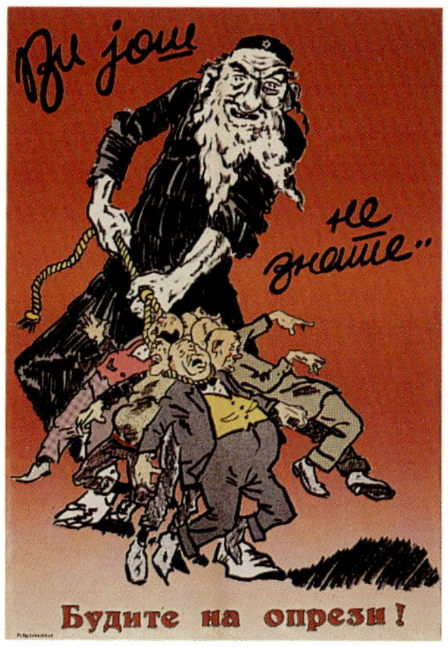

NATALIA GONTCHAROVA (1881-1962)

350. Bal de Nuit. 1920.
30^1/8 x 46^3/4 in./76.5 x 118.8 cm
Imp. Joseph-Charles, Paris
Cond B/Slight staining in background; unobtrusive tears near folds and paper edges.
Ref: Art Deco, 55; Weill, 322; PAI-XXVI, 306
Gontcharova's long and productive career spans several countries and many styles. She could be very expressionist, or be in the midst of futurism, or, as in this poster, at the very core of cubism. After a successful career of painting and teaching in Russia, as well as exhibiting in all the major European avant-garde shows, including the 1911 Blaue Reiter and the 1913 Der Sturm, she went to Paris in 1914 where she settled permanently. There she was involved in all facets of theatrical work, including designing sets for Diaghilev. Illustration also preoccupied her, but she did little in the medium of the poster. This one for the Grand Bal de Nuit at the Salle Bullier is a spectacular evocation of the cubist style that was little used in posters. Whether one sees in it a couple under a tree or some other image, one gets an impression of a vivacious "happening."
Est: $17,000-$20,000.

GRAND ANTI-MASONIC EXHIBITION

351. Three Posters. 1941.
Each Approx: 19 x 27^1/2 in./48.4 x 70 cm
Various Belgrade printers
Cond B+/Slight tears at folds and edges.
Ref: PAI-XLI, 298 (a) & 299 (a & c)
The Nazi regime occupied most of Yugoslavia by April of 1941. After a Serbian uprising in July of that year, a "Grand Anti-Masonic Exhibition" opened in Belgrade on October 22nd, funded by SS occupiers and supported by Milan Nedic, the collaborationist local ruler. The language used in these posters is Serbian, even though the Cyrillic alphabet hadn't been used there for many years and Serbia had become part of the newly-created Yugoslavia in 1918. The images on display were hardly new, however, and had been seen before during "The Eternal Jew" exhibitions in Munich and Vienna between 1937 and 1939.

The main thrust of the exhibition, which ran for three months, was to intensify hatred against the Jews, a fact made abundantly clear by the graphics even though the name of the exhibition vaguely attempts to make the viewer believe otherwise. Since the sentiment of these posters is immediately obvious, we will provide textual translation of the text in the posters with no other commentary.

a: Even if you're paying attention . . . Be on the lookout!
b: The Jewish dream of world domination is now disappearing under the attack from finally awakened nationalism! How? Learn about it at the Anti-Masonic Exhibition.
c: His weapons: Democracy, Masonry, Capitalism and Communism.
Est: $1,700-$2,000. (3)

350

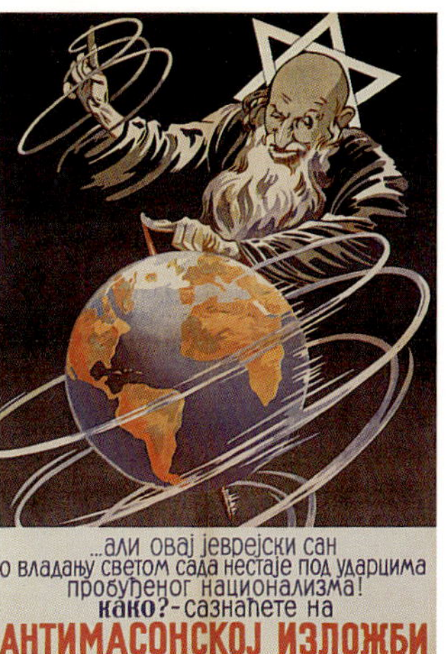

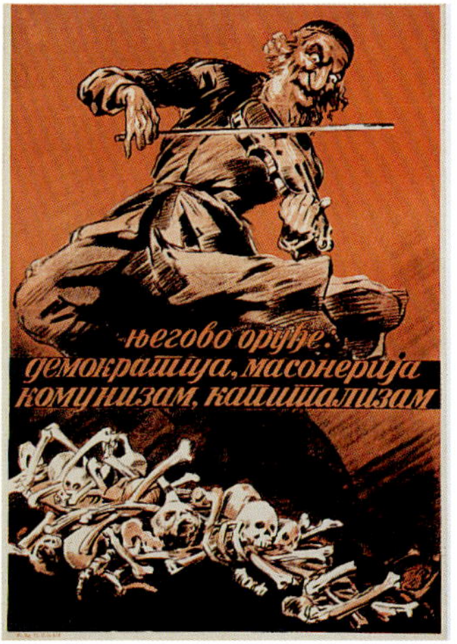

a   b   c   **351**

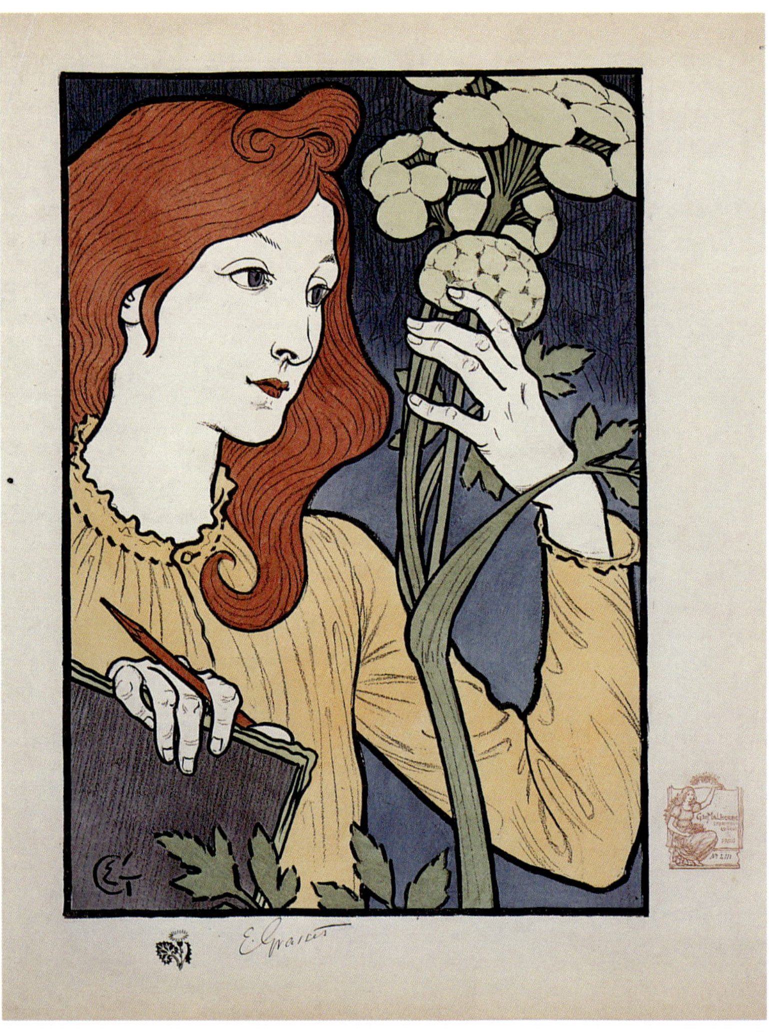

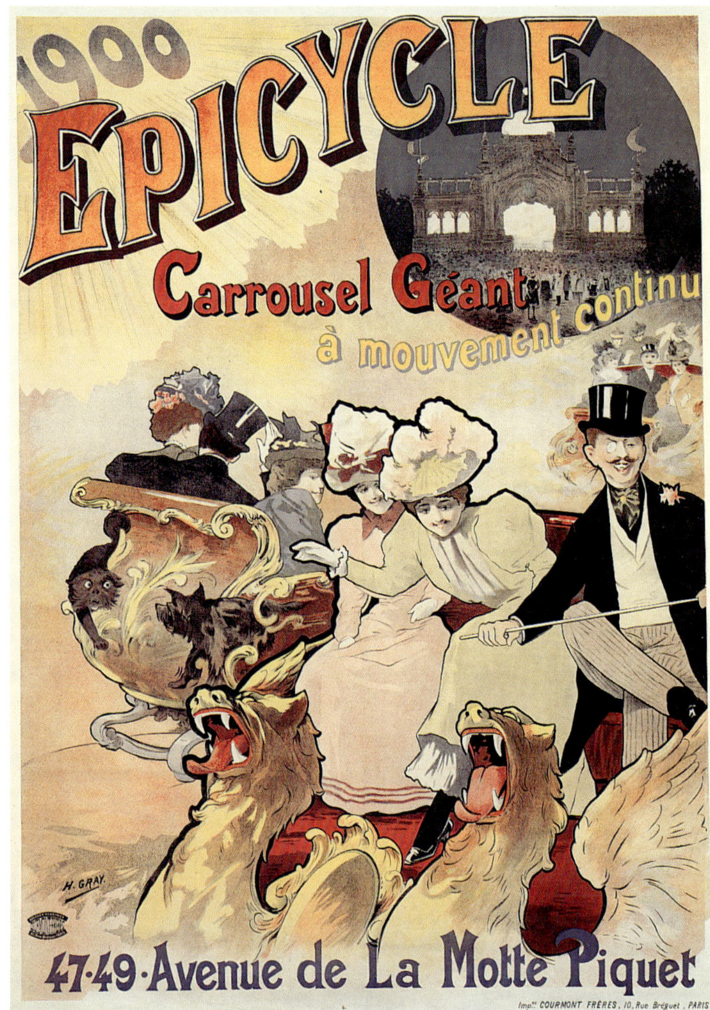

352

354

EUGENE GRASSET (1841-1917)

352. Salon des Cent/Exposition E. Grasset. 1894.
$19^3/_8$ x $25^1/_8$ in./49.4 x 63.8 cm
Imp. G. de Malherbe, Paris
Cond B+/Slight tears and stains, largely near paper
    edges.
Ref (All Var but PAI): Salon des Cent, p. 19;
    Salon des Cent/Neumann, p. 38; DFP-II, 410;
    Reims, 684; Wagner, 54; Berthon & Grasset, p. 6;
    Weill, 39; Gold, 274; PAI-V, 190
*Hand-signed proof from the numbered edition of
100 copies before letters on Chine paper with publisher's stamp.*
For his own exhibition at the Salon des Cents—seen
here in a rare before-letters proof—Grasset shows a
chestnut-tressed artiste soulfully contemplating a tall-
stemmed flower—a pose that is almost medieval in
its conception—and provides us with a rare glimpse
straight into the heart of the moment when observation becomes inspiration. Grasset did much to introduce the concept and practice of Art Nouveau in France.
In fact, Grasset "brought Art Nouveau to the aid of the
poster: it was to become a worldwide vehicle of the
art of advertising. In France, Grasset was the pioneer
of an attempt, like that of William Morris in England,
to reconcile art and industry . . . Interested as he was
in all the applied arts, he came naturally to the poster"
(Weill, p. 32).
Est: $5,000-$6,000.

353. Exposition Internationale de Madrid. 1893.
42 x $57^3/_4$ in./106.7 x 146.6 cm
Imp. Lemercier, Paris
Cond A.
Ref: DFP-II, 407; Berthon & Grasset, p. 32; Hiatt, p. 51;
    Reims, 673; Chaumont/Exposons, p. 23;
    PAI-XXXVII, 332
This justly famous image is a crazy quilt of patterns—
not just in the figure's gown and cloak, but in her
serpentine hair, the embellishment of her throne, the
muchness of ribbons, fold creases and drapes. The
setting has a nervousness as well, with clouds pulled

into shreds, repeated arches, fluttering pennants and
eerie shadows. But key to this slightly disturbing design
is the low perspective and skewed angle of the figure
as she steps down to trumpet the event. Fabulous!
This is the French-language version.
Est: $2,000-$2,500.

H. GRAY (Henri Boulanger, 1858-1924)

354. Epicycle. 1900.
$37^5/_8$ x 54 in./95.6 x 137 cm
Imp. Courmont Frères, Paris
Cond B/Restored tears at folds and edges.
Ref: PAI-XLI, 312
One of the many attractions of the 1900 World's Fair
was the Epicycle, essentially a merry-go-round for
grown-ups. Judging from the reactions of the three
patrons aboard the griffin-clad car, though it may
seem rather tame by today's thrill-seeking standards,
the ride was a totally enjoyable diversion.
Est: $2,000-$2,500.

JULES-ALEXANDRE GRÜN (1868-1938)

355. La Jolie Cliente. 1900.
$12^3/_4$ x $18^1/_8$ in./32.5 x 46.2 cm
Cond A. Framed.
Isn't she lovely? Isn't she wonderful? And she's an
active consumer to boot. With Montmartre serving as
a backdrop, it's safe to assume that this coquette might
know a thing or two about painting the town red; however, surrounded as she is by others who appear to
have made a few purchases themselves, it seems likely
that this easy-on-the-eyes shopper is making the scene
in order to promote one of Paris' finer department
stores. Regrettably our research yielded no information
as to which emporium these citizens might be patron-
izing. In an interview featured in the March, 1899 edition of *The Poster*, Grün summed up his graphic goals
as follows: "Since (1891), I believe that I have done
about fifteen (posters), in which I have tried to find
new and simple effects. Two or three colors are quite
sufficient to produce something interesting. Black and

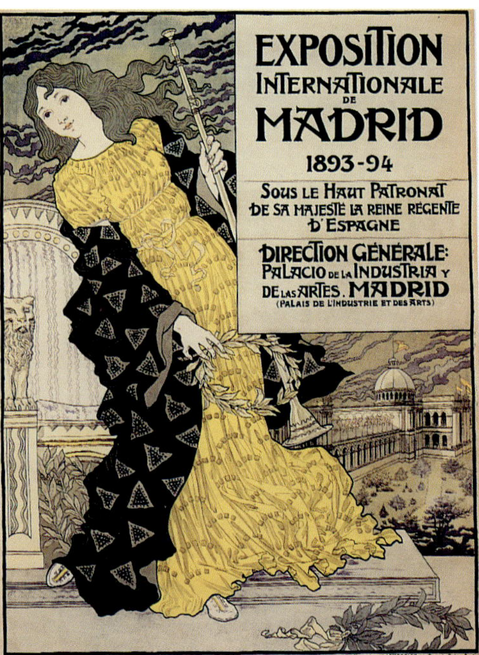

353

white, with a touch of red or green . . . As for my subjects, I search for them always in the same places: in
the theatres or café-concerts, for which I have done all
my affiches" (p. 100).
Est: $1,700-$2,000.

356. Concert Européen/Veux-tu Grimper? 1898.
$33^1/_4$ x $48^1/_4$ in./84.3 x 122.6 cm
Imp. Chaix, Paris
Cond A.
Ref (Both Var): Grün, p. 55; PAI-XL, 354
"The Concert Européen, located on Rue Biot close to

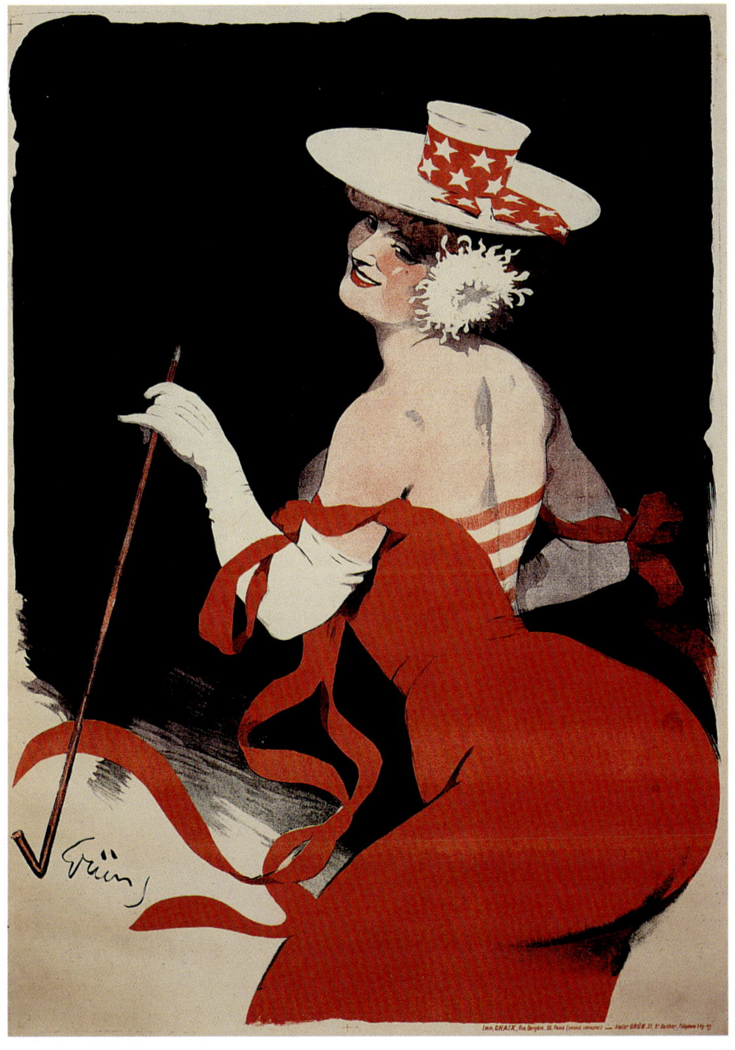
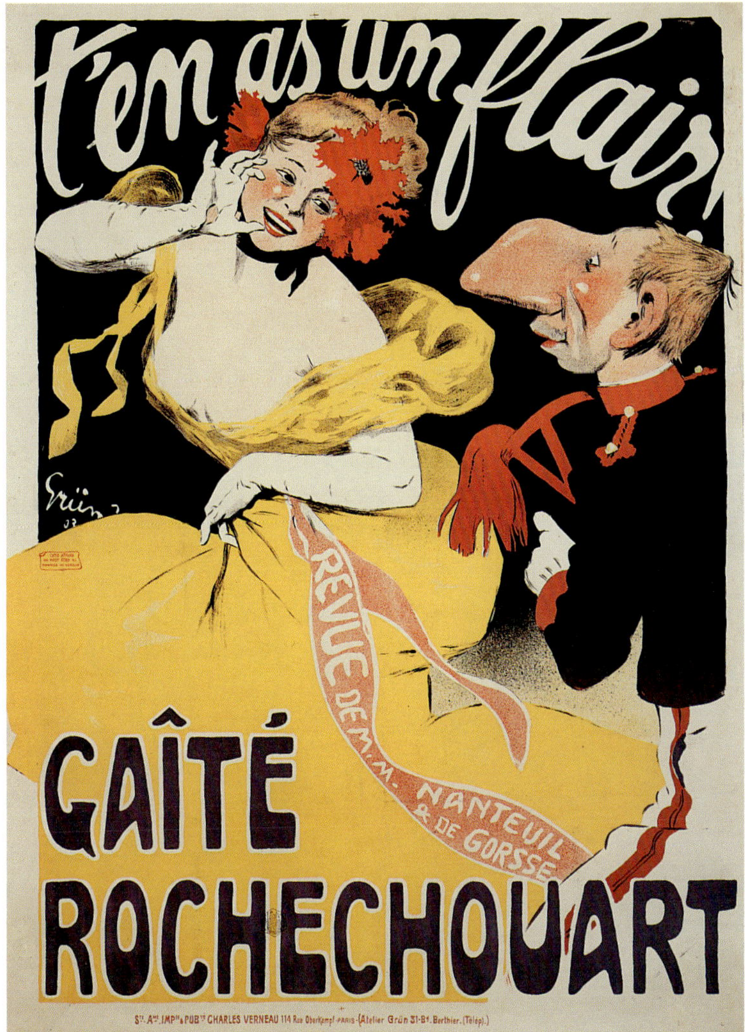

356

357

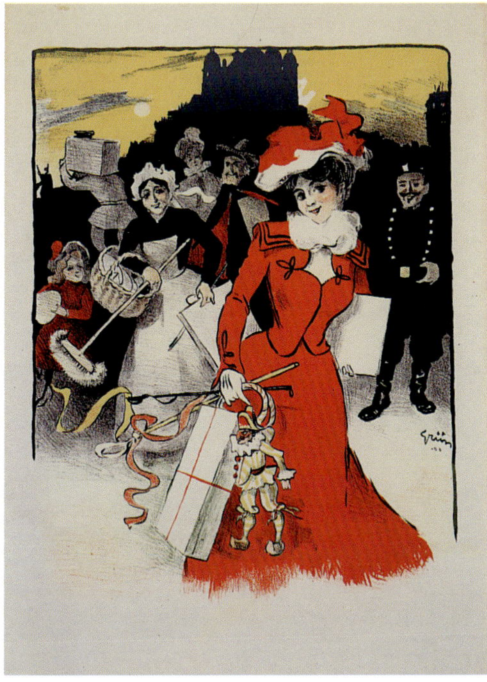

355

358

the Place Clichy, was primarily known as a realist theatre (which it became after 1905). Although barely mentioned in its time, it staged at least one revue written by P.L. Flers with Marville, a star in those days, as captain. Wearing a boater and dressed all in red she displays her generous bum presumably suggesting ideas to the passerby—especially given the title of the revue ("Want to Climb up?") (Grün, p. 55). *This is the larger format before the addition of letters.*
Est: $5,000-$6,000.

357. Gaîté Rochechouart/T'en as un Flair. 1903.
34¹/4 x 47¹/2 in./87 x 120.6 cm
Imp. Charles Verneau, Paris
Cond A–/Slight tears in upper text area.
Ref: Grün, p. 70; PAI-XXX, 516
"Opened in 1867, the Gaîté Rochechouart is taken over in 1892 by a dynamic duo, the Varlets. During the following twenty-four years they stage revues, which by the richness of the productions and interpretations are on level with La Scala. This doesn't mean that the intellectual level of these shows were very different— laughter, saucy expressions were offered at the Gaîté on par with other concert establishments. Wearing a yellow, low-cut dress as usual and facing the spectator, this cheeky young lady mocks a poor soldier who, given the size of his nose, must actually have excellent perception! Leading us to imagine the rest" (Grün, p. 70).
Est: $3,000-$4,000.

358. Chemins de Fer de le l'Ouest. 1901.
22⁵/8 x 40⁵/8 in./72.7 x 103 cm
Imp. Chaix, Paris
Cond B/Slight tears at folds and edges.
Ref: Grün, p. 123
"At sunset, a Breton in local costume scans the horizon, reminiscent of the Paimpolaise by Théodore Botrel, waiting for her husband to return from fishing. A gracious and elegant poster à la Grün—and in the corner, at the bottom left of the picture, the endless presentation of reduced rates" (Grün, p. 123).
Est: $1,500-$1,800.

359. A la Cigale Général. 1899.
34¹/2 x 48³/4 in./87.6 x 123.8 cm
Imp. Chaix, Paris
Cond B+/Tears at folds.
Ref: Grün, p. 50; DFP-II, 433 (var); PAI-XLI, 317
"On July 27, 1899 P. L. Flers creates a new revue at the Cigale: 'A la Cigale Général, à la Cigale'. Grün, once again in demand, returns to his favorite black background with the heroine dressed in red in the foreground. Behind the horse that she is reining in, stands a coachman, losing his hat and a well-accompanied old dandy. The rosette of the Legion of Honor he is wearing may well indicate that he is a general. As usual, everything is well laid out, funny and done with brio" (Grün, p. 50). *This is the larger format.*
Est: $2,500-$3,000.

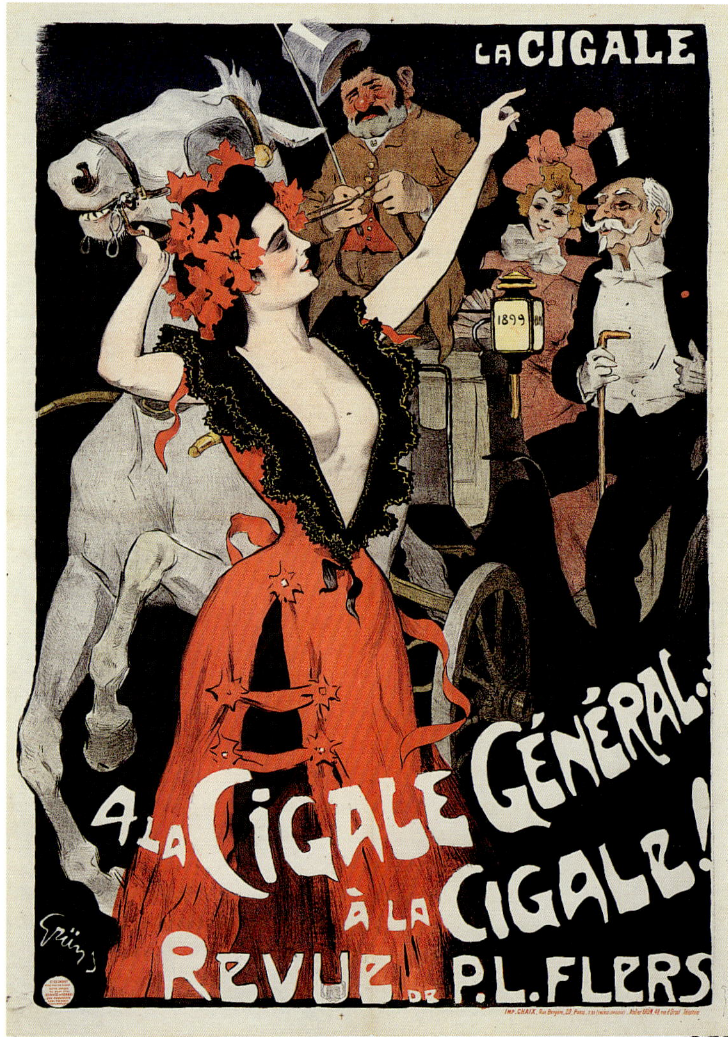

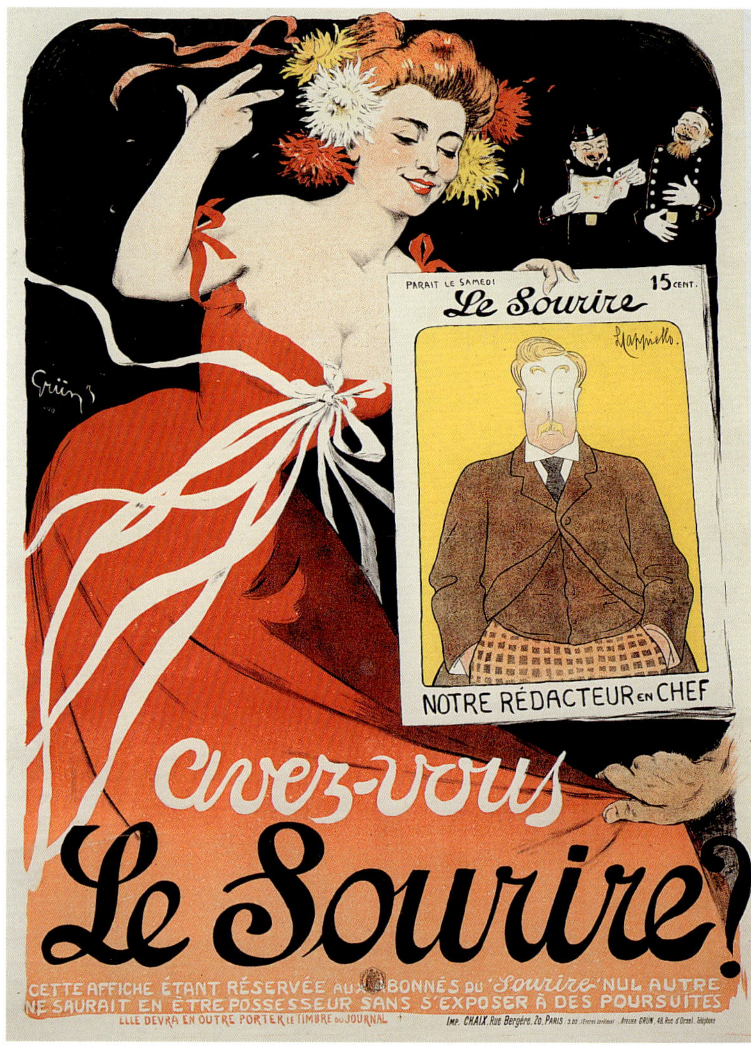

359   **360**

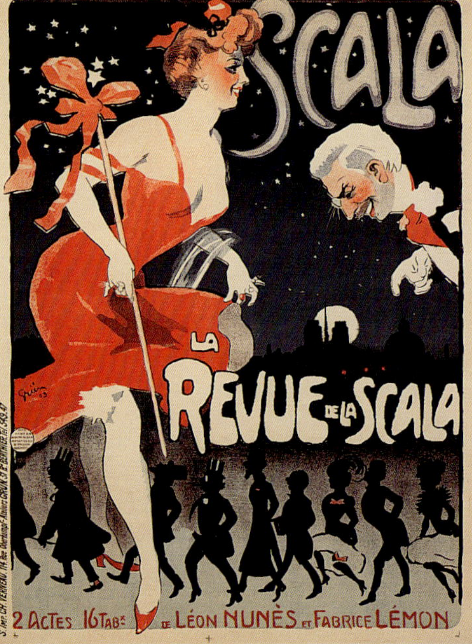

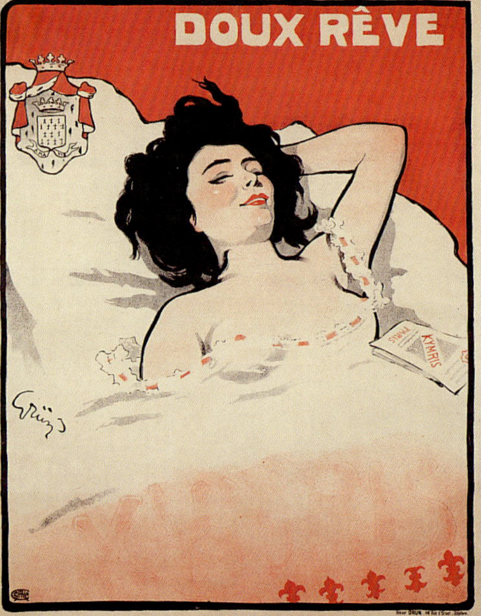

361   **362**

GRÜN (cont'd)

360. Avez-vous Le Sourire? 1900.
35x 48³/₄ in./88.9 x 123.9 cm
Imp. Chaix, Paris
Cond B+/Unobtrusive tears, largely at folds.
Ref: Grün, p. 108; Cappiello, 229; PAI-XXXII, 336
"On October 28, 1899 Maurice Méry launches *Le Sourire*, to compete against *Le Rire*, which was very successful since its inception in 1894. As editor he hires Alphonse Allais, one of the masters of French humor and ex-manager of the Chat Noir from 1886 through 1891. Allais becomes the driving force of *Le Sourire* until his death in 1905. In order to increase sales, the magazine publishes a poster in 1905 in which a Grünette displays an issue of *Le Sourire* showing Alphonse Allais, caricatured by Cappiello, enthroned on the cover page. In the rear, on a black background, two town councilors are doubled up with laughter. A peculiar and unusual detail: A man's clenched fist is pulling on her red dress. In May 1905 *Le Sourire* announces the publication of a special plate: 'A Bonus-poster! We are pleased to offer this plate free of charge to our subscribers. No copy will ever be sold in the stores and it will attain additional value since it is the result of rare collaboration, especially with artists of such caliber.' One notes that the value of the posters was already a sales argument. Oddly enough, in view of what is said in the ad, this poster should have been relatively common—which is far from being the case. The answer lies perhaps in the fact that one was charged for the 'bonus' plate" (Grün, p. 108).
Est: $2,500-$3,000.

361. Scala/La Revue de la Scala. 1905.
23³/₄ x 31³/₄ in./60.4 x 80.6 cm
Imp. Ch. Verneau, Paris
Cond A–/Slight tears at paper edges.
Ref: Grün, p. 64; DFP-II, 238; PAI-XL, 350
"Drawing its inspiration from the Folies Bergères in 1905 and again in 1906 (the revue opens in January), La Scala decides to avoid provocative headings and to offer a revue that sticks to mocking current affairs.

Two accomplices lead the revue. La Belle Otéro opens the show, followed by 12 acts and 16 scenes. Akin to shadow theater puppets, the men and women who epitomize current affairs parade between the legs of the female accomplice under the beaming gaze of the powers that be" (Grün, p. 64).
Est: $2,000-$2,500.

362. Kymris. ca. 1900.
33¹/₄ x 44⁷/₈ in./87 x 114 cm
Imp. Chaix, Paris
Cond B+/Restored tears at paper edges.
Ref (All Var): Grün, p. 96; Dodge, p. 116; PAI-XXIX, 68

"While commenting on this poster in *L'Estampe et l'Affiche*, de Crauzat notes: 'An ad for a bicycle without even showing the bicycle—that's rather unusual! The delightful imagination of the artist enabled him to create a graceful character who will do more to promote the product than all the cyclists or the bikes of the world!' In addition to its mysterious name this brand uses a royal coat of arms with the ironic motto 'To my life', and decides to take the opposite course of the hundreds of posters promoting the numerous brands of velocipedes vying with one another for a share of the market. Sensually languid, this young brunette is content with dreaming—and most likely making the public dream. After this advertising cam-

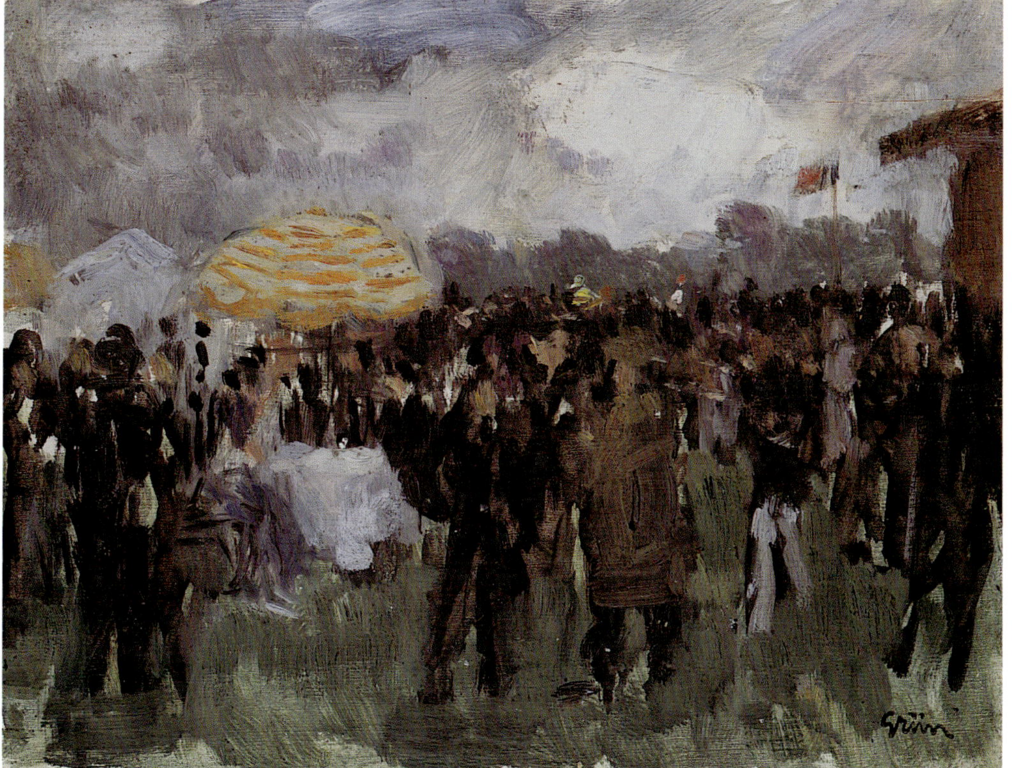

363

paign, Kymris was never heard of again" (Grün, p. 96). *This particular version of the poster appears without the bulk of the lower promotional text.*
Est: $1,400-$1,700.

363. À Longchamp.
9$^1/_2$ x 7$^1/_4$ in./24 x 18.4 cm
Hand-signed oil painting on wooden board. Framed.
Provenance (verso): Vente Grün, M. Dupuy, J. P. Camard, Exp.
"Grün . . . was meant to become a tradesman. A compromise was reached with his family where he first studied decoration, doing a stint at Lavastre's atelier at the Opéra, and finally joining Guillemet—a dominant figure of academic painting, who nevertheless was linked to the Impressionist School. Grün's talent was precocious. As early as 1886, one of his paintings was accepted at the Salon des Artistes Français, a laudable success as he was merely eighteen years old. His work became a feature of the Salon and was awarded an honorable mention in 1897, before rapidly being declared ineligible to compete. He charted a perfect course, rapidly becoming the accredited official painter. By the end of his career he served as a member of the committee and of the jury, and received the Legion of Honor" (Grün, p. 7). In other words, Grün was a respected painter long before he became a formidable posterist. And as proof we offer this splendid Impressionist painting of a day at the races, where, without a horse in sight, one gets the distinct impression that being seen was equally as important as taking in "The Sport of Kings." The Hippodrome de Longchamp is a fifty-seven hectare horse racing facility located on the Route des Tribunes in the Bois de Boulogne in Paris. Built on the banks of the Seine, it's used for flat racing and is noted for its variety of interlaced tracks, as well as a famous hill that provides a real challenge to competing thoroughbreds.
Est: $2,500-$3,000.

364. A Typical Night in Montmartre.
25$^1/_4$ x 14 in./64.2 x 35.6 cm
Gouache and ink artwork on paper. Framed.
To Grün, setting down the wicked Montmartre nightlife for posterity was more than a shrewd marketing technique—it was a way of life. It's not hard to see that he has a genuine fondness for the lecherous men, crooked cops and women of ill-repute that fill his artwork. And why wouldn't he—these folks weren't sermonizing or talking about what they wanted, they were out there grabbing life with both hands and having fun, morality be damned. Far less exaggerated than some of his promotional work, this Grün evening out certainly appears to accurately reflect your run-of-the-mill Montmartre round of debauchery, from the voyeurism to the exhibitionism to the donnybrook breaking out down-left.
Est: $4,000-$5,000.

365. Descent de la Butte.
25$^1/_2$ x 19$^1/_2$ in./64.7 x 49.5 cm
Cond A. Framed.
A rare lithographic proof whose lower-right remarque is just as informative with regard to the bawdy retreat seen above it as is its title—perhaps even more so. With "Descent from the Hillock" unobtrusively appearing in the lower-right hand corner, our focus is left free to take note of the remarque's *au naturel* courtesan, who awakes from her slumber to mutter a phrase that roughly translates—after being sanitized a bit—as "What a screwed-up nightmare!" In other words, what we're being shown is a mass exodus from Montmartre, where all the wonderfully sleazy, corrupt and libidinous elements that made the area a licentious destination have taken flight. Perhaps Grün set the idea to the page as a response to constant moralizing or a specific critique against the fountainhead of his inspiration. Perhaps it was nothing more than an actual dream experienced by the artist that led to its creation. We may never know for sure; however, whatever inspired this salacious abandon yielded superior results. *Hand-signed by the artist.*
Est: $1,700-$2,000.

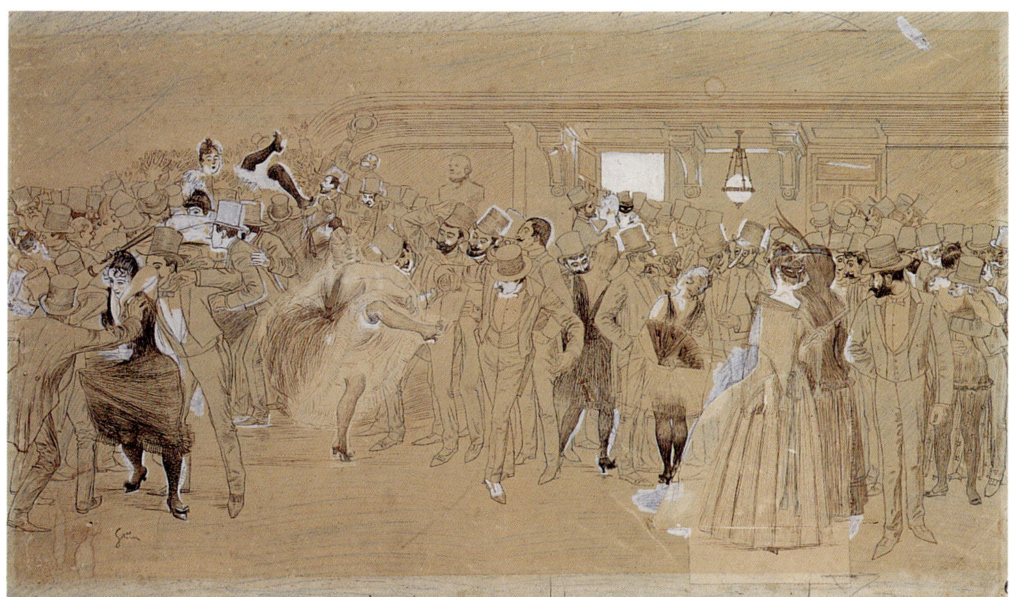

364

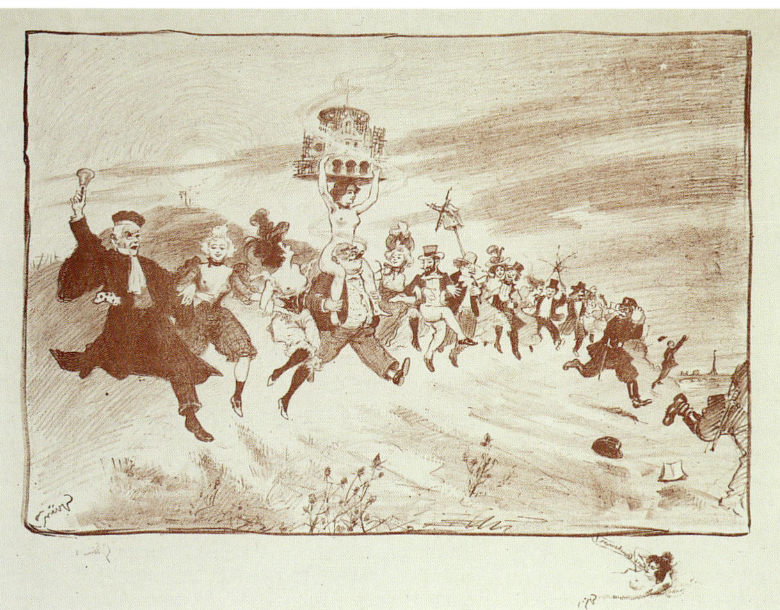

365

For a delightful Grün book cover, *see* "Les Chansonniers de Montmartre" in the "Books and Periodicals" section at the end of the catalogue.

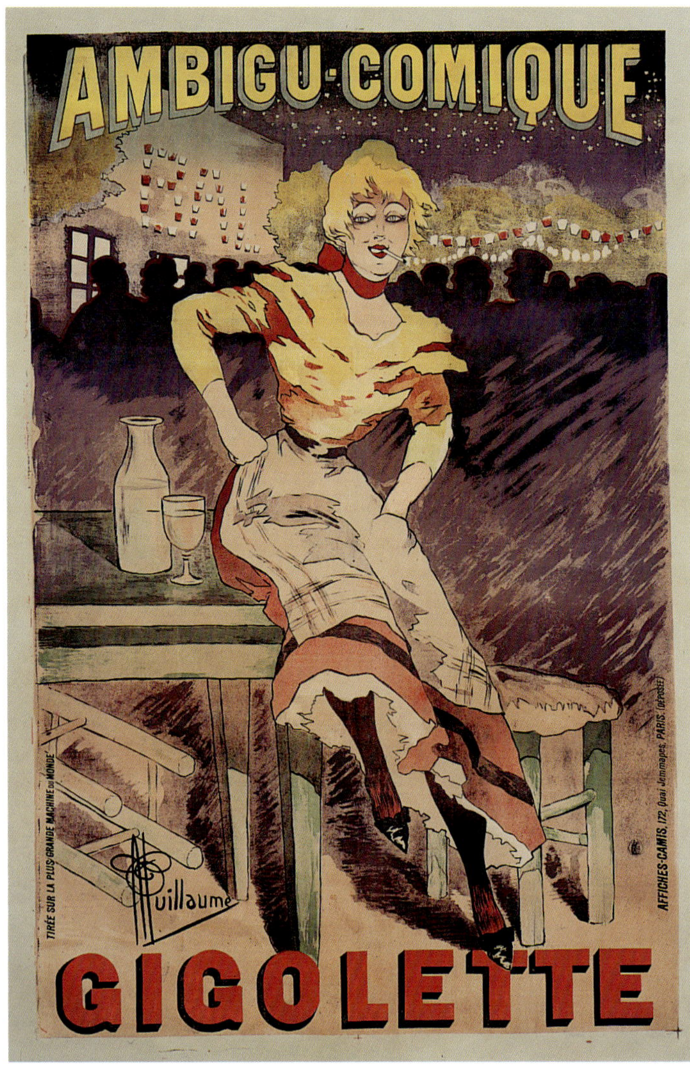

366

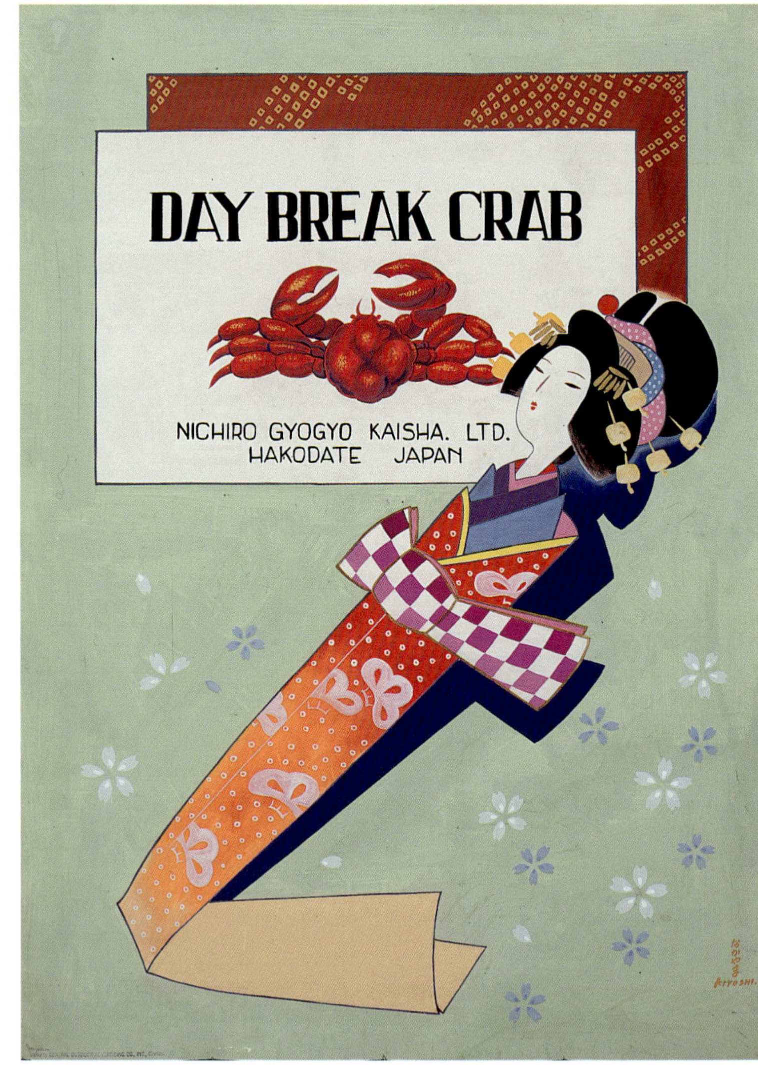

367

ALBERT GUILLAUME (1873-1942)

366. Ambigu-Comique/Gigolette. 1894.
$49^1/2$ x $74^3/4$ in./125.7 x 189.9 cm
Affiches-Camis, Paris
Cond B/Recreated borders; tears at folds and edges.
Ref: DFP-II, 452; Maitres, 30; Maindron, 6;
    PAI-XXXIII, 365 (var)
"I don't see an exception: all the posters of M. Guillame have value; they're perfect in that their designer has chosen to set his subjects down in the hottest and most lively colors." Thus spake Maindron (p. 74) on the subject of Guillame and we couldn't be more inclined to agree. His poster for Pierre Decorcelle's "Gigolette," playing at the Ambigu-Comique, takes us on a tour of the more intoxicated side of theater, its twinkling of lights and blur of a crowd the perfect backdrop for the table-topped barmaid, a tipsy vision of female carnality. *This is the larger format.*
Est: $2,000-$2,500.

HAKODATE

Hakodate is a small, charming city on the southern tip of the island of Hokkaido, famed for its hot spring resorts, tourist attractions and squid fishing. The region was in the hands of the indigenous Ainu for centuries, despite many Japanese attempts to gain control of the natural deep-sea port. In 1789, it was made a base for Japanese deep-sea fishing, and into the pre-war years, was considered the capital of Hokkaido. When Japan was forcibly opened to outside trade in the 1800s, Hakodate drew in Western imperial powers from all over the world, and their influence can still be seen today. Hakodate is home to Goryokaku, a star-shaped Western-style fort that was later converted to a park, a Russian Orthodox Church, the old British Consulate, and the only Trappist convent for women in Japan, built in 1898.

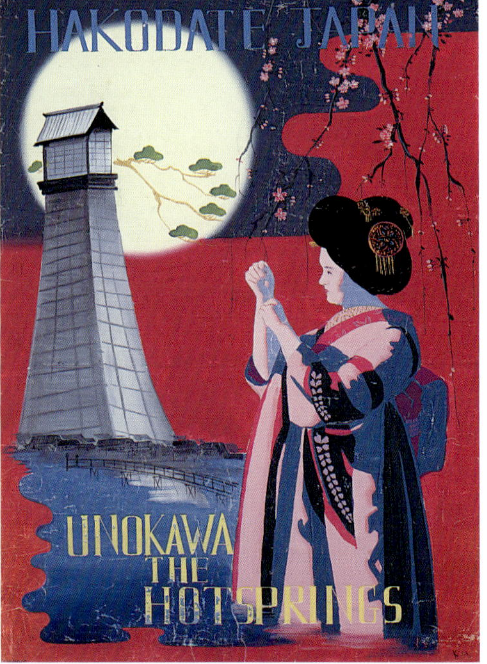

368

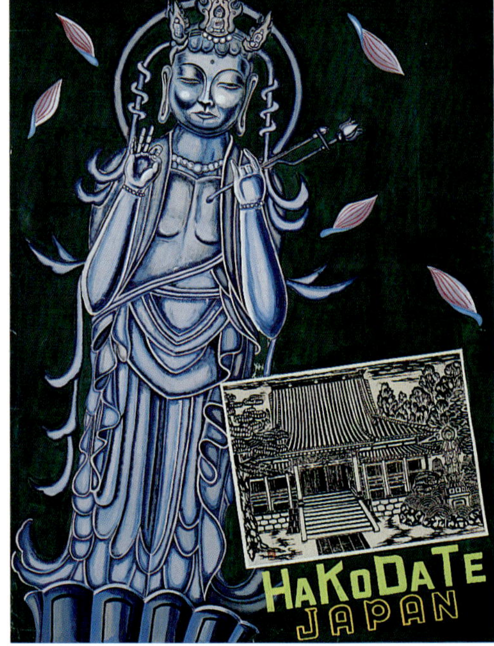

369

Hakodate's influence declined after World War II, but it's still a popular tourist destination, especially for the beaches, hot spring resorts and fresh seafood. There is a famous open-air Asa-ichi morning market on the bay, where the local fishermen cram into over 360 booths to hawk their goods. Hakodate added an airport in the 1960s, and the world's longest tunnel, the Seikan Tunnel (connecting the northern tip of Aomori in Honshu with the southern tip of Hokkaido in Hakodate) was completed in the 1990s. The night view of

Hakodate, along with Naples and Hong Kong, is considered to be one of the world's three most scenic. A cable car can take you to the top of Mt. Hakodate, the tallest peak in the city, with a commanding view of the city below and the twinkling lights of the fishing boats searching for squid, crab and salmon.

These three maquettes provide a rare glimpse into the life of the lovely Japanese city that otherwise may have escaped unaware contemporary Western eyes.

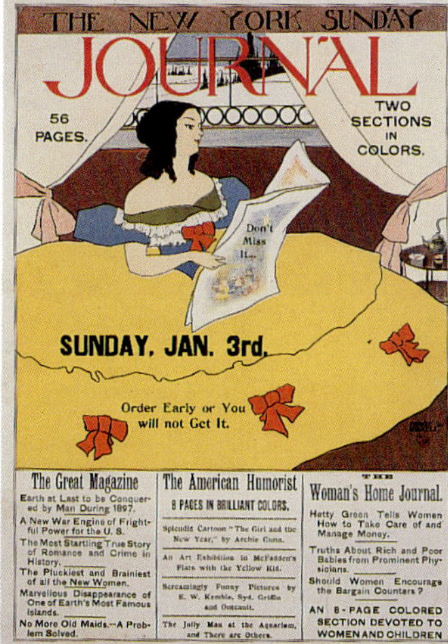

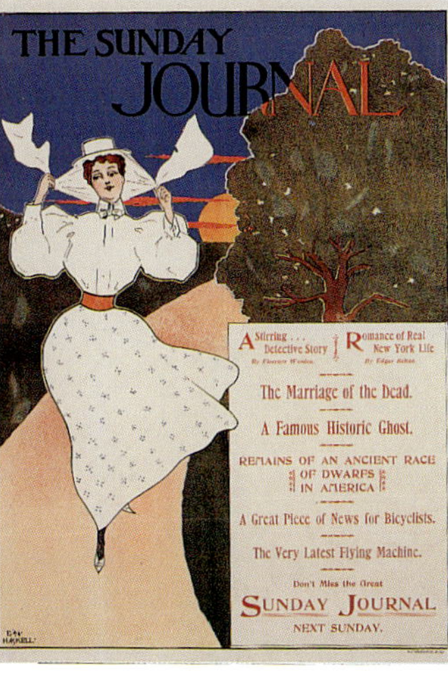

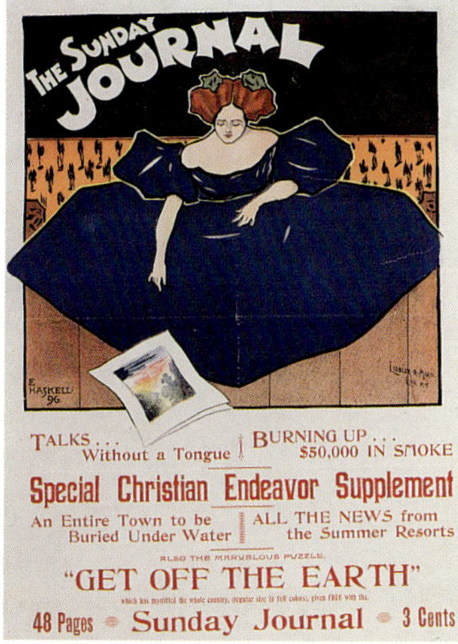

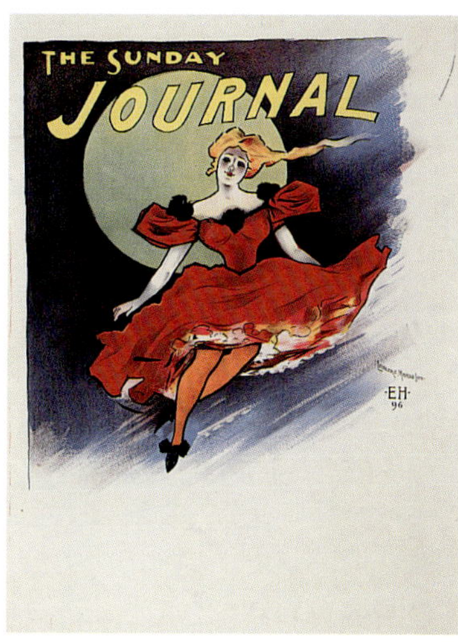

370

371

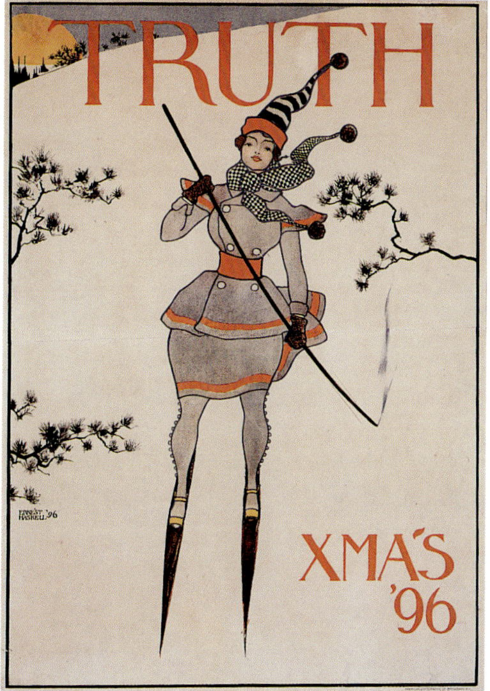

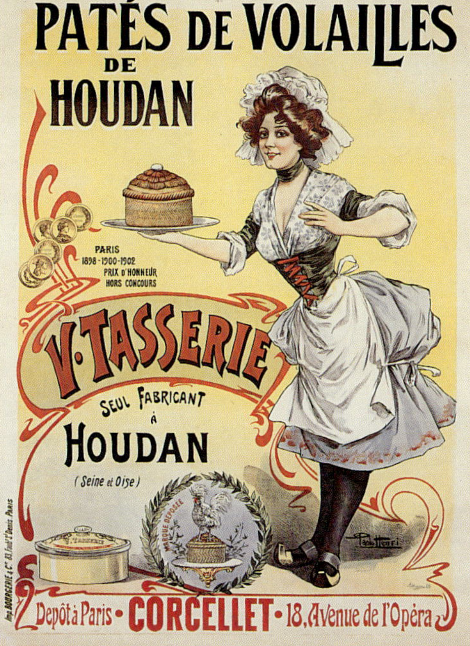

372

373

reading, that is) and some of the contents. Though the weather outside may be frightful, the articles inside are delightful for the January 3rd edition, which features not one, but two color sections. And in the advertisement for the summery edition, it appears as if a bonnet-tying lass is off to get her hands on a copy of the paper at the crack of dawn. And with such divergent articles as news on the "Very Latest Flying Machine" and the "Remains of an Ancient Race of Dwarfs in America," who can blame her for getting an early start. **Est: $1,700-$2,000.** (2)

371. The Sunday Journal: Two Posters. 1896.
Each: 15 x 20$^7/_8$ in./38 x 53 cm
Liebler & Masse, N.Y.
Cond B+/Slight tears at folds.
Ref: PAI-I, 21 (a & d; var)
Another lovely Haskell promotional pair for *The Journal*. The belle in the blue dress is definitely getting her three-cents worth with a forty-eight-page edition that features both a "Special Christian Endeavor Supplement" as well as "All the News from the Summer Resorts." And though her broom isn't visible, you have to imagine that the bewitching lass floating in front of the full moon promoted an autumnal issue of the newspaper. Though the textual portion remains blank, one has to imagine that the accompanying stories were equally as fascinating.
Est: $1,700-$2,000. (2)

372. Truth/X-Mas '96.
13$^1/_4$ x 19 in./33.6 x 48.3 cm
Amereican Lithographic Co., N.Y.
Cond B/Restored tears at folds and edges. Framed.
Ref: Lauder, 96; Margolin, p. 63; PAI-XXXV, 336
The Truth be told, this utterly coordinated ski maven makes for an alluringly crisp—albeit cinched—calling card for the magazine's Christmas installment. Born in Woodstock, Connecticut, Haskell studied in Paris, where he was greatly influenced by Whistler. He designed posters for many publications, including *New York World*, *The Critic* and provided illustrations for *Harper's* as well.
Est: $1,000-$1,200.

PAOLO HENRI

373. V. Tasserie/Patés de Volailles. ca. 1903.
39$^1/_4$ x 54$^3/_4$ in./99.6 x 39 cm
Imp. Bourgerie, Paris
Cond A.
Located sixty-three kilometers west of Paris in the Yvelines *département*, Houdan was once an important poultry market for the French capital. A breed of chicken was even named after the town, and that ornamental fowl is featured in the laurel-ensconced trademark for the oft-decorated V. Tasserie brand of poultry paté. And though awards certainly don't hurt sales, it helps to have a different sort of bird, complete with waist-cinching corset and plunging neckline, on hand to call the public's attention to a product as well.
Est: $1,700-$2,000.

---

367. Day Break Crab.
Artist: **Kiyoshi Nakayama**
30$^3/_8$ x 43 in./77.2 x 109 cm
Gouache and ink maquette.
This Nakayama artwork was prepared for one of the fishing companies that had a presence at the morning market in Hakodate: the Nichiro Seafood Company. Its delicate custom-made paper execution may seem a bit dainty for a commercial fishing operation, yet the cherry-blossom and traditional folded paper doll motifs identify the national origin of the creation with quiet restraint and unobtrusive subtlety.
Est: $1,200-$1,500.

368. Unokawa/The Hot Springs.
Artist: **Anonymous**
30$^5/_8$ x 43$^1/_8$ in./78 x 109.5 cm
Gouache maquette.
Yunokawa—literally "hot spring river" shown in this maquette with an older spelling—is the oldest hot spring resort on the island of Hokkaido. Located just five kilometers from the center of Hakodate, this resort is certainly one of the area's main attractions. Like many volcanic hot springs, the water has a bit of a sulfur smell, but the mineral-laden waters are purported to be good for one's health. For a modest fee, you can stay at an inn, eat a fantastic meal of fresh seafood, wallow in the hot springs and pamper yourself to the

utmost. And though the specifics may be absent from this impressive anonymous maquette, the sentiment of self-indulgence is more than admirably conveyed.
Est: $1,200-$1,500.

369. Hakadote Japan.
Artist: **Anonymous**
30$^1/_2$ x 42$^3/_4$ in./77.5 x 108.6 cm
Gouache maquette.
Whereas the other two Hakodate maquettes celebrate more commercial aspects of the city, this uncredited artwork leans toward the spiritual. The temple in the design is most likely Kyoruji—founded in 1633 as the last branch of Hogenji—while the statue is of Kanon, a Buddhist goddess of mercy. Floating lotus petals—the oft-used flower of Buddhist imagery—complete the design.
Est: $1,200-$1,500.

ERNEST HASKELL (1876-1925)

370. New York Sunday Journal: Two Posters. 1896.
Each: 14$^1/_2$ x 21$^1/_8$ in./37 x 53.7 cm
H. A. Thomas Wylie, NY
Cond B+/Slight tears at folds and edges.
Ref: PAI-I, 21 (b & c; var)
Haskell created a number of posters to promote the Sunday edition of the *New York Journal*, featuring women in rather extravagant attire (for newspaper

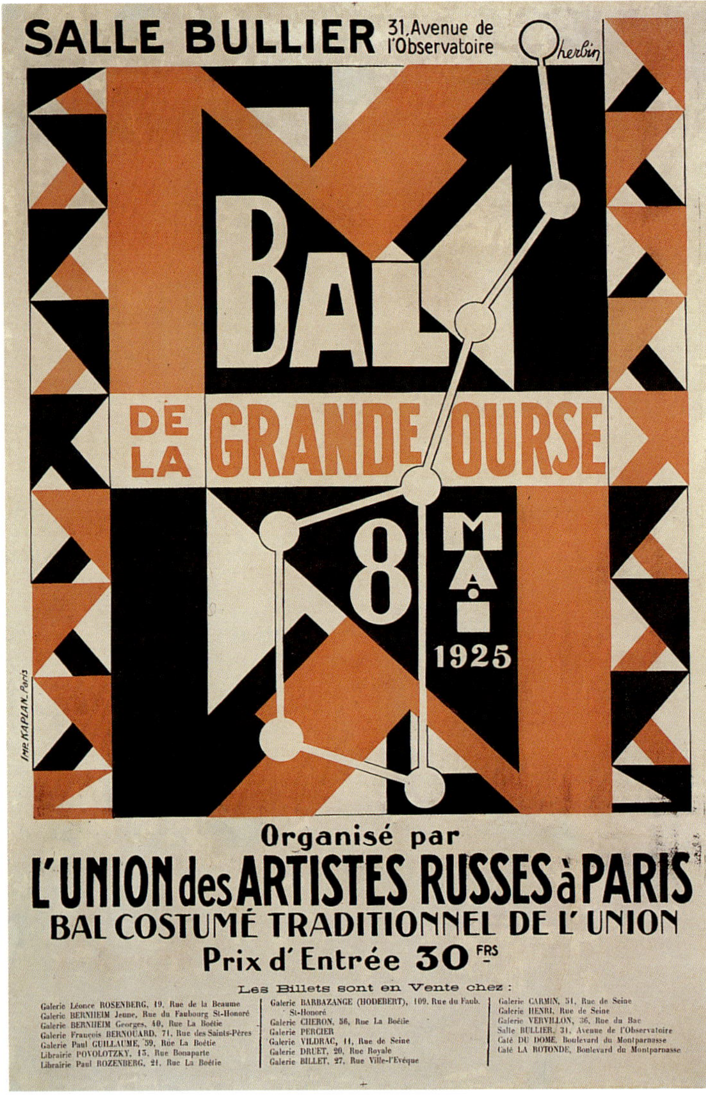

375

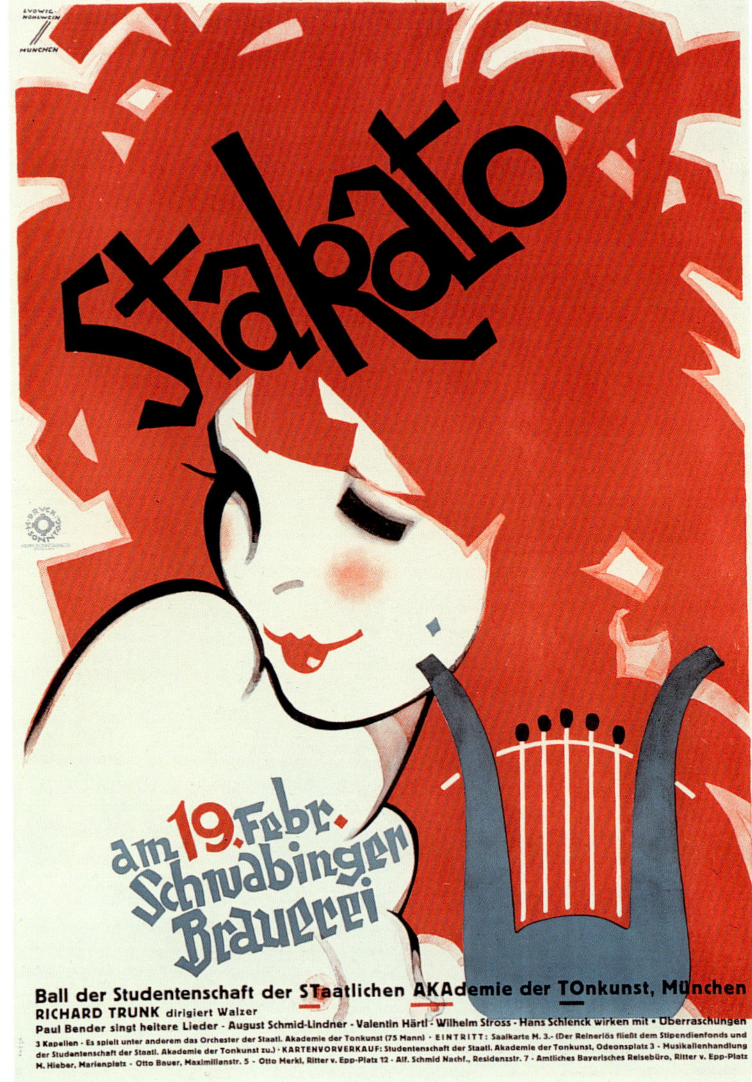

377

374

376

H. A. HENRIET

374. Kunst en Techniek Tentoonstelling. 1930.
22 x 33 in./55.8 x 83.7 cm
Cond A.
Henriet stays elementally pure in his promotion for a Dutch exhibition at the Stedelyk Museum whose focus is on lithographic art and technique: a press, a stone, a nib and, most importantly, the steady hand of an artist at work. Though accurate and effective, the entire feeling of the poster borders on the religious, a sanctified placard to the art of the poster.
Est: $1,500-$1,800.

AUGUSTE HERBIN (1882-1960)

375. Bal de la Grande Ourse. 1925.
$30^1/2$ x 47 in./77.5 x 119.3 cm
Imp. Kaplan, Paris
Cond B/Slightly light-stained; unobtrusive tears.

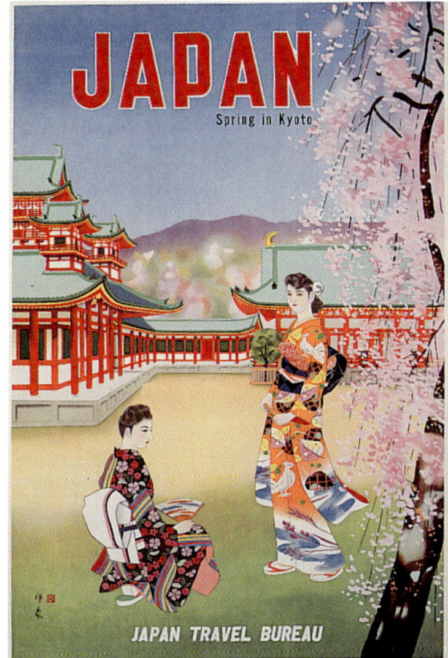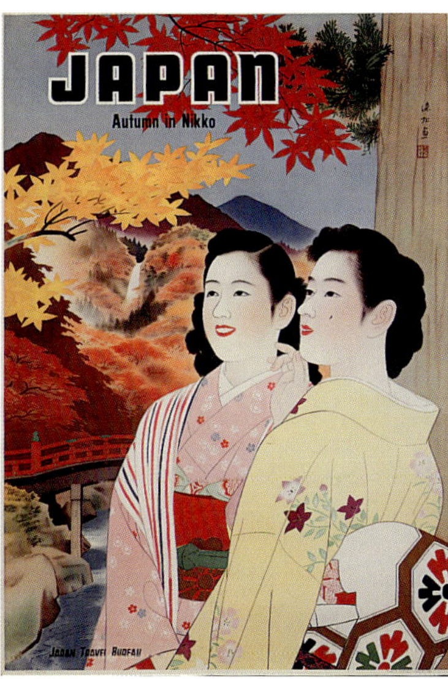

378

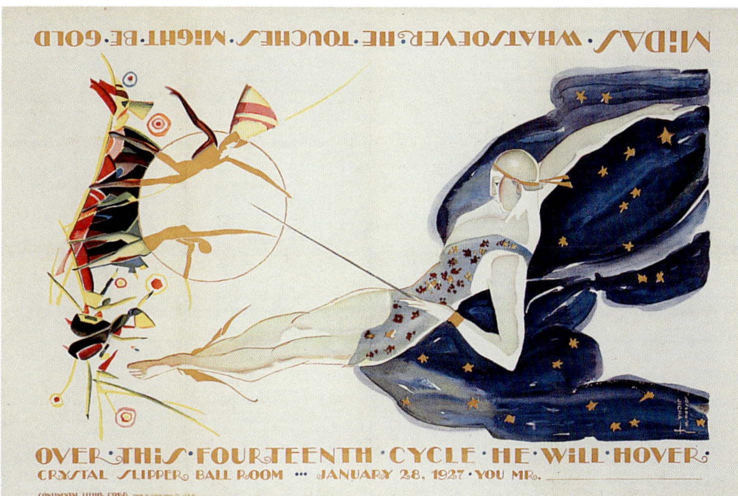

379

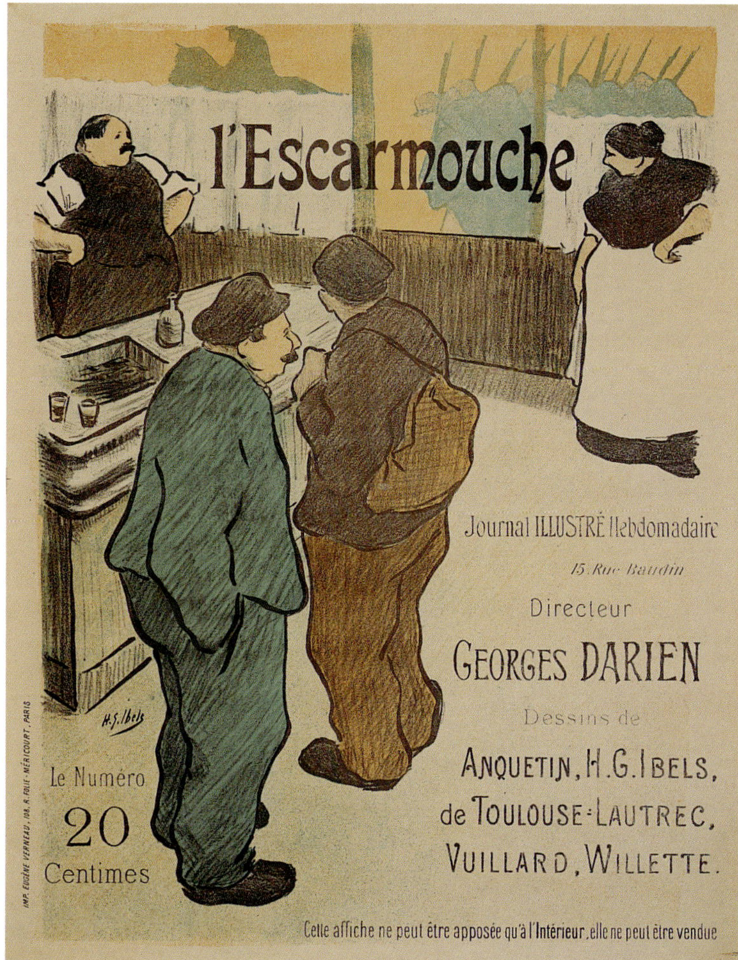

380

Ref: Weill, 191; Art Deco, p. 103;
Müller-Brockmann, 182; PAI-VII, 175
The Great Bear Ball, organized by the Union of Russian Artists in Paris, is announced, appropriately, by a poster executed in the Constructivist style that was at the time all the rage in Russia—and parts west.
Est: $6,000-$7,000.

LUDWIG HOHLWEIN (1874-1949)

376. Engleder & Finkenzeller Büro. ca. 1913.
$47^1/_2$ x $35^5/_8$ in./120.5 x 90.5 cm
Dr. C. Wolf V. Sohn, München
Cond A–/Unobtrusive folds.
Ref: DFP-III, 1442; PAI-I, 128
Weill comments that "Beginning with his first efforts, Hohlwein found his style with disconcerting facility; it would vary little for the next forty years. The drawing was perfect from the start . . . nothing seemed alien to him, and in any case, nothing posed a problem for him" (pp. 107-110). His "special way of applying colors, letting them dry at different times, and printing one on top of the other, producing modulations of shading, has often been copied, but never equaled. He belonged to no school or group, his art and personality are an unprecedented phenomenon in the history of German poster art" (Rademacher, p. 22). For a firm that proclaims to have everything that you may need for your office space at their Munich outlet, Hohlwein takes a rather ingenious promotional tack: instead of reproducing a storefront or a mass of inventory, he clearly points out what streetcar one needs to board in order to arrive at the Engleder and Finkenzeller establishment. *Rare!*
Est: $5,000-$6,000.

377. Stakato. 1935.
$33^1/_8$ x $48^1/_8$ in./84.2 x 122.2 cm
Sonntag, München
Cond B+/Recreated right margin.
Ref: PAI-XXXVI, 355

There's nothing abrupt or disjointed about this free-spirited Hohlwein invitation to set the night ablaze at this pre-Lenten revelry at the Schniabinger Brewery, a musical shindig sponsored by a student organization from the institution of higher artistic learning that gives the ball its acronymic title: Munich's **ST**atlichen **AK**ademie der **TO**nkunst. A fiery Hohlwein vision, far more free than a great number of his designs, and one whose flat planes of vibrant color create a feeling of pyrotechnic flirtation. *Rare!*
Est: $5,000-$6,000.

JAPAN TRAVEL BUREAU

378. Spring in Kyoto/Autumn in Nikko: Two Posters.
Each: 28 x $42^1/_2$ in./71 x 108 cm
a: Mitsumura Printing Co., Tokyo
b: Dai-Nippon Printing Co. Japan
Cond A–/Slight tears at edges/P.
In terms of sheer manpower, JTB remains the world's largest travel company. At the time of these posters' production, Japan Travel Bureau was still a part of the Japanese government, and the posters were designed to promote Japan as a destination to Westerners. It's hard to imagine now, but until the 1960s, Japanese people didn't engage in leisure travel. With a shift in policy coinciding with the Tokyo Olympics, the pent-up desire to roam abroad began, and Japan Travel Bureau was eventually privatized, handling both inbound and outbound travelers. Despite heavy competition, the Internet and many other innovations, JTB continues to garner the lion's share of Japanese travelers overseas, while serving as a primary conduit for bringing the rest of the world to Japan. The posters here celebrate arguably the two most agreeable seasons anywhere in the world. Spring falls to Kyoto, the old capital of Japan and perhaps that country's tourist Mecca. And what better to place directly in the public eye than the historic and lovely Heian Shrine, whose beautiful gardens, filled with many weeping cherry trees make it an espe-

cially popular destination in springtime. Fall takes us to Nikko, an extremely popular tourist destination just 135 kilometers north of Metropolitan Tokyo. The promotion features two traditional beauties in the foreground and Kegon Falls in the background—one of the most photographed sites in all Japan, spilling ninety-seven meters straight down into Lake Chuzenji below.
Est: $1,200-$1,500. (2)

JOSEPH W. JICHA (1901-?)

379. Midas/Crystal Slipper Ball Room. 1927.
$25^1/_8$ x $37^5/_8$ in./63.6 x 95.7 cm
Continental Litho. Corp., Cleveland, O., U.S.A.
Cond B/Tears along folds.
An American artist and illustrator, Joseph Jicha is today best remembered for his great Art Deco landscapes and figure studies that emphasized bold designs and colorations. He studied art in Cleveland and began exhibiting there around 1921. Later his paintings and watercolors were included in major exhibitions at such institutions as the Cleveland Museum of Art, the Chicago Art Institute and venues in New York, Philadelphia and Texas. In his hometown of Cleveland, Jicha was a member of the notorious 'Kokoon Club'. According to the *Cleveland Artists Foundation Newsletter* of February 2004, "For artists who spent their days making advertisements and posters, the Kokoon Club provided a venue for subverting the traditional expectations of pictorial art. Their clubhouse became the epicenter of the true Bohemian lifestyle in Cleveland, and the name of the club became known for radical art." The Club also became famous for its masked balls and bizarre costume dances that were rather notorious affairs. Jicha's topsy-turvy poster for the fourteenth Kokoon Club Ball features Midas, in a flowing blue cape, descending on a crowd of Cubist-inspired dancers, his wand literally turning their gyrations into golden silhouettes. Renowned for their debauchery, these costumed balls were actually banned by the city of Cleveland in 1923 based on charges of "drunkenness" and "immorality." However, the city reinstated the event the following year with the stipulation that the attendees wear decent clothing.
Est: $2,000-$2,500.

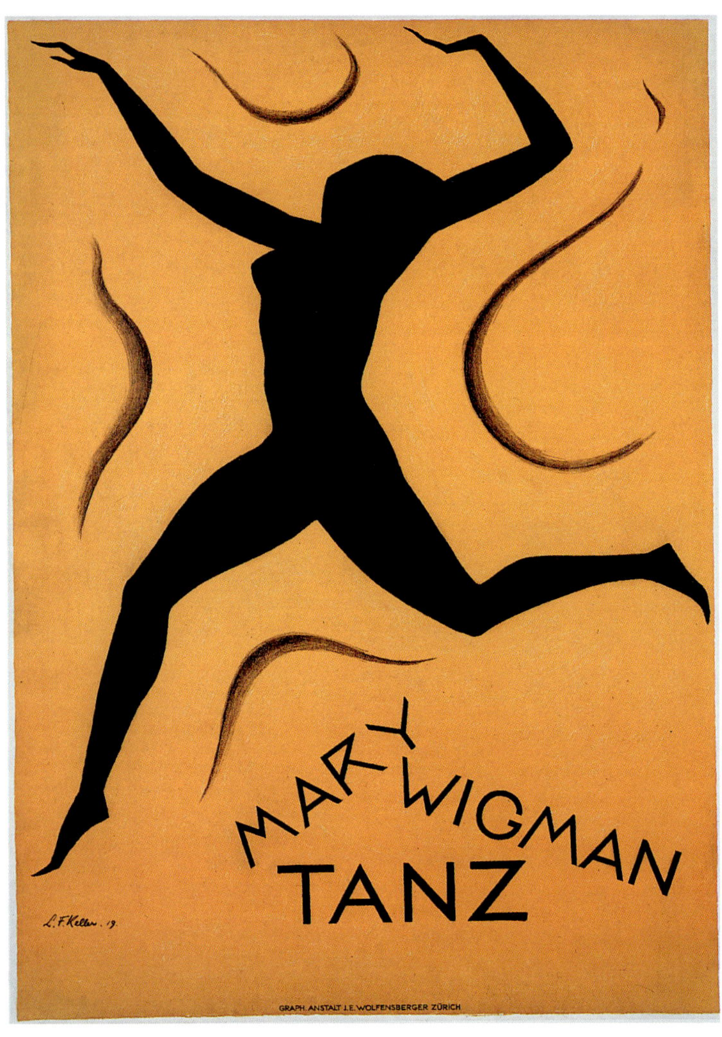

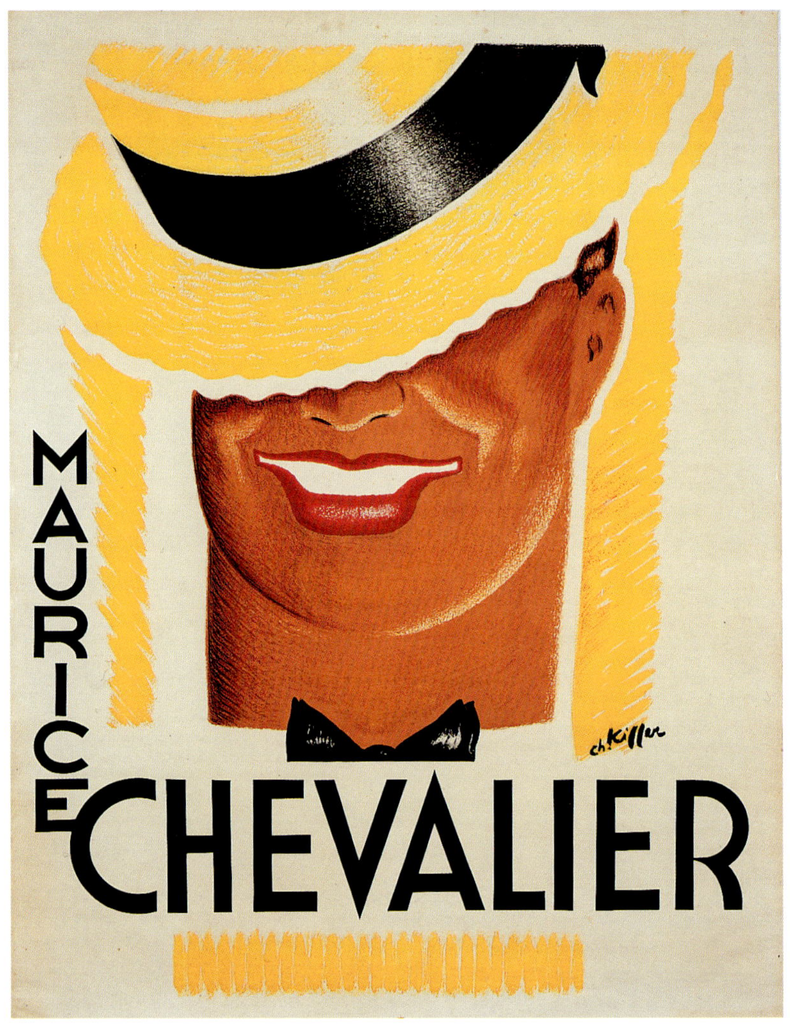

382

383

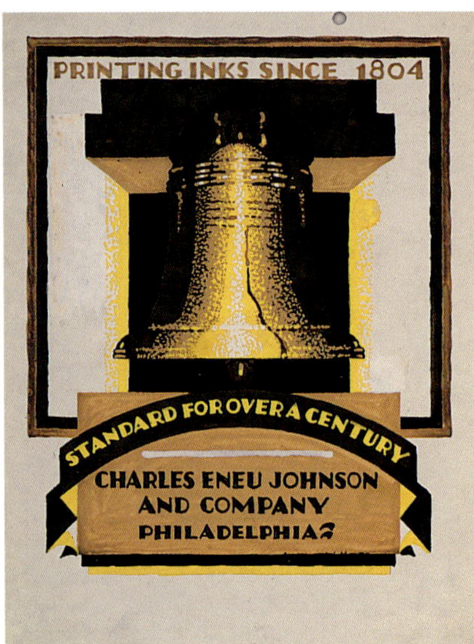

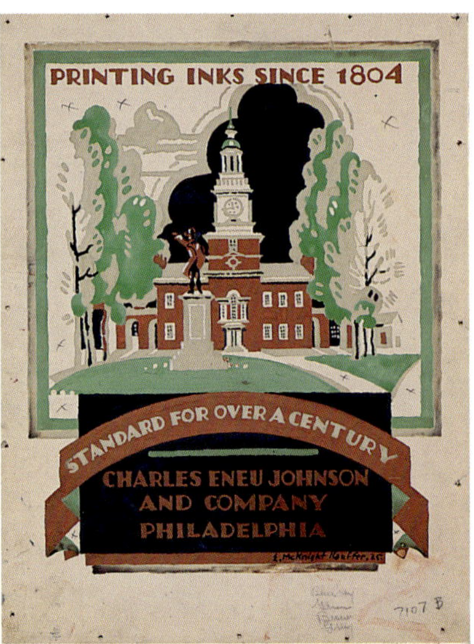

381

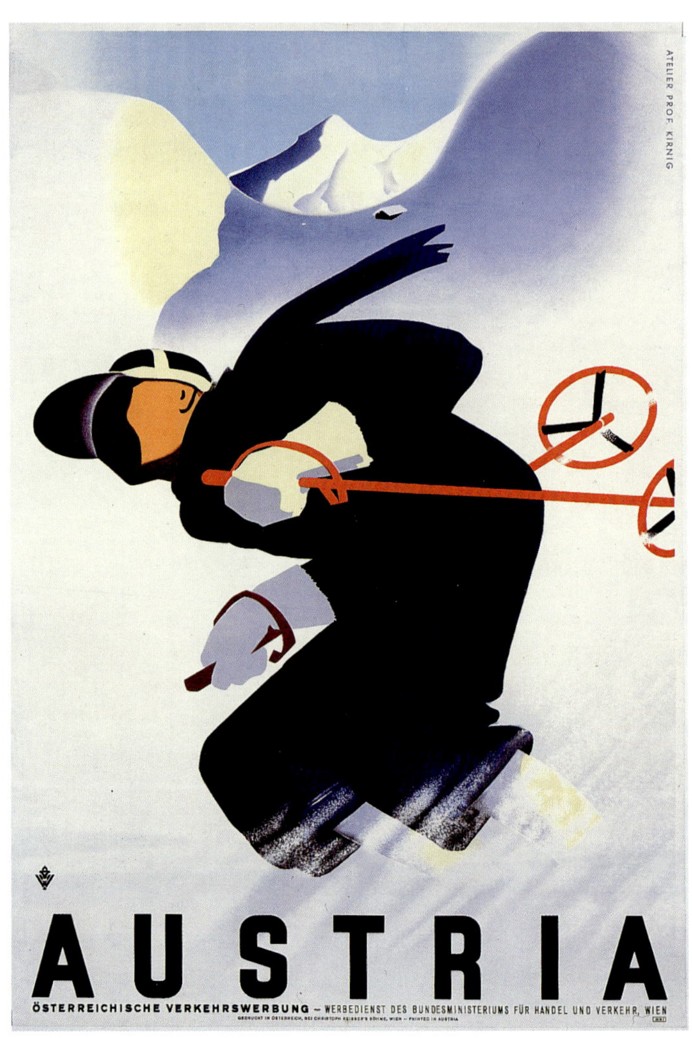

HENRI-GABRIEL IBELS (1867-1936)

380. L'Escarmouche. 1893.
19$^1/_2$ x 25$^1/_4$ in./49.5 x 64.2 cm
Imp. Eugène Verneau, Paris
Cond A. Framed.
Ref: DFP-II, 471; Wine Spectator, 56; Reims, 745; Schardt, p. 58; Maitres, 6;
    Weill, 44; Color Revolution, 104; PAI-XXVII, 460
A barroom scene in subdued cool colors advertises a magazine with illustrations
by Ibels himself as well as by other notable artists. This kind of portrayal of the
leisurely, everyday activity of the working people of Paris was typical of Ibels, as
well as of his friend Lautrec; both often imparted a good deal of social commentary in the process, subtly but incisively. Ibels is one of the most notable posterists of the Belle Epoque.
Est: $2,500-$3,000.

385

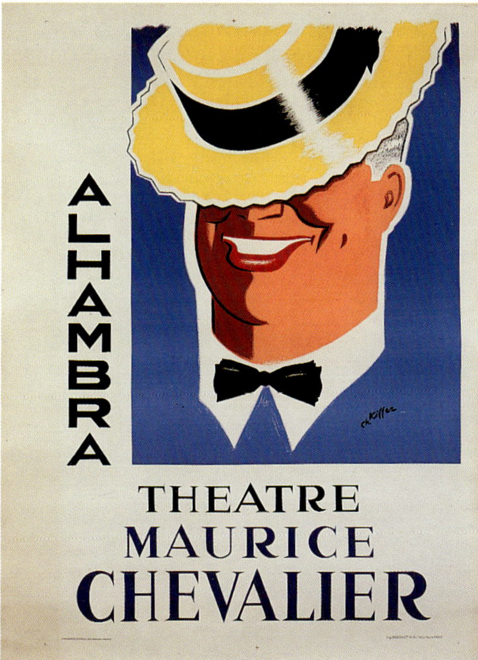

384

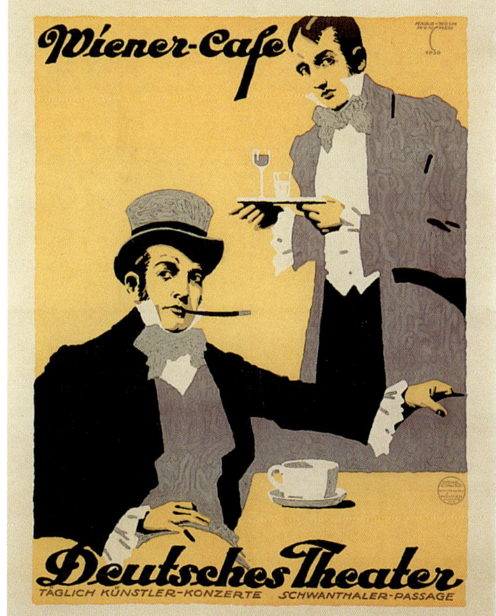

386

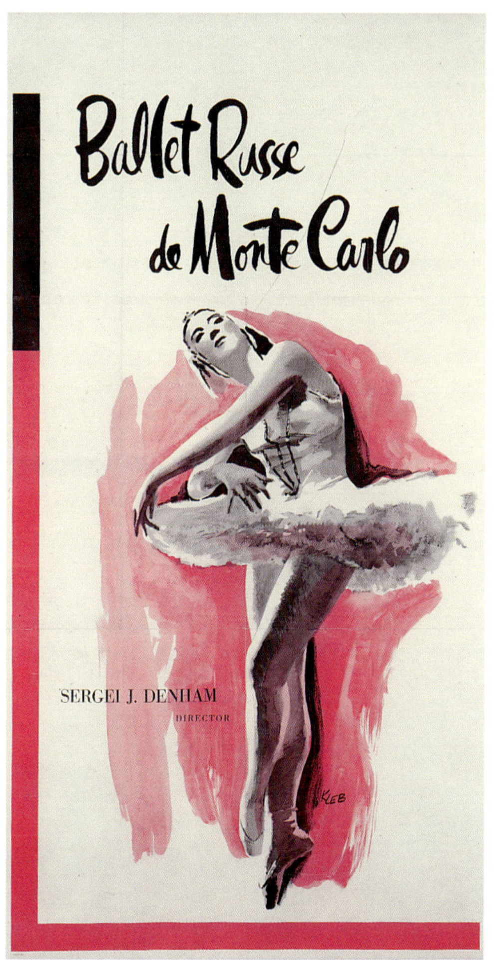

387

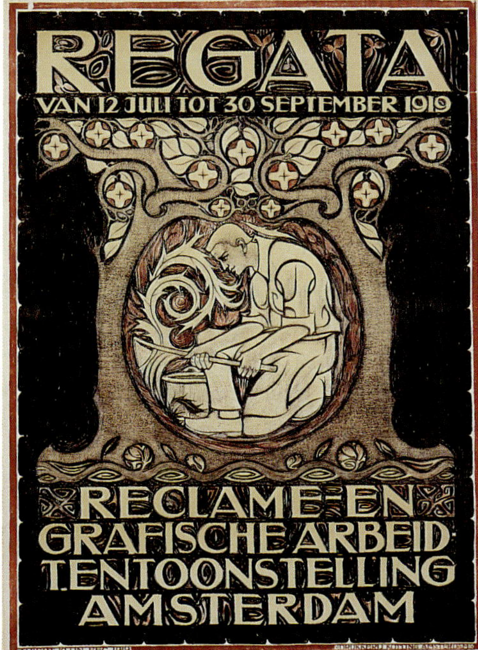

388

E. McKNIGHT KAUFFER (1890-1954)

381. Charles Eneu Johnson: Two Maquettes. 1926.
Each: 10 x 12⅝ in./25.3 x 32 cm
Gouache and ink maquettes. Framed.
Charles Eneu Johnson opened the first printing ink works in Philadelphia in 1804, so it only stands to reason that the firm would want to associate itself with other historic landmarks in "The Birthplace of the Nation." These two maquettes feature two of Philadelphia's most frequented destinations: the Liberty Bell and Independence Hall. Although he was a native of the United States, born in Montana, McKnight Kauffer spent most of his creative years in England. Returning home for the last fifteen years of his life, he designed posters in a New York studio, where his biggest clients were book publishers—Random House, Harcourt Brace, Alfred A. Knopf, Doubleday, Pantheon and Modern Library—and American Airlines. *Both maquettes ink-signed by McKnight Kauffer and dated verso.*
Est: $2,000-$2,500. (2)

L. F. KELLER

382. Mary Wigman Tanz. 1919.
35¾ x 50⅜ in./90.8 x 128 cm
J. E. Wolfensberger, Zürich
Cond A–/Slight tears at edges.
Ref: Dance Posters, 35 (var)
"This towering genius of European modern dance in-

fluenced dancing not only in her homeland, Germany, and in Central Europe where schools and teachers provided students with Wigman technique, but also in America where her own performances and the teaching of her major assistant, Hanya Holm, had a profound impact on the American modern dance movement. Wigman, born in 1886, first studied the music-rhythm-movement methods of Emile Jacques-Dalcroize and later became a pupil and assistant of Rudolf von Laban, a pioneer modern dancer and inventor of the dance script now in worldwide use and called Labanotation. Subsequently, Wigman outstripped her teacher in both fame and influence . . . Not much is known about the artist . . . But the poster so well captures the 'free dance' and acrobatics of Wigman that she used it frequently and it became her stock poster and trademark" (Dance Posters, p. 7). *This is the original version of the poster, seen here in its larger format.*
Est: $2,000-$3,000.

CHARLES KIFFER (1902-1992)

383. Maurice Chevalier. 1936.
47¼ x 62¾ in./120 x 159.2 cm
Richier-Laugier, Paris
Cond B+/Slight stains at paper edges.
Ref: Musée d'Affiche, 82; Weill, 320; Kiffer
(unnumbered); PAI-XLI, 341
One of the all-time great images associated instantly with its subject. The lettering, then as now, is wholly redundant: straw hat at a rakish tilt, prominent lower lip—voila, Chevalier! *This is the larger format.*
Est: $2,000-$2,500.

384. Theatre Maurice Chevalier/Alhambra. 1948.
46¾ x 62¾ in./118.7 x 159.3 cm
Imp. Bedos, Paris
Cond A–/Slight tears and stains at edges.
Ref: Folies-Bergère, 101 (var); PAI-XXX, 538
From 1925 on, Kiffer designed almost all of Chevalier's posters for a period of forty years. And although twelve years may have passed in the life of the Chevalier pictured in the previous number, it's clear that a little snow on the roof couldn't cool the jaunty magnetism of France's music-hall ambassador to the world.
Est: $1,700-$2,000.

PAUL KIRNIG (1891-1955)

385. Austria.
24¾ x 37¼ in./62.8 x 94.7 cm
Christopher Reisser's Söhne, Wein
Cond B+/Slight tears, largely at top paper edge.
Ref: PAI-XL, 84
The cobalt form of a skier schussing down a pristine slope evokes an instant image of the winter pleasures to be enjoyed in the Austrian Alps, and thus makes for an extremely effective travel poster. *This is the English-language version.*
Est: $2,500-$3,000.

RICHARD KNAB & HANS HEINRICH KOCH

386. Deutches Theater/Wiener-Cafe. 1920.
29¾ x 39¼ in./75.5 x 99.7 cm
Oscar Consée, München
Cond B+/Slight tears at folds.
We imagine that Munich's Deutsches Theater is advertising its Viennese cafe as yet another reason to frequent the venue in addition to their daily artist concerts. The design is composed with such skill that it easily piques the interest of even the most casual observer. Knab and Koch's lithographic partnership was formed in the 1920s.
Est: $1,700-$2,000.

KLEB

387. Ballet Russe de Monte Carlo.
39¾ x 76¾ in./101 x 95 cm
Cond B/Tears at folds.
Even more so than Derain (*see* No. 299), Kleb takes an extremely traditional pictorial approach in his 2-sheet promotion for the Ballet Russe de Monte Carlo with a graceful ballerina frozen mid-pirouette for all eternity. When Léonide Massine departed the company, Sergei Denham (1897-1970) assumed the position of director, a post that he would hold for twenty-four years. He also began the Ballet Russe School of Ballet in 1956.
Est: $2,500-$3,000.

ALBERT KLIJN (1895-1981)

388. Regata/Reclame-en Grafische Arbeid. 1919.
31 x 43⅛ in./78.8 x 109.5 cm
Drukkerij Kotting, Amsterdam
Cond B+/Slight tears at edges.
Ref: Dutch Poster, 167; PAI-XI, 24
The announcement of an exhibition of advertising and graphic work features a centerpiece of a man tilling a decidedly decorative, yet thorny garden, surrounded by a framework in earthen tones of brown and burnt umber. A talented graphic designer, Klijn later devoted himself mainly to landscapes and still lifes.
Est: $1,500-$1,800.

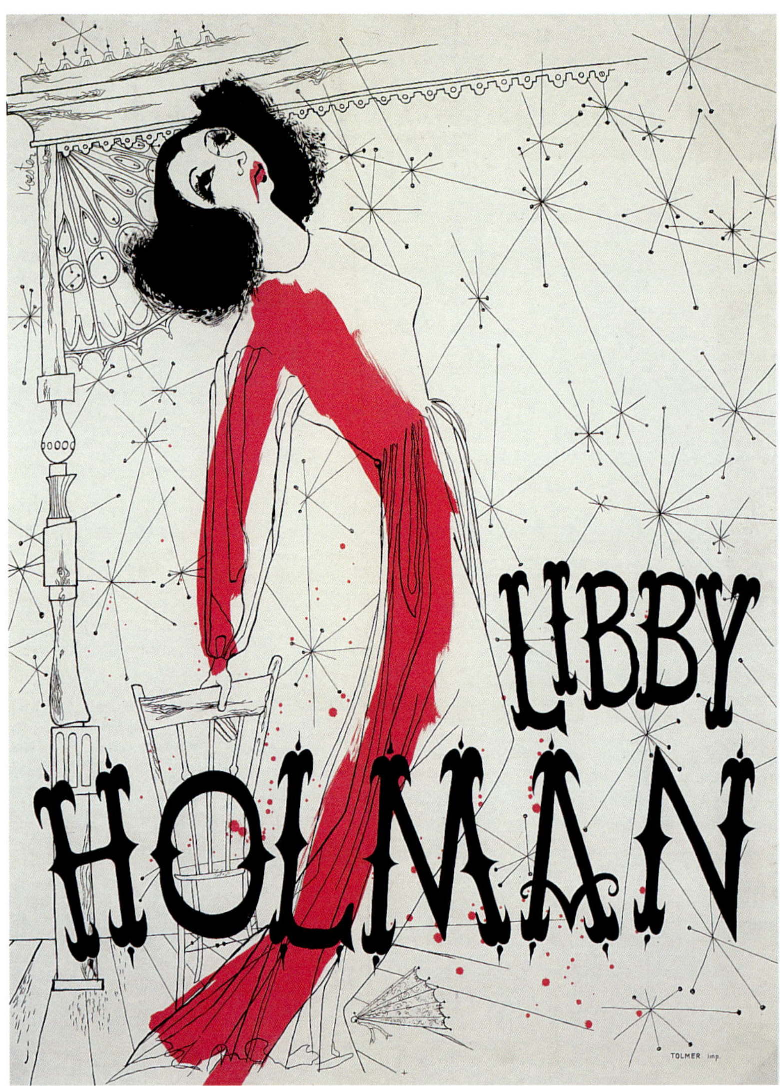

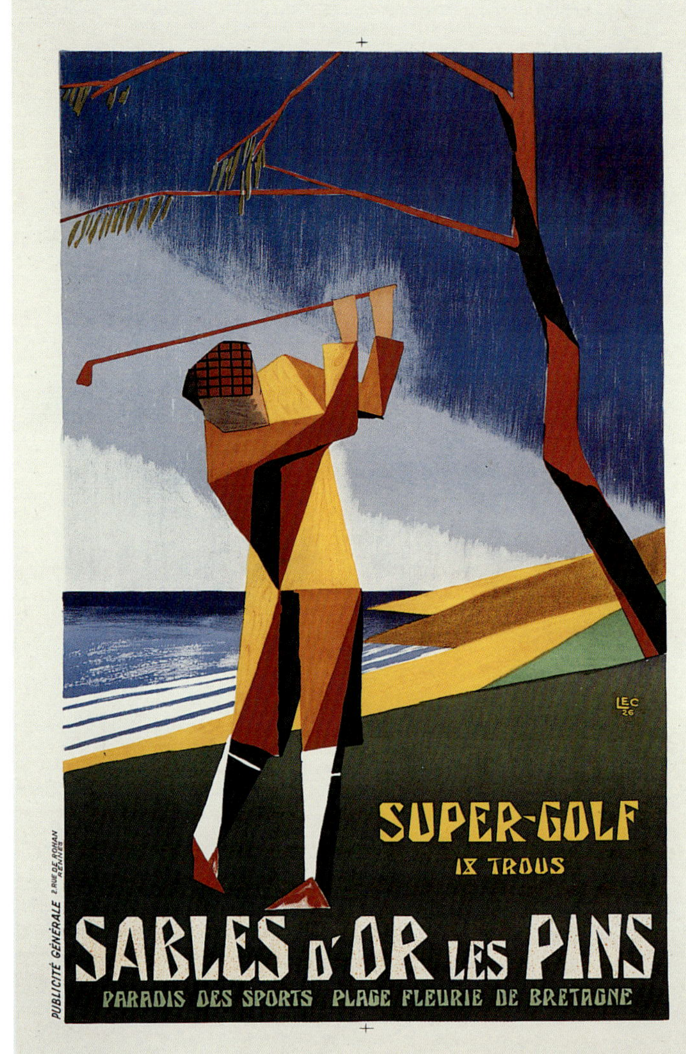

389

392

FRED W. KOESTER (1952-2000)

389. Libby Holman.
44$^7/_8$ x 62$^1/_4$ in./114 x 158.2 cm
Tolmer, Paris
Cond A-/Slight tears at folds and edges.
With its stars-and-splatter background, not to mention
the five-drinks-too-many perspective and claret-soaked,
Whatever-Happened-to-Baby-Jane-style melodrama,
it's difficult to ignore this Koester promotion for Libby
Holman. The manner of execution certainly matches the
notoriety of the subject seeing as Libby Holman (1904-
1971) has taken her place alongside Zelda Fitzgerald,
and Judy Garland in the pantheon of doomed American
women. Nee Elisabeth Holzman, she is regarded by some
as the first great Caucasian torch singer and by others
as a "dark purple menace" because of her tempestuous
private life. After playing minor roles in Broadway musi-
cals, she would become a major star thanks to her lan-
gourous, sultry renditions of songs such as "I Want a
Man," "Moanin' Low," "Body and Soul" and "Am I Blue?"
Her career went into a freefall after the shooting death of
her husband, Zachary Smith Reynolds. Though she was
accused in his murder, the case never went to trial. Holman returned to Broadway, but she never reclaimed her
former heights. In the 1940s she caused a furor by appearing as a double-act with black folk singer Josh White
in an era when this sort of interracial pairing was frowned
upon by bookers and critics. She continued to tour
throughout the 1950s presenting a program titled "Blues,
Ballads and Sin Songs," but subsequently remained in-
active. Turbulent to the end, it is rumored that Holman
died of carbon monoxide poisoning. Fred Koester
started as a window designer for Gimbels department
store and went on to become a regional theater designer.
Est: $2,000-$2,500.

HERMANN KOSEL (1896-1985)

390. Austria.
24$^3/_4$ x 37$^3/_8$ in./63 x 95 cm
Alfred Wall, Graz
Cond A.

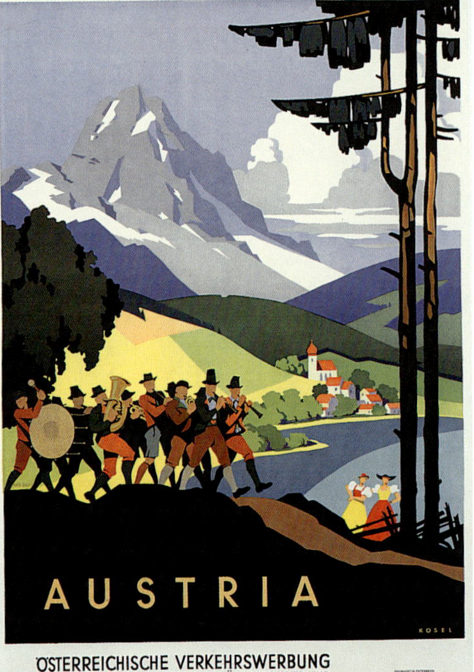

390

You can almost hear the oompahs echoing off the Alps
in this Kosel design for the Austrian Tourist Board. As
is the case with the lion's share of this designer's work,
flat colors and clean lines convey the message with striking clarity. His use of easily identifiable shapes goes
somewhat beyond graphic shorthand to arrive at a
promotional statement that erects contemporary sign-
posts for mass consumption and appreciation. Kosel
began his studies at the Vienna Academy before being
called into military service. After serving as an artillery

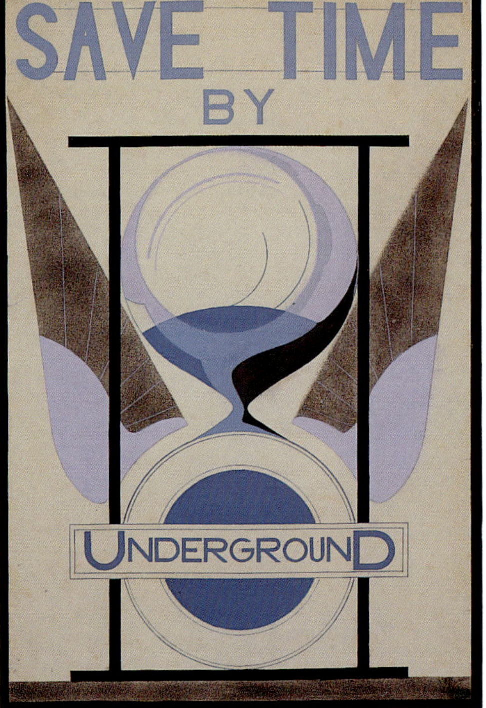

393

officer during WW I, he turned his attention to portraiture and graphic design, eventually being hired by
Julius Klinger as an instructor at Klinger's private school.
He would go on to run several design studios before
relocating to Aix-en-Provence in 1938 to paint landscapes. Upon his return to Vienna in 1948, he partici-
pated in several exhibitions and worked mainly on
designs for cultural and humanitarian events.
Est: $1,200-$1,500.

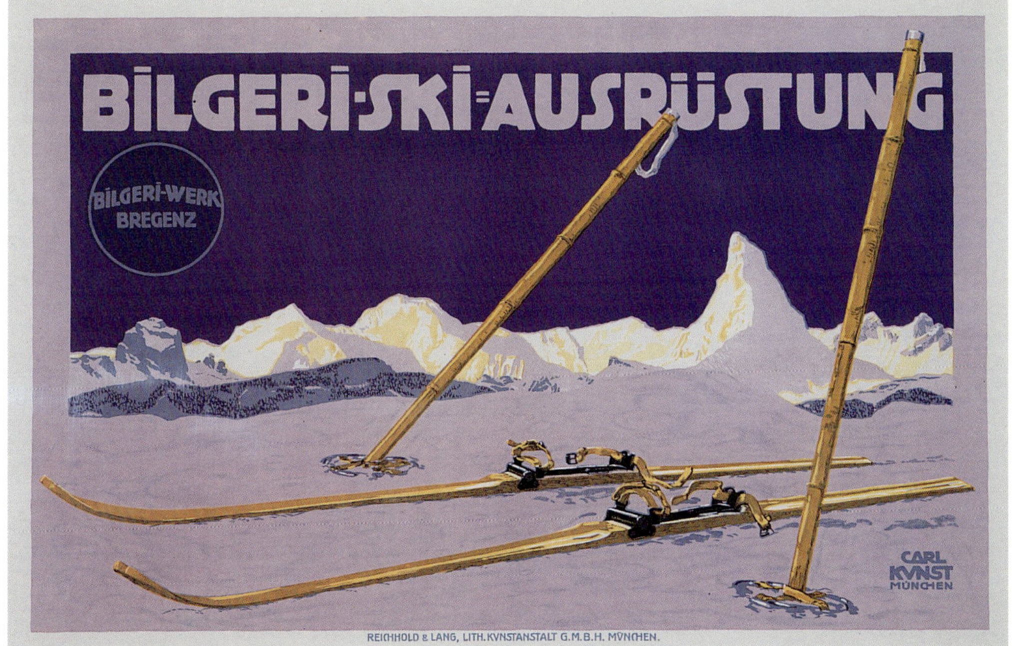

391

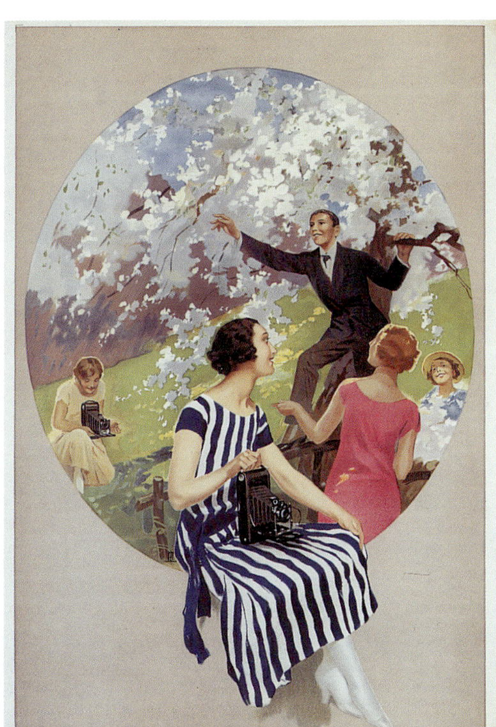
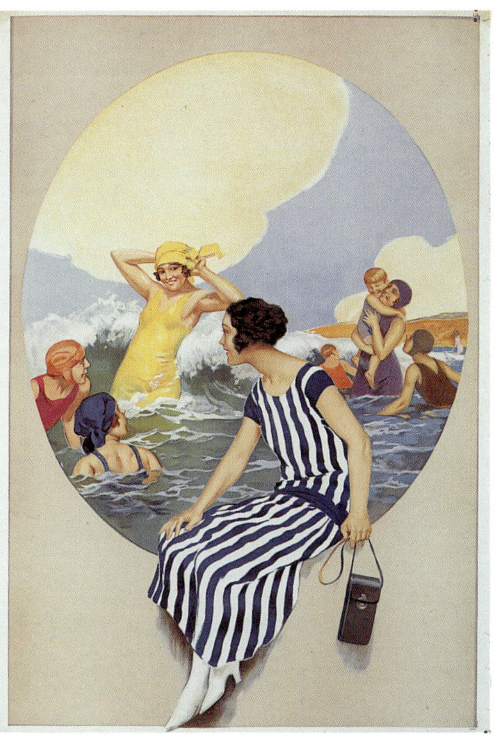

394

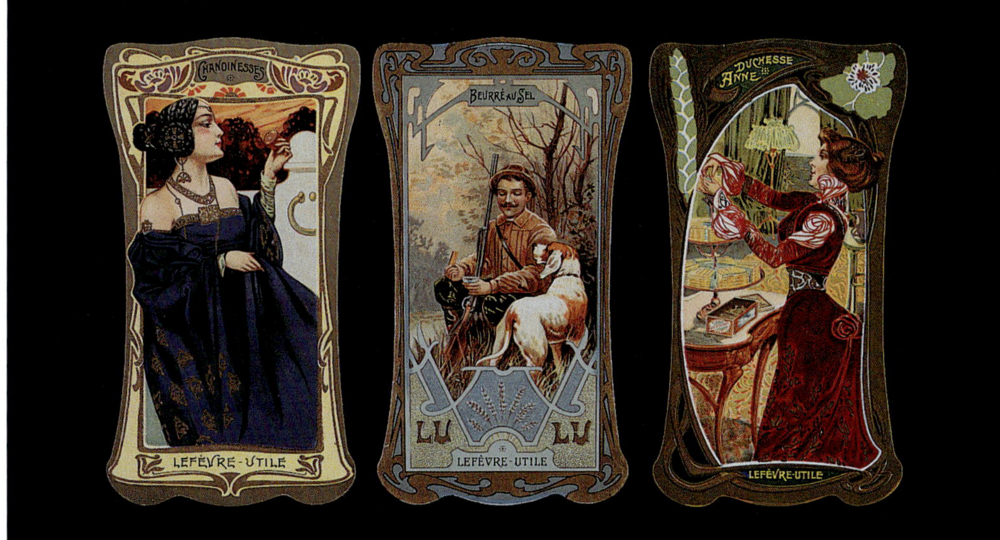

395

CARL KUNST (1884-1912)

391. Bilgeri-Ski Ausrüstung. ca. 1910.
29³/₄ x 19⁵/₈ in./75.5 x 50 cm
Reichhold & Lang, München
Cond A. Framed.
Ref: Voyage, p. 193; Takashimaya, 84; PAI-XXXVIII, 393
Kunst was not only a painter and graphic designer but also an enthusiastic mountaineer—a logical designer choice for this Munich ski equipment poster. A year or so later, he adapted the design for a ski equipment dealer in Berlin by simply adding a skier fastening his bindings and changing the mountains to snow-covered pines (*see* PAI-XVIII, 326).
Est: $1,200-$1,500.

LEC

392. Sables d'Or les Pins. 1926.
25 x 39 in./63.5 x 99 cm
Publicité Générale, Rennes
Cond A.
For many golfers, their sport of choice transcends mere sport to become something of a religious experience, each manicured green a shrine, every well-laid out course a cathedral. Hence, Lec's advertisement for Sables d'Or les Pins' nine holes of "Super-Golf" strikes a thematic chord with its geometric stained-glass " window-style approach, a seaside fairway shot for the true acolytes of the game. *Rare!*
Est: $4,000-$5,000.

THERYE LEE-ELLIOT (1903-1988)

393. Save Time by Underground.
18 x 27¹/₈ in./45.6 x 68.8 cm
Gouache and ink maquette. Framed.
A pair of outstretched wings and the slowly drifting sands of an hourglass are all the oppositional elements needed to convey the fact that you'll arrive at your destination before you realize that time has passed when you ride the London Underground. A concise, imaginative construct from Lee-Elliot, a designer who worked in England primarily in the 1930s whose work was influenced by McKnight Kauffer.
Est: $2,500-$3,000.

RENÉ LELONG (1860-?)

394. Kodak: Two Posters. ca. 1925.
Each: 17¹/₄ x 25¹/₄ in./44 x 64.2 cm
Cond A/P.
Though the text has yet to be added to these two Lelong designs—one a playful springtime romp and the other a splashy summer scene—the woman in the blue-and-white striped dress makes it clear that these are Kodak promotions. The wholesome, family and outdoor-life loving "Kodak Girl" was born in England in 1910, and was soon gracing Kodak posters and ads around the world. Lelong was chosen to redesign and adapt her in 1923. In all of these images, the breezy shutterbug is placed in the foreground, typically in profile, always wearing the blue-and-white striped dress and holding a camera. She looks smilingly into the framed "family picture," which itself always includes people either taking snapshots or in the process of posing for them. Thus, "little by little, the camera established itself as 'omnipresent witness to and participant in life's great moments'" (Affiche Reclame, p. 45).
Est: $1,700-$2,000. (2)

LEFÈVRE-UTILE

395. Cartes Publicitaires: Fourteen Chromolithos.
ca. 1901.
Each: 3 x 5¹/₄ in./7.5 x 13.7 cm
Cond A.
Ref: PAI-XLI, 357
These publicity cards advertise a variety of Lefèvre-Utile products—from the discerning "Duchess Anne" to the tasty "Chablis LU" to the numerous treats in between. Each card contains a rendering of the Art Nouveau female-client-most-likely-to-enjoy that particular cookie, as well as a brief description of the product verso in many cases (the "Chanoinesses" was a little spice cake with a rum glaze; the "Sans Pareil" was a "recommended" almond desert). There is one exception: the "Beurré au Sel," a salty little number promoted by a hunter and his faithful hound. The one steadfast constant remains the attention to detail, which in the end is what produces amazing advertising.
Est: $800-$1,000. (14)

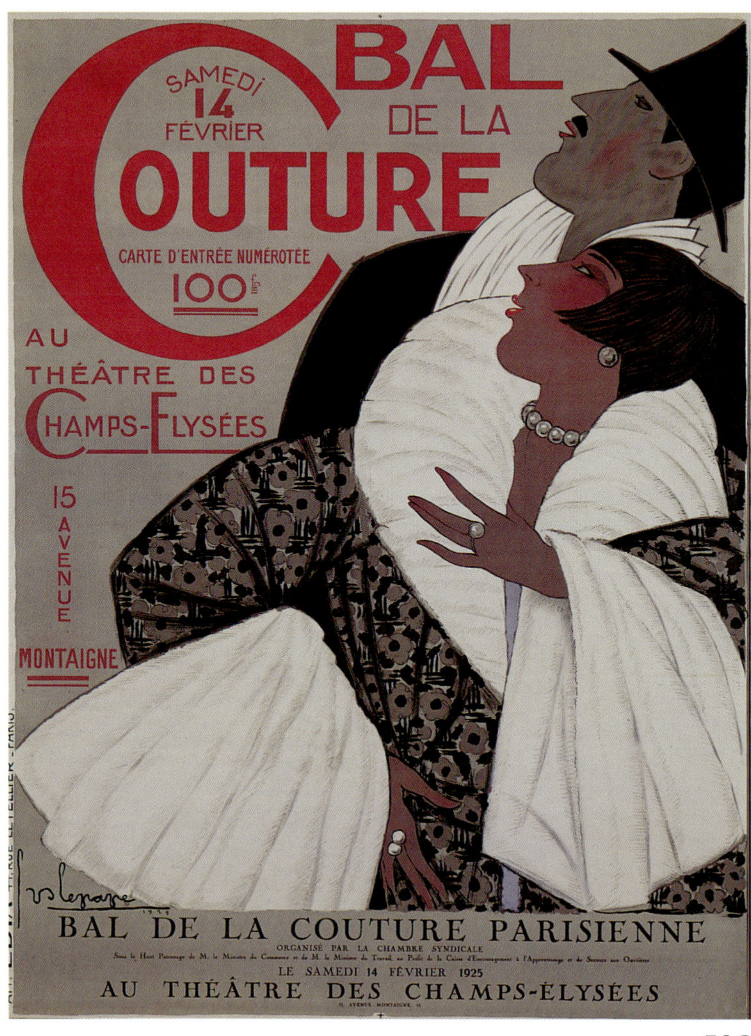

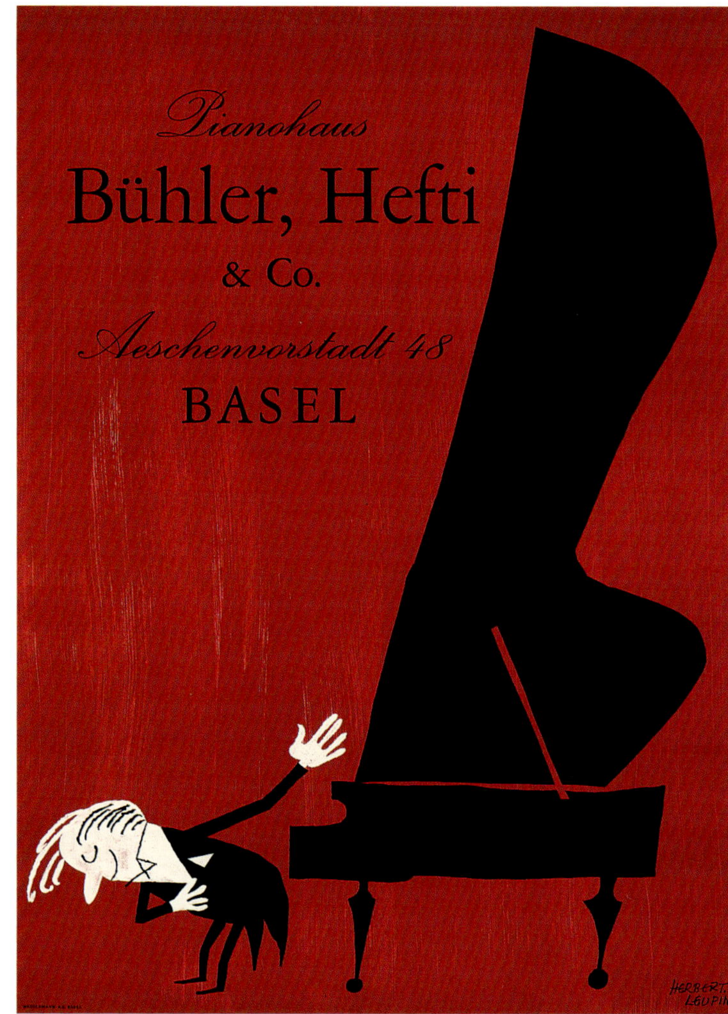

396

397

GEORGES LEPAPE (1887-1971)

396. Bal de la Couture Parisienne. 1925.
$45^{1}/_{2}$ x $62^{1}/_{4}$ in./115.6 x 158 cm
Imp. EDIA, Paris
Cond A–/Slight tears, largely at edges. Framed.
Ref: Art Deco. p. 62; Timeless Images, 127; PAI-XIV, 312
Cool colors and a hot design: the combination makes for
Lepape's finest poster and one of the most spectacular ones
by any artist of this period. "Created . . . for the famous fashion
ball at the Théâtre des Champs- Elysées, (this poster) sums up
much of the French high style. It was produced in 1925, the
year of the Paris exposition. In it, the couple's elegance, aloof-
ness and pride at being among the fashionable set are beautifully rendered" (Art Deco, p. 620). *This is the larger format.*
Est: $7,000-$9,000.

HERBERT LEUPIN (1916-1999)

397. Pianohaus Bühler, Hefti & Co. 1953.
35 x $49^{3}/_{8}$ in./89 x 125.5 cm
Wasserman, Basel
Cond A.
Ref: Leupin, p. 130
Leupin was simply the most prolific, influential and award-
winning of the postwar Swiss graphic designers. A combination
of all that's best in his French colleagues Savignac and Villemot,
he created long-running campaigns for his country's favorite
products—textbook classics filled with endless variety and
delicious humor. Here, in his clever, yet subtle poster for Basel's
Bühler, Hefti and Company, a virtuoso takes a deep bow to an
unseen appreciative audience, while at the same time indicating the grand piano behind him—an instrument that indubit-
ably came from the Bühler establishment—without which he
would be a far lesser musician.
Est: $2,000-$2,500.

CHARLES LEVY

398. L'Horloge.
34 x $48^{7}/_{8}$ in./86.5 x 124 cm
Affiches Ch. Levy, Paris
Cond B/Slight tears, largely at folds.
Ref: PAI-XLI, 360

Founded in 1855, the small garden pavilion café-concert on
the Champs-Elysées called L'Horloge ran into hard times in the
1870s, and by 1875 it was taken over by the city of Paris. That
same year, it was purchased from the city government by a
Viennese businessman by the name of Stein who was looking
to place his disabled daughter in just such a tranquil setting.
Stein kept the garden atmosphere and hired a stable of some of
the period's top personalities to perform there. And not only
did L'Horloge book the finest entertainers of the day, it was
the only establishment of its kind on the Champs-Elysées to
provide its audience with a summer rain cover so that the
music could continue regardless of the weather. Levy trots
out a cavalcade of Horloge stars in this general promotion for
the establishment, placing a name-tag of sorts somewhere on
each performer just in case the passerby doesn't instantly
recognize them—on a bonnet, on more than one fan, even on
a wine bottle. Charles Levy was a designer as well as one of
the major printers of show posters at the turn of the century.
His single most famous job was Toulouse-Lautrec's 1891
poster for the Moulin Rouge (*see* PAI-XXXVII, 524).
Est: $1,400-$1,700.

C. LICHT

399. Le Suez. ca. 1900.
$23^{1}/_{4}$ x 71 in./59 x 180 cm
B. Sirven, Toulouse
Cond B–/Restored tears and losses in margins and folds.
Ref: PAI-XIV, 313
For some reason, cigarette posters around the turn-of-the-
twentieth-century seemed to bring out the best in Art Nouveau
designers. Mucha's two designs for the Job brand (for his 1896
design, *see* No. 436) are notorious for rich decorative embellishments; here, an otherwise obscure graphic designer, working for an otherwise obscure brand of rolling papers, produced
a magniloquent composition with a flourish that does owe
some debt to Mucha, but stands on its own merit in the main.
Est: $1,200-$1,500.

PRIVAT LIVEMONT (1861-1936)

400. Tropon Chocolat-Cocoa. 1900.
$13^{5}/_{8}$ x 23 in./34.5 x 58.4 cm
O. de Rycker & Mendel, Bruxelles

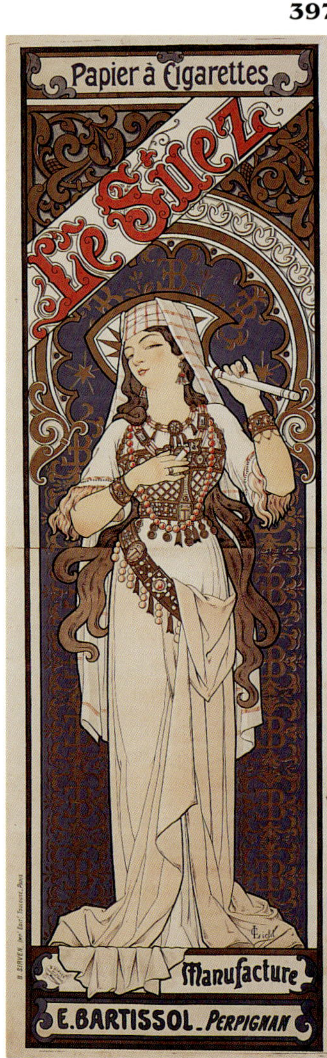

399

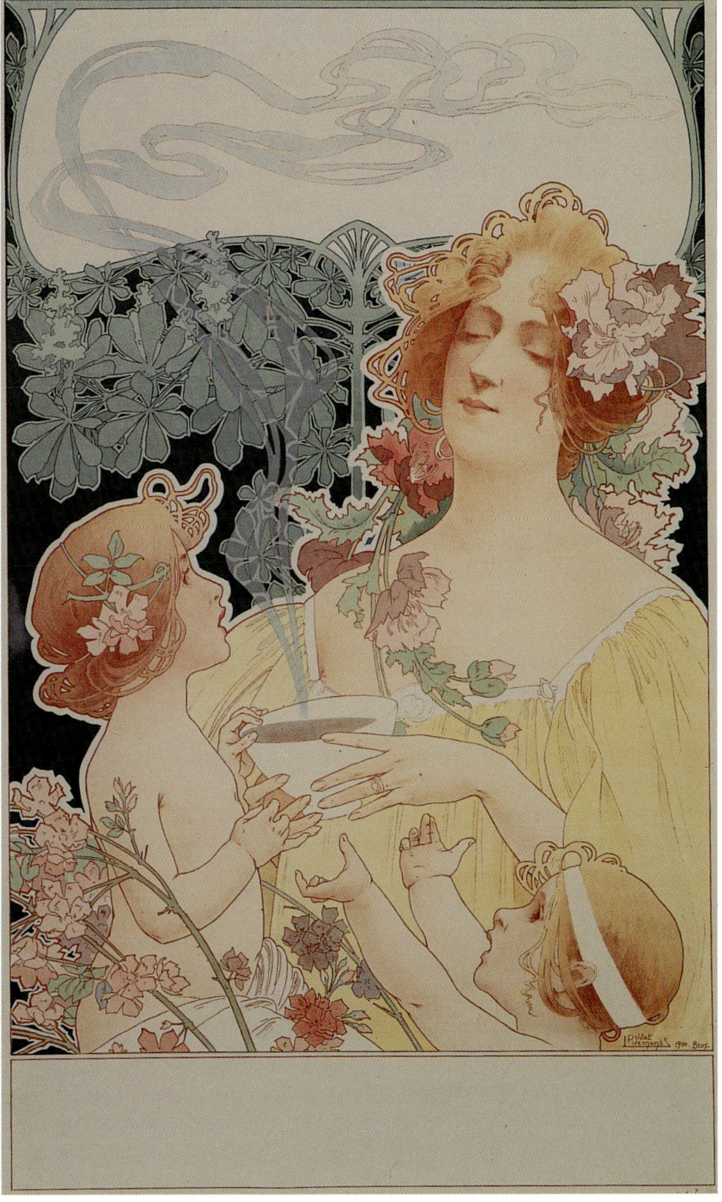

400

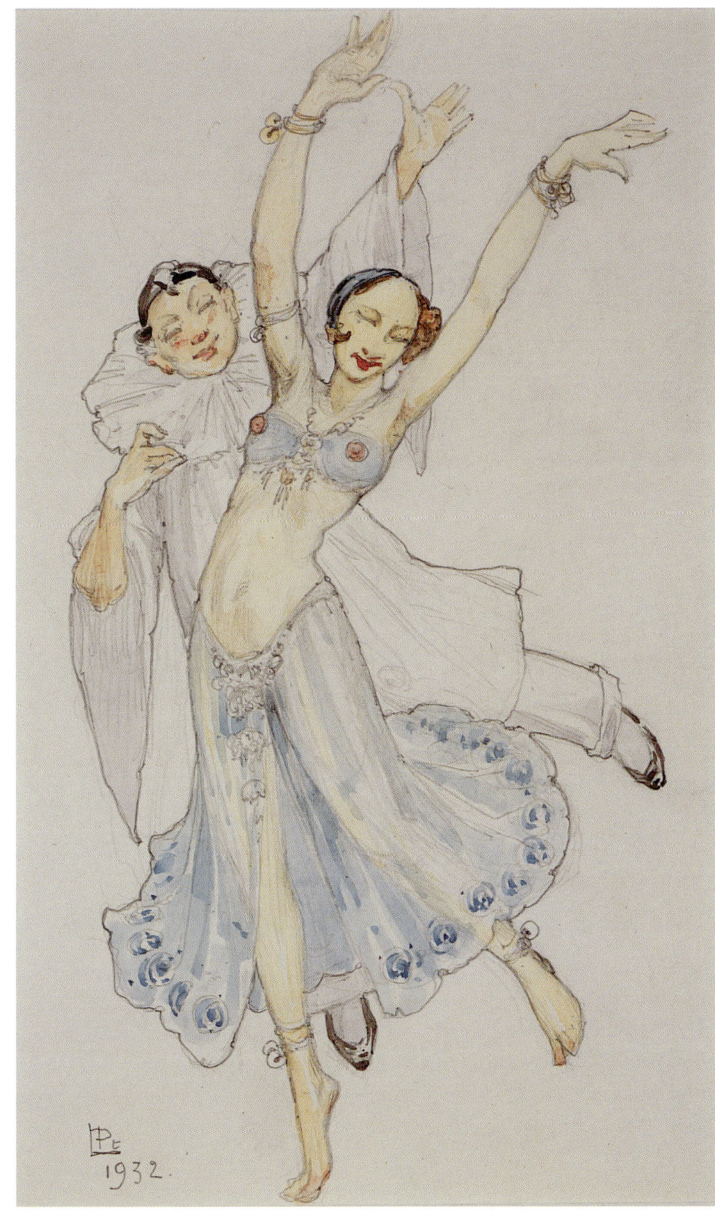

401

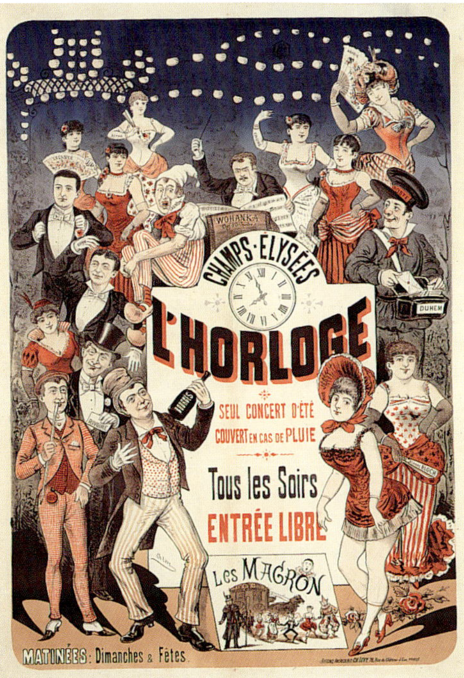

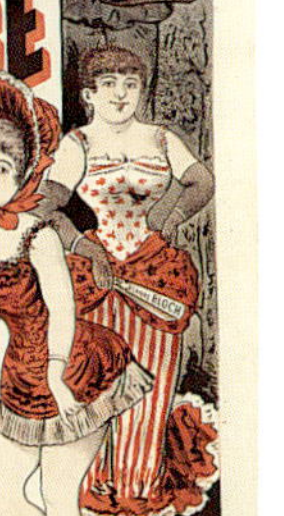

398

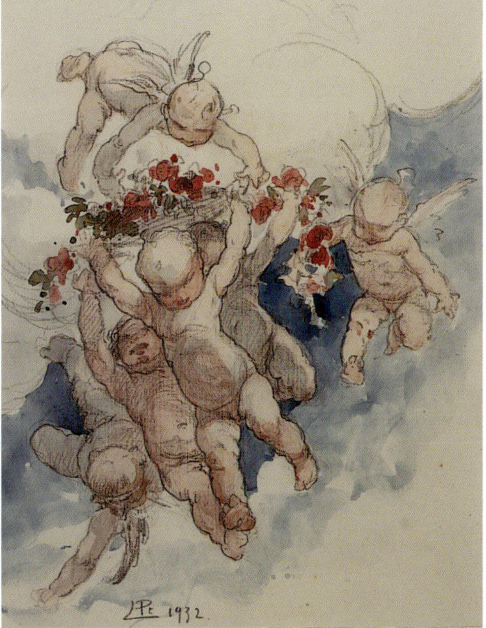

402

Cond A. Framed.
Ref: PAI-XVIII, 346
A serene, reassuring scene, with cheruby children and mother, awaiting the taste of Tropon cocoa. The only place that we've been able to locate a reference to

this poster is on Page 144 of the December 1900 issue of *The Poster*, where it is illustrated, also without text, but identified. Edgar Wenlock, who provides an essay on Belgian posterists in that issue, calls this a "window bill" and although he confesses to not being an admirer of Livemont—or Mucha "upon whom he has very obvi-

ously founded his style"—he admits that "both of these artists have invented very beautiful things, but it seems to me that internal decoration, rather than street advertisement, is the field in which their talent would have its fullest scope" and he goes on to nonetheless praise Livemont as superior to his mentor, for he concludes that "his work is bolder and his colour contrasts more effective" (p. 144). Very interesting!
Est: $5,000-$6,000.

401. Rhythmic Abandon. 1932.
$6^7/8$ x $11^1/4$ in./17.4 x 28.6 cm
Gouache and crayon artwork.
Though their movement implies classical training, their outfits hint at far more libidinous gyrations. And not that Livemont was a puritanical artist, but did you ever imagine that you'd come across a drawing of his that featured a peek-a-boo bandeau? Also, though it's purely suppositional, the less-than-Caucasian features of the dancers and the artwork's era of execution makes one wonder if it was inspired by or intended to promote an act capitalizing on "The Black Craze." An enthralling creation to be sure.
Est: $1,700-$2,000.

402. Heavenly Cherubs. 1932.
$6^1/2$ x $8^1/2$ in./16.5 x 21.5 cm
Gouache and crayon drawing. Framed.
Far from the first time that Livemont indulged in the playful antics of otherworldly toddlers, this boisterous group of cherubs provides ample speculative evidence that not all celestial activity need be solemn—in fact, sometimes its downright rambunctious.
Est: $1,700-$2,000.

403. 'Tis The Season: Two Promotional Christmas Drawings. 1932.
Each: 6¹/₂ x 10 in./16.5 x 25.3 cm
Gouache and crayon (a), and crayon (b) artwork.
A pair of Yuletide drawings from Livemont, overflowing with the artist's expected romanticism and a seasonal sense of giving. The first, executed in gouache and crayon, shows a mother passing out dolls to her two children in the presence of Saint Nicholas, an un-bridled joy evident on the faces of every individual. In the second crayon drawing, the mythical figure that served as the inspiration for Santa Claus has vanished from the scene, but the holiday fascination remains. And though the scene undoubtedly is one of a mother passing out presents to her children, a certain melan-choly permeates the design, creating a narrative alle-gory that hints at innocence lost.
Est: $2,000-$2,500. (2)

404. Diplôme pour l'Académie Royale des Beaux Arts de Bruxelles. 1896.
24¹/₄ x 15⁵/₈ in./61.6 x 39.6 cm
Cond A.
Ref: Schoonbroadt, p. 50
Of the many requests made of a talented graphic de-signer, one that doesn't immediately pop to mind is coming up with pictorially interesting diplomas. But at the turn of the Twentieth Century, Livemont was asked to create quite a few of these graduation documents. "The most remarkable among these diplomas was the one conceived in 1896 for the Royal Academy of Beaux-Arts and School of Decorative Arts of Brussels . . . where classical female allegories embody the aca-demic disciplines against a background of Brussels architecture. As is the case with other diplomas . . . the style, not surprisingly, raises more than one inter-pretation of the antiquated types in this subtle Art Nouveau creation" (Schoonbroadt, p. 49).
Est: $1,200-$1,500.

405. Woman Sculpting/Woman Painting. 1901.
Each: 17⁵/₈ x 25 in./44.8 x 63.5 cm
L. Van Leer, Amsterdam (not shown)
Cond A.
Ref: Belle Epoque 1980, 71 & 72; PAI-XXXV, 364
Two of Livemont's graphic works designed as decorative panels: one is a particularly tender study of an artist critically examining her sculpture, and the companion piece features a young lady intent on her painting. Both have a similar ornamental background. Livemont started out as an interior designer in his home town of Schaer-beek, Belgium. He came to poster art after entering a poster contest on a whim and winning it. By 1898, *The Poster* magazine was calling him "the uncontested mas-ter of Belgian posterists." Though one of several poster-ists often assumed to be disciples of Mucha, Livemont's version of Art Nouveau was in fact well-developed before Mucha burst onto the scene in the 1890s.
Est: $6,000-$7,000. (2)

GUSTAVE LORAIN (1882-?)

406. Ecole du Dessin. ca. 1900.
25¹/₂ x 35³/₄ in./64.8 x 90.9 cm
Gouache and ink maquette on paper. Framed.
Ref: PAI-XXXVIII, 407 (var)
One would certainly expect excellence in original art-work done for a poster promoting an art school—espe-cially one where Eugène Grasset taught. And excellence is precisely what we get in this lovely Art Nouveau design by Lorain—identified at the bottom as himself "a pupil of the school Guerin-Grasset." It features a lady in med-ieval dress surrounded by rose bushes, an orange tree and visible fanfare. Interestingly, at age sixteen, Lorain earned first prize in a poster contest for the monthly art magazine *Art et Decoration* (see PAI-XXXIII, 426). The style, subject and even the title "banner" and letter-ing are nearly identical. Both designs also have a text panel in the lower corner, which here is still blank. Both owe a considerable debt to Grasset. Lorain went on to win medals at the Salons des Artistes Français of 1921 and 1925.
Est: $3,000-$4,000.

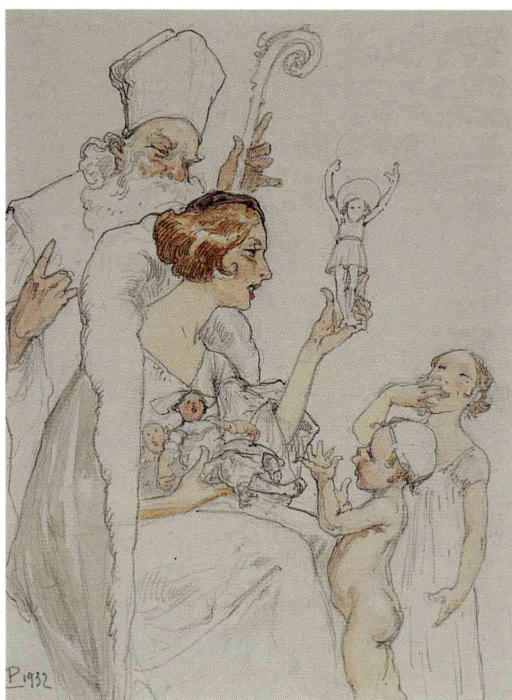
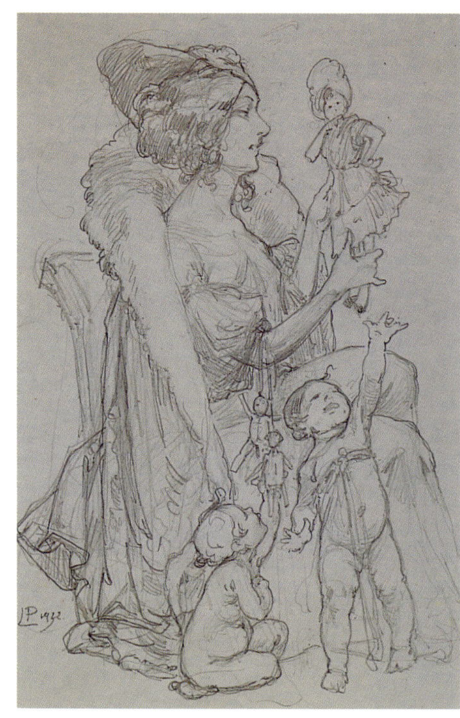

403

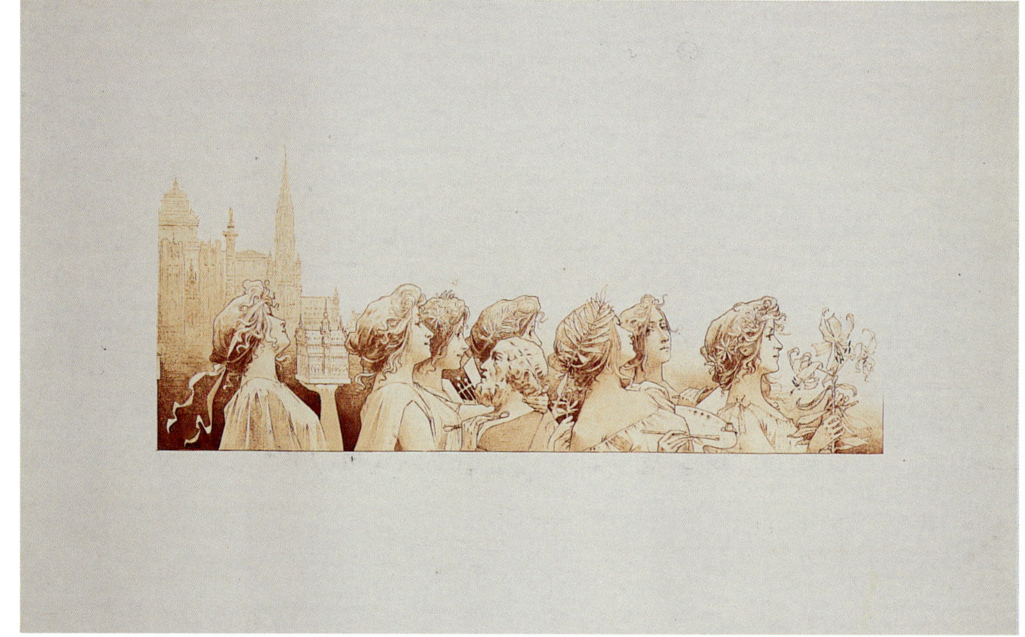

404

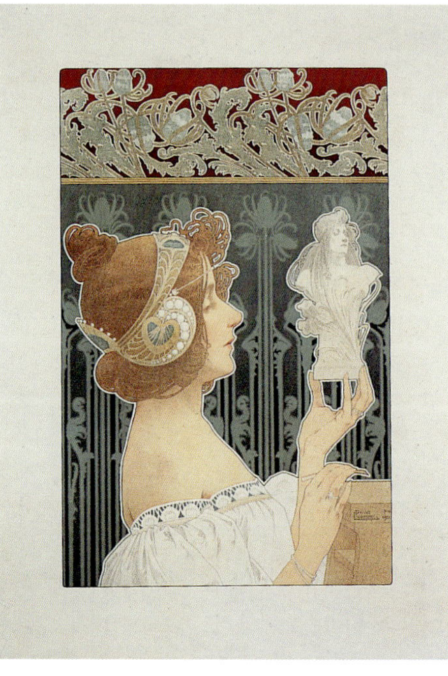
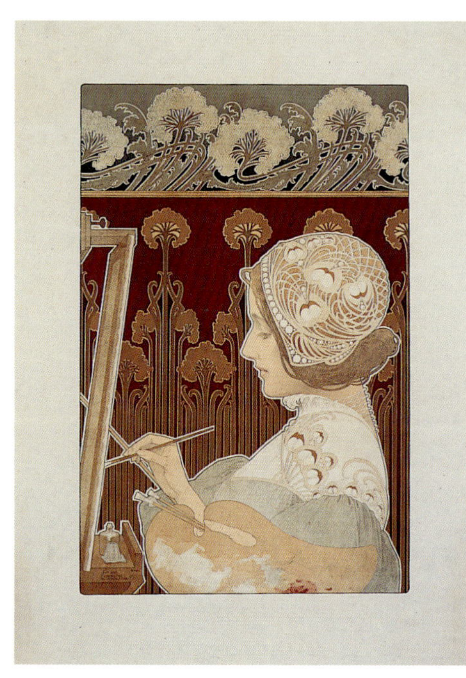

405

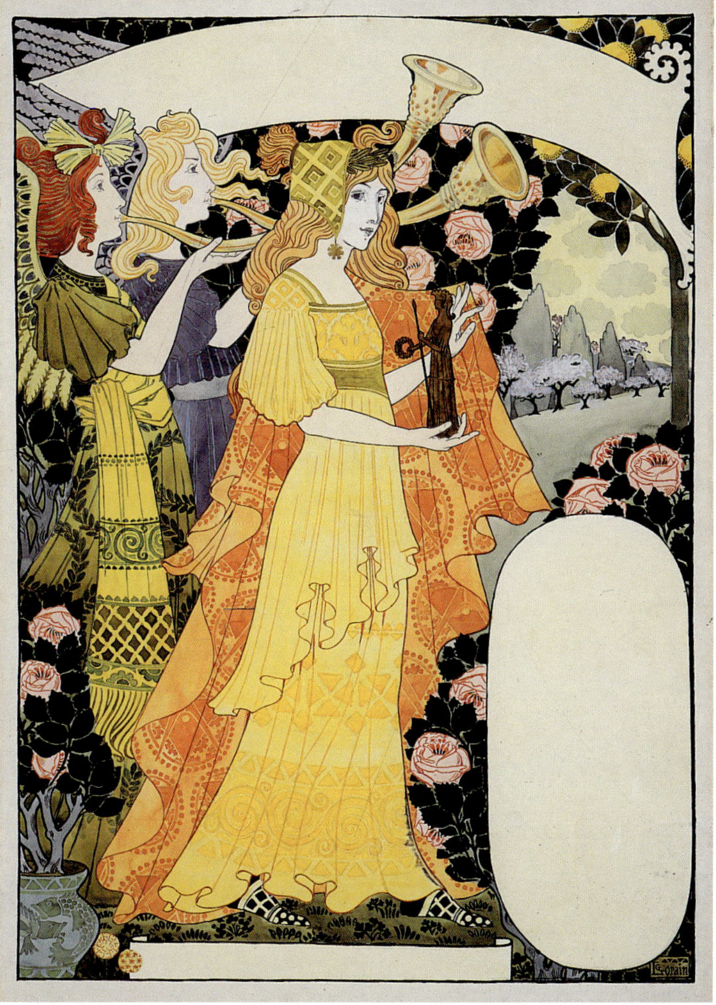

406

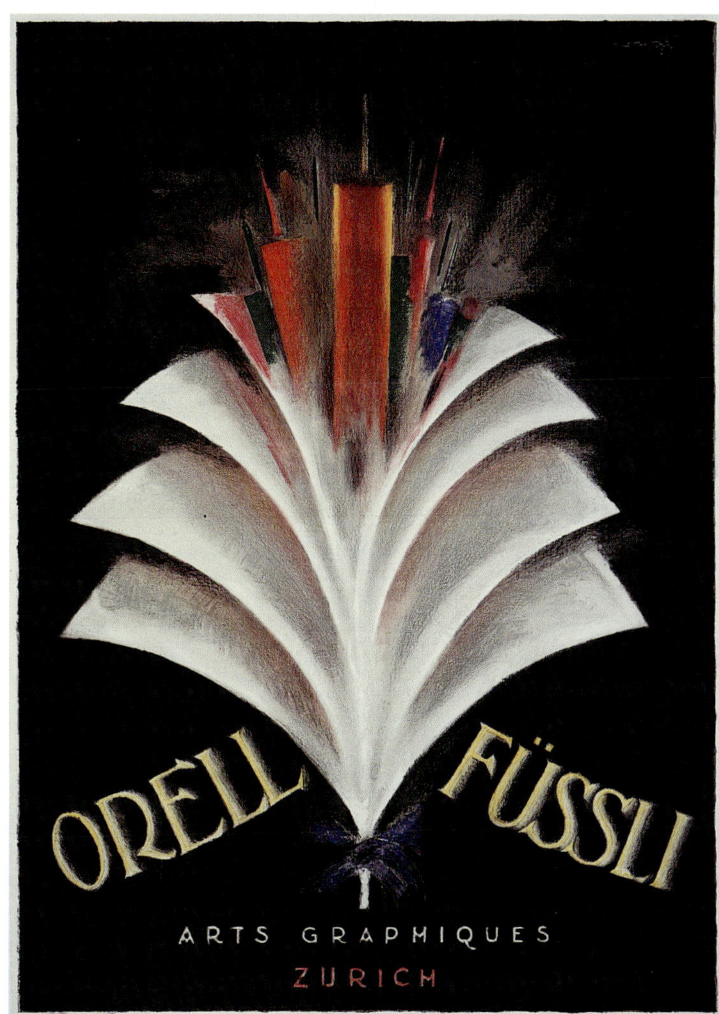

407

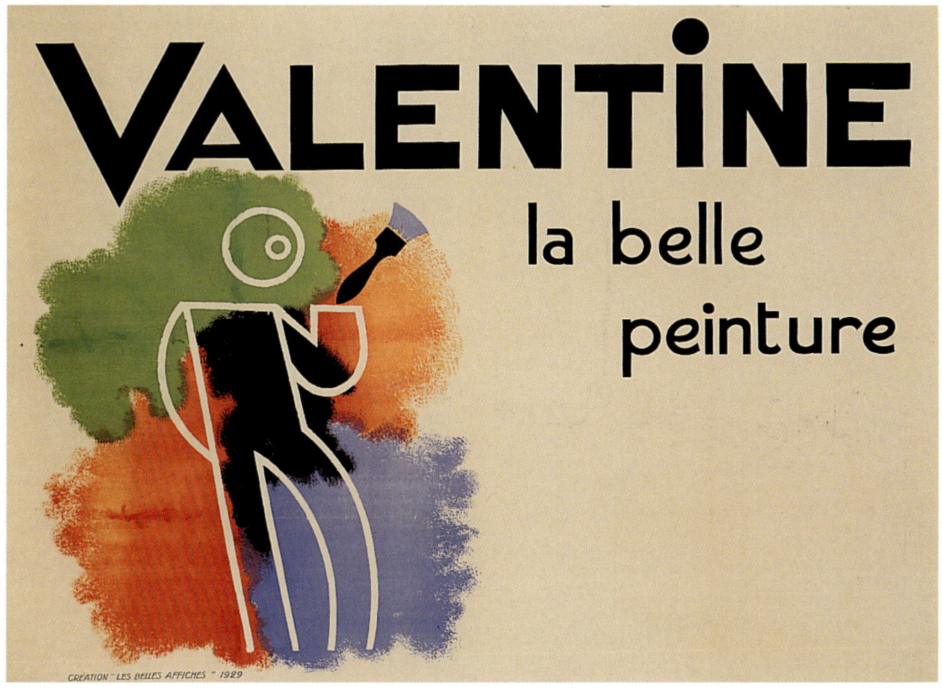

408

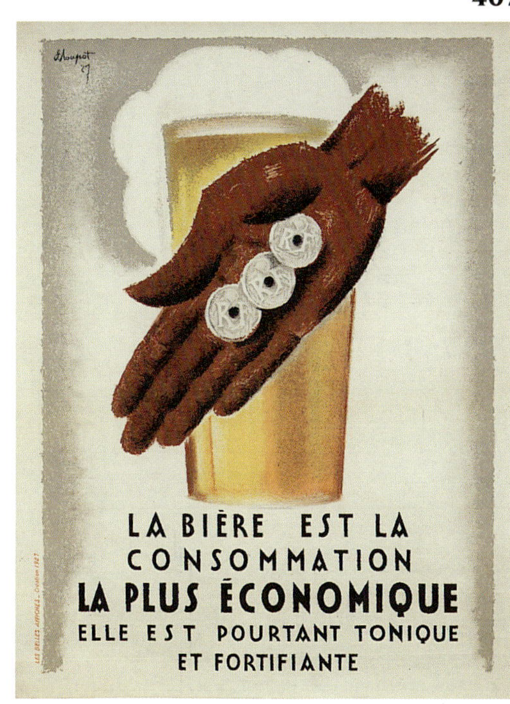

409

CHARLES LOUPOT (1892-1962)

407. Orell Füssli. 1922.
36 x 50^1/$_2$ in./91.5 x 128.2 cm
Orell Füssli, Zurich (not shown)
Cond A–/Unobtrusive tears near edges.
Ref: Loupot/Zagrodzki, 48; PAI-VII, 209
A bouquet made from sheets of paper and colored ink rollers is a perfect way to advertise a commercial lithographer. One of Loupot's last posters printed in Switzerland before returning to France.
Est: $7,000-$9,000.

408. Valentine. 1929.
62^7/$_8$ x 46^1/$_2$ in./159.6 x 118 cm
Création "Les Belles Affiches"
Cond B/Slight tears at folds.
Ref: PAI-XIII, 345 (var)
One year after Loupot created an inspired harlequin figure with a spraygun as a logo for this paint company (*see* PAI-XV, 365), he impossibly topped himself. Adopt-

ing the figure's outline, he replaced the gun with a paintbrush and then used the brush to have the figure daub on loose areas of color that replace the original clearly-delineated harlequin diamonds. A neat conceit from the master colorist who can make even black look brilliant. The figure of the jolly painter himself is still used by the company today. *Rare!*
Est: $4,000-$5,000.

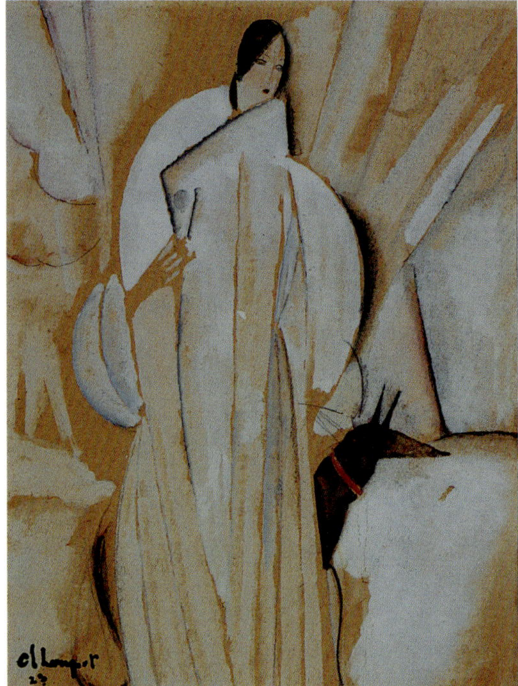

410

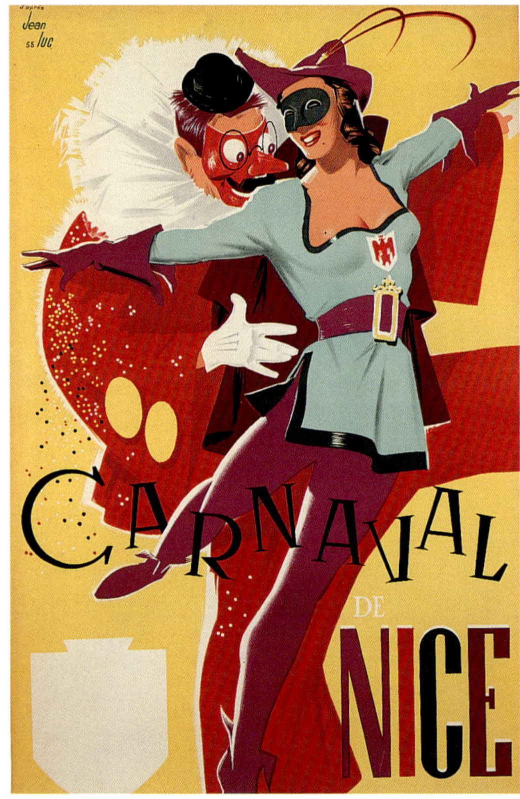

412

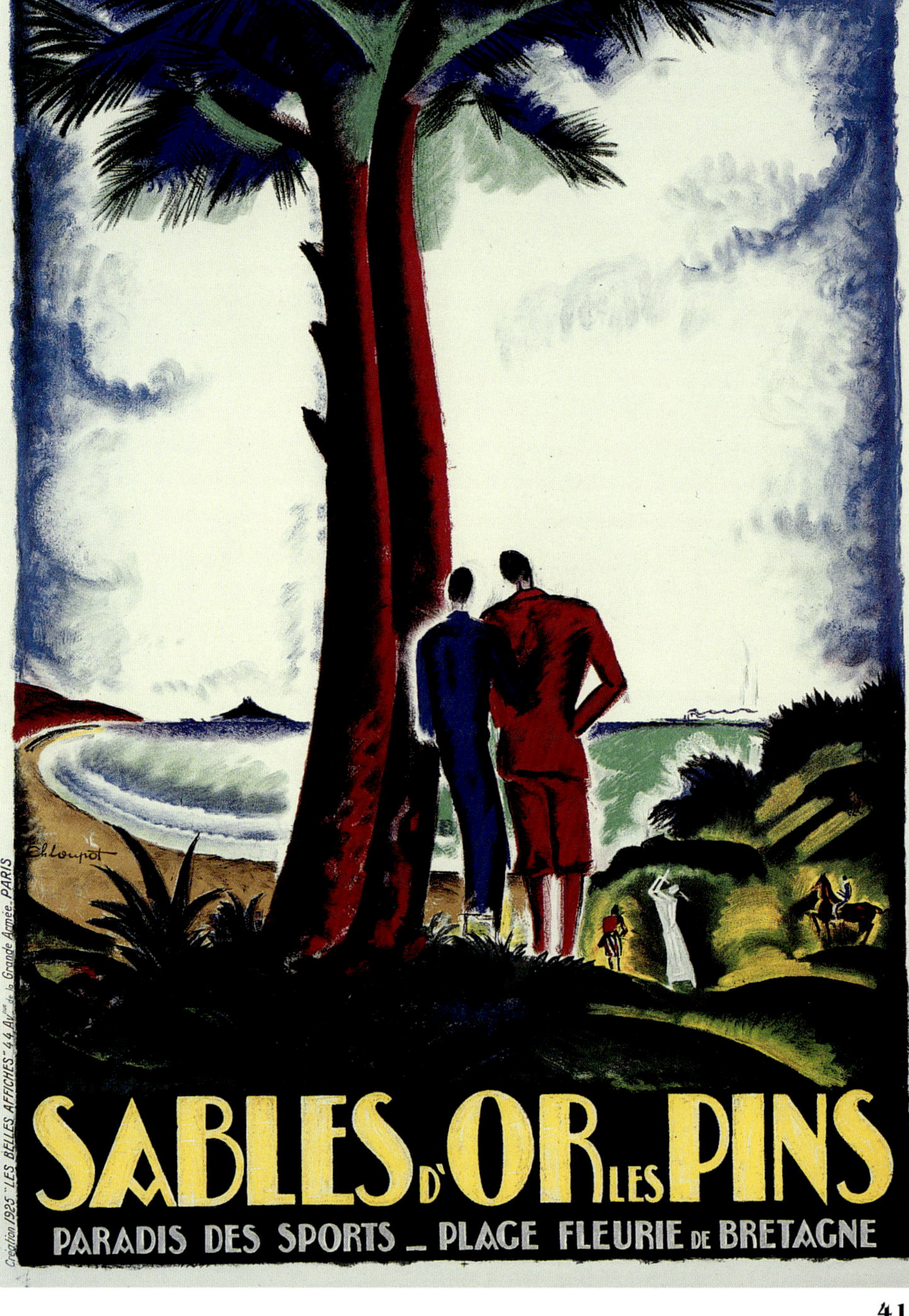

411

CHARLES LOUPOT (cont'd)

409. La Biere/La Plus Economique. 1927.
$23^3/_4$ x $31^3/_4$ in./60.4 x 80.7 cm
Les Belles Affiches, Paris
Cond A–/Slight stains at paper edges.
Ref: Loupot/Zagrodzki, 67; PAI-XXXI, 520
Loupot studied art at Lyon, but produced his first
posters in Switzerland where he stayed for seven years,
between 1916 and 1923. He then returned to Paris at
the invitation of the printer Devambez, and became
one of the top designers of his time. Between 1925
and 1930, most of his work was executed for the agency
Les Belles Affiches, founded by two brothers named
Damour. He was also Cassandre's partner in the Alliance Graphique. This rarely-seen specimen is an institutional ad for the beer industry, providing sound advice
—through straightforward graphic shorthand—about
the economic and health benefits of the delectable
amber liquid.
Est: \$2,500-\$3,000.

410. Exacting Couture. 1923.
$4^5/_8$ x $6^1/_4$ in./11.5 x 15.8 cm
Hand-signed gouache and crayon drawing. Framed.
Upon Loupot's return to France from Switzerland in
1923, he set out to reestablish himself in the illustrative scene by providing *La Gazette du Bon Ton* and
Femina with elegant fashion plates such as the crystal-
line Art Deco number seen here. The design is a con-
centrated thing of beauty, a study in contrasts perfectly
suited to a glamorous obsession that indulges itself in
both its cutting-edge and its luxurious wallow. And the
inclusion of the Doberman was stroke of genius—elegant, sleek and potentially savage, a subtle—not to
mention accurate—reflection of fashion itself.
Est: \$2,000-\$2,500.

411. Sables d'Or les Pins. 1925.
$29^1/_2$ x $41^1/_2$ in./74.9 x 105.4 cm
Les Belles Affiches, Paris
Cond A.

Ref: Loupot/Zagrodzki, 59; Loupot, 20; PAI-VIII, 438
A couple leaning against a palm tree take in the view
of a strong, lushly depicted landscape on the "flow-
ered beach of Brittany." A rider and golfer below reinforce the sales message that the locale is a "Sports
Paradise." Loupot joined Cassandre's Alliance Graphique shop in 1930, but as Patricia Kery points out, he
was "totally different in style and work habits. In contrast to Cassandre's geometric hard edges were Loupot's
gentle, painterly qualities. Although subtle in his technique, Loupot was more direct than Cassandre in presenting ideas. He depicted real objects and people, as
opposed to Cassandre's allusive floating windshields,
telegraph wires, and railroad tracks" (Art Deco, p. 591).
It is this painterly style that we see so masterfully executed in this travel poster.
Est: \$10,000-\$12,000.

JEAN LUC

412. Carnaval de Nice. 1955.
$24^1/_2$ x $37^5/_8$ in./62.3 x 95.5 cm
Cond A–/Slight tears and creases at paper edges.
You can't say that Luc errs on the side of decorum in
his design for Carnaval in Nice, but then again the city's
annual pre-Lenten festival hasn't been celebrated since
the thirteenth century because of its strict adherence
to propriety. This masked pair throws themselves into

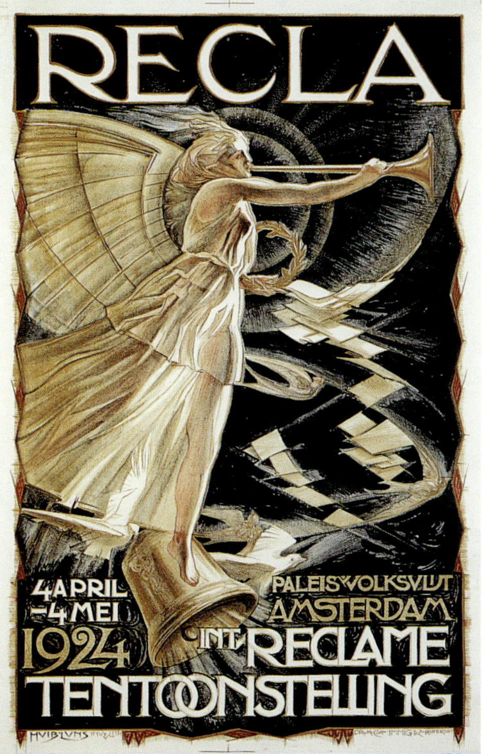

413

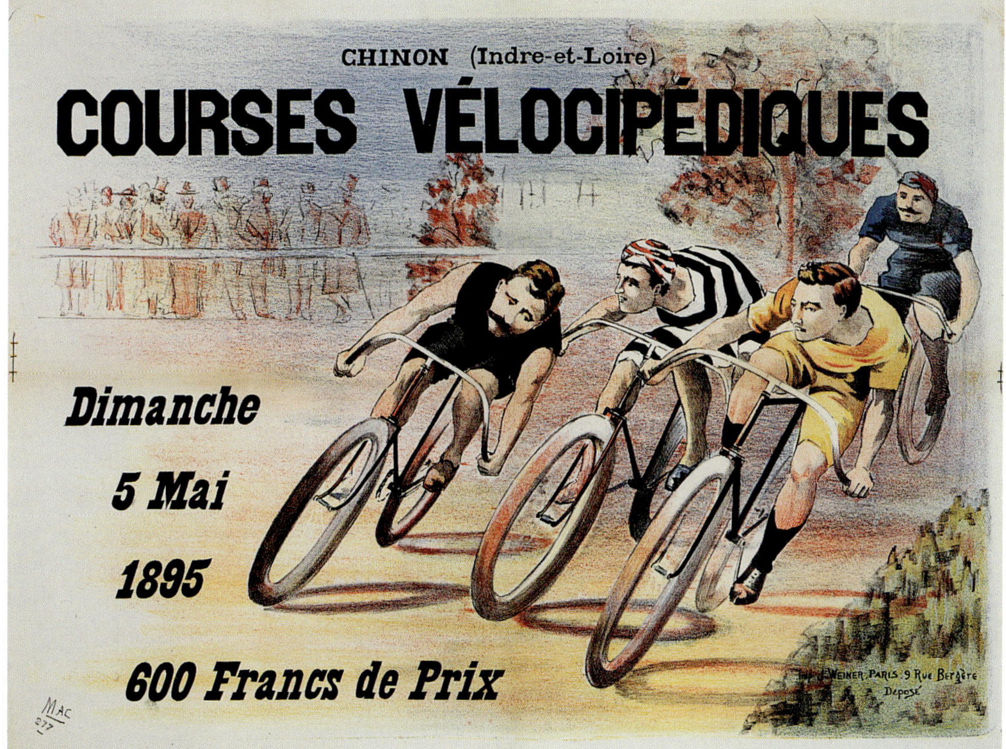

414

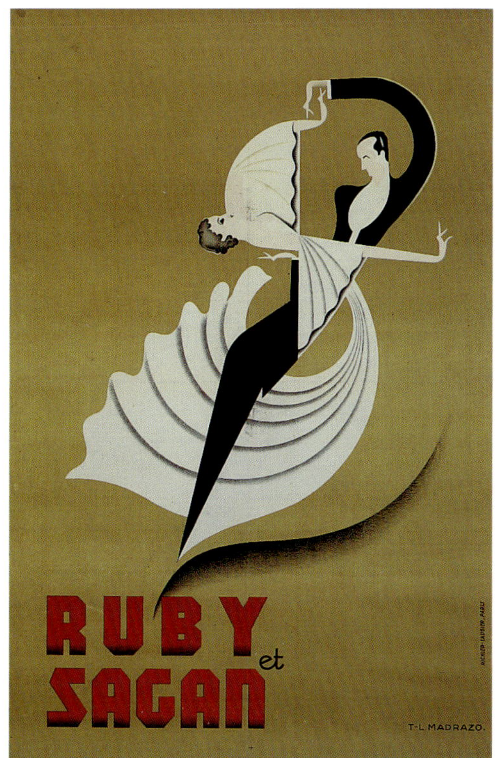

415

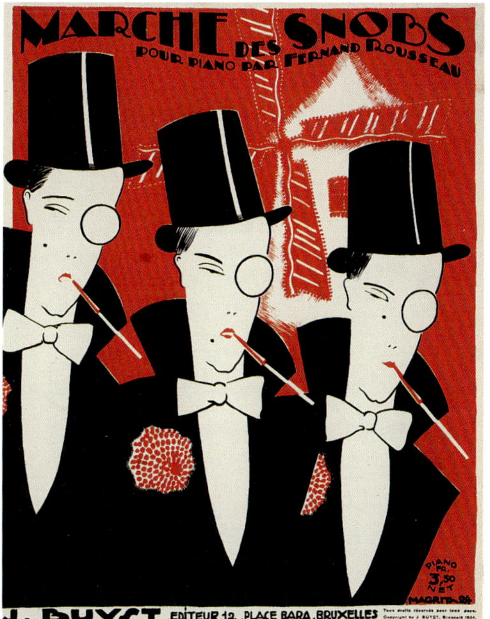

416

their promotional role with infectious abandon, with the libidinous portent of the event played up with a well placed coat of arms and a none-too-subtle stare. After all, it doesn't take much imagination to find the word "carnal" in "carnaval."
Est: $1,000-$1,200.

HUBERT M. LUNS (1881-1942)

413. Recla/Tentoonstelling. 1924.
$30^3/_4$ x $47^7/_8$ in./78 x 121.7 cm
Druck Corn Immig & Zn., Rotterdam
Cond B/Slight tears and stains, largely at edges.
Inspirational advertising for a month-long international publicity exhibition at Amsterdam's Paleis Wolksvlist. This gilded angelic herald of the promotional arts couldn't possibly be doing more to draw attention to the presentation, but perhaps the most stirring inclu-

sion is the spray of handbills that transform themselves into the winged messengers of consumerism. Luns was a painter, graphic artist, draftsman and art historian.
Est: $1,700-$2,000.

MAC

414. Courses Vélocipédiques. 1895.
$31^1/_2$ x $24^1/_2$ in./80 x 62.1 cm
Imp. J. Weiner, Paris
Cond A–/Unobtrusive tears at paper edges.
Head-to-head competition—pure and simple—is the order of the day in this Mac design for a day of mid-spring bike races in Chinon, a town situated in France's Vienne River valley. No allegory, no far-flung symbolism, just the testosterone-laced exploits (from the days before blood doping became a household phrase and any unfair advantages weren't as pharmaceutical in nature) of man versus man. And if this is what comes across in lithographic form, just imagine the intensity of seeing it in the flesh.
Est: $2,500-$3,000.

TITO LIVIO DE MADRAZO (1899-1979)

415. Ruby et Sagan.
$29^7/_8$ x $46^1/_2$ in./75.8 x 118.2 cm
Richier-Laugier, Paris
Cond B/Slight tears and stains at folds and edges.
Ref: PAI-XXXIV, 439
Exemplifying deftness, Madrazo renders Ruby's gown as a fluted shell while turning her partner into an Art Deco exclamation. Some of the most beautiful theatrical and dance posters of the 1930s were executed by the Spanish painter Madrazo, who arrived in Paris in 1923. He takes all the graphic liberties necessary to achieve motion with a singular clarity. There are about a dozen posters for various performers that Madrazo created, each sharing the same flair—terse, eloquent caricatures that capture the essence of the personality in sparse, fluid lines and shapes. Now very sought and very rare, these works mark a glorious end to the Art Deco style.
Est: $2,500-$3,000.

RENÉ MAGRITTE (1898-1967)

416. Marche des Snobs. 1924.
$10^5/_8$ x $13^3/_4$ in./27 x 35 cm
Imp. J. de Vleeschouwer, Bruxelles
Cond A–/Slight stains and edges.
Telling you that the name of this complete four-page song sheet for Fernand Rousseau's "March of the Snobs" seems completely redundant, what with these effete triplets descending upon us like a trio of dandies who have sworn their allegiance to Mr. Blackwell. Still, you can't fault them for their appearance, which is impeccable, naturally.
Est: $1,700-$2,000.

417. Primevère. 1926.
$33^5/_8$ x 49 in./85.3 x 124.5 cm
Lith. Fuytynck, Bruxelles
Cond B+/Unobtrusive folds; slight tears at paper edges.
Ref: Wallonie, 179; PAI-XXIII, 351
One wishes that this master of surrealism, who had an immense influence on advertising art, had produced more poster designs of his own. This is one of his first and most interesting, executed for the singer Marie-Louise Van Emelen who went under the spring-y stage name of Primevère. She makes her appearance here against a background of a checkered floor.
Est: $3,000-$4,000.

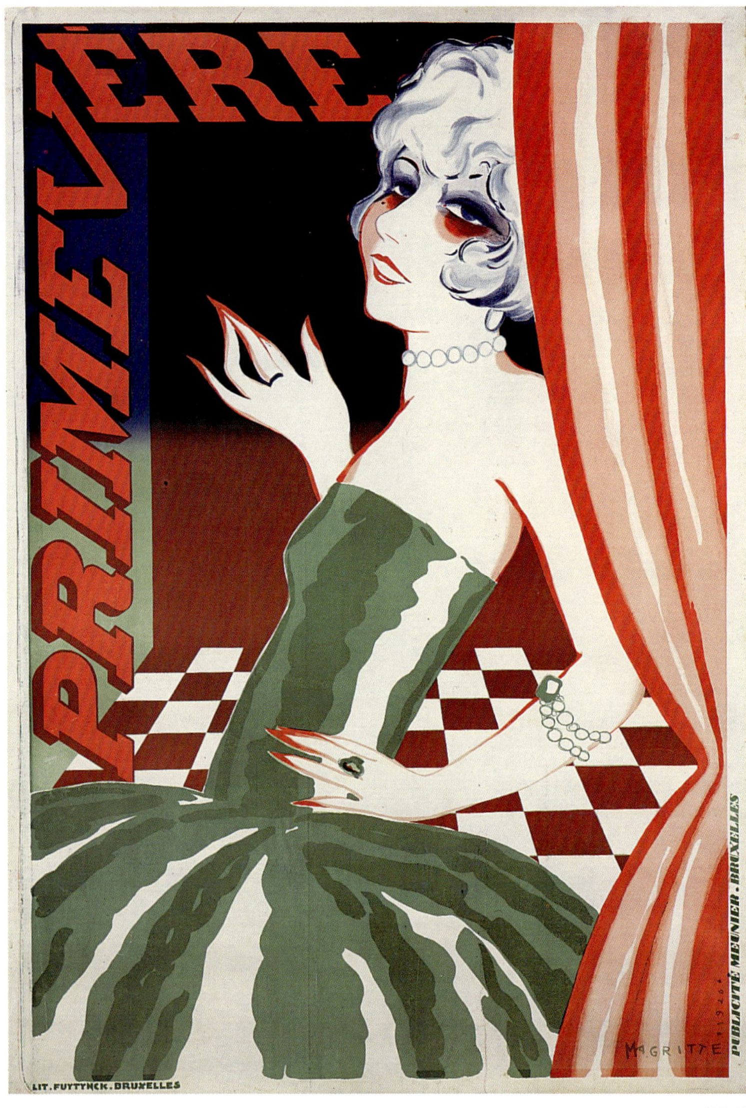

417

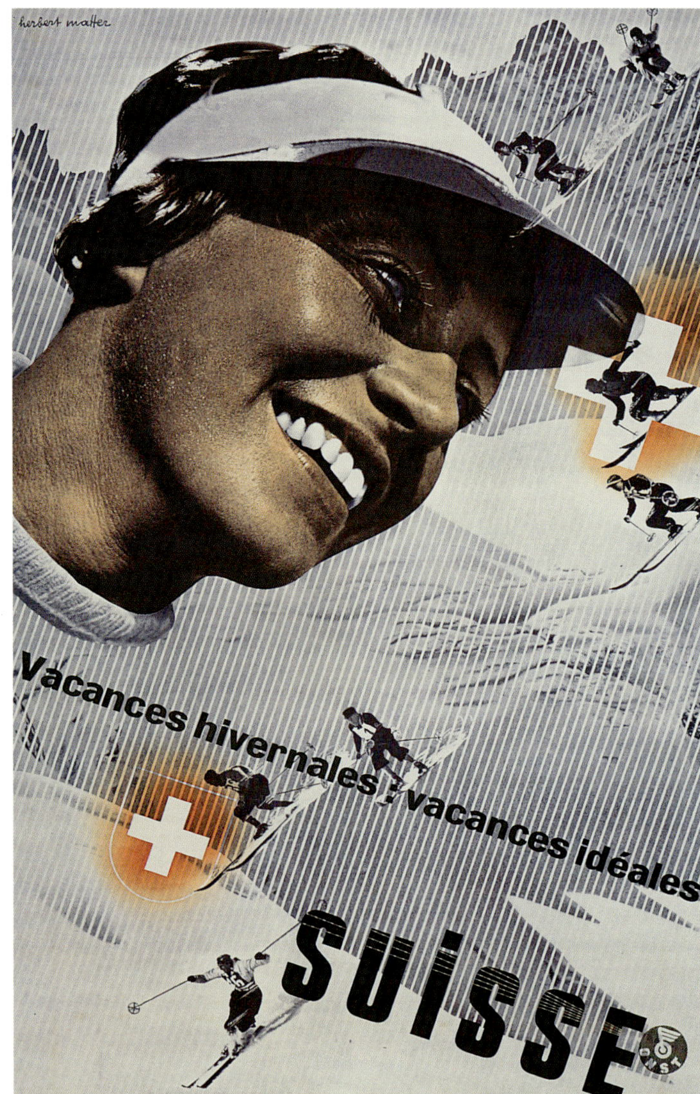

419

LEO MARFURT (1894-1977)

418. Belga. 1928.
12³/₄ x 39¹/₈ in./32.3 x 99.3 cm
Cond A–/Unobtrusive folds.
Ref (All Var): Belgique/Paris, 65; Galerie GCER, 69;
  PAI-XXI, 306
Swiss-born and educated Marfurt worked closely with
Belgian painter and decorator, Jules de Praeter, with
whom he came to Belgium in 1921, where he settled
and opened an Antwerp studio. He founded and opened
his own agency in 1917 and produced varied works,
including some magnificent posters for Chrysler, Remington, Minerva, Purfina and the British railways. Marfurt was by far the most innovative Belgian graphic
artist between the wars. He first used this sedate redhead to promote Belga cigarettes in 1925 (*see* PAI-XXI,
306), executed appropriately and entirely in the colors
of the Belgian flag. This version, however, casts her in
a cameo set into a field of green just above an oversized, smoldering cigarette; it's also unsigned, which
would seem to imply that this just may be a "d'après"
edition, executed by an uncredited designer working
from Marfurt's original. However, there's still no reason
to show the enchanting young woman smoking in
order to make it clear that Belga is her favorite brand.
Est: $1,400-$1,700.

HERBERT MATTER (1907-1984)

419. Suisse. 1934.
26⁵/₈ x 40¹/₄ in./65 x 102.2 cm
Cond A–/Slight tears at edges.
Ref (All Var but PAI): Margadant, 282; Fotoplakate, 130;
  Art Deco, p. 64; Word & Image, p. 74;
  Muller-Brockmann, 262; Matter, p. 99; PAI-X, 306
One of the early and important posters combining photos
and graphics, this design by the man who would perfect
the art of photomontage was widely distributed through-
out Europe in several languages, this being the rare
French-language version.
Est: $2,000-$2,500.

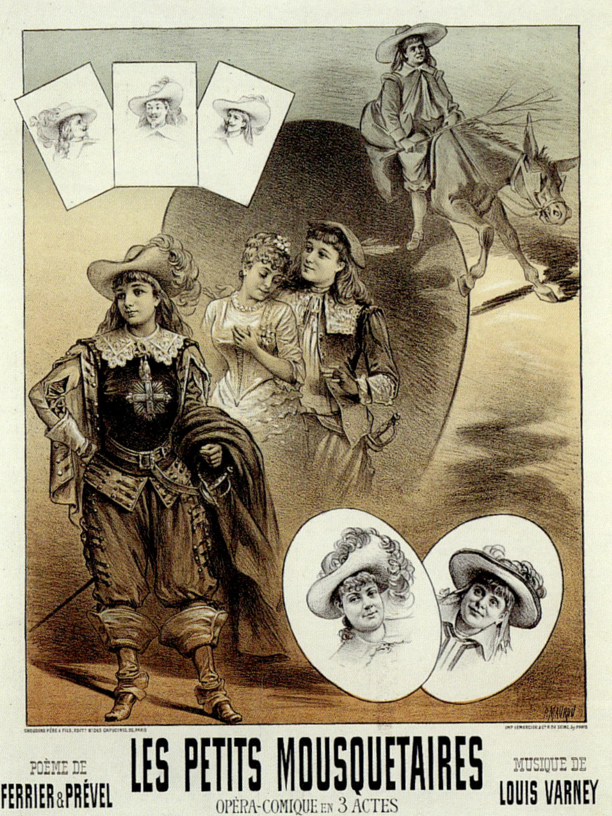

420

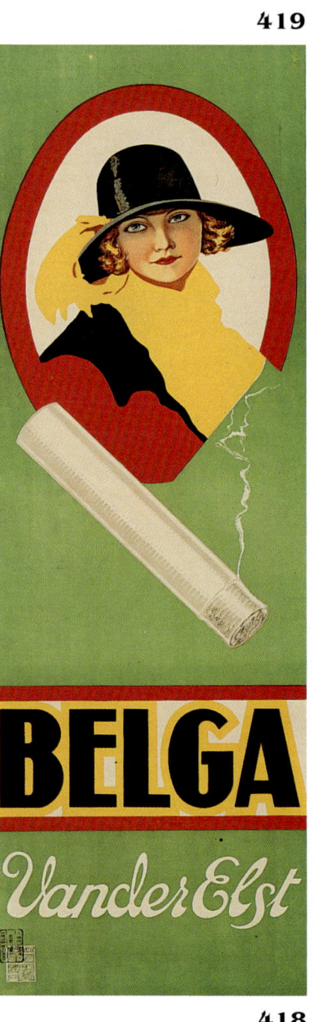

418

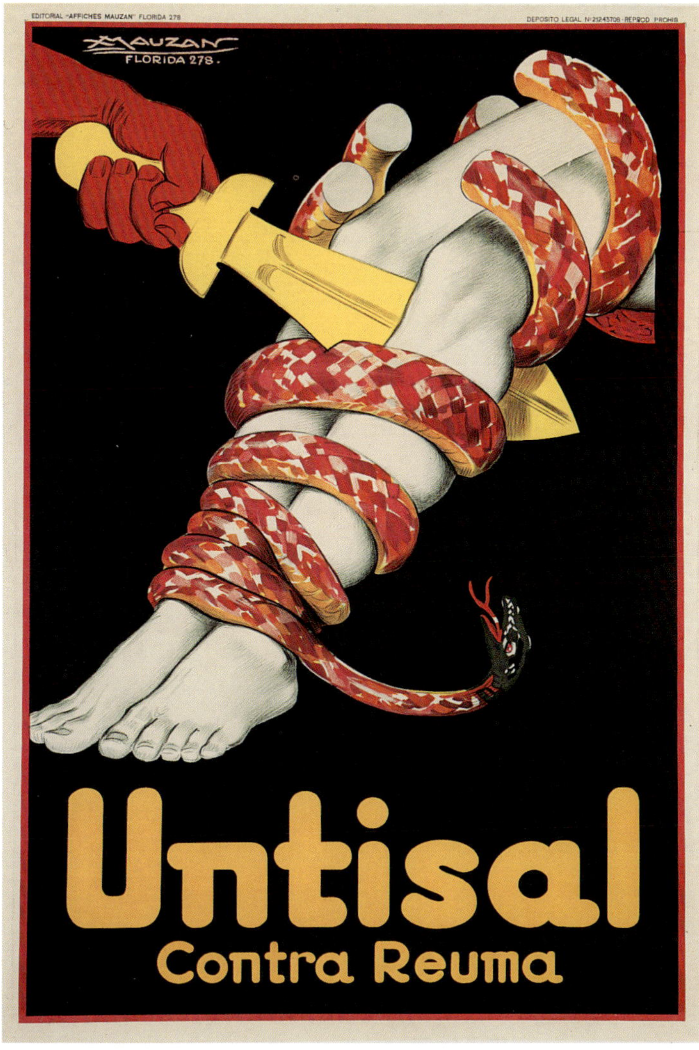

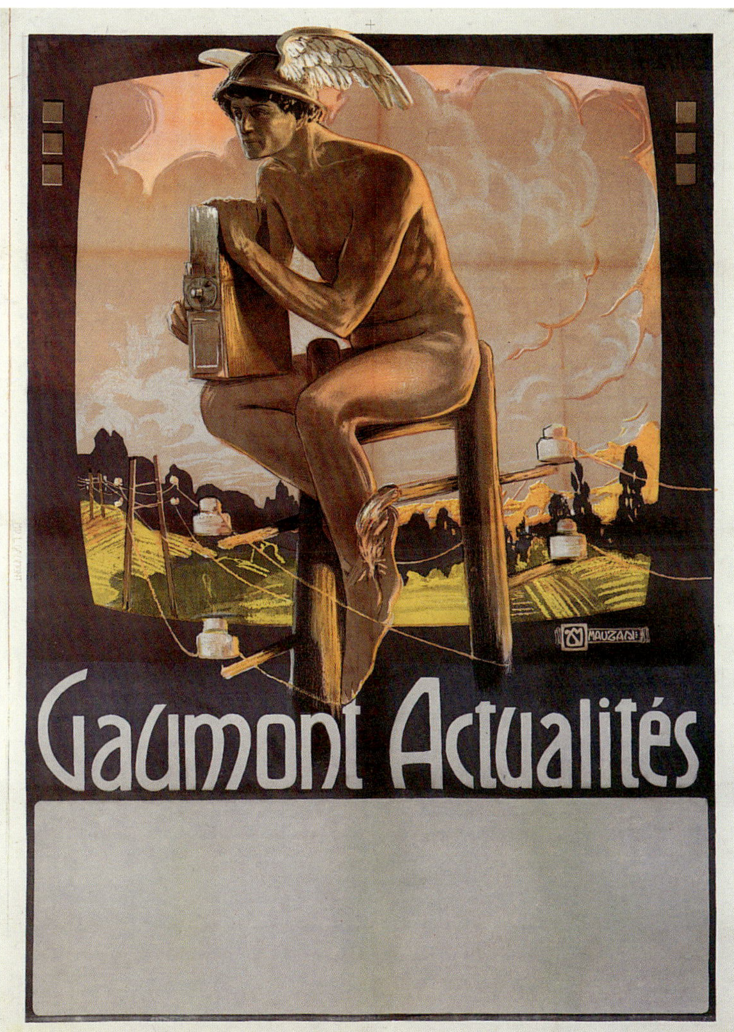

422

423

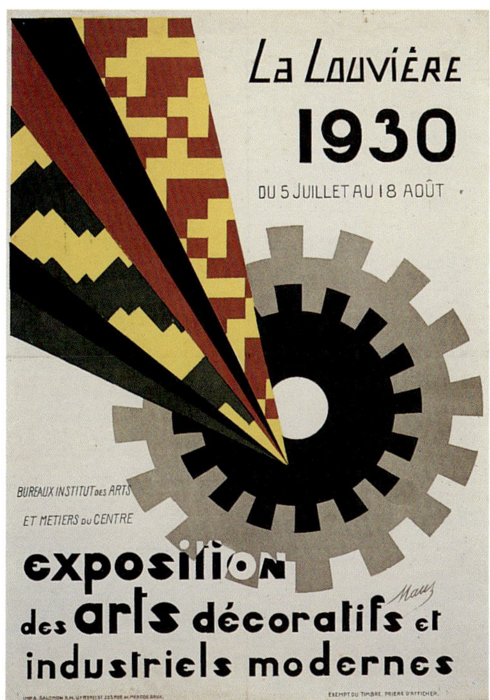

421

PAUL MAUROU (1848-1931)

420. Les Petits Mousquetaires. 1885.
$22^1/8$ x $30^1/8$ in./56 x 76.5 cm
Imp. Lemercier & Cie., Paris
Cond B+/Slight tears at bottom paper edge.
"An expected operetta appeared in 1885: a musical version of the popular dramatization of Dumas's *The Three Musketeers . . .* This was *Les petits Mousquetaires* (5 March, Folies-Dramatique), libretto by Ferrier and Prével, and there was nothing little about its success—149 performances, attributable not only to the familiar exploits of Athos, Porthos, and Aramis and to Varney's carefree tunes, but also to a gorgeous cast, including Marguerite Ugalde, *en travesti* as D'Artagnan, Mlle. Desclauzas, and Simon-Max. It was the first of several operettas based on this durable classic, and one, by virtue of its story, that might stand a modern producer's inspection" (Operetta, p. 97). The Maurou poster—executed primarily in sepia tones—provides finely-detailed portraiture of all the featured players.
Est: $1,000-$1,200.

PAUL MAUS

421. La Louvière/Expositions des arts décoratifs. 1930.
$14^1/8$ x $20^3/8$ in./35.7 x 51.7 cm
Imp. A. Solomon & Uytterelst, Bruxelles
Cond B/Slight tears at folds and edges.
The Belgian municipality of La Louvière located in the Hainaut province played host to this exhibition of modern decorative and industrial art. Maus's publicity gets directly to the point, summing up the expo's content with brevity and colorful clarity. Something of a departure for Maus, a Belgian painter better known for portraits and landscape paintings noted for their detail and burning lyricism. *Rare!*
Est: $1,400-$1,700.

LUCIANO ACHILLE MAUZAN (1883-1952)

422. Untisal. 1929.
$41^1/4$ x $61^1/2$ in./105 x 156.2 cm
Affiches Mauzan, Buenos Aires
Cond A.
Ref: Mauzan, A451; Mauzan/Paris, 31;
    Mauzan Cartellonista, p. 87; Health Posters, 76;
    PAI-XXVI, 386
Anyone who suffers from arthritis or rheumatism can testify that this exquisitely simple Mauzan design is not that much of an exaggeration. The powerful serpent has coiled itself tightly around the pale legs, its grip crippling the victim with ever increasing pressure and pain. But just when things look their worst, the liberating hand of Untisal appears, brandishing its golden sword, slicing through the merciless viper and relieving the discomfort with one fell swoop. The war against pain is never over, but Untisal is there to provide a welcome respite. Mauzan produced well over 2,000 posters during the course of his long, prodigious career. His boundless imagination is a landscape of ingenious concepts and incongruous associations working in harmony. He lays on color freely, but what marks his designs as unique is his sense of humor, by turns witty, grotesque, mad, pungent, charming and openly affectionate.
Est: $3,500-$4,000.

423. Gaumont Actualités. 1909.
$42^1/2$ x $59^1/8$ in./107.9 x 150 cm
Imp. L. Gaumont, Milan
Cond B+/Slight staining and tears at folds.
Ref: Mauzan, C02 (var)
Léon Gaumont (1864-1946) was a French inventor, engineer, and industrialist who became a pioneer of the film industry. Initially, L. Gaumont et Cie. just sold camera equipment and film, but in 1897 they made the jump into the motion picture production business. Gaumont rapidly expanded the business into cinematographic equipment for amateurs and within a few years his company ranked second only to Pathé Frères in the field. In 1906, the Etablissements Gaumont was founded to handle film production and distribution, as well as building a chain of movie theaters including the giant Gaumont Palace in Paris, which at that time was the largest movie house in the world. In this poster for Gaumont newsreels, Mauzan astutely perches Mercury—the fleet-footed Roman god of trade, profit and commerce —atop the wires of the fastest conveyor of current events at the time—the telegraph—in order to convey how rapidly news from the outside world makes its way into the Gaumont projection booth. The Gaumont company has survived in one form or another over the years to become the world's oldest surviving film company extant.
Est: $5,000-$6,000.

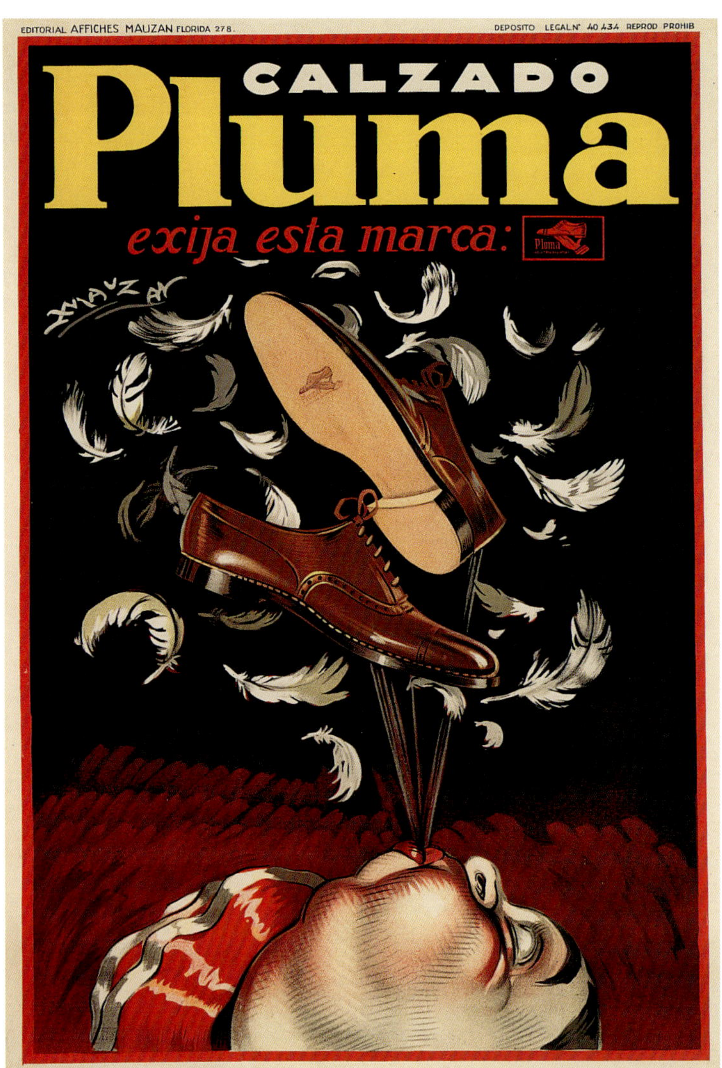

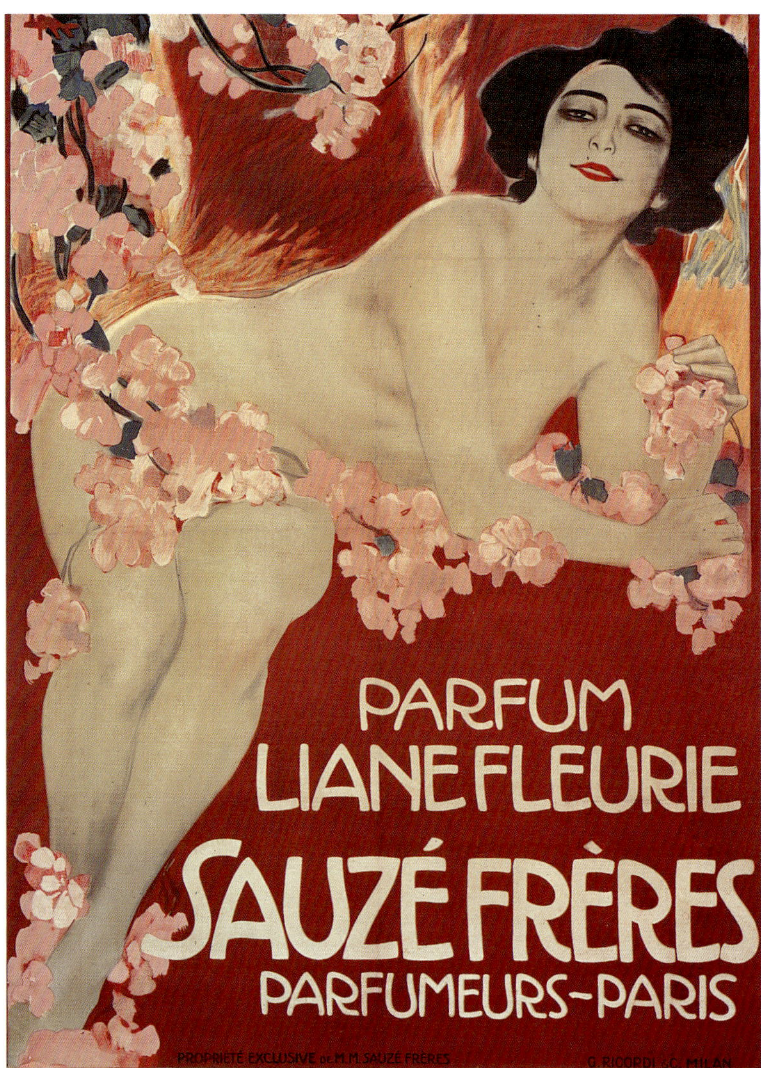

425

427

MAUZAN (cont'd)

424. Novaresi/Divano-Letto. 1940.
$39^1/_8$ x $55^1/_2$ in./99.4 x 141 cm
Tettamanti, Milano
Cond A.
Ref: Mauzan, 199; Mauzan Affiches p. 69 (var);
 PAI-XXXV, 378
Someone looks as if they need a good night's sleep and
the good folks at Novaresi have just what the sandman
ordered: a reader-sofa with built-in bookshelves, guaranteed to put you in the mood for quality shuteye. The
snooze-inducing couch is beautifully rendered, but it's
almost secondary to the picture of exhaustion in the
foreground, his mouth gaping in a yawn of such magnitude that you have to have some concern over whether
or not the attempt at politeness will cost the sleepy-
head his hand.
Est: $1,200-$1,500.

425. Calzado Pluma. 1930.
29 x 43 in./73.5 x 109.2 cm
Affiches Mauzan, Buenos Aires
Cond A–/Unobtrusive tears, largely at edges.
Ref: Mauzan, A424
Seeing as they're light as a feather, Pluma is an aptly
named brand of footwear. A single puff from a portly
buffoon is all it takes to send a pair of Plumas and a
spray of feathers skyward—not to mention the artist's
name, which he incorporates into the downy pyrotech-
nics with sly dexterity.
Est: $3,000-$4,000.

426. Prestito della Liberazione. 1917.
$39^3/_8$ x $56^1/_4$ in./100 x 143 cm
G. Ricordi, Milano
Cond B/Slight tears at folds and edges.
Ref: Mauzan, A075; Menegazzi-I, 57; Menegazzi-II, 18;
 Mauzan/Pinerolo, p. 11; Mauzan/Treviso, p. 19;
 Mauzan/Paris, p. 37; Bocca, p. 97; PAI-XXXI, 529
During World War I, in which Italy was on the Allied side,
Mauzan designed a number of posters for Italian war
bonds. In this one, for what best can be translated as

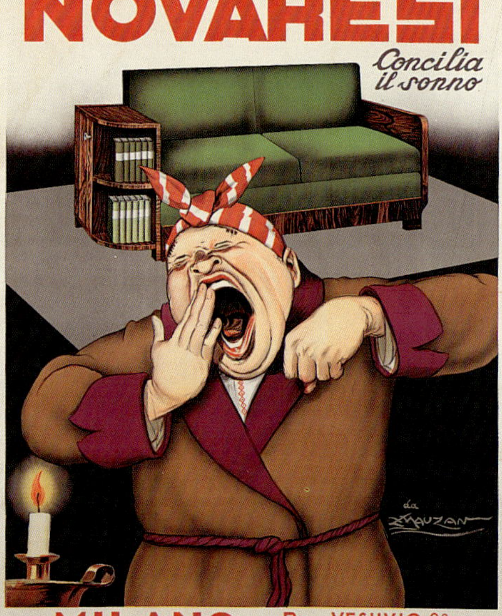

424

Liberty bonds, a solemn-faced allegorical figure of Italy,
winged and laurel-wreathed, extends a sword to which
arms reach in the ancient Roman oath-swearing gesture.
On a banner, a quote from Italy's wartime leader Orsini
obliquely refers to "the return of what was ours"—con-
quered Italian territory, and, perhaps, Italian pride.
Est: $1,200-$1,500.

LEOPOLDO METLICOVITZ (1868-1944)

427. Parfum Liane Fleurie/Sauzé Frères.
$30^1/_8$ x $42^1/_2$ in./76.5 x 107 cm

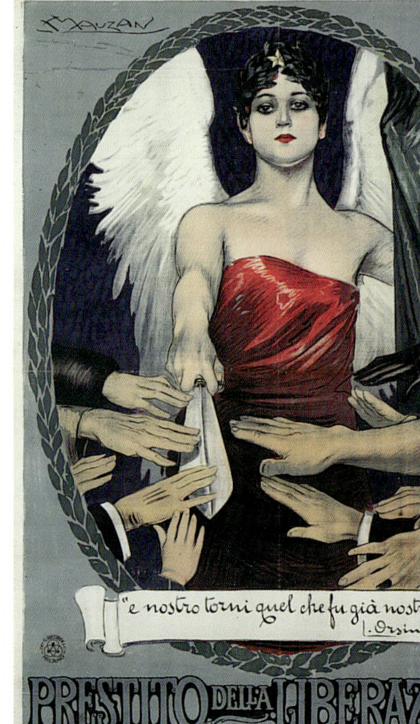

426

G. Ricordi, Milan
Cond B–/Restored tears at folds. Framed.
Ref: PAI-XLI, 387
A voluptuous raven-haired nude reclines erotically in
a bed of pink flowers against a crimson background.
Though discreet, there's no doubt that this perfume
was being marketed at women who were, shall we say,
on the prowl. A bold, lush design for Liane Fleurie, one
of the fragrances from Paris' Sauzé Frères. Metlicovitz
was born in the Adriatic port city of Trieste, and appears
to have become a painter and portraitist without any

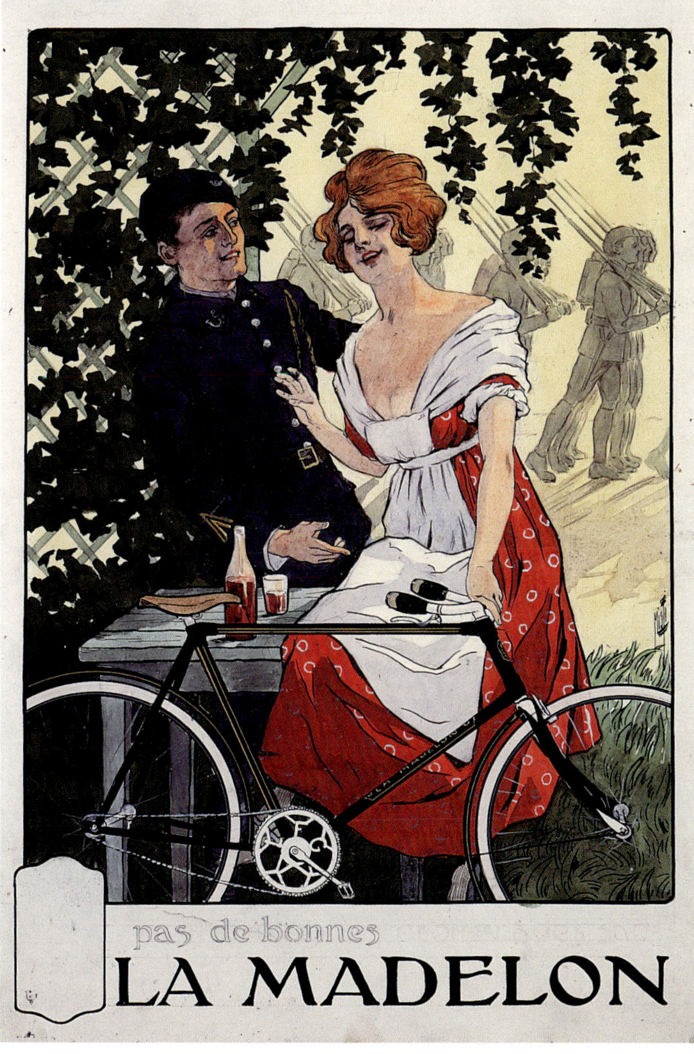

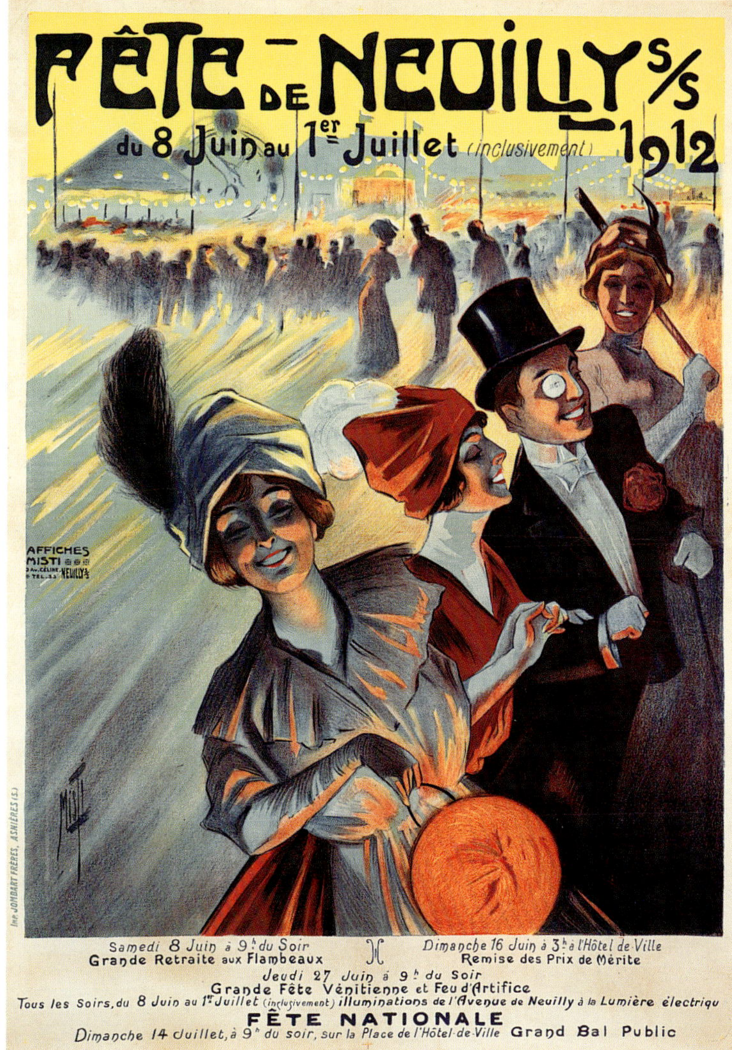

430   431

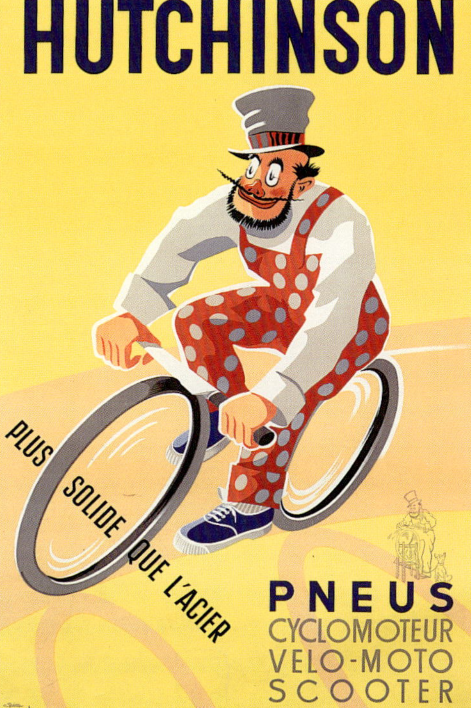

428   429

formal training. In 1891, he showed up in Milan at Ricordi's print shop as a lithography trainee, proving to be such a quick study he was promoted to technical director within a year.
Est: $6,000-$8,000.

GEORGES MEUNIER (1869-1942)

428. A la Place Clichy/Ètrennes. ca. 1896.
34 x 49 in./86.4 x 124.5 cm
Imp. Chaix, Paris
Cond B/Restored tears at folds and edges; colors very fresh.
Ref: Meunier, 29 (var); PAI-XXXVI, 428
Meunier executed several designs for Christmas sales at the Place Clichy department store, all featuring a woman or girl on a rocking horse. This one is perhaps the liveliest and certainly one of the rarest. However, this time it's a rocking *mule* called upon to serve as the stationary steed, with a clown and a lady in red

riding through a shopper's fantasy field of gifts represented by Japanese dolls, masks and assorted trinkets.
Est: $1,500-$1,800.

MICH (Michel Liebeaux, 1881-1923)

429. Hutchinson. 1958.
$30^1/4$ x $46^5/8$ in./77 x 117.8 cm
Imp. Gaillard, Paris
Cond A-/Slight tears at edges.
Ref: PAI-XXXV, 390 (var)
An artist named C. Guion draws inspiration from Mich's famous electrified mason (*see* PAI-XXXV, 390) in this "d'après" design for Hutchinson tires. Disposing of everything but the barest essentials (the man's canine companion can still be seen in the discreet line drawing to the right of the rider), our focus falls directly to the rubber-to-the-road meat of the promotion—tires, which if the promotional copy is to be believed, are "more solid than steel." The manufacturer remains a staple of the tire community, now as a member of Atofina, the chemical branch of the TotalFinaElf Group.
Est: $1,500-$1,800.

MISTI (Ferdinand Mifliez, 1865-1923)

430. La Madelon. ca. 1919.
$13^3/4$ x $20^3/4$ in./35 x 52.7 cm
Gouache and ink maquette. Framed.
It doesn't look like soldier boy is getting anywhere significant with this maiden fair beneath a shading arbor. She might be from the country, but it's going to take a bit more than a silver tongue and some drink to keep her from hopping aboard her Madelon bicycle—which the text informs us is the only good ride in the picture anyway—and pedaling away. And besides, shouldn't our charmer be a bit more concerned with getting back to his regiment that's clearly marching off in the background? A lyric little number from Misti, which as far as we know never saw its way to poster fruition.
Est: $1,700-$2,000.

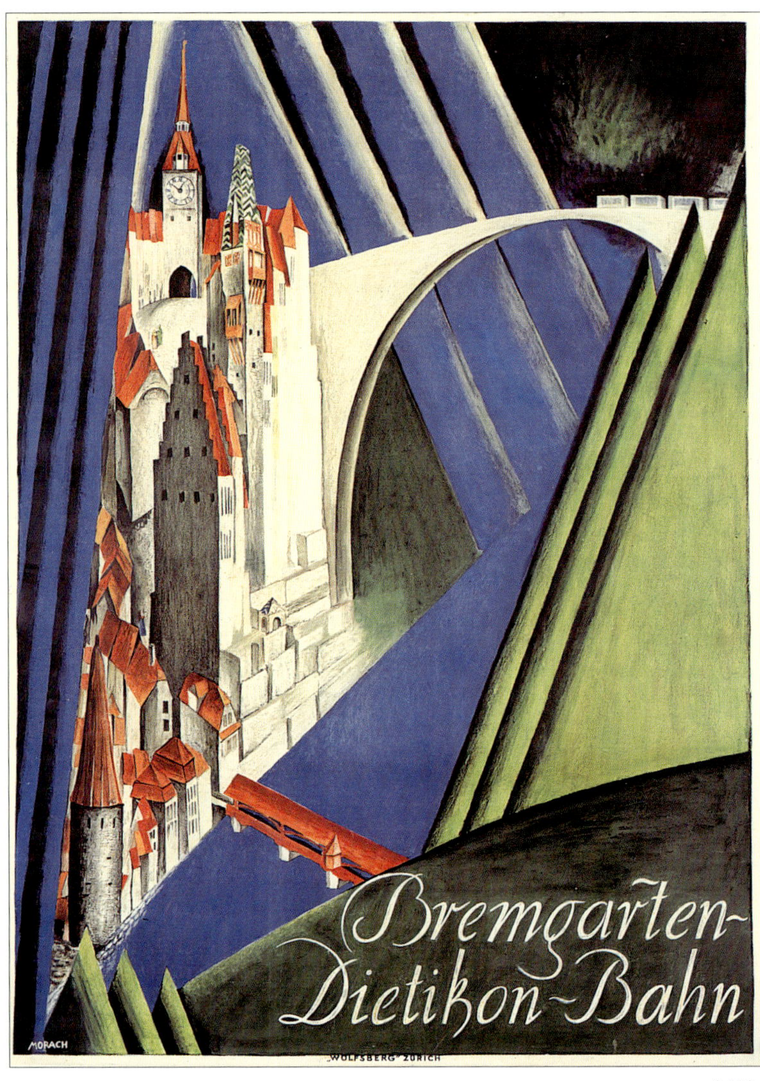

434

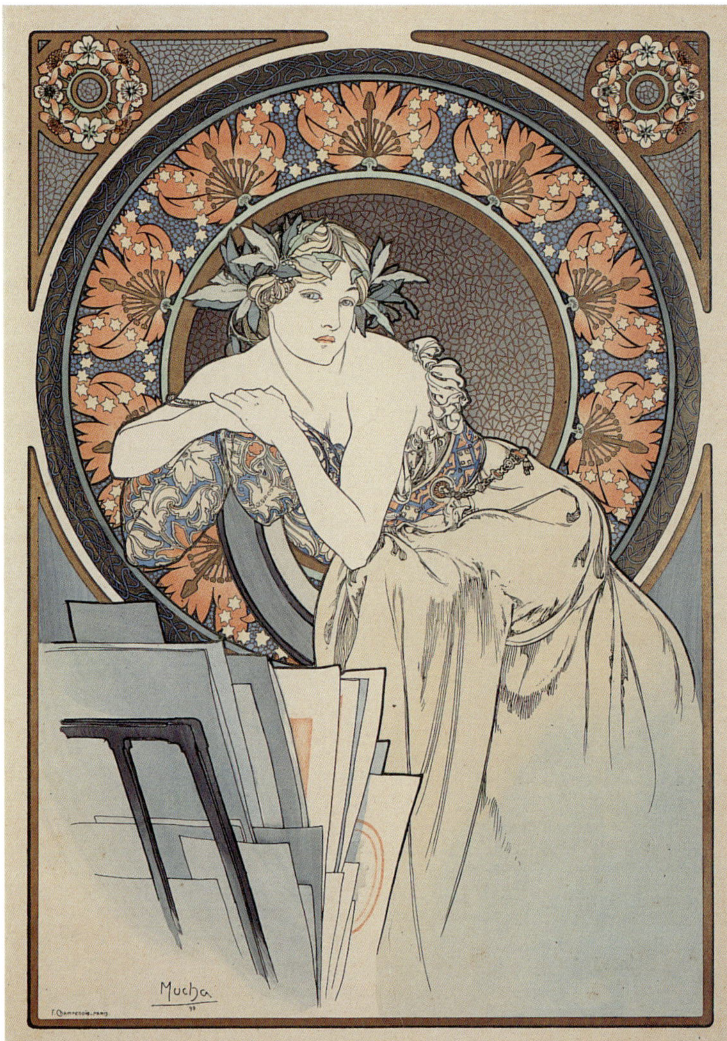

435

MISTI (cont'd)

431. Fête de Neuilly. 1912.
$38^5/_8$ x $54^3/_4$ in./98 x 139 cm
Imp. Jombart Frères, Asnières
Cond B+/Slight tears at folds and edges.
This quartet of revelers, all smiles and sophistication, doesn't look like they're even close to calling it an evening as they make their way from the annual fair in the Paris suburb of Neuilly. Perhaps illuminating one's way with a Chinese lantern isn't as in vogue as once it was, but its inclusion here creates both cozy intrigue and glowing satisfaction, which is in turn echoed in the implied movement of the carnival background.
This is by far the rarest of the Misti Neuilly series!
Est: $2,000-$2,500.

432. Cycles Clément. ca. 1898.
$36^3/_4$ x 83 in./93.5 x 211 cm
Imp. Bougerie, Paris
Cond B/Slight tears at folds and egdes.
Ref: Ailes, p. 40; PAI-XLII, 380
Beneath the glow of a Chinese lantern that bears the company name, a comely rider pauses midway through her evening Clément excursion, phosphorescing with upward trademark recognition as she does. Over the course of 2-sheets, Misti presents a spectacularly unique, near-mythic design, one that appears to draw inspiration from Japanese woodblock prints, while at the same time presaging the advent of the black-light poster. This version of the poster appears without the top text banner that announces that Clément produced both bicycles and motorcycles.
Est: $1,200-$1,500.

PAUL MOHR

433. Auto-Perco-Thermos. 1946.
$38^1/_4$ x $58^1/_2$ in./97.2 x 148.7 cm
Affiches Paul Mohr, Asnières
Cond B+/Slight tears at folds.
Ref: Négripub, 193; Célébrités, 216

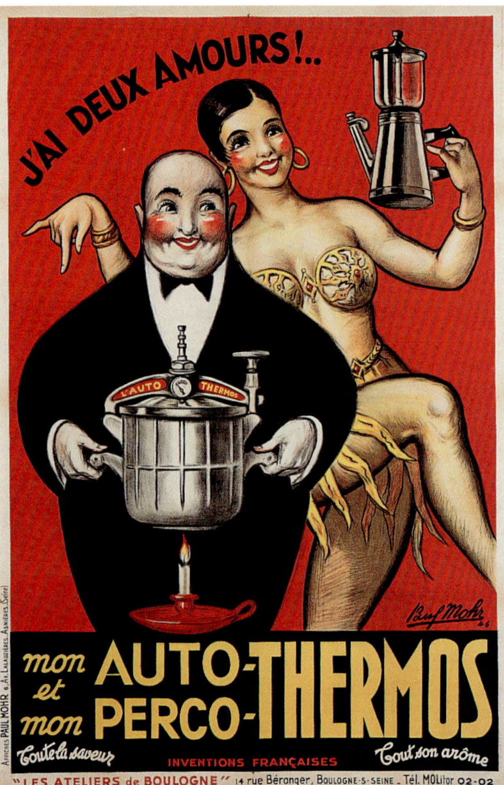

433

Josephine Baker premiered what would become her signature song, "J'ai deux amours, mon pays et Paris," at the Casino de Paris in 1930. Sixteen years later, it's neither the United States nor the French capital that Baker is referring to in this endorsement—rather her "Two Loves" have become an insulated pair of coffee

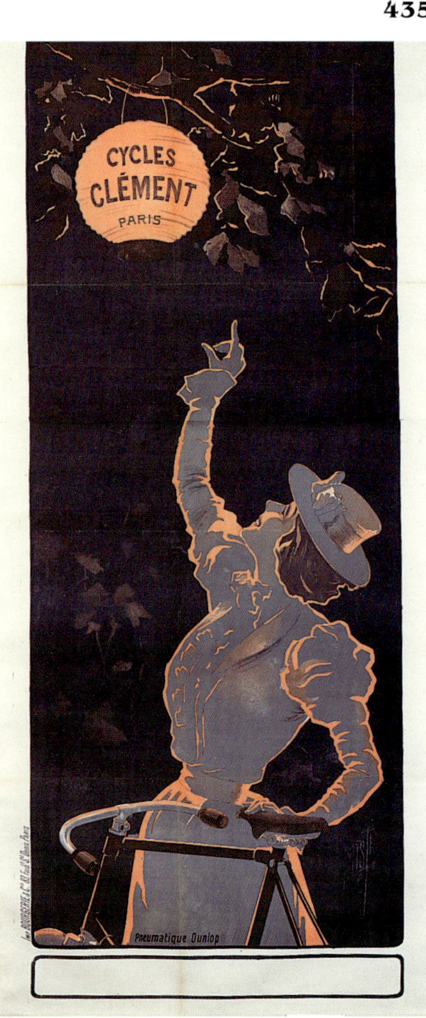

432

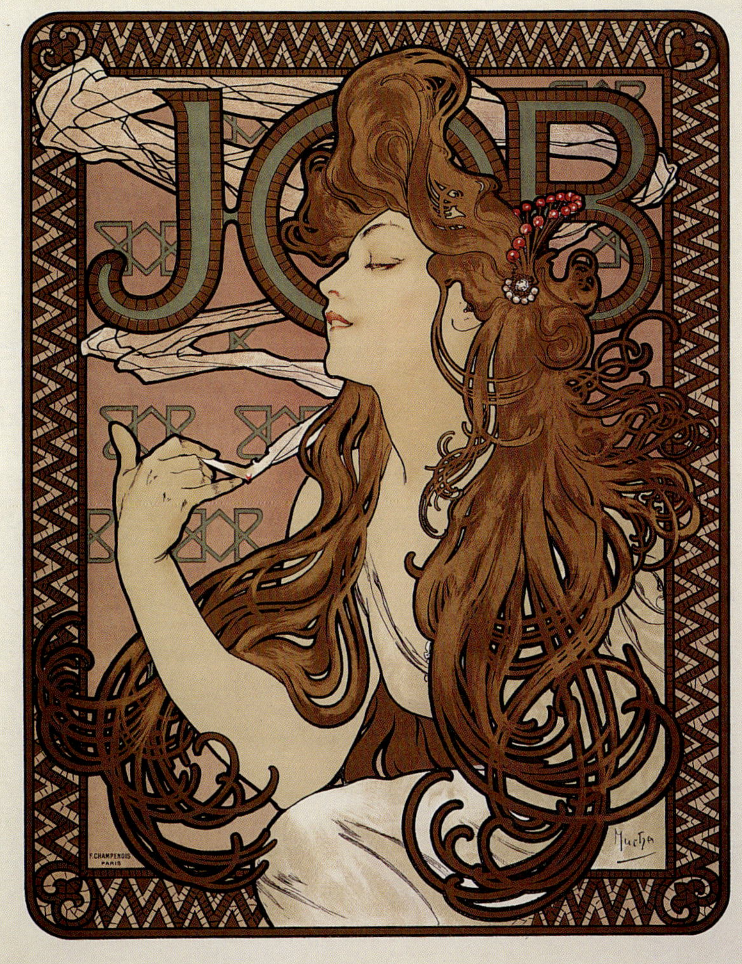

436

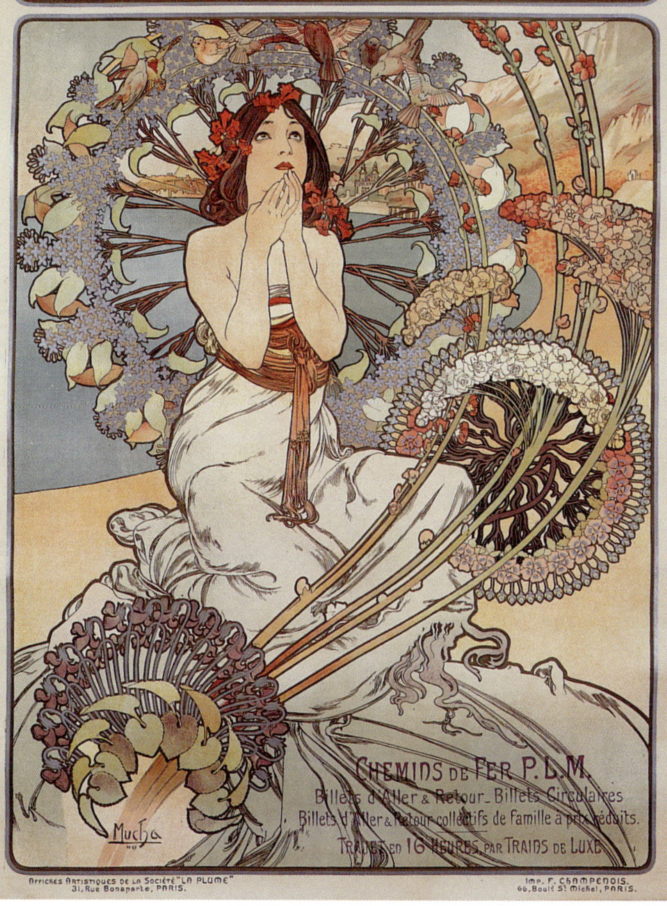

437

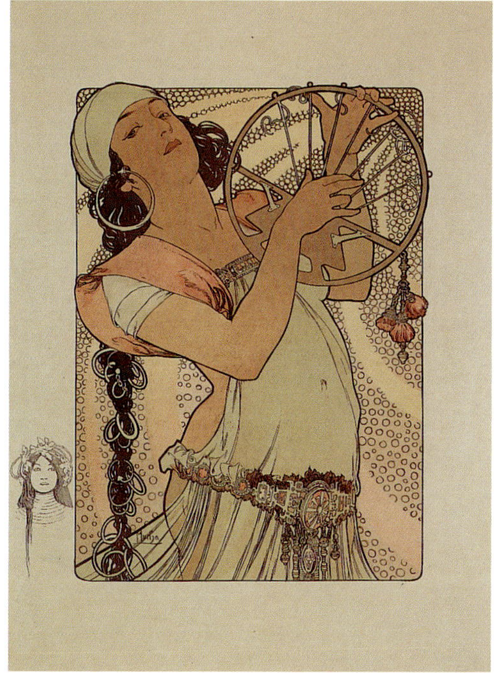

438

makers. Cheeky and amusing, the Mohr poster demonstrates that not only was Baker still a commercially-attractive celebrity, but that her greatest hit was also a recognizable commodity as well.
Est: $1,700-$2,000.

OTTO MORACH (1887-1973)

434. Bremgarten-Dietkon-Bahn. 1928.
$36^1/_8$ x $50^1/_8$ in./91.7 x 127.4 cm
Wolfsberg, Zurich
Cond B/Restored tears at edges.

Ref: Wobmann, p. 100; Margadant, 241; PAI-XLI, 414
It's interesting to compare Morach's dizzying, vertiginous promotion for this railway to the work of other posterists for the same line. Whereas Plinio Colombi took an Impressionistic approach (*see* PAI-XXV, 281) and Albert Rüegg indulged in fluid symbolism (*see* PAI-XXI, 391), Morach attacks with angular, geometric force, thrusting architecture and a spiking mountainscape into the face of the passerby, making the train a secondary feature while daring the viewer not to pay attention to the destination. It's nearly impossible not to pay heed to the graphic upheaval, which for all its aggressive qualities, doesn't repel the eye, but instead wins it over with unapologetic bravado. Morach was involved with cubism, dada and the Bauhaus movement, eventually arriving at an abstract style. He worked on murals, mosaics, carpet fabric design, glass painting and also taught applied painting from 1918 to 1953. In Switzerland's highly poster-conscious environment, Morach was a truly inspired posterist and one of the best.
Est: $5,000-$6,000.

ALPHONSE MUCHA (1860-1939)

435. Toutes les Oeuvres de Mucha. 1898.
$16^1/_4$ x 24 in./41.3 x 61 cm
Imp. F. Champenois, Paris
Cond A–/Slight tear near bottom. Framed.
Ref: Rennert/Weill, 56; Lendl/Paris, 99 (var);
    PAI-XXV, 428
This image advertised the sale of the works of Mucha at the offices of *La Plume* magazine. Without text, it was offered under the title of "Femme aux Coquelicots" ("Woman with Poppies"). "It is a good example of Mucha's quintessential ingredients: a languid girl, a long garment descending in graceful folds to the ground, a circular motif like a halo, plentiful flowers, and a carefully executed ornamental pattern . . . An unusual feature is that all known copies have hand coloring in a few areas" (Rennert/Weill, pp. 219-220). *Rare!*
Est: $14,000-$17,000.

436. Job. 1896.
$16^3/_4$ x $21^3/_4$ in./42.5 x 55.2 cm
Imp. F. Champenois, Paris
Cond A. Framed.
Ref: Rennert/Weill, 15; Lendl/Paris, 48;
    Mucha/Art Nouveau, 20; DFP-II, 635;
    Maitres, 202; Masters 1900, p. 18; Weill, p. 41;
    Timeless Images, 33; PAI-XXXIX, 396
More than any other work of Mucha's, this beauty established him as the master of convoluted hair and the creator of unforgettable popular images; the poster was used for years in many variants all over the world, sometimes with marginal text in various languages. A classic by any standard.
Est: $14,000-$17,000.

437. Monaco-Monte-Carlo. 1897.
$29^3/_4$ x 43 in./75.5 x 109.2 cm
Imp. F. Champenois, Paris
Cond A.
Ref: Rennert/Weill, 31; Lendl/Paris, 40; DFP-II, 639;
    Wagner, 76; Wine Spectator, 73; Affiches Azur, 194;
    Voyage, p. 15; Train ' l'Affiche, 114; Mucha/Art
    Nouveau, 24; Affiches Riviera, 92; PAI-XLII, 594
"Mucha went all out with a most opulent design. The shy maiden, kneeling, enraptured with the tranquility of the bay of Monte Carlo, is completely encircled by the curving stalks of lilacs and hydrangeas, featuring some of the most intricate conflorescences ever painted by Mucha. Since the client was a railroad—Chemin de Fer P.L.M.—it is probable that the design is meant to suggest the tracks and wheels that convey the public to Monte Carlo. The maiden is probably Spring herself, enraptured with the beauty of the seascape" (Rennert/Weill, p. 136). *Please note the exceedingly fresh colors of this poster. Even in the finest specimens, the railway information at bottom-right is usually faded—here, however, it's day-it-was-printed fresh!*
Est: $17,000-$20,000.

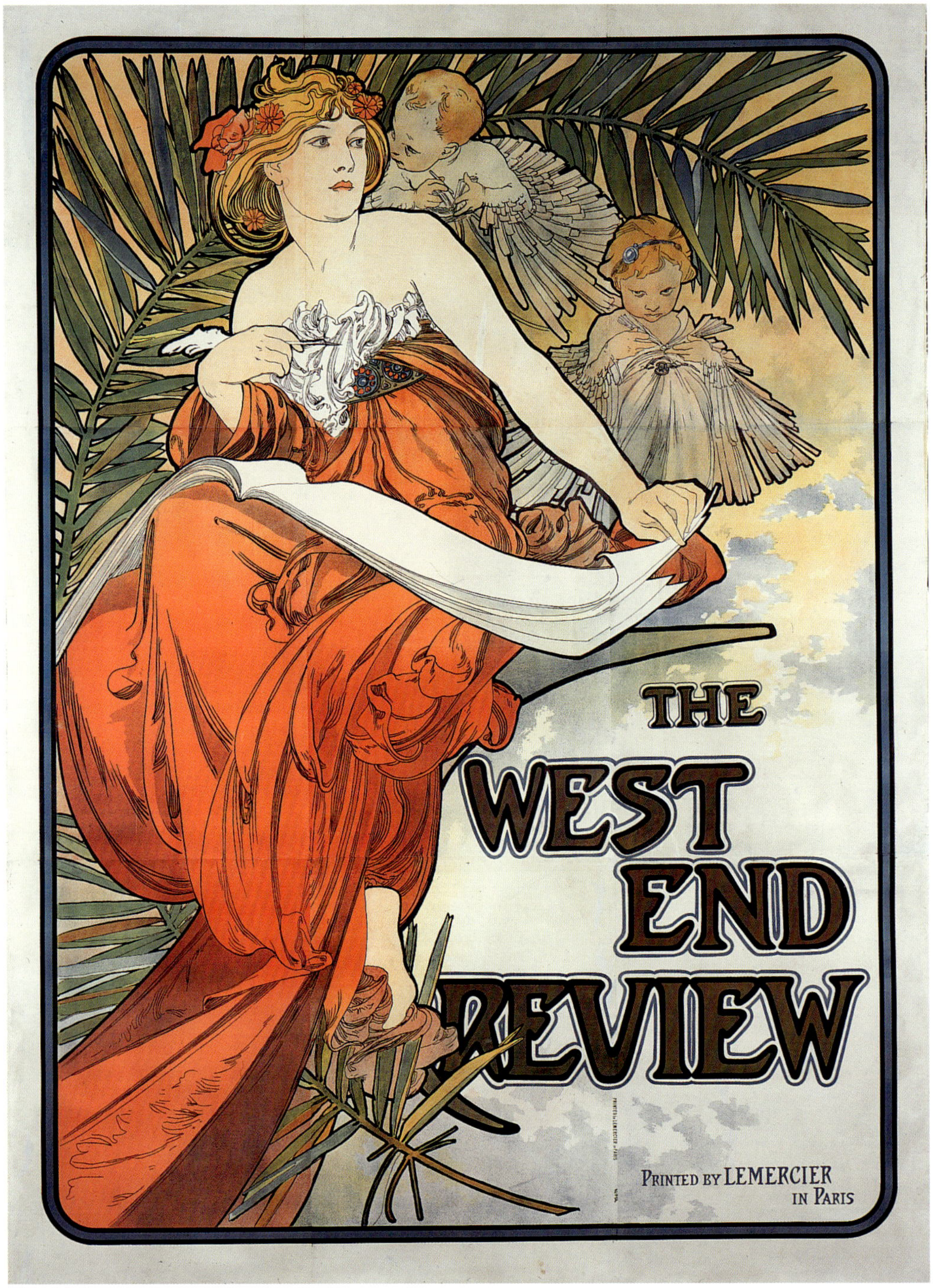

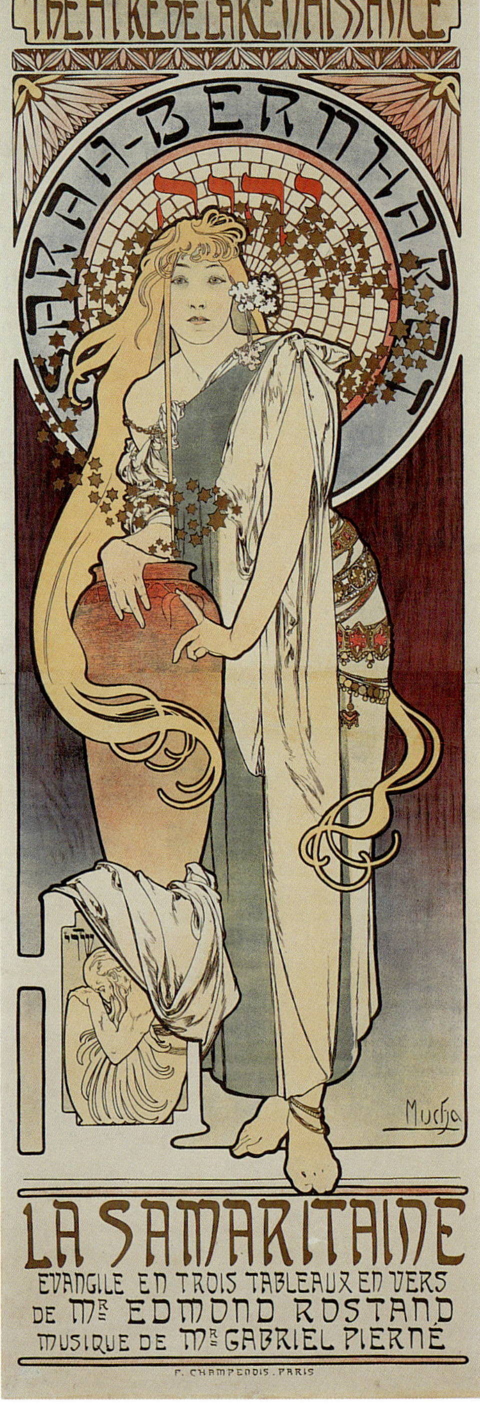

439

440

ALPHONSE MUCHA (cont'd)

438. Salomé. 1897.
15³/₈ x 20⁵/₈ in./39 x 52.4 cm
Imp. F. Champenois, Paris (not shown)
Cond A. Framed.
Ref (Both Var): Mucha/Bridges, R10c; PAI-XII, 329
Mucha created this unbelievably seductive lithograph expressly for the *L'Estampe Moderne*, a monthly portfolio of four lithographs issued between 1897 and 1899. His rendering of Salome presents the legendary temptress as a Byzantine gypsy—diaphanous apparel, raven tresses hung with rings, plucking an ancient stringed instrument, no doubt to accompany herself in the "Dance of the Seven Veils." *An extremely rare version of this design printed on chine paper, with both the publisher's blindstamp in the lower right and an exquisite remarque to the left!*
Est: $2,500-$3,000.

439. The West End Review. 1898.
86¹/₂ x 121¹/₂ in./219.5 x 309.5 cm
Imp. Lemercier, Paris
Cond A–/Slight tears and stains at folds and seams.
Ref: Rennert/Weill, 50; Lendl/Paris, 36 (var)
"One of the many small literary magazines which proliferated around the turn of the century, this one started as *The West End* in London in April of 1897, changing its name to *The West End Review* with the June number of that year, and continuing publication until its September, 1899 issue. The lady in red, an oversized portfolio on her lap, is obviously ready to jot down some interesting notes with a quill pen. The circular motif is provided this time by a huge palm frond forming a semi-circle of green to complement the color of the dress. Note the delightful touch of the two cherubs, one whispering in the girl's ear, the other sulking off by herself, apparently feeling left out of the proceedings. This is an unsigned work, printed by Lemercier. Exactly how this happened we cannot tell. Because of its exceptionally large size—it is in fact, the largest of all Mucha posters—it was printed in nine sheets" Rennert/Weill, p. 202). *Spectacular and rare!*
Est: $15,000-$20,000.

440. La Samaritaine. 1897.
23¹/₂ x 69³/₈ in./59.7 x 176.2 cm
Imp. F. Champenois, Paris
Cond B+/Slight tears and stains at seam and bottom text area.
Ref: Bernhardt/Drama, p. 3; Rennert/Weill 24; Lendl/Paris, 6; Mucha/Art Nouveau, 10; Wine Spectator, 72; PAI-XLII, 47
This "was a play with a biblical theme . . . (Bernhardt) played Photina, a girl from the Samaria district of ancient Palestine, who becomes a supporter of Jesus and leads her whole tribe in converting to Christianity" (Rennert/Weill, p. 118). "Bernhardt's mother was a Jew. For the actress, this was both a blessing and a curse. In biblical roles such as Photine . . . she turned her Semitic exoticism into an alluring attribute. In the poster by Alphonse Mucha for the play, the Hebrew inscription 'Jahwej' appears behind Bernhardt's head, while 'Shaddai,' another Hebrew word for God, accompanies the inset picture. Playing to the public's appetite for beautiful Jewesses redeemed by their conversion to Christianity, Bernhardt in the role of the Samaritan woman adheres to a faith resembling-pre-rabbinical Judaism. Almost Jewish, but not quite, Photine is a sort of surrogate for Bernhardt and her equivocal religious identity" (Bernhardt/Drama, p. 2).
Est: $15,000-$18,000.

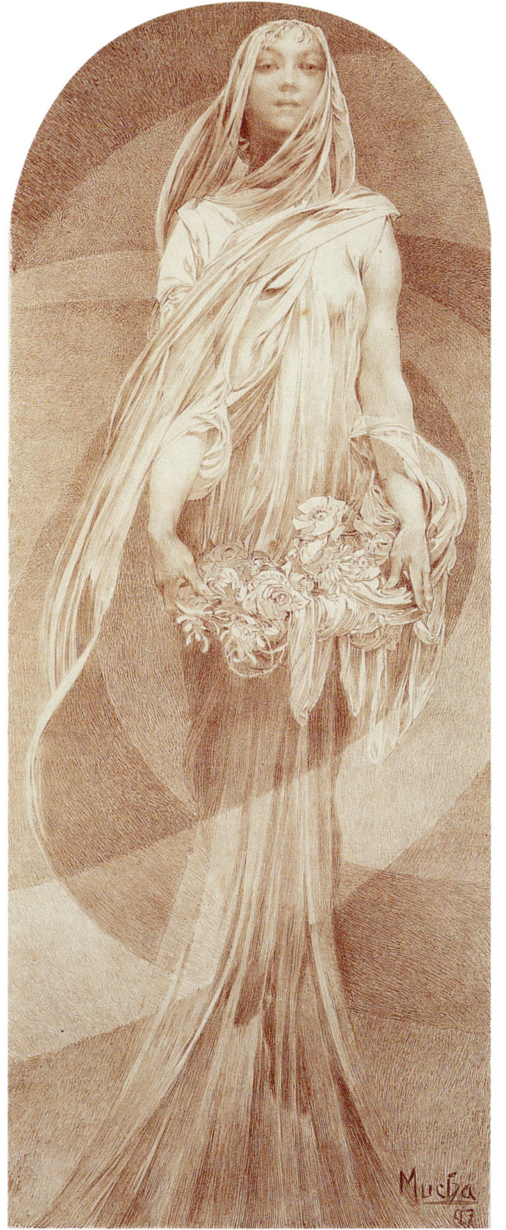

442

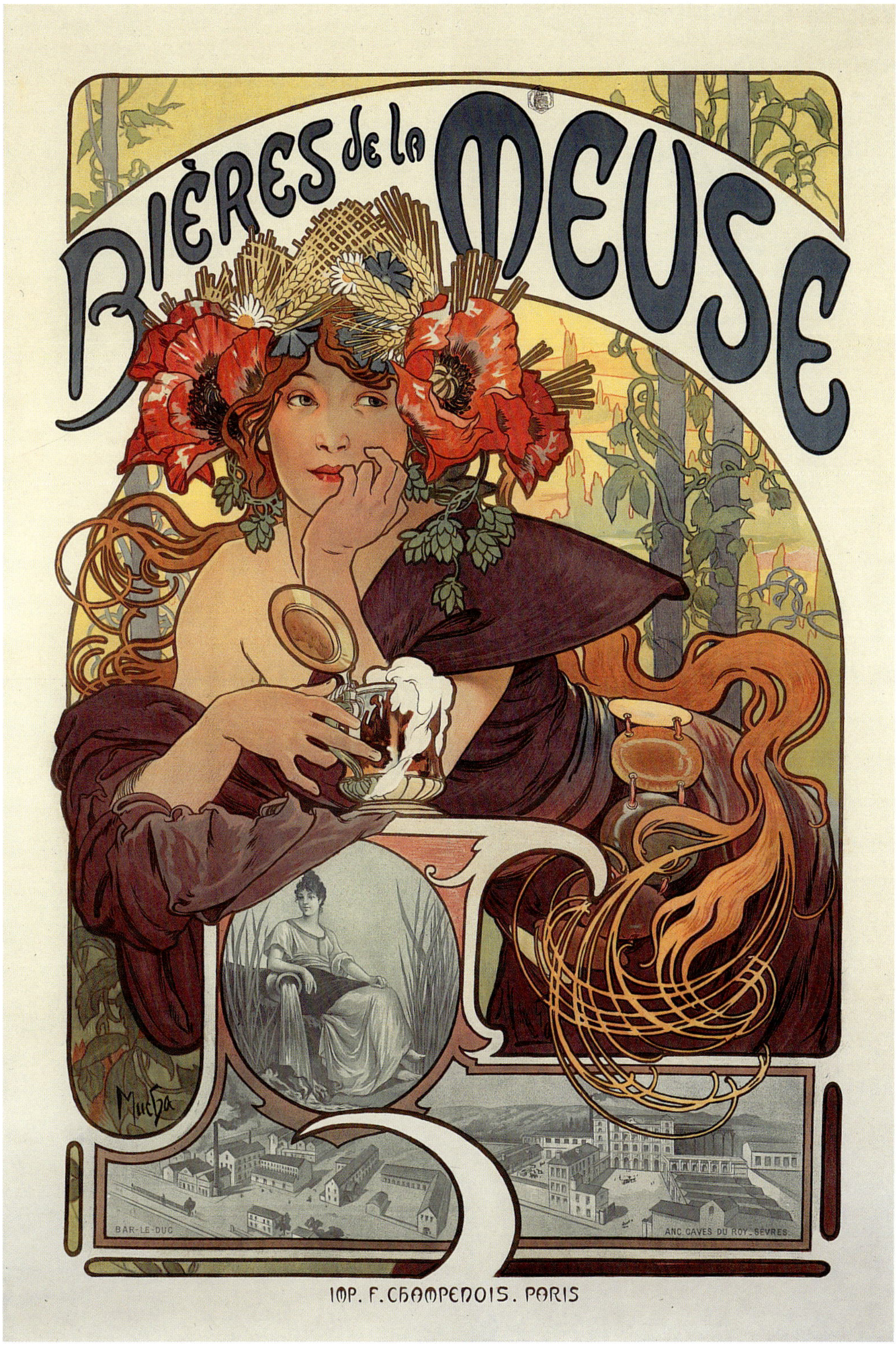

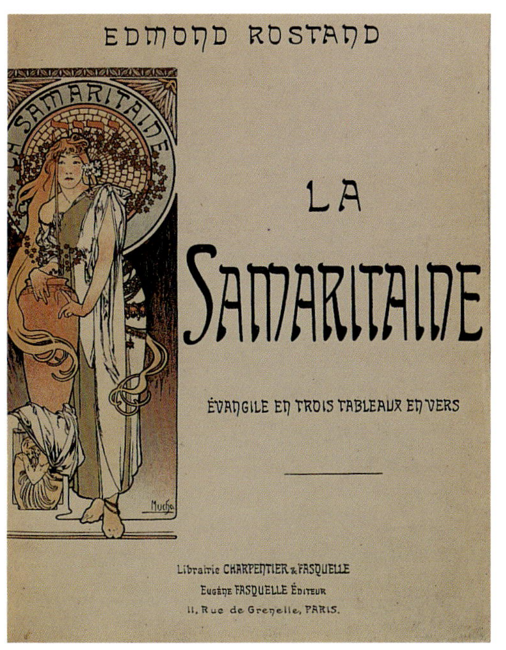

441

443

441. La Samaritaine: The Book. 1897.
$7^1/2$ x $9^3/8$ in./19 x 23.8 cm
In hardcover binding; in excellent condition.
The entire 120-page script of the Edmond Rostand
play, published by Eugene Fasquelle, Paris. Mucha's
poster design is featured on the cover.
Est: $800-$1,000.

442. Evocation. 1897.
$9^1/2$ x $24^1/2$ in./24.1 x 62.2 cm
Imp. F. Champenois, Paris (not shown)
Cond A. Framed.
Ref: Rennert/Weill, 46, Var. 1; PAI-XLI, 420
"L'Année qui vient" (The Coming Year) was a calendar
project with an image showing an alluringly eerie vision
of a wisp of a woman carrying a bouquet through swirls
of mist, in sepia monotones, surrounded by an elaborate decorative frame (*see* Rennert/Weill, 46). It was
also produced as a print, as shown here, without the
calendarium. This print was sold under the title "Evocation," quite apropos in light of the design's dream-
like enticement.
Est: $4,000-$5,000.

443. Bières de la Meuse. 1897.
$41^1/2$ x $61^1/8$ in./105.2 x 155.2 cm
Imp. F. Champenois, Paris.
Cond A.
Ref: Rennert/Weill, 27; Lendl/Paris, 37;
     Mucha/Art Nouveau, 23; Timeless Images, 36;
     Maitres, 182; DFP-II, 633; PAI-XXXIX, 382
Finest specimen ever seen!
"The jovial beer drinker has her long flowing tresses
adorned with some appropriate beer ingredients, including barley stalks and green hops, and field poppy
flowers indigenous to northeastern France. This is another one of Mucha's characteristic designs featuring a
beauty, semi-circular motifs, and artfully meandering
hair" (Rennert/Weill, p. 126). *This is the larger format.*
Est: $30,000-$35,000.

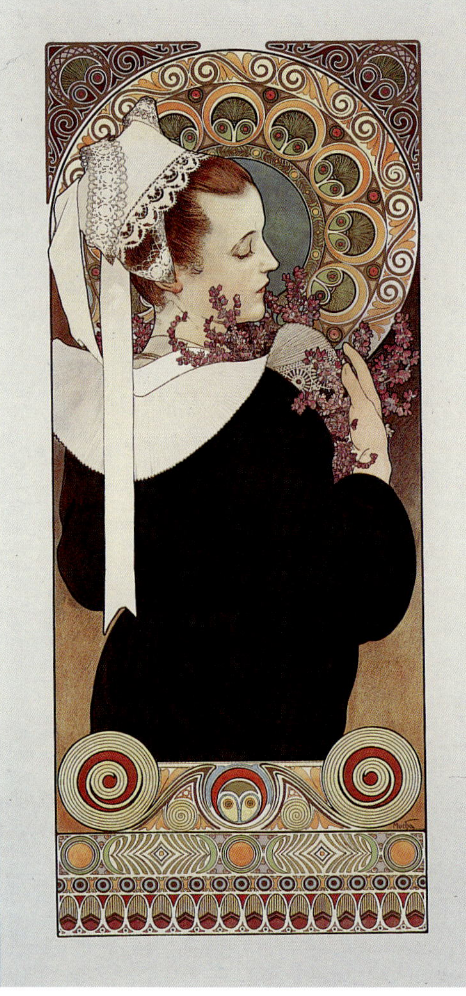

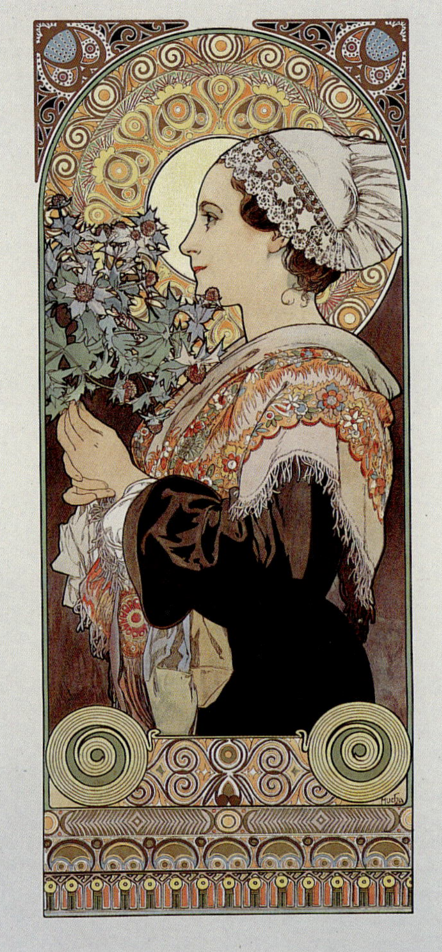

444

ALPHONSE MUCHA (cont'd)

444. Heather & Sea Holly. 1902.
Each: 14 x 29^3/$_8$ in./35.5 x 74.5 cm
Imp. F. Champenois, Paris (not shown)
Cond A.
Ref: Rennert/Weill, 80; Lendl/Paris, 77 (var);
    PAI-XXX, 590
"Both the plants and the costumes worn by the ladies
are representative of two ancient seacoast provinces
of northwestern France, Brittany and Normandy. Mucha
himself, according to his son Jiri, always referred to
the pictures as 'la Bretonne' and 'la Normande.' Their
official names are *Chardon de Greves* (Thistle of the
Beach) and *Bruyere de Falaise* (Heather of the Cliffs).
The thistle depicted here, however, is a common European plant of the eryngo family named Sea Holly—the
real thistle would be too prickly for the girl to carry in
her hands without discomfort" (Rennert/Weill, p. 290).
The set was reprinted with calendars for various years
as well, proving to be one of Mucha's most popular
designs. *Rare!*
Est: $14,000-$17,000. (2)

445. Paris 1900/Austria at the World's Fair. 1899.
28 x 39^7/$_8$ in./71 x 101.2 cm
Kunstanstalt Czeiger, Wien
Cond A.
Ref: Rennet/Weill, 66; Lendl/Paris, 41; DFP-II, 649; PAI-
    XL, 445
"Mucha's design shows a handsome youth lifting a veil
off the standing lady—'Paris revealing Austria to the
world,' according to contemporary publicity. The her-
aldic symbol of Austria-Hungary, a two-headed eagle,
may be seen behind the girl's head on both sides"
(Rennert/Weill, p. 248).
Est: $6,000-$7,000.

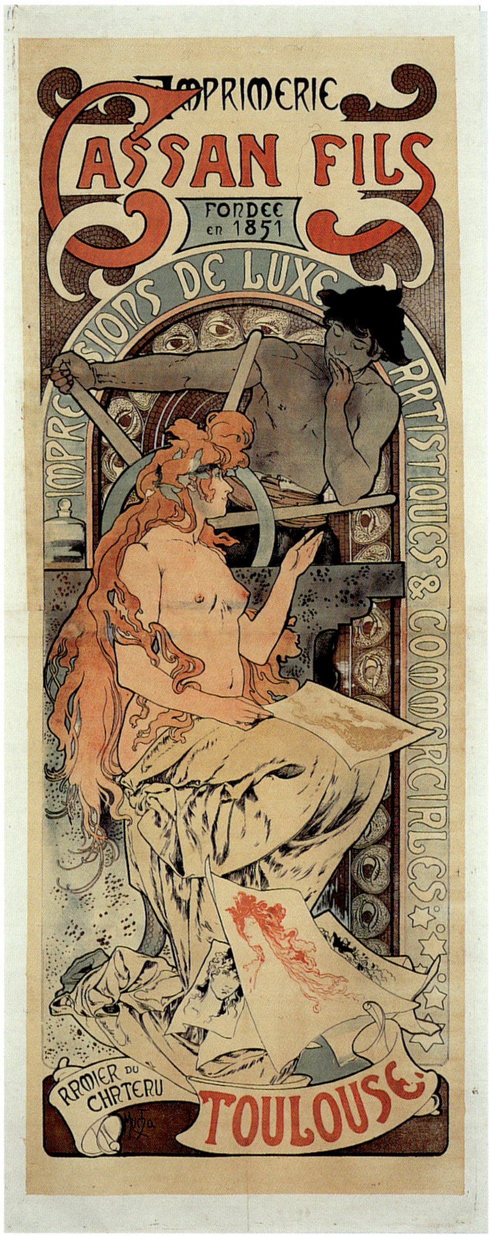

446. Cassan Fils. 1895.
28^1/$_4$ x 72^1/$_4$ in./71.7 x 183.5 cm
Imp. Cassan Fils, Toulouse
Cond B/Slight tears and stains at folds and edges.
Ref: Rennert/Weill, 11; Lendl/Paris, 37; DFP-II, 640;
    Reims, 897; PAI-IX, 380

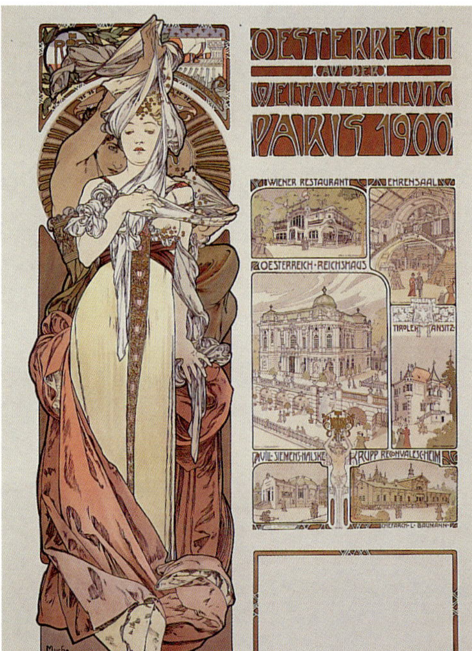

445

446

"Mucha's tendency to combine the real with the imaginary may be witnessed in this design where the semi-
nude model is a real person whereas the muscular
printer is an allegorical figure, representing the printing industry. An unusual border of eyes in the mosaic
background probably is meant to indicate the multitude of readers for whom the printing trade works. It
is also one of the mystic symbols used by Mucha in
several other works" (Rennert/Weill, p. 70). *This is the
largest format. Rare!*
Est: $9,000-$11,000.

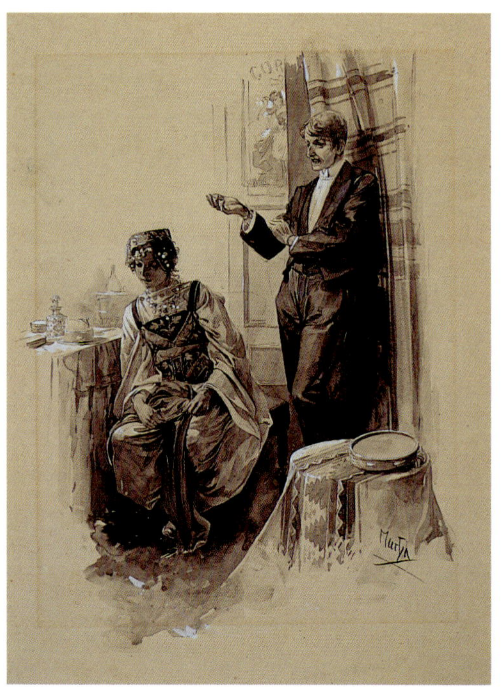

447

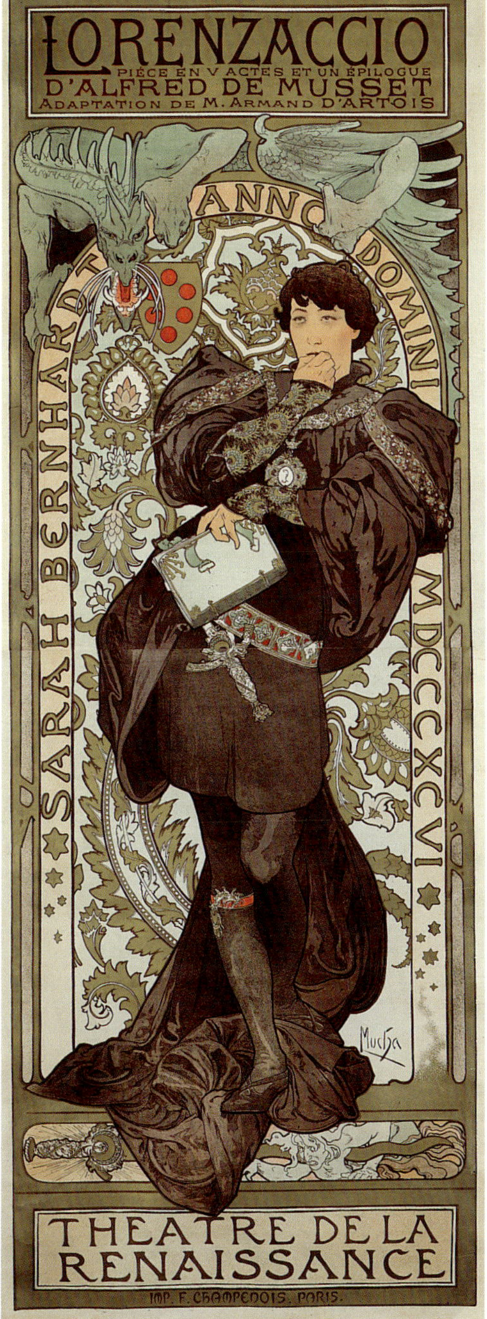

448

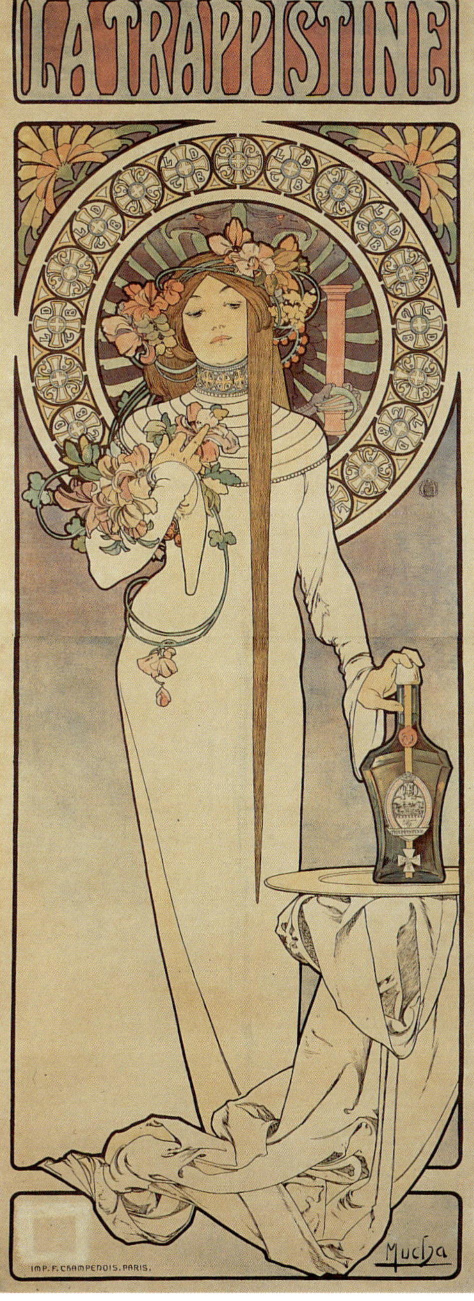

449

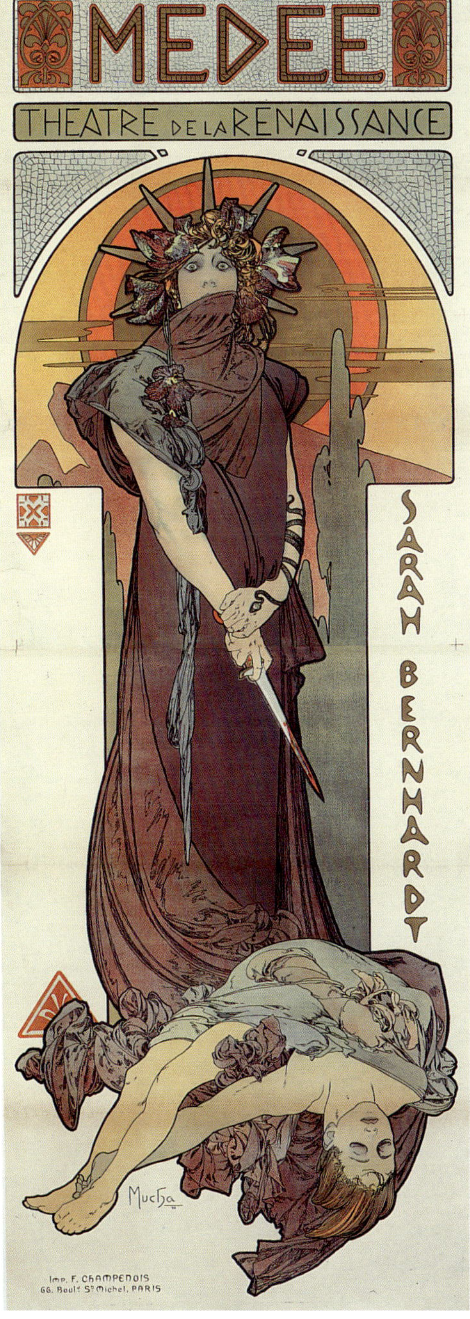

450

447. Model Behavior. ca. 1890.
8¹/₄ x 11 in./21 x 28 cm
Gouache, crayon and ink maquette. Framed.
Though this artwork predates Mucha's poster work by several years, it's interesting to take note of the fact that there's a poster hanging in the background. However, background presaging aside, the situation certainly seems somewhat unpleasant for the young woman at the vanity, who bows her head as she receives a tongue-lashing from the emphatic gentleman discreetly barring her only exit. Chances are that this gypsy dancer is receiving a terse critique after a particularly uninspiring performance from her director. Not the most cheerful spot at the moment, but Mucha fills the uneasy scene with detailed specificity and narrative clarity.
Est: $2,500-$3,000.

448. Lorenzaccio. 1896.
29¹/₂ x 81¹/₄ in./75 x 206.5 cm
Imp. F. Champenois, Paris
Cond A–/Slight tears, largely at edges.
Ref: Rennert/Weill, 20; Lendl/Paris, 4; DFP-II, 626;
    Maitres, 144; Mucha/Art Nouveau, 7;
    Bernhardt/Drama, p. 62; PAI-XXXVII, 431

"The character of Lorenzaccio, in the play by Alfred de Musset, is based on Lorenzo the Magnificent (1449-1492), the most powerful of the Medicis, who ruled the city state of Florence. In the play, Lorenzaccio struggles desperately to save Florence, which had grown rich during his reign, from the grip of a power-hungry conqueror. Mucha represents this tyranny by a dragon menacing the city coat of arms and portrays Lorenzaccio pondering the course of his action. Sarah Bernhardt adapted the play, first written in 1863, for herself, and the new version, for which this poster was produced, opened December 3, 1896. Never afraid to tackle a male role, Bernhardt made Lorenzaccio into one of the classic roles of her repertoire" (Lendl/Paris, p. 18).
This is the larger format.
Est: $15,000-$20,000.

449. La Trappistine. 1897.
29³/₄ x 80⁵/₈ in./75.5 x 204.7 cm
Imp. F. Champenois, Paris
Cond A–/Slight tears and stains.
Ref: Rennert/Weill, 30; Lendl/ Paris, 29; DFP-II, 631;
    Schardt, p. 50; PAI-XL, 422
"Once again we have a slender young lady in a grace-

fully draped pose, her head encircled by a halo which in this case has circles within it to reinforce the circular motif. This time, the hair is entirely orderly and hangs down in a single thick strand, but that is because it has the function to lead our eyes to the tabouret in the foreground which holds the bottle" (Rennert/Weill, p. 134).
Est: $17,000-$20,000.

450. Medée. 1898.
29³/₄ x 82¹/₈ in./75.3 x 208.7 cm
Imp. F. Champenois, Paris
Cond B/Slight tears at folds and edges.
Ref: Bernhardt/Drama, p. 102; Rennert/Weill, 53;
    Lendl/Paris, 7; DFP-II, 645; Mucha/Art Nouveau, 13;
    PAI-XLII, 46
In this 2-sheet poster, "Mucha's exquisite design used Medea's arm and the dagger as a giant exclamation point, emphasized by the look of stark horror in her face as she extracts gothic vengeance. It is one of his most powerful posters and an unusual departure from his normal choice of tranquil, sunny scenes" (Lendl/Paris, p. 20).
Est: $13,000-$16,000.

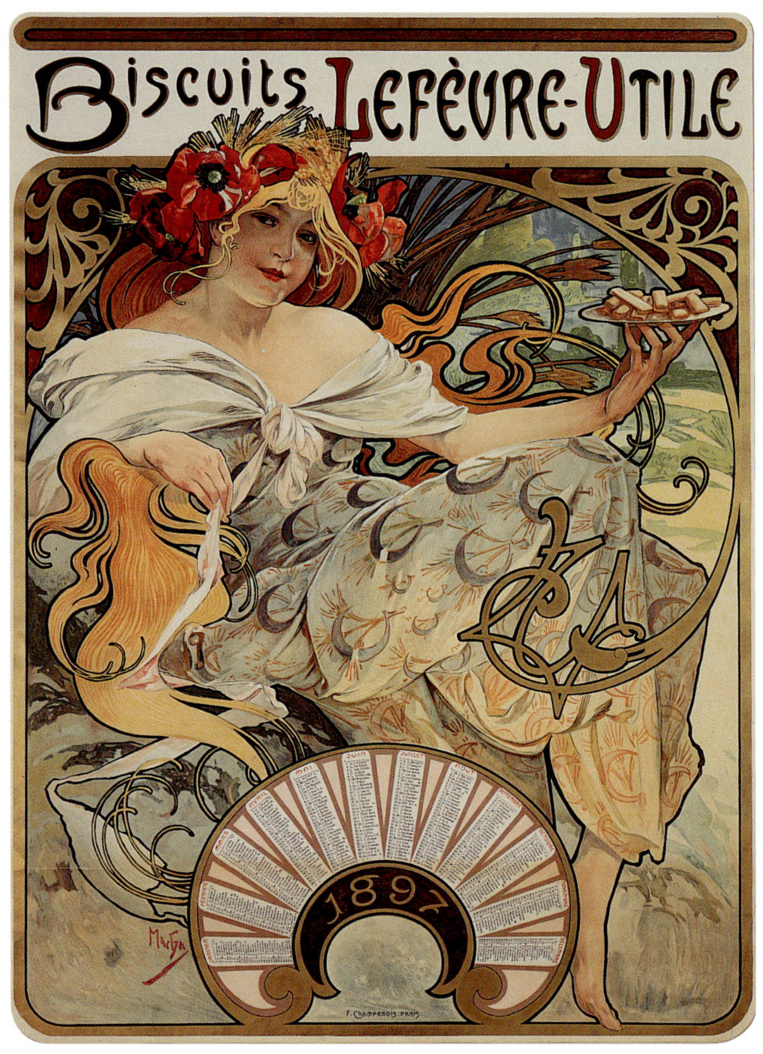

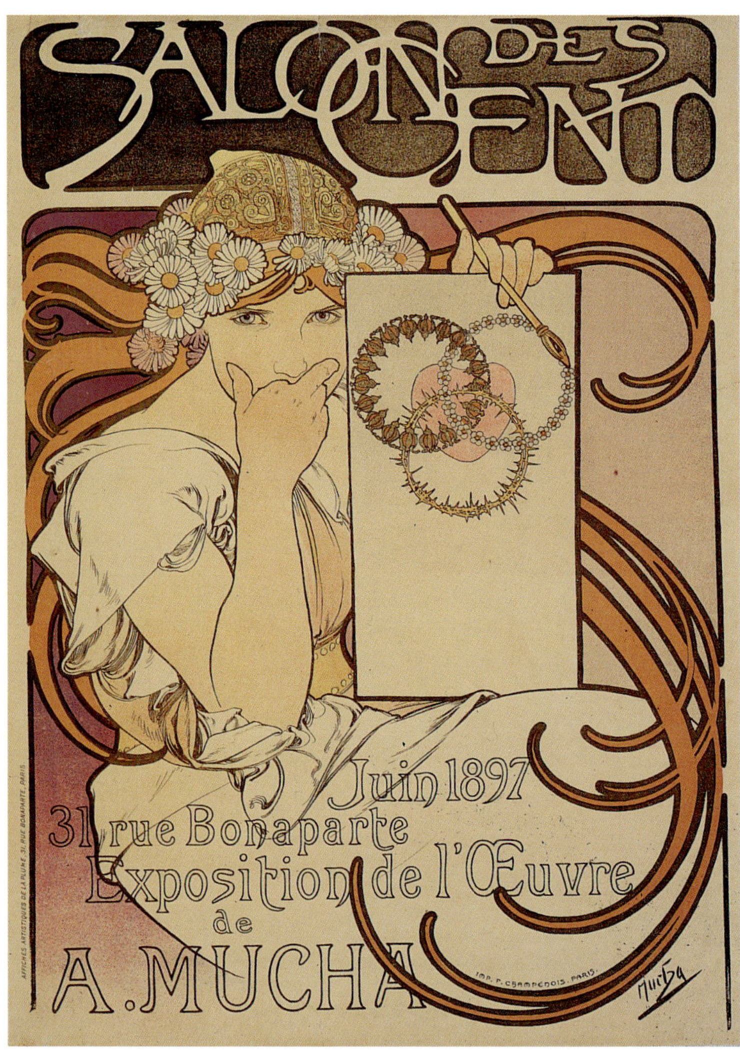

451

452

ALPHONSE MUCHA (cont'd)

451. Biscuits Lefèvre-Utile. 1896.
$17^1/_2$ x $24^1/_8$ in./44.4 x 61.1 cm
Imp. F. Champenois, Paris
Cond B+/Unobtrusive tear near bottom left edge; slight staining at bottom.
    Framed.
Ref: Rennert/Weill, 22; Lendl/Paris, 17; Weill, p. 42; Gold, 59 (var);
    PAI-XLII, 389
"One of Mucha's most personable young ladies, her hair cascading irre-
pressibly in fine style, is offering a dish of wafers in this exquisite design.
The calendar for 1897 is imprinted on a semi-circular base. Note the ini-
tials LU in that part of the golden ornamental border that protrudes into
the picture at right. The design of the girl's dress incorporates sickle and
wheat emblems . . . appropriate to the subject" (Rennert/Weill, p. 113).
Est: $10,000-$12,000.

452. Salon des Cent/Juin 1897.
$18^1/_8$ x $25^1/_2$ in./46 x 64.7 cm
Imp. F. Champenois, Paris
Cond A–/Slight tears at paper edges. Framed.
Ref: Rennert/Weill, 36; Lendl/Paris, 101; Mucha/Art Nouveau, 25;
    DFP-II, 638; Maitres, 114; Salon des Cent, p. 65;
    Salon des Cent/Neumann, p. 49); PAI-XXXII, 429
Mucha, for his own exhibition at the Salon des Cent, drew a "life-like girl
with a twinge of homesickness; it is a decidedly Slavic face, with a bonnet
featuring one of the embroidered regional patterns that distinguish the
folk costumes in his part of the world, and her hair is adorned with daisies
—symbol of the Moravian fields where Mucha spent his youth" (Rennert/
Weill p. 150).
Est: $7,000-$9,000.

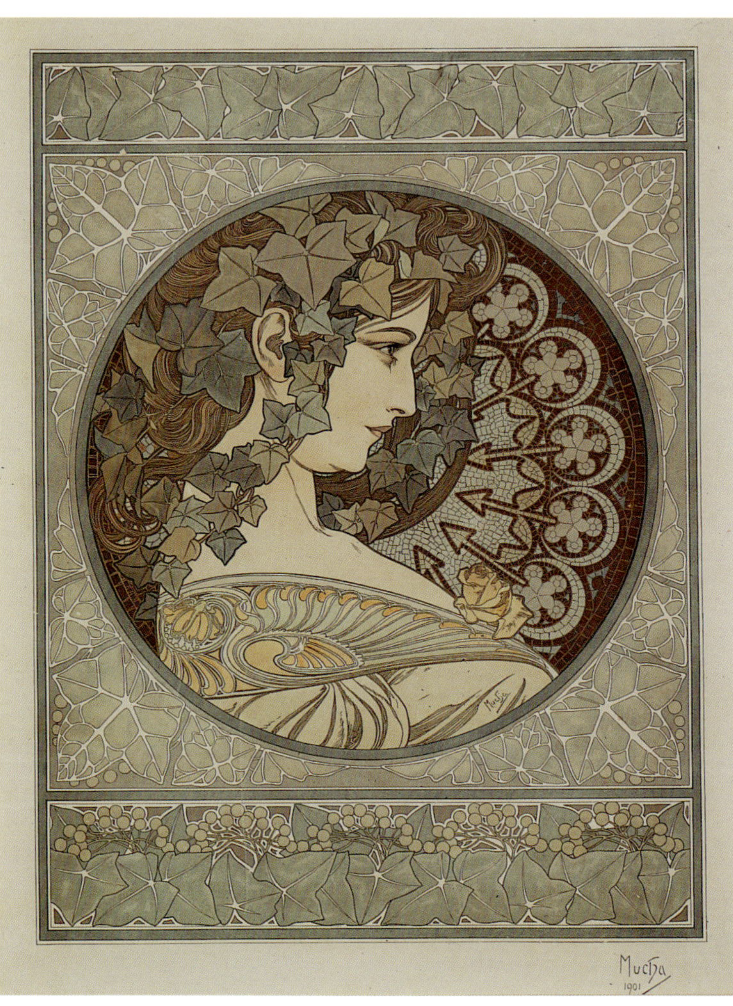

453

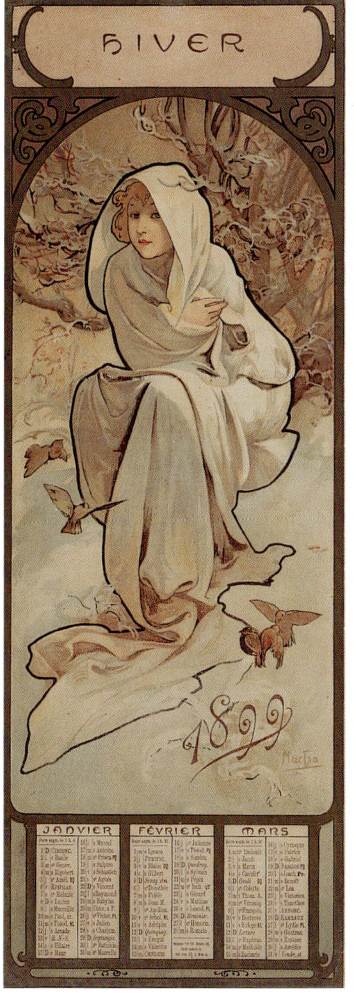

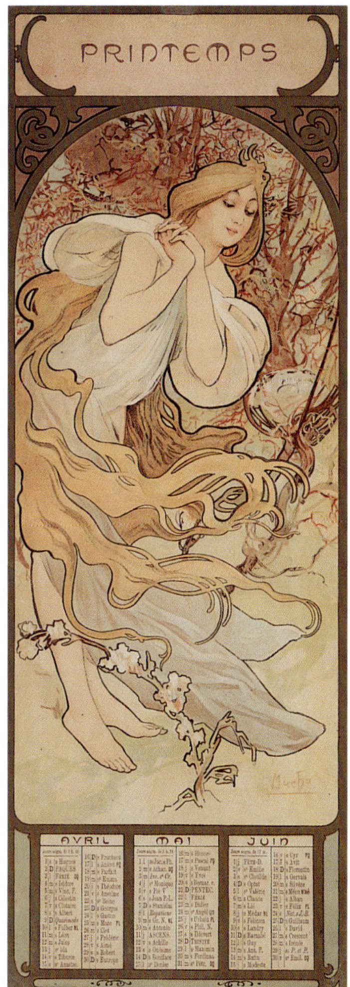

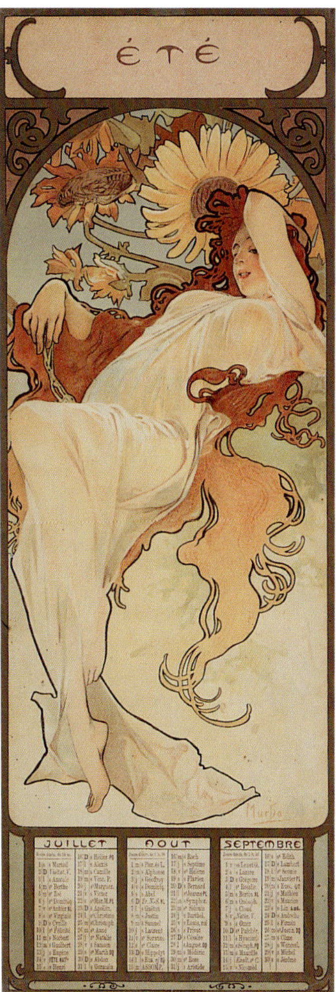

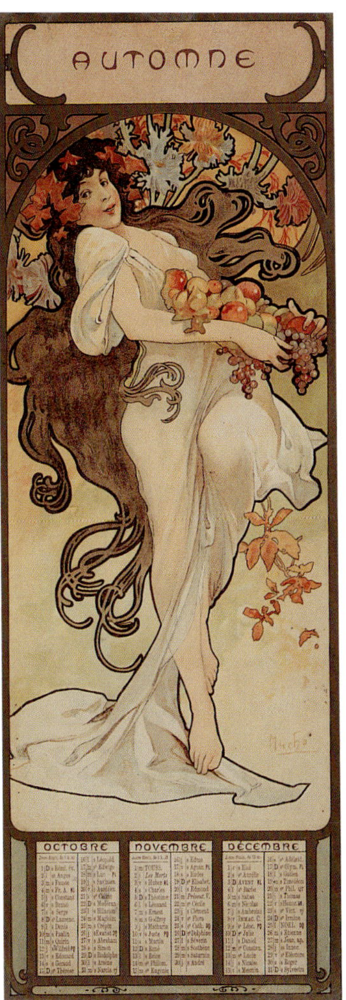

454

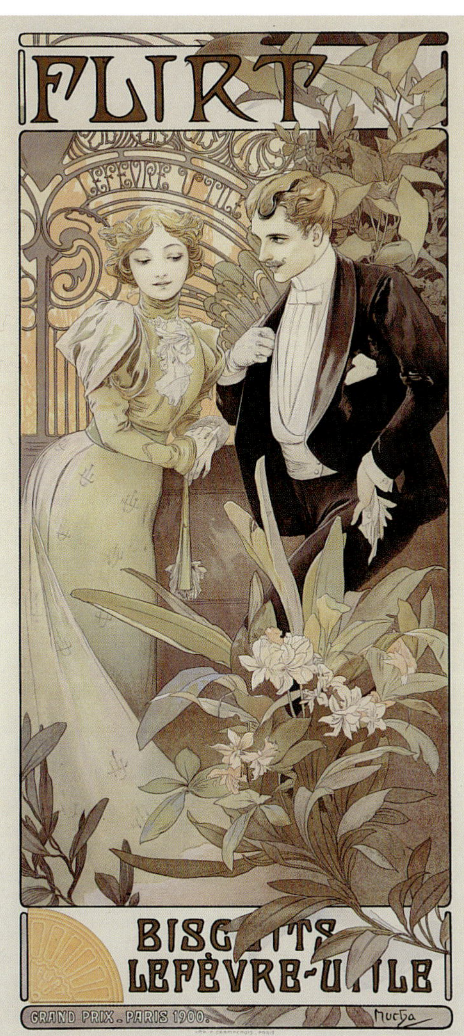

453. Laurel. 1901.
18 x 24³/₈ in./45.6 x 62 cm
Imp. F. Champenois, Paris
Cond A. Framed.
Ref: Rennert/Weill, 76; Lendl/Paris, 75;
   Mucha/Art Nouveau, 53b; PAI-XXX, 594
One half of the *Ivy and Laurel* set of decorative panels, produced at the same time as Mucha was designing the interior of George Fouqet's jewelry shop, utilizing a similar design of female heads placed within circular borders adorning the windowpanes. The embodiment of laurel is framed by a decorative area of rich foliage and backed by a mosaic pattern with "the repetitive motif of a stylized letter M as we know it from Mucha's alphabet." (Mucha/Art Nouveau, p. 203).
Est: $8,000-$10,000.

454. The Seasons. 1898.
Each: 5⁷/₈ x 16⁷/₈ in./14.9 x 43 cm
Imp. F. Champenois, Paris
Cond B+/Slight staining, largely in calendariums and
   top paper edges.
Ref (All Var): Rennert/Weill, 37; Lendl/Paris, 63;
   PAI-XXIII, 385
"With the decorative panel set of THE SEASONS of 1896 a proven success, Champenois had Mucha repeat the idea in a new design in 1897, and the result are four more lovely nymphs in arresting poses. Other than WINTER who sits all wrapped up and huddled against the cold, they frolic about in diaphanous clothes, their buoyant hair roaming freely in the best Mucha tradition.

WINTER and SPRING are blondes, SUMMER is auburn, and FALL is a brunette" (Rennert/ Weill, p. 151). This particular new variant of the panel series uses the 1897 images, with the specific season appearing above its respective breathtaking embodiment with 1899 calendarium appearing at their feet.
Est: $10,000-$12,000. (4)

455. Flirt. 1899.
11³/₈ x 24¹/₂ in./28.8 x 62.2 cm
Imp. F. Champenois, Paris
Cond A. Framed.
Ref: Rennert/Weill, 72, Var. 1; Lendl/Paris, 18;
   L'Art du Biscuit, p. 9 (var); Gold, 63 (var);
   PAI-XLII, 397
"Flirt" was not only the name of one of the biscuits sold by the firm Lefèvre-Utile, but also the theme of Mucha's design. The romantic couple engages in a flirtatious encounter in a setting of Victorian elegance. Just to remind us that this is not an illustration in a bodice-ripping novel but a poster, the demure young lady's dress is faintly decorated with the initials LU, and the company's full name appears on a wrought-iron grille behind them. Other than that, however, there is no blatant intrusion of the company, which always conducted its advertising campaigns with understatement and good taste. Originally published in 1899, this in-store display was reprinted, as shown here, to announce that the company won the "Grand Prix" at the Paris 1900 World's Fair.
Est: $6,000-$8,000.

455

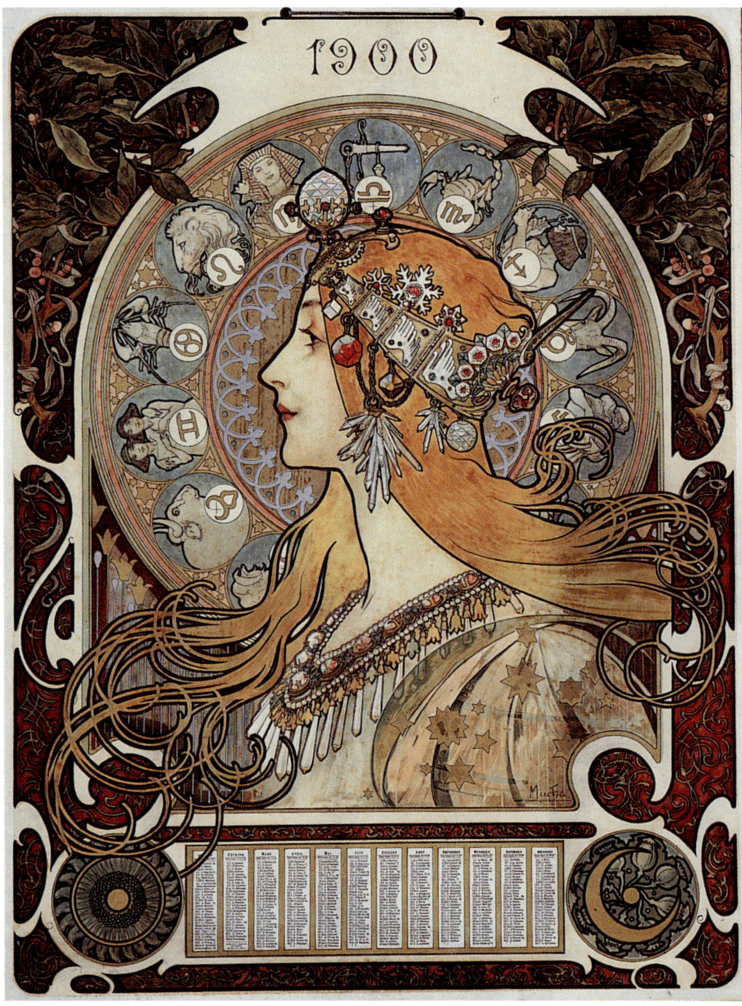

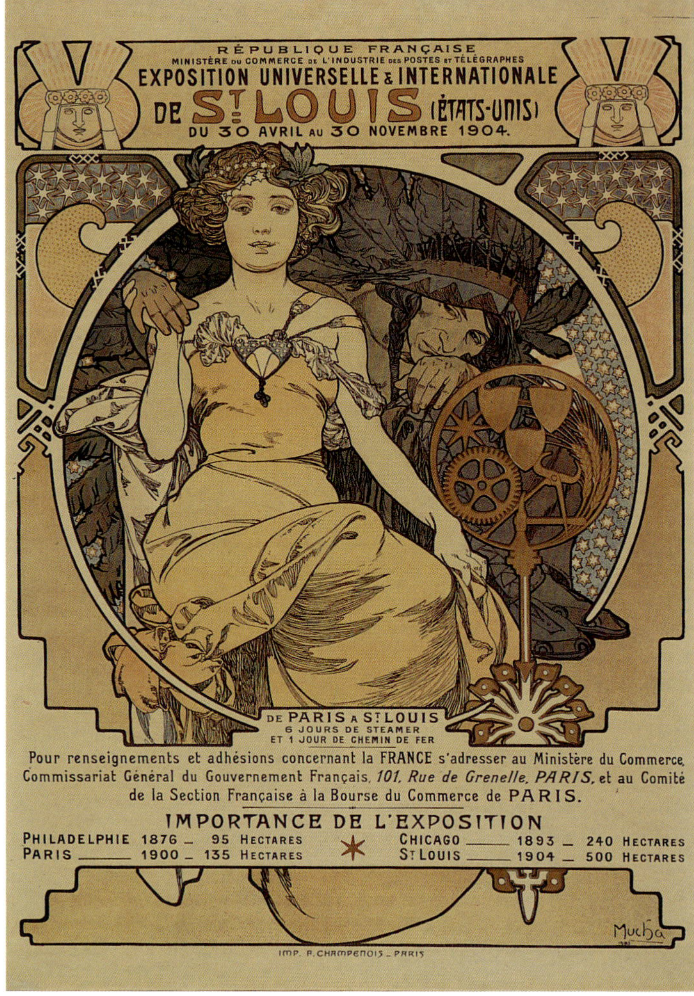

456

457

ALPHONSE MUCHA (cont'd)

456. Zodiac. 1899.
$13^3/_8$ x $17^3/_4$ in./34 x 45 cm
Imp. F. Champenois, Paris (not shown)
Cond A/Mounted on board with grommets at top.
Ref (All Var): Rennert/Weill, 19, Var. 9;
   Lendl/Paris, 43; Mucha/Art Nouveau, 46;
   DFP-II, 629; Wagner, 72; Gold, 97; PAI-XLII, 393
"This is one of Mucha's most frequently used designs.
Originally it was produced for the publisher Champenois
for an 1897 calendar (*see* PAI-XLI, 417) and almost
immediately it was chosen as well by the editor of *La
Plume* for a calendar for the same year (*see* PAI-XXXV,
410). After that the lithograph appeared without text
as a decorative panel and again as calendars . . . The
great success of this composition is due to several fac-
tors. First is the beauty of the central figure. Mucha's
contemporaries perceived her to be an oriental princess, desirable and at the same time unreachable. Next
is the remarkable connection between the stylization
of the figure . . . and the naturalistic drawing of the
foliage in the upper part of the lithograph. This is one
way that Mucha created subtle tension . . . Last but not
least is the harmony of the composition and the colors
as a whole." (Mucha/Art Nouveau, p. 189). This particular variant of the poster comes complete with a 1900
calendarium. *This is the smaller format.*
Est: $8,000-$10,000.

457. Exposition de St. Louis. 1903.
$28^5/_8$ x 41 in./72.6 x 104 cm
Imp. F. Champenois, Paris
Cond A–/Slightly light-stained. Framed.
Ref: Rennert/Weill, 87, Var. 1; Lendl/Paris, 43 (var);
   Mucha/Art Nouveau, 30; DFP-II, 650 (var);
   PAI-XXXVII, 434
"The Mucha maiden holding hands with the Indian chief
advertises the 1904 World's Fair at St. Louis, Missouri,
and invites the French traveler to take a journey involving six days by steamer and one day by train . . . The
theme of the fair was science and industry, as shown
in the circle at right. The star in it represents the rather
unusual first day of the Fair, which demonstrated the
sensitivity and scientific value of a rather new discovery
of the time, the photocell. A photocell at the bottom of

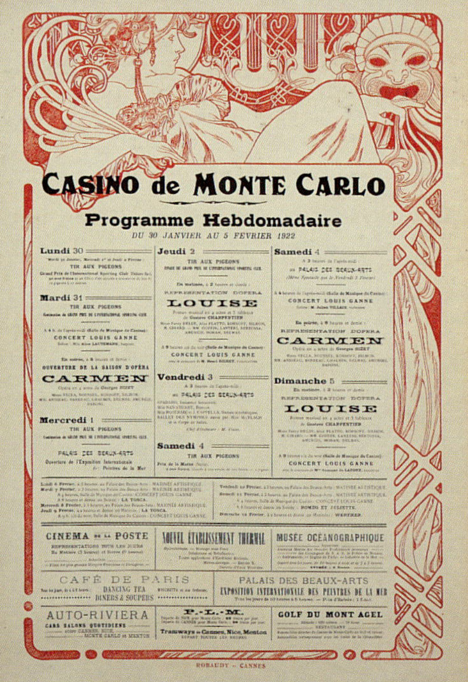

458

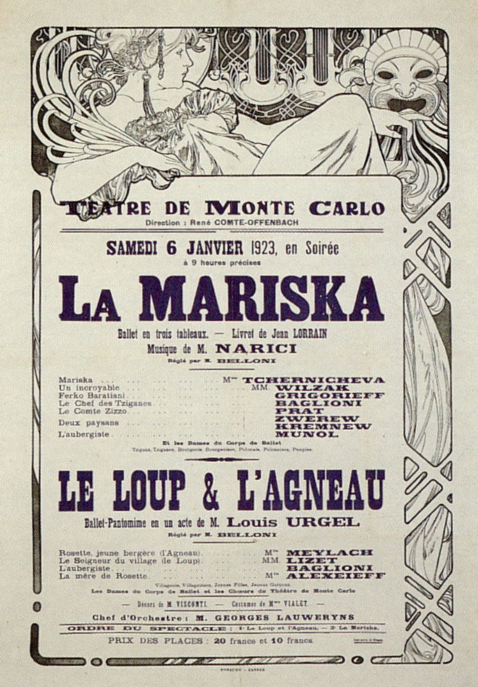

459

a long tube was aimed at a spot in the heavens where a
bright star—Arcturus—would appear at the exact opening hour of the Fair. As the star's light reached the
photocell at the precise moment, it activated a switch
which lit all the lights in the fair grounds" (Rennert/Weill,
p. 310). *This is the rare version of the poster with
complete train info listed in the bottom text area.*
Est: $10,000-$12,000.

458. Casino de Monte Carlo. 1922.
$20^3/_8$ x $30^3/_4$ in./52 x 78.2 cm
Robandy, Cannes
Cond A.

Ref (Both Var): Rennert/Weill, 33; PAI-XXVII, 518
Though the original appearance of this border design
dates back to 1897 (*see* PAI-XXVII, 518), it first shows
up in *La Plume*, "on the title page of the special Mucha
edition . . . Thereafter, it appears to have lain dormant
for a few years until the printer Robaudy of Cannes
printed a quantity of the borders and sold them to
Imprimerie de Monaco, who in turn used them subsequently on numerous occasions to advertise various
events in Monte Carlo by filling in the appropriate letter-
print text. The design no longer had the artist's signature on it, however. How the design suddenly showed
up in Monaco is a bit of a mystery" (Rennert/ Weill, p.

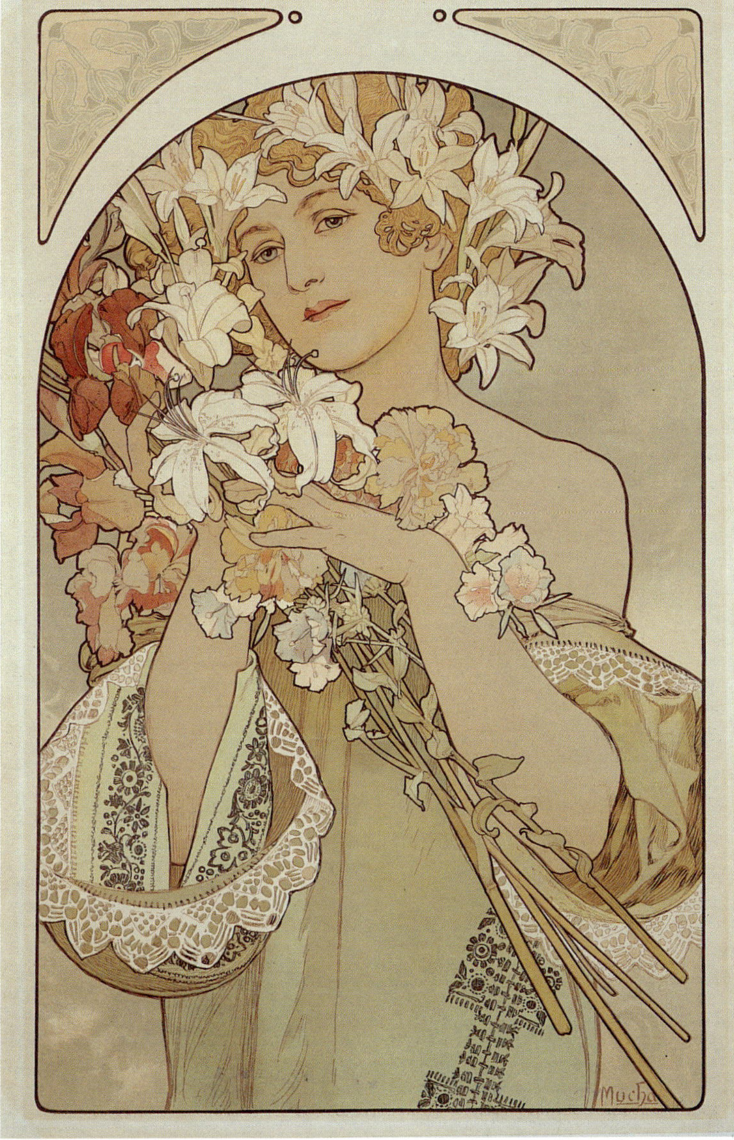

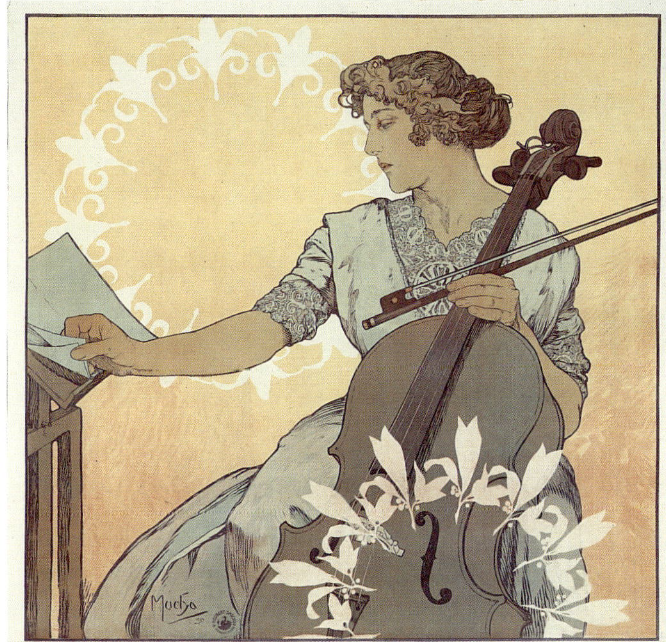

460

461

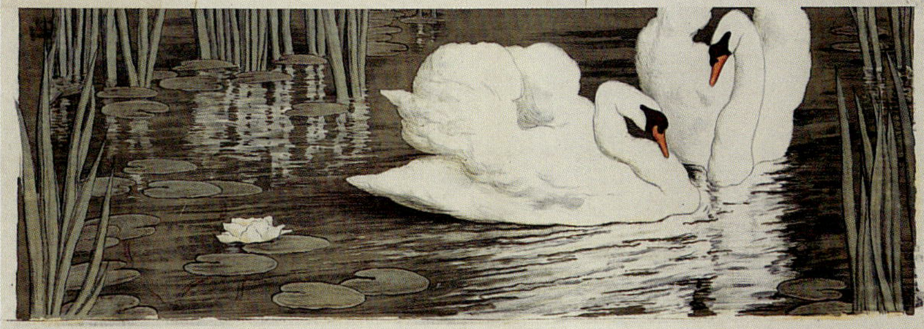

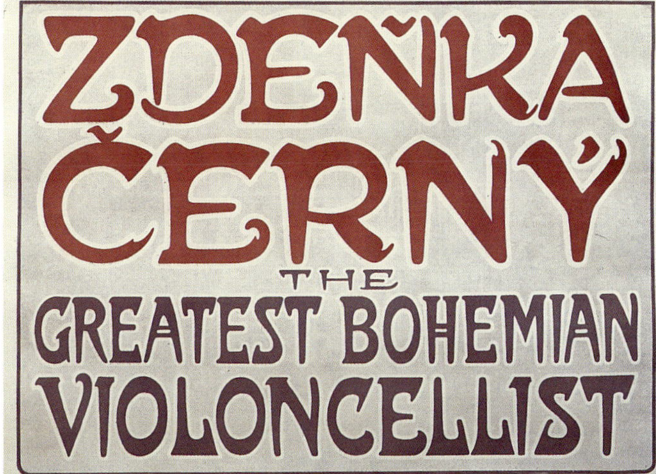

462

463

141). No matter how the design arrived in Monaco, it's important to note that it was such a recognizable and well-loved image that it was subsequently used into the 1920s for various Monte Carlo cultural events. Such as the details of this "Weekly Program" at the Casino de Monte Carlo in the winter of 1922. *This is the smaller format printed with red ink.*
Est: $1,700-$2,000.

459. Teatre de Monte Carlo. 1923.
33⅝ x 48¾ in./85.5 x 123.6 cm
Robandy, Cannes
Cond B/Slight tears at folds.
Ref (Both Var): Rennert/Weill, 33; PAI-XXVII, 518
Once more we're presented with Mucha's popular border design, this time promoting—with artwork in green and letterpress text in navy—a pair of balletic works being staged at the Theatre de Monte Carlo (which has been conspicuously misspelled). *This is the larger format.*
Est: $1,700-$2,000.

460. Flower. 1897.
14⅝ x 24 in./37 x 61 cm
Imp. F. Champenois, Paris
Cond B/Slightly light-stained. Framed.

Ref: Rennert/Weill, 44; Lendl, 68; PAI-XVIII, 379 (var)
This rather melancholic young woman represents one half of the "Fruit and Flower" decorative panels. The somber faced mademoiselle is "presented to us in a simple, straightforward design with a minimum of embellishments, which in this early period is a departure from Mucha's usual style. There is, however, a great delicacy and tenderness in the way he pays tribute to nature's bounty—the flowers at their fullest bloom . . . the (maiden) representing the finest flowering of womanhood" (Rennert/Weill, p. 179).
Est: $10,000-$12,000.

461. Zdenka Cerny. 1913.
43¼ x 73½ in./109.8 x 186.7 cm
V. Neubert, Smichov/Prague
Cond A.
Ref: Rennert/Weill, 102; Lendl/Paris, 88; Mucha/Art
  Nouveau, 39; Gold, 177; PAI-XXI, 341
This poster was prepared for Ms. Cerny's European tour planned for the fall of 1914; when war broke out that spring, the tour was canceled, and the poster was not used. Cerny was the daughter of a Czech-American music teacher who befriended Mucha during the artist's stay in Chicago. "Mucha worked from a photo-

graph of Zdenka with a cello, but idealized her face by investing it with a spiritual quality, her love of music. He created a unique poster-portrait by adjusting the slant of her head, softening her expression, lightening the hair, lifting the hand turning the sheet music, and elongating the body. Two circles, one with lilies symbolizing Zdenka's youthful innocence, the other with laurels of her past triumphs, complete the design suffused with warm light" (Mucha/Art Nouveau, p. 180).
Est: $8,000-$10,000.

ALFRED MULLER (1869-1940)

462. Swans.
60¾ x 22¾ in./154.5 x 58 cm
Cond A–/Recreated top border.
Ref: PAI-XXXI, 560
The romance of the only feathered paramours who mate for life is reflected by Muller with Art Nouveau grace amidst the calming quietude of lily pad and rush. Born in Livorno in 1869, Italian-native Alfred (or Alfredo) Muller was active as a painter and watercolorist in both his homeland and France, specializing graphically in the production of decorative panels.
Est: $2,000-$2,500.

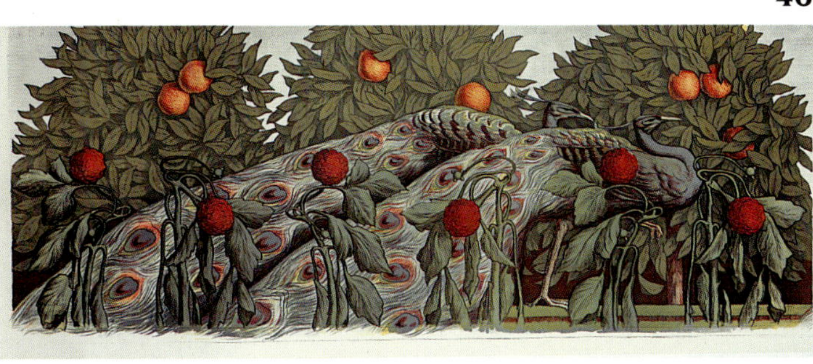

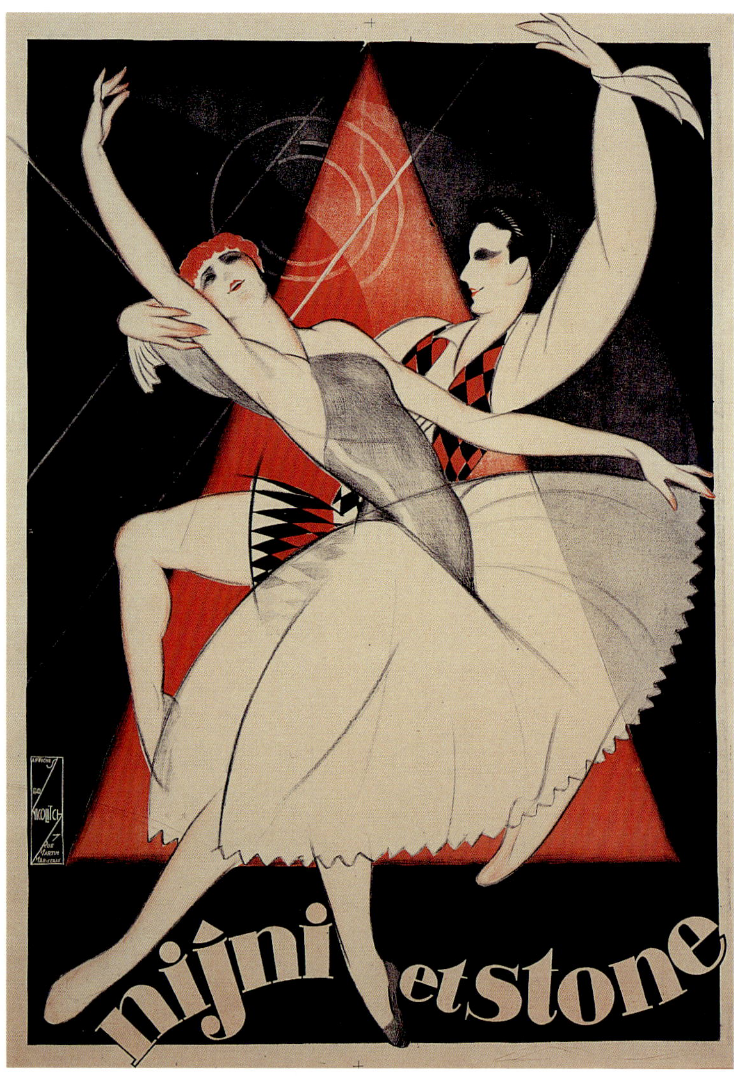

464

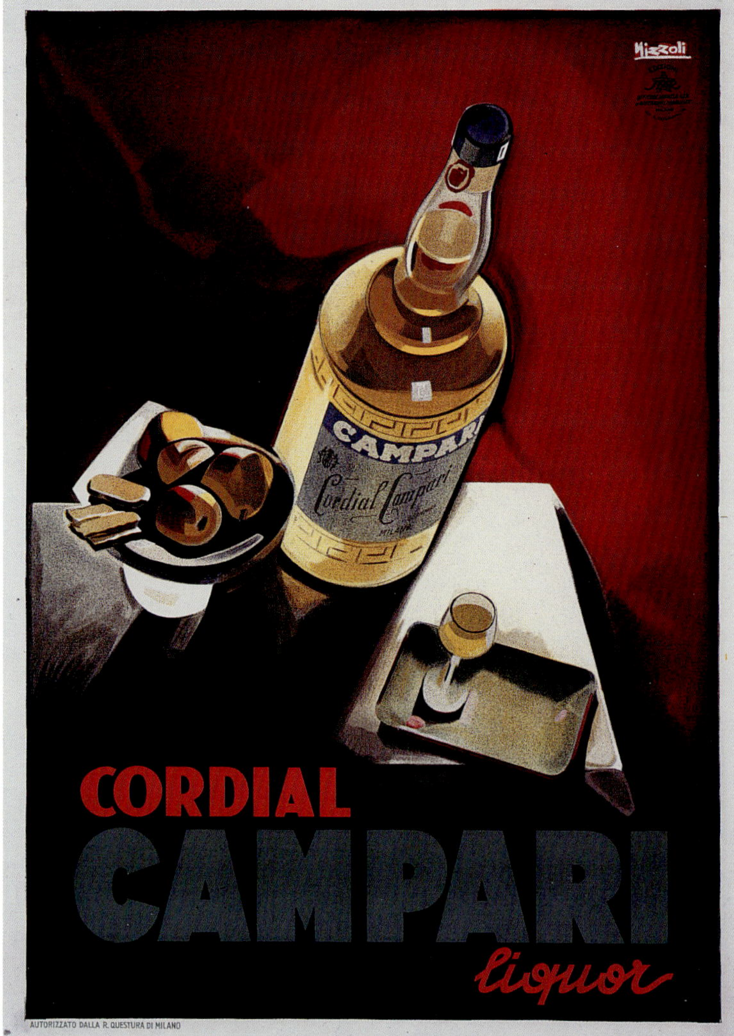

465

MULLER (cont'd)

463. Peacocks.
60$^1/_2$ x 24 in./153.7 x 61 cm
Cond A.
Ref: PAI-XXXII, 451
These colorful and elegant peacocks, at once both integrated into and decorously separate from their lush surroundings, amply demonstrate Muller's natural flair. Steinlen, in his poster for the magazine "Cocorico" indicated that Muller was one of its contributors, but no work of his appears in any issue.
Est: $2,000-$2,500.

OBRAD NICOLITCH

464. Nijni et Stone.
37$^7/_8$ x 54$^1/_4$ in./96.2 x 137.7 cm
Affiches Nicolitch, Marseille
Cond A. Framed.
Ref: PAI-XXXIX, 412
A very effective, Constructivist rendering of the dancers in red and black. It's not clear if the "Stone" of this pair is Bentley Stone, the famous chore-ographer, dancer and teacher who was the premiere danseur with many companies in the 1930s and '40s, including the Chicago Grand Opera Ballet, the Page-Stone Ballet and others.
Est: $2,500-$3,000.

MARCELLO NIZZOLI (1887-1960)

465. Cordial Campari. 1926.
27$^1/_8$ x 39 in./69 x 99.1 cm
R. Questura, Milano
Cond A.
Ref (All Var): Nizzoli, p. 11; Weill, 478; PAI-VII, 461
A cozy still life, the bottle and glass glowing warmly against subdued tones of brown and red, makes an inviting advertisement for Campari. There's something deliberately precarious about the arrangement and perspective that creates just enough tension to further hold our attention. Nizzoli was a most versatile artist, being a painter, decorator, textile designer and pos-terist. Many of his posters were for automobile companies. In 1938, he

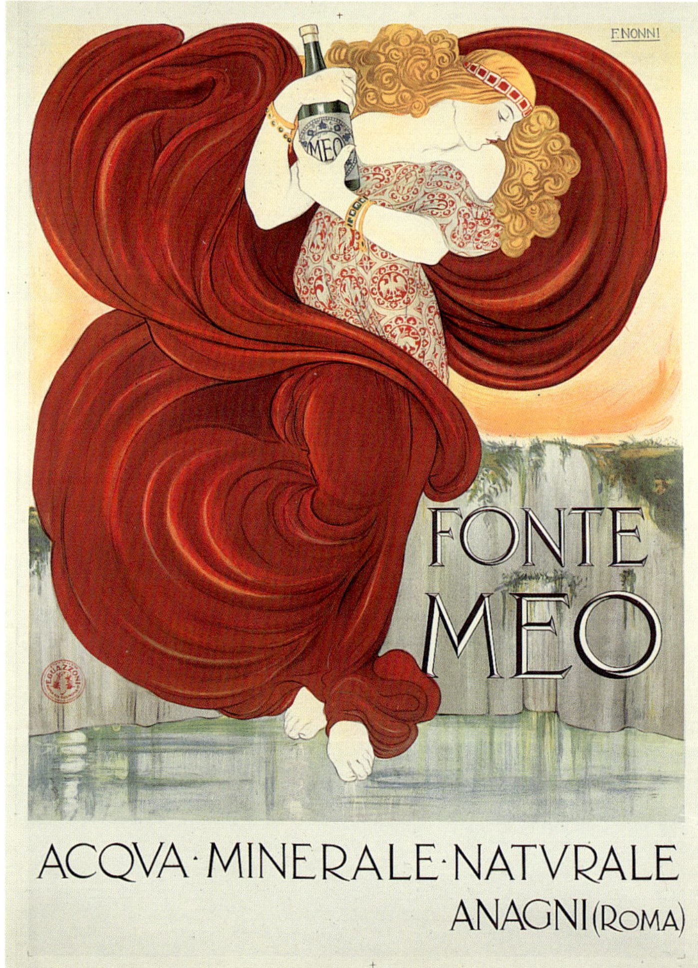

466

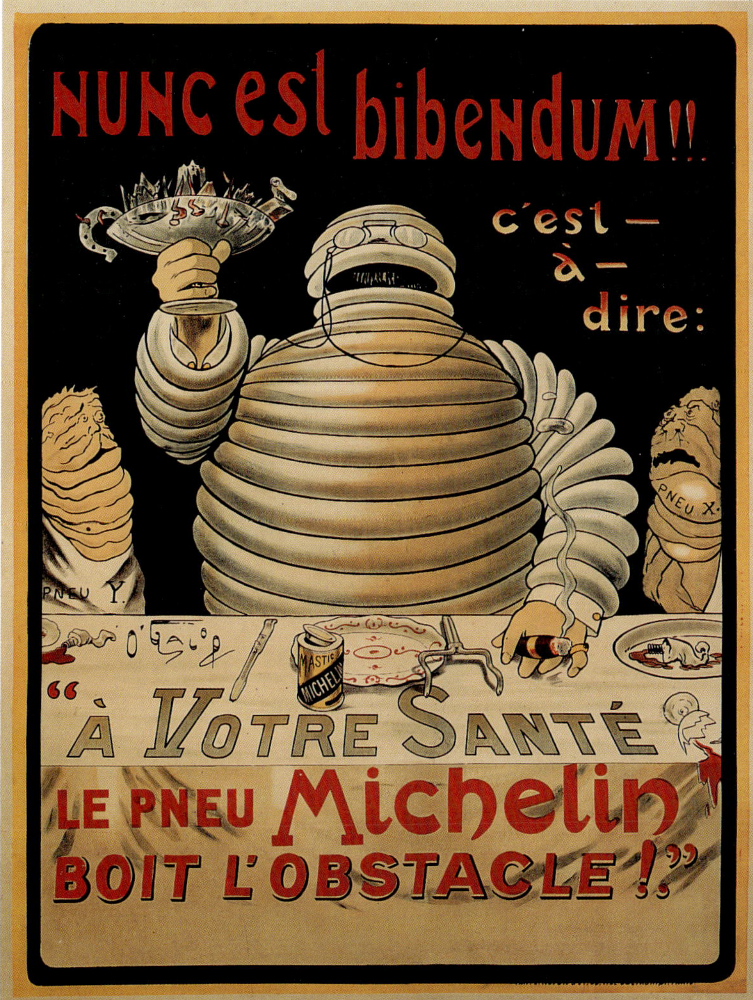

467

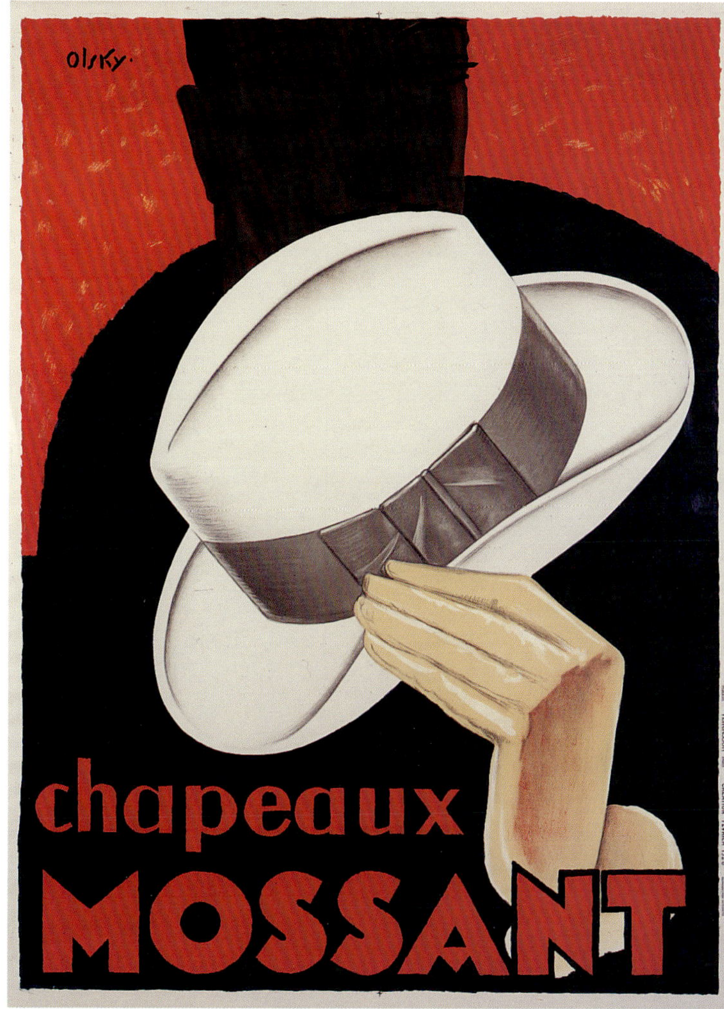

469

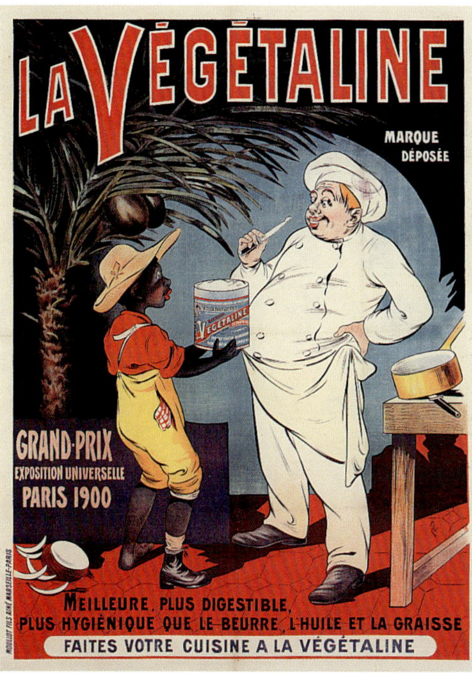

468

joined Olivetti and was responsible for some of the finest images in the 1940s and '50s. *This is the smaller format.*
Est: $6,000-$8,000.

F. NONNI (1885-1976)

466. Fonte Meo. 1924.
$39^1/_8$ x 55 in./99.2 x 146.3 cm
E. Guazzoni, Roma
Cond A.
One of the most honestly wonderful things about posters is the way that they elevate completely mun-

dane commercial products into an altogether different and altogether more rarefied air—the way that a bottle of drinking water, for example, can suddenly be transformed into a nectar worthy of the gods. Such is precisely the case in this Nonni poster for Fonte Meo mineral water, a design that combines such disparate elements—Byzantine quasi-idolatry, placid naturalism and seductive commerce—with such flair that he creates a splendiferous hybrid, an advertisement of sancro-sexy portent from which one can hardly look away without feeling as if one is missing out on something spectacular, most especially in the hypnotic swirl of the bottle embraceor's flowing crimson wrap. *Rare!*
Est: $6,000-$7,000.

O'GALOP (Marius Rossillon, 1867-1946)

467. Le Pneu Michelin/Nunc est bibendum. 1896.
$47^1/_2$ x $63^3/_8$ in./120.6 x 161 cm
Imp. L. Revon, Paris
ond B+/Slight tears, largely at edges.
Ref: Bicycle Posters, 38; Collectioneur, p. 243;
PAI-XXIX, 44
The first of all the Bibendum designs. To show that Michelin tires can take it, O'Galop in 1896 showed the personified tire about to down a cup of rusty nails and broken bottles, presumably with no ill effects, and for a heading he used, mockingly, the venerable Latin phrase, "Let us drink." Many people apparently believed that "Bibendum" was the figure's name, and that's how he's been known in France for over a century. It's one of the world's longest lasting advertising images, one still enjoying widespread popularity today. The company was started by André and Edouard Michelin in 1892 when they obtained a patent for a pneumatic bicycle tire. *Rare!*
Est: $12,000-$15,000.

EUGENE OGÉ (1869-1936)

468. La Végétaline. ca. 1910.
$44^3/_4$ x $61^7/_8$ in./113.5 x 157 cm
Moullot Fils, Marseille-Paris
Cond B+/Slight tears at folds.
Ref: Ogé, 139; Négripub, 170
"Topped with a large straw hat and dressed in short trousers held up by a single shoulder strap . . . a young black boy gives a head chef a taste of his Végétaline, extracted from coconuts. In his haste, he forgot to put on one of his shoes" (Négripub, p. 124). And from the satisfied look of things, this substitute may very well replace butter, oil and grease in the gourmand's preparations—a fact not-so-coincidentally mentioned in the poster's text. Ogé's principal claim to fame was his long tenure as house artist for the printer Charles Verneau around the turn of the century; he also, however, produced numerous drawings that were well-received in fine-art circles. A retrospective exhibition of all his posters drew a large audience at the Bibliothèque Forney in Paris during the summer of 1998.
Est: $1,700-$2,000.

OLSKY

469. Chapeaux Mossant. 1928.
$45^3/_8$ x $62^1/_4$ in./115.2 x 158.2 cm
Imp. Vercasson, Paris
Cond A. Framed.
Ref: Deco Affiches, p. 69; PAI-XLII, 414
The Mossant hat firm's product pops off the paper, an ivory *objet d'art* against a shadowy backdrop. Olsky's near-photographic rendering of the chapeau makes for effective marketing, but his artistic instincts utilize intrigue to keep the viewer locked-in with the shady gigolo who claims the fedora as his own.
Est: $4,000-$5,000.

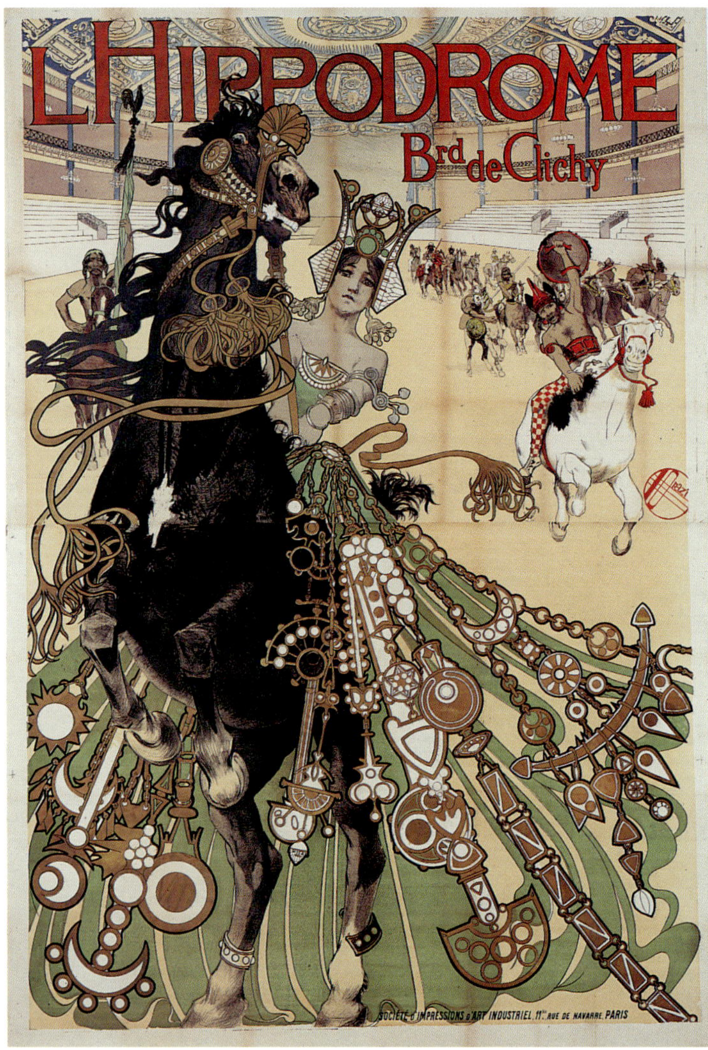

470

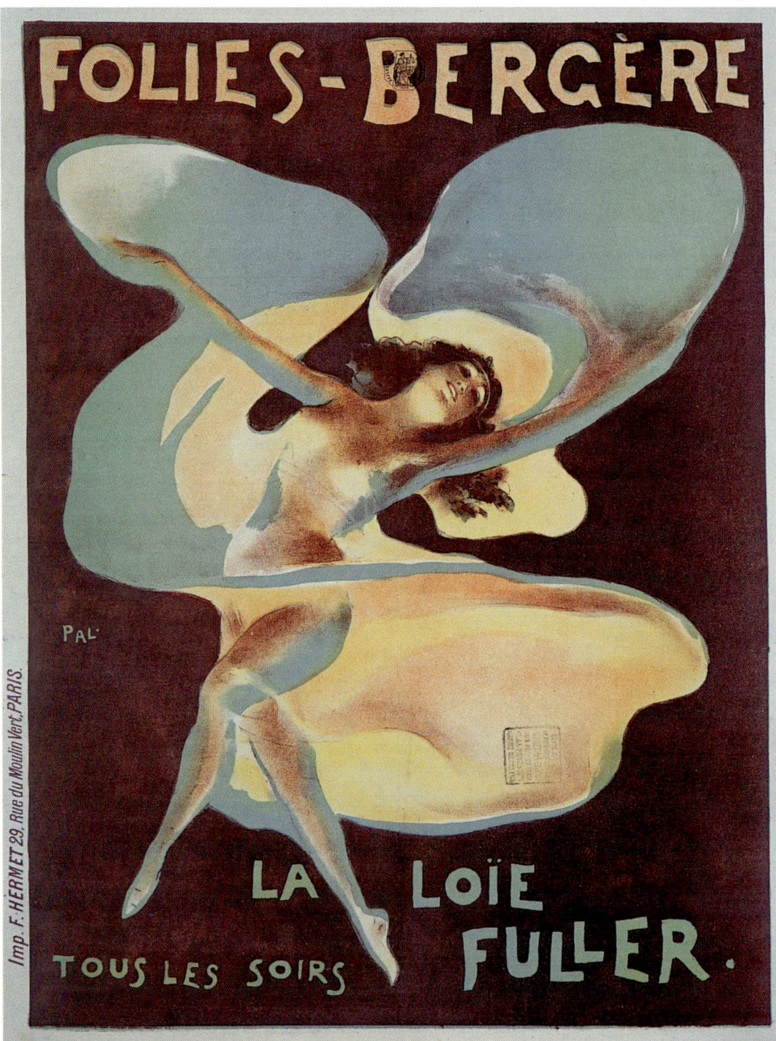

476

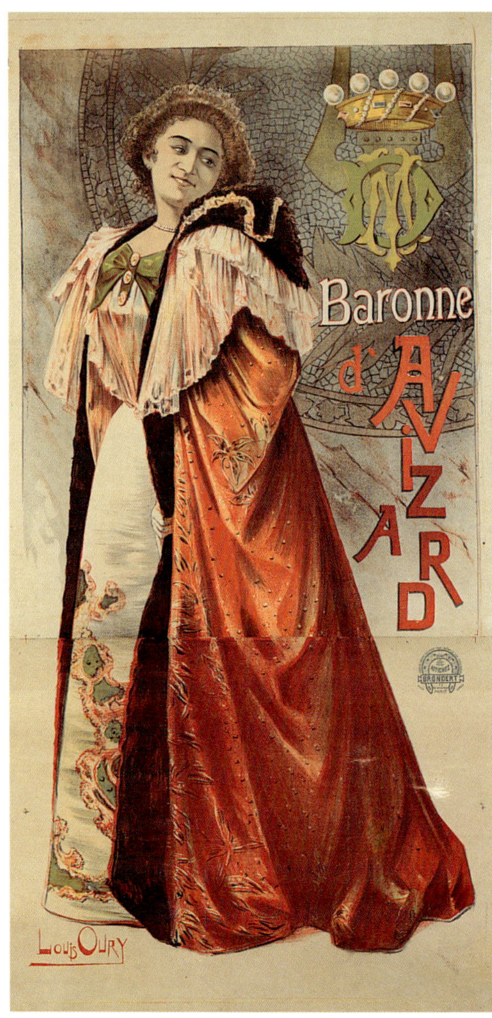

471

MANUEL ORAZI (1860-1934)

470. L'Hippodrome. 1905.
63 x 93³/₈ in./160 x 237 cm
Société d'Impressions d'Art Industriel, Paris
Cond B/Slight tears and stains at folds and edges.
Ref (All Var but PAI): DFP-II, 676a; Circus Posters, 30;
 Gold, 150; PAI-XLII, 416
Maindron properly calls Orazi "the master lithographer" and this is one of his best posters. It is for a show at the new, ornately-roofed Hippodrome (the old one was open-air) on the Boulevard de Clichy in Paris. The advertised event recreates a barbarian invasion featuring a flamboyantly bedecked horse ridden by a pagan princess. Orazi places her front and center in all her saber-rattling splendor. The mosaic-like approach was used by Orazi in an earlier poster for Sarah Bernhardt's "Theodora" (*see* PAI-XLII, 43). *This is the larger,*
2-sheet format.
Est: $7,000-$9,000.

D'ORNELLAS

471. 13e. Salon des Arts Ménagers. 1936.
24³/₈ x 39 in./62 x 99 cm
Imp. Chaix, Paris
Cond A–/Slight stains.
D'Ornellas advertises this home improvement expo with an at-work domestic contrasted off a black-and-blue checkered background. The show opened on January 30, 1937, at the Grand Palais exhibition hall in Paris. Certainly there have to have been some advancements in domestic science on display to make this woman's job somewhat less arduous. It's interesting to compare this with a like motif of Francis Bernard from five years earlier (*see* No. 166).
Est: $1,000-$1,200.

LOUIS OURY (1846-?)

472. Baronne d'Avizard.
36 x 75³/₄ in./91.5 x 192.4 cm
Affiches Brondert, Paris
Cond B/Slight tears and stains at folds and edges.
Apart from being a regal presence on a 2-sheet poster, it's difficult to say much about the "Baroness of Avizard."

472

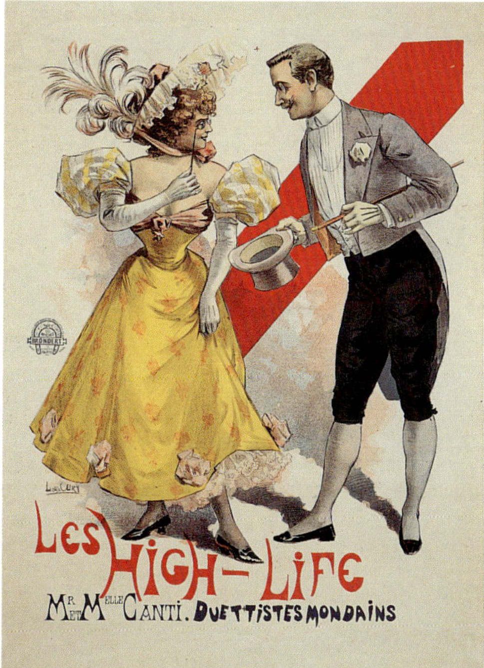

473

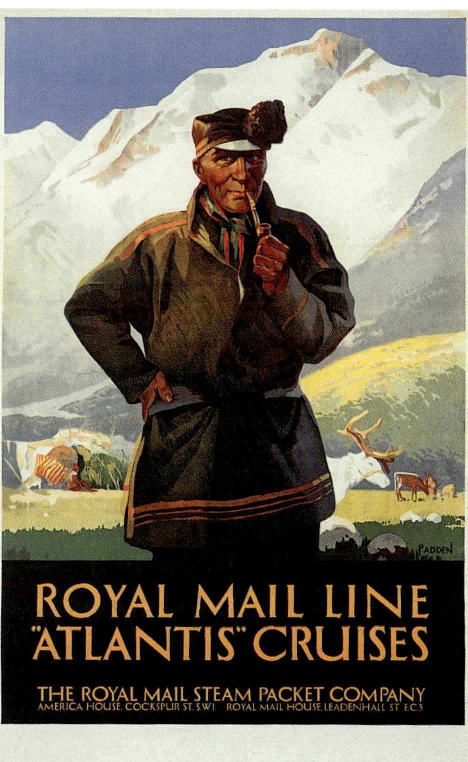

474

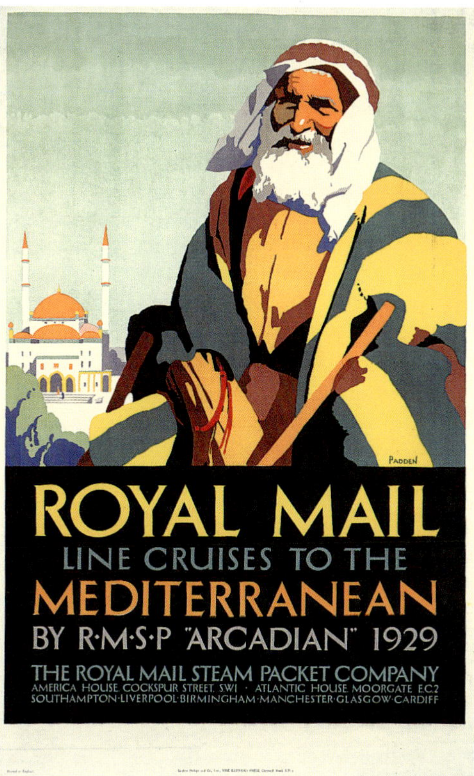

475

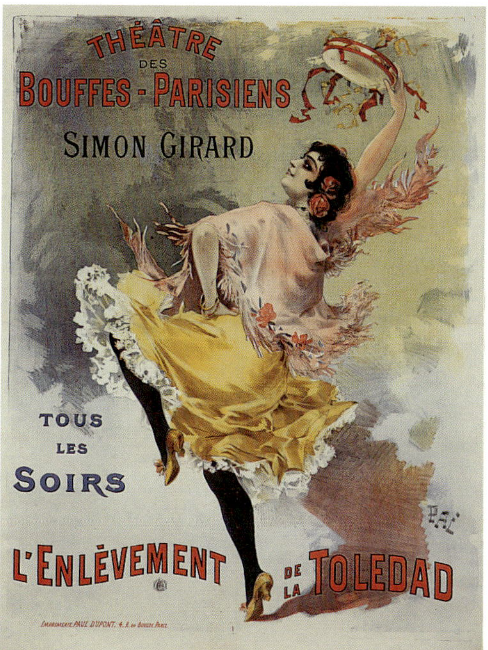

477

If she was an actual historical personage, she was one that made no impression whatsoever. So, chances are good that this poster was executed for a lesser theatricality that explored the travails and triumphs of an imaginary noblewoman. Where the play may not have succeeded, Oury's creation triumphs impressively, conveying grace and breeding with artful fluency. Oury was born in the town of Montauban and exhibited his paintings at the Salon des Artistes Français where he received Honorable Mention in 1898. Aside from that, nothing is known of him.
Est: $1,500-$1,800.

473. Les High-Life. ca. 1898.
$29^3/8$ x $41^3/4$ in./74.5 x 106 cm
Affiches Brondert, Paris
Cond A.
Oh, what a tony time it must have been meandering through the "High-Life" in the company of the Cantis, a father/daughter pair of "Urbane Duetists." And though few specifics are given, Oury fills the page with a whimsical sense of decorum and civility that has all but disappeared from today's in-your-face entertainment scene.
Est: $1,200-$1,500.

DAPHNE PADDEN

474. Royal Mail Cruises/"Atlantis". ca. 1936.
$24^3/4$ x $39^1/2$ in./62.9 x 100.4 cm
Baynard Press, London
Cond A–/Slight tears in background.
Ref: PAI-XXXV, 428 (var)
Padden creates an irreverently wide open destination poster for the Royal Mail Line, a British steamship company serving far-flung locations not on the routes of the major carriers of the time. With the aid of a puffing Sami herdsman and his reindeer, the lithographic mountainous environs lure the viewer with a landscape that's a far cry from the less altitudinous options of the island sovereignty from whence the cruise service originates. The "Atlantis," the ship singled out for her Scandinavian destinations, also served the R.M.L.'s Caribbean service.
Est: $1,500-$1,800.

475. Royal Mail Line/Mediterranean. 1929.
$24^1/2$ x $39^1/2$ in./62.4 x 100.1 cm
Baynard Press, London
Cond B+/Tears, largely near top margin.
A colorful North African tribesman serves as Padden's singular drawing card, calling upon his anything-but-British appeal to inject some adventure into the regimented lifestyle of anyone in need of time away from their routine. And, as usual, the "Arcadian" is nowhere to be found. In fact, not a single salty Mediterranean drop appears anywhere in the design.
Est: $1,500-$1,800.

PAL (Jean de Paléologue, 1860-1942)

476. Folies-Bergère/La Loïe Fuller. ca. 1894.
$23^3/8$ x $31^1/8$ in./59.3 x 79 cm
Imp. F. Hermet, Paris
Cond A.
Ref (Both Var): Masters 1900, p. 41; PAI-XLII, 421
"Loïe Fuller's meteoric rise to fame is one of the oddest success stories of the 1890s. Coming from a small Midwestern town in the United States . . . she studied singing, dancing and acting . . . In one play, she noticed how the spotlights, with various color filters, created a rainbow effect on the material of her dress. Fascinated, she experimented with the effect, eventually working up a specialty dance wearing diaphanous materials on

which the colored lights played with dazzling results" (Gold, p. 116). Probably the rarest of at least five posters Pal created for Fuller's appearance—seen here with slight variations in text and colorization from the referenced poster—at the Folies-Bergère, which because it shows her virtually bare-breasted, is also the most sensuous. Pal wasn't the only one to go overboard about her—Toulouse-Lautrec did a whole series of lithographs trying to capture her dazzling terpsichorean show on paper, and many others took their turn.
Est: $4,000-$5,000.

477. L'Enlèvement de la Toledad. 1894.
$43^1/8$ x $58^1/4$ in./109.5 x 148 cm
Imp. Paul Dupont, Paris
Cond B+/Slight tears at folds.
Ref: Spectacle, 121; Reims, 935; PAI-XXIII, 416
The original moving force behind the Bouffes-Parisiens was Jacques Offenbach. Without competing directly with the Opéra Comique, he wanted to create a kind of theater that joined fantasy and burlesque. His first production opened in 1855 in the former offices of a doctor on the Champs-Elysées, but it took several moves and many years before the theater came to have real success—under the manager known only as Cantin who began staging operettas there around 1879. One of Cantin's most dependable composers was the talented Edmond Audran. "Unlike most of his contemporaries, who were survived by only one great hit . . . Audran left several" (*Operetta*, p. 90). He created *L'Enlèvement de la Toledad* (The Abduction of Toledad) in collaboration with lyricist Fabrice Carré. Pal's poster features its star (Juliette) Simon Girard (1859-1954), one of the lights of the French operetta world. She had made her career as the lead in *Les Cloches de Corneville*—perhaps the most popular French operetta ever written—and originated the role of Stella in the famed Offenbach-Carré work, *Les Contes d'Hoffman*. Here, Pal depicts Girard as Toledad with flashing eyes and swishing ruffles—enticement in every inch (no wonder she was abducted). The Reims catalogue indicates that Pal did a second poster for the production, showing cast members Félix Huguenet and Rosine Maurel "doing a popular Spanish dance."
Est: $1,400-$1,700.

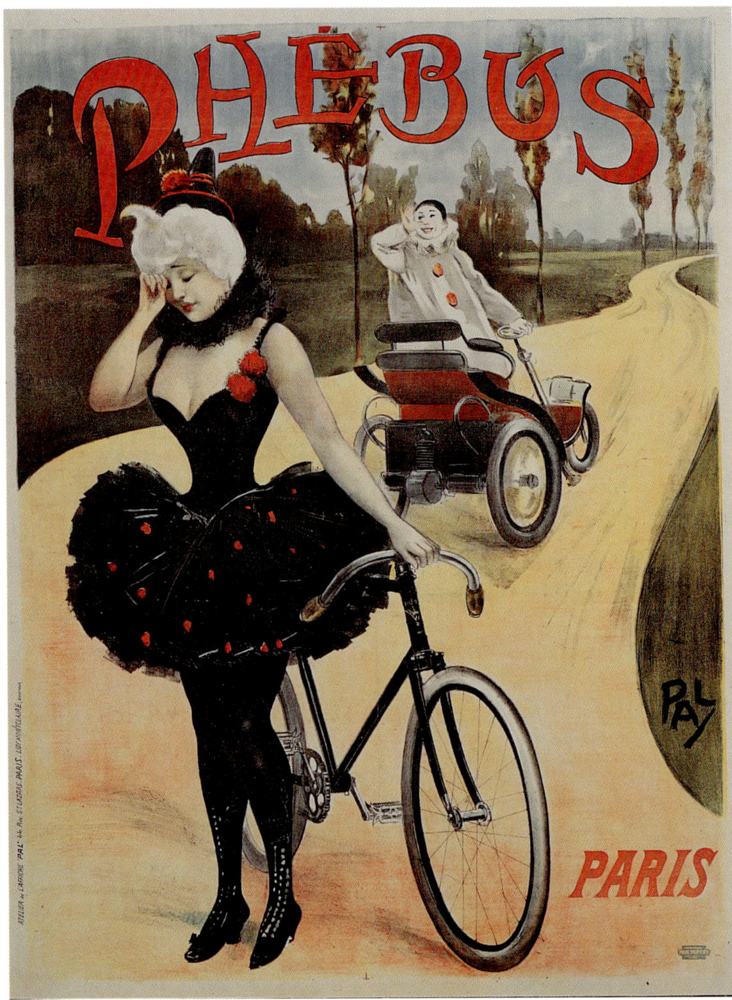

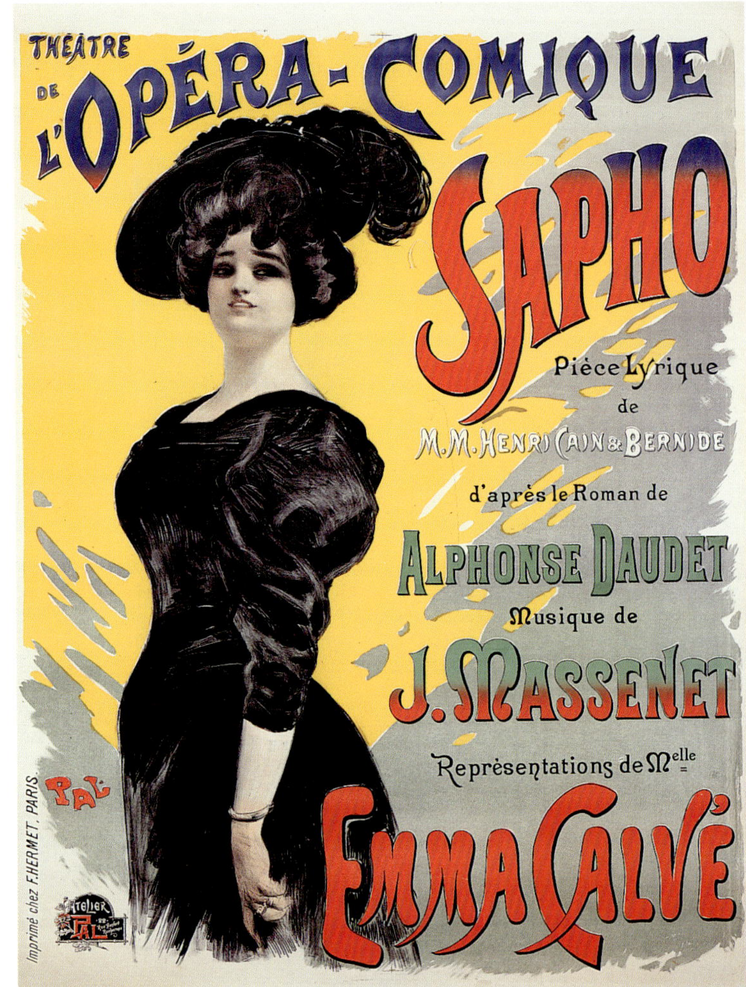

478

479

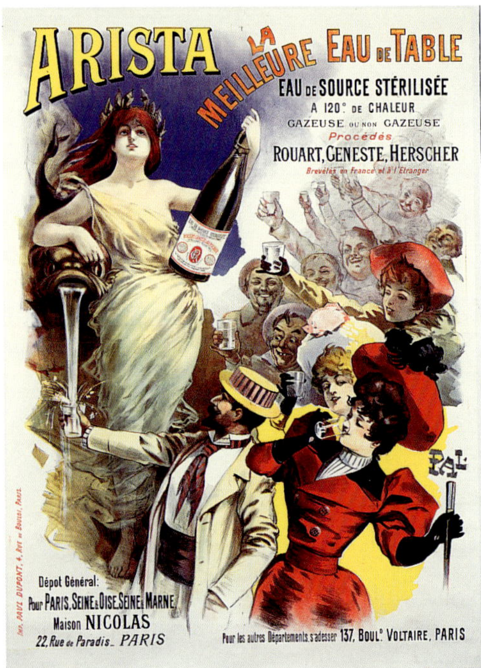

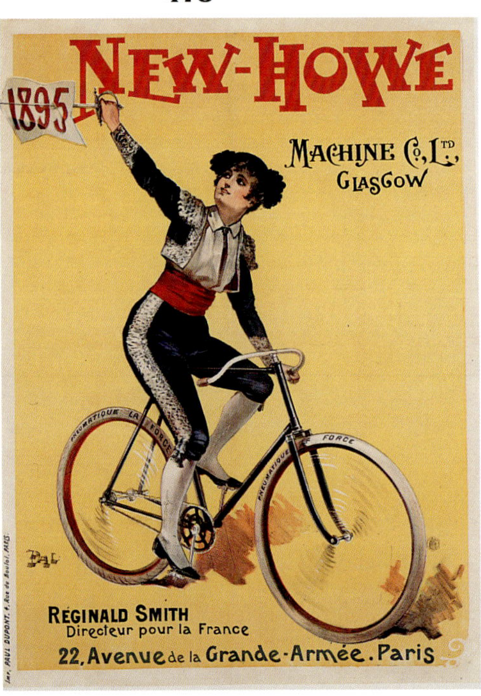

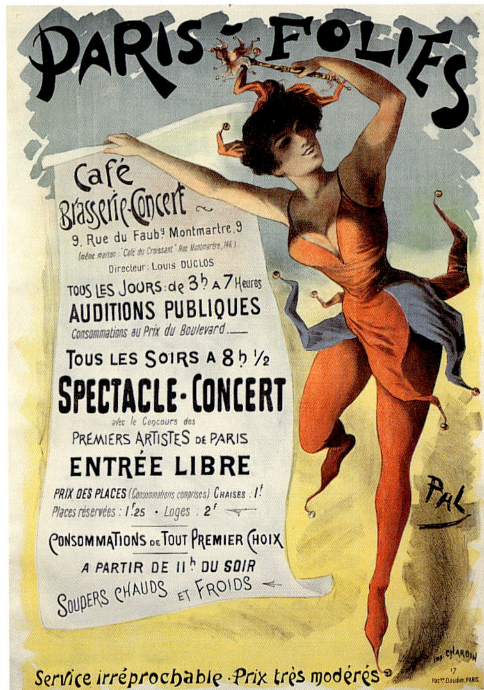

480

481

483

PAL (cont'd)

478. Phébus. ca. 1898.
43 x 57in./109 x 144.6 cm
Imp. Paul Dupont, Paris
Cond A–/Unobtrusive folds.
Ref: Petite Reine, 28; Collectionneur, p. 232; Pierrot,
69; PAL-XL, 53
A poignant scene on a deserted country road: the
female biker—from her get up one can only guess that
she's a circus trouper—has grown weary and dis-
mounted, so that the clown, who has presumably
been racing her in a motorized three-wheeler, was

able to overtake her. Far from sympathizing with her,
he's thumbing his nose at her in the flush of victory. A
peculiar, yet strangely appealing narrative for a brand
of bicycles—one in which Pal simply had to include
one of his charming women somehow!
Est: $5,000-$6,000.

479. L'Opéra Comique/Sapho/Emma Calvé. 1897.
39¼ x 53½ in./99.7 x 135.9 cm
Imp. F. Hermet, Paris
Cond B/Restored lower right margin; tears at bottom
edge.

Ref: Affiche Opéra, 52; PAI-XXXVII, 456
A smashing poster for the Massenet opera, "Sapho,"
starring the famed Emma Calvé, beautifully
designed—and decorously so in light of the potentially
salacious subject matter—by Pal. Colorfully audacious
lettering adds to the impact.
Est: $1,500-$1,800.

480. Arista.
41¾ x 58⅝ in./106 x 149 cm
Imp. Paul Dupont, Paris

482

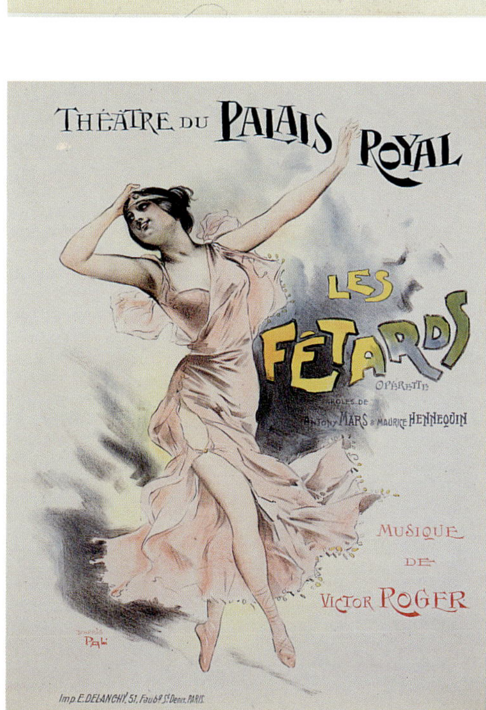

484

Cond B+/Unobtrusive tears at folds; image and colors
      excellent.
Ref: PAI-XL, 458
Seen in the full-text version, this alabaster nymph per-
sonifies the salutary properties of Arista mineral
water, as the water itself rushes forth from the seal-
faced fountain to the clamoring throng below.
Est: $1,700-$2,000.

481. New-Howe. 1895.
$41^3/4$ x $56^1/4$ in./106 x 142.7 cm
Imp. Paul Dupont, Paris
Cond B+/Slight tears at folds.
Ref: PAI-XXXIX, 430
Atop her pedal-powered steed, this breezy toreador
skewers a banner emblazoned with the year "1895,"
boldly staking the claim that this year belongs to the
New-Howe bicycle and no other. Exactly why Pal chose
to advertise a Scottish bike being sold in France with a
Spanish theme is a continental riddle probably best
left to the ages. It does, however, allow the artist once
more to inveigle a female into a design without seemingly any other reason than it never hurts to attach a
pretty face to an everyday product. And in the end, is
that such a bad thing? We think not.
Est: $1,700-$2,000.

482. Folies-Bergère/Tous les Soirs. ca. 1899.
$59^1/4$ x $43^3/8$ in./150.5 x 110.2 cm
Imp. Paul Dupont, Paris
Cond B+/Unobtrusive folds.
Ref: Gold, 147 (var); PAI-XXXVI, 483
"In the seven years Pal spent in Paris, the city's best
known music-hall availed itself of his services at least
a dozen times, recognizing his superior talent for showing women performers at their best. In this case, however, it's not the showgirls but the patrons who are being
used to attract customers. Elegant and apparently out
for the evening on their own, these two women assure
prospective visitors of the showplace's high repute"
(Gold, p. 103). *This is the rare larger format.*
Est: $8,000-$10,000.

483. Paris-Folies. ca. 1898.
$33^3/8$ x 49 in./85 x 124.5 cm
Imp. Chardin, Paris
Cond A–/Slight stains at paper edges.
Ref: PAI-XII, 355
It must have been a very busy café-concert: there were
public performances in the afternoon; in the evening
you got in free, but then paid one or two francs for a
seat, drink included, to see the show; hot and cold
suppers were served from 11 P.M. Most importantly,
the "Service is impeccable; very moderately priced."
Est: $1,500-$1,800.

484. Les Fêtards.
$23^7/8$ x $31^1/2$ in./60.6 x 80 cm
Imp. E. Delanchy, Paris
Cond A.
Ref: French Opera, 44; Spectacle, 673 (var);
      Gold, 160 (var); PAI-XXXVI, 478
"The Palais Royal was an early version of a shopping
mall—an arcade with a number of stores, a bistro or
two, and even a theater, which on this occasion was
presenting a light musical revue. Pal comes through,
as usual, with a delectable dancing damsel, obviously
one of the 'roisterers' of the title" (Gold, p. 112). This
is second edition of this design; the "d'après" designation denotes it as a printing based on Pal's initial design.
Est: $1,200-$1,500.

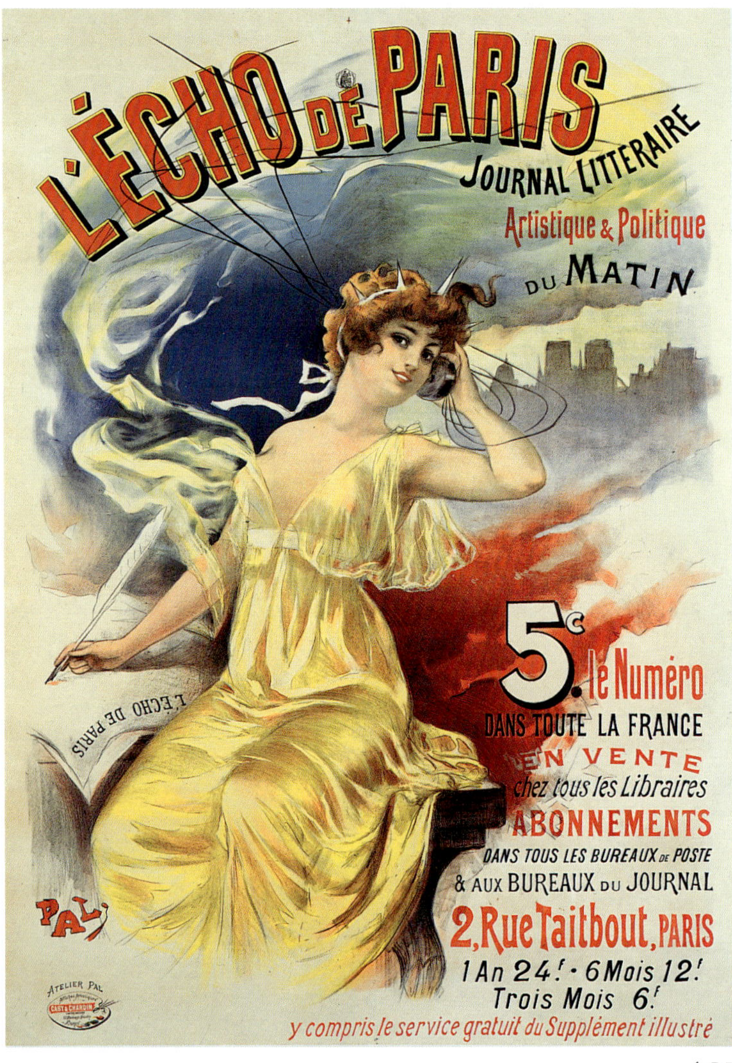

485

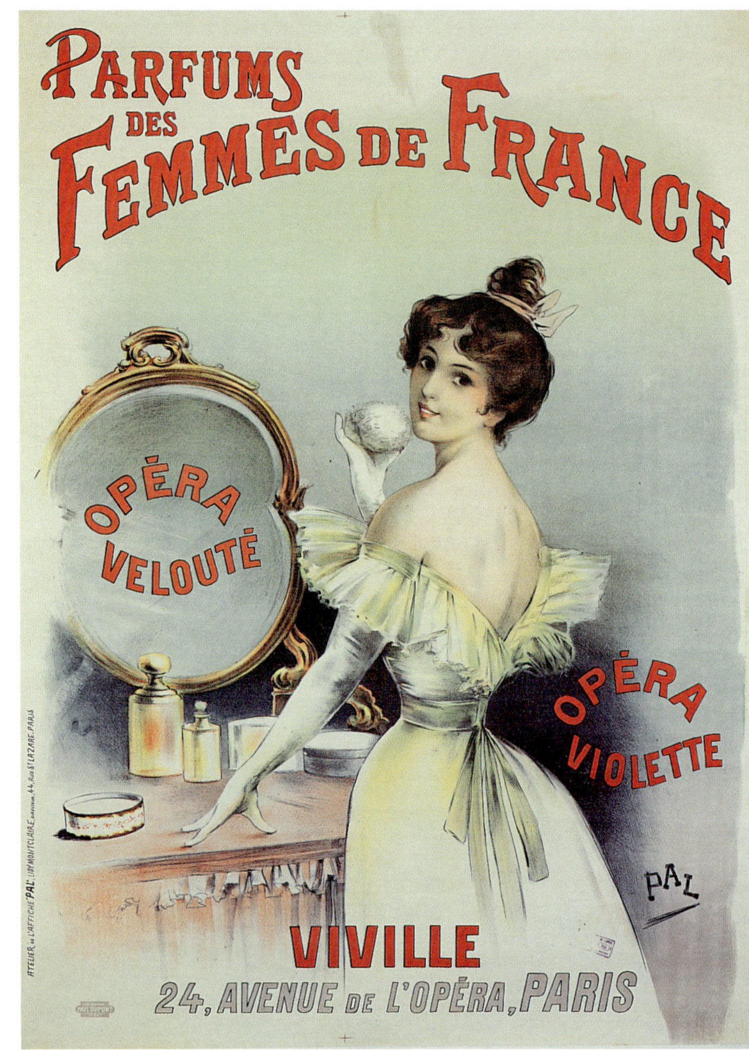

486

PAL (cont'd)

485. L'Echo de Paris. ca. 1899.
$43^1/2$ x $61^3/4$ in./110.5 x 157 cm
Imp. Caby & Chardin, Paris
Cond A-/Unobtrusive folds.
Ref: Fit to Print, 107; PAI-XXI, 362
One of Pal's divine creatures, togged-out in a filmy golden gown, takes plume in hand to transcribe the morning's literary, artistic and political news for this Paris newspaper. But one does have to wonder from which cloud her information comes from.
Est: $2,500-$3,000.

486. Parfums des Femmes de France. 1900.
36 x $51^1/8$ in./91.5 x 130 cm
Imp. Paul Dupont, Paris
Cond B/Slight tears and stains at edges.
Ref: PAI-XXXVI, 476
Pal was wont to embody anything in the form of a woman; here, he legitimately was promoting a product that made it all but unavoidable. But the one area in which Pal excels, even surpasses those considered to be the greatest posterists of all time, is the sheer accessibility of his women, who in their admittedly idealized form still appear breathtakingly attainable. At least that's what the gifted Pal wanted us to believe. For another treatment for the same perfume producers, *see PAI-XX, 355.*
Est: $1,700-$2,000.

487. Mrs. Harry Wilson.
$17^1/8$ x $22^3/8$ in./43.5 x 56.8 cm
Original hand-signed pastel. Framed.
A rather restrained vision of female pulchritude from Pal. Perhaps that might have something to do with the fact that he didn't want to make the wife of a friend look too much like a strumpet, seeing as he considered Mister Wilson a "pal," a detail that we learn from the lower-right hand dedication ("To Mrs. Harry Wilson from Pal—a pal of her husband"). Regardless of his motivation, Pal's pal's wife stands as a lovely, demure reminder of the artist's sincere appreciation of all things feminine.
Est: $8,000-$10,000.

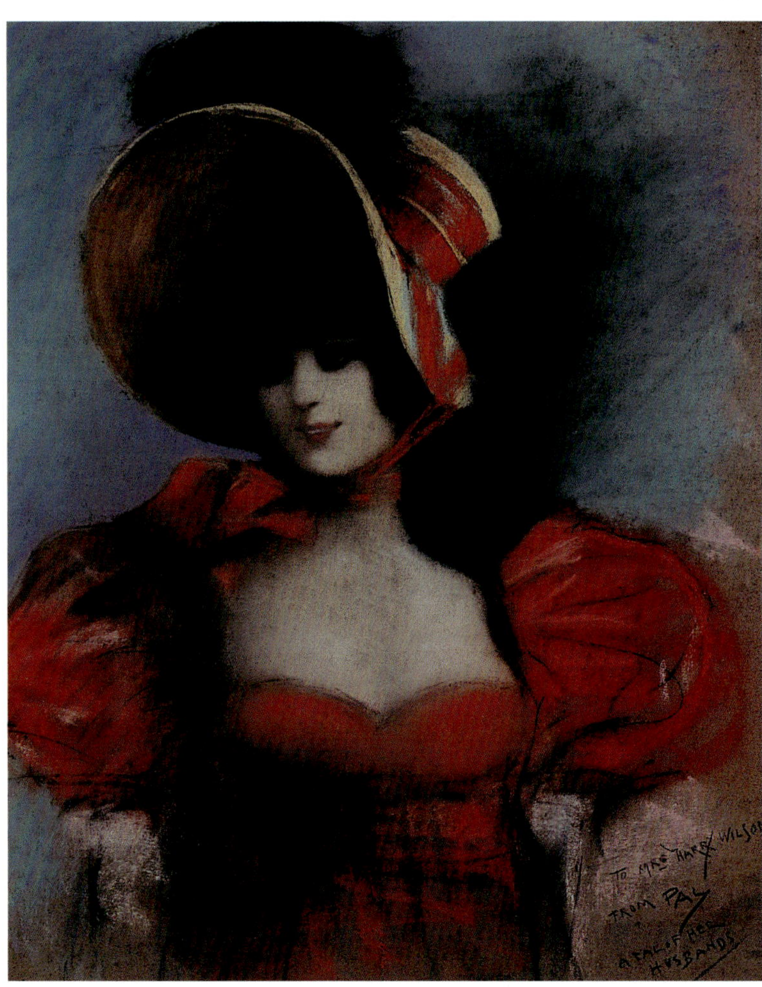

487

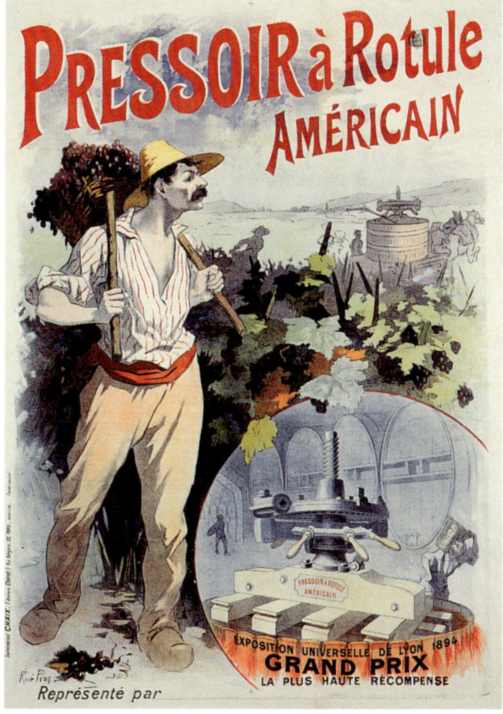

488

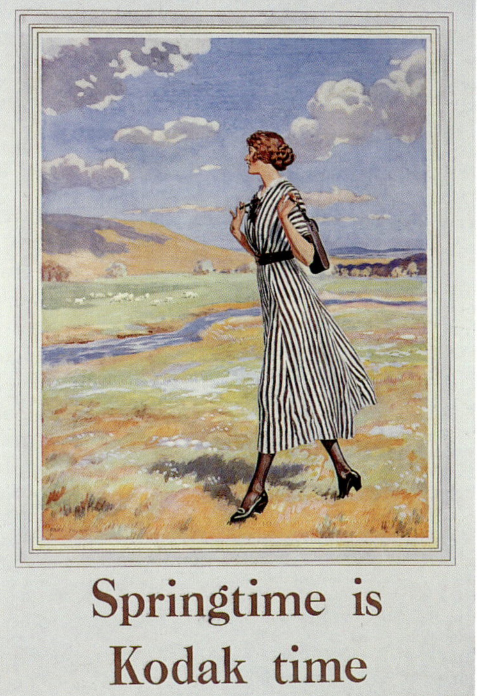

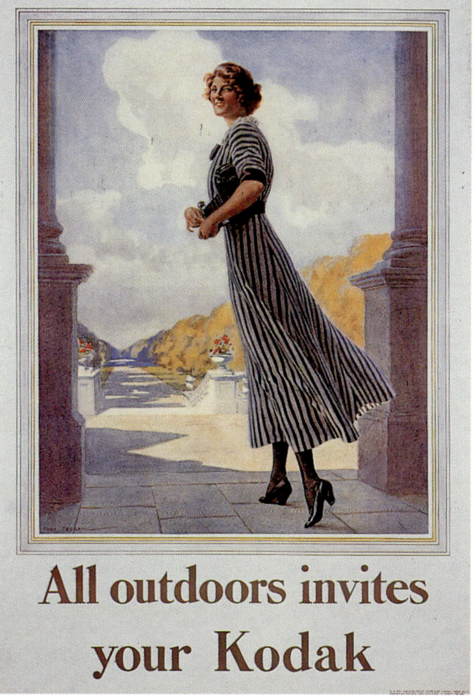

489

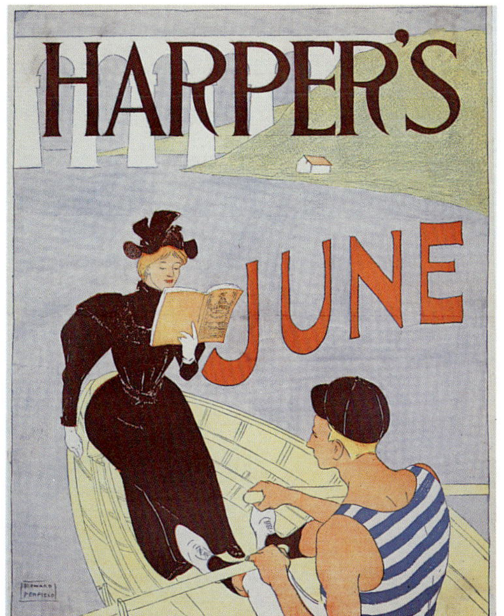
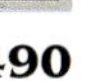

490

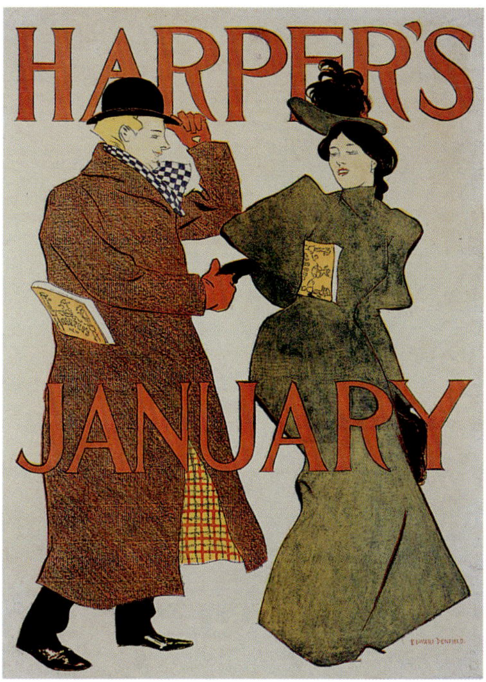

491

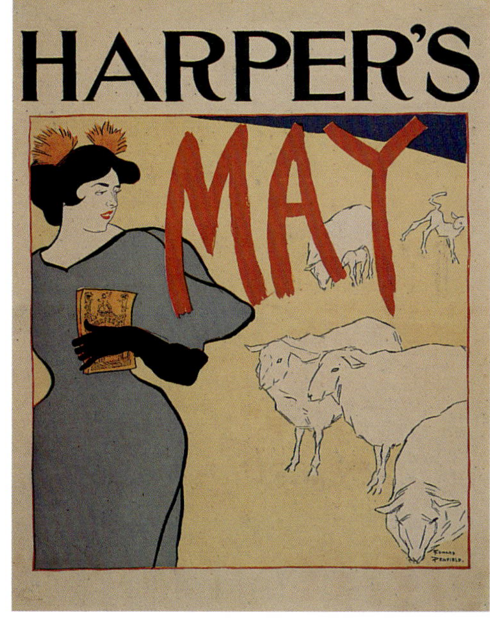

492

RENÉ PÉAN (1875-1940)

488. Pressoir à Rotule Américain. 1895.
33⁷/₈ x 48⁵/₈ in./86 x 123.6 cm
Imp. Chaix, Paris
Cond A–/Unobtrusive folds.
Péan delivers an unexpectedly wistful advertisement for an American ball-joint wine press that, though ultimately provincial in nature, doesn't shy away from its industrial side. Péan was a pupil of Chéret, working under him at the Chaix printing firm. He specialized in theater and cabaret posters from around 1890 to 1905. After being among the first to produce posters for the fledgling movie industry, he faded into obscurity.
Est: $1,700-$2,000.

FRED PEGRAM (1870-1937)

489. Kodak: Two Posters.
Each: 20 x 30¹/₄ in./50.8 x 76.8 cm
Henry Stone, Banbury
Cond A–/Slight tears at paper edges.
With a spring in her step, there's nowhere the "Kodak Girl" won't go for a gripping pic, especially if that potential photo op features nature in all its glory. In

fact, the text on one of these posters sums up Pegram's approach succinctly: "All outdoors invites your Kodak." Though he doesn't stray far afield from the Lelong parameter (*see* No. 394)—striped dress, profile pose, camera in-hand—Pegram has no qualms about making his "Girl" a liberated, on-the-go figure, capable of discovering photogenic moments all by herself. A native of London, Pegram is most recognized for his book illustrations and etchings.
Est: $1,700-$2,000. (2)

EDWARD PENFIELD (1866-1925)

490. Harper's/June. 1894.
12⁷/₈ x 16⁵/₈ in./33 x 42.2 cm
Cond B/Slight tears and stains, largely at edges.
Ref: DFP-I, 333; Lauder, 150; PAI-XXV, 453b
Summer reading, one of life's little pleasures, gets the Penfield treatment for *Harper's*. And though black may not be the ideal color to refract the summer sun, this rapt reader does have the luxury of being nothing more than a passenger on this rowboat excursion.
Posters from the 1894 series are exceedingly rare.
Est: $1,200-$1,500.

491. Harper's/January. 1895.
12⁷/₈ x 18 in./32.7 x 45.6 cm
Cond B+/Unobtrusive tears at edges.
Ref: DFP-I, 340; Reims, 1257; Lauder, 161;
    PAI-XXXVI, 498
Penfield is one of America's premier posterists. For a ten-year period, from 1891 to 1901, he was an art director at *Harper's*, and from 1893 he produced a series of monthly posters for its magazine. These were largely used as in-store displays for bookshops as well as newsstands. Most are deliciously irrelevant; all are interesting. Here, a copy of the magazine carried by the woman appears to be sufficient grounds to facilitate an introduction.
Est: $1,000-$1,200.

492. Harper's/May. 1895.
13 x 16⁵/₈ in./33 x 42 cm
Cond B+/Slight tears and stains, largely at paper edges.
Ref: DFP-I, 344; Reims, 1261; Lauder, 165;
    Margolin, p. 66; Keay, p. 80; PAI-XL, 463
This May lass clutches her *Harper's* in defense against the wanton appetites of approaching ruminants.
Est: $800-$1,000.

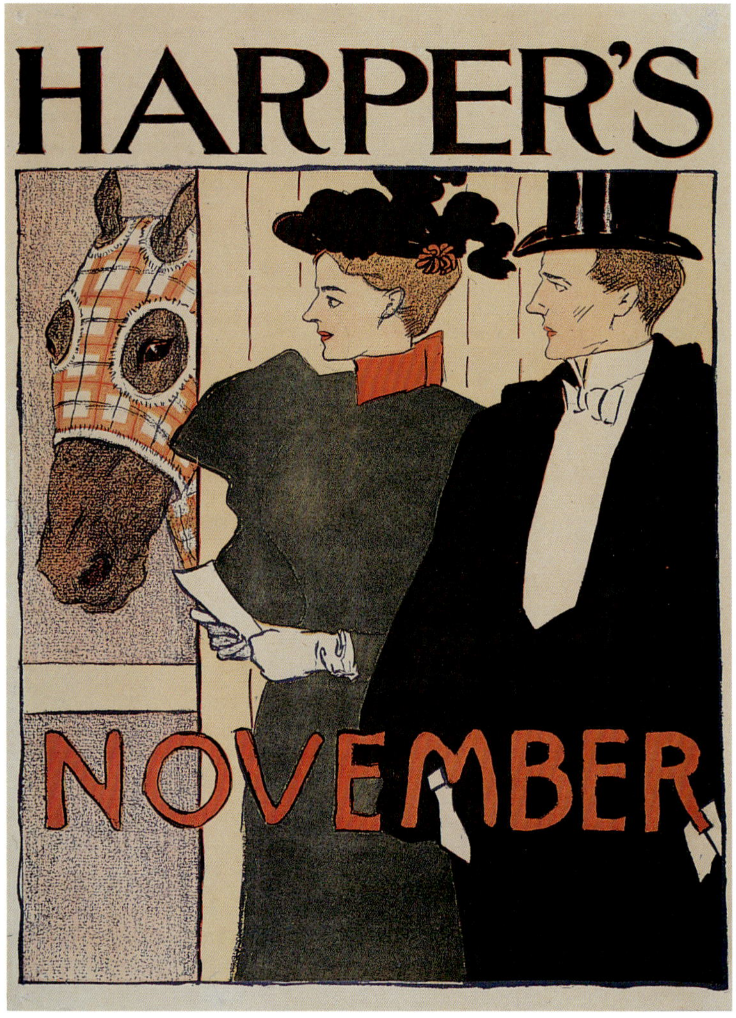

494

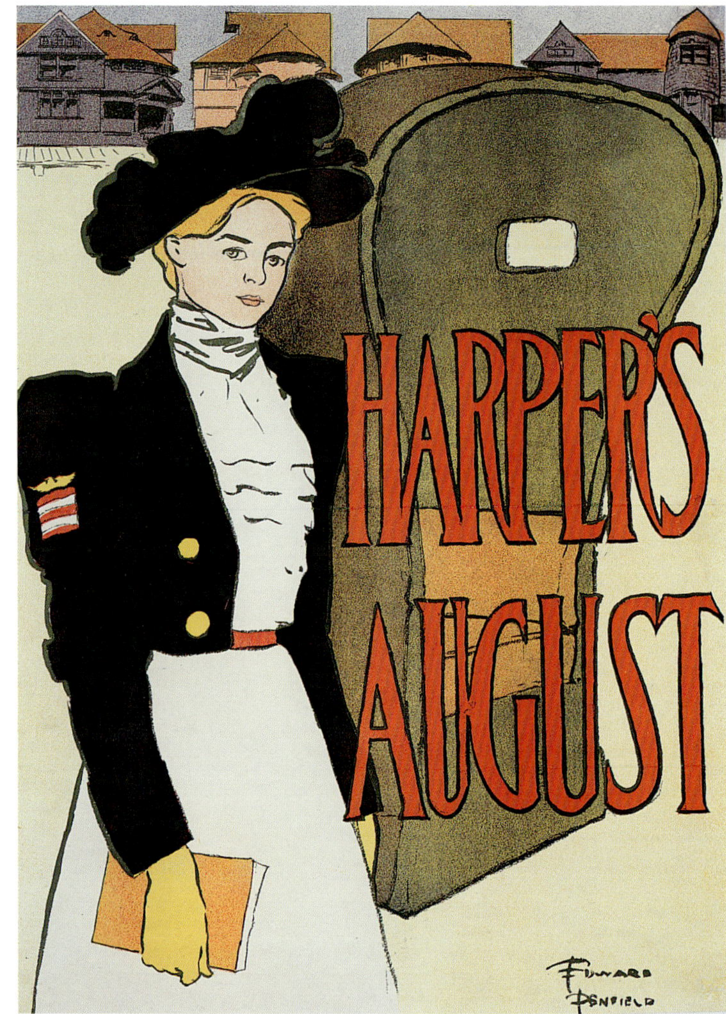

497

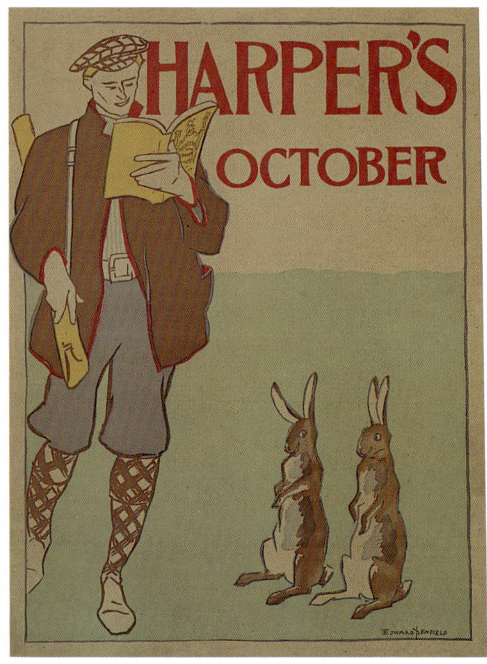

493

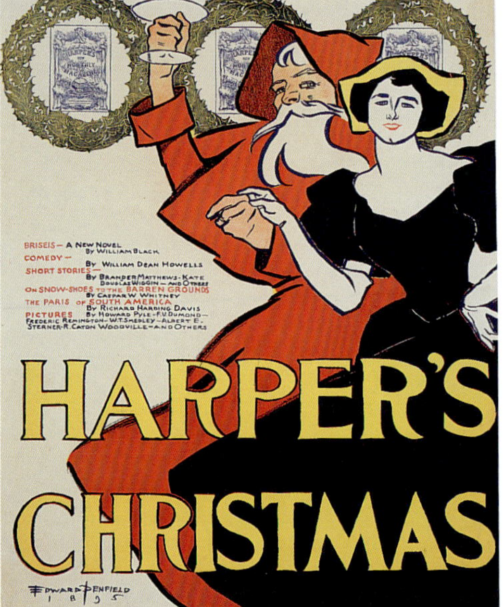

495

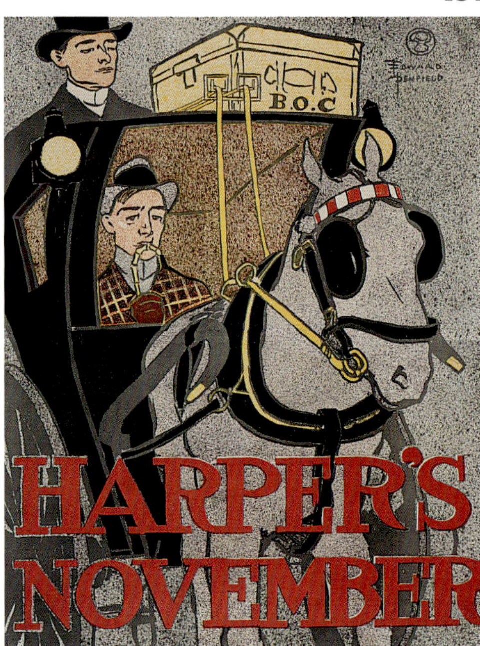

496

EDWARD PENFIELD (cont'd)

493. Harper's/October. 1895.
$11^1/8$ x $15^1/8$ in./28.2 x 38.5 cm
Cond A–/Slight tears at paper edges.
Ref: DFP-I, 349; Reims, 1266; Lauder, 170;
    PAI-XXXIV, 106
Fear not, fluffy bunnies. No season is ever hunting season with a *Harper's* in hand.
Est: $800-$1,000.

494. Harper's/November. 1895.
$11^7/8$ x $16^1/4$ in./30 x 41.3 cm
Cond A–/Unobtrusive tears at corners.
Ref: DFP-I, 350; Lauder, 171; Reims, 1267; PAI-XL, 464

Here, an elegant couple appraises a thoroughbred—as always a subtle suggestion that people of breeding read the magazine.
Est: $1,200-$1,500.

495. Harper's/Christmas. 1895.
20 x $25^1/8$ in./51 x 64 cm
Cond A–/Unobtrusive horizontal fold.
Ref: DFP-I, 351; Reims, 1268; Lauder, 172;
    PAI-XXXIV, 108
One of the few posters in the *Harper's* series with the contents spelled out; note that Howard Pyle and Frederick Remington are among the contributors in the "Picture" section.
Est: $1,200-$1,500.

496. Harper's/November. 1896.
$13^1/2$ x $17^7/8$ in./34.3 x 45.4 cm
Cond B+/Tears along horizontal fold.
Ref: DFP-I, 362; Lauder, 186; PAI-XXXV, 444
No matter what thoughts this pensive gentleman is preoccupied with, Penfield makes it clear that that the magazine's readers are top-drawer.
Est: $1,200-$1,500.

497. Harper's/August. 1897.
$13^1/4$ x $18^1/2$ in./33.6 x 47.1 cm
Cond B+/Unobtrusive tears along horizontal fold and
    corners.

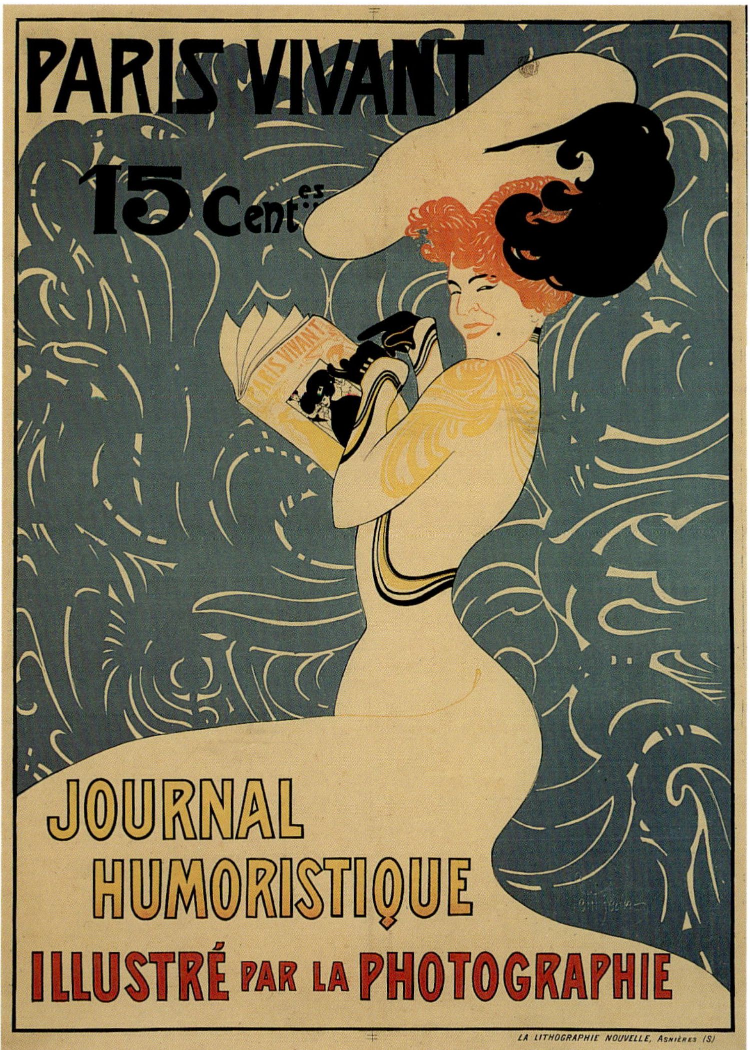

499

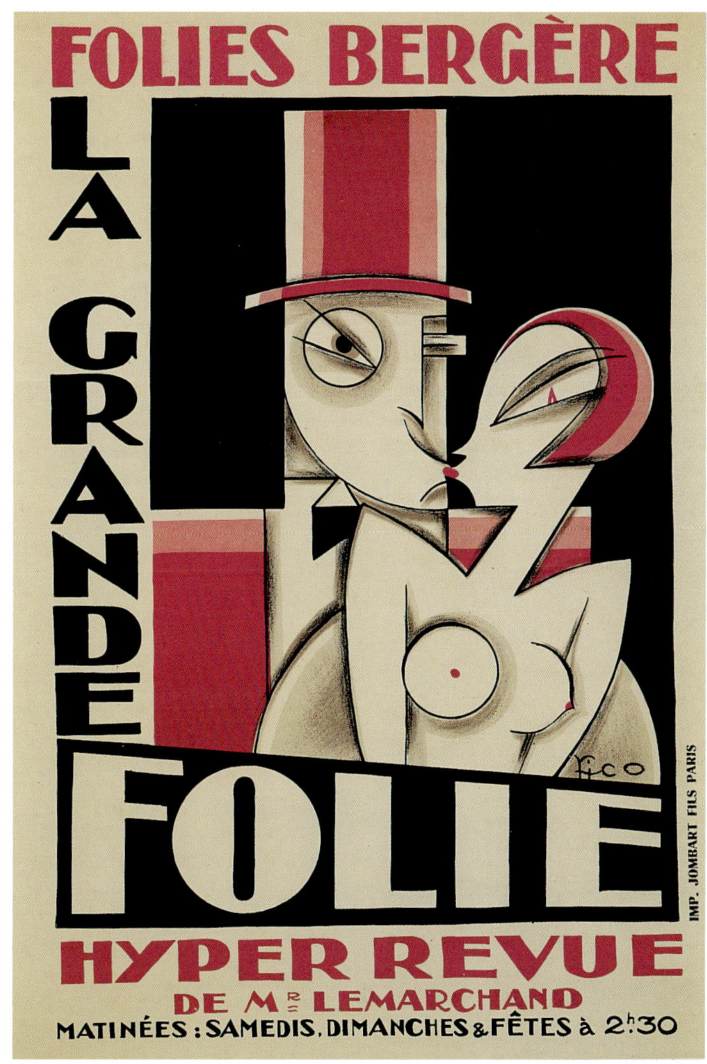

500

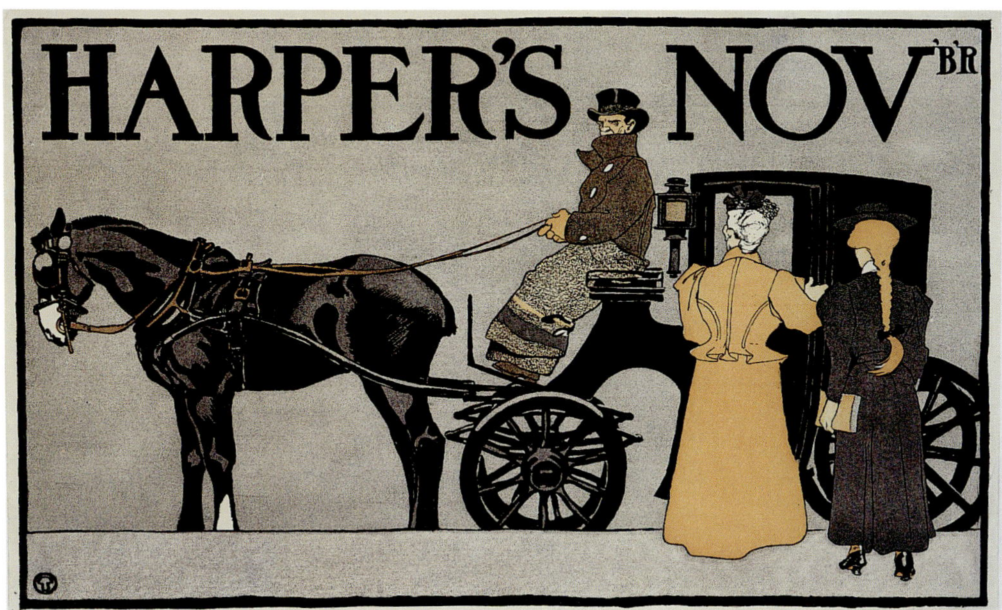

498

EDMOND M. PETITJEAN (1844-1925)

499. Paris Vivant.
$41^3/8$ x $58^1/2$ in./105.2 x 148.7 cm
La Lithographie Nouvelle, Asnières
Cond B+/Slight tears and stains, largely at folds.
Ref: PAI-XXVIII, 490
Petitjean was an oft-exhibited landscape painter whose
work won him numerous jury prizes, election to the
Legion of Honor in 1892 and a place in the permanent
collections of museums throughout France. In what we
suspect was a rare foray into graphic art, he created
this poster for the Parisian humor magazine, graced by
a reader who is obviously tickled by its contents. Petitjean certainly knew whom to emulate: the serpentine
forms and caricaturistic treatment of the face show his
admiration for Aubrey Beardsley and the early work of
Cappiello.
Est: $2,000-$2,500.

PICO

500. Folies-Bergère/La Grande Folie. ca. 1927.
$13^3/4$ x $20^5/8$ in./35 x 52.5 cm
Imp. Jombart Fils, Paris
Cond A.
Ref: Folies-Bergère, 89 (var); PAI-XLII, 435
"'La Grande Folie' (The Great Folly) remained faithful
to Paul Derval's principles: a title of thirteen letters, the
same number as all his other revues, lavish decors and
costumes but no superstar. The poster on the other
hand is surprising. The Folies rarely produced anything
as 'art deco-ish' (and it is difficult to imagine anything
more art-deco in style than this poster!). The image of
this couple embracing, where we discover, as if in a
cocktail, a mixture of cubism, some of Halouze's style
and some of Colin's, appears to be a 'practical work'
of the 1920's . . . The letters, the people, are hurled
into our faces with a bluntness that is a far cry from
the mannered elegance of most music hall posters"
(Folies-Bergère, p. 13).
Est: $7,000-$9,000.

Ref: DFP-I, 381; Lauder, 199; PAI-XXIII, 423
A young woman prepares to occupy a beach chair with
her copy of *Harper's* for company. An interesting look
at seaside attire (stifling) and architecture (turreted
boxes) of the 1890s.
Est: $1,200-$1,500.

498. Harper's/November. 1898.
$18^1/2$x $11^1/2$ in./47.2 x 29.3 cm
Cond B/Unobtrusive tears at edges and top text.
Ref: DFP-I, 396; Lauder, 216; PAI-XX, 376

Though most of the *Harper's* posters tend to place the
spotlight on the goings-on of the upwardly mobile, Penfield could slyly inject a bit of humor with the inclusion
of a working class stiff who didn't wholly appreciate
these shenanigans. Case in point, this coachman with
the less-than-accommodating expression. The power
of the design comes from its unspoken narrative and a
curiosity as to what could have transpired to put that
puss on his face.
Est: $1,400-$1,700.

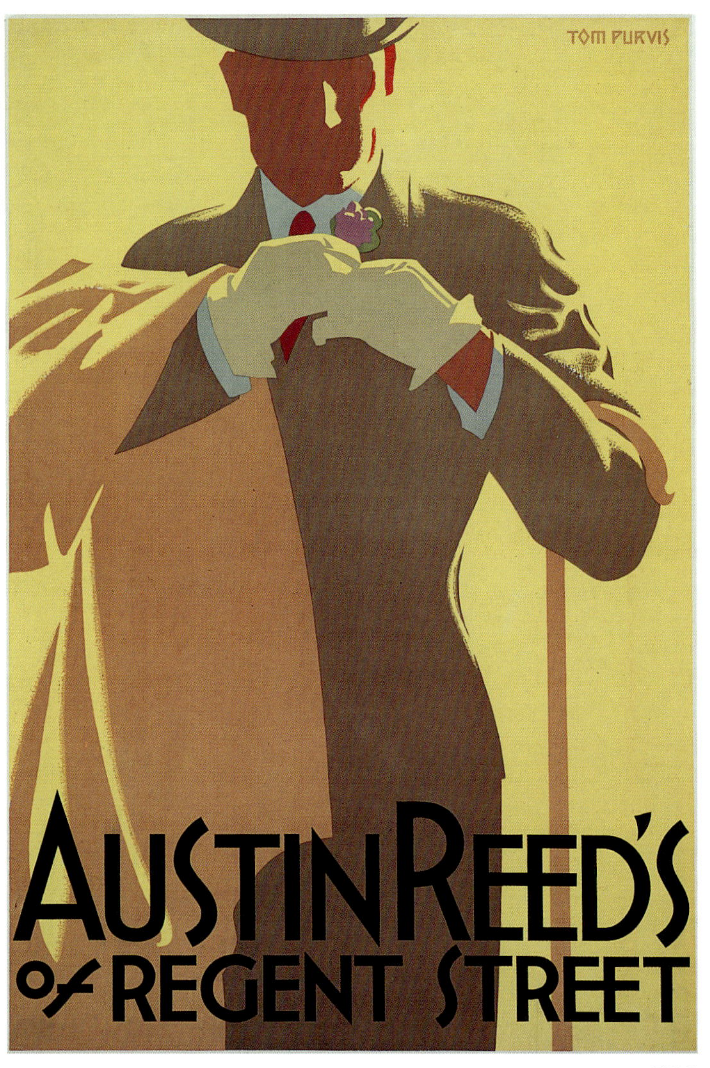

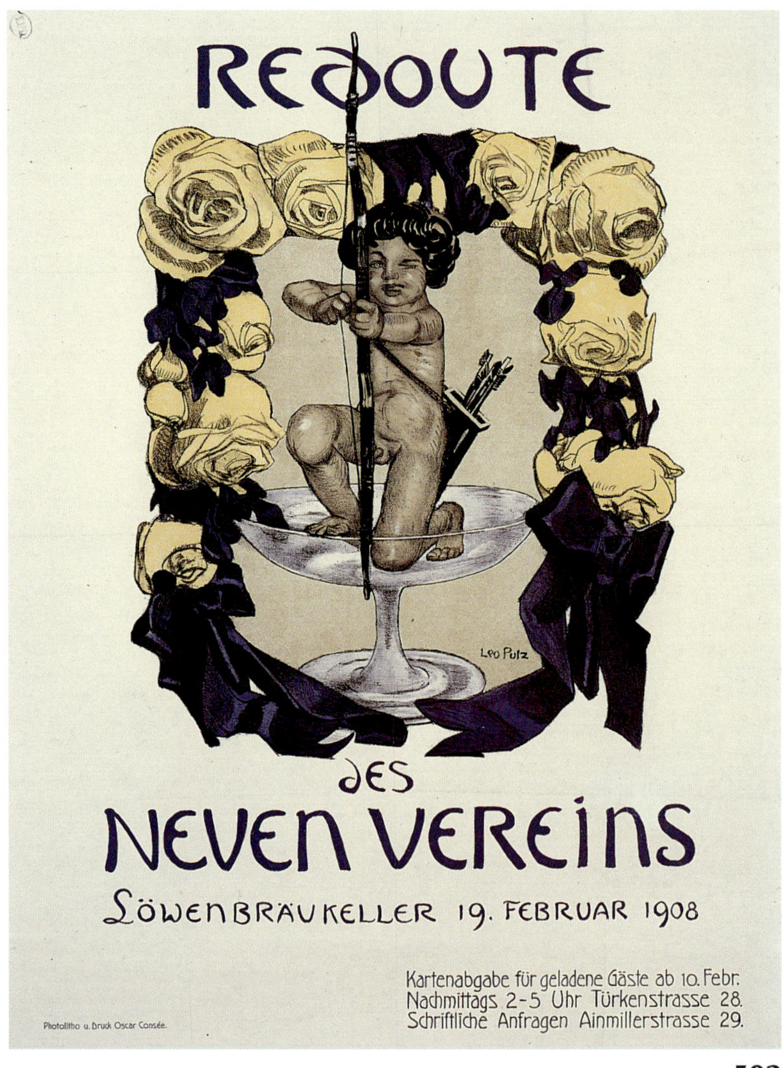

501

502

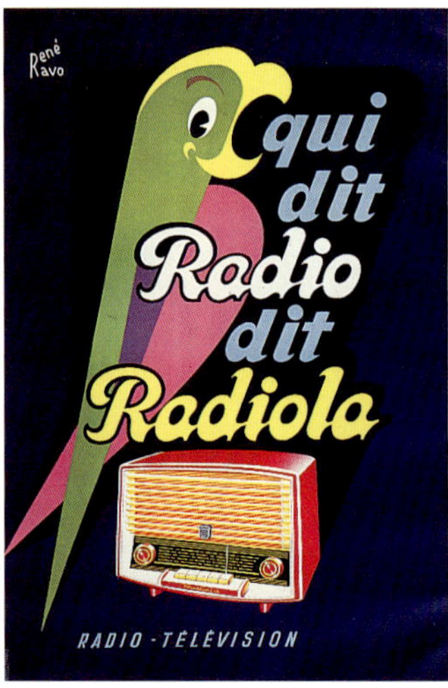

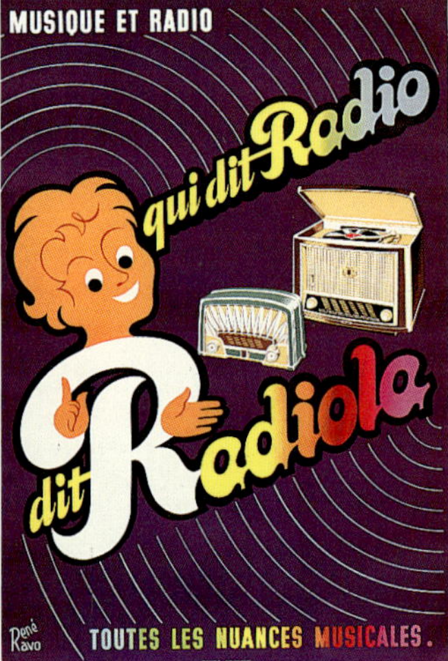

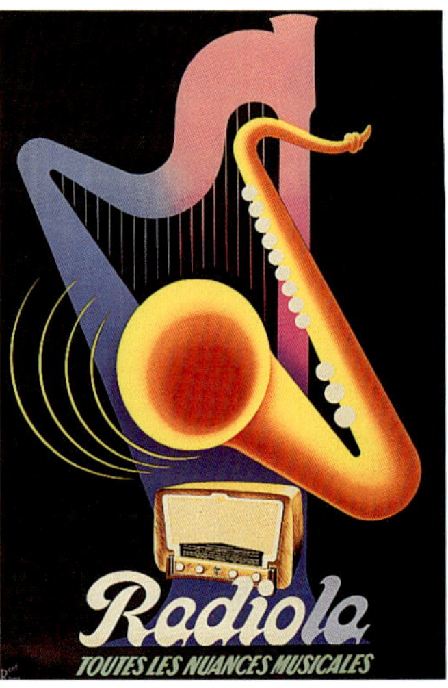

505

TOM PURVIS (1888-1959)

501. Austin Reed.
19³/₄ x 29⁵/₈ in./50 x 75.2 cm
Cond B+/Slight tears at bottom paper edge. Framed.
Though somewhat less formal than another poster he
created for Austin Reed of Regent Street (*see* PAI-XVIII,
414), Purvis doesn't fail to communicate the clothier's
impeccable sense of style in this design that not only
features a fashion sense to which all gentlemen should
aspire, but sumptuous fabric folds and creases that all
but beg to be felt firsthand. Best known for his British
railway posters, the artist ranks among the best of all
posterists working between the Wars, making dramatic
impact with his use of flat colors and simplified design.
Est: $1,500-$1,800.

LEO PUTZ (1869-1940)

502. Redoute de Neven Vereins. 1908.
28⁷/₈ x 38¹/₈ in./73.3 x 97 cm
Oscar Consée (München)
Cond B+/Unobtrusive folds.
Ref: DFP-III, 2614; Plakate München, 193
His credentials are impeccable: studies at the Munich
Academy and at the Julian in Paris; member of the
Secession in Berlin, Vienna and Munich, work on the
Jugend. Most active as a painter, Putz nevertheless
produced a few posters, such as this rosy little num-
ber for a gala whose proximity to Valentine's Day still
allows its Cupid to directly take aim at the heart of the
viewer. The design was also used as a title page in *Der
Jugend* that same year.
Est: $1,700-$2,000.

LESLIE RAGAN (1897-1972)

**503. New York Central System/For the Public
Service.** 1946.
15⁷/₈ x 21¹/₄ in./40.3 x 54 cm
Cond A–/Slight tears at edges.
Ref: PAI-XXXVIII, 506
In 1867, American railroad magnate, Cornelius Vander-
bilt, became president of the New York Central Railroad
and through a series of mergers, formed the New York
Central and Hudson River Railroad. By 1930, having
absorbed other large rail companies and reverted back
to its original name, the New York Central was one of
the leading lines connecting the Eastern seaboard with
Midwestern cities. This powerful image, set at Chicago's
La Salle Street Station with the Ceres-topped Board of
Trade Building towering in the background, proudly
displays each engine model of the Central fleet, from
the old-fashioned steam engine to the post-war marvel
of the Diesel and the Streamlined Steam marvel, The
Twentieth Century Limited, designed by Henry Dreyfus,
its front crest actually inspired by the Mohawk haircut.
An inspired Ragan design that promotes both the glitz
of passenger service and the bread-and-butter of the
freight lines.
Est: $3,000-$3,500.

**504. New York Central System/The Century in the
Highlands of the Hudson.** ca. 1938.
16 x 21¹/₄ in./40.6 x 54 cm
Cond A.
Ref: PAI-XXXIX, 486
Cognizant of the fact that superior graphics can be
transplanted into different surroundings with an equally
stunning impact, Ragan transposed his streamlined
locomotive previously seen on the banks of the Hudson
(*see* PAI-XXXVIII, 504) into the autumnal splendor of
the Hudson Highlands. Very few changes have been
made to the *20th Century*—the design was also used
as a calendar—but the change in location highlights
the technological marvel of design and transportation
as it simultaneously generates a panoramic reason to
ride the rails.
Est: $3,000-$3,500.

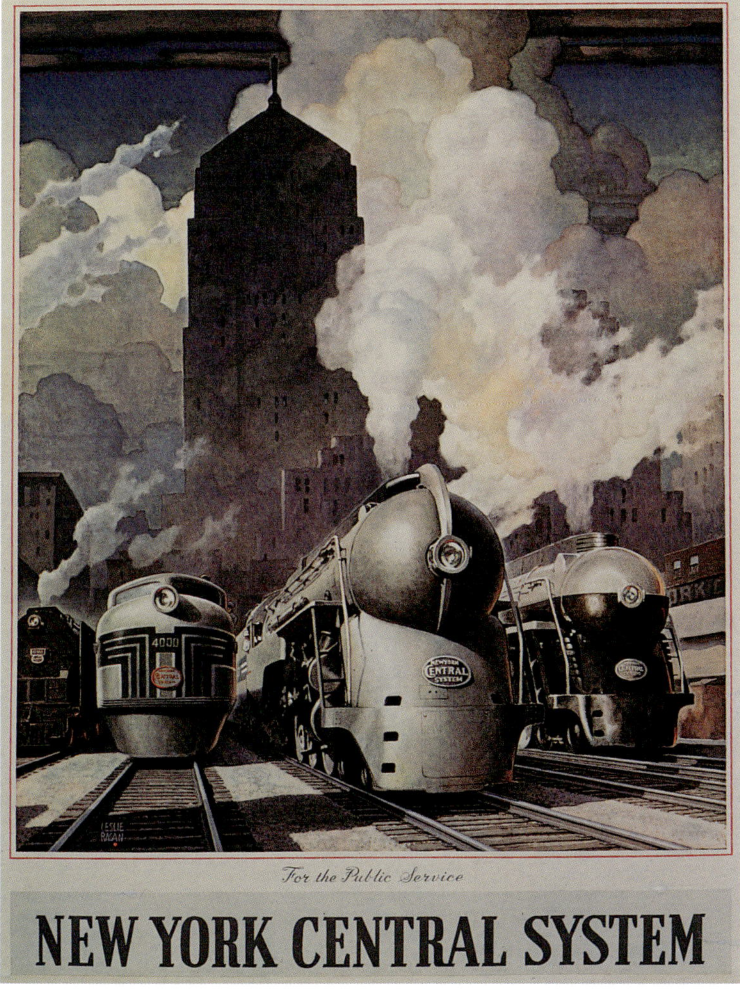

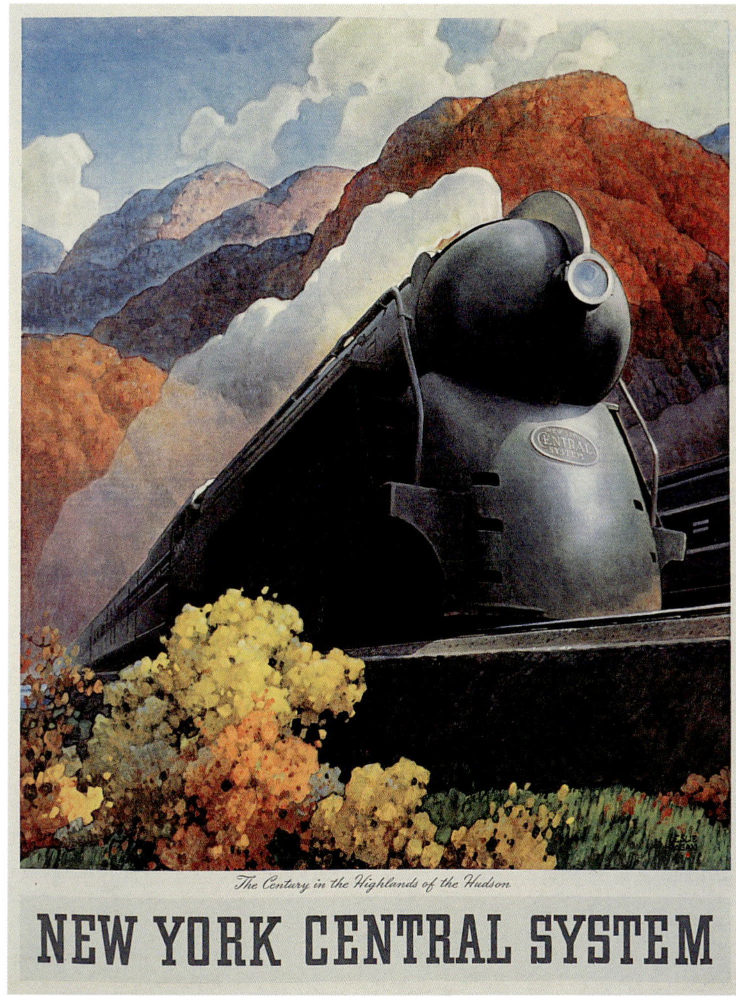

503

504

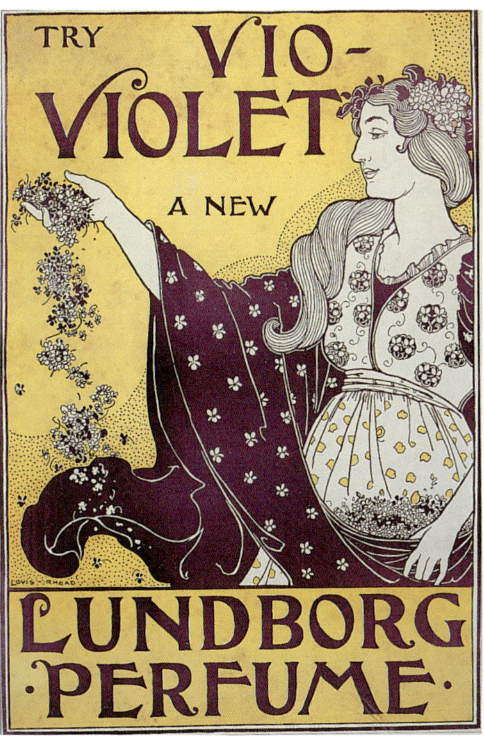

506

507

RENÉ RAVO (1904-1998)

505. Radiola: Three Posters.
Each: 30^1/$_8$ x 45^5/$_8$ in./76.5 x 115.8 cm
Imp. Bedos, Paris
Cond A–/Slight tears at edges.
Ref: PAI-XXIX, 590 (c only)
As their name implies, Radiola was a brand of equipment that produced tubes, sets and the like for both television and radio reception. This trio of Ravo promotions for the company utilizes soothing prismatic composition along with two catch phrases—"When you say radio you say Radiola" being the most clever—to relay that their products deliver all the musical goods for which one could ever wish. Whether they call upon the services of a squawking parrot, a humanized "R" or a pair of contrasting instruments, it's perfectly clear that the nuanced technology of wireless transmission comes across best on a Radiola.
Est: $2,000-$2,500. (3)

LOUIS J. RHEAD (1858-1926)

506. Lundborg Perfume/Vio-Violet. 1895.
11 x 16^1/$_2$ in./28 x 42 cm
Cond B+/Slight staining in text areas; tears in top margin.
Ref: DFP-I, 459; PAI-XIX, 472c
An illustrator and decorator, Rhead came to the United States from England in 1883 and forged an active career designing posters for publications and other clients. He was heavily influenced by Grasset, whom he admired and met while in Paris. He was just as popular in Europe as in the United States, and his posters formed a major body of work in all the leading poster exhibitions in England, France and Germany during this period. He created several posters for Lundborg Perfumes, the relation of the product to its floral origins depicted quite literally in very rare, delicately conceived designs. Here, for Vio-Violet, a lavender Byzantine princess scatters a handful of namesake blossoms, captured in the sweet melancholy of the moment.
Est: $1,000-$1,200.

507. The Gentlewoman. 1895.
19^3/$_4$ x 29^5/$_8$ in./50.2 x 75.2 cm
Marlborough, Pewiress Lith., London
Cond B+/Unobtrusive tears at folds and edges.
Ref: DFP-I, 469 (var); PAI-I, 57
This stock poster design, used for several years by this publication, features a woman in a red dress with flowing blonde hair. Today, it's one of Rhead's rarest designs. Published in London between 1890 and 1926, when it was merged with "Eve," this magazine reached a huge circulation of 250,000 by the mid-1890s. One of their announcements makes their formula for success quite clear: "Astute advertisers will observe *The Gentlewoman* is bought by women and read by women, and as women spend nine-tenths of what men earn, the moral is obvious."
Est: $1,000-$1,200.

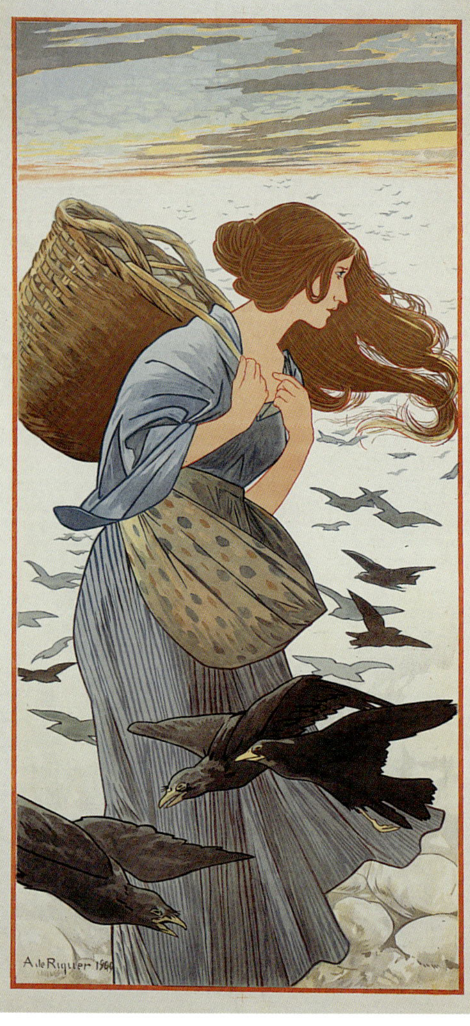

509

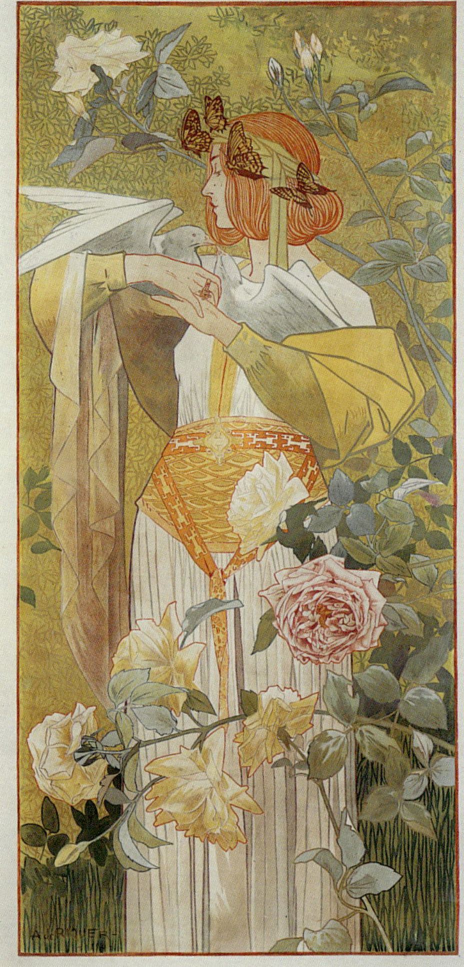

510

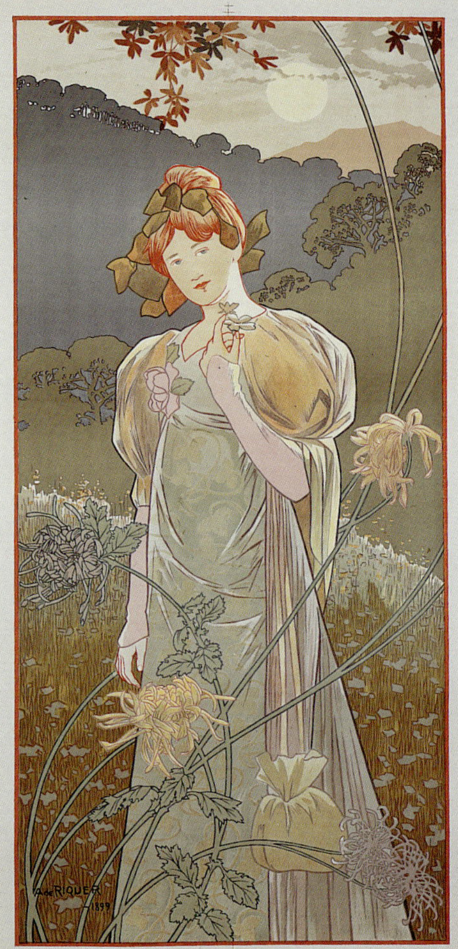

511

LOBEL RICHER

508. Peugeot Bycles.
44$^1/_2$ x 58$^1/_2$ in./113 x 148.5 cm
Affiches Camis, Paris
Cond B–/Restored tears at folds.
Ref: Ailes, p. 95
"At the end of the XIXth century, terrestrial transport was the prerogative of the railroad, which represented speed, luxury, comfort and safety. Illustrators sometimes used railway themes, taking on or opposing these characteristics on behalf of the cycles, as this poster . . . is an example, the quantity of energy spent by the steam engine played-off of the apparent displacement facility of the bicycle. While the smiling foreground couple glides by on the road, one sees, rejected in the background, an engine climbing a steep slope. A plume of smokes testifies to the effort being produced by the engine, and the gleaming vapor emitting from the cabin makes one think that the engine is continually being stoked. In this twilight environment, the color being cast by the woman's Venetian lantern echoes the reddening reflections of the engine . . . If the representation of the bicycles and the differences between the men's and women's models are well looked after, the drawing of the engine, apparently of type 120, is on the other hand whimsical. One identifies, however, that this idealized steam engine has many of the elemental characteristics associated with the PLM speed machines: the wind-cutter smokestack, the *hirondelle* cabin and large-diameter drive wheels masked by wheel covers on which one distinguishes the prestigious company's initials" (Ailes, p. 94).
Est: $1,500-$1,800.

ALEJANDRO DE RIQUER (1856-1920)

509. The Seasons/Winter. 1900.
21$^7/_8$ x 45$^3/_4$ in./55.5 x 116.2 cm
Cond B+/Slight tears at folds and edges.
Ref: PAI-IV, 257 (var)
De Riquer embodied the harshest season of year with a windswept brunette, hefting her basket through a barren land as crows swoop about her. Though the artwork isn't overly dramatic, a certain desperation and

chill pervades the design, a far cry from the snugly, bird-warming vision of winter presented by Mucha (*see* PAI-XXXVI, 444). Writing the year after the publication of this lithographic panel set, British critic Rogers made these comments about the artist: "Of Spanish placardists, undoubtedly A. de Riquer stands first. He has produced more work than any of his countrymen, and that all of the best quality. His posters have the important qualities of strong decorative effect, cleverness and originality in colour scheme, and of delicate and pleasing line" (p. 71).
Est: $1,700-$2,000.

510. The Seasons/Summer. 1900.
21$^7/_8$ x 45$^3/_8$ in./55.5 x 115.3 cm
Cond B/Several restored tears; recreated margins; image and colors excellent.
Ref: PAI-IV, 257 (var)
Gentle and genteel, "Summer" is so thoroughly integrated into her sultry halcyon environs that even the most skittish of creatures are drawn to the safe haven of her bosom. Beginning in 1879, the artist traveled widely, from Rome to Paris to London. He became associated with the Arts & Crafts Movement, inspired by William Morris, becoming a protégé of Walter Crane, who admired his attempts to enhance the esthetic value of industrial design, such as window displays, textiles and books. He worked as an illustrator, art director of publications and graphic designer, becoming one of the foremost graphic art stylists and innovators of the Art Nouveau movement upon on his return to Spain. De Riquer is particularly well-known for his engravings of ex libris, a specialty which he introduced practically single-handed to his native Catalonia.
Est: $2,500.-$3,000.

511. The Seasons/Spring. 1900.
22$^5/_8$ x 46 in./57.5 x 117 cm
Cond A.
Ref: PAI-IV, 257 (var)
Writing specifically about this 1900 seasonal panel series, Rogers states that "In Spain, de Riquer has executed some charming decorative panels, which are worthy to rank with the best efforts of Mucha. The set

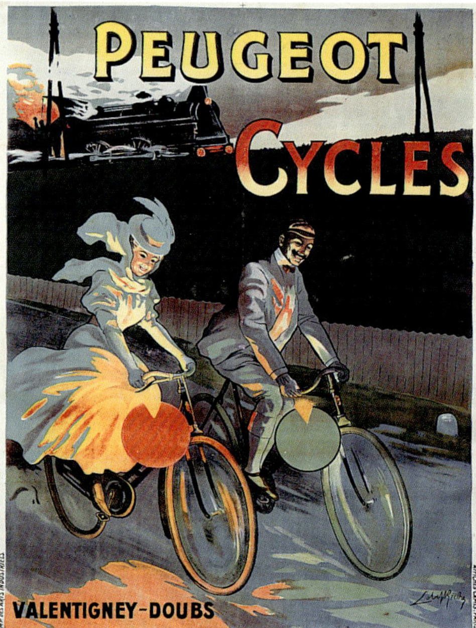

508

representing the four seasons, of which 'Spring' is undoubtedly the best, are single-figure studies in the open air, and treat the subjects from an original and unconventional point of view" (p. 127). And here is that "best" panel, a dreamy, thought-provoking composition done with such ease that not only is the redhead experiencing the rebirth of the world around her, she is irrefutably an essential part of it. And note the date at the artist's signature in this panel is 1899, while "Winter" is dated 1900, proving that great allegory takes time.
Est: $2,500-$3,000.

ROBYS (1916-)

512. Savon Lesieur. 1935.
46$^1/_8$ x 62$^3/_8$ in./117.2 x 158.4 cm
Creation L. Marboeuf, Paris

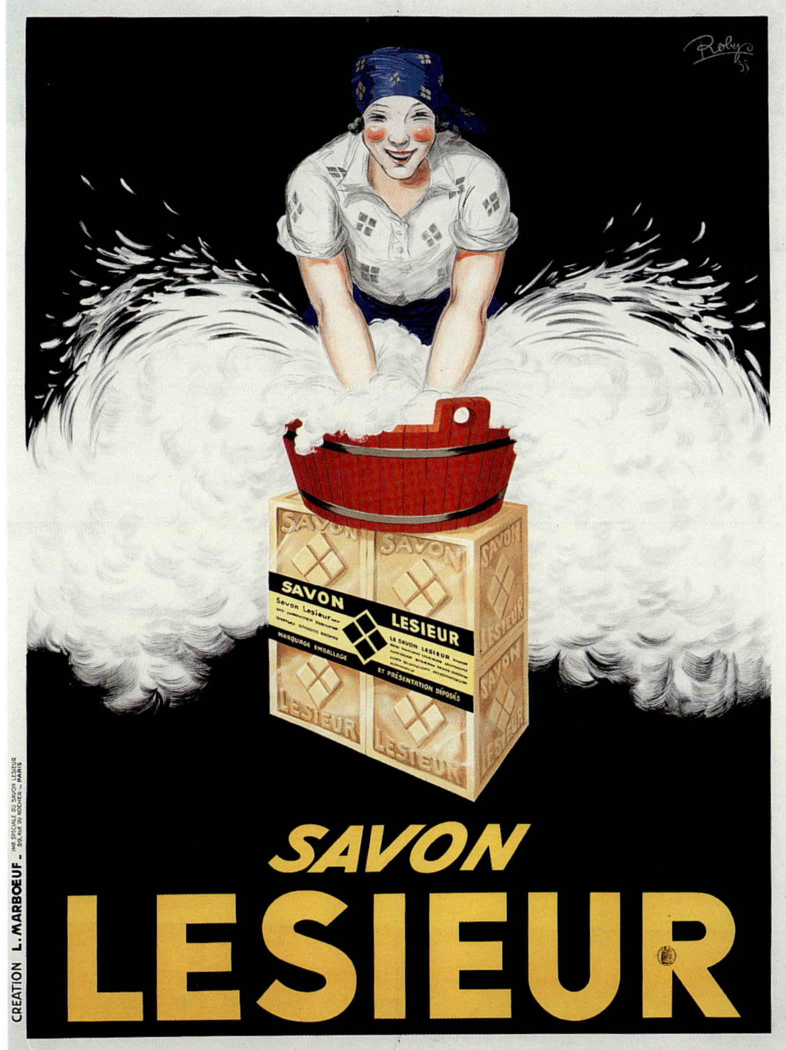

512

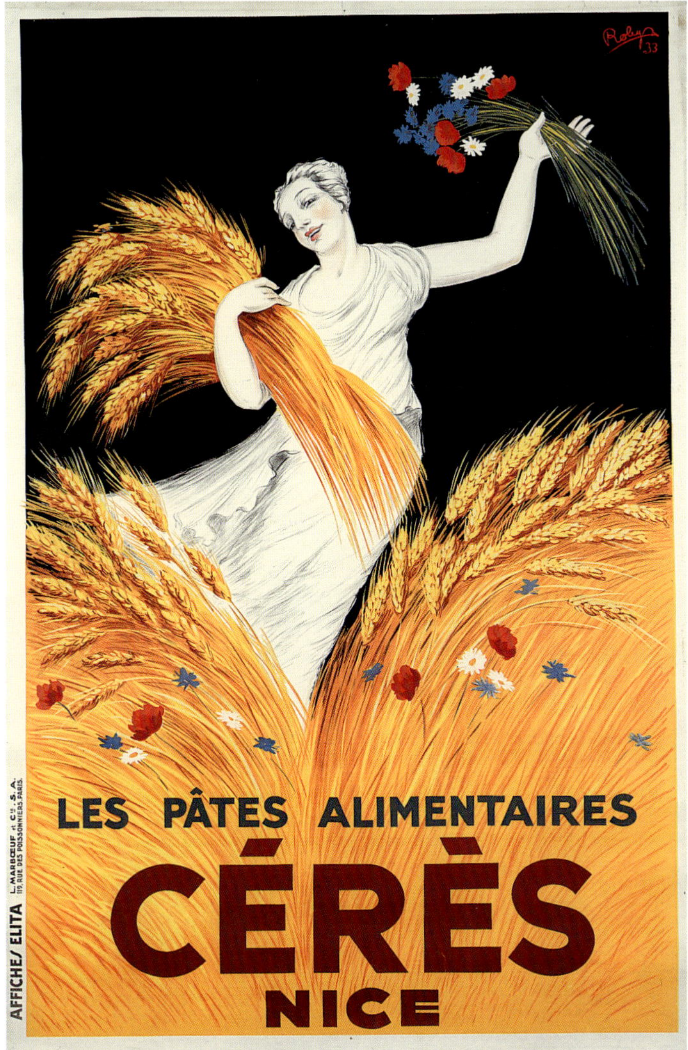

513

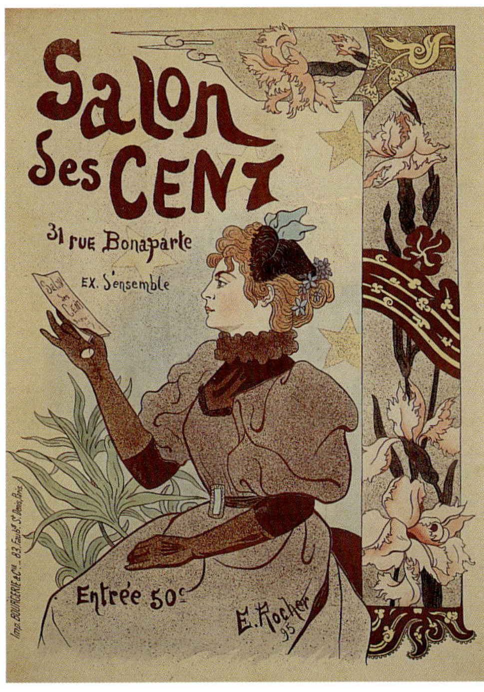

514

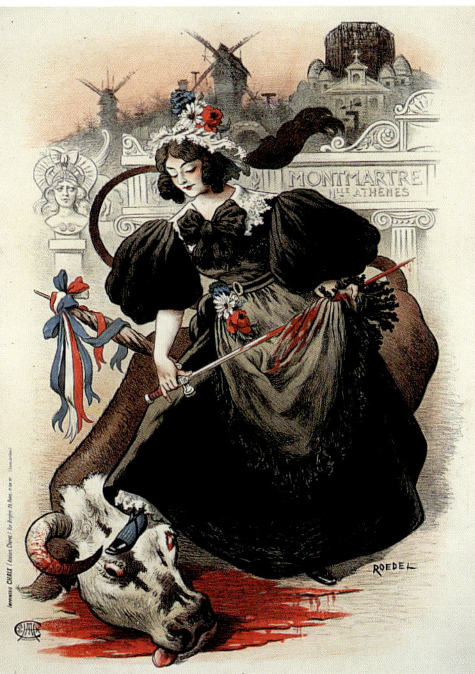

515

Cond B+/Unobtrusive folds.
This androgynous, clown-faced washer-person is really working themselves into a lather thanks to the sudsy superiority of Lesieur detergent. And apparently having a fine time doing so. Robys' simple conceit is that laundry needn't be a laborious endeavor and he presents it with persuasive brio. *Rare!*
Est: $2,000-$2,500.

513. Cérès. 1933.
51¹/₈ x 78 in./129.7 x 198.2 cm
Affiches Elita/L. Marboeuf, Paris
Cond A-/Six-inch tear at top edge.
Ref: PAI-XXV, 469
Whoever Robys was—he seems to not have left a clue —he must have been a charter member of Cappiello's fan club: in virtually all the posters he left us, he borrowed the nestor's various devices to create visual excitement for even the most mundane causes. A case in point is this maiden merrily skipping among the wheat stalks, against Cappiello's patented stark black background (and this is daytime!), inducing us to buy a brand of pasta. The bulk of Robys' work hales from the 1930s.
Est: $1,700-$2,000.

EDMOND A. ROCHER (1873-?)

514. Salon des Cent. 1895.
17¹/₈ x 23⁷/₈ in./43.5 x 60.8 cm
Imp. Bourgerie, Paris
Cond A.
Ref: DFP-II, 756; Reims, 995; Salon des Cent, p. 26; Gold, 194; PAI-XXXV, 60
"The woman is examining the print with intensely critical concentration—she might be an art student or even a painter herself" (Gold, p. 132). This was the only poster by Rocher in the historic 1896 Reims exhibition. The brown-on-beige gives the piece a duotone effect that is achieved by printing pochoir over letterpress. In addition to his work as an illustrator, lithographer and engraver, Rocher also indulged his muse by way of poetry.
Est: $1,000-$1,200.

ROEDEL (1859-1900)

515. La Vache Enragée. 1897.
34⁷/₈ x 49¹/₂ in./88.7 x 125.7 cm
Imp. Chaix, Paris
Cond A.
Ref: Maîtres, 179 (var); PAI-XXXII, 489
Roedel was a caricaturist, illustrator, watercolorist and lithographer; he aligned himself in Paris with a group of artists of Montmartre such as Willette, Léandre and Caran d'Ache, supplied drawings for *Le Courrier français* and produced posters, mostly for the local cabarets and theaters. When Willette started the magazine *La Vache enragée* (*The Angry Cow*), Roedel contributed several designs. The name of the publication refers to the artists' life: "manger de la vache enragée" is a French idiom for "eking out a miserable existence." Clearly this mock-serious design pokes fun at the expense of its subject. (For Lautrec's version of this subject, *see* PAI-XLII, 488). *This is a rare proof before letters.*
Est: $1,700-$2,000.

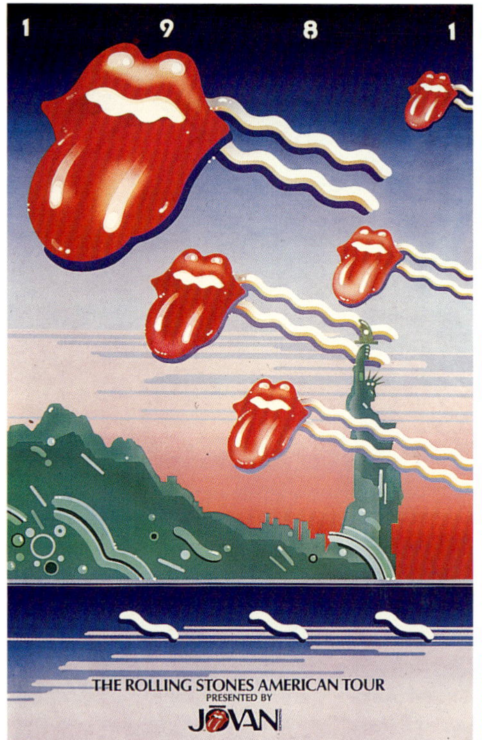

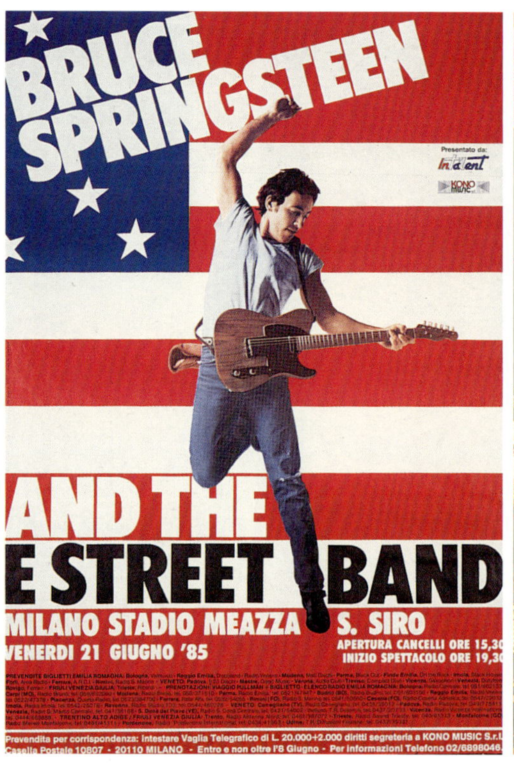

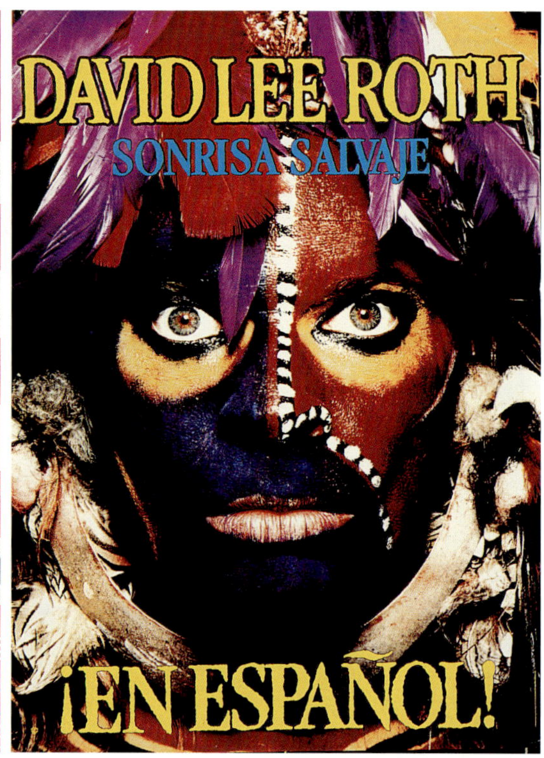

516

ROCK AND ROLL

516. Collection of 100 Posters. 1977-1992.
Smaller: 22 x 22 in./55.9 x 55.9 cm
Larger: 26 x 37 in./66 x 94 cm
Cond A/P.
Ref: PAI-XXII, 487
Rock and roll delivers the image of American popular culture to the ears of the world. Nobody does it—the creation, production and promotion—better. This rare collection of promotional posters published by the recording companies covers a sixteen-year span in the life of the industry—encapsulating a wide range of singers and bands, represented in an equally broad range of visual modes. Virtually every big name that you love (or love to hate) from the era is represented here—Ozzy Osborne, Elvis Costello, The Go-Gos, Motorhead, Diana Ross, Crowded House, Guns n' Roses, Siouxsie & the Banshees, Rolling Stones, The Cramps, Elton John, Duran Duran, Danzig, Hall & Oates, The Clash, and that's just scratching the surface. Designs include LP jacket-cover blow-ups and tour posters (hard-to-find images for German, Italian and Japanese tours), personality portraits and abstract expressions in styles from photography to pure graphics. None of these posters were available for sale, and all were obtainable solely through industry sources. Each is shrink-wrapped. *List of posters available on request.*
Est: $2,500-$3,000.

ERIK ROHMAN (1891-1949)

517. Sapho. 1918.
23³/₈ x 35³/₈ in./59.3 x 90 cm
A.-B. Sätherland & Krook, Stockholm
Cond B/Slight tears at folds.
An appropriately bacchanalian design promotes the Swedish release of *Sapho*, a Famous Players (which would become Paramount) production from 1917. In the original version of the Greek myth, Sappho (spelled with two Ps) was a female poet living on the Isle of Lesbos who, after being jilted by her younger lover for a woman his own age, threw herself into the Aegean Sea. By the time Alfred Daudet adapted this story as a novel, play and movie, Sapho (spelled with a single P) was the tale of a good-life seeking social climber named Fanny who goes through a series of artistic types—a sculptor, a poet, an engraver—before settling upon a lover from the country who she loses to the gal she stole him away from, after which she decides to turn over a new leaf. Go figure. Rohman, a highly productive Swedish graphic artist with his own studio, executed the body of his work between 1916 and 1949.
Est: $1,700-$2,000.

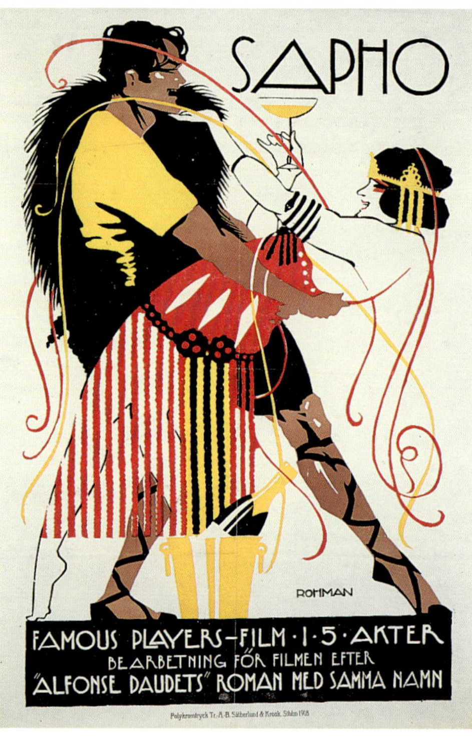

517

PABLO ROÏG

518. Au Cirque—Seventeen Prints. 1907.
Each: 15 x 19³/₄ in./38.1 x 50.2 cm
Cond A/P.
Ref: PAI-XXXV, 458
Roïg, a contemporary and friend of Toulouse-Lautrec, produced this series that, with a deft touch, transfers circus life from the sawdust to the page. However, seeing as they went largely uncirculated at the time of their production, they remain a fairly unknown quantity to the contemporary collector. The similarities to Lautrec are undeniable—evocative graphic musings with a minimum of clutter and subtle use of color. Seeing as the far better-known artist went on to also produce a series of big top panels late in his short life, it's a curious proposition to attempt to determine who influenced who, or whether their mutual attraction to the circus yielded a somewhat unified vision of life in the spotlight. I am indebted to my colleague, Mirelle Romand, for informing us that this group of prints comes from the suite of twenty original lithographs published by Sagot in 1907 and printed by Monroq. The edition

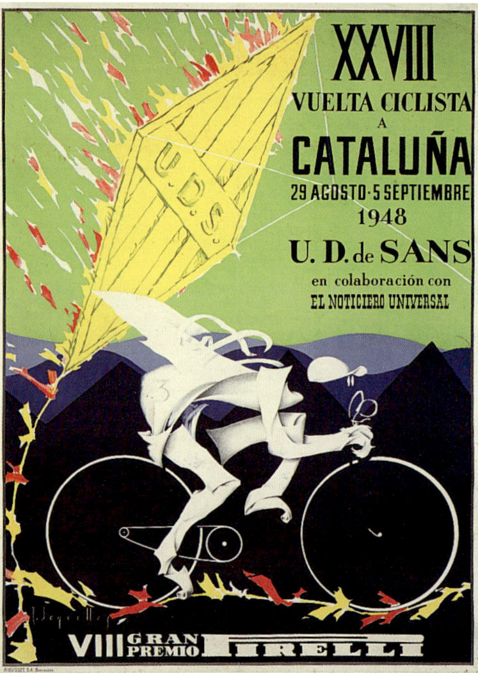

521

was limited to fifteen copies on japan paper and one-hundred on regular white stock.
Est: $5,000-$6,000. (17)

WALTER SCHNACKENBERG (1880-1961)

> For Schnackenberg's magnificent portfolio, *Ballet und Pantomime*, see No. 601.

519. Die Heilung der Prinzessin Pierapinka. 1920.
7⁵/₈ x 9³/₄ in./19.4 x 24.7 cm
Oscar Consée, München
Cond A–/Slight tears and stains at paper edges. Framed.
Ref: PAI-XXIX, 610 (var)
Schnackenberg's involvement with the graphics end of the Berlin theatrical scene is a well-documented fact. But apparently, his participation went a little deeper than that of a visual artist as this program insert can attest. "The Cure of Princess Pierpinka" was a "stylish play" created by the artist and Erik Charell, the producer/director of Berlin's Grosses Schauspielhaus, known throughout the world for his lavish musical productions who in the early 1930s, was banished by Nazi authorities. Though it's informative to know that Schnackenberg was more than just an avid fan, any

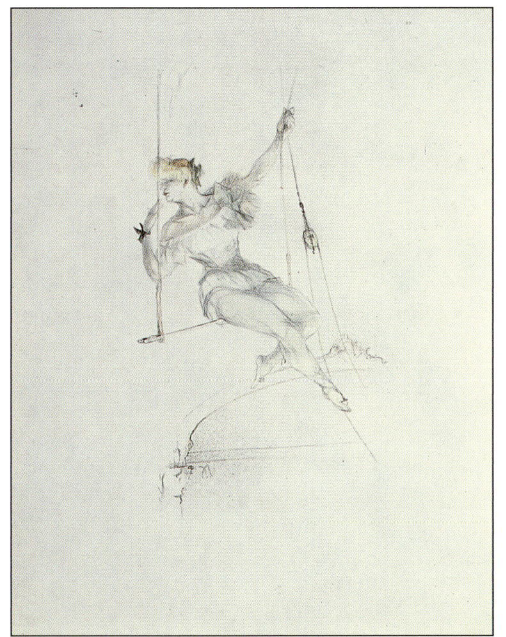

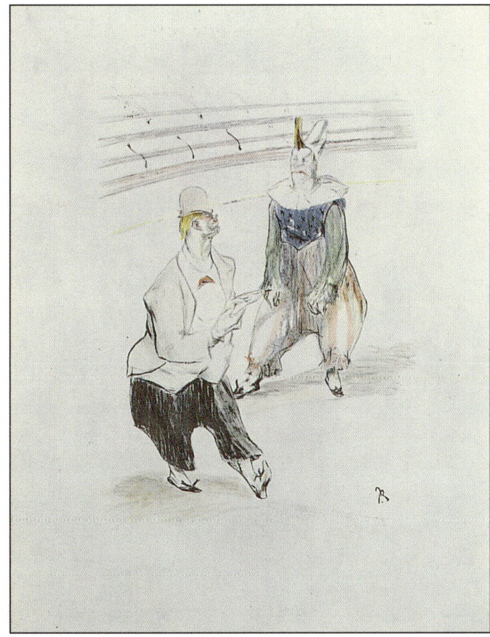

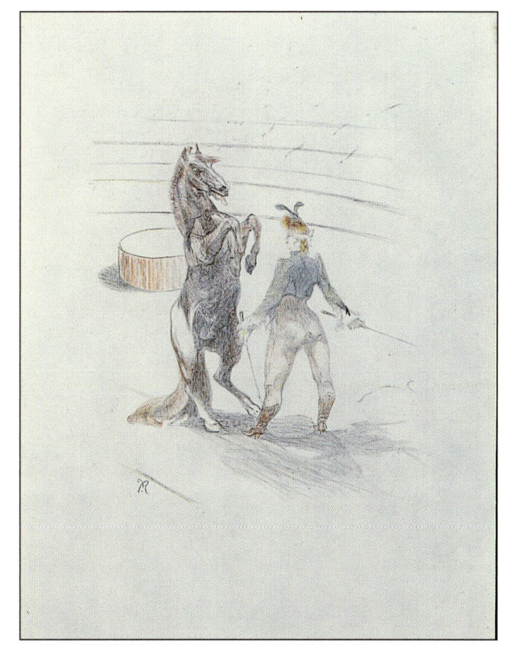

518

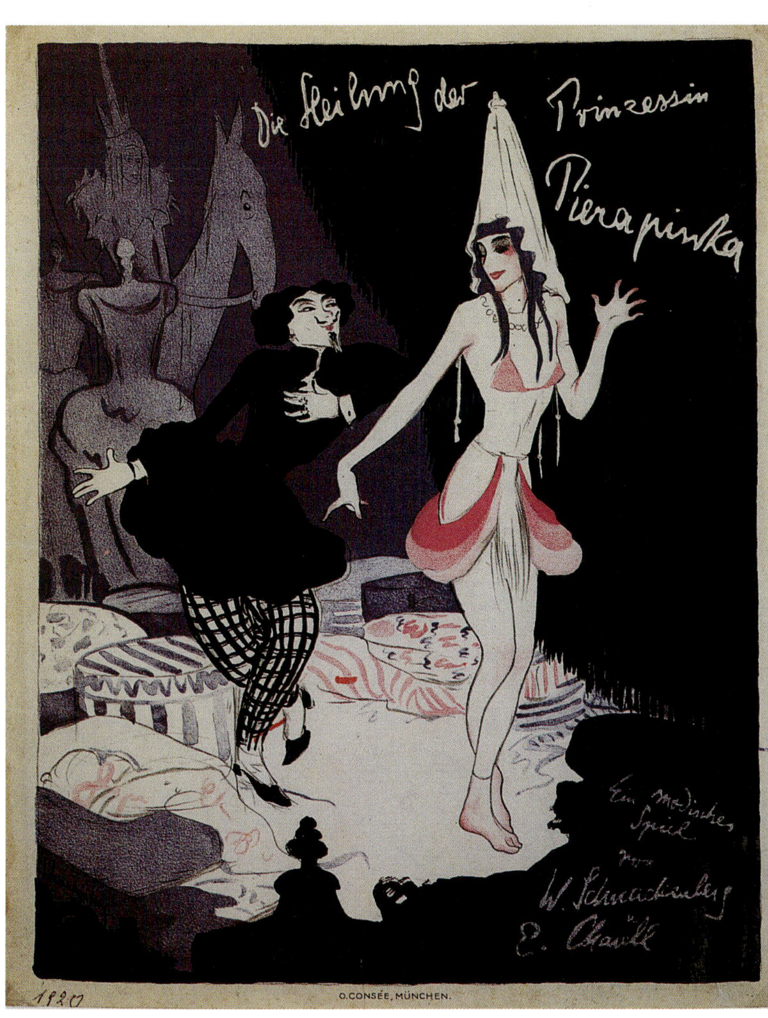

519

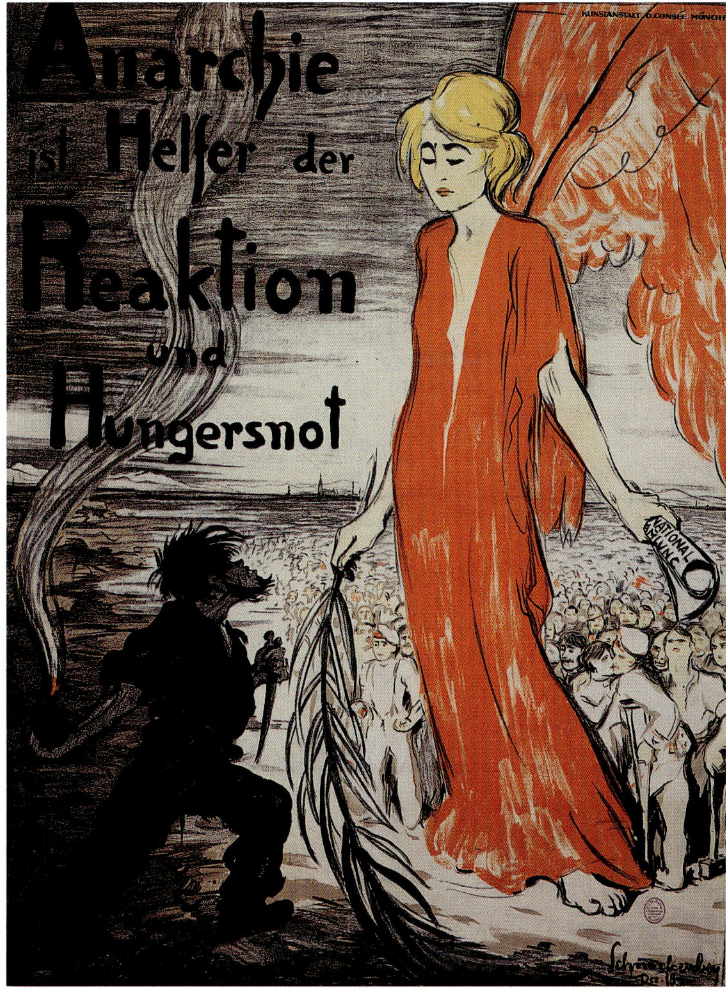

520

details of this tour de force are long since lost to the ages. The artwork is, however, quite fitting for this fashionable affair, practically a costume design itself in execution. *This lot includes a program from the performance.*
Est: $2,000-$2,500.

520. Anarchie ist Helfer der Reaktion und Hungersnot. 1918.
36 x 48$^1/4$ in./91 x 122.5 cm
Oscar Consée, München
Cond A.
Ref: Plakate München, 422
Schnackenberg was an unusual graphic artist—a cultured and sophisticated esthete who created only a handful of posters, mostly for his acquaintances in Munich theatrical circles. His sense of design was highly individual, a quaint amalgam of caricature and fantasy that he called "suggestive dreams." Though this politically charged creation could never be described as "quaint," the artist's adherence to fantastical presentation remains in tact, calling upon an angelic herald of national unity and a soot-encrusted bearer of destruction to deliver the message that "Anarchy is the Aide of Reaction and Famine." To say that the time following World War I was chaotic and filled with upheaval is something of an understatement, but Schnackenberg's split vision—prosperity versus despair, an angel red with the blood of a nation torn apart confronting the embodiment of ongoing ruin, unthinkable waste contrasted off the hope of a better tomorrow—delivers that message with force and clarity.
Est: $4,000-$5,000.

JOSEP SEGRELLES (1885-1969)

521. XXVIII Vuelta Ciclista a Cataluña. 1948.
26$^1/8$ x 36$^1/2$ in./66.5 x 92.5 cm
Rieusset, Barcelona
Cond B/Slight tears and stains at folds and edges.
Viewed as an important Tour de France preparation race for Spanish cyclists, the Tour of Catalonia is a popular bicycle road race that has been held annually since 1911. Here, Segrelles advertises the pedal-powered contest with a rider comprised entirely of ribbon who appears as if he's about to be swept away by a fiery kite that bears the initials of the governing body of Spanish bicycle racing, which makes this design metaphorically clever on two levels—1) that the riders in this race move like the wind; and 2) that the competition will be scorching.
Est: $1,200-$1,500.

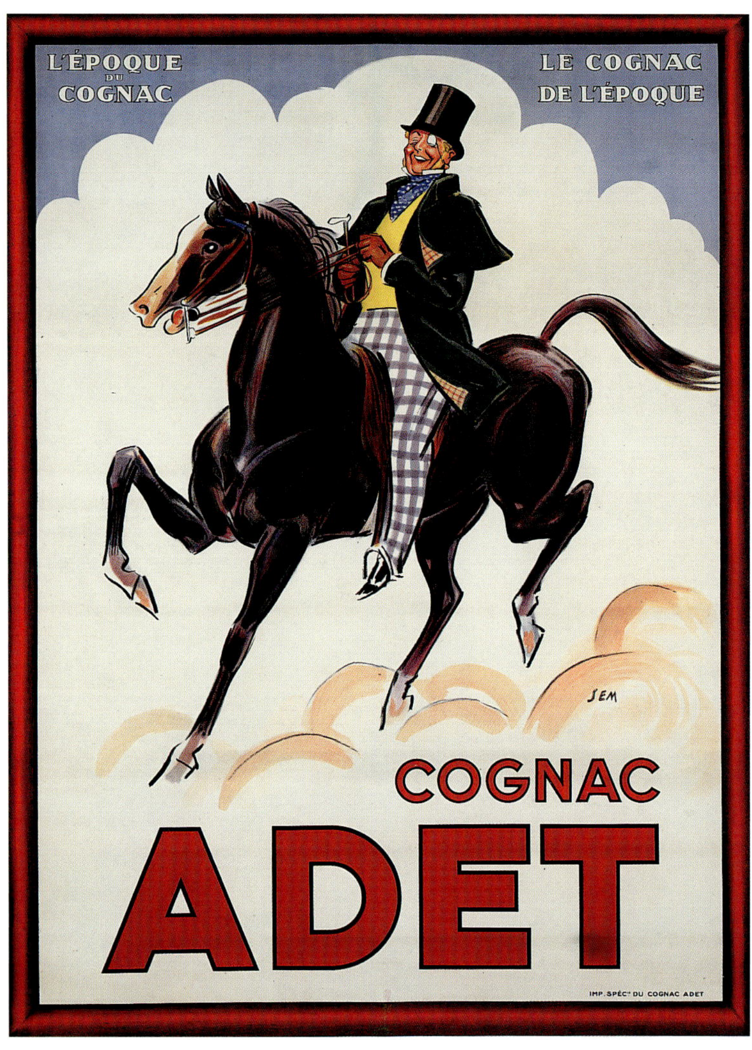

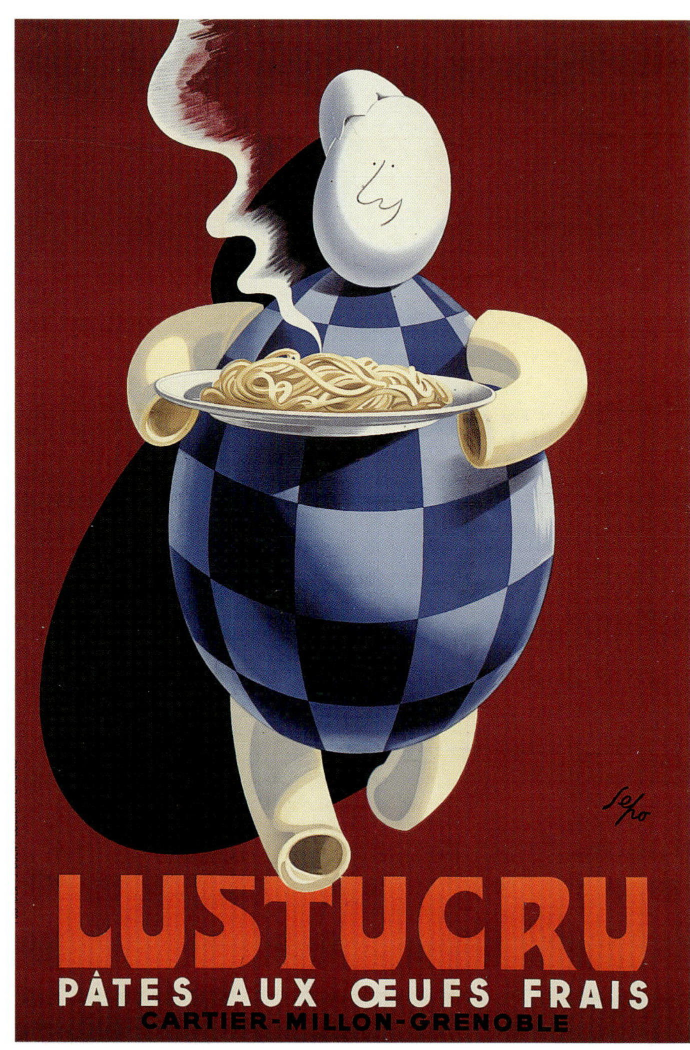

522

523

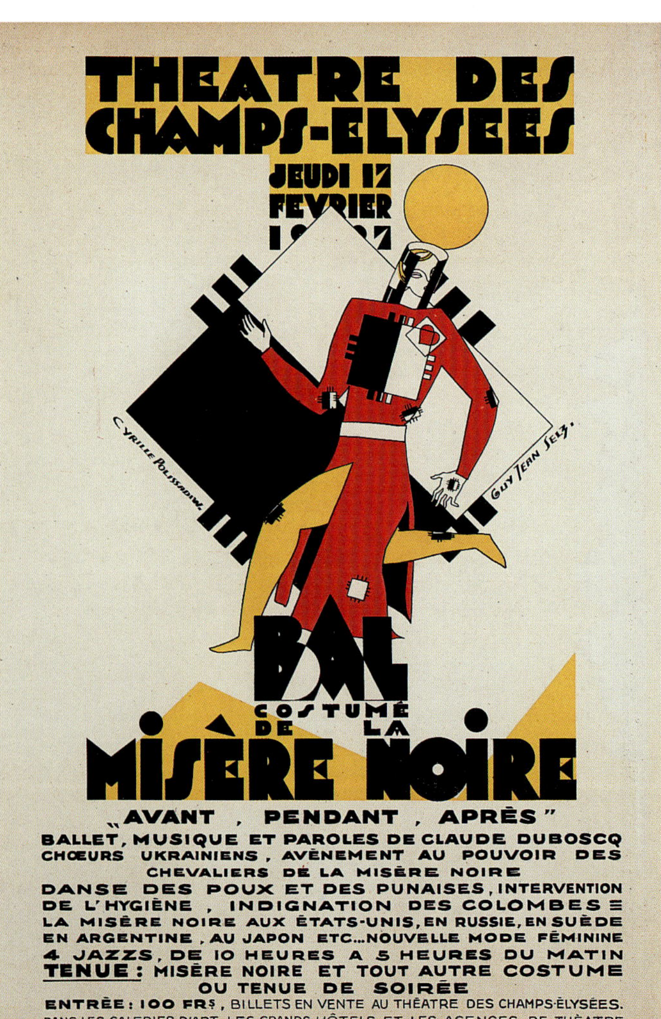

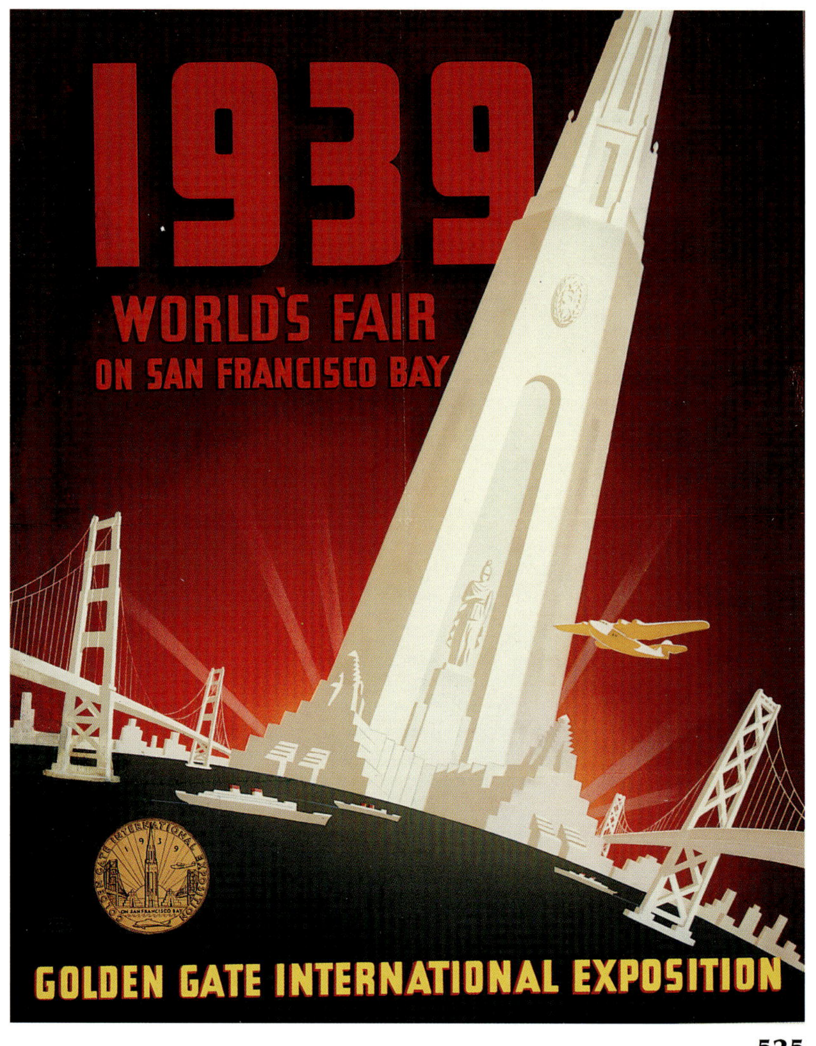

524

525

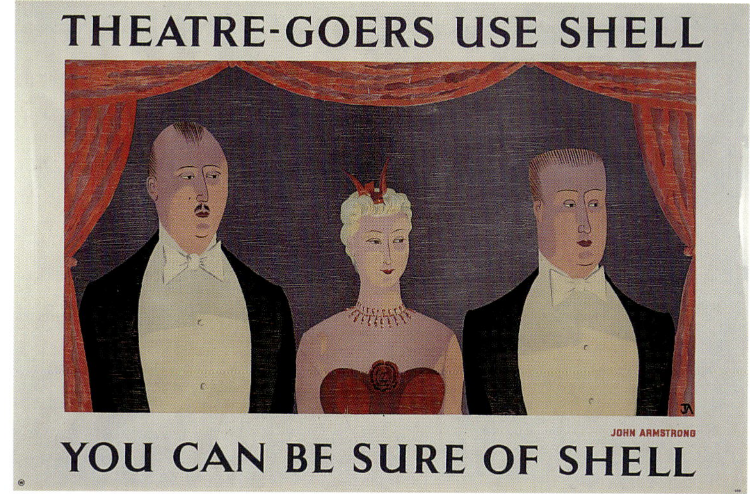

526

527

SEM (Georges Goursat, 1863-1934)

522. Cognac Adet.
$45^5/_8$ x $62^5/_8$ in./116 x 159 cm
Imp. Spécle. du Cognac Adet
Cond A–/Unobtrusive tears.
Who needs to show a bottle of Adet cognac when an artist can make it effortlessly clear that a few sips of the stuff will make you feel as if you're riding a stallion through the sky? And we're not even talking about Pegasus here! And what's not to love about a slogan as pure and engaging as "The Era of Cognac, the Cognac of the Era." The career of caricaturist Sem started modestly enough in his home town of Perigueux where he published his first collection of local celebrities' portraits in 1895. Only after doing the same for Bordeaux in 1897 and Marseilles in 1898 did he venture to Paris where he charmed the city folk with his talent. Hardly anyone of note escaped being captured for posterity.
Est: $2,000-$2,500.

SEPO (Severo Pozzati, 1895-1983)

523. Lustucru. 1951.
$38^7/_8$ x 59 in./98.7 x 149.7 cm
Pub. Idea/Coudert et Dino, St. Oven
Cond B/Slight tears at folds and edges; some printer's
    creases.
Ref: Sepo, 302; Marques, p. 76 (var); Alimentaires, 68;
    PAI-XXIX, 625
This jovial egghead doesn't seem bothered in the least that someday his time for a noodling comeuppance may arrive. But for the moment, he's happy as can be to deliver a steaming tray of spaghetti with the assistance of macaroni limbs. A spectacularly charming Sepo image for Lustucru pasta, the brand made from only the freshest eggs and wise enough to use the services of only the finest graphic designers. Born near Ravenna, Pozzati grew up in Bologna where he studied sculpture at the Academy of Fine Arts, then took up painting. In 1917, he joined the "Maga" agency of Giussepe Magagnoli, ex-director of Vercasson in Paris. (Along with its stable of Italian artists, "Maga" had the Italian contracts of Mauzan and Cappiello, the chief influence on Pozzati's early style.) He moved to Paris in 1920 and was soon exhibiting widely and winning recognition. In 1923, he adopted the name Sepo.
Est: $4,000-$5,000.

GUY JEAN SELZ & CYRILLE POLISSADIM

524. Theatre des Champs-Elysees/Misère Noire. 1927.
$15^3/_4$ x $23^3/_4$ in./40 x 60.5 cm
Imp. H. Chachoin, Paris
Cond A.
Ref: Spectacle, 192, Color Plate, p. 288; PAI-XXXIII, 48
Get out your glad rags—and we do mean rags. The shabbiest chic and dirtiest patches are requested for the Dadaesque "Utter Poverty" costume ball. It's going to be a don't-miss night: fox-trotting (that's what the lice-ridden do) to four jazz bands until 5 a.m., a dreadful theatrical presentation, a fashion show and other things we're too embarrassed to translate. Don't shave, don't shower, just slum. The place must have been mobbed: this Cubist announcement by the unknown Selz and Polissadim couldn't fail but bring them in by the motley droves.
Est: $3,000-$4,000.

SHAWL NYELAND & SEAVEY

525. 1939 World's Fair/San Francisco Bay.
$26^1/_2$ x $34^1/_4$ in./67.5 x 87 cm
Schmidt Litho., S.F.
Cond B/Tears at folds and edges. Framed.
Held from February 19 to October 29, 1939, the Golden Gate International Exposition had a hard act to follow seeing as it came close on the heels of 1937's Pan-Pacific International Exposition, which was considered by many at the time to be the quintessential expo. However, the "Pageant of the Pacific," with its distinctive environment, reflecting the dreams and aspirations of the epoch, became a sensation in its own right. The Golden Gate Exposition presented an eclectic blend of European, Eastern and Latin American architectural, landscape and artistic styles, evoking the exoticism of Pacific Rim cultures such as the Mayas, Incas, Malaysians and Cambodians, which reflected a nostalgic look at past civilizations. This bent was contrasted off a streamlined, international theme of modernism and technological innovation that celebrated the earlier completion of the Golden Gate and San Francisco/ Oakland Bay Bridges. The design team of Shawl, Nyeland and Seavey incorporate the Tower of the Sun and Elephant Towers with the pair of bridges, as well as a Pan American clipper ship, to create a Treasure Island destination of monolithic proportions in their monumentally futuristic poster.
Est: $2,000-$2,500.

SHELL OIL POSTERS

The British Branch of Shell Oil was one of the biggest —and most open-minded—advertisers in Britain. Its publicity director, Jack Beddington, didn't believe in hamstringing creative people by forcing them to show the product (Shell's, after all, isn't much to look at); he gave them freedom to advertise not the product, but the company—what we now call image advertising. And his virtual motto was, "advertising is the one sphere in which true originality always pays."

The Shell approach was to pick a theme and create a series around it—the best known and most successful being the one shown here that featured the kinds of people and professions that use Shell. The reasons for some of these are clear enough: motorists, racers and farmers. Others take some thinking, and even after a bit of thought still leave us puzzled, such as "theatre-goers" and explorers. Because *everyone* does, of course, is the idea that this famous series implies, with a low-key humor that still seems fresh today.

526. These Men Use Shell/Farmers. 1939.
Artist: **John Armstrong (1893-1973)**
44 x $29^1/_2$ in./117.8 x 75 cm
Weiner, London
Cond A. Framed.
Ref: Shell, 82; PAI-XVIII, 5
One of Armstrong's classic harrumphing Englishmen— a prosperous farmer—stands stolidly before a map of his lands. Shell images like these, along with the landscapes, identified the product with the people and the land itself, and appealed to the public's sense of Englishness. "Shell appropriates the country . . . Motoring, and therefor Shell, give you the whole of Britain" (Shell, Introduction). Armstrong himself was a one-man "These People" series: law student, soldier in World War I, then painter, posterist, set and costume designer, and muralist. Eight of his murals decorated Shell headquarters.
Est: $1,700-$2,000.

527. Theatre-Goers Use Shell. 1938.
Artist: **John Armstrong (1893-1973)**
$43^3/_4$ x $29^3/_4$ in./113.6 x 75.5 cm
Weiner, London
Cond A. Framed.
Ref: PAI-XVIII, 6
This charming design in the famous series stresses snob appeal, right down to the blasé facial expressions. In fact, these three "theatre-goers" are so striking in their appearance that they might very well be actors taking a bow on stage.
Est: $1,700-$2,000.

528. Magicians Prefer Shell. 1934.
Artist: **E. McKnight Kauffer (1890-1954)**
42^1/$_8$ x 29^1/$_4$ in./112.2 x 74.3 cm
Cond B–/Paper losses at top edge; slight tear at
      bottom edge; image excellent. Framed.
Ref: Kauffer, 45; Word & Image, p. 79;
     Müller-Brockmann, 202; Modern Posters, 164;
     Purvis, p. 21; PAI-IX, 132
Alain Weill indicates that "While France shone between
the wars thanks to a few first-quality artists who worked
for many clients, the poster situation in Great Britain
was characterized by a few large advertisers—the London Underground, the railway companies, Shell-Max —
who could retain a high level in their campaigns. They
provided work for a whole generation of artists, but
the only true star to stand out from the lot was
E. McKnight Kauffer" (Weill, p. 223). And the proof that
this comment wasn't simply hollow praise lies right before our eyes, where a magician's sleight of hand makes
for one of the most effective of all the McKnight Kauf-
fer-designed Shell posters.
Est: $3,000-$4,000.

529. Motorists Prefer Shell. 1935.
Artist: **J. S. Anderson**
44^3/$_8$ x 29^1/$_2$ in./112.7 x 75 cm
Weiner, London
Cond A. Framed.
Ref: Shell, 57; Avant-Garde, p. 173; Purvis, p. 54;
     Word & Image, p. 84; Art Deco, p. 88; PAI-XXIV, 60
In one of the finest designs in this distinguished Shell
series, Anderson poses pistons and the fuel line against
the front profile of an automobile. A cool composition
that gives us the mechanical essence of auto—inside
and out.
Est: $3,500-$4,000.

530. These Men Use Shell/Racing Motorists. 1939.
Artist: **Richard Guyatt (1914-)**
42^1/$_8$ x 29^3/$_4$ in./112.2 x 75.6 cm
Cond A. Framed.
Ref: Shell, 83; PAI-XXIV, 67
In this poster for Shell's "People" series, it's racing
motorists who endorse the product, and the devil-may-
care tilt of the cigarette in the mouth of the speedster
in his coveralls tells us that they are indeed a special
breed. Guyatt was a longtime and much-honored professor at the Royal College of Art's School of Graphic
Design in London.
Est: $3,000-$4,000.

531. Explorers Prefer Shell. 1934.
Artist: **E. McKnight Kauffer (1890-1954)**
44^1/$_8$ x 29^1/$_4$ in./112 x 74.3 cm
Cond A–/Unobtrusive folds. Framed.
Ref: PAI-XII, 52
Explorers are always looking beyond the blue horizon,
so McKnight Kauffer makes it clear that its time for
the everyday adventurer to gas-up with Shell and write
their own page in the big book of sights-unseen. Deft
brevity justly expressed.
Est: $1,700-$2,000.

532. Summer Shell/May to October. 1939.
Artist: **E. McKnight Kauffer (1890-1954)**
44^1/$_2$ x 29^1/$_2$ in./112.3 x 75 cm
Weiner, London
Cond A. Framed.
Ref: Shell, 84; PAI-XVIII, 19
A straw hat, photomontaged in black-and-white onto a
bucolic background, is enough to associate Shell with
happy thoughts of summer. One of the simplest, best
and last of McKnight Kauffer's great posters for Shell.
He executed a companion poster, "Winter Shell," later
the same year (see PAI-XVIII, 20).
Est: $1,700-$2,000.

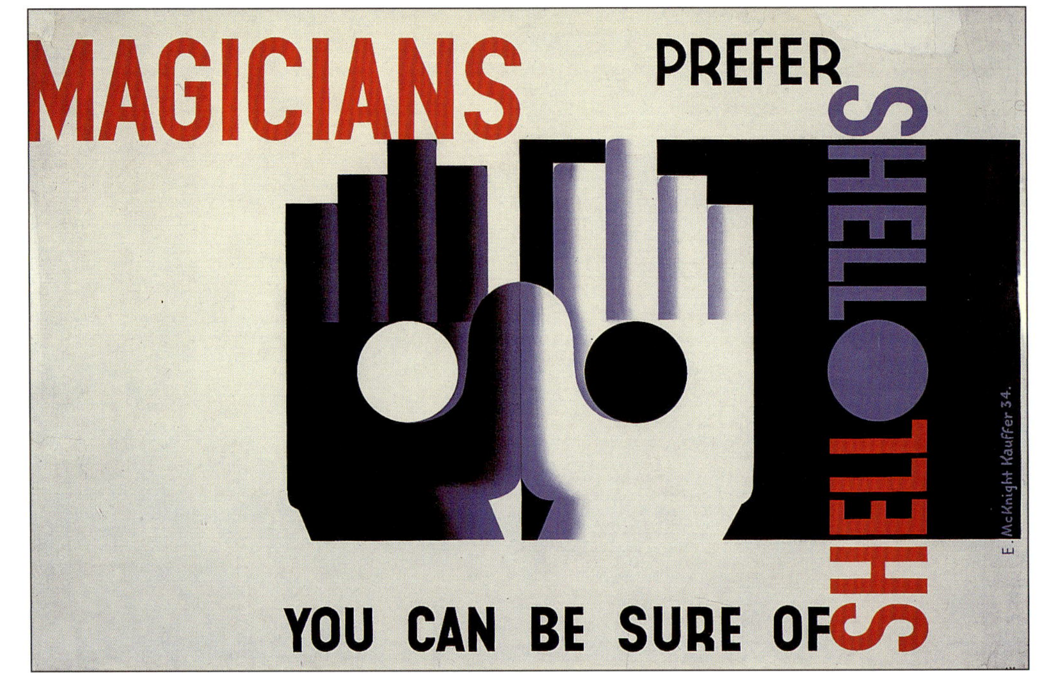

528

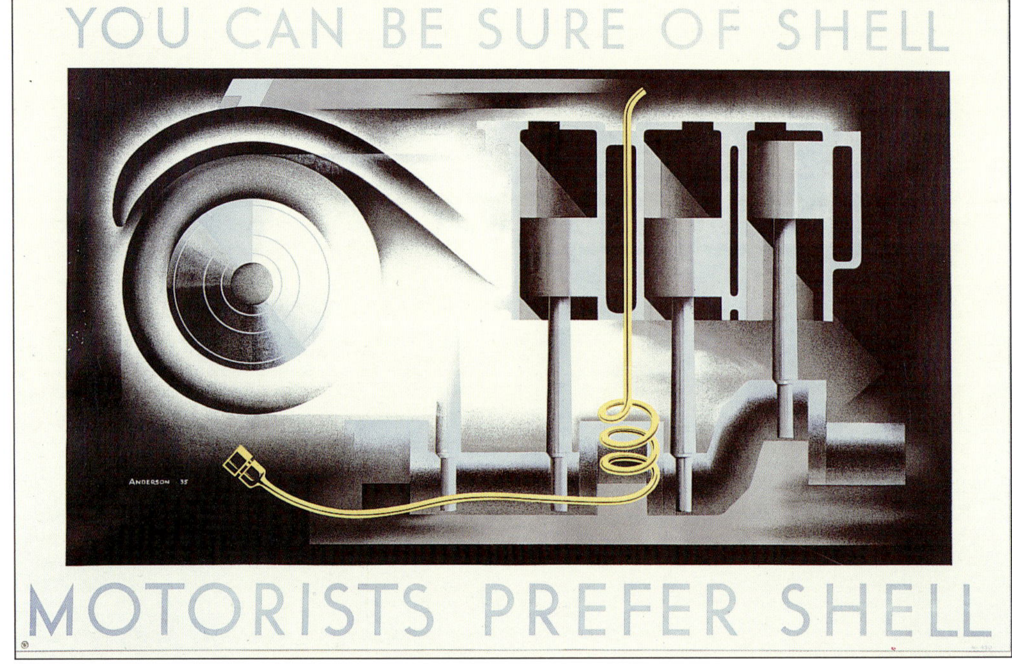

529

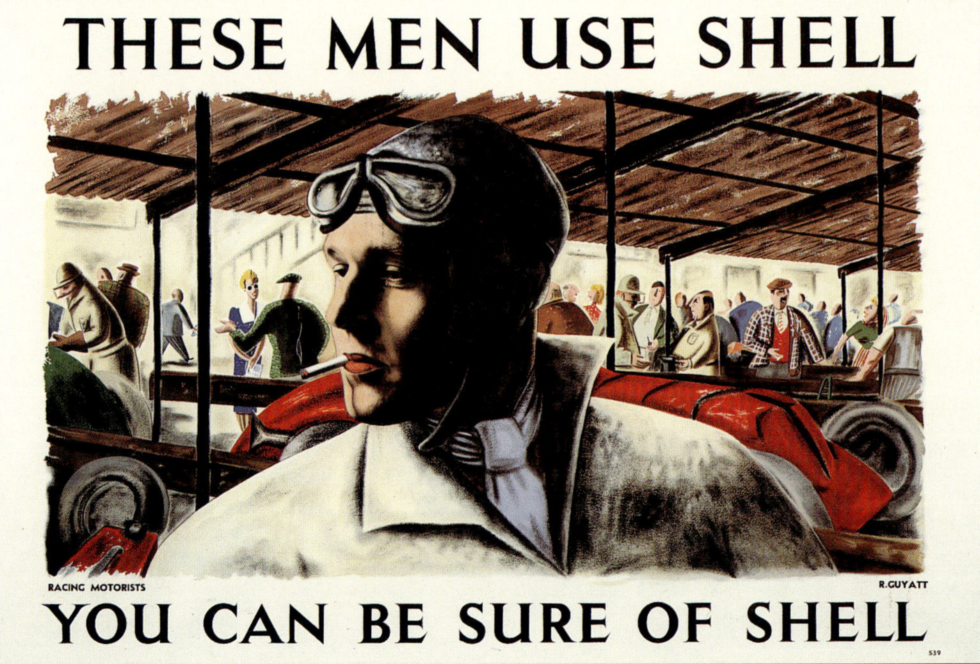

530

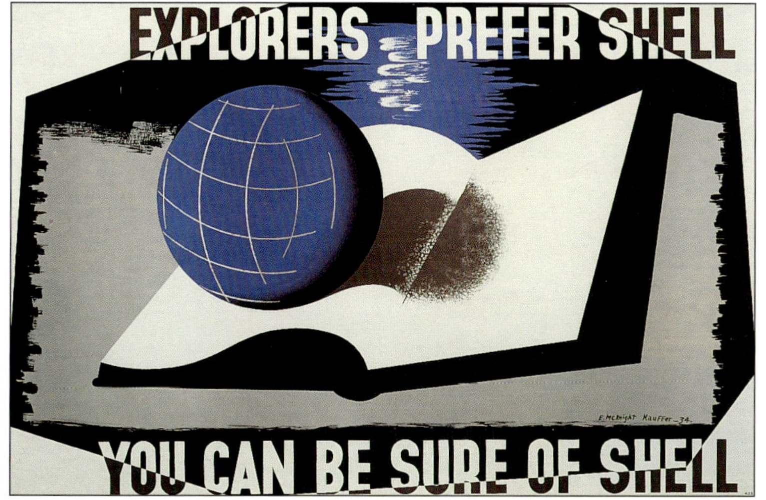

531

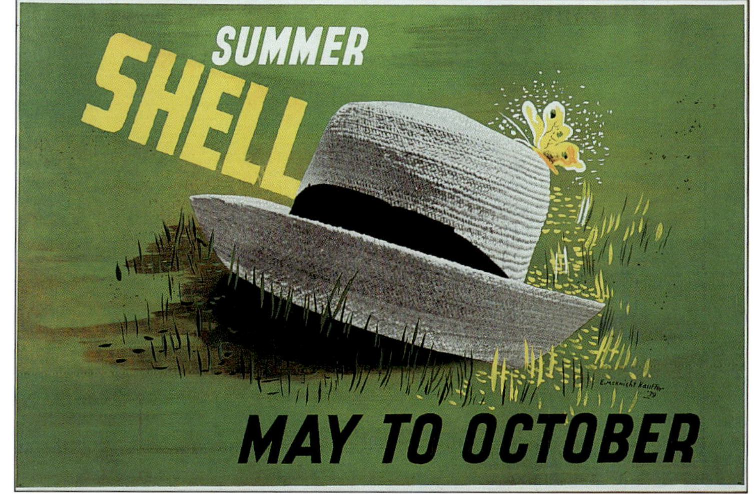

532

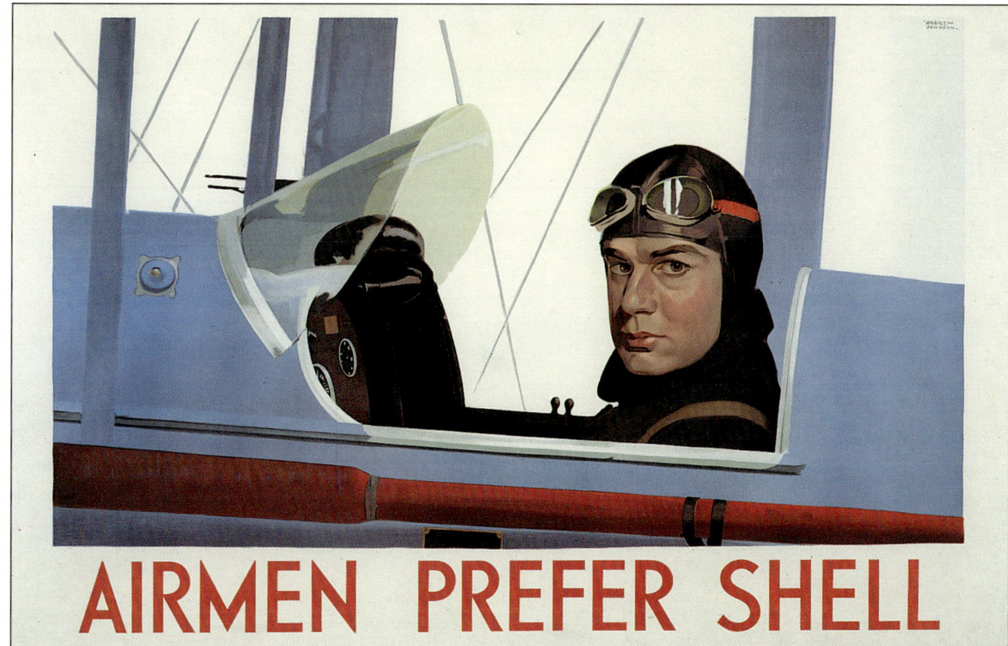

533

533. Airmen Prefer Shell.
Artist: **Andrew Johnson**
$44^3/_4$ x $29^1/_8$ in./113.6 x 74 cm
Chorley & Pickersgill, Leeds
Cond A–/Slight tears at bottom edge. Framed.
Ref: PAI-XII, 49
Johnson was best known as "an agreeable landscape painter (who) expertly rendered the scenic views he was entrusted with" (Weill, p. 226). The designer himself, however, had some simple ground rules for poster making that he adhered to no matter what the designated subject matter: "If the poster forces attention by its dramatic presentation or its 'newness' its first object is achieved. It has been seen" (Richmond, p. 149). Certainly one would have difficulty disputing the veracity of his goals after catching a glimpse of the direct, nononsense gaze of the young flier that lends his visage to the service of promoting Shell, who comes across as a textbook demonstration of sincerity in advertising.
Est: $3,000-$4,000.

SHEPARD

534. Catalina.
50 x $38^1/_4$ in./127 x 97 cm
Cond A. Framed.
Over the course of its history, the island of Santa Catalina has been inhabited by a number of disparate groups—the Native American Tongva tribe, Portuguese and Spanish explorers, Russian otter hunters, Chinese pirates, Franciscan monks, Spanish smugglers and even the Chicago Cubs, who used the island for the team's spring training. However, in 1891, William, Hancock and Joseph Banning, the sons of Phineas Banning —American businessman, stagecoach driver, entrepreneur and the "Father of the Port of Los Angeles"—purchased Santa Catalina and the island's age of tourism began. The town of Avalon became the primary destination for vacationers and it's this area that Shepard chose as the focal point for his lush, Colorform tourism bauble for the "Scenic Riviera of the U.S.A.," located a scant twenty-six miles off the coast of Southern California, which at this point in time was reachable exclusively by ferry. Today, approximately one-million tourists arrive on the island every year via ferry, small plane (at Catalina's "Airport in the Sky") or express helicopter service.
Est: $2,500-$3,000.

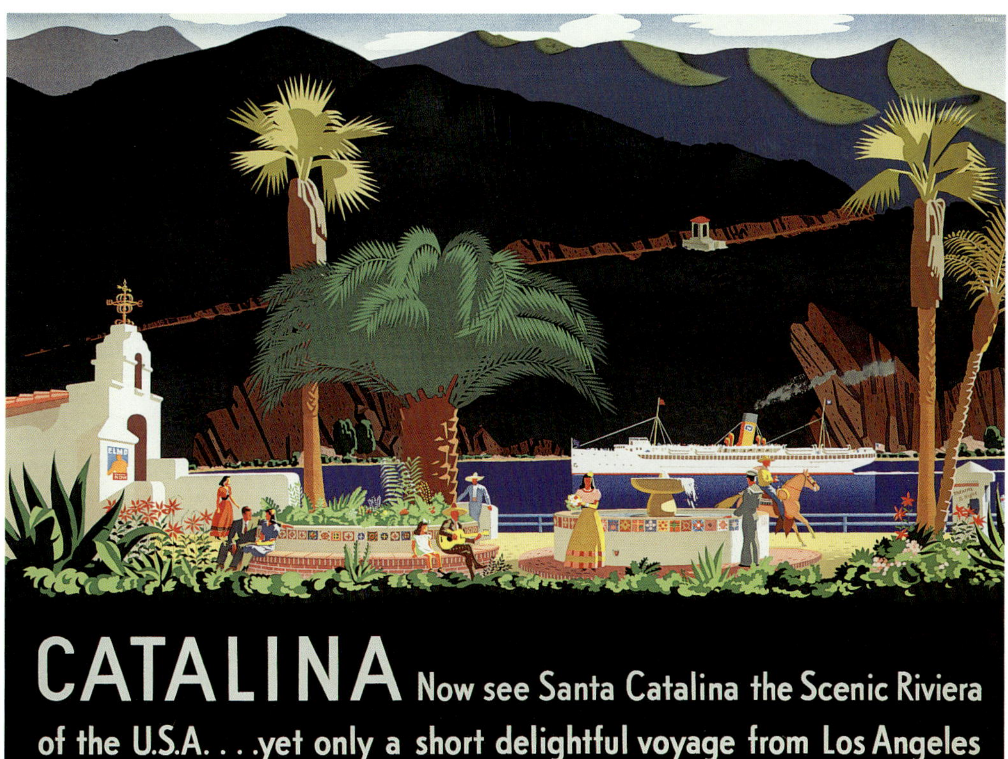

534

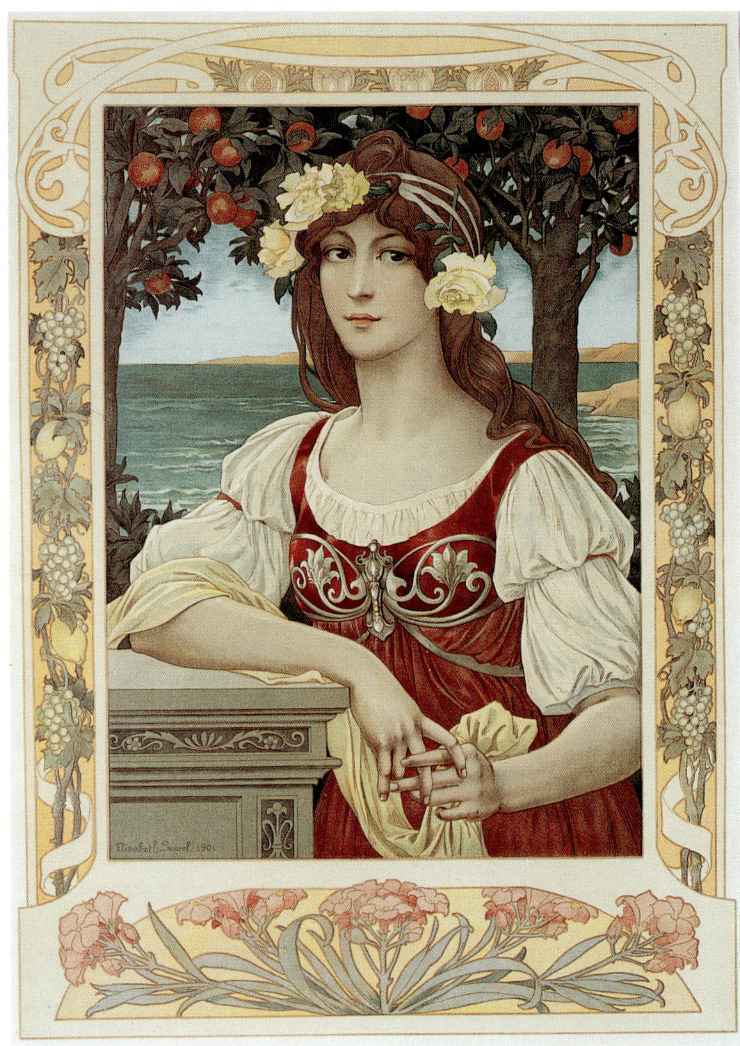

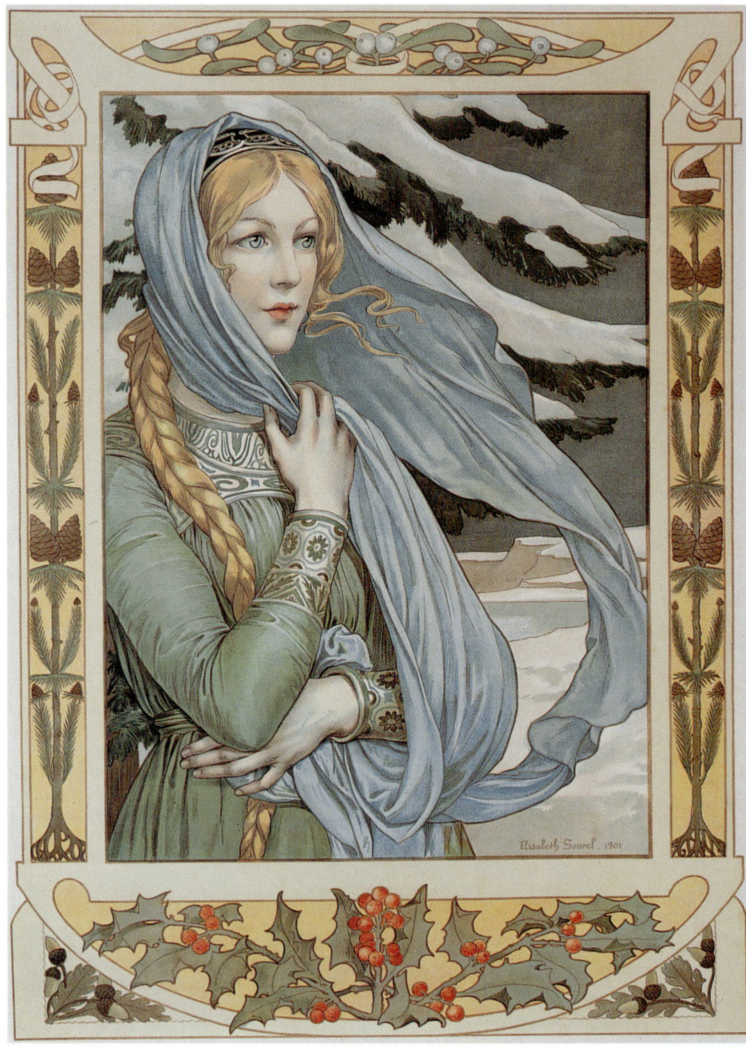

537

538

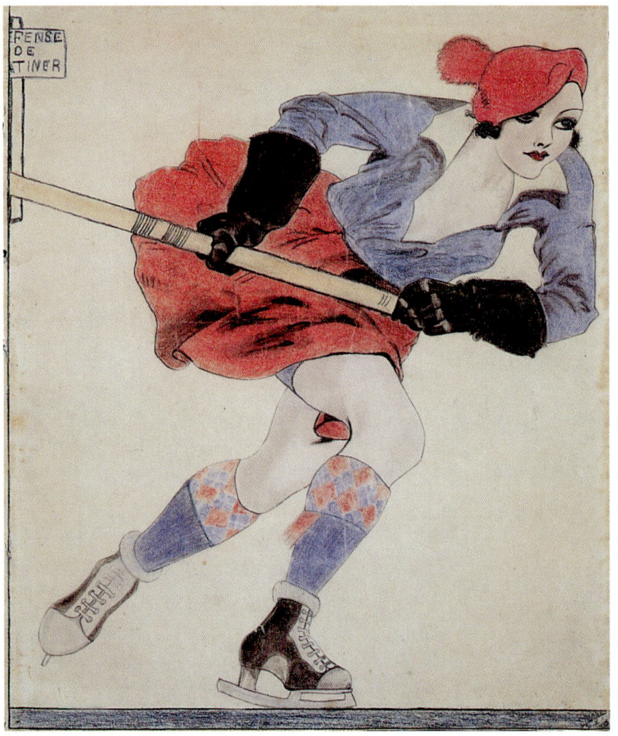

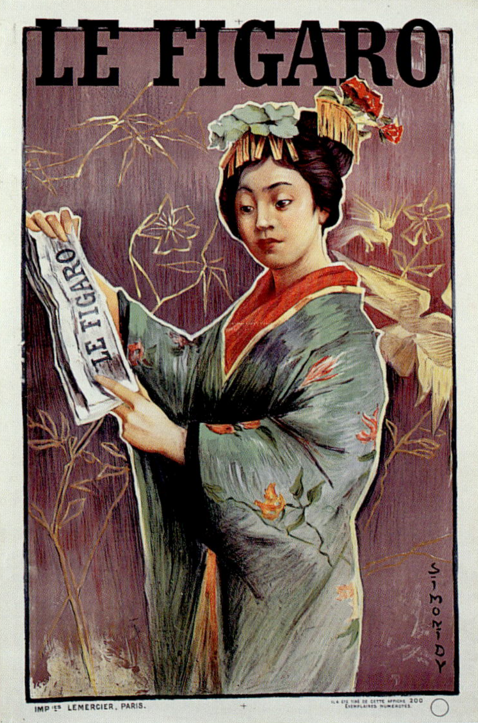

535

536

SIMONE

535. Determined Pucker. ca. 1935.
17^1/$_2$ x 21 in./44.4 x 53.4 cm
Crayon and pencil on paper. Framed.
My, how times have changed. Granted, there's not a contact sport in the world whose gear hasn't been modified in the name of safety (goaltenders in ice hockey and catchers in baseball now look as if they're employed by bomb squads, for example), but this stick-wielding cover-girl certainly serves as an eye-opener as to just how much has changed in the past seventy years. But even taking safety into account it's difficult to imagine that there ever was a defencewoman alive willing to show this much cleavage. The temperature alone would seem to preclude this sort of thing. Couture aside, her focus and athleticism make it obvious that she's hellfire on blades regardless of what she's wearing. Currently, ice hockey is one of the fastest growing women's sports in the world, with the number of participants increasing 400 percent in the last ten years.
Est: $1,500-$1,800.

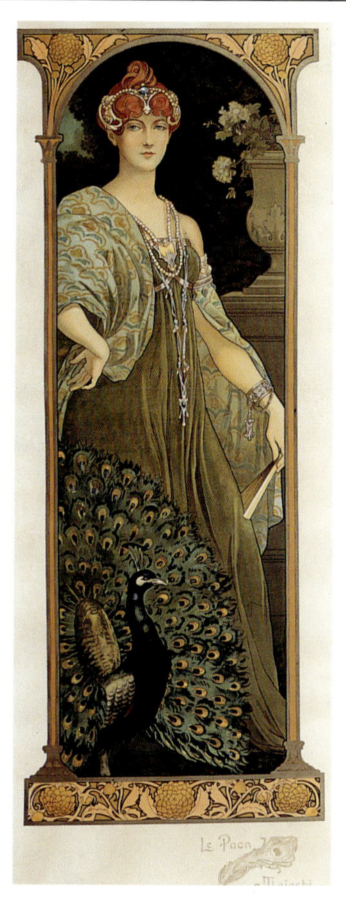

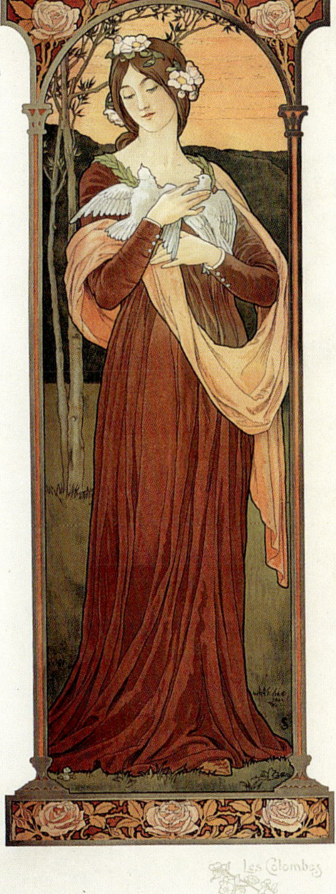

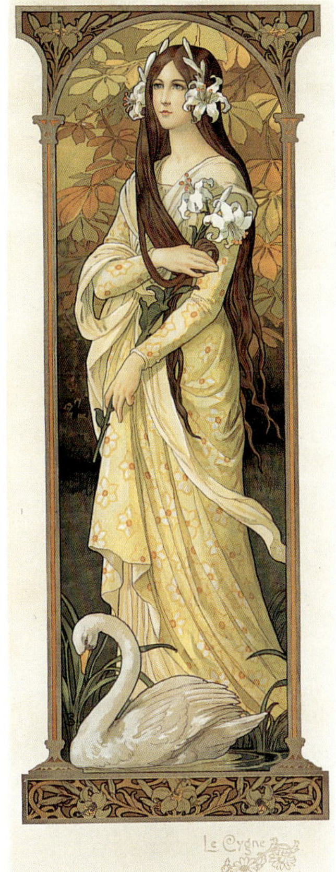

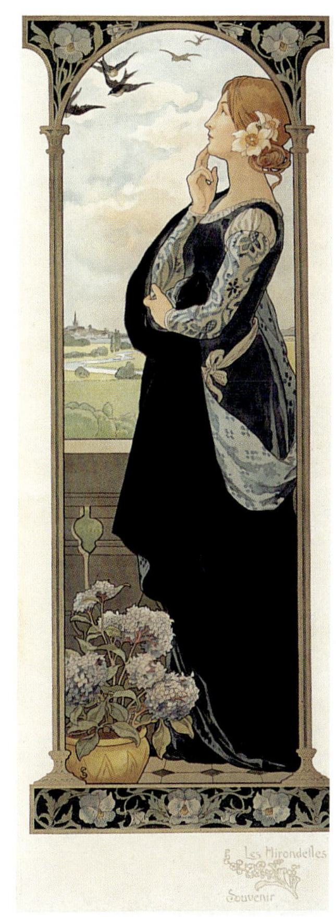

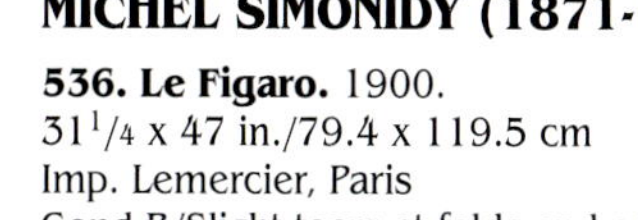

539

MICHEL SIMONIDY (1871-1929)

536. Le Figaro. 1900.
31$^1/_4$ x 47 in./79.4 x 119.5 cm
Imp. Lemercier, Paris
Cond B/Slight tears at folds and edges.
Ref: PAI-II, 217
In 1900, Simonidy created six charming posters for the newspaper *Le Figaro* that showed women from around the globe reading their publication. It's a distinguished—and rare— series (for three other worldly women, *see* PAI-II, 214-216). Here, a traditionally-garbed Japanese woman peruses her copy of *Le Figaro* in an altogether reverent manner, holding with her fingertips as if it were an object of fragile significance.
Est: $1,200-$1,500.

ELISABETH SONREL (1874-1953)

537. Été . 1901.
15$^3/_4$ x 22 in./40 x 55.8 cm
Cond A.
Sonrel's decorative panels are a bit more painterly than Mucha's, but they're equally as effective as the better known artist's work. Having previously applied her talents to flowers (*see* PAI-XXXII, 507) and birds (*see* No. 539), she turns her attention to seasonal concerns, the second such personifica-tions we've seen from the artist (the first came in PAI-XXXIX, 469). Here, she explores the quiet soli-tude of summertime solemnity with the casual lovel-iness of a thought-absorbed, long-necked beauty pausing in an apple grove by the sea. Born in Tours, Sonrel was quite possibly the daughter of painter Stephane Sonrel, from whom she received her early artistic guidance. To further her artistic studies, she moved to Paris where she became the pupil of Jules Lefebvre at his Ecole des Beaux-Arts. Begin-ning in 1893, she exhibited her work at the Salon des Artistes français, especially large watercolors of idealized women that have both a certain Pre-Raphaelite intensity and an affinity for French sym-bolism, inspired by Arthurian romance, biblical subjects, archaic legends and medieval love. Al-though Sonrel's output was known during her life-time, it's only in the past twenty years or so that her work has again received the attention it deserves.
Est: $2,000-$2,500.

538. Hiver. 1901.
15$^3/_4$ x 22 in./40 x 55.8 cm
Cond A.
And here we're presented with the frosty flip-side of the previous panel's allegorical midsummer stunner, a Nordic beauty whose frigid environs do little to distract the viewer from the porcelain sen-suality of her isolated musings. As was the case with summer, seasonal-appropriate flora frames the central image.
Est: $2,000-$2,500.

539. Les Oiseaux: Four Decorative Panels.
Each: 9$^5/_8$ x 26$^3/_8$ in./24.5 x 67 cm
Cond A. Framed.
Ref: PAI-XLI, 531
Sonrel completely outdoes herself with these four flights of fancy—exquisite birds whose special qualities are mirrored in the women they inspire: the Majestic Peacock (Le Paon/Majesté), a pair of Tender Doves (Les Colombes/Tendresse), the Inno-cent Swan (Le Cygne/Innocence) and the Swallows of Remembrance (Les Hirondelles/Souvenir). The respectful treatment is shown not only in the poses and the frames around each subject, but also in the great attention to detail, most especially in the elaborate gowns.
Est: $8,000-$10,000. (4)

540. Vve. L. Brancher/1901. 1900.
13$^1/_8$ x 28$^1/_4$ in./33.3 x 71.6 cm
L. Brancher, Paris
Cond A–/Slight stains and creases.
Though not typically inclined to lend her consider-able talent to the arena of crass commercialism, Sonrel turns in a striking promotional calendar for the Brancher widow's ("Veuve") printing inks and materials, featuring a positively stunning Byzantine flower gatherer. What lovely deception, because even with first-rate ink and material, one requires talent on par with Sonrel's in order to achieve such superlative results.
Est: $2,500-$3,000.

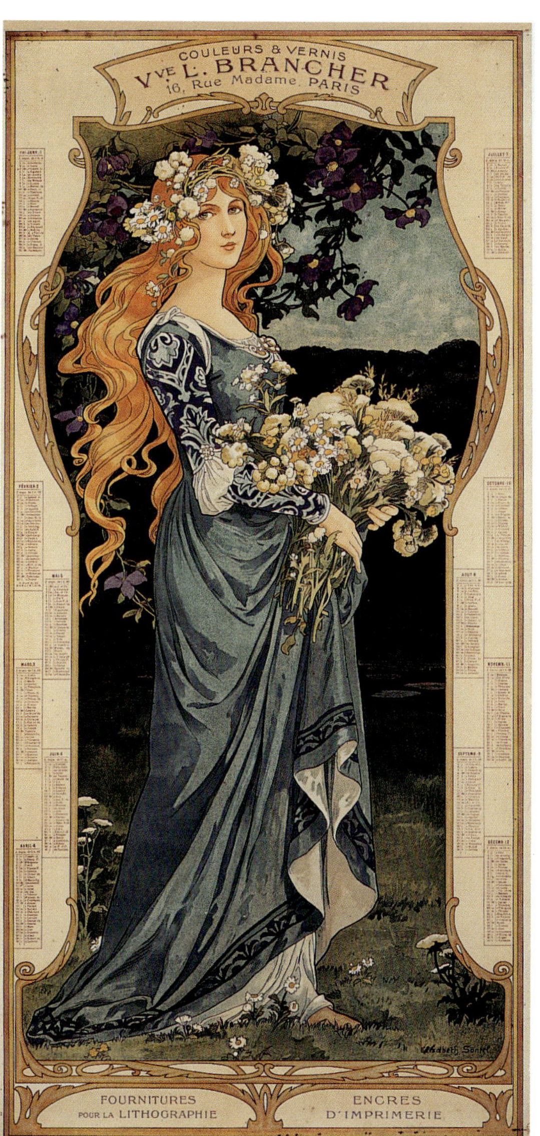

540

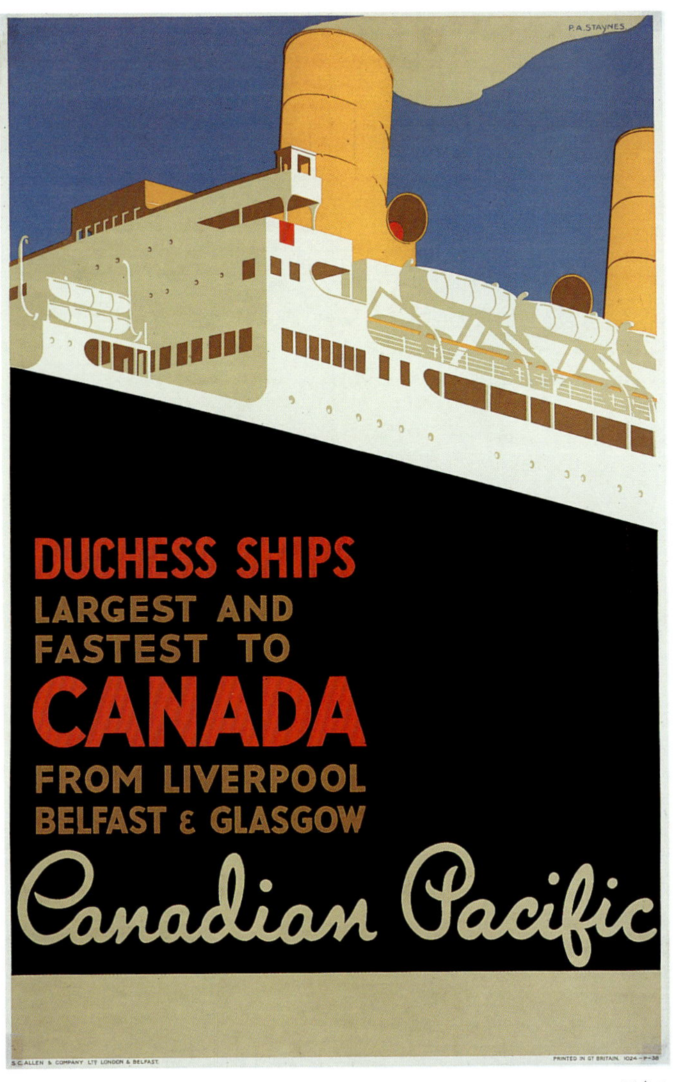

541

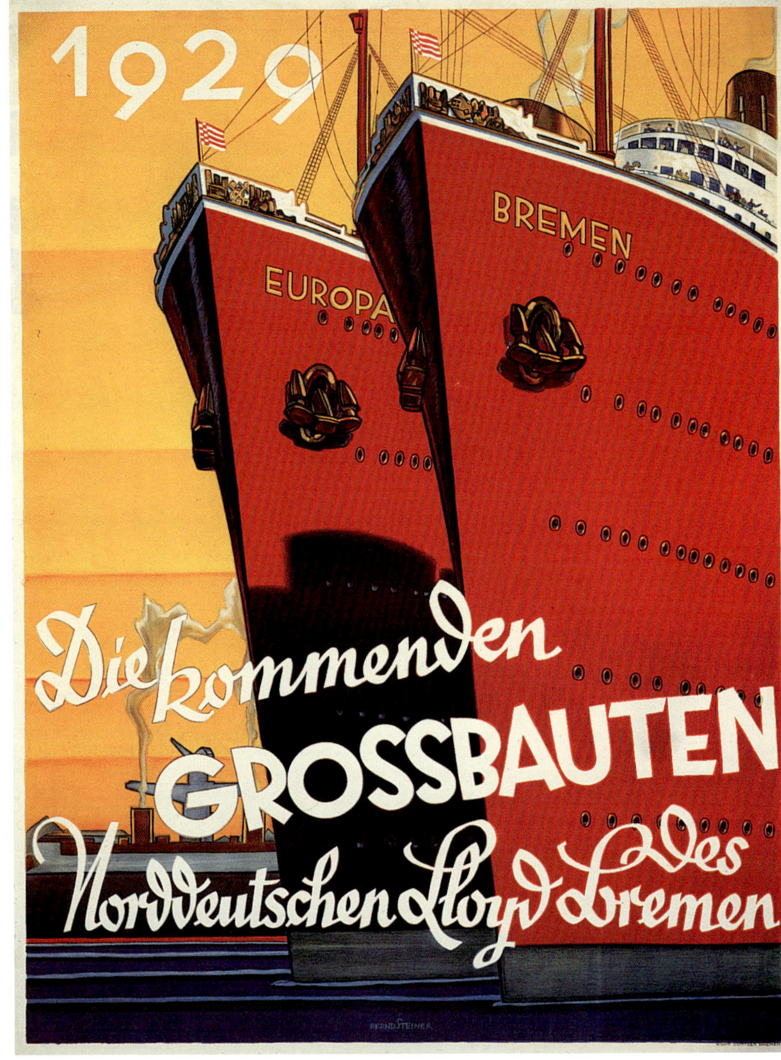

542

PERCY ANGELO STAYNES (1875-1953)

541. Canadian Pacific. ca. 1928.
$24^7/_8$ x 39 in./62.5 x 99 cm
S. C. Allen & Co., London
Cond B+/Restored tears at corners.
The period between the two World Wars was the hey-day of luxury cruising. During these years, Canadian Pacific operated more than 350 cruises to the West Indies, the Mediterranean, the Canary Islands, Scandinavia and around the world, as well as Great Lakes' voyages on the domestic front. "In 1927 and 1928, the four 'Duchess' steamships were launched for the Quebec to Liverpool service. In the same vein as the 'Empresses of the Pacific' these vessels were often referred to as 'Duchesses of the Atlantic.' 'Newest and Largest to Montreal and Quebec,' trumpeted the posters" (Canadian Pacific, p. 44). Here, Staynes promotes the line's service with stark, uncluttered majesty. All four of the two-funneled ships—the *Duchess of Atholl,* the *Duchess of Bedford,* the *Duchess of Richmond* and the *Duchess of York*—were converted into troop ships during World War II, but only two would survive: the *Duchess of Bedford*—which would be rechristened the *Empress of France*—and the *Duchess of Richmond*—renamed the *Empress of Canada.* Staynes "studied at the Manchester School of Art, the Royal College of Art, and the Academie Julian, in Paris. Staynes established himself in London as an oil and water-color painter, as well as an illustrator and designer . . . During World War II, Staynes designed posters for the British campaign against the German U-boats" (Canadian Pacific, p. 74).
Est: $1,700-$2,000.

BERND STEINER (1884-1933)

542. Norddeutscher Lloyd Bremen/Grossbauten.
$37^3/_4$ x 52 in./96 x 132 cm
Dontzen, Bremen
Cond B+/Slight tears at edges.
Ref: PAI-XVIII, 4554 (var)
Steiner became the house graphic designer for Norddeutscher Lloyd in the 1920s, creating many memo-rable designs for the vessels in their service. The line's behemoth sister ships *Europa* and *Bremen* are practically Siamese twins in Steiner's striking image. This German-language version announces that the wondrous ships are under construction. Steiner was to pair them again in other images for his employer (*see* Hillier, p. 260). *Rare!*
Est: $3,000-$4,000.

543. Wiener Mode. 1919.
$36^1/_2$ x $49^1/_2$ in./92.6 x 125.8 cm
Gesellschaft für Graphische Industrie, Wien
Cond B/Restored tears at folds and edges.
Using 18th-Century couture to promote contemporary chic may seem a bit counterproductive. However, in Steiner's capable hands, this triumvirate of well-bustled women creates magnetic commercial potential for the "Viennese Fashion" magazine, putting forth the time-less notion that comportment is just as vital as the clothes one wears. Steiner was for a time the art director for Bremen's City Theater and in 1919 began doing posters for *Motor* magazine and became the house graphic designer for Norddeutscher Lloyd in the 1920s. He died in Vienna in 1933.
Est: $1,400-$1,700.

THÉOPHILE-ALEXANDRE STEINLEN (1859-1923)

Deceptively simple, Steinlen's designs have a surpris-ing vigor—somehow they insinuate themselves into your consciousness, whether you like it or not. What he can do with a little girl and a couple of cats is irre-sistible; he creates an instant appeal, engages our emotions, involves us in the image and the very life he breathes into the poster.

Such a quality is, of course, highly prized in a posterist; it's a pity that he produced comparatively few commer-cial posters. The bulk of his work was book and maga-zine illustration (more than a thousand of them), as well as war and political images in poster and print media.

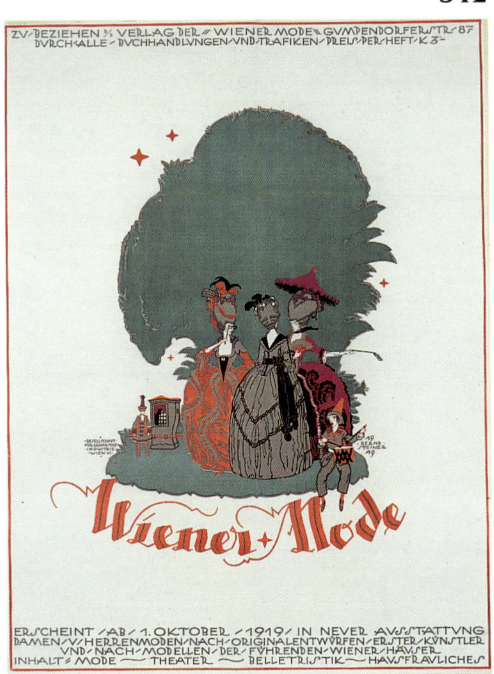

543

We call your attention to the five volumes of "Gil Blas" in the "Books and Periodicals" section—they are replete with Steinlen's finest illustrations. Also, Crauzat's catalogue raissoné of Steinlen's prints.

544. A la Bodinière/Exposition T. A. Steinlen. 1894.
$32^1/_2$ x $23^3/_4$ in./82.7 x 60.3 cm
Imp. Charles Verneau, Paris
Cond B/Restored tears at folds and edges.
Ref: Bargiel & Zagrodzki, 14; Crauzat, 492;
DFP-II, 782; PAI-XLII, 470

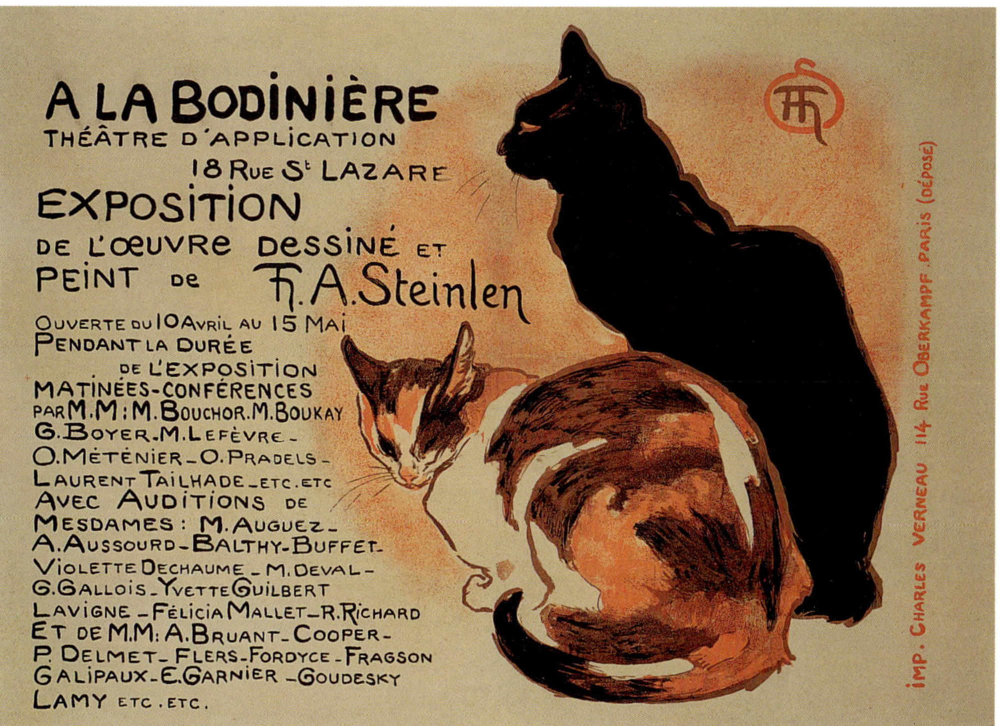

544

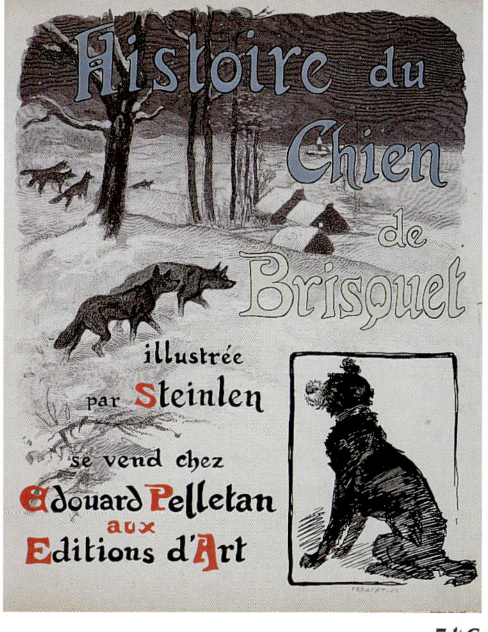

546

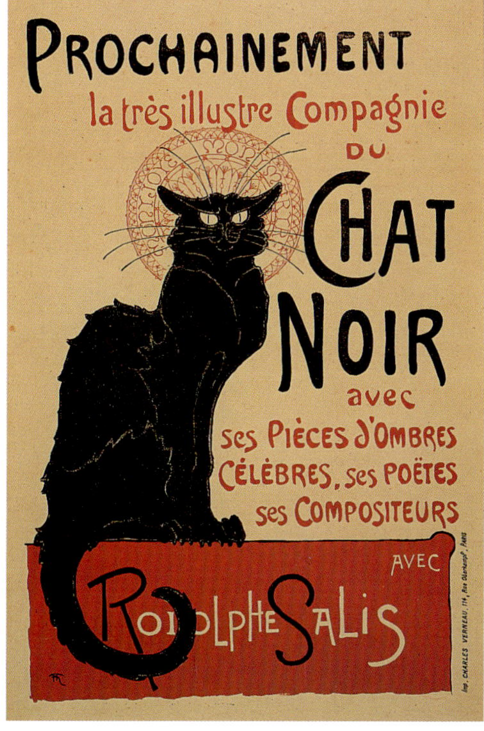

547

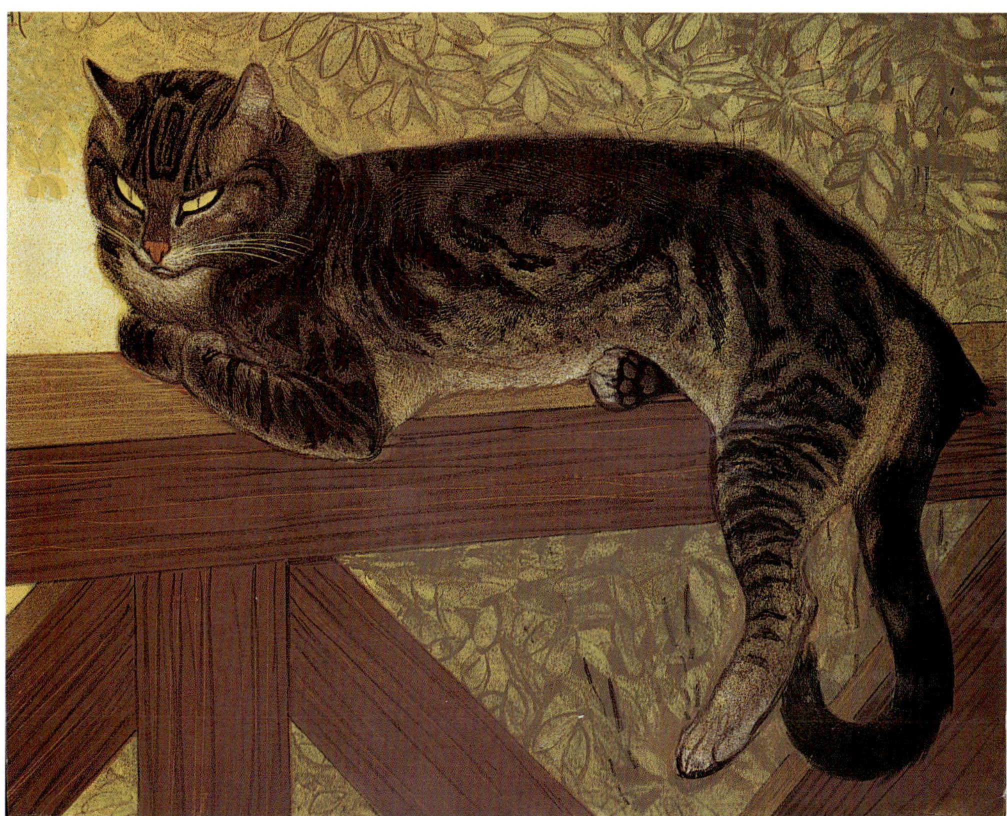

545

To advertise his important first exhibition of paintings, drawings and posters at the Bodinière gallery, Steinlen returns to a favorite subject: his cats. The simple but masterful sketch justly remains one of the great poster-ist's most famous and beloved images. This is the rare edition with text at left indicating the various celebrities who will make appearances during this exhibition. **Est: $5,000-$6,000.**

545. Summer Cat. 1909.
22 x 18 in./55.8 x 45.6 cm
Imp. R. Engelmann, Paris
Cond C/Trimmed into image at top left.
Ref: Crauzat, 282; Steinlen, 43; Steinlen's Cats, 16; PAI-XLII, 475
Titled "L'Été Chat sur un Balustrade," this "cheetah-like cat of summer drops a hind leg and its tail over the edge of the railing to catch a breeze. Its yellow eyes squint less with ferocity than with lassitude" (Steinlen's Cats, p. 48). This lithographic kitty was decoratively paired with a comfortably reclining feline originally used to announce an exposition of artists who paint animals at the Cercle International des Arts known as "L'Hiver Chat sur un Coussin" ("Winter Cat on a Pillow," *see* PAI-XL, 540).
Est: $3,000-$4,000.

546. Histore du Chien de Brisquet. 1899.
9 x 11³/₈ in./22.7 x 28.7 cm
Published by Éditions d'Art ƒduoard Pelletan, Paris
Cond A–/Slight horizontal fold. Framed.
Steinlen brings his animal mastery into play for a new edition of Charles Nodier's classic tale of a beloved and devoted mongrel being published by Éduoard Pelletan in a special edition for the 1900 Paris World's Fair. Steinlen, in addition to presenting the title mutt, shows the literal wolves-at-the-door moment that transpires moments before the story's climax. In addition to informing us of all the prices for the various states in which this edition will be available, the verso side of this prospectus mentions that there will be a total of twenty-five Steinlen compositions gracing its pages, including five color illustrations.
Est: $1,200-$1,500.

547. Chat Noir/Prochainement. 1896.
15³/₄ x 24¹/₈ in./40 x 61.2 cm
Imp. Charles Verneau, Paris
Cond A.
Ref: Bargiel & Zagrodzki, 22.B1; PAI-XXXIX, 476
This is the smaller format of the classic design for the Black Cat cabaret; the text here promotes the opening of a tour of the venue's resident performers, boasting of a "highly illustrious troupe" presenting shadow plays, poetry readings and songs. This represents the initial printing of the "Prochainement" poster; later, after Rodolphe Salis fell ill and was unable to perform with the company, the "avec" preceding his name was re-placed with "de," both as a tip-on and in a new edition of the poster.
Est: $10,000-$12,000.

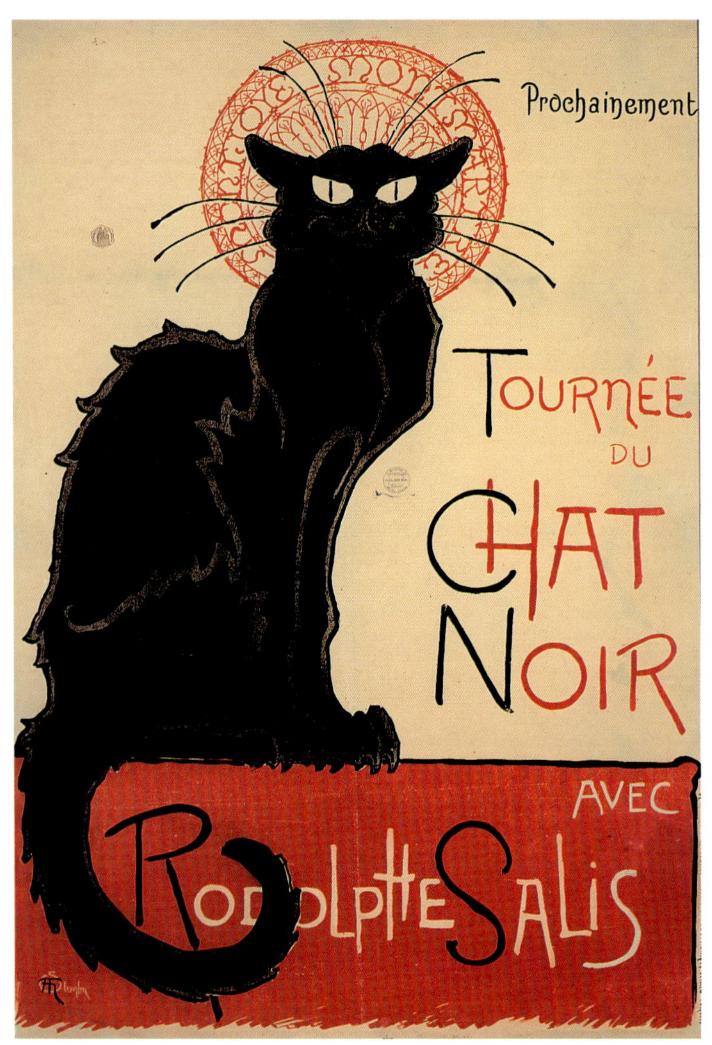

548

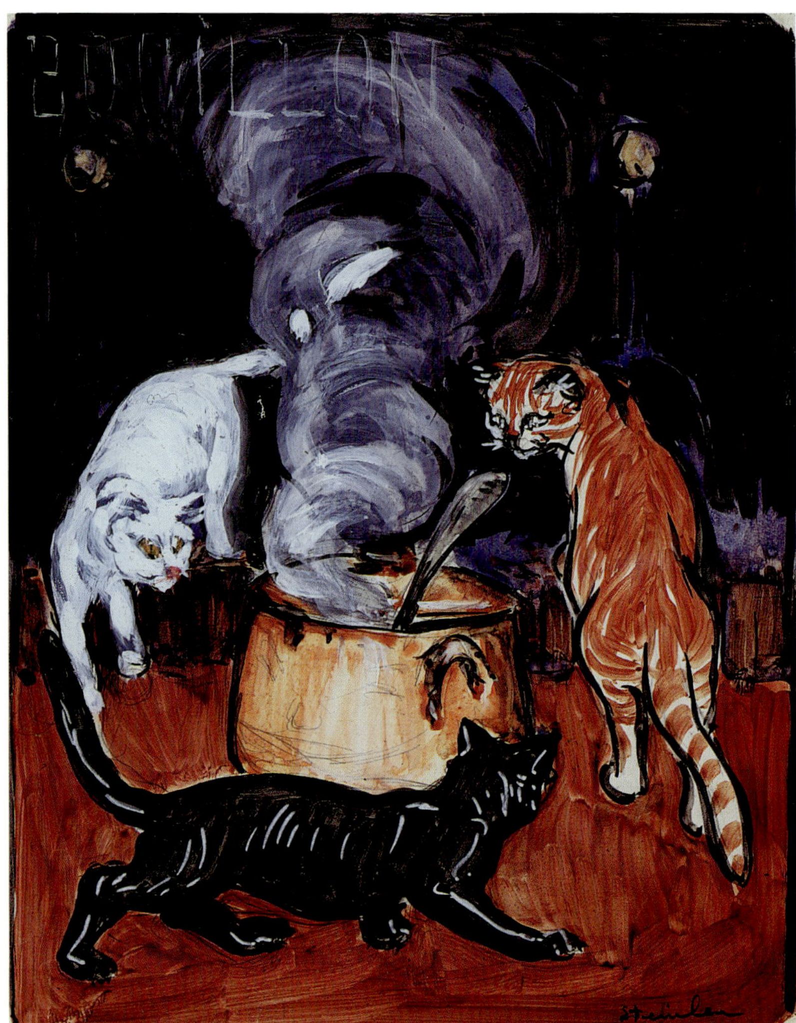

549

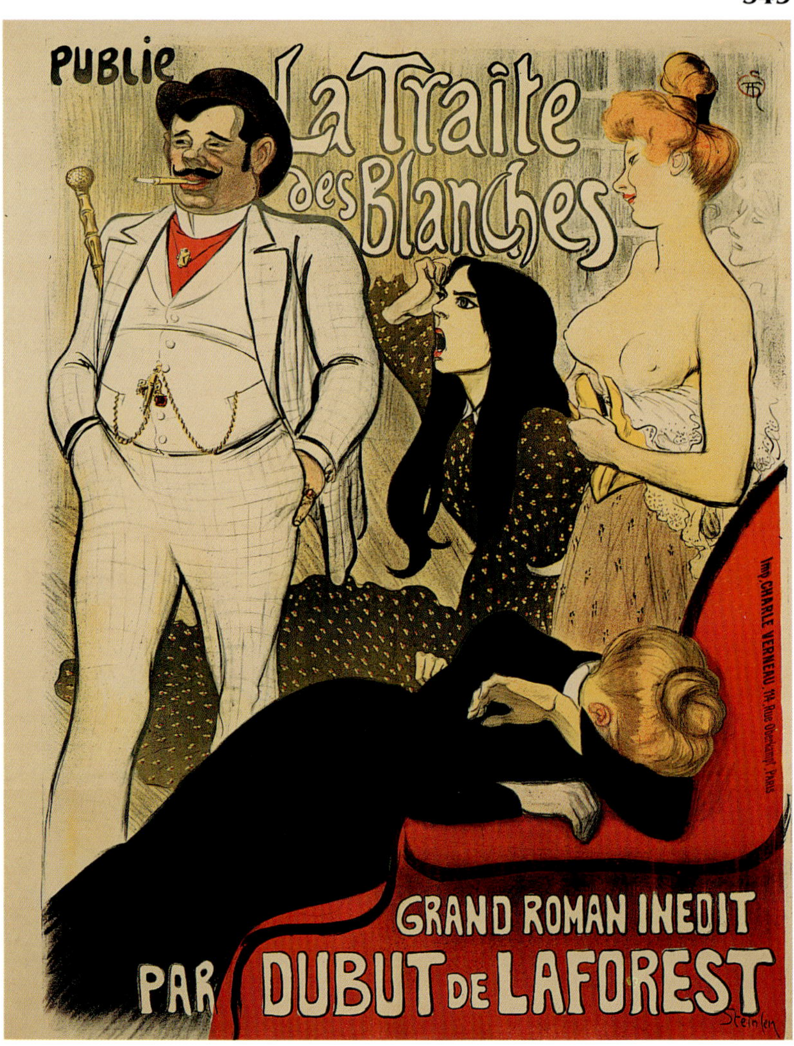

550

STEINLEN (cont'd)

548. Tournée du Chat Noir. 1896.
$37^1/_4$ x 54 in./94.6 x 137.2 cm
Imp. Charles Verneau, Paris
Cond B+/Slight tears at folds and in bottom text area.
Ref: Bargiel & Zagrodski, 22; Crauzat, 496; DFP-II, 787; Wagner, 63;
    Timeless Images, 51; Lautrec/Montmartre, 104; PAI-XLI, 534
That darn cat is at it again in the promotional service of the Chat
Noir cabaret. The design was no doubt meant as a satirical comment
on Mucha's posters, with Steinlen's well-traveled cat's long tail replac-
ing the long tresses in Mucha's images and the halo here having the
inscription "Mont-Joye-Montmartre." *This is the larger format.*
Est: $15,000-$20,000.

549. Bouillon.
$9^3/_8$ x $12^1/_8$ in./23.7 x 30.7 cm
Gouache and crayon maquette. Framed.
Like lionesses circling a gazelle before going in for the kill, this trio
of prowling felines close-in on their prey—a cauldron of steaming
broth. While Steinlen's cats can hardly be accused of always appearing completely domesticated, this is certainly a walk on the feral
side. A superb blend of the mundane and the untamed—so much
so that it's hard to imagine why this artwork never saw its way to
poster fruition.
Est: $6,000-$8,000.

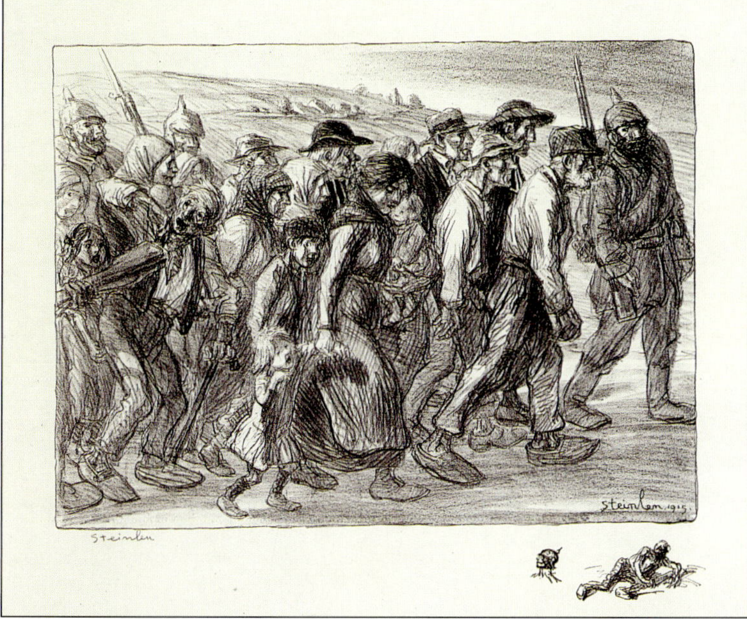

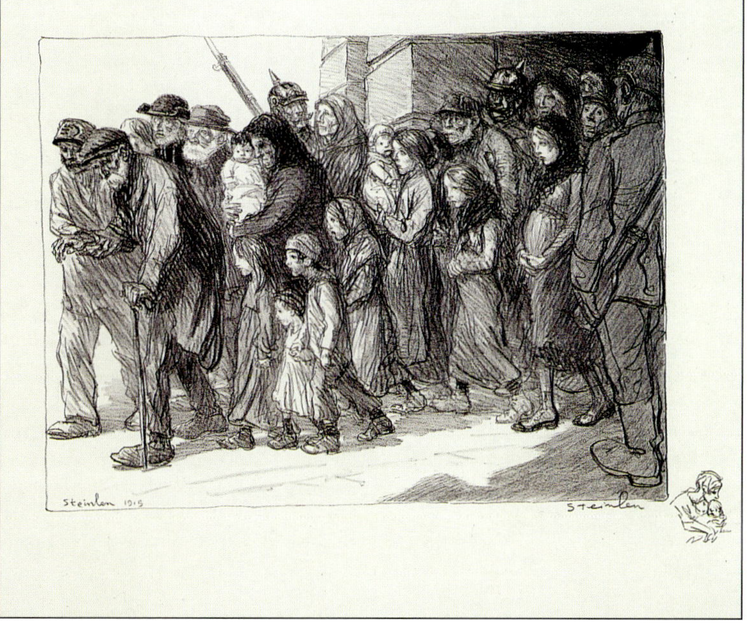

551

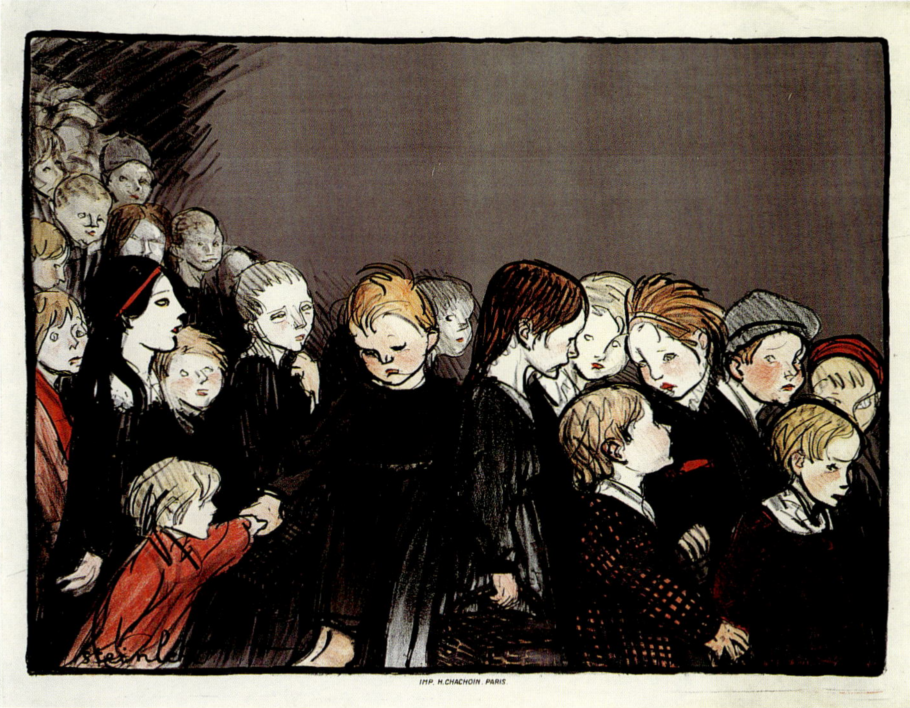

552

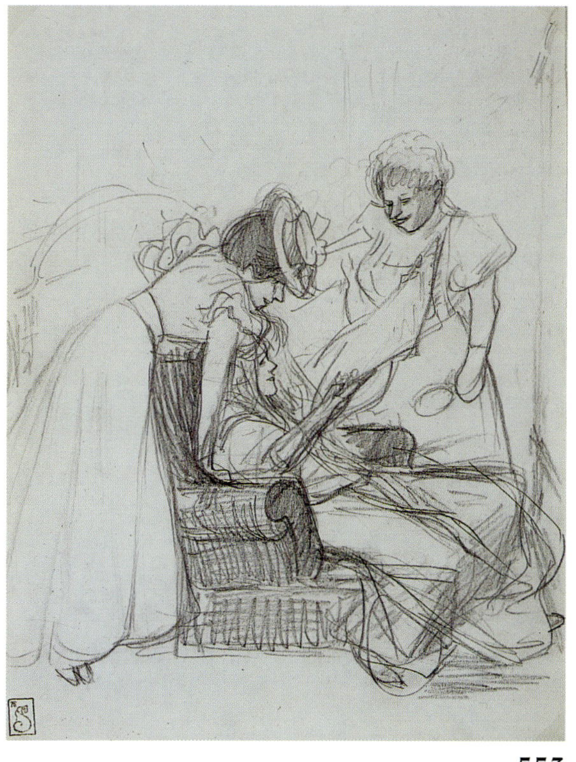

553

550. Le Journal/La Traite des Blanches. 1899.
$48^7/_8$ x $63^3/8$in./124.2 x 161 cm
Imp. Charle Verneau, Paris
Cond A.
Ref: Bargiel & Zagrodzki, 35; Crauzat, 503;
    DFP-II, 792; PAI-IV, 264
"Quite a few literary works of this era first saw the light of day as installments printed in daily or weekly papers . . . A major novel appearing in a trickle would hold readers for several months, with the hope that (readers) would get used to the paper's other features and remain loyal afterwards. The lure of a new sensational novel was often used to advertise the paper itself. And sensational is the word for this poster advertising installments of "White Slavery." It depicts a heartless pimp with three of his victims. One is arguing passionately for her freedom, one seems resigned to her fate, and one in utter despair" (Gold, p. 66). *This uncensored, larger format of the poster–seen here without top text banner–is the rarest of all versions–and this is the finest specimen of the design that we have ever seen!*
Est: $10,000-$12,000.

551. Refugees of War: Two Prints.
Each: $30^1/_4$ x $25^3/_4$ in./36.7 x 65.3 cm
Cond A.
Steinlen is always at his best when providing social commentary. Here, the compassionate artist presents not the soldiers who take up arms, but rather the citizens whose lives their conflicts impact. Steinlen doesn't heighten the situation, because there's no need to—the raw reality speaks volumes without augmentation. Women, children, the elderly and the infirm, all displaced by the ravages of war. As with all of his work, it's the sincerity with which Steinlen imbues his art that elevates it above the ordinary. *Hand-signed with remarques.*
Est: $1,500-$1,800. (2)

552. La Maternelle. 1920.
$43^1/_2$ x 34 in./110.5 x 86.3 cm
Imp. H. Chachoin, Paris
Cond A.
Ref: Bargiel et Zagrodzki, 72A2; PAI-XII, 402
Initially, "La Maternelle" was a 1904 novel that Steinlen illustrated. By 1920, it was turned into a stage play, and the author, Léon Frapié, asked Steinlen to prepare a poster, which was printed in two ways: with a buff background and red lettering, or with a dark background and yellow lettering. *This is the former version before the addition of letters.*
Est: $1,500-$1,800.

553. Le Journal.
$10^1/_2$ x $13^5/_8$ in./26.5 x 34.7 cm
Crayon drawing. Framed.
Steinlen, ever the keen observer of humanity, an illustrator of complexities without judgment or condescension, produced this drawing of three women, representative of different social strata gathered together in a single spot. With its sketch-style execution, one has to imagine that it was a promotional First Step that went no further than this. But what was it intended to promote precisely? After all, it's not an unusual scene, one that could easily have taken place in any parlor. Well, considering that all three women appear to be focused on the seated woman's newspaper, it seems as if the most likely answer is that it was done for a publication that appealed to all women, regardless of their age or where they fit into the era's socioeconomic continuum. *Estate stamp in the lower left corner.*
Est: $2,500-$3,000.

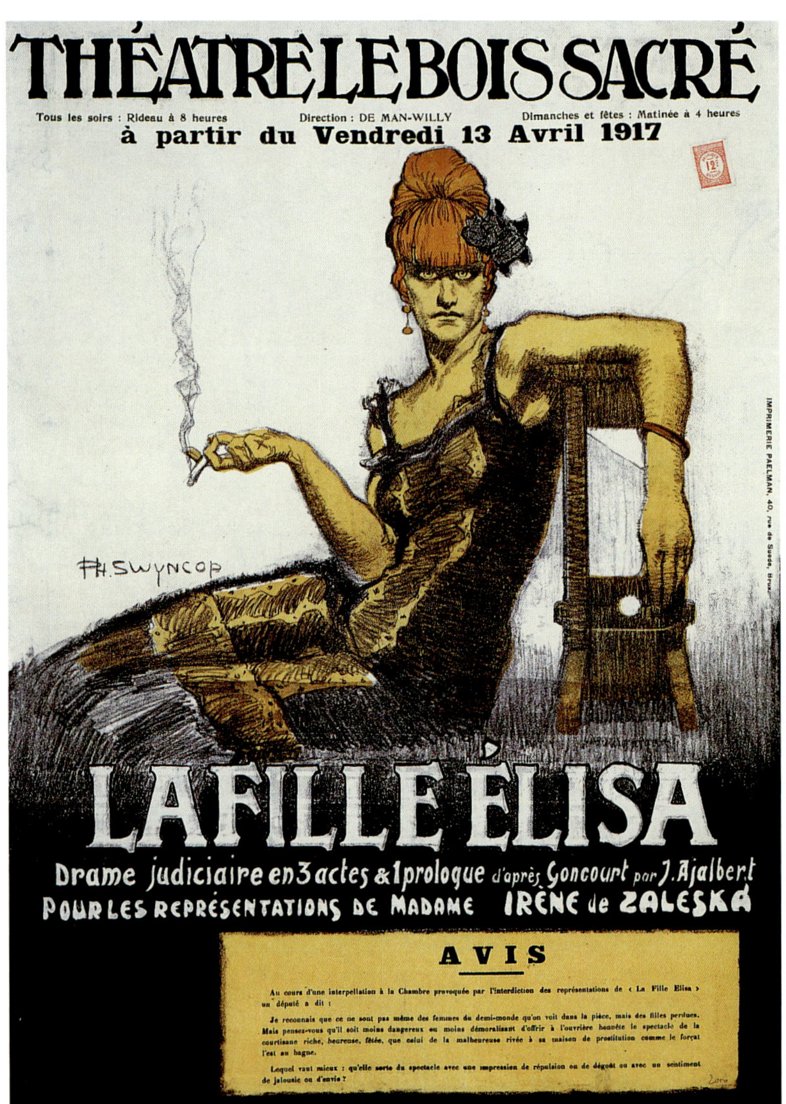

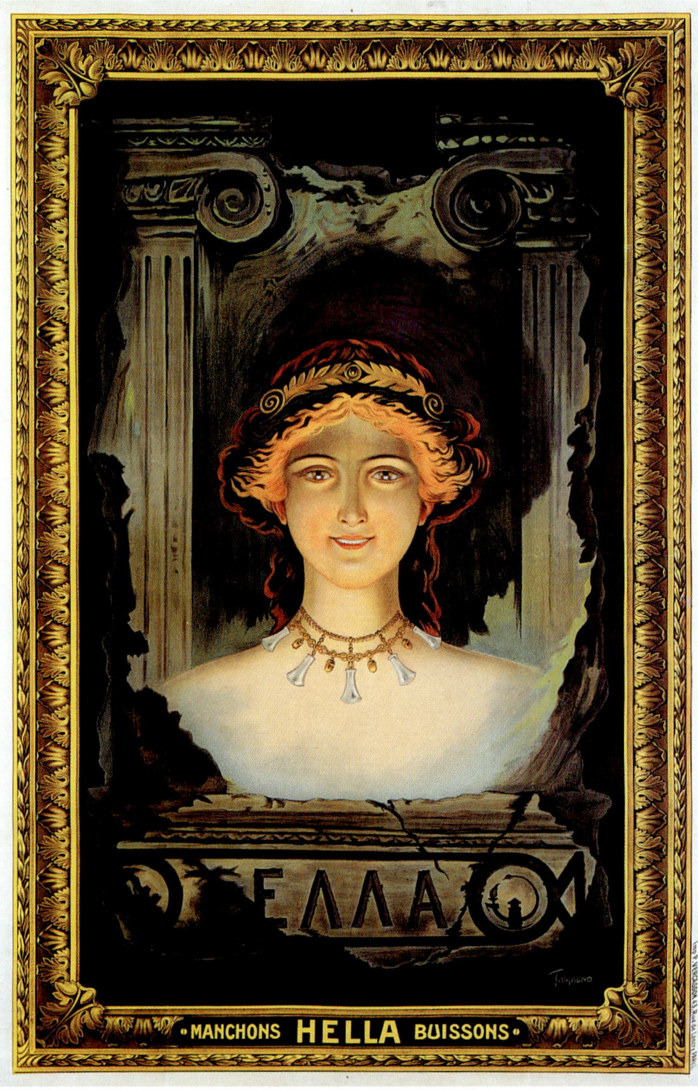

555

556

FRANK STELLA (1936-)

554. Lincoln Center Festival '67.
$29^1/2$ x $44^1/4$ in./74.8 x 112.3 cm
Cond A–/Slight stains at edges/P.
Ref: Lincoln Center, 38; Images of an Era, 68;
     Word & Image, p. 135;
     Modern American Posters, 171; PAI-XLI, 545
This photo-offset poster gives us Stella's minimalist
geometric patterns interlocked in vibrant Magic Marker
tones on graph paper. Commissioned by the List Foundation, these brightly-colored spinning shapes are definitely responsible for attracting our attention to the
existence of the 1967 Lincoln Center Festival, but the
question remains that for all their effectiveness—as is
often the case with Stella designs—in what way do
these patterns promote Lincoln Center? The results
are inconclusive, but it would seem that the conceptual conceit behind the design had to be that once
you've got someone's attention, the text takes care of
the informative end of the bargain, whether the image
is connected to the words or not.
Est: $1,200-$1,500.

PHILIPPE SWYNCOP (1878-?)

555. Théatre le Bois Sacré/La Fille Élisa. 1917.
$23^1/2$ x $33^1/8$ in./59.6 x 84.1 cm
Imp. Paelman, Bruxelles
Cond B/Restored tears, largely near paper edges.
This broad looks as if she's been around the block a
time or two. Or ten or twelve. In fact, she may even
own part of the block. It's certainly not likely that one
will find a "Pretty Woman" resolution in this adaptation
of Edmond de Goncourt's prostitution novel playing at
the Théâtre le Bois Sacré. However, this thought pro-
voking notice appears beneath the tough cookie known
as "The Girl Élisa"—"During a period where the theater
was shut down due to a ban being placed on performances of "La Fille Élisa" a deputy said: I recognize that
they aren't the same women of the demimonde that
one sees in the play, but they are lost women. But, do
you think that it's less dangerous or less demoralizing
to offer honest working-class people the spectacle of
the rich courtesan, happy, celebrated, than it is to show
an unhappy soul attached to a house of prostitution as
a convict is to a prison. Which is better: those who
leave the spectacle with an impression of repulsion or
disgust or those who depart with a feeling of jealousy
or envy?" An interesting query to be sure. Little is known
about etcher Swyncop other than he studied at the

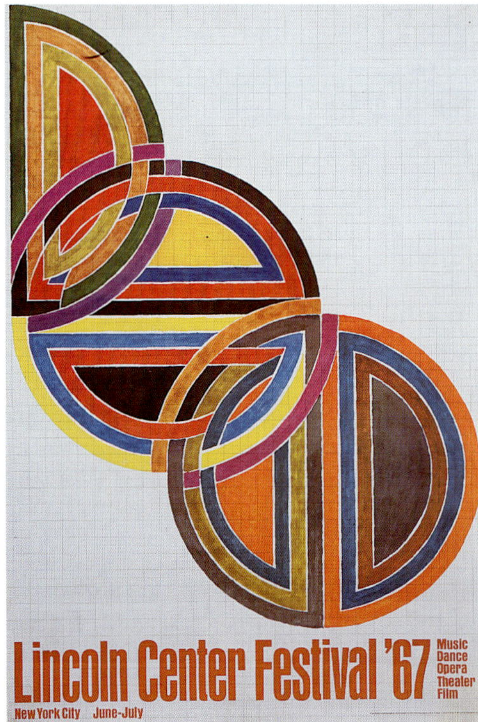

554

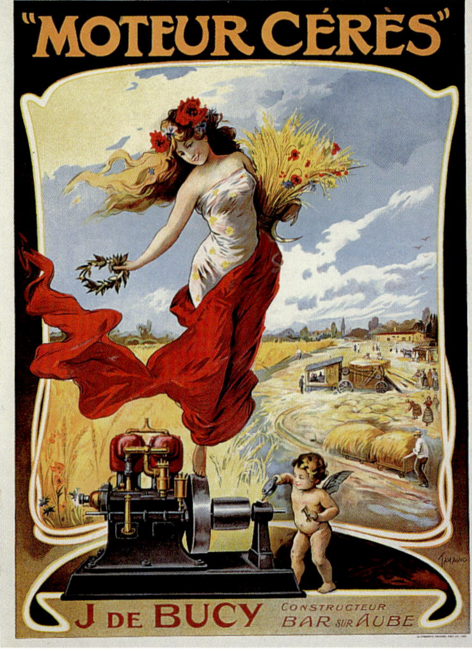

557

Academy of Brussels and that he traveled extensively
throughout France, Spain and Italy.
Est: $1,700-$2,000.

FRANCISCO TAMAGNO (1851-?)

556. Hella.
$50^1/8$ x $77^1/2$ in./127.3 x 196.9 cm
Imp. P. Vercasson, Paris
Cond B/Slight tears at folds.
Tamagno created this genuinely intriguing poster for

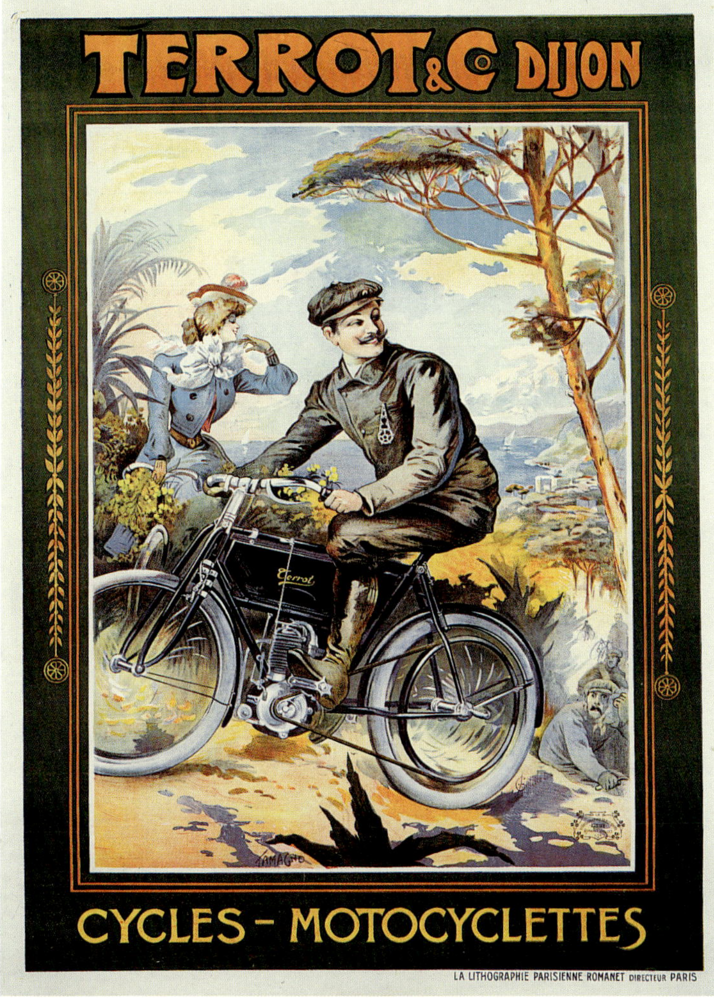

558

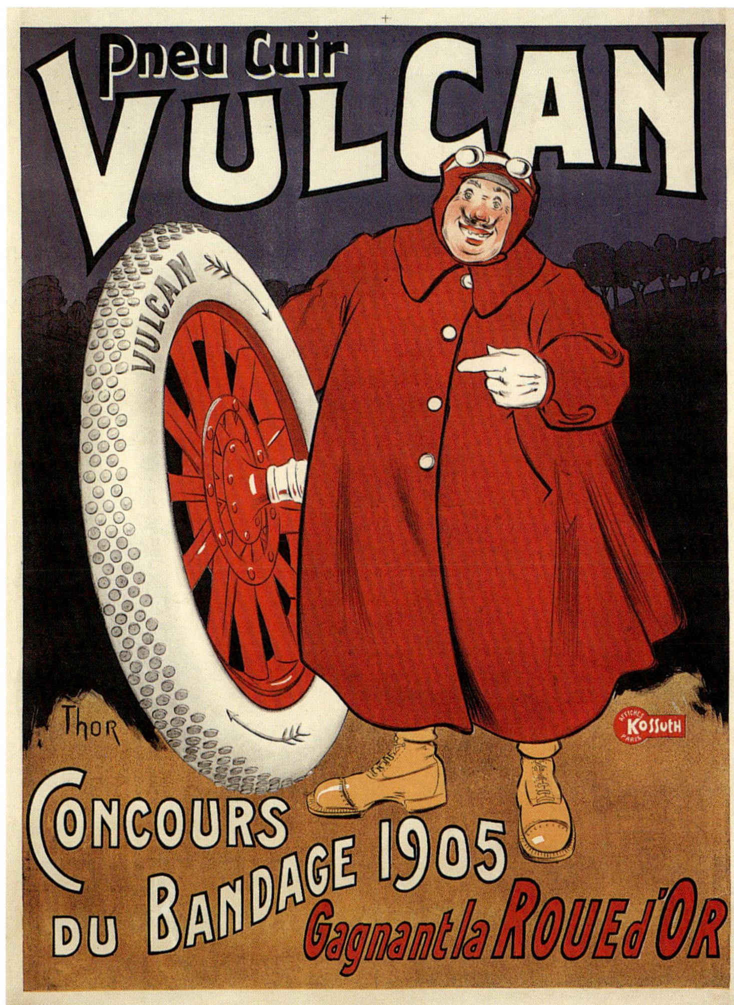

559

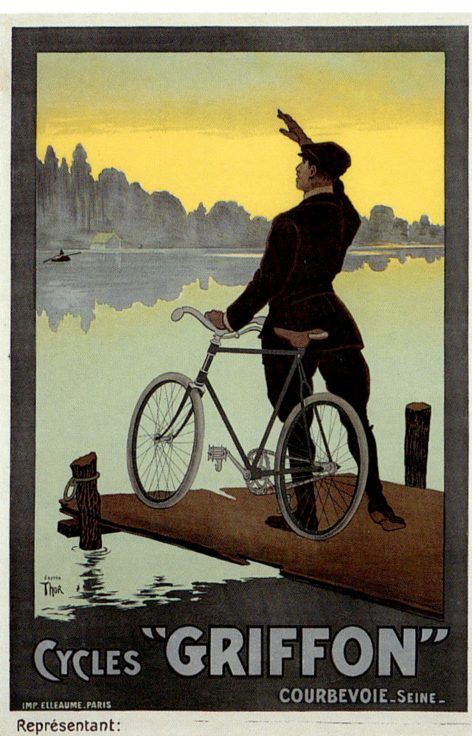

560

Hella, an establishment that we have to assume was a restaurant based on its subtle urging to eat and drink included at the base of the lithographic frame. Steeped in mythology and presented with classical decline, the centered dazzler places a sublime face to Hella, which, judging from the crumbling Ionic columns that flank her and the Cyrillic lettering beneath her, was an enterprise named for the goddess of Crete's oracular caves. However, no divination is required to comprehend the charming appeal of Tamagno's poster. *Rare!*
Est: $2,000-$3,000.

557. "Moteur Cérès"/J. de Bucy.
19$^1/_2$ x 27 in./49.5 x 68.5 cm
La Lithographie Parisienne, Paris
Cond A.
Farm machinery never looked so good. The central figure—poised, pleased and bounteous—represents, Ceres, the Roman goddess of agriculture and motherly love after which the engine was named. Not surprisingly, the golden hue of a plentiful harvest dominates the design. It's interesting to compare this Tamagno poster with a Charles Tichon creation for the same company (*see* PAI-XVI, 486)—whereas the Tichon goddess is austere and businesslike, Tamagno's vision conjures forth an image of benevolence and attraction.
Est: $1,200-$1,500.

558. Terrot/Dijon/Cycles-Motocyclettes.
39$^1/_4$ x 54$^3/_4$ in./99.7 x 139 cm
Lithographie Parisienne, Paris
Cond A–/Unobtrusive folds.
Ref: PAI-XXXIV, 567
Attitude is everything in the several Terrot bicycle posters Tamagno created at the turn of the century. In all of them a young lady makes it to the top of a hill way ahead of the competition (*see* PAI-XXII, 32 & PAI-XIX, 53), effortlessly outdistances an airplane (*see* PAI-XXVI, 545), beats a locomotive coming on at full speed (*see* PAI-XXX, 296 & PAI-XXXIV, 567) and, as seen here, keeps pace with a male companion atop a Terrot motorbike—although she appears to have taken some sort of shortcut through the underbrush. Her gentleman friend is the picture of good sportsmanship as he outpaces the other riders, but this feisty female, as is always the case in a Tamagno Terrot poster, doesn't neglect to let the competition know in no uncertain—if not precisely ladylike—terms who's the champ.
Est: $2,500-$3,000.

WALTER THOR (1870-1929)

559. Vulcan/Pneu Cuir.
45$^5/_8$ x 61$^3/_4$ in./116 x 157 cm
Affiches Kossuth, Paris
Cond B+/Slight tears at folds.
Leather isn't typically associated with pneumatic tires. And yet, before John Boyd Dunlop, the father of the modern tire, created the inflatable tires for his son's tricycle, Robert William Thomson, another Scottish innovator, invented the "Aerial Wheel," which consisted of a canvas inner tube surrounded by a leather outer tire. Even Dunlop's tire at first had a modified leather hosepipe as an inner tube under rubber treads. So even though it isn't commonplace, we shouldn't be surprised to see the use of leather in early tire production, as is the case with Vulcan, the winner of the "Golden Wheel" at a 1905 binding competition. And seeing as this overjoyed driver has opted to drape himself in a driving coat that matches his tire of choice, we have to assume that at least for a brief period of time, the French automotive public was pleased to roam the roads upon Vulcan leather tires. Thor, a member of the Salon des Artistes Français, is best known for his humorous turn-of-the-century transportation posters.
Est: $2,000-$2,500.

560. Cycles Griffon.
30$^1/_4$ x 45$^7/_8$ in./77 x 116.5 cm
Imp. Elleaume, Paris
Cond B+/Slight tears at folds and edges.
Ref: PAI-XXXI, 671
Thor designed several other posters for Griffon bicycles (*see* PAI-XXVII, 26, PAI-XXIX, 81 and PAI-XL, 64), which, though charming, don't even begin to approach the evocative nostalgia of this lakeside encounter. The namesake mythological winged-lion of the chain-driven transport is nowhere to be found; what is clearly present is a sense of anticipation and camaraderie in a tale primarily told in earth tones. Thor's composition is nothing short of brilliant, creating a splendid visual tension smattered with enough details so as to allow the viewer the opportunity to create a narrative of their own for the imminent meeting.
Est: $1,700-$2,000.

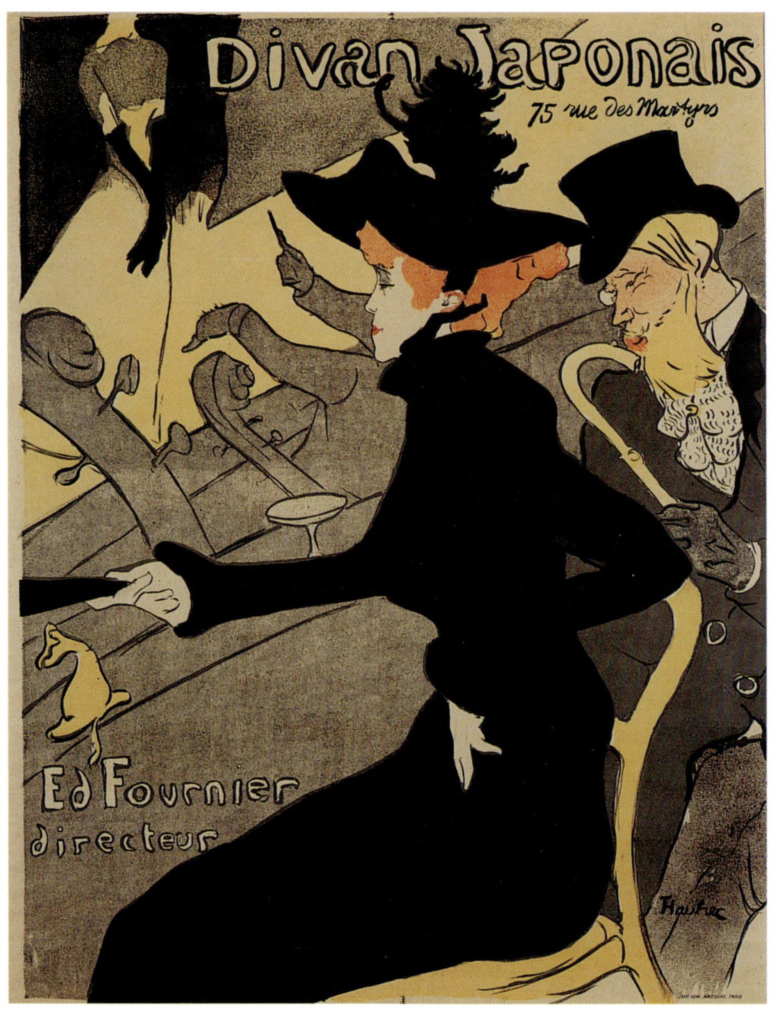

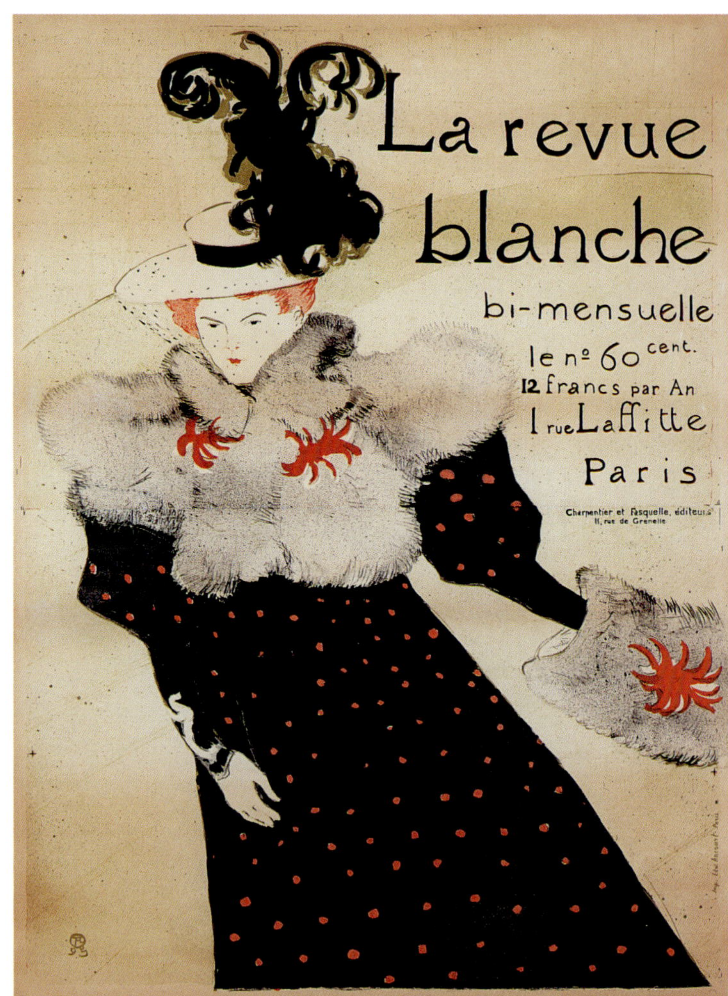

561

562

HENRI DE TOULOUSE-LAUTREC (1864-1901)

561. Divan Japonais. 1893.
$24^{1}/_{8}$ x $31^{1}/_{4}$ in./61.2 x 79.4 cm
Imp. Edw. Ancourt, Paris
Cond A-/Slight creases at edges. Framed.
Ref: Wittrock, P11; Adriani, 8; DFP-II, 824; Maitres, 2; Wagner, 3;
Modern Poster, 5; Wine Spectator, 42; Lautrec/Montmartre, 164;
PAI-XLI, 553

"Of all the female entertainers Lautrec celebrated in his posters, Jane Avril
and Yvette Guilbert were the two with whom he maintained the longest
friendships. He portrayed them both together in one of his most brilliant
posters, *Divan Japonais* . . . Although Guilbert was the performer at this
rather shabby cabaret when it opened in the spring of (1893), Lautrec made
the half-Italian Avril the focal figure in his composition. Under a shock of
red-orange hair topped with a pagoda-shaped hat and towering plume, her
black, silhouetted figure dominates the frontal plane as she assumes a
regal pose and an attitude of hauteur. Neither she nor her companion,
Edouard Dujardin, the distinguished founder of the Symbolist *Revue Wag-
nerienne*, deign to look at Guilbert on stage, whom Lautrec has portrayed
as acephalous, probably as a witty response to her complaint that he caricatured her and made her ugly" (Wagner, p. 21).
Est: $50,000-$60,000.

562. La Revue Blanche. 1895.
$37^{1}/_{8}$ x $51^{1}/_{4}$ in./94.3 x 130.2 cm
Imp. Edw. Ancourt, Paris
Cond A. Framed.
Ref: Wittrock, P16B; Adriani, 130-II; Maitres, 82 (var); DFP-I, 835 (var);
Gold, 92; PAI-XLI, 557

When Toulouse-Lautrec chose to advertise the art and literary magazine
"La Revue Blanche" by using a portrait of Misia Natanson, wife of coeditor
Thadée Natanson, it was because the brainy, redheaded beauty was the
real mover behind the throne. Her house was the mecca of the literati, and
it was she who coaxed some of the major celebrities of the day—Catulle
Mendès, Paul Valéry, Léon Blum, Octave Mirbeau, Claude Débussy, André
Gide, Colette and Toulouse-Lautrec himself—to contribute to the publication's success. The original design for this poster had a small remarque
printed at left that made it clear that Misia was being shown skating. In

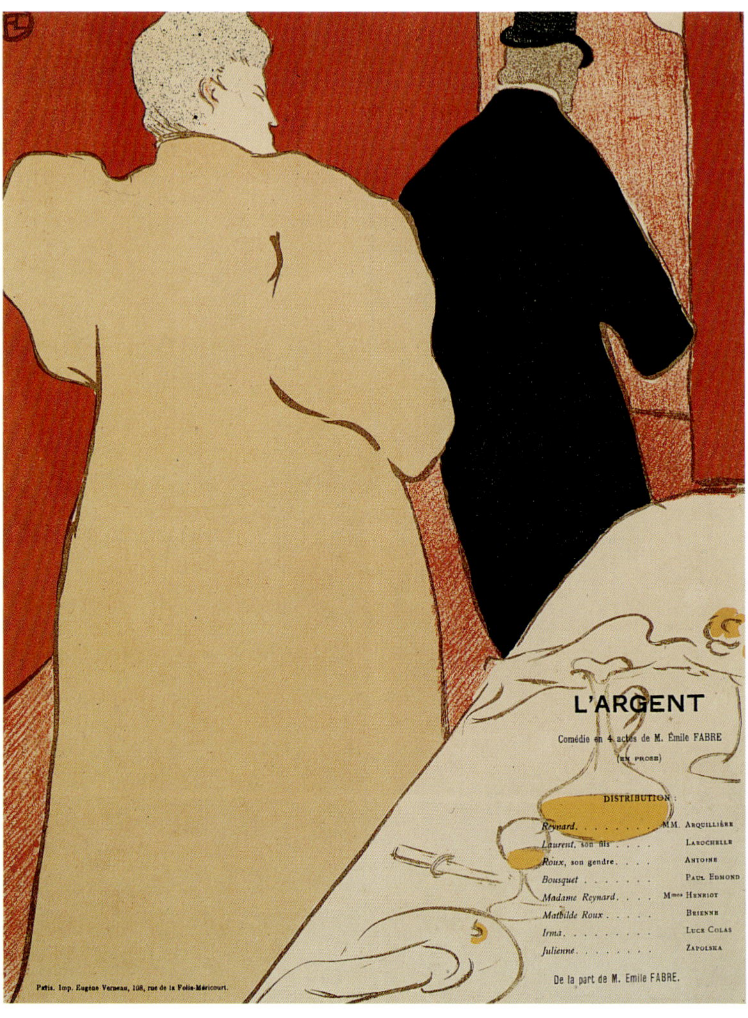

563

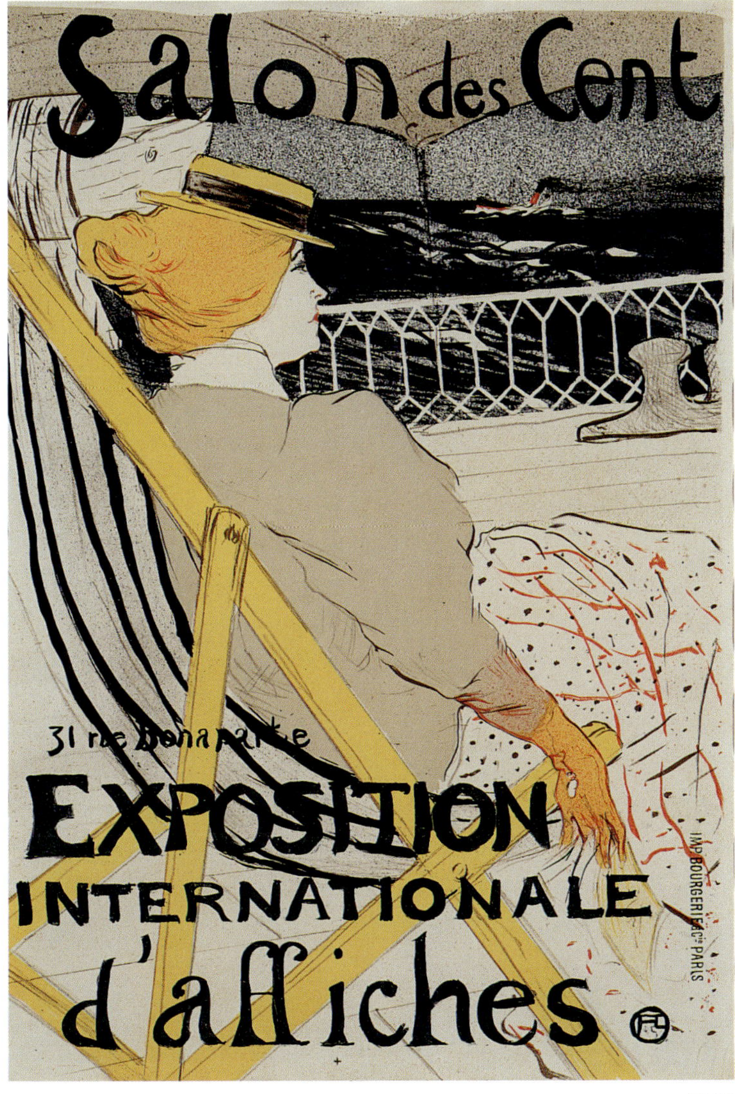

564

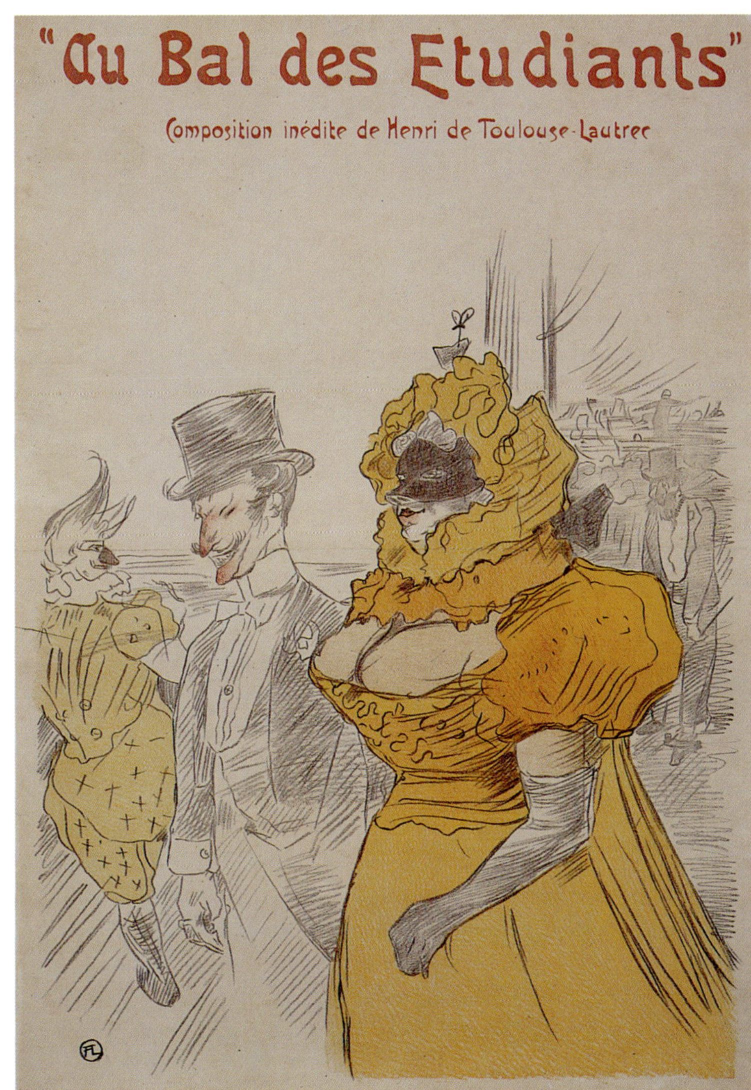

565

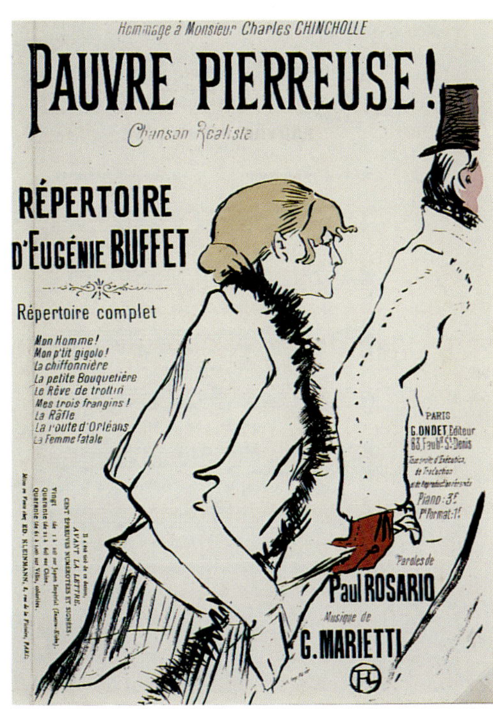

566

her biography of the artist, Frey writes that "many people feel [this poster] is [Toulouse-Lautrec's] strongest individual work . . . The strength of this work comes in large part from the fact that, as in many of Henry's posters, the figure is cut off by the lower edge just below the knees . . . The entire poster is like a little joke, as if Henry were amusing himself by proving that he could show an ice skater without ever showing her skates" (p. 408).
Est: $30,000-$35,000.

563. L'Argent. 1895.
$9^{1}/_4$ x $12^{1}/_2$ in./23.5 x 31.7 cm
Imp. Eugene Verneau, Paris
Cond A. Framed.
Ref: Wittrock, 97 (theater program edition);
    Adriani, 133-II; PAI-VII, 340
"On this coloured programme for the comedy *L'Argent* (Money) by Emile Fabre, the large figures—Henriot and Arquillière as Monsieur and Madame Reynard—are only coloured shapes and there is no indication of modeling in the bodies. Since the play had its première on 5 May 1895 at André Antoine's Théâtre Libre, the lithograph was presumably made just before that date. The composition and details of the place-setting on the table are reminiscent of the Reine de Joie poster (*see* PAI-XXXIII, 575) . . . the dimensions of which are almost the same as the larger first state of this lithograph" (Adriani, p. 186).
Est: $5,000-$6,000.

564. Salon des Cent. 1896.
$15^{3}/_4$ x $23^{1}/_2$ in./40 x 59.7 cm
Imp. Bougerie & Cie., Paris
Cond A. Framed.
Ref: Wittrock, P20; Adriani, 137-III;
    Salon des Cents, p. 37; Chaumont/Exposons, p. 18;
    Gold, 195; PAI-XXXV, 484
The model lounging on deck (the poster is sometimes called "La Passagère du 54"—the number being that of her cabin) is an elusive woman whom Lautrec fleetingly glimpsed aboard a ship bound from Le Havre to Bordeaux; he pursued her to Portugal where he gave up the chase. He did manage to get a photograph of her and, on that basis he executed a lithograph and subsequently a poster to advertise an Exhibition of International Posters at the Salon des Cent. "The woman's hair, which the artist characteristically drew as red with splatter . . . is pulled back in a low chignon, upon which sits her little straw boater. The forward tilt of the hat accents the profiled diagonality of the composition, continuing in the geometric frame of the yellow deck chair. The gentle dip of the ship is conveyed by the slant of the deck chair counterpoint the lightly parallel lines of the floor, while the billowing plaid blanket balances the figure's sag on the canvas seat. The great poise and composure of the woman is unparalleled among Lautrec's posters" (Wagner, p. 30). *The finest specimen of this rare poster that we have ever offered!*
Est: $70,000-$90,000.

565. Au Bal des Etudiants. 1901.
$14^{1}/_2$ x $21^{1}/_4$ in./36.8 x 54 cm
Cond A–/Slight tears and stains at edges; usual
    horizontal fold. Framed.
Ref: Wagner, p. 34; Delteil, Vol. X, Intro;
    Dortu, D.4.636, Vol. VI; Joyant, p. 240;
    Lautrec by Lautrec, p. 71; PAI-XLII, 499
With a self-satisfied smirk, a gentleman escorts an extremely over-endowed lady to a social event where they are bound to create quite a stir. Lautrec knows that once we catch a glimpse of the lady's ample charms, we won't take notice of anything else—and so everything else is, quite appropriately, almost indistinct and insignificant. This is Lautrec's last poster; he designed it a few months before his death for a students' ball in Bordeaux, where he was living at the time. He wasn't involved in the printing process nor did he create the lettering.
Est: $7,000-$9,000.

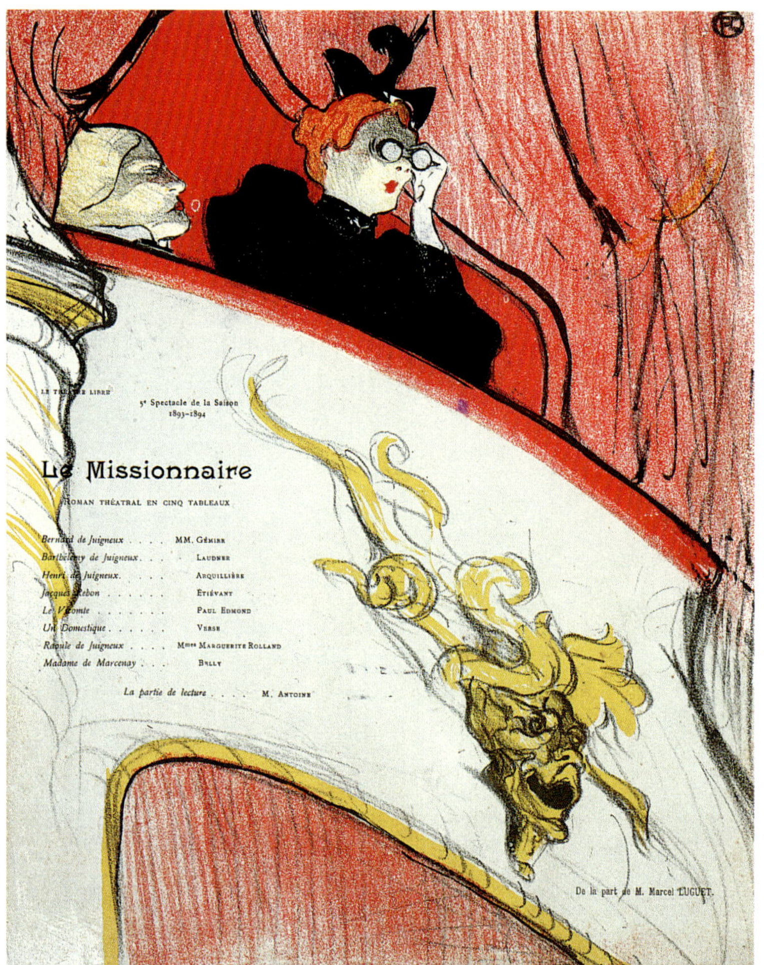

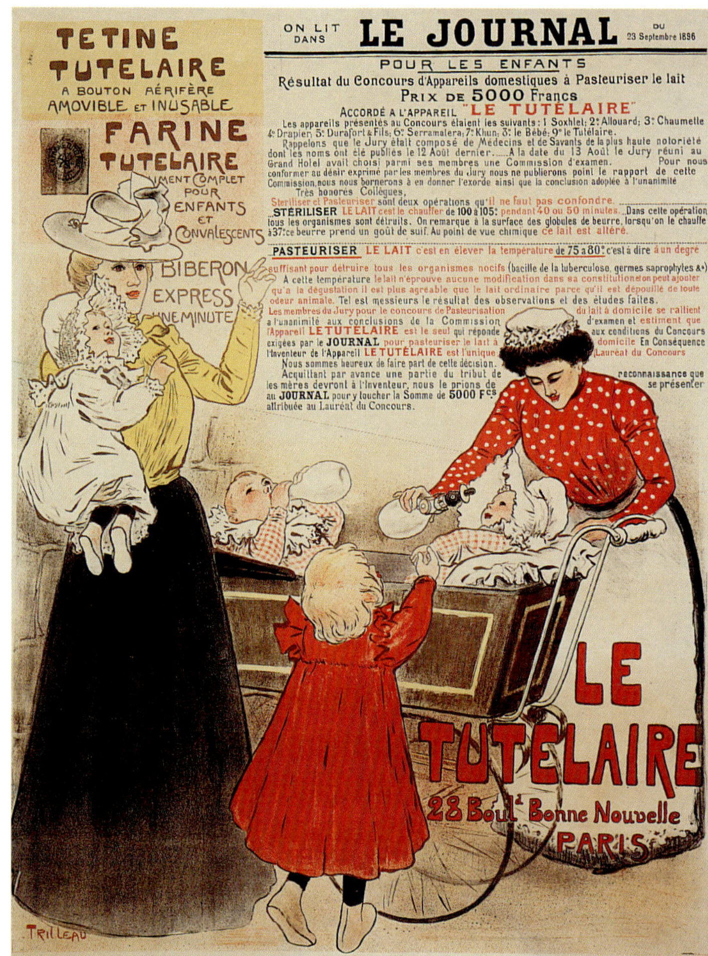

567

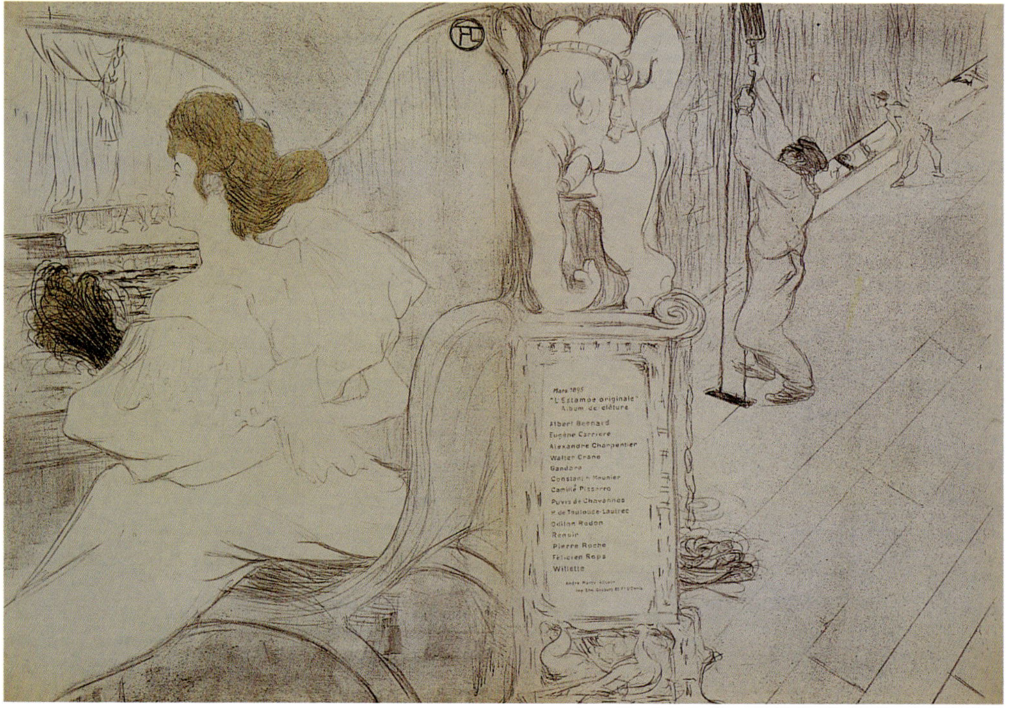

568

TOULOUSE-LAUTREC (cont'd)

566. Pauvre Pierreuse. 1893.
6³/₄ x 9⁵/₈ in./17 x 24.3 cm
Cond A. Framed.
Ref: Adriani, 35-II; Delteil, 26-II; Adhemar, 27-II;
   Witrock, 13
The two-page song sheet for "Poor Streetwalker" not only lists the other songs that make up the repertoire of Eugénie Buffet, "la chanteuse populaire" of the Parisian music hall scene, it informs the reader where they can acquire signed-and-numbered textless poster versions of the design. As always, Lautrec presents the target of his artistry without glamorization or condescension, presenting the dire, dour situation in an altogether unromantic fashion. *The cover is a lithograph with stencil coloring.*
Est: $3,000-$4,000.

567. La Loge au Mascaron Doré. 1894.
9¹/₂ x 12¹/₈ in./24 x 30.7 cm
Imp. Ancourt, Paris
Cond A. Framed.
Ref: Wittrock, 16; Adriani, 69-II; PAI-XXXVIII, 551
"For Lautrec the theatre was to be found in the boxes as much as on stage. One of his best known inventions, *La Loge au Mascaron Doré* (The Box with the Gilded Mask) was a programme for Marcel Luguet's play *Le Missionnaire* (The Missionary), which had its première at the Théâtre Libre on 24 April 1894. With its economical use of colour, this is one of Lautrec's greatest achievements in the field of small scale colour lithography . . . Above left we see the profile of the English illustrator Charles Edward Conder (1868-1909), who had met Lautrec at the Moulin Rouge" (Adriani, p. 110). Julia Frey, who calls this "one of his best-known lithographs," makes the interesting point that by focusing on the audience rather than the play, Lautrec was making a reactionary statement, as his friend André Antoine, the actor/director and founder of the Théâtre Libre, was "the first to turn out the house lights and insist that the audience instead of watching each other, watch the actors on stage" (Frey, p. 368).
Est: $14,000-$17,000.

568. L'Estampe Originale/Cover. 1895.
32¹/₄ x 22⁵/₈ in./82 x 57.5 cm
Cond A–/Slight stain at vertical fold. Framed.
Ref: Wittrock, 96; Adriani, 129-III; PAI-XXXIX, 497
An unsigned proof of the cover, apart from the edition of 100 signed copies.
"The scenery for the unsuccessful play *Le Chariot de Terre Cuite* makes another appearance in this cover for the ninth and last edition of *L'Estampe Originale* in March 1895, printed by Ancourt, Paris. On the left half of the large sheet, which is used in horizontal format, Lautrec has varied the motif of the Divan Japonais poster (*see* No. 561), though the much-feted Misia Natanson (1872-1950) is now seated in the box instead of Jane Avril" (Adriani, p. 181).
Est: $15,000-$20,000.

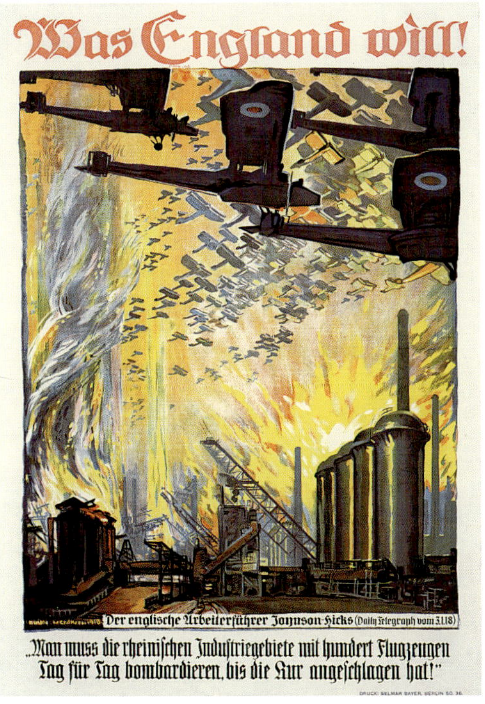

570

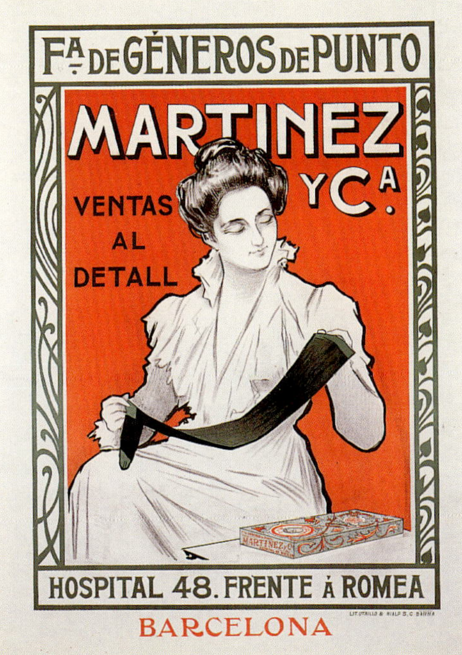

571

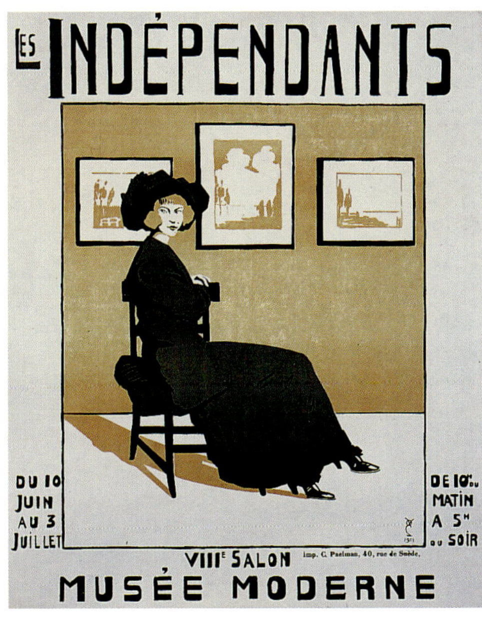

572

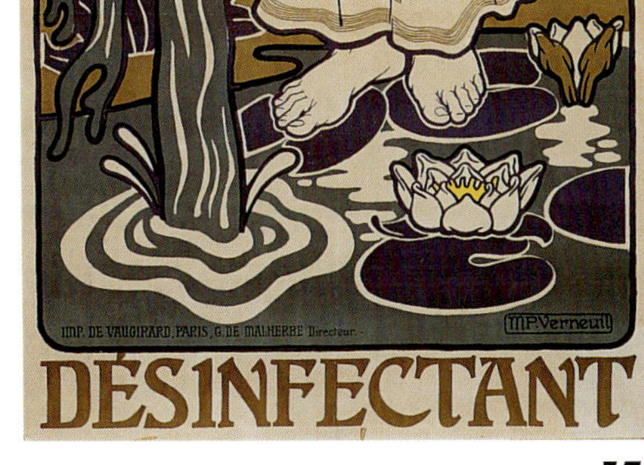

573

TRILLEAU

569. Le Journal/Le Tutelaire. 1896.
45 x 61^{1}/$_8$ in./114.3 x 155.2 cm
Atelier Trilleau, Paris
Cond B+/Unobtrusive folds.
Though we may not be overly-familiar with Trilleau's work, it would appear as if the lesser-known artist was fairly well-acquainted with Steinlen's output. Not that this advertisement for Tutelaire formula is an out-and-out copy of Steinlen, but the composition, on-view domesticity and color-scheme certainly have an air of familiarity. Regardless of artistic inspiration, these ready-to-use, fast-heating bottles—whose name roughly trans-lates as "The Guardian"—look to be a hit with infants, nannies and mothers alike, thanks to their portability and durability, not to mention an easy-to-suckle venti-lated nipple. The upper text goes on at length about the merits of the product—including its top prize in the *Le Journal* competition for the very best way to pas-teurize milk—but make no mistake: it's the vision of all-around instant gratification that carries the promo-tional load.
Est: $1,700-$2,000.

EGON TSCHIRCH (1889-1948)

570. Was England Will! 1918.
26^{5}/$_8$ x 38^{1}/$_4$ in./7.7 x 97.3 cm
Selmar Bayer, Berlin
Cond A-/Unobtrusive folds.
RAF bombers fill the skies like a plague of biblical pro-portions, raining down destruction in seemingly limit-less quantities. As accustomed as we've become to seeing posters that warn the British and American publics about the ruthless nature of their foes, here we're presented with the opposite side of the argument, proving that in war one sole constant endures—fear. According to the Tschirch poster, "What England Wants" is to see the German industrial complex bombed out of existence. And in order to provide the whiff of an immediate threat so necessary for effective propaganda, a quote from British Labour Party leader Johnson-Hicks that appeared in the *Daily Telegraph* on January 3 of that year is included: "One must bomb the Rhine indus-trial area day by day with hundreds of airplanes, until the cure has occurred." In addition to his graphic work, Tschirch dabbled in fine art and scenic design. *Rare!*
Est: $1,500-$1,800.

ANTONI UTRILLO (1864-1944)

571. Martinez y Ca. 1900.
16^{1}/$_4$ x 22^{3}/$_8$ in./41.3 x 56.8 cm
Lit. Utrillo & Rialp, Barcelona
Cond A.
Ref: Cataluña, 98; PAI-XLI, 58 (var)

Soft, subtle Spanish Art Nouveau is called into play in this promotion for a Barcelonan stocking manufacturer. Nothing is forced about this silken inspection that is at once realistic and somehow quietly seductive. Antoni Utrillo i Viadera (not to be confused with posterist Miguel or painter Maurice, no relations) was one of Spain's most productive early posterists, as well as an accomplished painter, muralist and illustrator. He was flexible as to style, and in fact lived long enough to experience several trends in poster design starting with Art Nouveau. *This is the smaller format.*
Est: $1,700-$2,000.

VANO

572. Les Indépendants. 1911.
15^{3}/$_4$ x 19^{3}/$_4$ in./40 x 50 cm
Imp. C. Paelman (Bruxelles)
Cond A.
This eighth annual unjuried exhibition of Belgian artists is brought to the public's attention by Vano with poised austerity, so much so that his sole observer becomes as much a part of the viewing as the pastoral scenes that hang behind her.
Est: $1,200-$1,500.

MAURICE P. VERNEUIL (1869-1942)

573. Laurénol. 1898.
21^{7}/$_8$ x 60^{3}/$_4$ in./55.5 x 154.2 cm
Imp. de Vaugirard, Paris
Cond B-/Slight tears at folds and edges.
Ref: Health Posters, 197; PAI-XLI, 577
"What a strikingly beautiful poster this is! The entire poster depicts a modern version of a classical naïad. The link between this nymph of springs and streams and Laurénal is not immediately apparent, however. Perhaps one might suggest that it resides in the notion of cleanliness: no doubt the artist wanted to suggest that use of the product allows one to return to a purity comparable to that of spring water? The text is kept to a strict minimum. The image is laden with ornamental swirls and stylized plant images that fill the picture. The design is also remarkable because of the monumental quality that its strongly vertical design accentuates. In a nutshell: this poster exemplifies every characteristic of Art Nouveau. Frozen in a kind of priestly stillness, the Laurénal nymph seems to defy the stress of centuries . . . At the time of this poster, there were various forms of Laurénal on the market: nr 1, medical, nr 2, a disin-fectant, and nr 3, for agricultural use" (Health Posters, p. 154). The influence of his mentor, Grasset, is evident in this Verneuil design. He also created works for *Le Monde Moderne* and Docteur Pierre toothpaste.
Est: $1,500-$1,800.

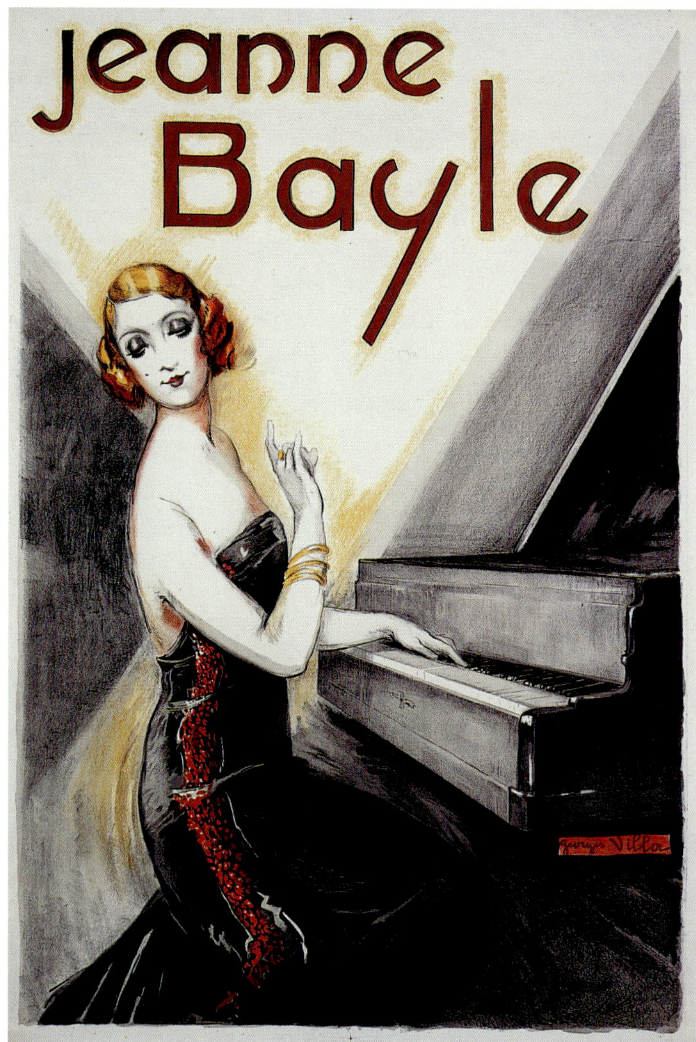

575

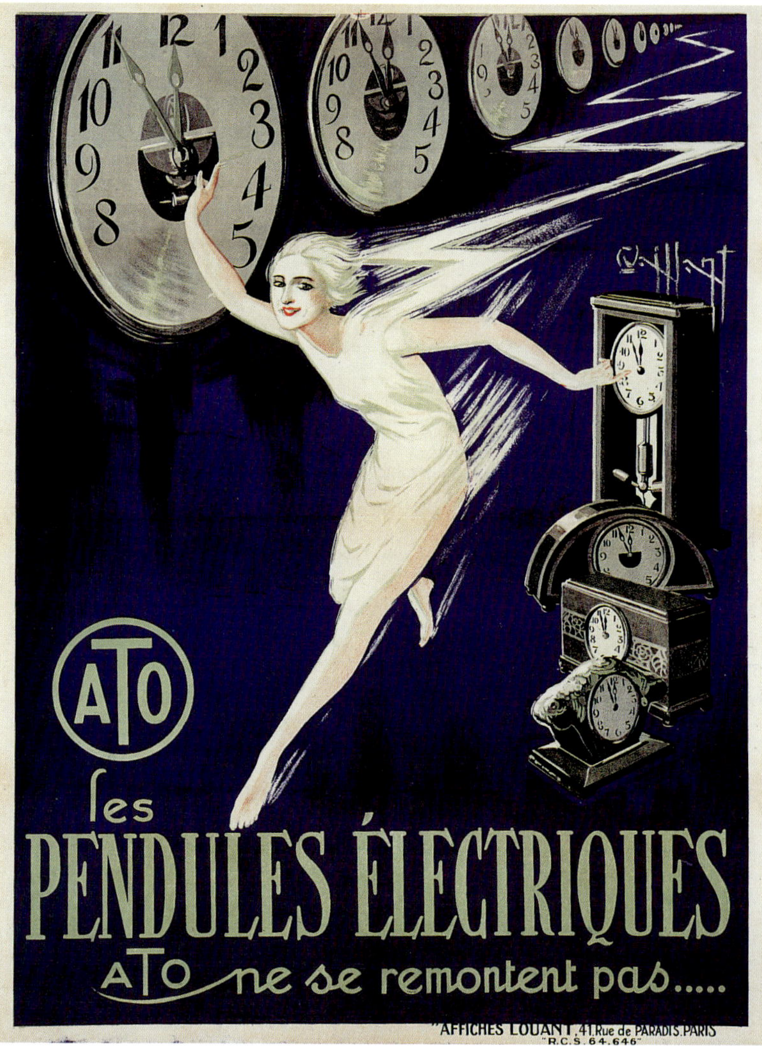

576

WALTER VAN DIEDENHOVEN (1886-1915)

574. Huis & Tuin. 1913.
$29^1/_2$ x $48^3/_4$ in./75 x 123.6 cm
N. V. Dieperink & Co.
Cond B+/Slight tears and stains at edges.
Ref: Dutch Posters, 98; PAI-XI, 12
Diedenhoven belongs to the Dutch romanticists, like Roland-Holst, Klijn (*see* No. 388) or Rot, who believed in elaborate decorative frames and borders. This 2-sheet poster for a home show charmingly centers a cozily snuggled house into the midst of all the ornate goings-on.
Est: $1,700-$2,000.

GEORGES VILLA (1883-?)

575. Jeanne Bayle.
$31^1/_4$ x $46^3/_4$ in./79.3 x 119 cm
Cond A-/Slight tears and stains at paper edges.
Ref: PAI-II, 243
No career specifics are known for this polished French pianist, but Villa turns in a dandy of a poster for her, an Art Deco nonpareil in which the gifted Ms. Bayle's talent shines so brightly that she herself has to look away. In a word: brilliant.
Est: $2,400-$2,800.

VILLANT

576. Ato/Pendules Électriques.
$45^7/_8$ x $62^3/_8$ in./116.5 x 158.4 cm
Affiches Louant, Paris
Cond B/Slight tears at folds.
Time waits for no man, or woman for that matter. And with every second zipping by with lightning-fast rapidity, why would anyone want to waste a single instant winding a clock? It's literally taking time to make time. Fortunately, the Ato firm has the answer—electric pendulums that never need to be wound. French inventor, Leon Hatot, named his company with the phonetic pronunciation of his last name: "Ah-Toe." His

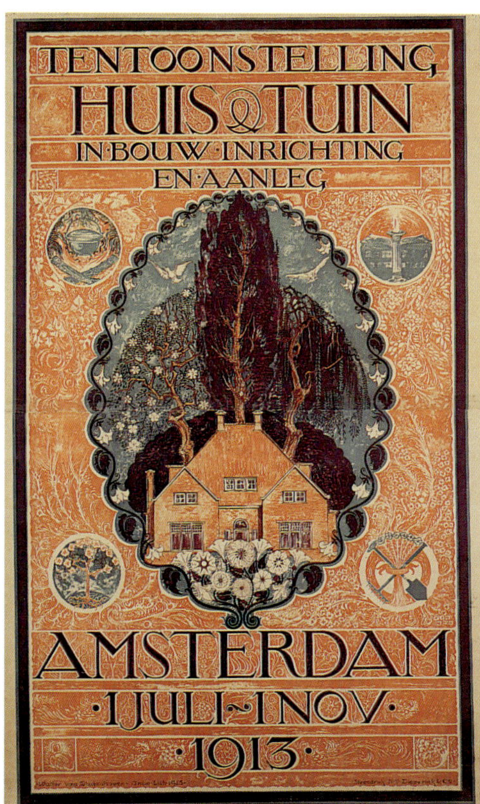

574

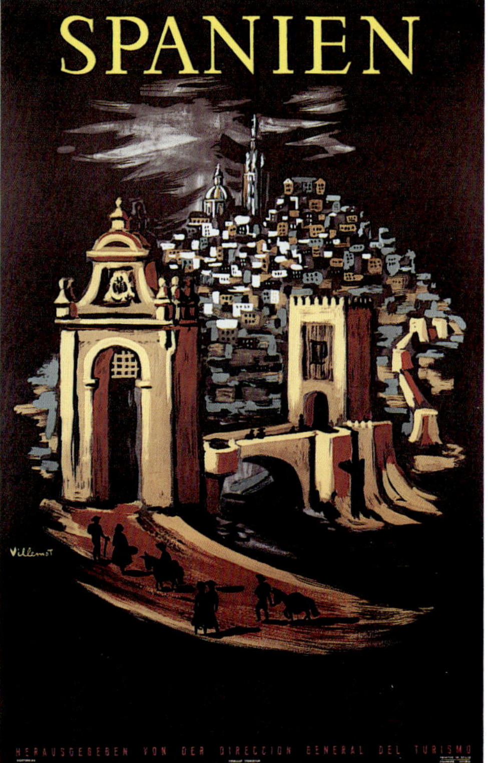

578

clocks were based on the electromagnetic principle that the solenoid is stationary and the simple permanent magnet serves as part of the pendulum mass. Ato clocks were offered in a variety of stylish cases,

many very small and in Lalique glass. Others were produced in metal utility cases to serve as master clocks controlling secondary or slave dials. It appears that Ato continued to make clocks until at least 1948.
Est: $3,000-$4,000.

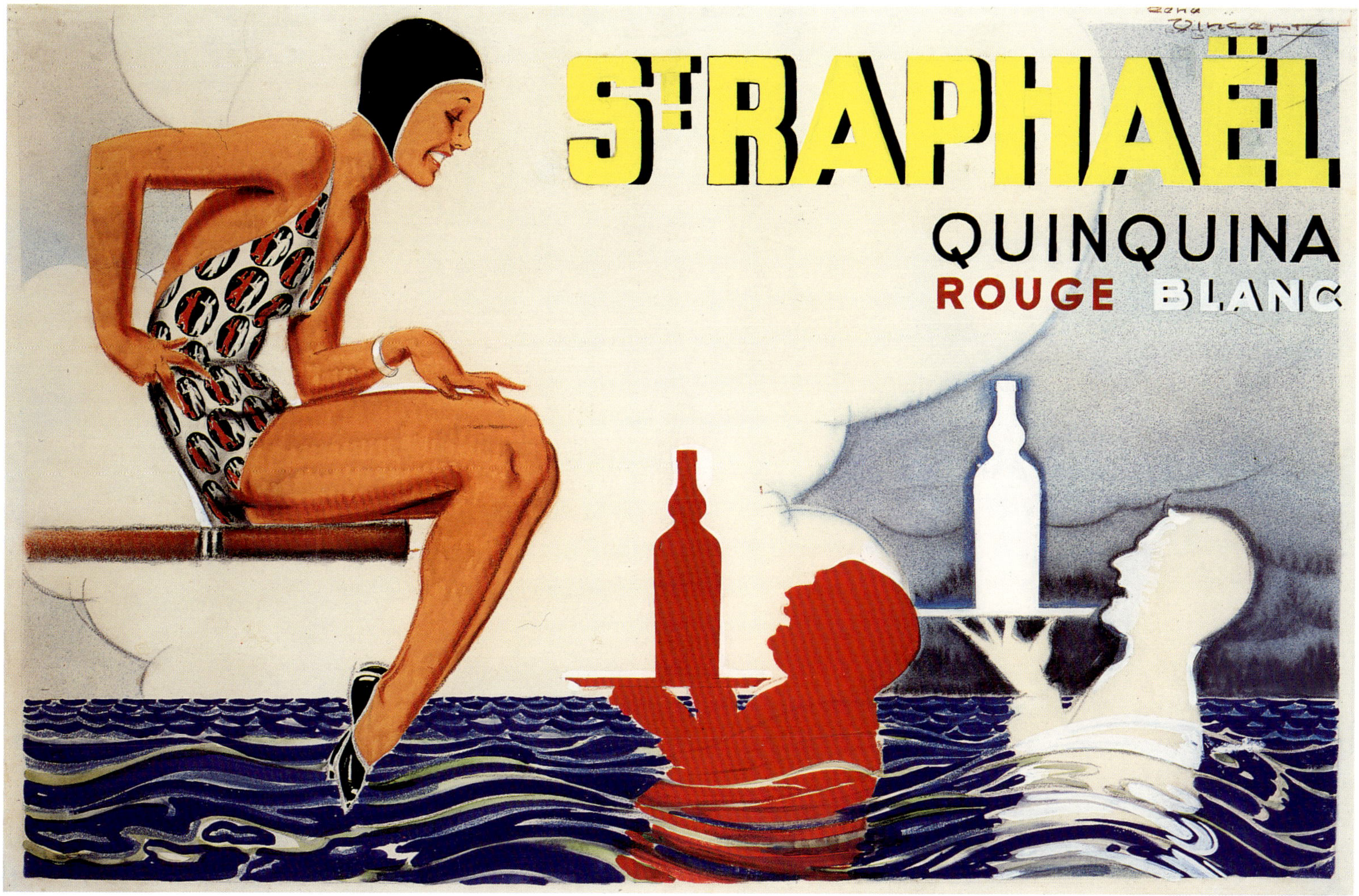

579

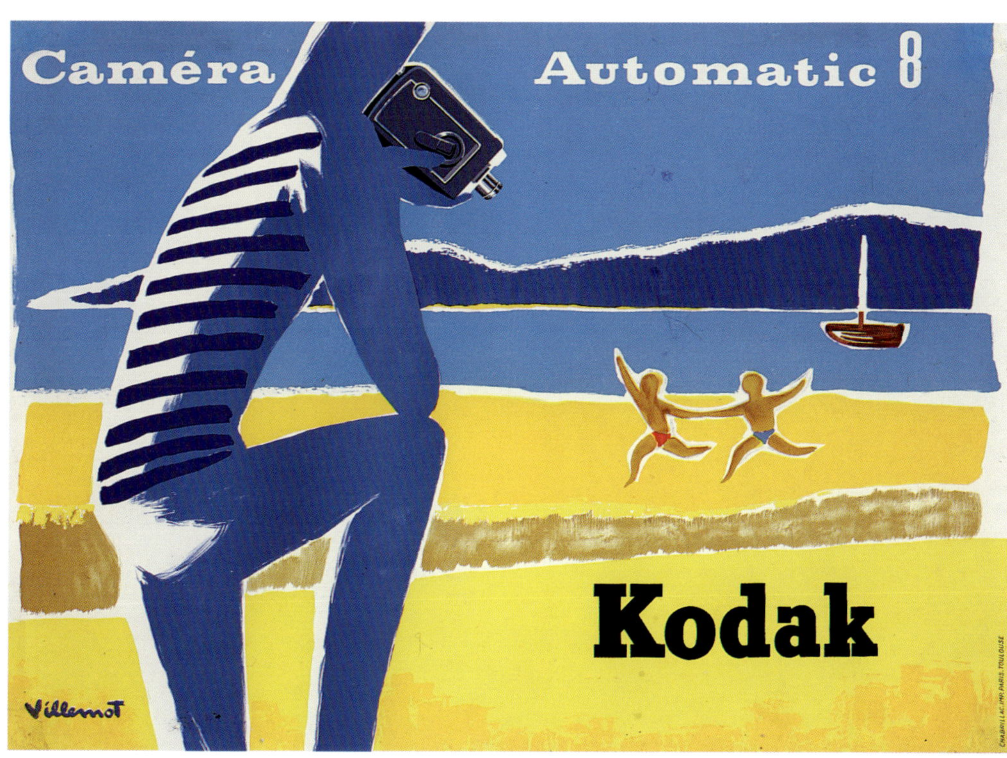

577

BERNARD VILLEMOT (1911-1989)

577. Kodak.
$23^3/_4$ x $17^1/_2$ in./60.4 x 44.5 cm
Imp. Chabrillac, Paris-Toulouse
Cond B/Slight tears and stains.
The "Kodak Girl" in the blue-and-white striped dress (see Nos. 394 & 489) may have disappeared from the scene, but Villemot has come up with an altogether appropriate replacement in his advertisement for a Kodak automatic movie camera: a fellow in a blue-and-white striped shirt, seen here filming his boys as they romp about the beach. A subtle shift to be sure, but one that serves both as an homage and a breezy clue to the consumer that times are a-changin'. The irrepressible Villemot could always be counted on to come up with something fresh, carefully calculated to create a riveting impression. "What allows one to recognize a Villemot poster without a shadow of hesitation is the powerful drawing, that seeks to be natural, spontaneous . . . and significant enough in itself to the point of not needing any slogan" (Villemot, p. 120).
Est: $1,400-$1,700.

578. Spanien. 1957.
$24^1/_8$ x $38^3/_4$ in./61.2 x 98.4 cm
Imp. Fournier, Vitoria
Cond A.
Ref (Both Var): Villemont, p. 65; PAI-XXI, 450
Around the same time that Villemot was creating his celebrated India poster for Air France (see PAI-XXI, 450), he was also working on behalf of the Spanish Government Tourist Office. Using a deep, earthy palette he produced a total of three images to promote travel in Spain to both natives and internationals. The member of that trio seen here utilizes a nighttime scene to suggest the cathedral-topped mountain of Toledo. This poster was released in German, English and French. *This is the German-language version.*
Est: $1,000-$1,200.

RENÉ VINCENT (1879-1936)

579. St. Raphaël Quinquina.
47 x 31 in./119.4 x 78.8 cm
Gouache and ink maquette on paper.
Now that's what I call service! Vincent remains fairly faithful to the spirit of the mono-toned pair of waiters first brought into advertising servitude by Loupot in 1937 (perhaps the facial features are a bit more defined), demonstrating that if there's nothing broken in a promotional campaign, there's nothing to fix. However, Vincent personalizes the conceit with a few simple touches: a leggy bathing beauty, an undulating sea and a sense of playfulness that's all his own.
Est: $7,000-$9,000.

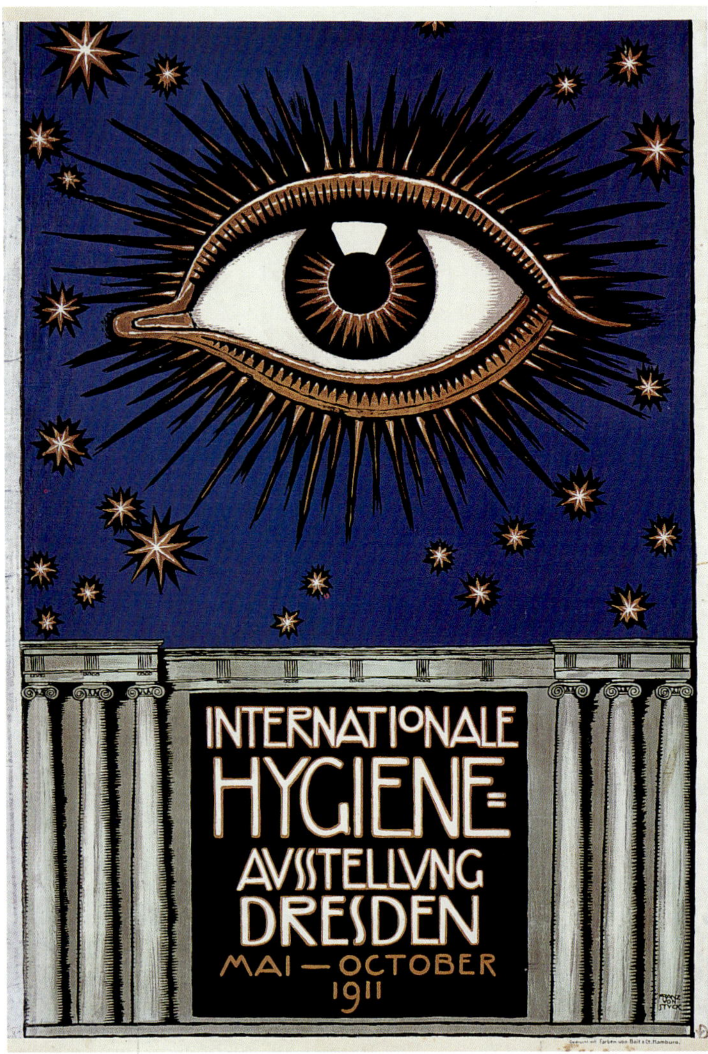

580

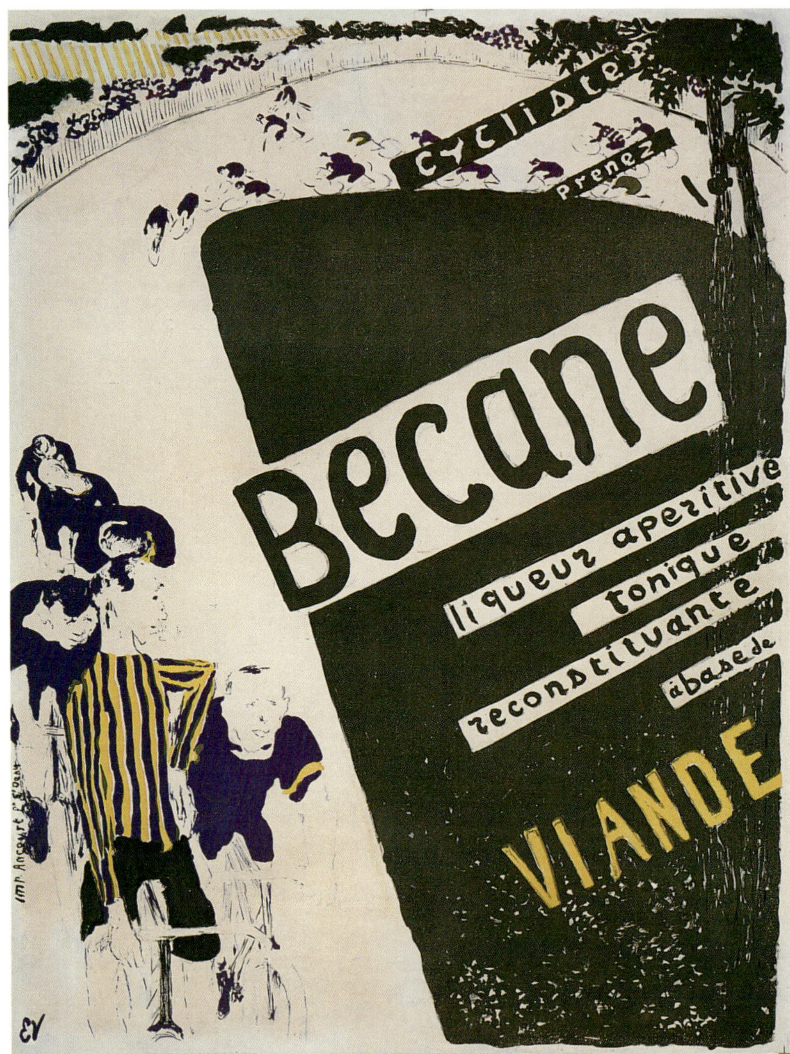

581

FRANZ VON STUCK (1863-1928)

580. International Hygiejne-Udstilling Dresden.
1911.
23³/₄ x 35¹/₄ in./60.4 x 89.6 cm
Bert, Hamburg
Cond B–/Slight creases and stains; recreated top margin.
Ref: DFP-III, 3221 (var); Rademacher, p. 60 (var);
   Plakate München, p. 32 (var); Internationale
   Plakate, 180 (var); Deutsche Plakat, 474;
   Affiches Miroir, 45; Sachs, 474; PAI-XXVII, 594
Von Stuck's eye motif became so popular that this
design was subsequently used for State Express cigarettes in 1912, for the *Lustige Blätter*, and for the
1930 Hygiene Exposition as well. The stylized eye is
seen in a midnight blue sky, surrounded by stars, with
Grecian architecture framing the text below—an interesting surrealist image. Von Stuck was the cofounder,
in 1893, of the Munich Secession, and his influence
on other artists of the period was extensive, not only
through his work in the group, but also as a frequent
contributor to the magazine *Jugend* and as a teacher
at the Munich Academy. He created several of the
Secession posters, including their first, which was
used for several years thereafter. *This is the German-
language version.*
Est: $1,700-$2,000.

EDOUARD VUILLARD (1868-1940)

581. Becane. ca. 1894.
23³/₄ x 32 in./60.4 x 81.2 cm
Imp. Ancourt, Paris
Cond B/Restored tears, largely near paper edges.
Ref: HTL/Rutgers, 178; Weill, 43; Sport à l'Affiche, 29;
   PAI-XVIII, 493
Cyclists are urged to take this health-giving tonic in one
of only two posters created by Vuillard. "Its focus on a
bicycle race encourages comparison with Lautrec's
poster *La Chaine Simpson*, done approximately two
years later. Vuillard's composition is considerably
bolder, depicting the track from a more extremely ele-

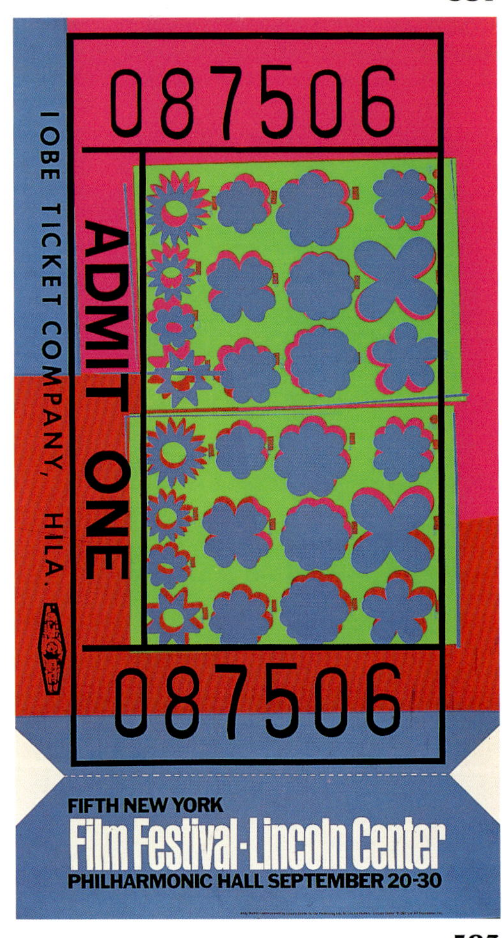

582

vated viewpoint. Physiognomies are simplified and dis-
torted to the point of caricature, and text is integrated
into the decorative scheme. Vuillard's layering of subtle hues contrasts with Lautrec's tendency to use flat
color or *crachis* in isolated areas" (HTL/Rutgers, p. 182).
Vuillard put a stamp of his individuality on everything
he did; in an appreciation of his forays into lithography,
André Mellerio wrote: "An exact artistic sense makes
him quickly appreciate his medium, both what one must
and what one can get out of it" (Color Revolution, p. 83).
Est: $3,000-$3,500.

583

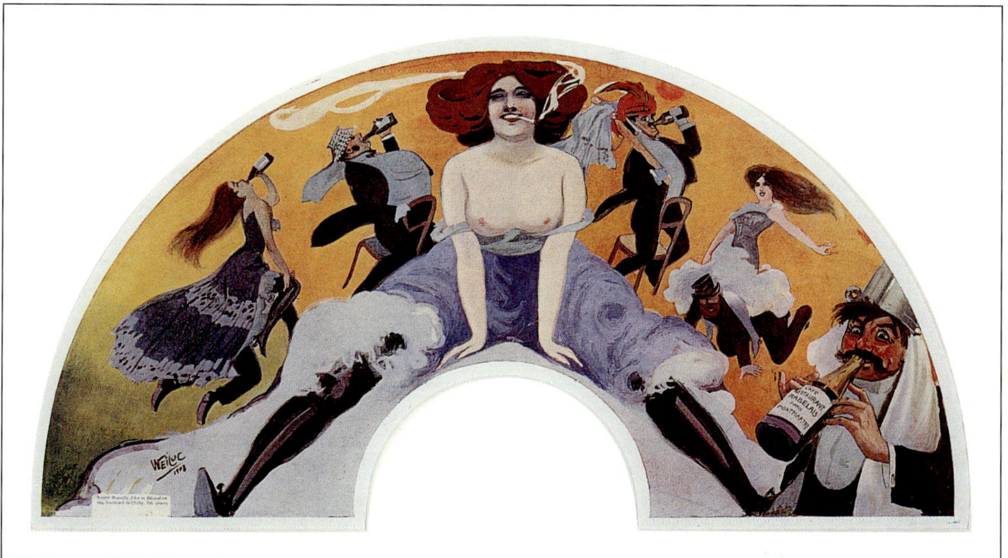

584

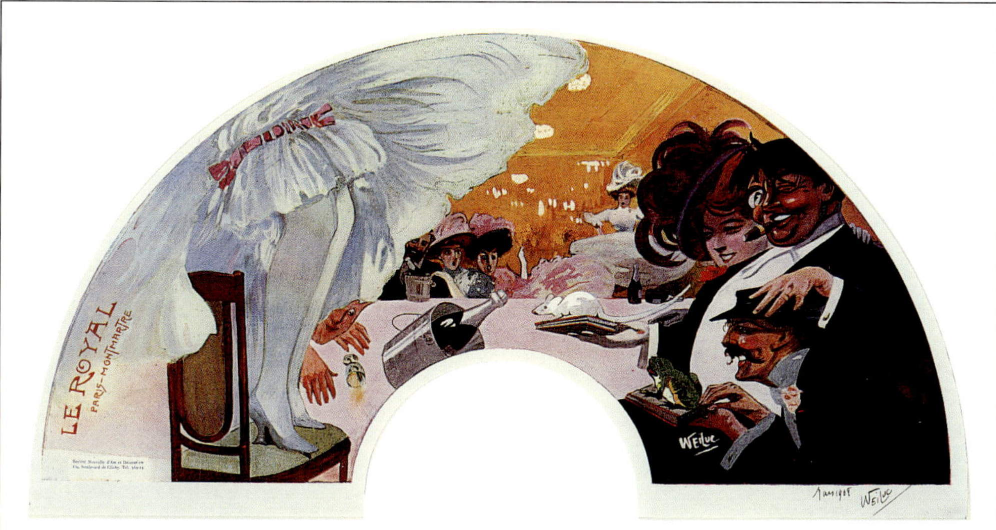

585

turned to Campbell's soup cans, Marilyn, cows and Mao. The work is one of the most interesting and relevant of all the posters commissioned by the List Art Foundation (*see also* No. 554).
Est: $1,000-$1,200.

WEILUC (Lucien-Henri Weil, 1873-1947)

584. Restaurant Rabelais. 1908.
17 x 9 in./43.3 x 22.8 cm
Société Nouvelle d'Art et Décoration, Paris
Cond A. Framed.
Weiluc was an illustrator and cartoonist who always tinged his work with humor. He first appeared in public in the magazine *La Caricature* in 1896, after which we find his drawings in many other similarly oriented publications of Paris. In 1907, he became involved with organizing the Salon des Humoristes, and in 1911, he joined the governing body of the Société des Dessinateurs Humoristes. His posters abound in good-natured fun; here, in a fan-shaped promotion for a Montmartre restaurant, he throws temperance to the wind. More accurately, he blows sobriety away with the force of a Category Five hurricane. But to be honest, the lascivious tableau that Weiluc puts on display looks like one helluva ride, a "What happens in Montmartre, stays in Montmartre" scenario into which one would be lucky to find oneself. Just as long as no questions needed to be answered the following morning.
Est: $1,700-$2,000.

585. Le Royal. 1908.
16³/₄ x 9 in./42.5 x 22.8 cm
Société Nouvelle d'Art et Décoration, Paris
Cond A. Framed.
Weiluc spawns another decadent fan-shaped promotion for Montmartre's Le Royal with a pair of lecherous gents not quite living-up to the establishment's regal appellation seeing as they intend to get a good look at a few frilly undergarments by any means necessary. As was apparent in the previous creation, Weiluc casts no aspersions regarding the goings-on at the establishments he promoted; rather, he seems to have the appreciation of one who may have personally indulged in a few shenanigans on more than one occasion.
Hand-signed by the artist.
Est: $1,700-$2,000.

JACQUES WELY (ca. 1875-1910)

586. Les Desmoiselles des St. Cyriens. 1898.
23¹/₂ x 31³/₄ in./59.8 x 80.8 cm
Imp. Ed. Delanchy, Paris
Cond A.
Ref: French Opera, 50; PAI-XXXVI, 569
Everything appears as prim and proper as can be—I mean, seriously, it takes a rather oversexed imagination to infer anything from a salute and a shuttlecock. But looks can be deceiving. "A girls' boarding school is conveniently located near the aristocratic officers' training school, Saint-Cyr. In the risqué plot typical of French operettas of the time, the heroine is not only involved romantically with a cadet, but is also faced with the prospect of an inheritance—provided she competes in a nude beauty contest" (French Opera, p. xxiv).
Est: $800-$1,000.

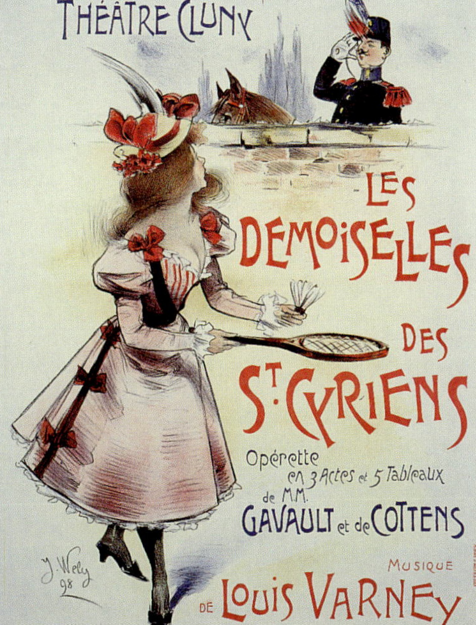

586

WAKHEVITCH

582. Ballets Américains de Ruth Page et Bentley Stone. 1950.
15³/₄ x 22³/₈ in./40 x 56.7 cm
Tolmer, Paris
Cond A.
Ref: Dance Posters, 64

Geometrized modernism and classical portent combine superbly in this Wakhevitch design for a Parisian appearance by the Ballets Américains. "Chicago owes much of its dance fame to Ruth Page who . . . made it her headquarters for half a century. Miss Page, a member of Anna Pavlova's company in 1918 and the Diaghilev Ballets Russes in 1925, established a major Chicago-based company with Bentley Stone . . . in 1938. In the ensuing years, Miss Page directed the Chicago Opera Ballet not only for opera performances but as an independent unit for international tours. Her troupes . . . varied their titles slightly—Ruth Page's International Ballet was one designation—but the key name has been Ruth Page's Chicago Ballet. Miss Page, a prolific choreographer . . . created a number of ballets on operatic themes; with Bentley Stone, the famous *Frankie and Johnny*; new stagings of classical ballets; and modern works not only for her own company but also for groups both American and European. Shown here is the excellent poster—used as a window card—for their appearance at the Théatre des Champs- Elysées and sponsored by the Bureaux de Concerts de Paris" (Dance Posters, p. 11).
Est: $800-$1,000.

ANDY WARHOL (1930-1987)

583. Film Festival-Lincoln Center. 1967.
24¹/₄ x 45 in./61.5 x 114.3 cm
Cond A/P.
Ref: Images of an Era, 72 (and cover);
    Müller-Brockmann, 121; Lincoln Center, p. 25;
    Plakatkunst, p. 173; PAI-XX, 509
For the fifth New York Film Festival held at Lincoln Center, Warhol produced a silkscreen image of a movie ticket in fluorescent inks, patterned with the flowers that were a favorite motif in the period before he

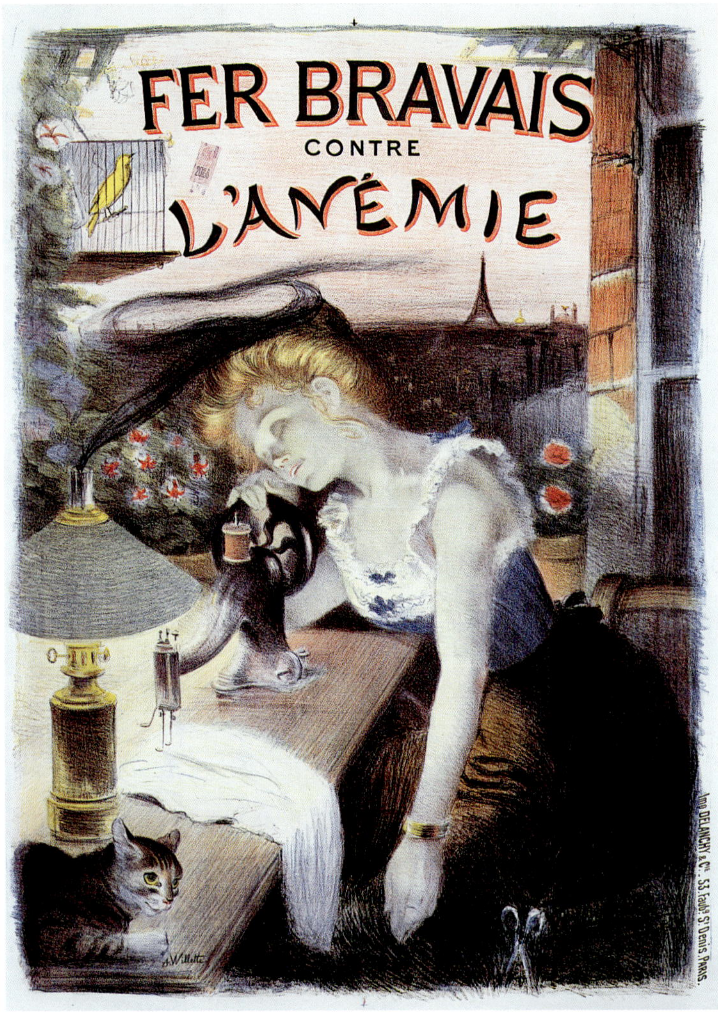

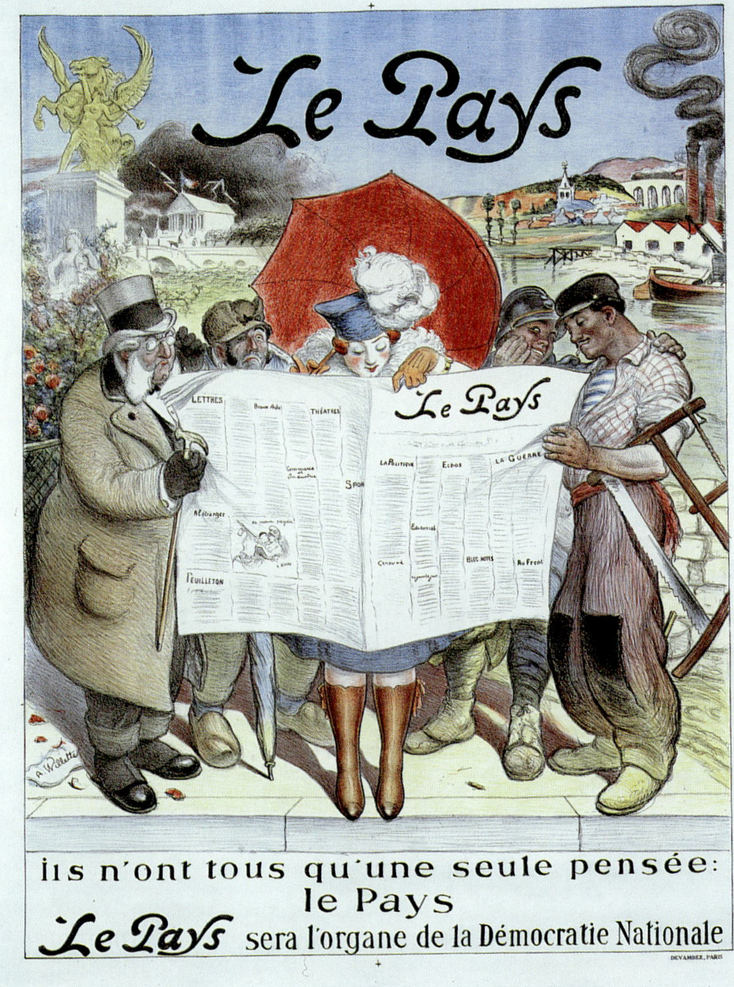

588

589

ADOLPH L. WILLETTE (1857-1926)

587. Le Boulou.
29³/8 x 41¹/4 in./74.7 x 105 cm
Imp. E. Baudelot, Paris
Cond A.
The Central and Orleans Railways' service to Boulou, the southern French resort with the year-round "Mediterranean Climate," is touted simply enough. Situated in the foothills of the Albères mountains, the serenity of the spot is adequately well-known to place the focus on the gentility of the clientele, which Willette achieves with a mid-ramble sip of alkaline water, even though the stroller's pooch doesn't quite seem to comprehend why he's not getting a little lap himself. A lilting charmer from Willette, a successful painter who in 1887 switched to drawing, lithography and poster design. He became a frequent contributor to satirical publications such as "Le Rire" and "Chat Noir," even founding three of his own magazines, as well as being one of the founders of "Les Humoristes."
Est: $1,200-$1,500.

588. Fer Bravais Contre L'Anemie. 1898.
34¹/2 x 48¹/2 in./87.6 x 123 cm
Imp. Delanchy, Paris
Cond A–/Unobtrusive folds.
Ref: DFP-II, 892; Affichomanie, 98;
   Color Revolution, p. 64; PAI-XXVII, 617
A sensitively drawn image in subtle colors advertising an iron supplement: the pale seamstress, exhausted from work and drained by anemia succumbs to sleep while resting her head on the sewing machine. The curling smoke from the lamp, the wide-eyed cat, the chirruping bird and the falling scissors are strikingly animated in comparison. It was reproduced as a supplement to the *Courrier Français* of March, 1898 (*see* PAI-XXXVII, 549).
Est: $2,000-$2,500.

589. Le Pays.
47 x 62⁷/8 in./119.3 x 159.7 cm
Imp. Devambez, Paris
Cond B/Restored tears, largely near edges.

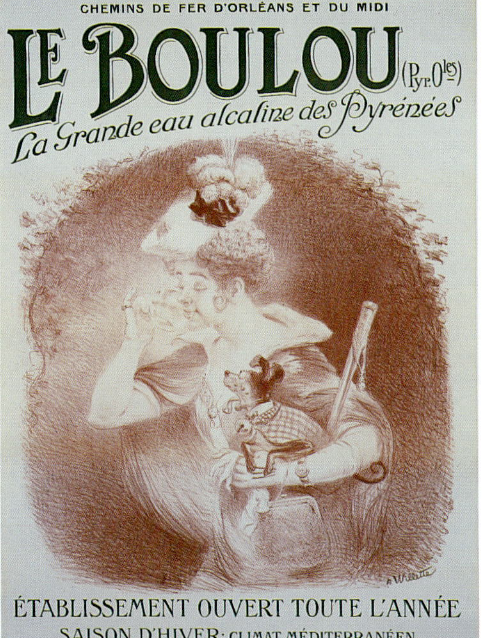

587

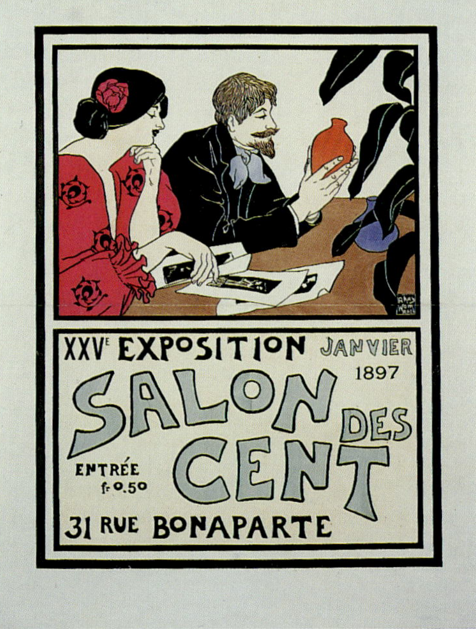

591

Ref: DFP-II, 894; Fit to Print, 132; PAI-XL, 526
Since it takes more than one type of person to create the diverse complexion of a nation, it only makes sense that the citizenry of said nation would have more than a single thought bouncing around in their collective consciousness. And what better compiled source of the issues occupying these good folks—from socialite to laborer—could there be than *Le Pays* (*The Country*), incidentally the editorial branch of the French National Democratic party. Gathered 'round its pages, complete with an inset cartoon by the artist, this diverse gather-

ing stands out against its amalgamated national backdrop, safe in the certainty that their interests are represented by the daily
Est: $1,700-$2,000.

WIMANAHL

590. Wintersport in Wien und Niederästerreich.
26 x 40¹/4 in./66 x 102.2 cm
Druck von Christoph Reisser's Sähne, Wien
Cond B+/Unobtrusive tears at folds and top text area.
The sheer abundance of winter sport destinations pointed out on the map of Lower Austria in the central panel of the lower quadrant is impressive, but what

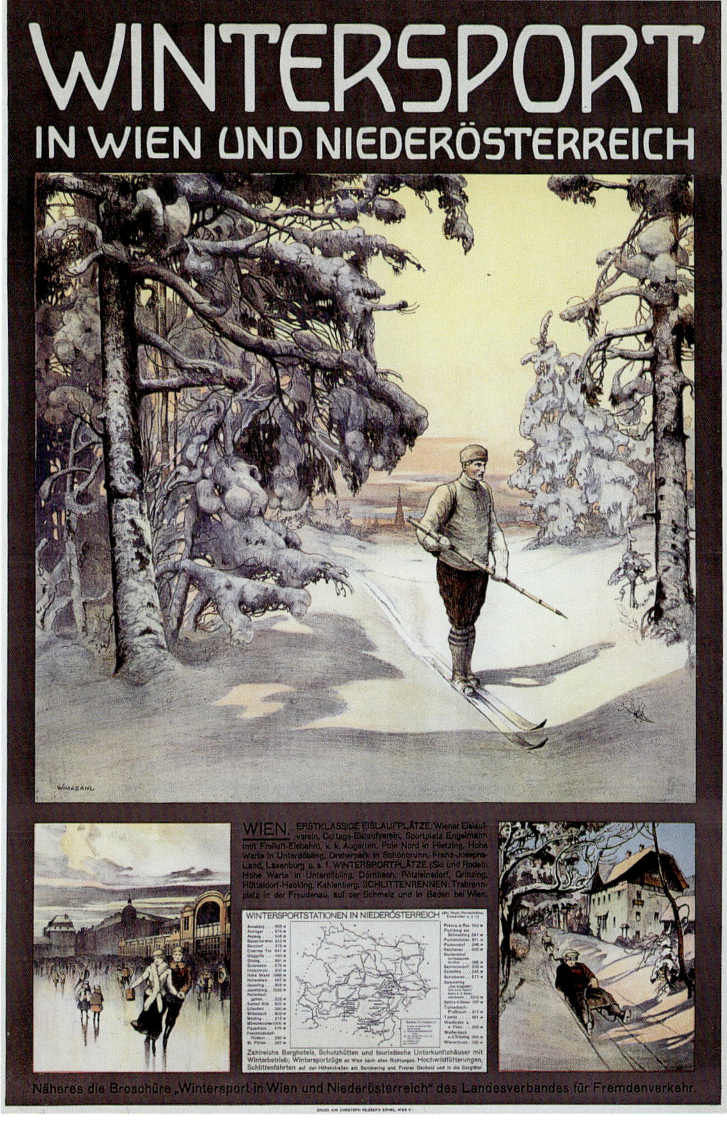

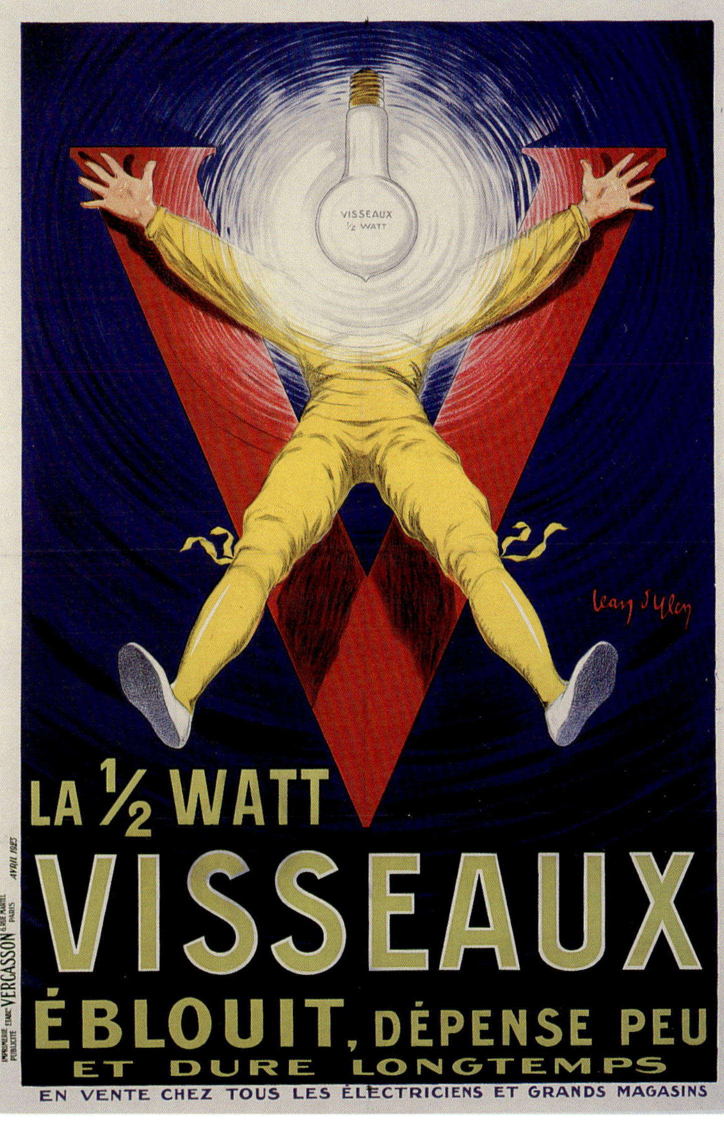

590

592

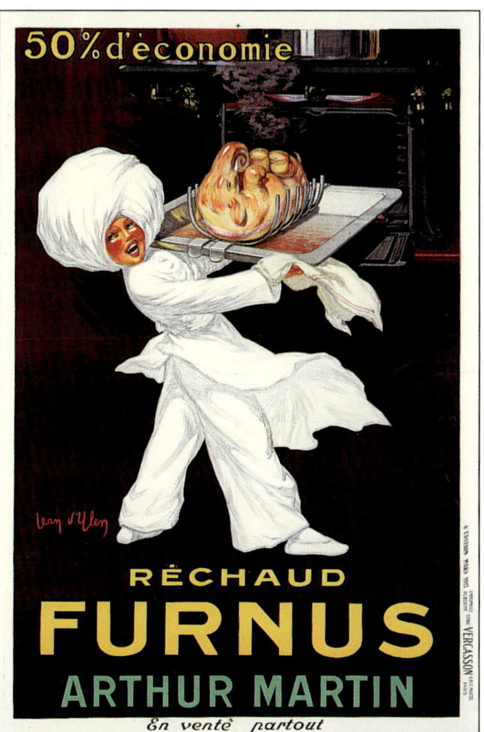

593

convinces the enthusiast to get themselves to one of these spots are the Wimazahl representations of cross-county skiing, ice skating and sledding. Though there's fun to be had by all ages, what makes the proposition so markedly attractive with widespread

appeal is the way in which Wimazahl portrays the out-doors—crisp, yet enjoyable, snow-laden, yet inviting. It's the joys of winter in lithographic form.
Est: $2,000-$2,500.

ANDREW K. WOMRATH (1869-?)

591. Salon des Cent. 1896.
$16^1/8$ x $21^3/4$ in./41 x 55 cm
Cond B+/Horizontal fold.
Ref (All Var but DFP): DFP-II, 895; Salon des Cent, p. 58;
    Salon des Cent/Neumann, p. 68; Gold, 196;
    PAI-XXXIV, 532
"Andrew Kay Womrath was an American artist who studied in New York, London and Paris. This is his only known poster, showing a woman leafing through some prints while a man admires a vase. She is dressed conventionally enough, while the man, judging by his Van Dyke and floppy cravat, is either an artist or would be bohemian" (Gold, p. 134). The broad appeal of the artwork on display hinted at is reinforced by fact that a February/March tip-on was included in a later version of the poster: Originally slated to run only for the month of January, the popularity of the event demanded a two-month extension (see PAI-XXXI, 634).
Est: $1,000-$1,200.

JEAN D'YLEN (1866-1938)

592. Visseaux. 1922.
$38^7/8$ x $58^1/4$ in./98.7 x 148 cm
Imp. Vercasson, Paris
Cond B+/Slight tears at folds.
Ref: PAI-XLI, 587 (var)
After several years as a designer of jewelry, d'Ylen became a full-time posterist in 1919 and signed an exclusive contract with Vercasson in 1922. He may

have owed the job offer to the fact he was a sincere admirer and disciple of Cappiello, who was the previous star of the Vercasson shop, and thus the firm was as-sured of an uninterrupted flow of designs of unbridled exuberance that had been Cappiello's trademark. In total, d'Ylen designed three posters for Visseaux light bulbs, of which this is the first. Dazzling and inexpen-sive, the half-watt Visseaux clearly intends to outshine the competition, and calling upon d'Ylen's talents was clearly a step in the right direction. The poster is a bright burst of inspiration—literally to the man behind the oversized bulb (or is he perhaps simply bulb-headed)—an exciting creative flare-up that contrasts the red Visseaux "V" off of the yellow "X" of the central figure's spread-eagled limbs. It's interesting—and instructive—to compare d'Ylen's design to Cappiello's earlier poster for the same product (see Cappiello/ Rennert, 255 & PAI-XL, 261). Both achieve the same end—grabbing our attention—with different, but equally effective means. *This is the smaller format.*
Est: $3,000-$4,000.

593. Réchaud Furnus. 1927.
$39^1/8$ x $58^3/4$ in./99.2 x 149.2 cm
Imp. Vercasson, Paris
Cond B+/Slight tears at folds. Framed.
Ref: PAI-XIX, 523
D'Ylen certainly had a talent for creating the startling image. Here, he illustrates the economy of a brand of compact stove by showing that it can cook even not-so-compact fare. A poster virtually assured of getting a resounding "tusk-tusk" from wildlife preservationists. Beautifully drawn, d'Ylen's work is reminiscent of Cap-piello's—which is precisely why Vercasson hired him after Cappiello's move to Devambez in 1919. *Rare!*
Est: $2,000-$2,500.

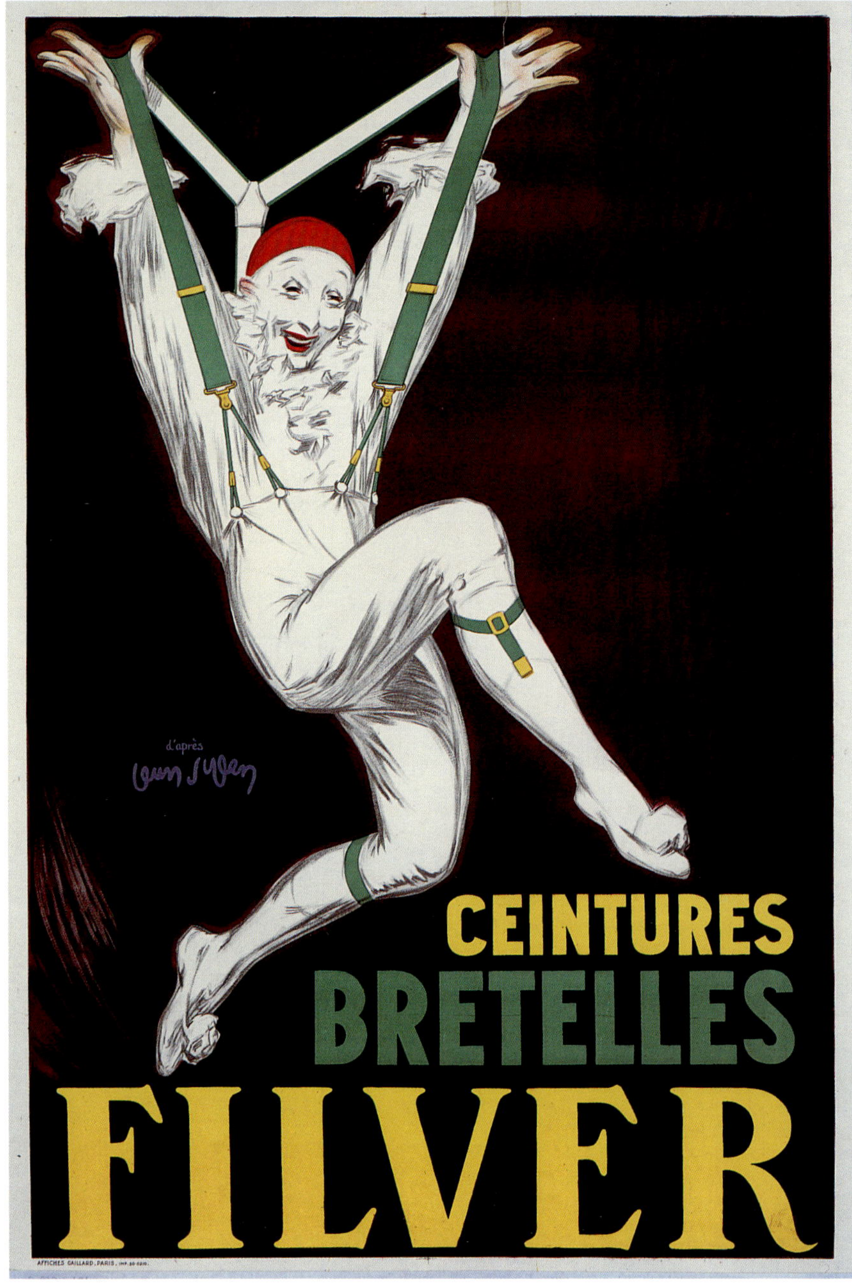

594

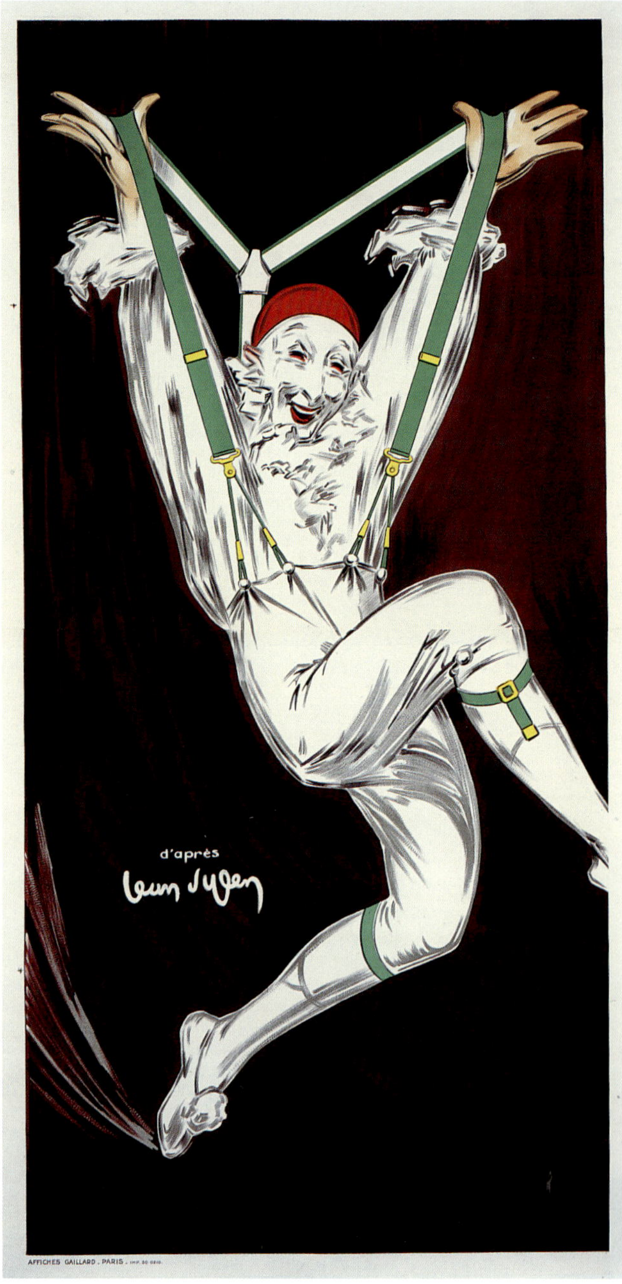

595

JEAN D'YLEN (cont'd)

594. Filver Bretelles. 1926.
$31^5/8$ x $47^1/4$ in./80.5 x 120 cm
Affiches Gaillard, Paris
Cond A–/Unobtrusive folds.
Ref: PAI-XL, 528 (var)
Taken from an original d'Ylen design ("d'après") and executed by an unnamed artistic collaborator, this prancing harlequin couldn't be happier with his choice of suspenders—Filver to be precise, a firm that not only keeps one's pants hiked to respectable heights with both suspenders and belts, but also produces sock garters as well. The design is nothing short of elastic exuberance.
Est: $2,000-$2,500.

595. Filver Bretelles. 1926.
$43^3/8$ x $88^7/8$in./110.2 x 225.7 cm
Affiches Gaillard, Paris
Cond A.
Ref: PAI-XL, 528
This is the 2-sheet format of the previous poster.
Est: $1,700-$2,000.

596. La Maison du Porte-Plume. 1928.
$42^3/4$ x $60^7/8$ in./108.6 x 154.6 cm
Publicité E. V. Ferdi, Bruxelles
Cond A.
Ref: PAI-XL, 529
Once more, disbelief rears its incredulous head in a d'Ylen design, this golden jester literally dumbfounded that anyone would shop anywhere other than Charleroi's "Fountainpen House" when it came to getting their hands on superior writing instruments. And in the face of such finely-detailed, oversized proof, frequenting any other longhand establishment does seem a bit ludicrous.
Est: $3,500-$4,000.

F. D. XHARDEZ

597. Catz-Elixer. 1897.
$24^1/2$ x $33^3/8$ in./62 x 84.8 cm
Affiches Vve. Al Strickaert, Bruxelles
Cond B/Slight tears at folds.
Though her coif more closely resembles a hand blown amber glass lampshade than an actual hairdo, this waitress appears unfazed and intent on delivering some Catz-Elixer to a pair of unseen patrons. Unfortunately, this brand of bitters has disappeared from today's marketplace, an apparent loss to the consumer seeing as it was a competition favorite and promoted here as "The Best Aperitif." Xhardez was a Brussels-based graphic designer, who in addition to his lithographic output created works for artistic and industrial catalogues, newspaper logos and illustrations for fashion magazines. Beyond his handful of known posters —all of them marked by his use of bold color—the artist also used his talents to create a series of small pen-and-ink drawings to illustrate a tourist guide distributed in 1905 on the occasion of Belgium's seventy-fifth anniversary of national independence entitled "Vade Mecum of the Traveler and Tourist in Belgium."
Est: $1,200-$1,500.

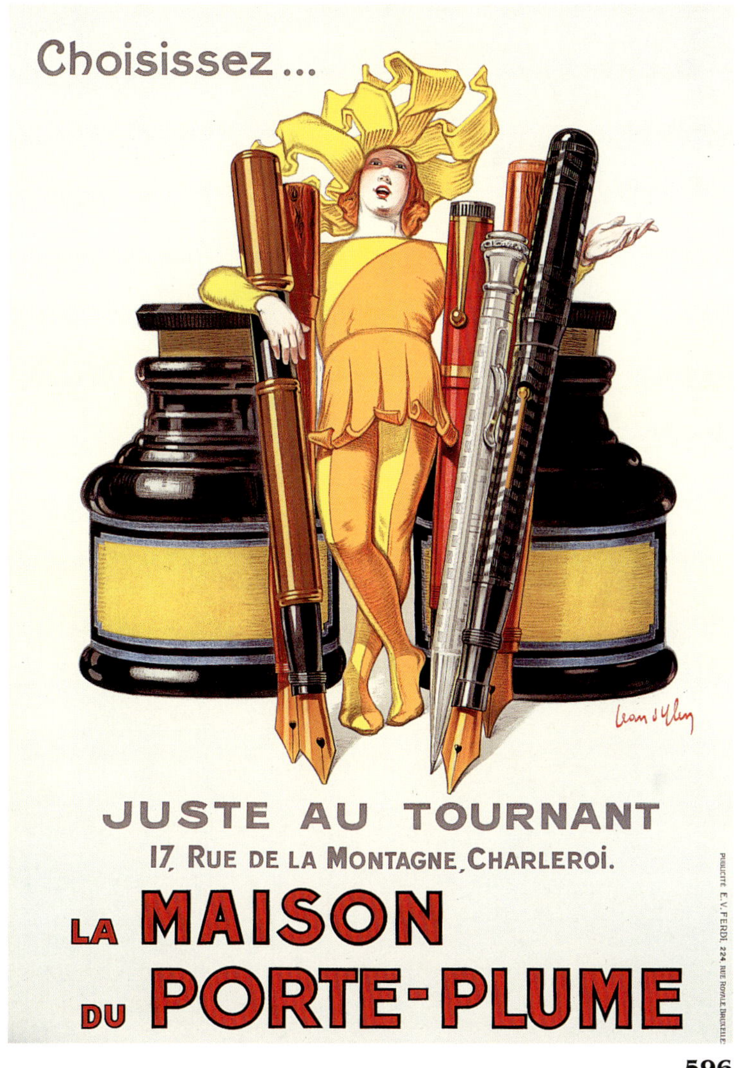

596

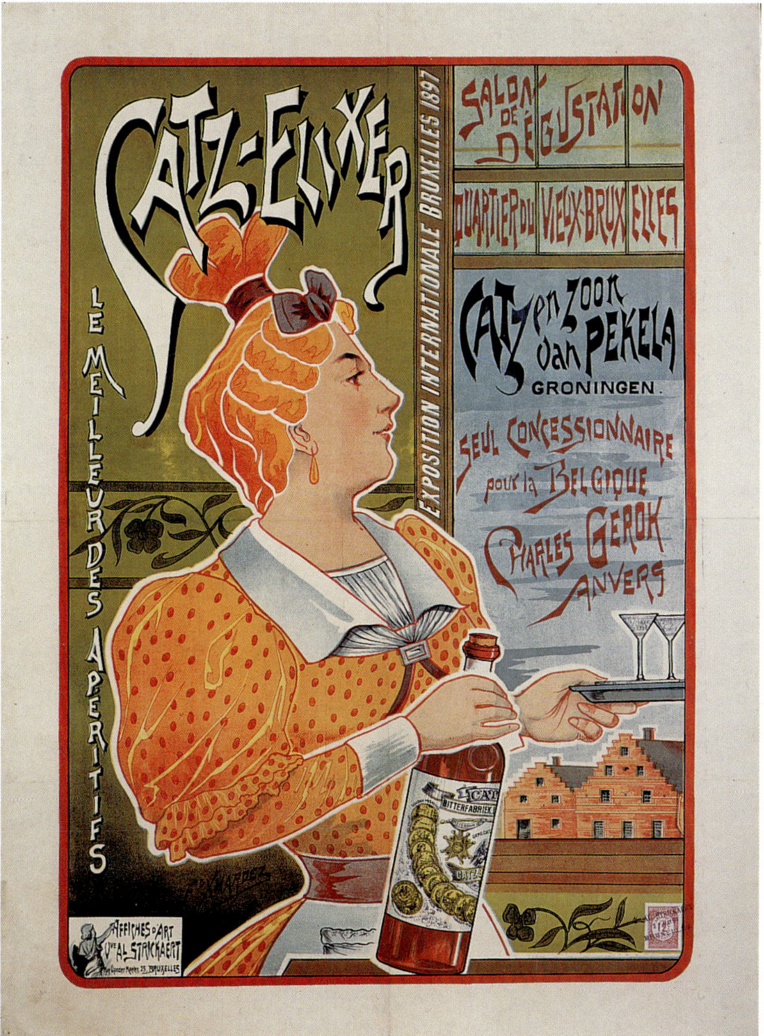

597

BOOKS AND PERIODICALS

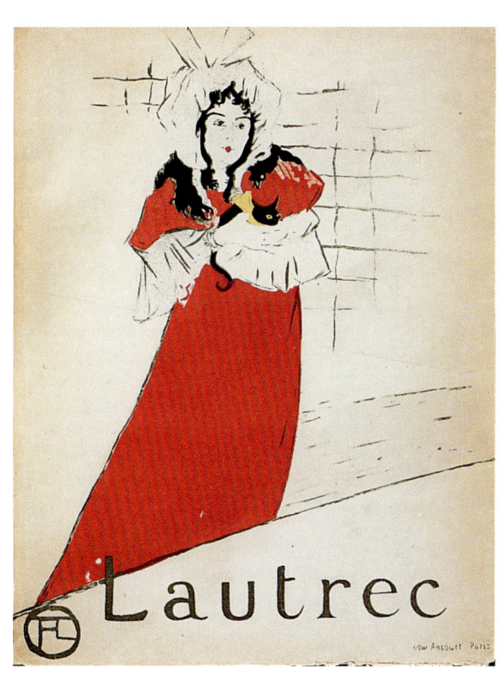

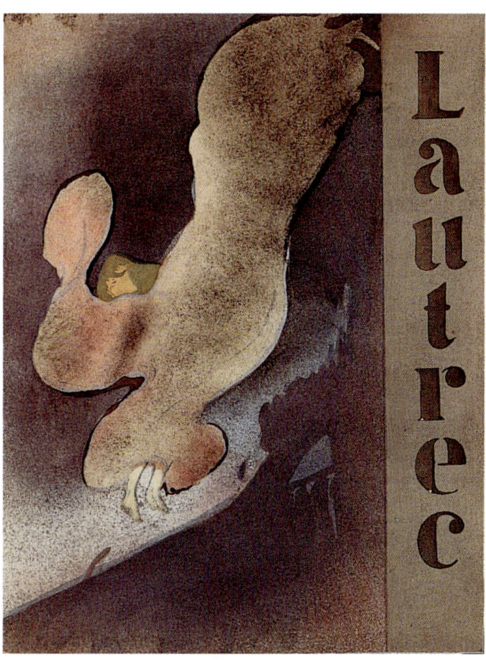

598

**598. Henri de Toulouse-Lautrec, 1864-1901,
by Maurice Joyant.**
Each: 8⅝ x 10⅝ in/22 x 27 cm
Published by H. Fleury, Paris
Ref: PAI-XLII, 492
*In fine period binding; includes two original dry-point
etchings.*
The hardcover-bound, 2-volume definitive work on
the artist by his lifelong friend and manager, Maurice
Joyant. Volume I, 312 pages and subtitled *Peintre*, was
published in 1926. It contains an original dry-point
etching of Charles Maurin (Wittrock, 242). Volume II,
284 pages and subtitled *Dessins-Estampes-Affiches*,
was published in 1927 and also contains one original
dry-point etching of "Monsieur X" (Wittrock, 246). Both
volumes contain numerous color plates. No one knew
Lautrec better than Joyant and it shows in the care
and detail of presentation.
Est: $2,000-$2,500.

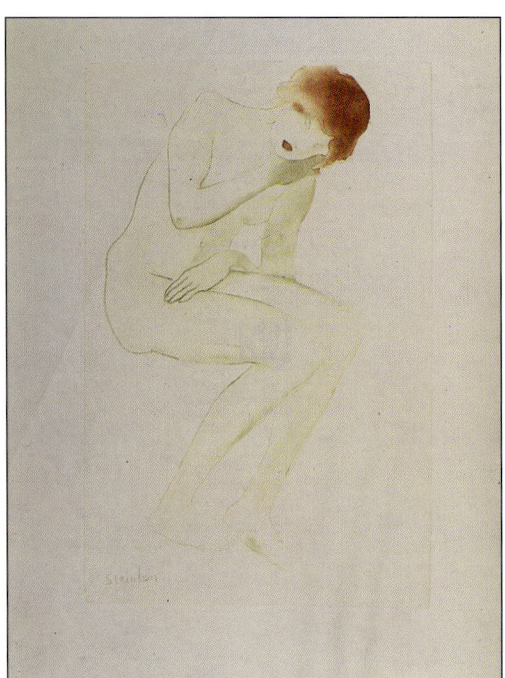

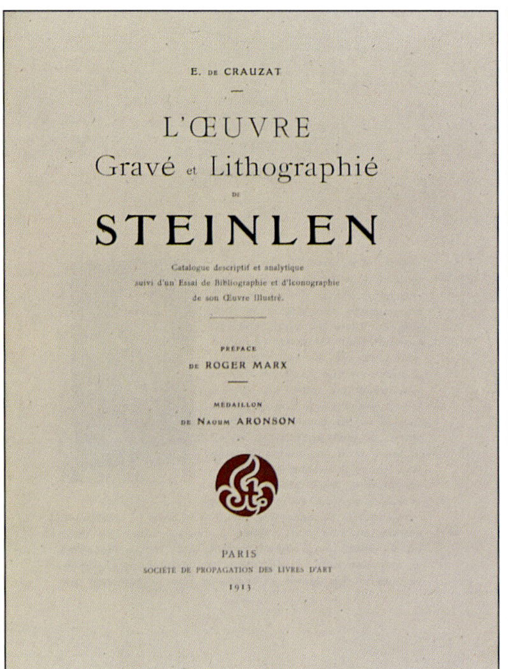

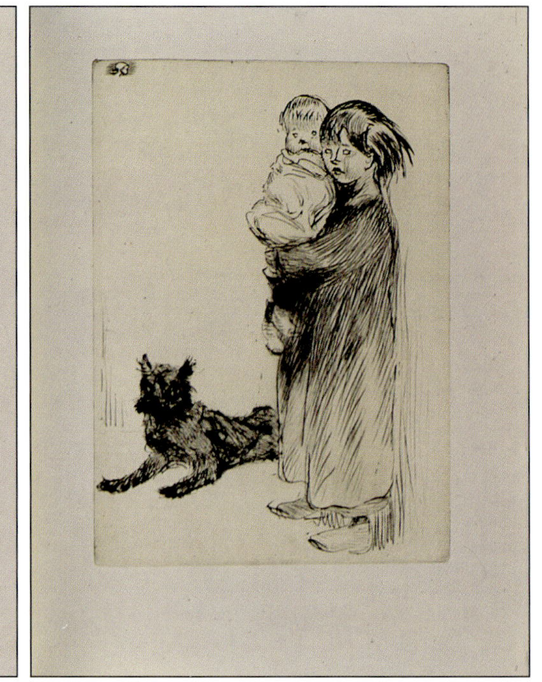

599

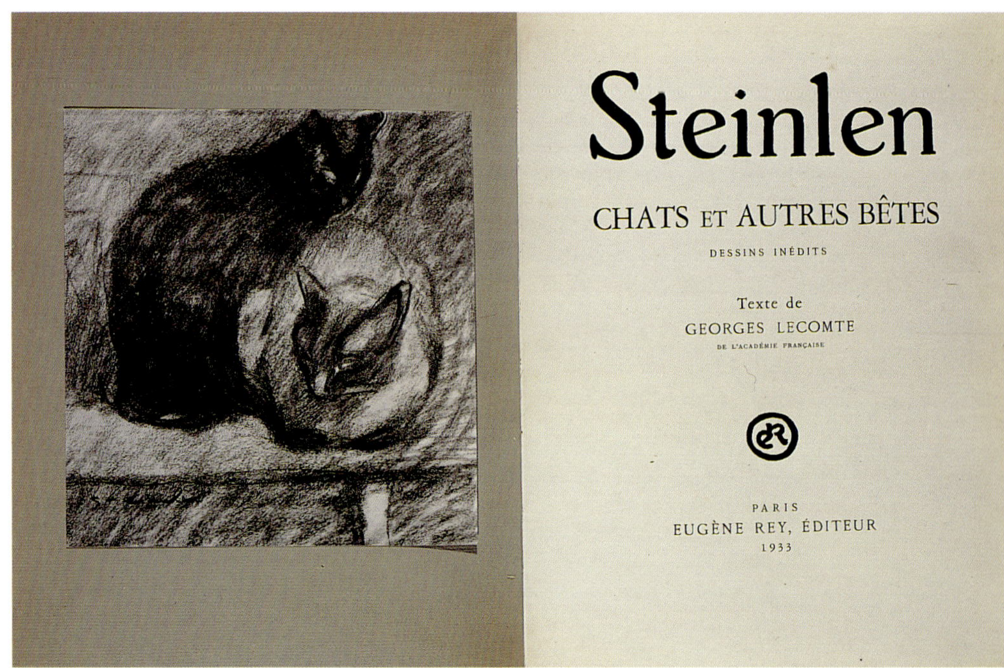

600

BOOKS AND PERIODICALS (cont'd)

599. L'Oeuvre Gravé et Lithographié de Steinlen.
1913.
10 x 13 in./25.5 x 33 cm
Ref: PAI-XXXVI, 540
*Steinlen's personal copy of the catalogue raisonné
of his work by E. de Crauzat.*
This deluxe edition, in leather boxed binding, consists
of 232 pages plus a special suite of seventeen full-page
etchings and lithographs ("Tirage Special Reserve").
Printed on chine paper, this very special edition was
created for the Society of XX and offered, with dedication of its president, to Steinlen. Published by the
Société de Propagation des Livres d'Art of Paris, it contains a preface by Roger Marx and is the only complete
catalogue raisonné of all the artist's work on paper. Of
special interest are the two additional original dry-point
etchings by the artist. The sweep of the publication is
incredible, containing every illustration and engraving
executed by the artist up to that point. It provides a
rare opportunity to see Steinlen's visionary insights
placed alongside one another, be they politic or commercial, from song sheet covers to the purely artistic.
Published during the artist's lifetime, the book serves
not only as a wondrous overview of his creative output, but also as a tribute to the genius he expressed to
the citizens of Paris via the democratic artistry of his
posters and prints. This is a most special reference
and art work for the serious Steinlen collector.
Est: $14,000-$17,000.

600. Steinlen: Chats et Autres Bêtes. 1933.
10 x 13 in./25.5 x 33 cm
Published by Eugène Rey, Paris
*Softcover book; 208 pages; overall excellent
condition with slight wear in binding.*
With text by Georges Lecomte, this book contains previously unpublished Steinlen designs, many of them
being tip-ons that could pass for originals of cats and
other animals. Chock full of the charm and whimsy we
have come to expect from the artist. *This is No. 458
of 500 copies on velin d'arches paper.*
Est: $1,700-$2,000.

**601. Ballet und Pantomime, by Walter Schnacken-
berg.** 1920.
15³/₈ x 20¹/₄ in./39 x 50.4 cm
Published by Georg Müller Verlag, München
*Foreword by Alexander von Gleichen-Russworm.
The complete portfolio of twenty-two plates, loose
in hardcover binding.
Slight wear in binding and cover; plates in excellent
condition.
No. 39 of 50-numbered copies printed on hand-
crafted paper.*
Nowhere is Schnackenberg's theatrical phantasmagoria
better exemplified than in these twenty-two costume
designs. Not only are the images exquisite—the fantastical amalgamation of Eastern inspiration, animalistic
animus and otherworldly envisioning all but defies
realistic description—but they are also rare and important, irreproachable artifacts from a distant performance
era. "When we remember this (dance renaissance)
movement (in Germany) we think of the Munich art
feasts and performances in theaters and concert halls,
which came out of this art-loving city thanks to the
collaboration of creative artists. Among those who
actively and knowingly took part in this movement, the
painter Schnackenberg attracted attention with his
creations. His planes, figures and drawings make it
clear that in dance and pantomime, we can reclaim
the right to rejoice in the beauty of the body, the striking pose and the animated movement. Glowing colors
delight the eye, joy of life shines in the lightness, and
the bright colors convey to us that the world need not
remain grey and colorless if we have the courage to be
guided by our yearnings" (*From the Foreword by Von
Gleichen-Russworm*).
Est: $30,000-$40,000.

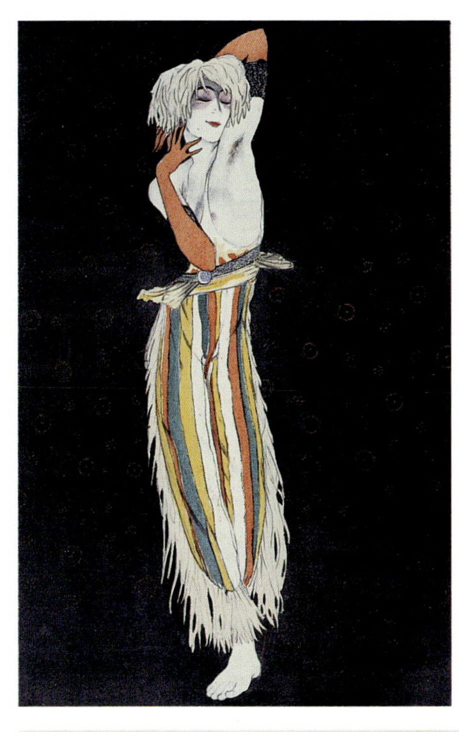
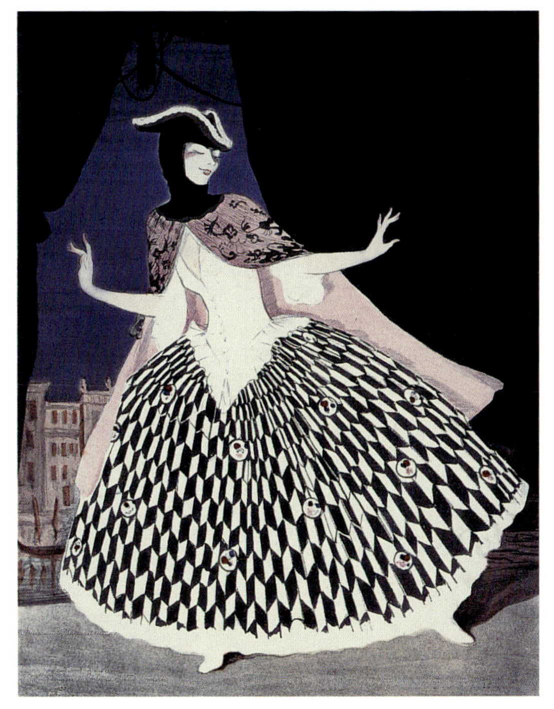
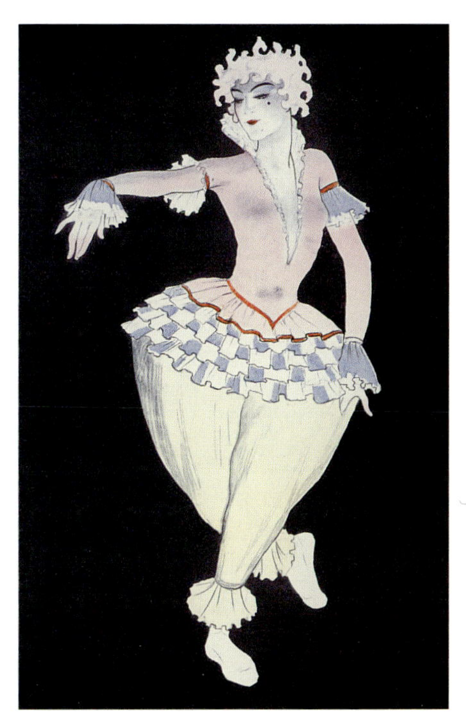
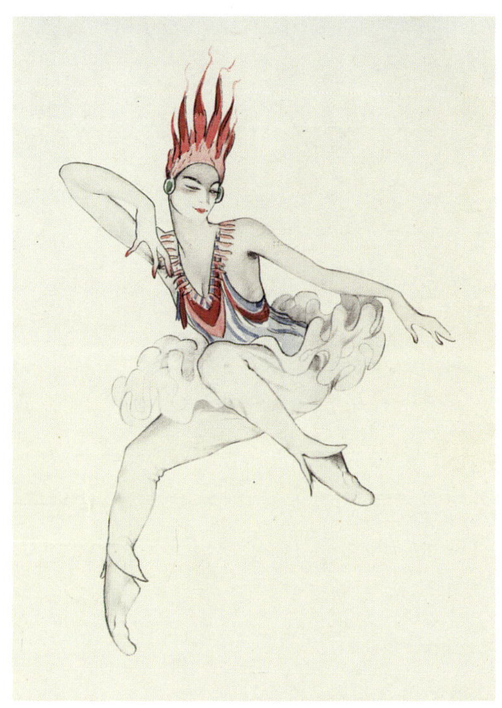
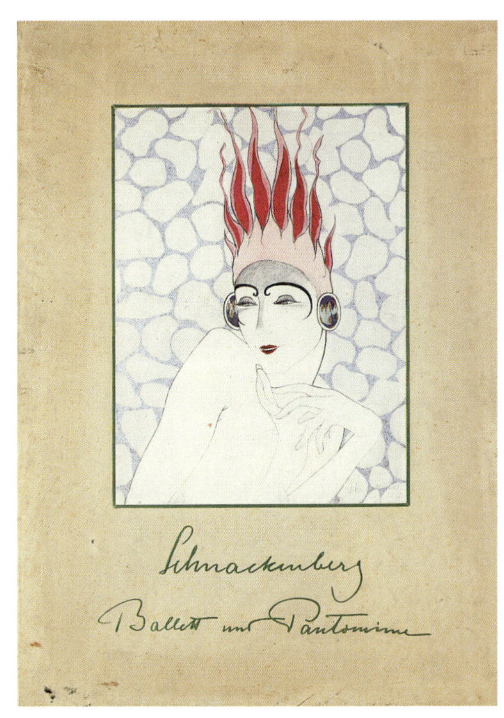
Schmackenberg
Ballett und Pantomime
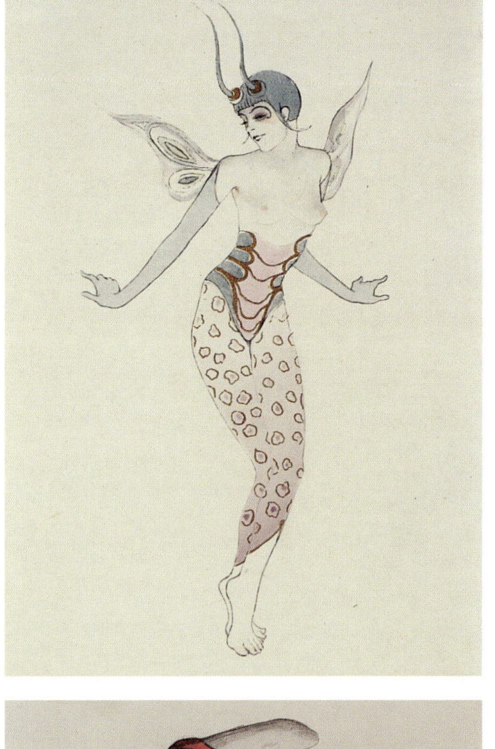
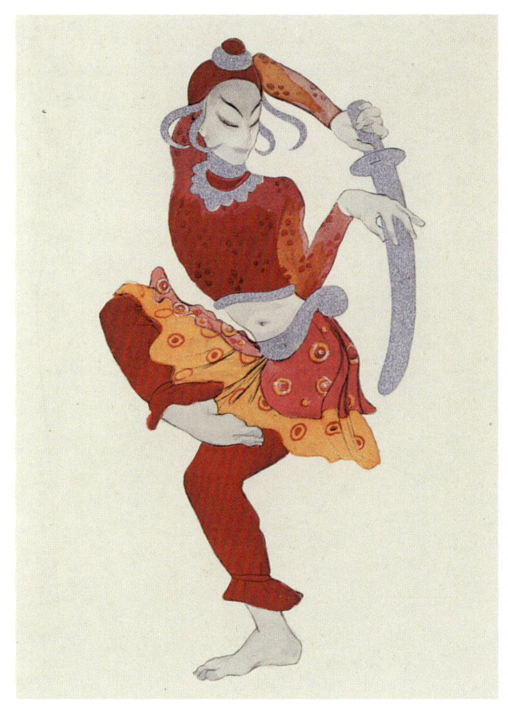
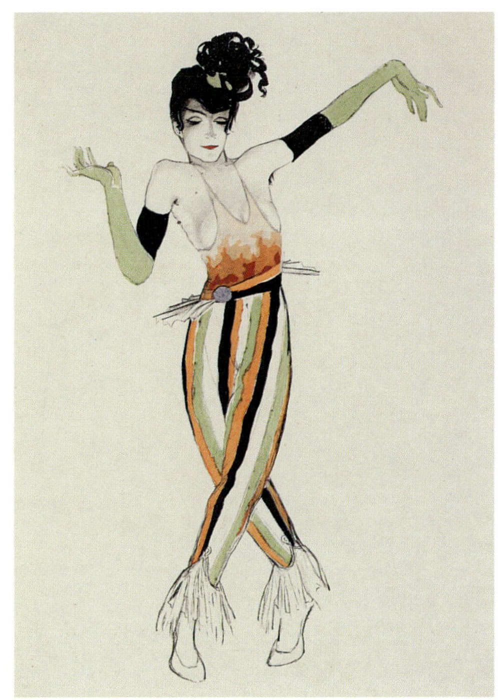
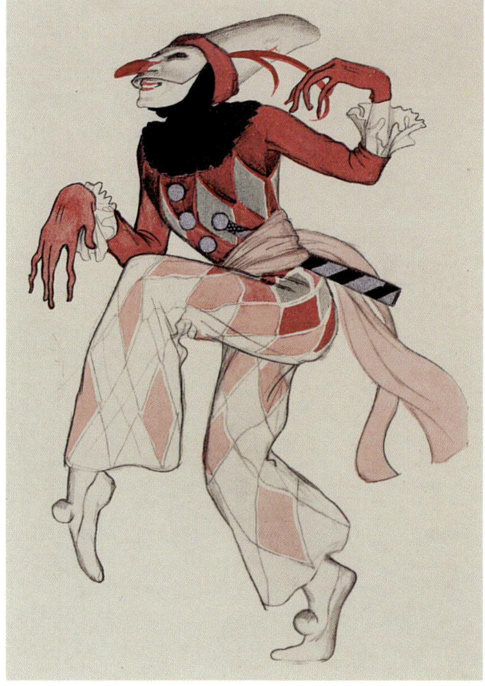

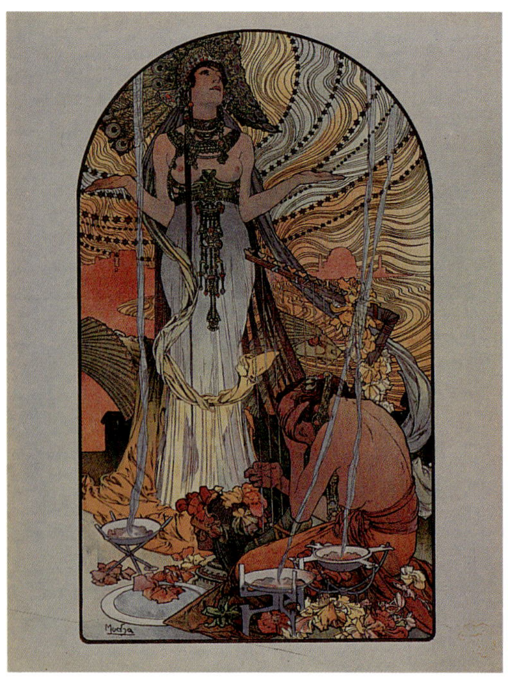 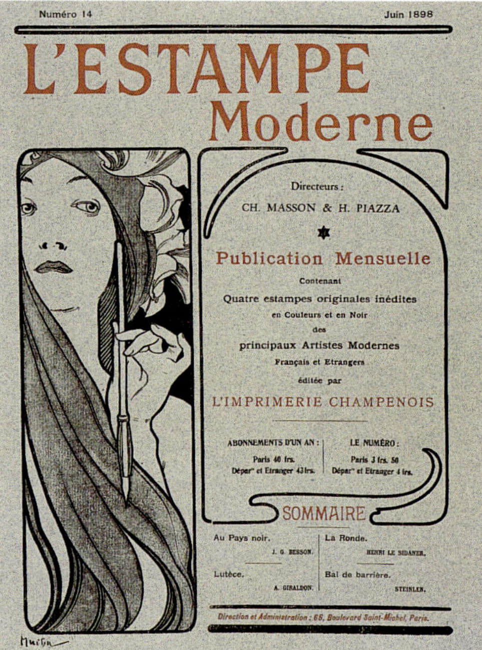 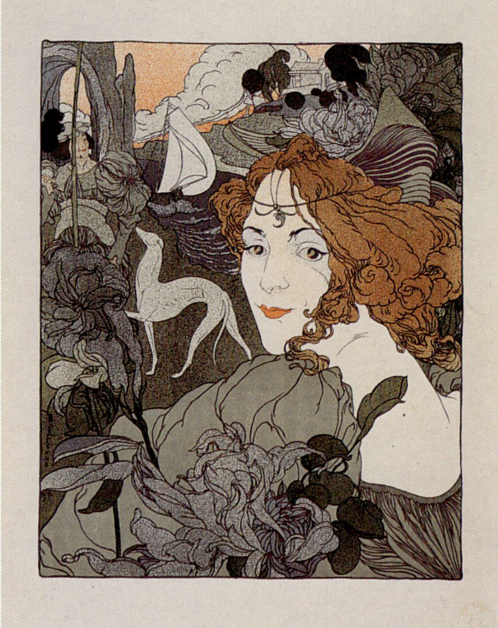

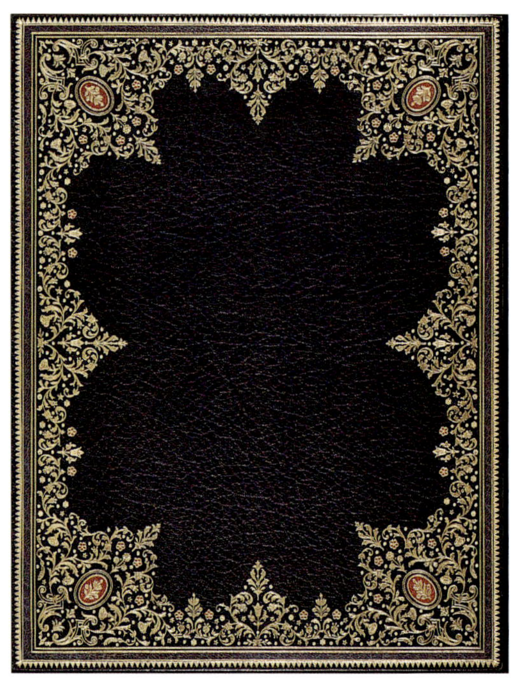 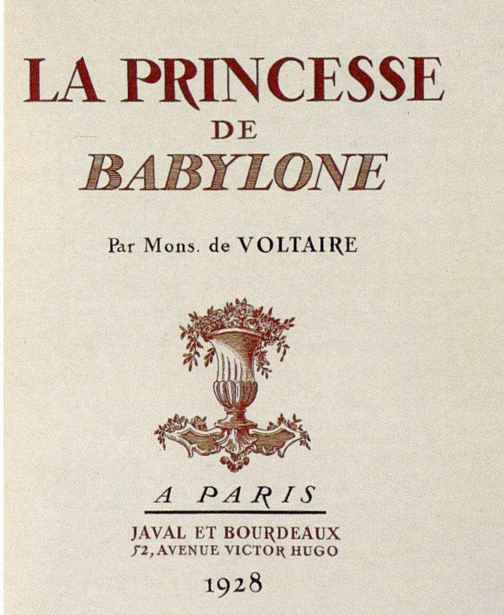 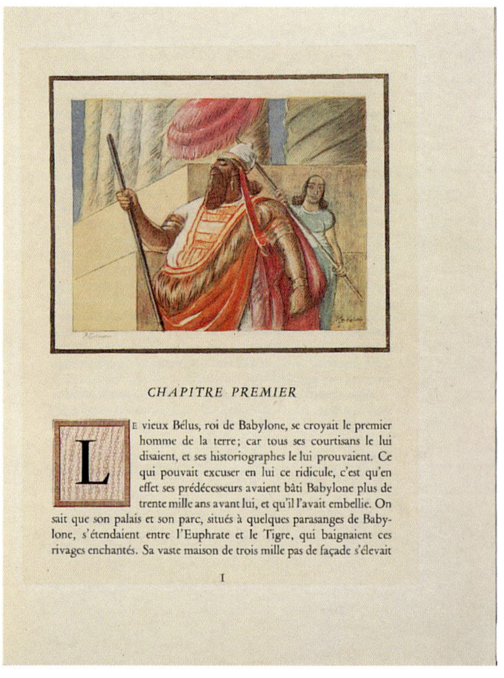

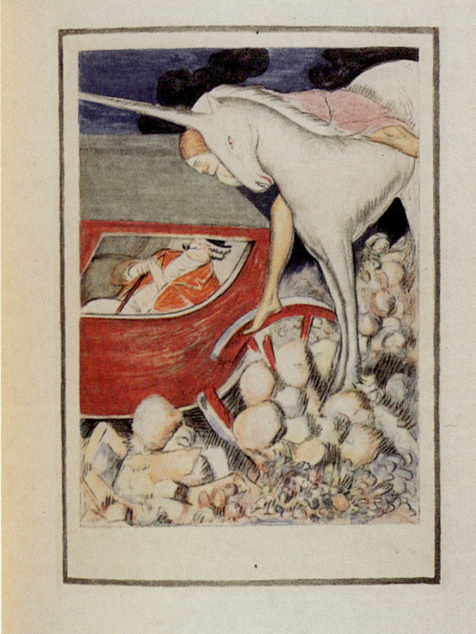 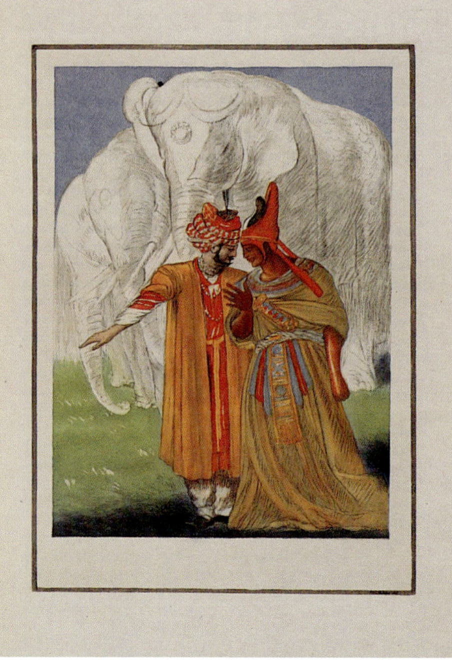 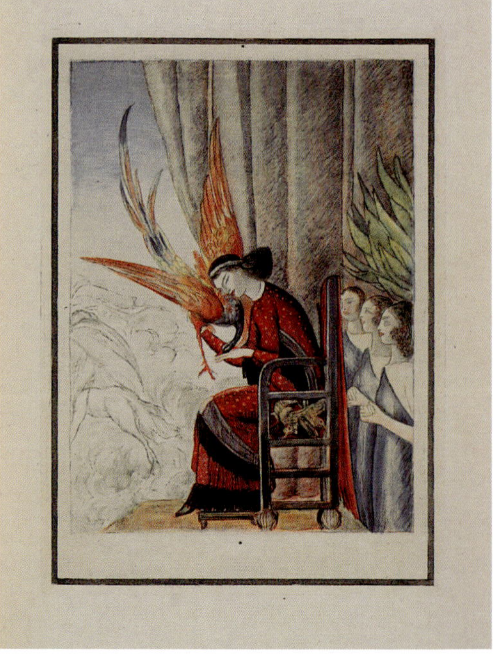

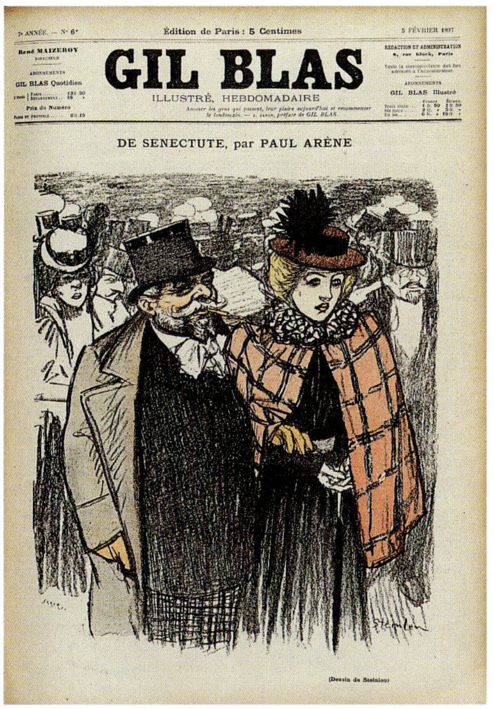
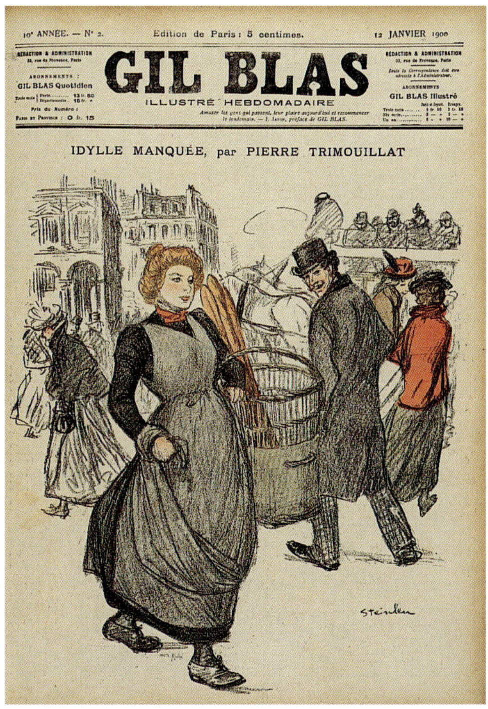
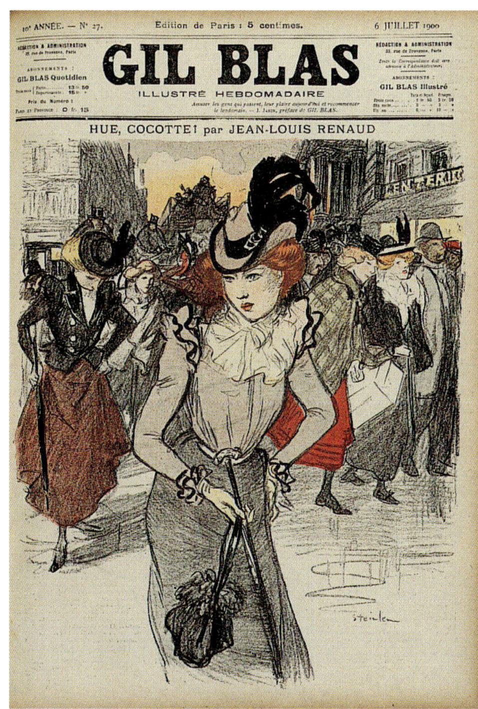

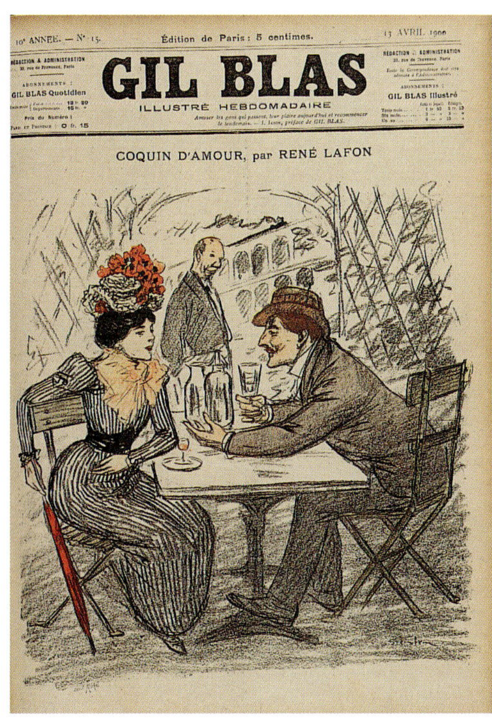
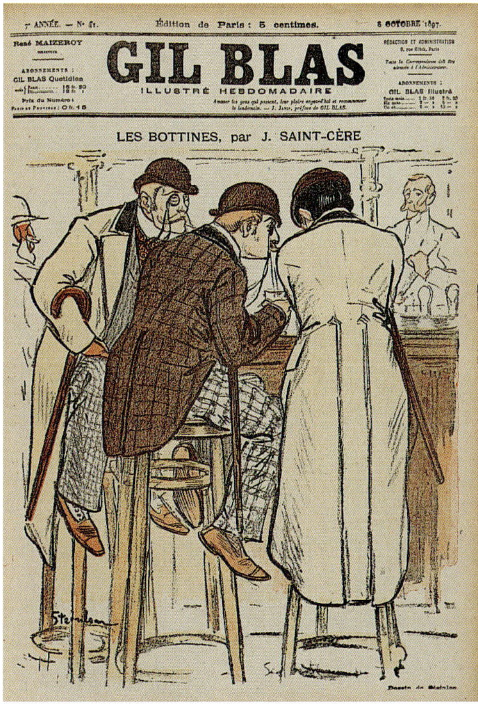
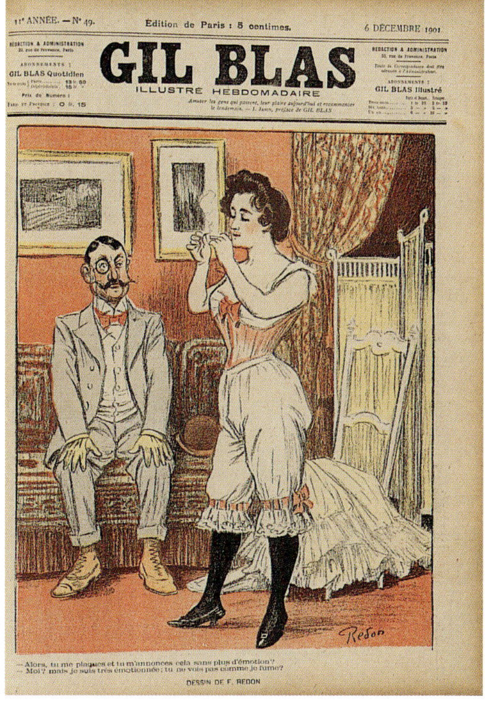

604

BOOKS AND PERIODICALS (cont'd)

602. L'Estampe Moderne. 1897-1899.
Each: 13 x 16 in./30.7 x 41 cm
Ref: PAI-XLII, 528
All 100 plates; includes tissue overlays with commentaries and twenty-four Mucha covers; complete set.
The publication distributed by Imprimerie Champenois, Paris, contains twenty-four monthly portfolios plus four bonus plates, with twenty-four original covers by Mucha, with four original lithographs in each. Almost all of these lithographs were commissioned especially for this series, featuring works by Mucha (2), Donnay, Evene-poele, Rassenfosse, Louis Rhead, H. Meunier, Léandre, Lepère, Grasset, Berchmans, Ibels, de Feure, Robbe, Helleu, Roedel, Steinlen, Bouisset, Gottlob, Détouche, Boutet, Bellery-Desfontaines, Lenoir and Willette.
Est: $20,000-$25,000.

603. La Princesse de Babylone, by Mons. de Voltaire. 1928.
*Illustrated by **Leonetto Cappiello**.*
10 x 12⁷/8 in./25.5 x 32.6 cm
Published by Javel et Bourdeaux
Ref: PAI-XXXVIII, 232
In mint condition!
One of a deluxe limited edition of forty copies printed on Japon Impérial vellum. The deluxe copy is the "Exemplaire imprimé spécialement pour Monsieur Robert Coulouma" and hand-signed by Cappiello. Comes with a separate folder containing four additional suites: one in color, one in two colors, one in blue and one in black-and-white. Leather cover design by Lorrain. In lavish presentation case. Voltaire's philosophical tale—originally published in 1752—gets a facelift in this 1928 special edition, thanks to Cappiello's fifteen color engravings. The

results are first-rate, with Cappiello, free of commercial constraints, celebrating his artistic freedom with an even broader palette clearly brought about by a narrative utterly devoid of product placement.
Est: $6,000-$7,000.

604. Gil Blas. 1891-1901.
10¹/2 x 15³/8 in./26.5 x 39 cm
Ref: PAI-XXXVI, 589
Five leather bound volumes; overall excellent condition; slight staining at paper edges.
Contains short stories, social commentary, music and poetry, but most importantly, about 1,000 illustrations of which more than 300 are color illustrations by Steinlen. Featured artists include Balluriau, Guillaume, Guydo, Grün, Bernard, Redon, Poulbot, Bac and other designers well-known to poster collectors.
Est: $8,000-$10,000.

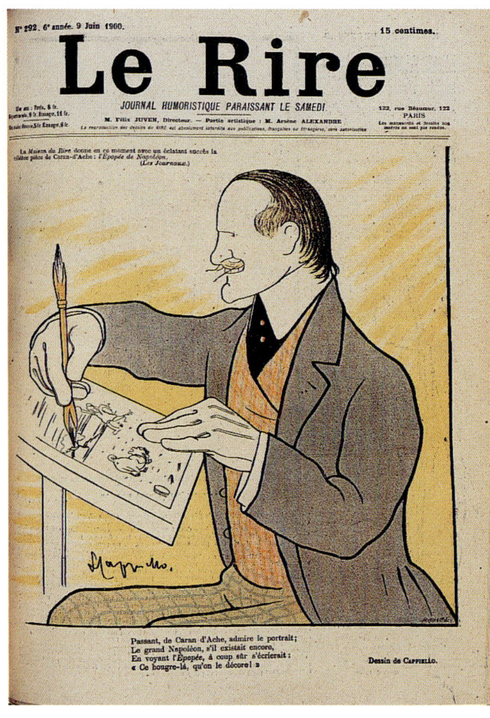
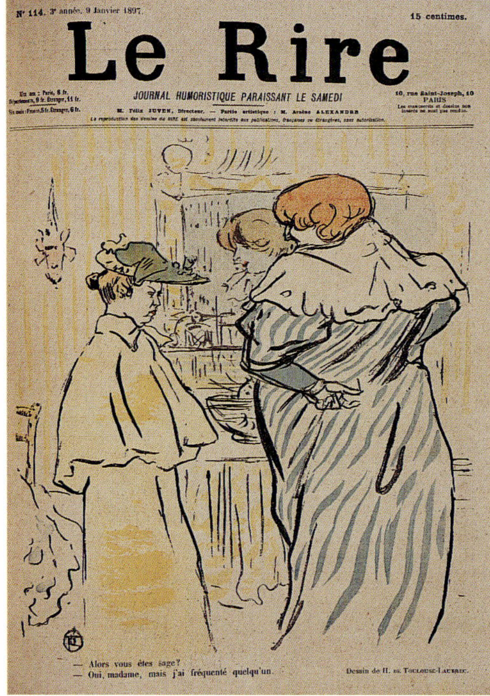
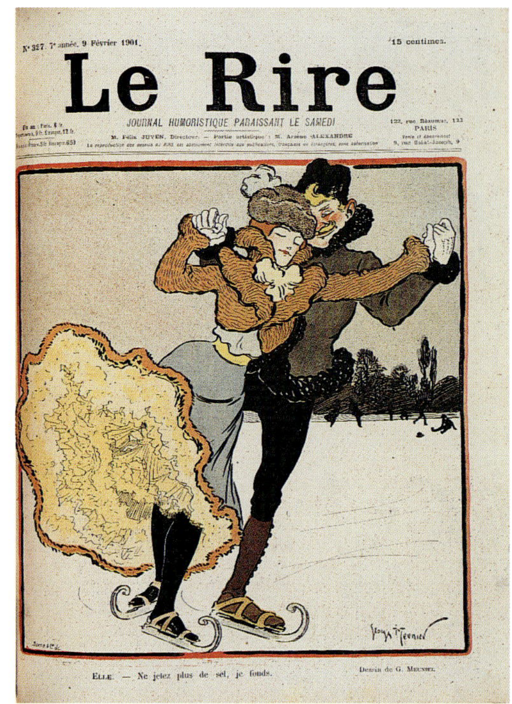

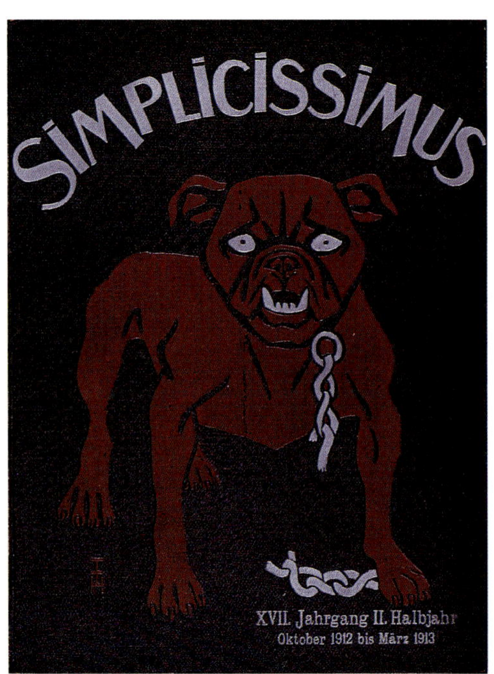
SIMPLICISSIMUS
XVII. Jahrgang II. Halbjahr
Oktober 1912 bis März 1913

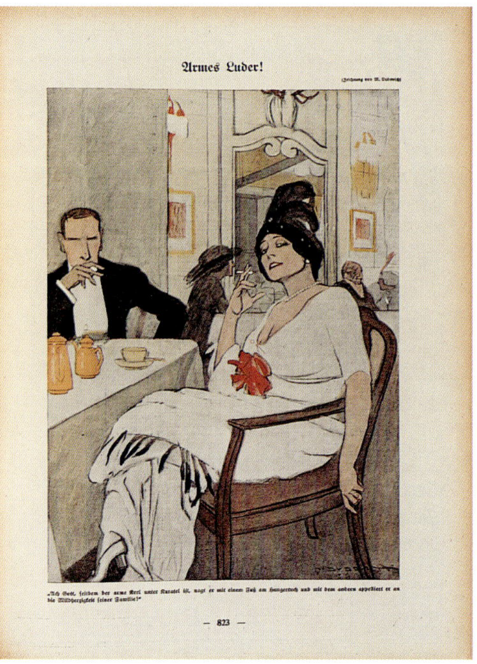

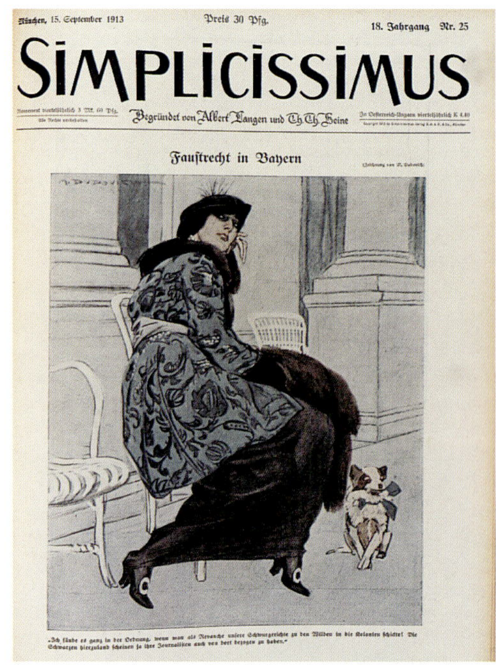
SIMPLICISSIMUS
Faustrecht in Bayern

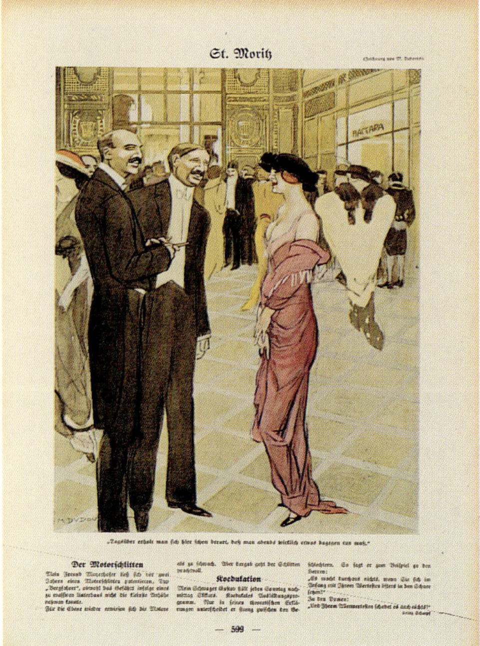

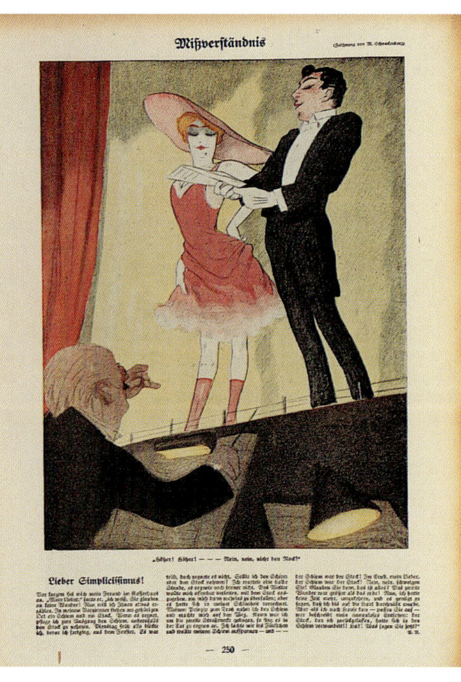

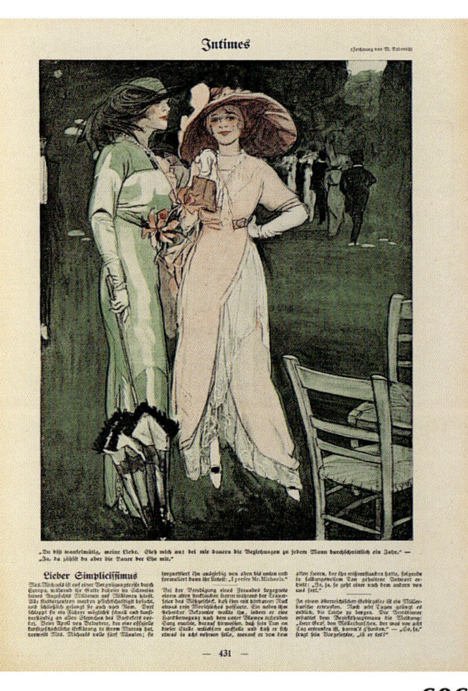

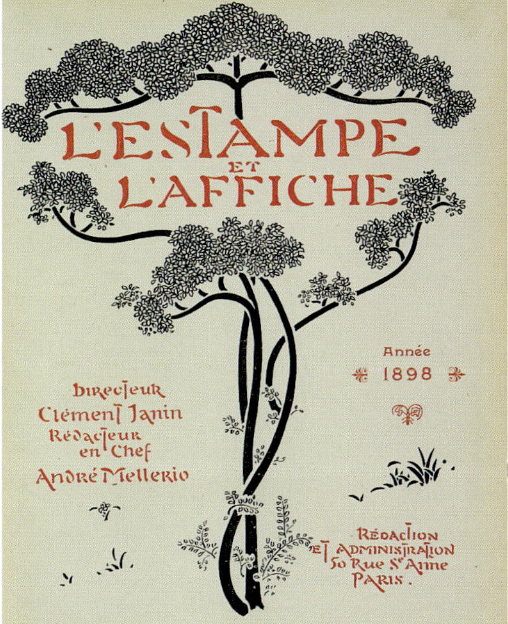

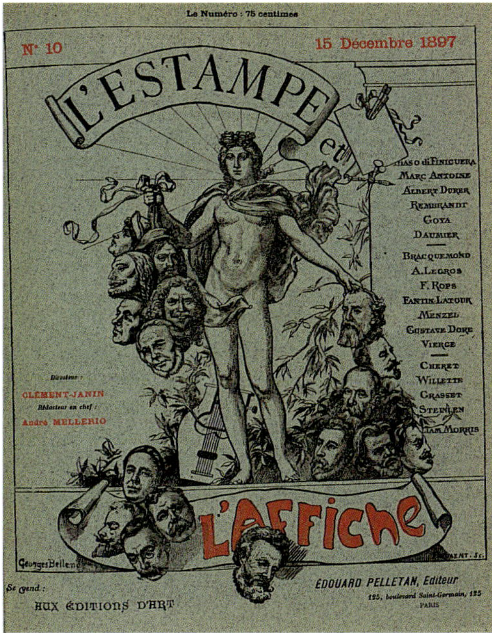

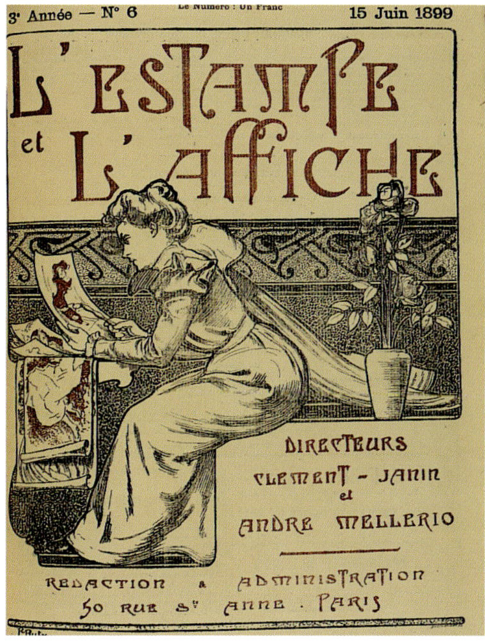

607

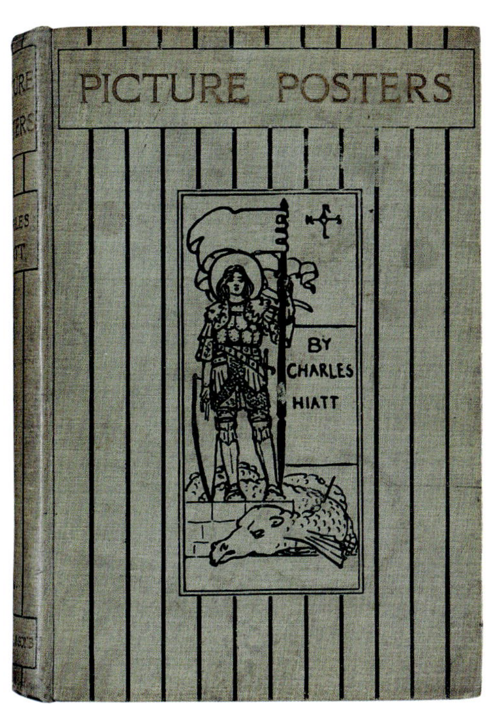

608

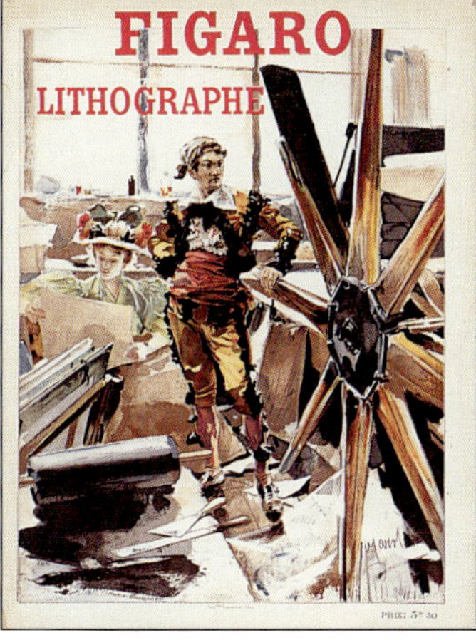

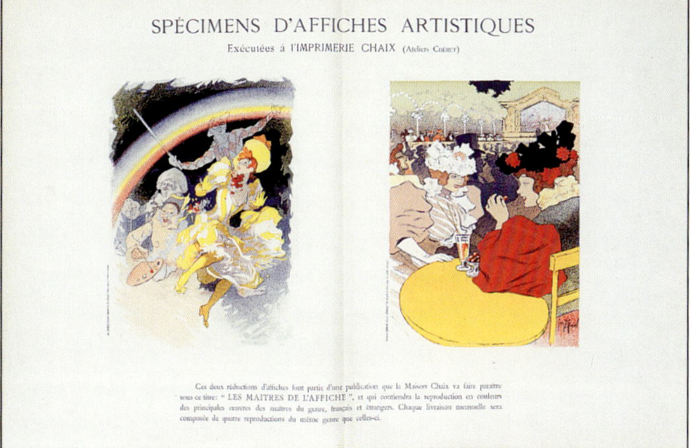

609

BOOKS AND PERIODICALS (cont'd)

605. Le Rire: 1894-1903.
9^1/$_2$ x 12^3/$_4$ in./24 x 32.5 cm
Ref: PAI-XLI, 591 (var)
Bound in nine volumes—the first decade of this journal.
This is the famous satirical weekly to which Lautrec contributed drawings, mostly in color and all eighteen appear here (beginning with Issue 1—November 10, 1894—and concluding with Issue 430—January 31, 1903). Also important (and delightful!) are the numerous fine caricatures by Cappiello, including his first published work—sketches of Puccini and Novelli—in the July 2, 1898, issue. Other artists represented include some of the top posterists of the period: Hermann-Paul, Jossot, Léandre, Forain, Willette, Vallotton, Métivet, Roedel, Faivre, Steinlen and Roubille.
Est: $6,000-$8,000.

606. Simplicissimus: Four Volumes. 1912-1914.
Each: 11^1/$_4$ x 15 in./28.5 x 38.2 cm
Overall good condition, with some stains at paper edges and some wear in the binding.
Simplicissimus was an influential Munich-based weekly humor magazine launched in 1896 to ridicule rigid official hierarchy, Prussian militarism and German *nouveau riche*. The magazine attracted the cream of German intelligentsia up until 1933, at which point the Nazi's seized control of the publication. The four volumes of the publication presented here encompass the years in which Marcello Dudovich was a major contributor. After many years of successful work in Italy, Dudovich accepted an invitation from his friend, Albert Langen, editor of *Simplicissimus*, to work for him. Some of the artist's finest work appears in these volumes—100 of his finest drawings to be exact. Other contributors include Schnackenberg and Thomas Heine—creator of the infamous red bulldog featured on the cover.
Est: $6,000-$8,000.

607. L'Estampe et l'Affiche. 1897-1899.
9 x 11^1/$_4$ in./23 x 28.5 cm
In good condition, in three hardcover bindings, with some wear on a few pages.
Articles on French and foreign posters, with several hundred reproductions on a total of 750 pages.
Artists include: Chéret, Combaz, Fraipont, Grasset, Gray, Hassall, Jossot, Meunier, Misti, Mucha, Pal, Penfield, Privat Livemont, Reed, Rhead, Roedel, Steinlen, von Stuck, Thiriet, Toulouse-Lautrec, Toussaint and Willette. Most articles are by country, but some were written regarding special topics, such as Crauzat's article on

the many new posters for Loie Fuller. There's news on poster shows and publications, as well as a price list for the latest posters published, dealer-by-dealer, which makes us want to weep—Bonnard's famous screen is 40 francs and Lautrec's entire "Elles" suite is 300 francs. *A must for the serious poster collector.*
Est: $4,000-$5,000.

608. Picture Posters, by Charles Hiatt. 1895.
5^1/$_2$ x 8^5/$_8$ in./14 x 22 cm
Published by George Bell, London
Ref; PAI-XXXIII, 625
Hardcover book.
"In the present volume an attempt has been made briefly to trace the history of the picture poster from the earliest times, and to comment upon and reproduce some of the most noteworthy examples in various countries. The English and American placards have received special attention, while the best examples of the French school have not been overlooked . . . The whole subject is treated from the point of view rather of art than of commerce." So begins the preface of Hiatt's 368-page overview of worldwide poster production, packed to the brim with wonderful contemporary opinions and appraisals of the global poster scene—not to mention one-hundred-fifty-one black-and-white illustrations—his textual analysis beginning in ancient Egypt and ending with the following axiom: "Art is generally supposed to be inimical to art, yet here we have the two combining to the advantage of both, and succeeding in making the beautiful an incident of the necessary." *Note: This particular copy was in the possession of poster historian Matlack Price, with his bookplate gracing the inside front cover!*
Est: $1,200-$1,500.

BOOKS AND PERIODICALS (cont'd)

609. Le Figaro lithographe. 1895.
13 x 18 in./33 x 45.8 cm
Imp. Lemercier, Paris
Overall excellent condition, with slight wear at edges.
Published to commemorate the one-hundred year
history of lithography, this special issue of *Le Figaro*
includes a two-page color spread for the upcoming
Maitres de l'Affiche, featuring Chéret and Meunier,
as well as a series of color progression proofs and a
wonderful indoor scene of the Lemercier printing
plant in the 1870s. *An essential acquisition for the
serious collector!*
Est: $800-$1,000.

610. Das Moderne Plakat, by Jean-Louis Sponsel.
1897.
8¹/₂ x 10⁷/₈ in./21.2 x 27.7 cm
Verlag von Gerhard Kuhtmann, Dresden
Ref: PAI-XXXVI, 583
*Deluxe edition: No. 12 of 40 copies printed on Japan
and Chine paper.*
A country-by-country survey of posters, published in
Germany in 1897. Its wide scope required a total of
316 pages and 318 illustrations, including fifty-two
plates in color. Coming a year after Mandron's 1896
classic, this monumental work is further proof of the
worldwide *affichomanie* ("poster craze") of the
period. *A rare and valuable reference for the serious
collector.*
Est: $5,000-$6,000.

611. Paris Illustré. 1883-1888.
13 x 17¹/₂ in./33 x 44.5 cm
*In five hardcover bound volumes; overall excellent
condition.*
Replete with hundreds of illustrations of worldwide
happenings and phenomenon. This weekly covered the
arts (a fine article on Bouguereau), music (including
illustrated song sheets) and drawings by Leloir, Raffaelli,
Grasset, Lunel, Chéret, Willette, Forain, Toulouse-Lautrec,
Steinlen, Fernand Fau, Outamoro and Caran d'Ache.
Est: $2,500-$3,000.

612. La Chanson a Montmartre. 1899.
10 x 13 in./25.5 x 33 cm
Ref: PAI-XXVIII, 337 (var)
This hardcover book contains music and lyrics for
twelve of the favorite songs from the Montmartre cabaret scene. Though the volume contains songsheets
by three artists—Numa, Matet and Gros—the cover
piece by Grün is priceless—a kitten with a whip doles
out richly deserved spankings—with a cat-o'-nine-tails
no less—to the lecherous officials who are nothing
more to her than wee, tiny playthings, as the police
throw back their heads with glee and the Moulin Rouge
sits enthroned in the moonlight.
Est: $1,200-$1,500.

613. Posters & Publicity/Modern Publicity.
1924-1938.
8³/₈ x 11¹/₂ in./21 x 29 cm
*14 volumes representing the complete run of this
most important reference published by The Studio,
London. Overall excellent condition; all hardcover
except 1929.*
Articles and illustrations on press advertisements and
posters, with excellent introductory texts to various
national sections. The very helpful and complete index
makes it easy to find the subject or artists that you're
looking for. Approximately 300 illustrations appear per
book.

Consists of:
    Posters & Their Designers 1924
    Art & Publicity 1925
    Posters & Publicity 1926-1929
    Modern Publicity 1930-1938

The introduction to the 1930 "Modern Publicity" ex-
plains the reason for the shift of titles and emphasis
and gives an excellent explanation of the perennial
tug-of-war between art and commerce:

"It is no longer possible to consider the poster as the
only or even necessarily the main feature of progressive
advertising as it was in the earlier days of the century,
when a great gulf existed between posters like those
of the Beggarstaff Brothers and the style of advertisement appearing in the newspapers and the magazines.

"Nor is it possible to consider art and advertising as
two separate things, which by some odd fluke have
managed to approach closely to one another, but still
remain as distinct as oil and water. The experiment of
employing academic artists, painters of easel pictures,
to design advertisements may be looked upon as an
instance of this temporary converging of different
functions. But when the experiment has been made
the results have not been successful. The oil and the
water have not mixed . . .

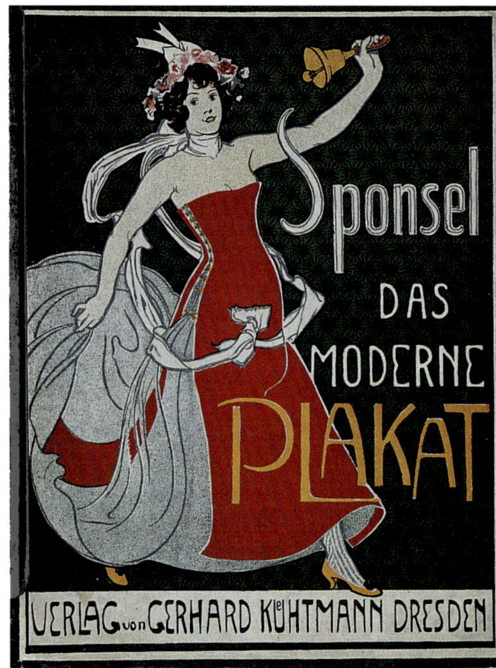

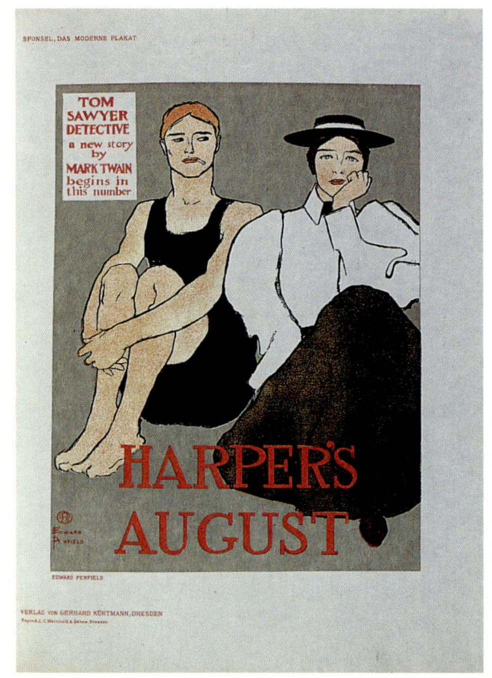

610

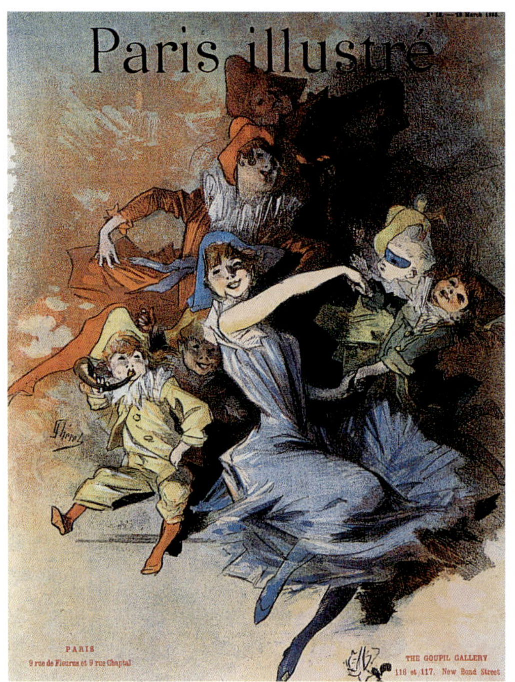

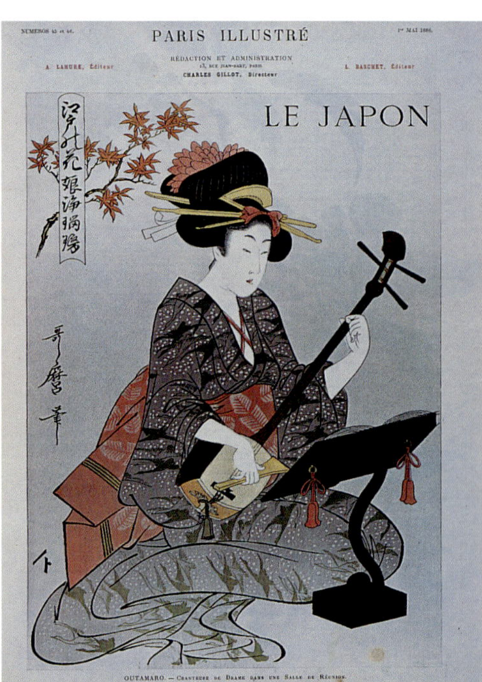

611

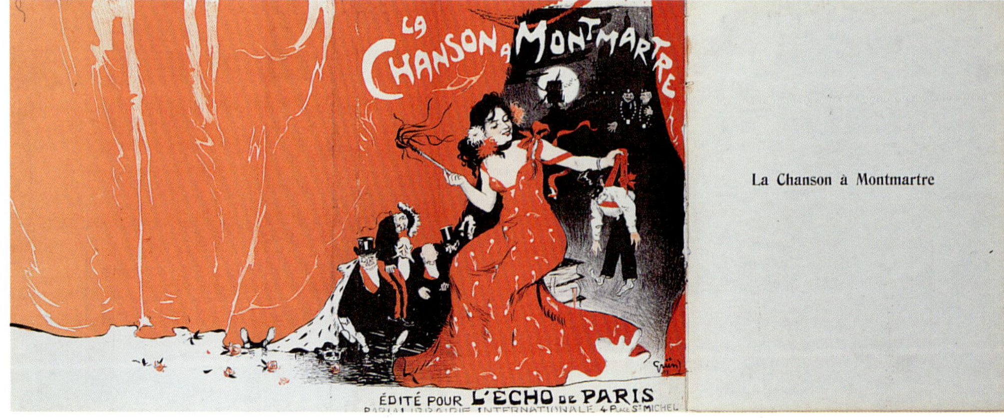

612

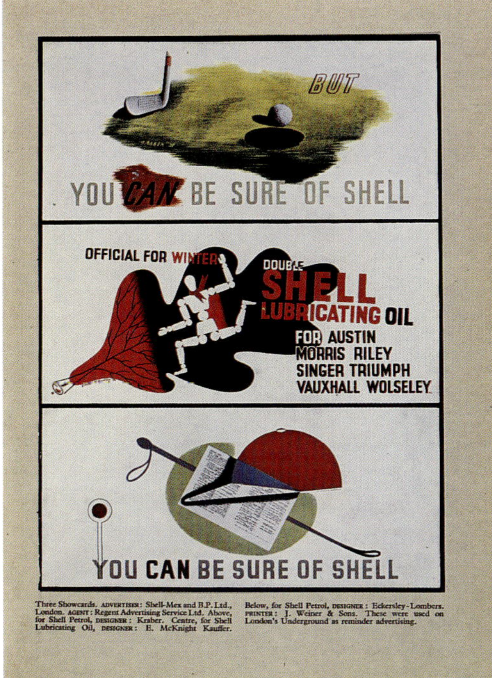
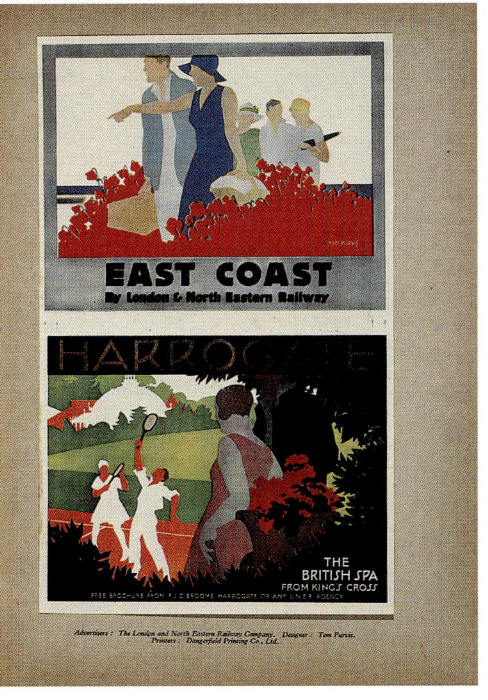
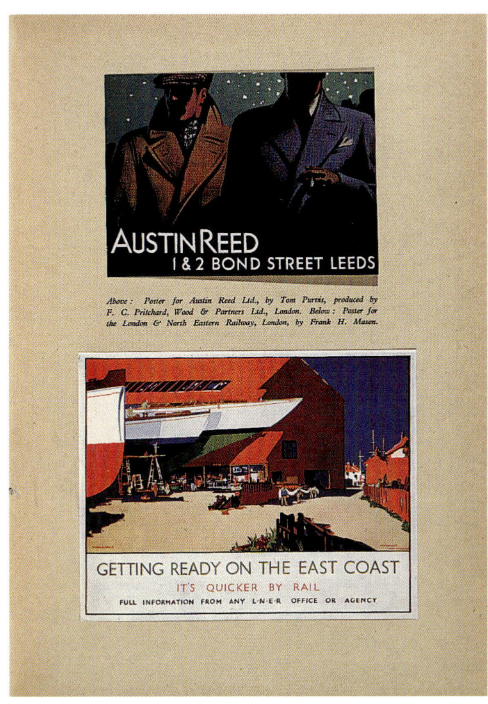

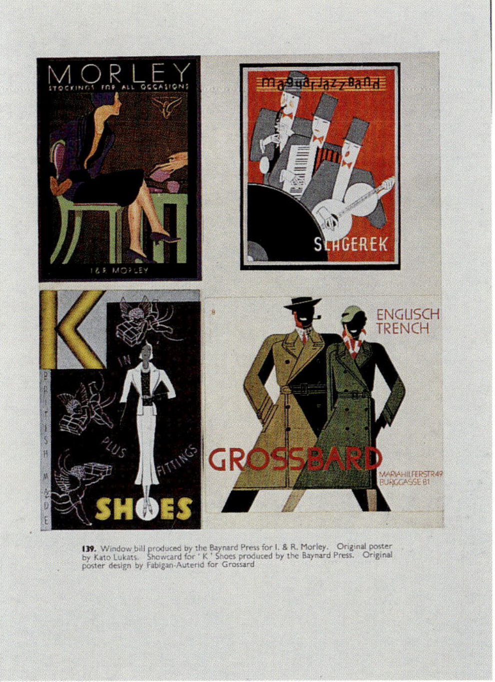
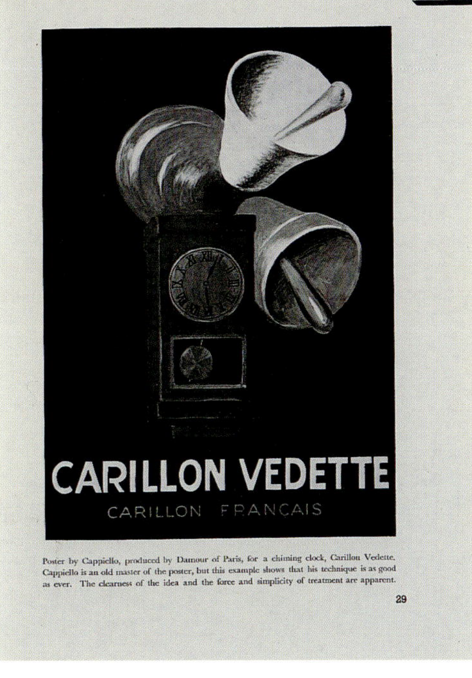
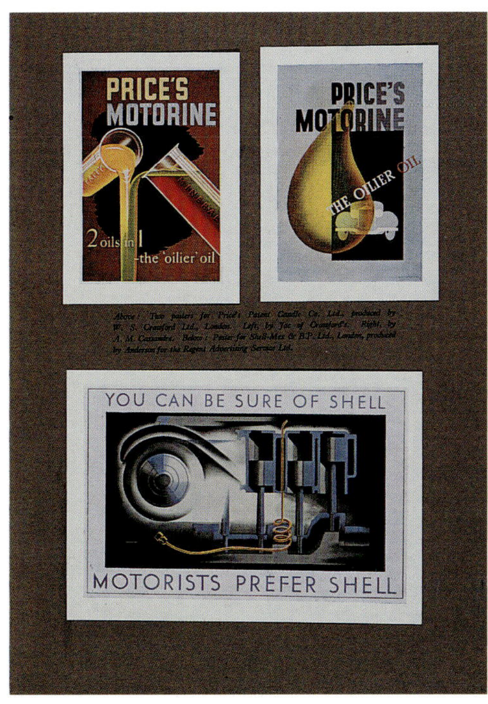

613

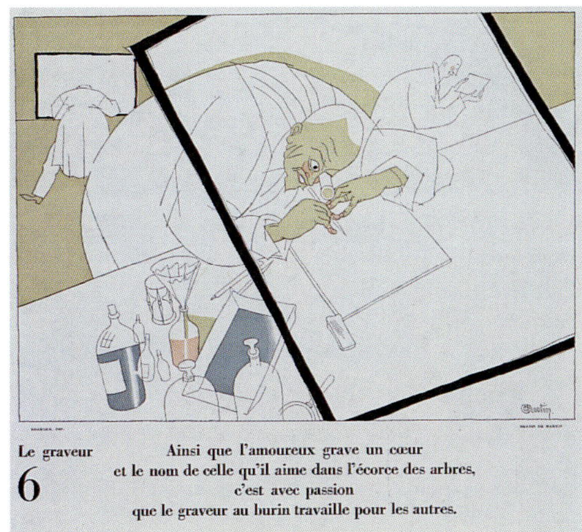
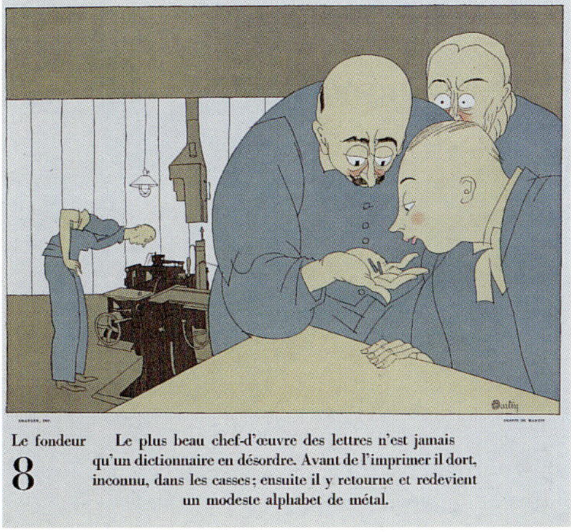

614

"Advertising . . . has a technique of its own. Whatever art there is in it merges from its very nature. It is not tacked on. Nor, to revert to our previous metaphor, does it float upon the surface. It is the product of a separate function. There is art in copy-writing, in typography, in the arrangement of designs and colours, but it proceeds naturally from the intention of the advertiser and is based on the psychological principles proper to advertising" (Modern Publicity, 1930, p. 9). Sound advice indeed for today's advertisers and designers. **Est: $6,000-$8,000.**

614. Draeger: Les Industries des Arts Graphiques.
12¼ x 15 in./31 x 38 cm
Ref: PAI-XXXI, 713
Overall excellent quality; slight stains at paper edges.
A portfolio of eleven lithographs by Charles Martin (1848-1934) that playfully bestow the printing process of the Draeger firm upon us, with accompanying text by Jean Cocteau. Intended to "glorify the graphic arts industry," the album was naturally printed and published by none other than the Draeger Frères. This particular copy has a dedication to Jacques-Émile Ruhlman (1879-1933), the famed Parisian cabinet-maker signed by Georges Draeger, one of the three Draeger brothers. Martin was a well-known fashion designer and magazine illustrator for *Gazette du Bon Ton, Femina* and *La Vie Parisienne.*
Est: $2,000-$2,500.

BIBLIOGRAPHY

The following is a list of books used in the preparation of this catalogue. In the interest of brevity, these works have been abbreviated in the Reference ("Ref:") section of the description of each lot. The abbreviations can be found below accompanied by the work's full title, publisher's name, city and date of publication. It should be noted that we have made no reference to the many magazines and annuals which are essential tools in this area, such as *The Poster, Estampe et Affiche, La Plume, Arts et Metiers Graphiques, Vendre, Das Plakat, Gebrauchsgraphik* and *Graphis Posters*.

NOTE: References to prior PAI books are limited to the last auction in which the poster was offered. We refer readers to our book, *Poster Prices VIII,* which gives the complete record of each poster offered at the first 40 PAI sales.

Abdy
The French Poster, by Jane Abdy. Clarkson N. Potter. New York, 1969.

Absinthe
Absinthe: History in a Bottle, by Barnaby Conrad III. Chronicle Books, San Francisco, 1988.

Absinthe Affiches
L'Absinthe: Les Affiches, by Marie-Claude Delahaye. Musée de l'Absinthe, Auvers-sur-Oise, 2002.

Adriani
Toulouse-Lautrec: The Complete Graphic Works, by Götz Adriani. The catalogue raisonné, featuring the Gerstenberg collection. Thames & Hudson, London, 1988.

Affiche Belgique
L'Affiche en Belgique, by Jean-Patrick Duchesne. Editions Labor, Bruxelles, 1989.

Affiche Miroir
L'Affiche-Miroir du Temps. Catalogue of the exhibition of the collection of Eric Kellenberger. Fondation Neumann, Gingins, 1995-96.

Affiche Opéra
L'Affiche Opéra. Catalogue of the exhibition at the Musée de la Seita, Paris, Oct. 1894-Jan. 1985.

Affiche Réclame
Quand l'Affiche Faisait de la Réclame! Editions de la Réunion des Musées Nationaux, Paris. 1991.

Affiches Azur
Affiches d'Azur–100 Ans d'Affiches de la Côte d'Azur et de Monaco, by Charles Martini de Chateauneuf. Editions Gilletta, Nice, 1992.

Affiches Riviera
Affiches de la Riviera, by Annie de Montry, Françoise Lepeuve & Charles Martini de Chateauneuf. Editions Gilletta, Nice-Matin, 2001.

Affichomanie
L'Affichomanie. Catalogue of the exhibition on the subject of the Postermania of the period 1880-1900 held at the Musée de l'Affiche, Paris, 1980. Text by Alain Weill.

Ailes
Voici des Ailes, affiches de cycles. Catalogue from the exhibition at the Musée d'Art et d'Industrie, Saint-Étienne, May 3-September 22, 2002.

Alimentaires
Un Siecle de Reclames Alimentaires, by F. Ghozland. Editions Milan, 1984.

Alpes
Les Alpes à l'Affiche, by Yves Ballu. Editions Glenat, Grenoble, 1987.

American Railroad
Travel by Train: The American Railroad Poster, 1870-1950, by Michael E. Zega and John E. Gruber. Indiana University Press, Bloomington, 2002.

Art & Auto
L'Art et Automobile, by Hervé Poulain. Les Clefs du Temps, Zoug, 1973.

Art Deco
Art Deco Graphics, by Patricia Frantz Kery. Harry N. Abrams, New York, 1986.

Art du Biscuit
L'Art du Biscuit, by Patrick Lefèvre-Utile. Éditions Hazan, Verona, 1995.

Auto Posters
100 Years of Auto-Posters, by Dominique Dubarry. Maeght Editeur, Paris, 1991.

Auto Show I
1er Salon de l'Affiche Automobile. Catalogue of the exhibition, compiled by Jacques Perier, and sponsored by the Automobile Club de France, Paris, October 1978.

Auto Show II
2eme Salon de l'Affiche Automobile. Catalogue of the exhibition at the Musée de l'Affiche, Paris, September to October 1979. Edited by Jacques Perier.

Auto Show III
L'Automobile et la Publicité. Catalogue of the exhibition at the Musée de la Publicité, Paris, 1984.

Avant Garde
The 20th Century Poster–Design of the Avant Garde, by Dawn Ades. The catalogue-book of the exhibition of the Walker Art Center, Minneapolis, 1984. Abbeville Press, New York, 1984.

Bargiel et Zagrodzki
Steinlen-Affichiste. Catalogue Raisonné, by Réjane Bargiel and Christophe Zagrodzki. Editions du Grant-Pont, Lausanne, 1986. (Distributed in the United States by Posters Please, Inc., New York City).

Baumberger
Otto Baumberger 1889-1961. Catalogue of the exhibition of Baumberger posters held at the Museum für Gestaltung Zurich, May-July 1988, and subsequently in Basel and Essen.

Beardsley
Aubrey Beardsley, by Brian Reade. The Viking Press, New York, 1967.

Belgique/Paris
L'Affiche en Belgique 1880-1980. Catalogue of the exhibition at the Musée de l'Affiche, Paris, 1980. Text by Alain Weill.

Belle Epoque 1980
La Belle Epoque. Catalogue of the loan exhibition from the Wittamer-De Camps collection, featuring the works of Combaz, Léo Jo and Livemont. Text by Yolande Oostens-Wittamer. International Exhibitions Foundation, 1980-81.

Bernhardt/Drama
Sarah Bernhardt: The Art of High Drama, by Carol Ockman and Kenneth Silver. Catalogue of the exhibition at the Jewish Museum, New York, 2005-2006. Yale University Press, New Haven, 2005.

Berthon & Grasset
Berthon & Grasset, by Victor Arwas. Academy Editions, London; Rizzoli, New York, 1978.

Bicycle Posters
100 Years of Bicycle Posters, by Jack Rennert. Harper & Row, New York, 1973.

Bocca
I Manifesti Italiani: fra belle epoque e fascismo, by Giorgio Bocca. Fratelli Fabri editori, Milano, 1971.

Boissons
Les Boissons/Un Siècle de Réclames, by F. Ghozland. Editions Milan, Toulouse, 1986.

Bolaffi
Catalogo Bolaffi Del Manifesto Italiano–Dizionario Degli Illustratori. Giulio Bolaffi Editore, Torino, 1995.

Broders
Voyages: Les Affiches de Roger Broders, by Annic de Montry and Françoise Lepeuve. Syros-Alternatives, Paris, 1991.

Broders Travel
Roger Broders/Travel Posters, by Alain Weill and Israel Perry. Queen Art Publishes, New York, 2002.

Broido
The Posters of Jules Chéret: 46 Full Color Plates and an Illustrated Catalogue Raisonné, 2nd ed., by Lucy Broido. Dover Publications, New York, 1992.

Brown & Reinhold
The Poster Art of A. M. Cassandre, by Robert K. Brown and Susan Reinhold. E. P. Dutton, New York, 1979.

Die Bugattis
Die Bugattis/Automobile-Mobel-Bronzen-Plakate, by Conway, Fersen, Jedding, Malhotra, Saldern and Spielmann. Christians Verlag, Hamburg 1983.

Café-Concert
Le Café-Concert 1870–1914. Catalogue of the poster exhibition at the Musée des Arts Décoratifs, Paris, 1977. Text by Alain Weill.

Canadian Pacific
Canadian Pacific Posters 1883-1963, by Marc. H. Choko and David L. Jones.

Cappiello
Cappiello. Catalogue of the exhibition at the Galerie Nationale du Grand Palais, Paris, 1981.

Cappiello/Rennert
The Posters of Leonetto Cappiello, by Jack Rennert. Poster Art Library, Posters Please, Inc., New York, 2004.

Cappiello/St. Vincent
Leonetto Cappiello–dalla pittura alla grafica. Catalogue of the exhibition in Centro Culturale Saint-Vincent. Text by Raffaele Monti & Elisabeth Matucci. Artificio, Firenze, 1985.

Caradec-Weill
Le café concert, by François Caradec and Alain Weill. Hachette/Marsin, Paris, 1980.

Carlu
Jean Carlu. Catalogue of the exhibition of the posters of Jean Carlu at the Musée de l'Affiche, Paris, 1980.

Cassandre/BN
A. M. Cassandre–Oeuvres Graphiques Modernes 1923-1939. Catalogue of the exhibition at the Bibliothèque Nationale de France in Paris, 2005.

Cassandre/Suntory
Cassandre: Every Face of the Great Master, 1901-1968. Catalogue of the exhibition held at the Suntory Museum, Osaka, June-August, 1995.

Cassandre/Weill
Cassandre, by Alain Weill. Bibliothèque de l'Image, Paris. 2005.

Cataluna
Cataluna en 1000 Cartelels: Desde los origenes hasta la Guerra Civil, by Jordi Carulla et al. Postermil, S.L , Barcelona, 1994.

Célébrités
Célébrités à l'Affiche, by A. C. Lelieur and R. Bachollet. Edita, Lausanne, 1989.

Chaumont/Exposons
Exposons Affichons: 300 affiches d'expositions. Catalogue for the 5th annual Poster Festival of Chaumont, France. Includes a section on "L'Affiche pour l'affiche" (Posters on Posters) from the Rennert collection. Somogy, Paris, 1994.

Chemins de Fer
100 Ans d'Affiches des Chemins de Fer, by Pierre Belves. Edition NM— La Vie du Rail, Paris, 1980.

Chocolate Posters
Chocolate Posters, by Israel Perry and Alain Weill. Queen Art Publishers Inc., New York, 2002.

Circus Posters
100 Years of Circus Posters, by Jack Rennert. Avon Books, New York, 1974.

Colin
100 Posters of Paul Colin, by Jack Rennert. Images Graphiques, New York, 1977.

Colin Affichiste
Paul Colin: Affichiste, by Alain Weill & Jack Rennert. Editions Denoel, Paris, 1989.

Collectionneur
Collectionneur d'Affiches, edited by Laurence Prod'homme. Editions Apogé, Musée de Bretagne, 1996.

Color Revolution
The Color Revolution. Catalogue of the exhibition at Rutgers University Art Gallery, Boston Public Library and Baltimore Museum of Art. Edited by Philip Denis Cate and Sinclair Hamilton Hitchings. 1978.

Cooper
Making a Poster, by Austin Cooper. The Studio, Ltd., London, 1938, 1945, 1949.

Côte Belge
Affiches de la Côte Belge 1890-1950, by Marie-Laurence Bernard. The collection of Roland Florizoone. Uitgeverij Marc van de Wiele, Brugge, 1992.

Crauzat
L'Oeuvre Gravé et Lithographié de Steinlen, by E. de Crauzat. Société de Propogation des Livres d'Art, Paris, 1913. Reprinted by Alan Wofsy Fine Arts, San Francisco, 1983.

Crayons
Et aussi des Crayons: Ecriture, Papeterie et Publicité. Edited by Thierry Devynck. Catalogue of the exhibition at the Bibliothèque Forney, 1996. Somogy, Paris, 1996.

Dance Posters
100 Years of Dance Posters, by Walter Terry & Jack Rennert. Avon Books, New York, 1973.

Darracott
The First World War in Posters, by Joseph Darracott. Dover Publications.

Deco Affiches
Affiches Art Deco, by Alain Weill. Inter-Livres, Paris, 1990.

Delteil
Le Peintre-Graveur Illustré, by Loys Delteil. (Volumes X and XI devoted to Lautrec). Paris, 1920. Reprinted by Collectors Edition Ltd.-Da Capo Press, New York, 1969.

Deutsche Plakat
Das deutsche Plakat—Von den Anfangen bis zur Gegenwart, by Hellmut Rademacher. VEB Verlag der Kunst, Dresden, 1965.

DFP-I
Das Frühe Plakat in Europa und den USA. Volume I. British and American Posters. Edited by Ruth Malhotra and Christina Thon. Mann Verlag, Berlin, 1973.

DFP-II
Das Frühe Plakat in Europa und den USA. Volume II. French and Belgian Posters. Edited by Ruth Malhotra, Marjan Rinkleff and Bernd Schalicke. Mann Verlag, Berlin, 1977.

DFP-III
Das Frühe Plakat in Europa und den USA. Volume III. German Posters. Edited by Helga Hollman, Ruth Malhotra, Alexander Pilipczuk, Helga Prignitz and Christina Thon. Mann Verlag, Berlin, 1980.

Dodge
The Bicycle, by Pryor Dodge. Flammarion, Paris-New York, 1996.

Dortu
Toulouse-Lautrec et son Oeuvre, by M. G. Dortu. Collectors Editions (6 volumes), New York, 1971.

Dryden
Divinely Elegant: The World of Ernst Dryden, by Anthony Lipmann. Pavilion, Books, London, 1989.

Dubout
Affiches Dubout. Editions Michele Trinckvel, Lausanne, 1985.

Dutch Poster
A History of the Dutch Poster 1890-1960, by Dick Dooijes and Pieter Brattinga. Scheltema & Holkema, Amsterdam, 1968.

España
España en 1000 Carteles, by Jordi Carulla and Arnau Carulla. Postermil, Barcelona, 1995.

Femme s'Affiche
La Femme s'Affiche. Catalogue of the exhibition of the Kellenberger Collection held in Montreux, 1990.

Ferrari
Piloti, Che Gente, by Enzo Ferrari. Conti Editore, Bologna, 1985.

Fiat
Cinquanta arnni immagini della pui importante industria italiana, by Alberto Arbasino and Gianni Bulgari. Edizioni de Autocritica, Rome, 1984.

Fit to Print
Fit to Print–The Newspaper and the Poster, by Marc Davidson. The News-Journal Corporation, Daytona Beach, Florida, 2004.

Fix-Masseau
Pierre Fix-Masseau: Affiches 1928–1983. Catalogue of the exhbition at the Bibliothèque Nationale, Paris, 1983.

Folies-Bergère
100 Years of Posters of the Folies Bergère and Music Halls of Paris, by Alain Weill. Images Graphiques, New York, 1977.

French Opera
French Opera Posters 1868-1930, by Lucy Broido. Dover Publications, New York, 1976.

Frey
Toulouse-Lautrec: A Life, by Julia Frey. Viking Penguin, New York, 1994.

Galerie CGER
L'Art de l'Affiche en Belgique 1900-1980. Catalogue of the exhibition at Galerie CGER. Brussels, 1980.

Gid
Raymond Gid/Affichiste et Typographe, edited by Anne-Claude Lelieur. Catalogue of the exhibition at the Bibliothèque Forney, Paris, 1992. Agence Culturelle de Paris.

Gold
First Ladies of the Poster: The Gold Collection, by Laura Gold. Posters Please Inc., New York City, 1998.

Golden Age of Travel
The Golden Age of Travel Posters: 1880-1939, by Alexsis Gregory. Cassell, London, 1998.

Golf
L'Affiche de Golf/Golf Posters, by Alexis Orloff. Éditions Milan, Toulouse, 2002.

Gourmand
Un Voyage Gourmand: 60 affiches de gastronomie, by Alain Weill. Catalogue of the exhibition at the Musée-Galerie de la Seita, Paris, 1984.

Graphicar
Graphicar, by Claudio Bertieri. Fratelli Fabbri, Milano, 1976.

Grün
Jules-Alexandre Grün: The Posters/Les Affiches, by Alain Weill and Israel Perry. Queen Art Publishers, New York, 2005.

Guerra Civil
La Guerra Civil en 2000 Carteles, by Jordi Carulla and Arnau Carulla. 2 volumes. Postermil, Barcelona, 1997.

Health Posters
Posters of Health, by Marine Robert-Sterkendries. Therabel Pharma, Brussels, 1996.

Hiatt
Picture Posters, by Charles Hiatt. George Bell and Sons, London, 1895.

Hillier
Posters, by Bevis Hillier. Weidenfeld and Nicholson, London, 1969; Stein & Day, New York, 1969; Spring Books, The Hamlyn Publishing Group, New York, 1974.

HTL/Rutgers
The Circle of Toulouse-Lautrec. Catalogue of the exhibition at the Zimmerli Art Museum, Rutgers University, 1986. Text by Phillip Dennis Cate and Patricia Eckert Boyer.

Images of an Era
Images of an Era: The American Poster, 1945-1975. Catalogue of the exhibition of the Smithsonian Institution, Washington. D.C., 1975.

Internationale Plakate
Internationale Plakate 1871-1971. Catalogue of the exhibition at the Haus der Kunst, Munich, 1971. Edited by Dr. Heinz Spielmann.

Josephine
Josephine Baker: The Hungry Heart, by Jean Claude Baker and Chris Chase. Random House, New York, 1993.

Joyant
Henri de Toulouse-Lautrec, by Maurice Joyant. 2 volumes. H. Floury, Paris, 1927.

Karcher
Memoire de la Rue–Souvenirs d'un imprimeur et d'un afficheur. Illustrated book of the archives of the Karcher printing firm of Paris with introduction by Alain Weill. WM Editions, Paris, 1986. (Distributed in the U.S.A. by Posters Please, Inc., New York, with a translation of text and the addition of an index).

Kauffer
E. McKnight Kauffer: a designer and his public, by Mark Haworth-Booth. Gordon Fraser, London, 1979.

Keay
American Posters of the Turn of the Century, by Carolyn Keay. Academy Editions, London, 1975.

Kiffer
Charles Kiffer et le Spectacle. Catalogue of the exhibition at the Centre de l'Affiche, Toulouse, 1900.

Lauder
American Art Posters of the 1890s (The Leonard A. Lauder Collection). Catalogue of the exhibition of the Metropolitan Museum of Art, New York, October 1987–January 1988. Text by David W. Kiehl. Harry N. Abrams, New York, 1987.

Lautrec by Lautrec
Lautrec by Lautrec, by Ph. Huisman and M. G. Dortu, Galahad Books, New York, 1976.

Lautrec/Montmartre
Toulouse-Lautrec and Montmartre. The book of the exhibition at the National Gallery of Art, Washington, D.C., and the Art Institute of Chicago. Text by Richard Thomson, Phillip Dennis Cate and Mary Weaver Chaplin. Princeton University Press, Princeton, NJ, 2005.

Lendl/Paris
Alphonse Mucha: La Collection Ivan Lendl. Catalogue of the exhibition at Musée de la Publicité, Paris, 1989. Text by Jack Rennert. Editions Syros/Alternatives, Paris.

Leupin
Herbert Leupin: Plakate, Bilder, Graphiken, by Karl Lüönd and Charles Leupin. Friedrich Reinhardt, Basel, 1995.

Lincoln Center
Lincoln Center Posters, by Vera List and Herbert Kupferberg. Harry N. Abrams, New York, 1980.

Litfass-Bier
Litfass-Bier: Historische Bierplakate-Sammlung Heinrich Becker. Edited by Gerhard Dietrich. Plakat/Konzepte, Hannover, 1998.

Looping the Loop
Looping the Loop: Posters of Flight, by Henry Serrano Villard and Willis M. Allen, Jr. Kales Press, San Diego, California, 2000.

Loupot
Charles Loupot. Catalogue of the exhibition at the Musée de l'Affiche, Paris.

Loupot/Zagrodzki
Charles Loupot: L'Art de l'Affiche, by Christophe Zagrodzki. Le Cherche-Midi, Paris, 1998. (Exclusive American distributor: Posters Please Inc., N.Y.C.)

Magic Posters
100 Years of Magic Posters, by Charles and Regina Reynolds. Grosset & Dunlap, New York, 1976.

Maindron
Les Affiches Illustrées, 1886-1895, by Ernest Maindron. G. Boudet, Paris, 1896.

Maitres
Les Maitres de l'Affiche 1896-1900, by Roger Marx. Imprimerie Chaix, Paris 1896-1900. Reprinted as "Masters of the Poster 1896-1900," by Images Graphiques, New York, 1977, and "The Complete 'Masters of the Poster,'" by Dover Publications, New York, 1990.

Margadant
Das Schweizer Plakat/The Swiss Poster, 1900-1983, by Bruno Margadant. Birkhaus Verlag, Basel, 1983.

Margolin
American Poster Renaissance, by Victor Margolin. Watson-Guptill Publications, New York, 1975.

Marques
Images de Marques/Marques d'Images: 100 marques du patrimoine français, by Daniel Cauzard, Jean Perret and Yves Ronin. Editions Ramsay, Paris, 1989.

Masters 1900
Masters of the Poster 1900, by Alan Weill. Bibliothèque de l'Image, Paris, 2001.

Matter
Herbert Matter/Foto Grafiker/Sehformen der Zeit, edited by Walter Binder, Adrian Battig and Armin Hofmann. Verlag Lars Muller, Baden, 1995.

Mauzan
The Posters of Mauzan–A Catalogue Raisonné, by Mirande Carnévalé-Mauzan. Exclusive North American distribution by Posters Please, Inc., New York, 2001.

Mauzan Affiches
Mauzan: Affiches/Oeuvres Diverses, by A. Lancellotti. Casa Editrice d'Arte Bestetle Tumminlelli, Milan, ca. 1928.

Mauzan/Cartellonista
Mauzan: Cartellonista degli anni ruggenti. Catalogue of the Mauzan collection in the Salce Collection of the Treviso Museum, edited by Eugenio Manzato. Edizioni Canova, Treviso, 1983.

Mauzan/Paris
Achille Mauzan. Catalogue of the exhibition held at the Musée de la Publicité, Paris, 1983.

Mauzan/Pinerolo
Omaggio a Luciano Achille Mauzan: Al'arte del manifesto. Catalogue of the exhibition titled "Omaggio a Luciano Achille Mauzan—l'arte del Manifesto," curated by Mario Marchiando-Pacchiola, and held in Pinerolo in 1984.

Mauzan/Treviso
Manifesti di A. L. Mauzan, by Antonio Mazzaroli. Editrice Canova, Treviso, 1983.

Menegazzi-1
Il Manifesto Italiano, by Luigi Menegazzi. Electa Editrice, Milan, ca. 1976.

Menegazzi-II
Il Manifesto Italiano, by Luigi Menegazzi. Arnoldo Mondadori Arte, Milan, 1989 (revised edition).

Meunier
Georges Meunier–affichiste 1869-1942. Catalogue of the exhibition at Bibliothèque Fourney, Paris, 1978.

Modern American Posters
The Modern American Poster, by J. Stewart Johnson. Catalogue of the Japanese exhibition of the posters from the N.Y. Musuem of Modern Art collection, 1983-84. Little Brown, Boston, 1983.

Modern Poster
The Modern Poster, by Stuart Wrede. Catalogue of the exhibition at the Museum of Modern Art, New York, 1988. New York Graphic Society/ Little Brown and Co., Boston, 1988.

Moderno Francés
El Cartel Moderno Francés. Catalogue for the Colin, Carlu, Loupot and Cassandre exhibition at the Museo Nacional Centro de Arte Reina Sofia, Madrid, 2001.

Modes & Publicité
Modes & Publicité 1885-1986—Le Regard de Marie Claire. Editions Hermé, Paris, 1986.

Mouron
A. M. Cassandre, by Henri Mouron. Rizzoli, New York, 1985.

Mucha/Art Nouveau
Alphonse Mucha: The Spirit of Art Nouveau. Catalogue of the touring exhibition organized by Art Services International, Alexandria, Virginia, 1998. Edited by Victor Arwas, Jana Brabcová-Orliková and Anna Dvorák.

Mucha/Bridges
Alphonse Mucha: The Complete Graphic Works, edited by Ann Bridges. Academy Editions, London, 1980.

Müller-Brockmann
History of the Poster, by Josef and Shizuko Müller-Brockmann. ABC Edition, Zurich, 1971 (in German, French and English).

Musée d'Affiche
Musée d'Affiche. Catalogue for the inaugural exhibition titled *Trois Siècles d'Affiches Françaises*, Paris, 1978.

Nectar/Nicolas
Nectar comme Nicolas, by Alain Weill. Editions Herscher, Paris, 1986.

Negripub
Negripub: L'image des Noirs dans la publicité, by Raymond Bachollet, Jean-Barthelemi Debost, Anne-Claude Lelieur and Marie-Christine Peyrière. The book of the exhibition at the Bibliothèque Forney, 1992. Editions Somogy, Paris.

Nizzoli
Marcello Nizzoli, by Germano Celant. Edizioni di Comunità, Milano, 1968.

Ogé
Eugène Ogé/Affichiste 1861-1936. Catalogue of the exhibition at the Bibliothèque Fourney, Paris, with text by its director, Anne-Claude Lelieur and Raymond Bachollet. Agence Culturelle de Paris, 1998.

Operetta
Operetta: A Theatrical History, by Richard Traubner. Doubleday & Company, Inc., Garden City, New York, 1983.

PAI – Books of the auctions organized by Poster Auctions International, Inc.

PAI-I
Premier Posters. Book of the auction held in New York City, March 9, 1985.

PAI-II
Prize Posters. Book of the auction held in Chicago, November 10, 1985.

PAI-III
Poster Impressions. Book of the auction held in New York City, June 1, 1986.

PAI-IV
Prestige Posters. Book of the auction held in New York City, May 3, 1987.

PAI-V
Poster Pizzazz. Book of the auction held in Universal City, California, November 22, 1987.

PAI-VI
Poster Splendor. Book of the auction held in New York City, May 1, 1988.

PAI-VII
Poster Potpourri. Book of the auction held in New York, November 13, 1988.

PAI-VIII
Poster Treasures. Book of the auction held in New York, May 7, 1989.

PAI-IX
Poster Palette. Book of the auction held in New York, November 12, 1989.

PAI-X
Elegant Posters. Book of the auction held in New York, May 20, 1990.

PAI-XI
Poster Passion. Book of the auction held in New York, November 11, 1990.

PAI-XII
Poster Panache. Book of the auction held in New York, May 5, 1991.

PAI XIII
Poster Jubilee. Book of the auction held in New York. November 10, 1991.

PAI-XIV
Poster Extravaganza. Book of the auction held in New York May 3, 1992.

PAI XV
Rarest Posters. Book of the auction held in New York, November 8, 1992.

PAI-XVI
Poster Parade. Book of the auction held in New York, May 2. 1993.

PAI-XVII
Poster Classics. Book of the auction held in New York, November 14, 1993.

PAI-XVIII
Winning Posters. Book of the auction held in New York, May 1, 1994.

PAI-XIX
Prima Posters. Book of the auction held in New York, November 13, 1994.

PAI-XX
Poster Panorama. Book of the auction held in New York, May 7, 1995.

PAI-XXI
Timeless Posters. Book of the auction held in New York, November 12, 1995.

PAIXXII
Positively Posters. Auction held in New York City, May 5, 1996.

PAIXXIII
Poster Delights. Auction held in New York City, November 10, 1996.

PAI-XXIV
Poster Pleasures. Auction held in New York City, May 4, 1997.

PAI-XXV
Sterling Posters. Auction held in New York City, November 9, 1997.

PAI-XXVI
Postermania. Auction held in New York City, May 3, 1998.

PAI-XXVII
Poster Ecstasy. Auction held in New York City, November 8, 1998.

PAI-XXVIII
Poster Vogue. Auction held in New York City, May 2, 1999.

PAI-XXIX
Posters for the Millennium. Auction held in New York City, November 4, 1999.

PAI-XXX
Poster Allure. Auction held in New York City, May 7, 2000.

PAI-XXXI
Poster Power. Auction held in New York City, November 12, 2000.

PAI-XXXII
Dream Posters. Auction held in New York City, May 6, 2001.

PAI-XXXIII
Swank Posters. Auction held in New York City, November 11, 2001.

PAI-XXXIV
Poster Pride. Auction held in New York City, May 5, 2002.

PAI-XXXV
Posters Perform. Auction held in New York City, November 10, 2002.

PAI-XXXVI
Posters Persuasion. Auction held in New York City, May 4, 2003.

PAI-XXXVII
Poster Holiday/The Wright Stuff. Dual-auction held in New York City, November 9, 2003.

PAI-XXXVIII
Poster Style. Auction held in New York City, May 2, 2004.

PAI-XXXIX
Poster Intoxication. Auction held in New York City, November 14, 2004.

PAI-XL
Posters Excel. Auction held in New York City, May 1, 2005.

PAI-XLI
Matchless Posters. Auction held in New York City, November 13, 2005.

PAI-XLII
Posters Charm. Auction held in New York City, May 7, 2006.

Petite Reine
La Petite Reine: Le Vélo en Affiches à la fin du XIXeme. Catalogue exhibition of bicycle posters of the end of the 19th century held at Musée de l'Affiche, Paris, May to September, 1979.

Phillips I
A Century of Posters 1870-1970. The catalogue of the Phillips Auction held November 10, 1979, in New York. Text by Jack Rennert.

Phillips II
Poster Classics. The catalogue of the Phillips Auction held May 10, 1980, in New York. Text by Jack Rennert.

Pierrot
Les 100 plus belles images de Pierrot, by Daniel Bordet. Editions Dabecom, Paris, 2003.

Plakate München
Plakate in München 1840-1940. Catalogue of the exhibition of Munich posters at the Münchner Stadtmuseum, 1975-76.

Purvis
Poster Progress. Introduction by Tom Purvis. Edited by F.A. Mercer & W. Gaunt. The Studio, London and New York, ca. 1938.

Rademacher
Masters of German Art, by Hellmut Rademacher. October House, New York, 1966 (Original German edition published in 1965 by Edition Leipzig).

Railway Posters
Railway Posters 1923-1947, by Beverly Cole and Richard Durack. Rizzoli, New York, 1992.

Rawls
Wake Up, America: World War I and the American Poster, by Walton Rawls. Abbeville Press, New York, 1988.

Reims
Exposition d'Affiches Artistiques Françaises et Etrangères. The catalogue of the November 1896 exhibition held in Reims. Reissued in a numbered edition of 1,000 copies by the Musée de l'Affiche in 1980.

Rennert/Weill
Alphonse Mucha: The Complete Posters and Panels, by Jack Rennert and Alain Weill. G. K. Hall, Boston, 1984.

Richmond
The Technique of the Poster, by Leonard Richmond. Sir Isaac Pitman & Sons, London, 1933.

Rogers
A Book of the Poster, by W. S. Rogers. Greening & Co., London, 1901.

Russian Films
Film Posters of the Russian Avant-Garde, by Susan Pack. Benedikt Taschen Verlag, Koln, Germany, 1995.

Sachs
Kunst Kommerz Visionen: Deutsche Plakate 1888-1933. Catalogue of the exhibition at the Deutsches Historisches Museum in Berlin, 1992, consisting of the Hans Sachs collection. Edition Braus, Heidelberg, 1992.

Salon des Cent
Le Salon des Cent: 1894-1900. Affiches d'artistes, by Jocelyne Van Deputte. Catalogue of the exhibition held at the Musée Carnavalet, Paris, 1995.

Salon des Cent/Neumann
Les Affiches du Salon des Cent. Catalogue of the exhibition sponsored by the Foundation Neumann in Paris at the Musée de Pont-Aven and the Musée des Arts decoratifs de Bordeaux in 2000-2001.

Schardt
Paris 1900, by Hermann Schardt. G P. Putnam's Sons, New York, 1970; reprinted in 1987 by Portland House, New York. (Originally published as *Paris 1900: Französiche Plakatkunst,* Belser Verlag, Stuttgart, 1968.)

Schoonbroadt
Privat Livemont: Entre Classicisme et Art Nouveau, by Benoit Schoonbroadt. C.I.D.E.P., Bruxelles, 2003.

Sepo
Sepo. Catalogue ("catalogo critico") of artist's work, edited by Vanja Strukelj and published by the Universita di Parma, 1979.

Shell
The Shell Poster Book. Introduction by David Bernstein. Hamish Hamilton, London, 1992.

Sparrow
Advertising and British Art, by Walter Shaw Sparrow. John Land/ The Bodley Head, London, 1924.

Spectacle
Les Arts du Spectacle en France–Affiches Illustrées 1850-1950, by Nicole Wild. The catalogue of the Bibliothèque de l'Opera (part of the Bibliothèque Nationale), Paris, 1976.

Sport à l'Affiche
Sport à l'Affche, by Jean Durry. Editions Hoebeke, Paris, 1988.

Steinlen
Théophile-Alexandre Steinlen, by Phillip Dennis Cate and Susan Gill. Gibbs M. Smith, Salt Lake City, Utah, 1982.

Steinlen's Cats
Steinlen's Cats, by Francois Fossier. Steinlen images from the Bibliothèque Nationale, Paris. Harry N. Abrams, New York, 1990.

Takashimaya
The Poster 1865-1969. Catalogue of the exhibition which opened at the Takashimaya Art Gallery, Nihonbashi, Tokyo, April 18, 1985, and consisted largely of posters from the Deutsches Plakat Museum of Essen, Germany.

Theaterplakate
Theaterplakate: ein internationaler historischer Überblick, by Hellmut Rademacher. Edition Leipzig, Leipzig, 1990.

Theofiles
American Posters of World War I, by George Theofiles. Dafran House, New York.

Timeless Images
Timeless Images. Catalogue of the touring exhibition of posters in Japan, 1984-85. Text by Jack Rennert; in English and Japanese. Exclusive American distributor: Posters Please, Inc., New York City.

Tolmer
Tolmer: 60 ans de création graphique dans l'Ile St. Louis. Catalogue of the exhibition at the Bibliotèque Fourney, Paris, 1986.

Toujours Plus Haut
Toujours Plus Haut: Affiches Aviation. Catalogue of the aviation poster exhibition at the Centre de l'Affiche in Toulouse, France, 2004-2005. Edited by François-Régis Gastou. Chorus Editions, Toulouse, 2004.

Train à l'Affiche
Le Train à l'Affiche: Les plus belles affiches ferroviaires française, by Florence Camard and Christophe Zagrodzki. La Vie du Rail, Paris, 1989.

Villemot
Les affiches de Villemot, by Jean François Bazin. Denoël, Paris, 1985.

Villemot/A to Z
Villemot–L'Affiches de A à Z, by Guillaume Villemot. Éditions Hoëbeke, Paris, 2005.

Voyage
L'Invitation au Voyage, by Alain Weill. Somogy, Paris, 1994.

Wagner
Toulouse-Lautrec and His Contemporaries: Posters of the Belle Epoque from the Wagner Collection. Book of the exhibition at the Los Angeles County Museum of Art, 1985.

Wagons-Lits
125 Years International Sleeping Car Company, by Albert Mühl and Jürgen Klein. The history in text and graphics of the Wagons-Lits company, with text in German, French and English. EK-Verlag GmbH, Freiburg, 1998.

Wagons-Lits II
Traveling in Luxury, by Albert Mühl and Jürgen Klein. Revised and expanded edition, published by EK-Verlag, Freiburg, 2006.

Wallonie
L'Affiche en Wallonie: À travers les collections de la Vie Wallonne. Edited by the students of the Seminaire d'Esthetique de l'Université de Liège, 1980.

Weill
The Poster: A Worldwide Survey and History, by Alain Weill. G.K. Hall, Boston, 1985.

Wember
Die Jugend der Plakate 1887-1917, by Paul Wember. Scherpe Verlag, Krefeld, 1961.

Wine Spectator
Posters of the Belle Epoque: The Wine Spectator Collection, by Jack Rennert. The Wine Spectator Press, New York, 1990.

Wittrock
Toulouse-Lautrec: The Complete Prints, by Wolfgang Wittrock. 2 volumes. Sotheby's, London, 1985.

Wobmann
Touristikplakate der Schweiz (Tourist Posters of Switzerland), by Karl Wobmann, introduction by Willy Rotzler. AT Verlag, Aarau, 1980.

Word & Image
Word & Image. Catalogue of the exhibition at the Museum of Modern Art, New York, edited by Mildred Constantine. Text by Alan M. Fern. New York Graphic Society, Greenwich, Connecticut, 1968.

CONDITIONS OF SALE

The Conditions of Sale in this catalogue, as it may be amended by any posted notice during the sale, constitutes the complete terms and conditions under which the items listed in this catalogue will be offered for sale. Please note that the items will be offered by us as agent for the consignor.

Every potential buyer should read these Conditions of Sale and it will be agreed, acknowledged and understood by such buyer that said buyer has consented to each and every term and condition as set forth herein.

1. Authenticity and Terms of Guarantee.
For a period of five years from the date of this sale, Poster Auctions International, as agent, warrants the authenticity of authorship of all lots contained in this catalogue as described in the text accompanying each lot.

This warranty and guarantee is made only within the five year period and only to the original buyer of record who returns the purchased lot in the same condition as when sold to said buyer; and, it is established beyond doubt that the identification of authorship, as set forth in the description in this catalogue as may have been amended by any posted signs or oral declarations during tire sale, is not correct based on a reasonable reading of the catalogue and the Conditions of Sale herein. Any dispute arising under the terms in this paragraph will be resolved pursuant to final and binding arbitration at the American Arbitration Association.

Upon a finding by an Arbitrator in favor of buyer, the sale will be rescinded and the original purchase price, including the buyers premium, will be refunded. In such case, Poster Auctions International and the purchaser shall be deemed released of any and all claims that each may otherwise have had against the other arising out of the sale of such item.

The benefits of any warranty granted herein are personal to the buyer and are not assignable or transferable to any other person, whether by operation of law or otherwise. Any assignment or transfer of any such warranty shall be void and unenforceable. The purchaser refers only to the original buyer of the lot from Poster Auctions International and not any subsequent owner, assignee, or other person who may have or acquire an interest therein.

It is understood, in the event of disputed authenticity of authorship of any lot results in a rescission of the sale and restitution of the original price and premium paid by such purchaser, stated aforesaid, such restitution is buyer's sole remedy and Poster Auctions International disclaims all liability for any damages. incidental, consequential or otherwise, arising out of or in connection with any sale to the buyer.

Poster Auctions International has provided as much background information for each item listed in this catalogue as possible and has made reasonable efforts to insure the accuracy of the descriptions provided; but Poster Auctions International disclaims any warranty with regard to such descriptions and statements which accompany the listings in this catalogue, including but not limited to, the year of publication, the size, the condition, the printer, the references or any other background information or fact. Accordingly, buyer has due notice that any such information and/or descriptions cannot and will not be considered as material facts to this transaction and will root affect any sales herein.

On the fall of the gavel, THE SALE IS FINAL.

All items are sold AS IS.

The consignor warrants good title to the buyer. Poster Auctions International and the consignor make no representations or warranty that the buyer acquires any reproduction rights or copyright in items bought at this sale.

Any statements made by Poster Auctions International, whether in this catalogue or by its officers, agents or employees, whether oral or written, are statements of opinion only and not warranties or representations of material facts as to each arid every transaction herein.

2. Auctioneers Discretions.
Poster Auctions International has absolute discretion to divide any lot, to combine any of them, to withdraw any lot, to refuse bids and to regulate the bidding. Poster Auctions International reserves the right to withdraw lots at any time prior to or during the sale. The highest bidder acknowledged by the auctioneer will be the purchaser of the lot. Any advance made on an opening bid may be rejected if the auctioneer deems it inadequate. In the event of any dispute between bidders, or in the event of doubt as to the validity of any bid, the auctioneer shall have the final decision either to determine the successful bidder or to re-offer and re-sell the lot in dispute. If any dispute arises after the sale, the auctioneer's sale record shall be deemed the sole and conclusive evidence as to the purchaser of any lot or item.

3. Transfer of title and property.
Upon the fall of the auctioneer's hammer, title to the offered lot shall pass to the highest bidder, who may be required to sign a confirmation of purchase; and, shall be required to pay the full purchase price. The purchaser shall assume full risk and responsibility for the lot purchased upon the fall of the auctioneer's hammer. Poster Auctions International, at its option, may withhold delivery of the lots until funds represented by check have been collected or the authenticity of bank or cashier checks has been determined. No purchase shall be claimed or removed until the conclusion of the sale. In the event Poster Auctions International shall, for any reason whatsoever, be unable to deliver the lots purchased by the buyer, its liability shall be solely limited to the rescission of the sale and refund of the purchase price end purchaser's premium.

Poster Auctions International disclaims all liability for damages, incidental, consequential or otherwise, arising out of its failure to deliver any lots purchased. Poster Auctions International does not charge extra or sell separately any frame if a poster is so offered; but it is clear that it is the poster and not the frame which is being offered for sale. Poster Auctions International shall not be responsible for any damage to the frame or to any poster within the frame. Generally, framed posters offered for sale were received framed, photographed that way, and Poster Auctions International can make no warranty or representations regarding the condition of the poster in unseen areas of any such frame. All items are sold strictly as is and the purchaser assumes full risk and responsibility for the purchased lot upon the fall of the hammer, as stated aforesaid.

All lots shall be paid for and removed at the purchaser's risk and expense by noon of the second business day following the sale. Lots not so removed will, at the sole option of Poster Auctions International and at purchaser's risk and expense, be stored at Poster Auctions International's office or warehouse or delivered to a licensed warehouse for storage. Purchaser agrees, in either event, to pay all shipping, handling and storage fees incurred. In the case of lots stored at Poster Auctions International's own warehouse, the handling and storage fee will be an amount equal to 2% of the purchase price for each such lot, per month, until removed, with a minimum charge of 5% for any property not removed within thirty days from the date of the sale.

In addition, Poster Auctions International shall impose a late charge, calculated at the rate of 2% of the total purchase price per month, if payment has not been made in accordance with these Conditions of Sale.

Poster Auctions International may, on the day following the sale, remove all unclaimed lots to its offices or warehouse.

Unless purchaser notifies Poster Auctions International to the contrary, purchaser agrees that Poster Auctions International may, at its discretion, use purchaser's name as buyer of the item sold. If the purchaser fails to comply with one or more of these Conditions of Sale, then, in addition to any and all other remedies which it may have at law or in equity, Poster Auctions International may, at its sole option, cancel the sale without notice to the buyer. In such event, Poster Auctions International shall retain as liquidated damages all payments made by the purchaser, or sell the item and/or lots and all other property of the purchaser held by Poster Auctions International, without notice. Such liquidation sale shall be at standard commission rates, without any reserve. The proceeds of such sale or sales shall be applied first to the satisfaction of any damages occasioned by the purchaser's breach, and then to the payment of any other indebtedness owing to Poster Auctions International, including without limitation, commissions, handling charges, the expenses of both sales, reasonable attorneys fees, collection agency fees, and any other costs or expenses incurred thereunder. The purchaser hereby waives all the requirements of notice, advertisement and disposition of proceeds required by law, including those set forth in New York Lien Law, Article 9, Sections 200-204 inclusive, or any successor statue, with respect to any sale pursuant to this section.

4. Buyer's Premium
A premium of 15% will be added to the successful bid price of all items sold by Poster Auctions International. This premium shall be paid by all purchasers, without exception.

5. Order Bids

Poster Auctions International shall make reasonable efforts to execute bids for those not able to attend the auction; and act on the prospective purchaser's behalf to attempt to purchase the item desired at the lowest price possible, up to the limit indicated by purchaser in writing as if the purchaser were in attendance. Poster Auctions International shall not be responsible for any errors or omissions in this matter. Poster Auctions International reserves the right not to bid for any such purchaser if the order is not clear; does not arrive in sufficient time; the credit of the purchaser is not established prior to the sale; or, for any other reason in its sole discretion. An Order Bid Form shall be provided on request.

6. Sales Tax

Unless exempt by law, prior to taking pssession of the lot, the purchaser shall be required to pay the combined New York State and local sales tax, or any applicable compensating tax of another state, on the total purchase price.

7. Packing and shipping

Packing and/or handling of purchased lots by Posters Auctions International is performed solely as a courtesy for the convenience of purchasers. Unless otherwise directed by purchaser, packing and handling shall be undertaken at the sole discretion of Poster Auctions International. Poster Auctions International, at its sole discretion as agent of the purchaser, shall instruct an outside contractor to act on its behalf and arrange for or otherwise transport purchased lots. Charges for packing, handling, insurance and freight are payable by the purchaser. Poster Auctions International shall make reasonable efforts to handle purchases with care, but assumes no responsibility for damage of any kind. Poster Auctions International disclaims all liability for loss, or damages of any kind, arising out of or in connection with the packing, handling or transportation of any lots/items purchased.

8. Reserves.

All lots are subject to a reserve, which is the confidential minimum below which the lot will not be sold. Poster Auctions International may implement the reserve by bidding on behalf of the consignor. The consignor shall not bid on consignor's property.

9. Notices and jurisdiction.

(a)   All communications and notices hereunder shall be in writing and shall be deemed to have been duly given if delivered personally to an officer of PAI or if sent by United States registered mail or certified, postage prepaid, addressed as follows:

From: Poster Auctions International
To: _________________________ (Seller)
    ____
    ____

From: _________________________ (Seller)
To: Poster Auctions International
601 W. 26th Street
NewYork, NewYork 10001

or to such other address as either party hereto may have designated to the other by written notice.

(b)   These Conditions of Sale contain the entire understandings between the parties and may not be changed in any way except in writing duly executed by PAI and buyer.

(c)   These Conditions of Sale shall be construed and enforced in accordance with the laws of the State of New York.

(d)   No waiver shalt be deemed to be made by any party hereto of any rights hereunder, unless the same shall be in writing and each waiver, if any, shall be a waiver only with respect to the specific instance involved and shall in no way impair the rights of the waiving party or the obligations of the other party in any other respect at any other time.

(e)   The provisions of these Conditions of Sale shall be binding upon and inure to the benefit of the respective heirs, legatees, personal representatives and successors and assigns of the parties hereto.

(f)   The Conditions of Sale are not assignable by either party without written permission of the other party; any attempt to assign any rights, duties or obligations which arise under these Conditions without such permission will be void.

DESCRIPTION OF THE POSTERS

I. Artist's name.
Unless otherwise indicated, the artist's name, mark or initials appear on the poster.

2. Year of the Poster.
The year given is that of the publication of the poster, not necessarily the date of the event publicized or the year that art for it was rendered.

3. Size.
Size is given in inches first, then centimeters, width preceding height. Size is for entire sheet, not just the image area.

4. Printer.
Unless otherwise indicated, the name of the printer is that which appears on the face of the poster. It should be kept in mind that frequently the establishment credited on the poster is, in fact, an agency, studio or publisher.

5. Condition of the Poster.
We have attempted a simplified rating of all the posters in this sale. It should be kept in mind that we are dealing in many cases, with 50 to 100-year-old advertising paper. The standards of the print collector cannot be used. Prints were, for the most part, done in small format, on fine paper, and meant to be immediately framed or stored in a print sleeve or cabinet. A poster, for the most part, was printed in a large format, on the cheapest possible paper, and was meant to last about eight weeks on the billboards.

Most important to the condition of a poster—not eight weeks but often eighty years later—is the image of the poster: is that image (the lines, the colors, the overall design) still clearly expressed? If so, it is a poster worth collecting.

While details of each poster's condition are given as completely and accurately as possible, blemishes, tears or restorations which do not detract from the basic image and impact should not seriously impair value.

All posters are lined, whether on linen or japan paper, unless otherwise indicated. But please note that posters received in frames are not inspected out of their frames and therefore no warranty can be made about them.

All photos are of the actual poster being offered for sale. A close look at the photo and a reading of the text should enable the buyer who cannot personally examine the item to make an intelligent appraisal of it.

The following ratings have been used:

Cond A   Designates a poster in very fine condition. The colors are fresh; no paper loss. There may be some slight blemish or tear, but this is very marginal and not noticeable. A+ is a flawless example of a poster rarely seen in such fine condition. A– indicates there may be some slight dirt, fold, tear or bubble or other minor restoration, but most unobtrusive.

Cond B   Designates a poster in good condition. There may be some slight paper loss, but not in the image or in any crucial design area. If some restoration, it is not immediately evident. The lines and colors are good, although paper may have yellowed (light-stained). B+ designates a poster in very good condition. B– is one in fairly good condition. The latter determination may be caused by heavier than normal light-staining or one or two noticeable repairs.

Cond C   Designates a poster in fair condition. The light-staining may be more pronounced, restorations, folds or flaking are more readily visible, and possibly some minor paper loss occurs. But the poster is otherwise intact, the image clear, and the colors, though possibly faded, still faithful to the artist's intent.

Cond D   Designates a poster in bad condition. A good part of such poster may be missing, including some crucial image area; colors and lines so marred that a true appreciation of the artist's intent is difficult, if not impossible. There are no D posters in this sale!

The above condition ratings are solely the opinion of Poster Auctions International, and are presented only as an aid to the public. Prospective purchasers are expected to have satisfied themselves as to the condition of the posters. Any discrepancy relating to the condition of a poster shall not be considered grounds for the cancellation of a sale.

Some other notes and designations relating to the condition of a poster:

Framed   Where a poster is framed, this is indicated. In many cases, we have photographed the poster in the frame and the dimensions given are those which are visible within the matting or edges of the frame.

Paper   All posters in this sale are linen- or japan-backed unless the designation "P" appears.

6. Bibliography.
An abbreviation for each reference (Ref) is given and can be found in the complete Bibliography. The reference is almost always to a reproduction of that poster. If a "p." precedes it, it means the reproduction or reference is on that page; if number only, it refers to a poster or plate number. Every effort has been made to refer to books that are authoritative and/or easily accessible.

7. Pre-Sale Estimate
These estimates are guides for prospective bidders and should not be relied upon as representations or predictions of actual selling prices. They are simply our best judgment of the fair market value of that particular poster in that condition on the date it was written.

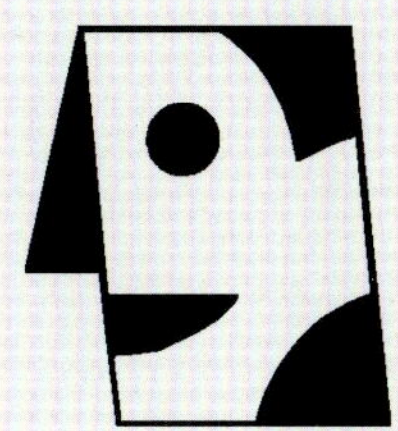

POSTER AUCTIONS INTERNATIONAL, INC.
601 WEST 26TH ST., NEW YORK, N.Y. 10001
TEL (212) 787-4000 FAX (212) 604-9175
www.posterauctions.com   Email: info@posterauctions.com

POSTERS VA-VA-VOOM
ABSENTEE BID FORM

Please bid on my behalf on the following lots up to the price shown. I understand that all bids are subject to the Conditions of Sale which are printed in the Catalogue.

Poster Auctions International will make every effort to execute bids for those not able to attend and act on the prospective purchaser's behalf to try to purchase the item desired at the lowest price possible up to the limit indicated by purchaser below as if the purchaser were in attendance, but Poster Auctions International cannot be responsible for any errors or omissions in this matter. Poster Auctions International may reserve the right not to bid for any such party if the order is not clear, does not arrive in sufficient time, or the credit of the purchaser is not established, or for any other reason in its sole discretion.

The purchase price will be the total of the final bid and a premium of 15% of the final bid together with any applicable sales tax. Unsuccessful bidders will not be informed but may telephone for sales results.

____   Date _________________
(Signed)

NAME ____

ADDRESS ____

City _______________________________State ________________Zip ____________

TEL: Home: (   ) _______________ Office: (   ) _______________ FAX: (   ) _______________

E-mail address____

BANK: Name ____Telephone (   )_____________

Address ____

Account Number ___________________________Officer_________________________

Credit Card # ____________________________________ Expiration: _________________________

☐ ORDER BID

☐ TELEPHONE BID—Telephone number where you can be reached on Sunday, Nov. 12 _______________

Lot #	Artist	Title	BID (excluding premium)
______	___________	________________________________	$ _________
______	___________	________________________________	$ _________
______	___________	________________________________	$ _________
______	___________	________________________________	$ _________
______	___________	________________________________	$ _________
______	___________	________________________________	$ _________